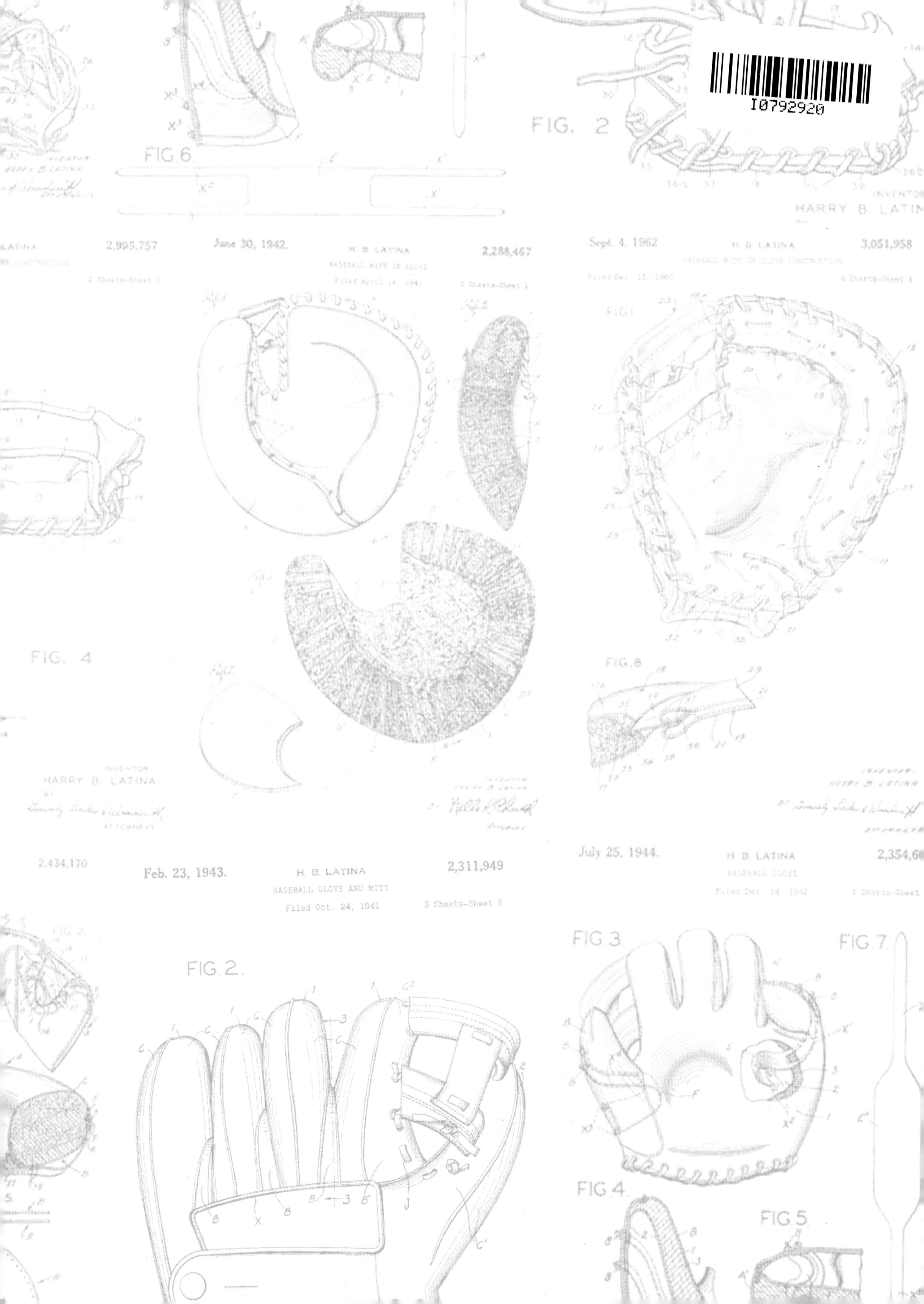
FIG. 6.
FIG. 2
INVENTOR
HARRY B. LATINA
2,995,757
June 30, 1942.
H. B. LATINA
2,288,467
BASEBALL MITT OR GLOVE
Filed April 14, 1941
2 Sheets-Sheet 1
Sept. 4, 1962
H. B. LATINA
3,051,958
BASEBALL MITT OR GLOVE CONSTRUCTION
4 Sheets-Sheet 1
FIG. 1
FIG. 4
FIG. 8
INVENTOR
HARRY B. LATINA
ATTORNEY
2,434,170
Feb. 23, 1943.
H. B. LATINA
2,311,949
BASEBALL GLOVE AND MITT
Filed Oct. 24, 1941
3 Sheets-Sheet 2
July 25, 1944.
H. B. LATINA
BASEBALL GLOVE
2 Sheets-Sheet
FIG. 2.
FIG. 3.
FIG. 7.
FIG. 4.
FIG. 5.

The Finest in the Field®

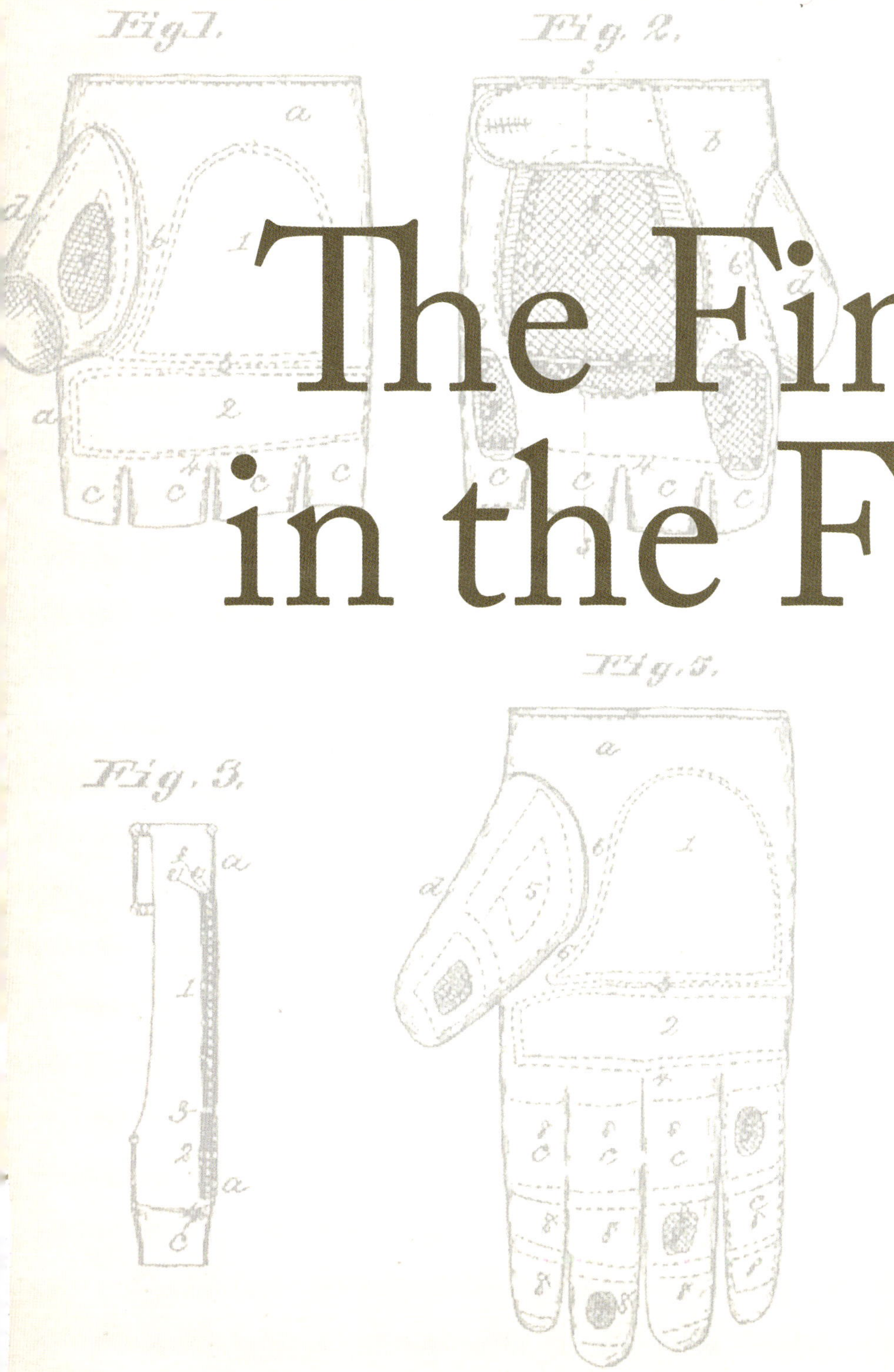

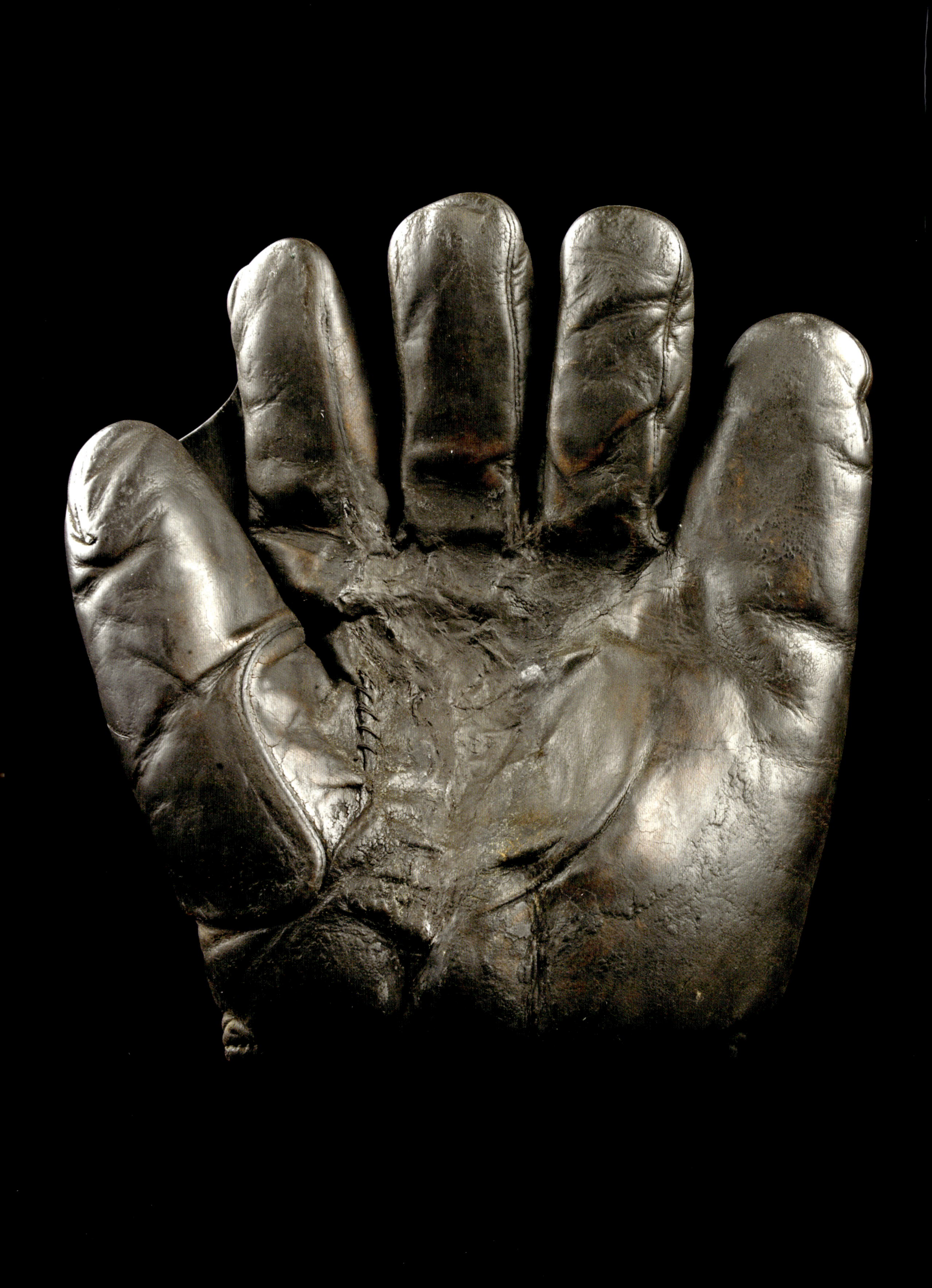

The Finest in the Field®

A HISTORY OF BASEBALL THROUGH 50 ICONIC GLOVES

Ed Wheatley

Foreword by Johnny Bench

Rizzoli
NEW YORK
New York · Paris · London · Milan

CONTENTS

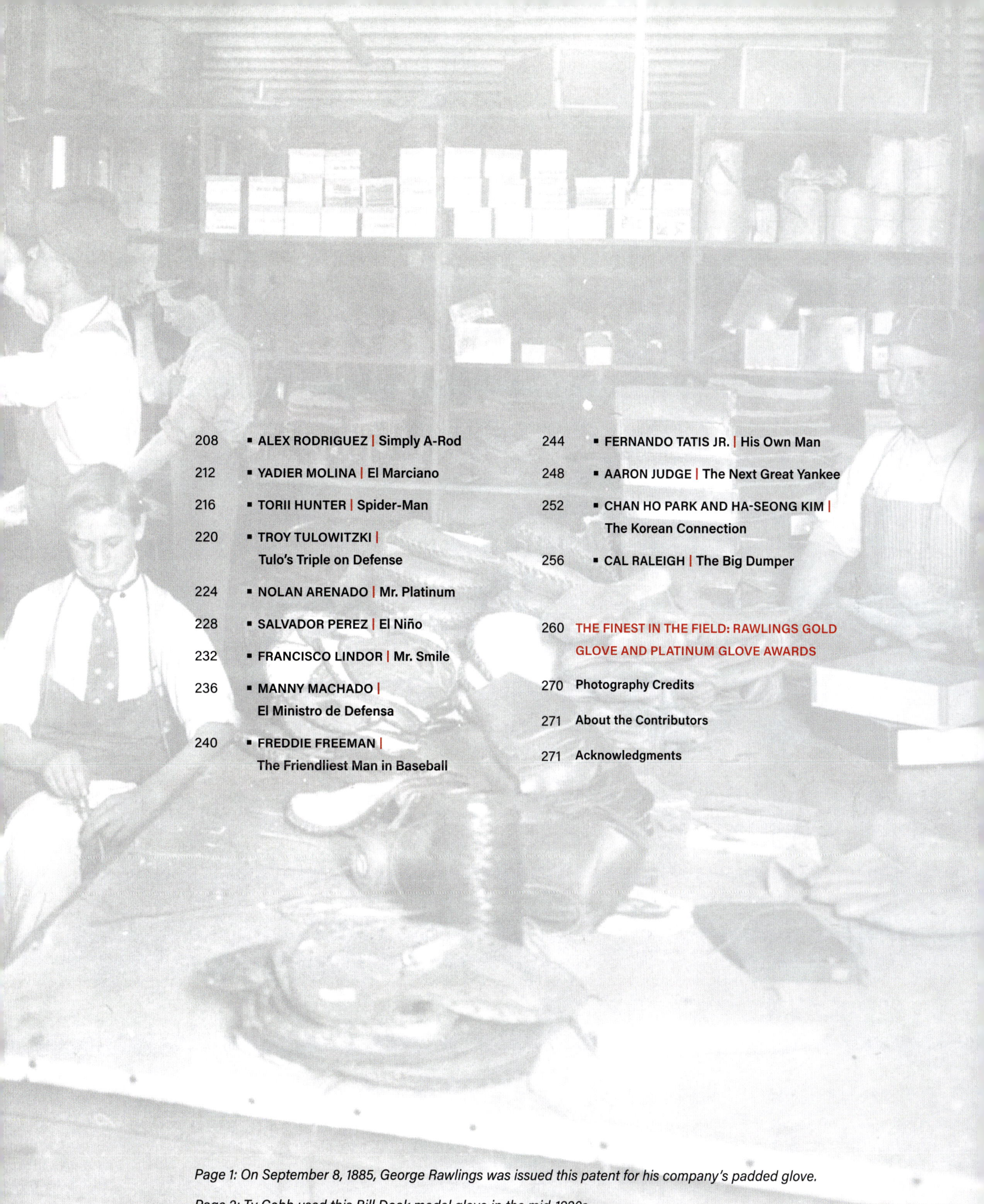

Page 1: On September 8, 1885, George Rawlings was issued this patent for his company's padded glove.

Page 2: Ty Cobb used this Bill Doak model glove in the mid-1920s.

A Rawlings team is hard at work making gloves in the 1920s (background image).

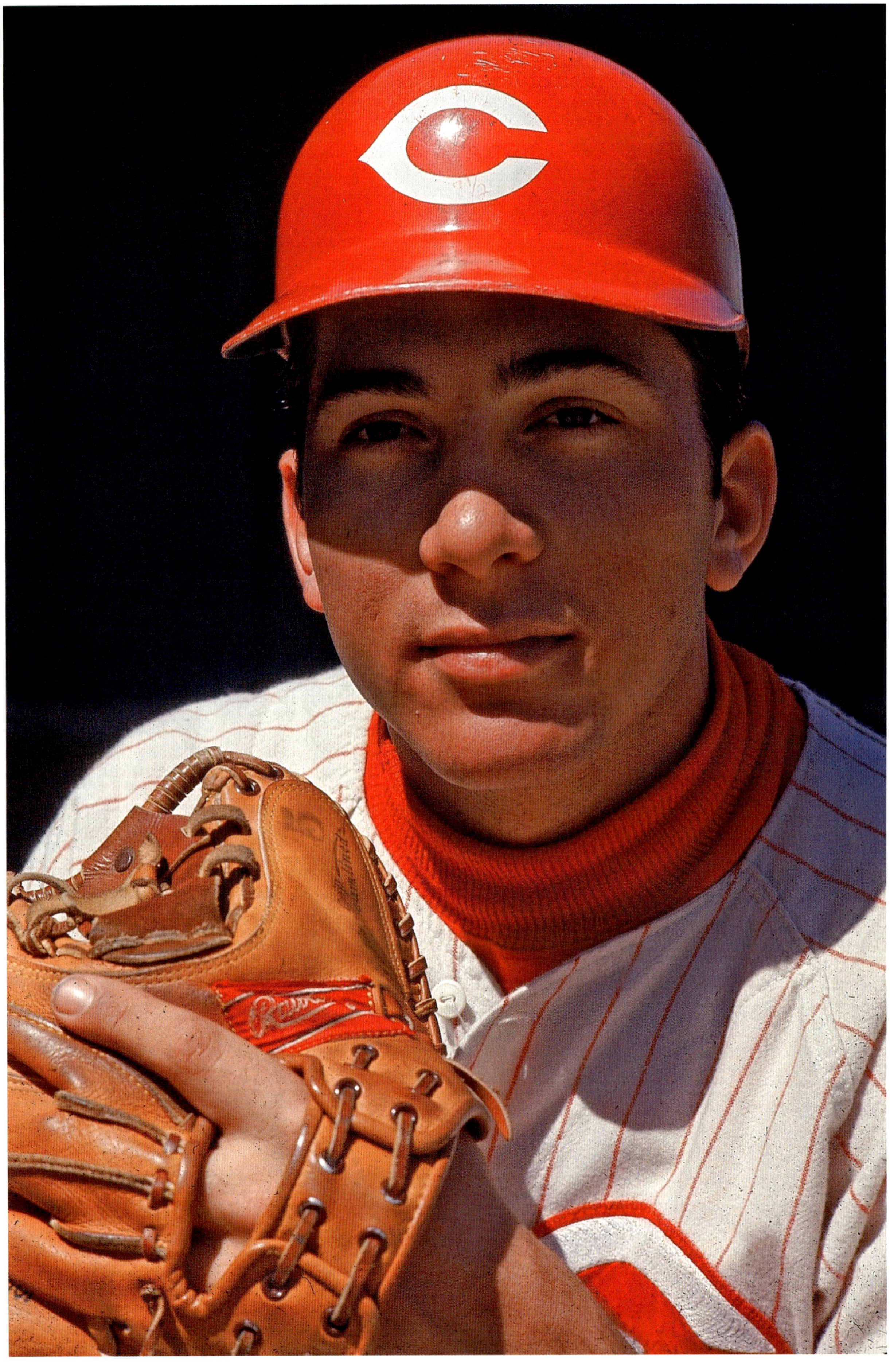

Johnny Bench of the Cincinnati Reds is a 10-time Rawlings Gold Glove Award winner.

FOREWORD

Johnny Bench
Hall of Fame Catcher, Cincinnati Reds

Baseball is a simple game. It is played with a ball, a bat, and a glove on a field with four bases. Throughout the past 150 years of Major League Baseball (MLB)'s history, the ball, the bat, and the field have undergone very few modifications. In contrast, the glove has evolved over these decades. It has witnessed changes in its purpose and style and has resulted in new rules that forever changed the game.

I saw some of those changes up close during the years when baseball was a central part of my life. I played in the big leagues for 17 seasons, appeared in four World Series, and was selected to 14 All-Star Games. I had the great honor of being chosen as the Rookie of the Year in 1968, and I won the NL MVP Award twice (in 1970 and 1972) and the World Series MVP Award once (in 1976). I also won 10 Rawlings Gold Glove Awards. It was a Hall of Fame career of hard work and always striving to be better. And the tool of my trade—my mitt—was always by my side during those seasons. For ballplayers, there is no greater memory than receiving your first baseball glove, and as I think back over my career accomplishments, I remember my own first glove. While people may assume it was a catcher's mitt, it was actually a Rawlings six-finger fielder's model—catching came later. I bought that glove with money I had saved up from working a paper route and picking cotton in the fields of Oklahoma.

Later, once I was behind the plate, I was able to witness the evolution of gloves and their impact on the game. Catcher's mitts were first designed like a big, circular, heavily padded pillow to swallow the pitcher's toss. For more than seven decades, there was not much change to the style of the glove or the role it played in shaping the game. My experience with broken fingers on my throwing hand led me to try an innovative design that helped revolutionize the position and the game. Randy Hundley, the Chicago Cubs catcher, had started using a hinged mitt the season before I first used it. The new model had less padding and a hinge within the palm of the mitt. I was almost like a first baseman, scooping and snapping at balls. Better yet, I improved my catching efficiency while protecting my throwing arm. The change of the mitt's design enhanced the athleticism of my play and defense. There are those today who talk about how this glove transformed the catcher's position, and I am proud to be a part of that transition.

My experience shows the impact a glove can have on the game of baseball. Within each glove is a unique story, and this book is a collection of many of those stories. Some of them are dramatic, with the player's glove in the forefront, like the great catches Willie Mays and Mickey Mantle made in the World Series. In others, the glove's role is more subtle, always remaining by each player's side or on their hand. As baseball looks forward to the next 150 years, the glove will remain a tool upon which many more memories will be built.

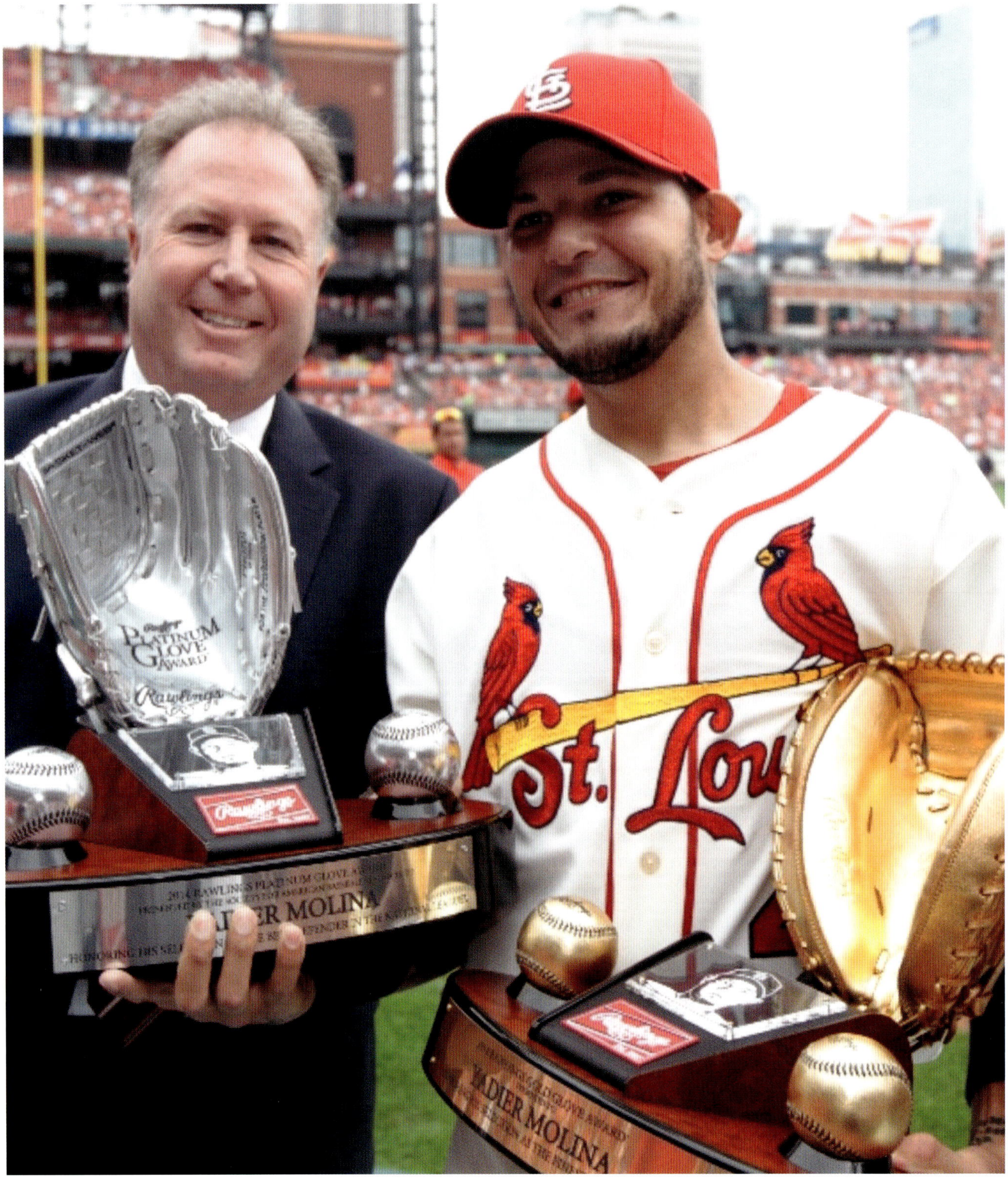

Mike Thompson presents the 2014 Rawlings Gold Glove and Platinum Glove Awards to Yadier Molina in a ceremony at Busch Stadium in St. Louis.

INTRODUCTION

Mike Thompson
Chief Marketing Officer, Rawlings

It has been 42 years since I began working for Rawlings Sporting Goods Inc. In a twist of fate, 1984 also become a magical year for the world of sports and particularly baseball. It was the year the Olympics came to Los Angeles, and baseball was featured as a demonstration sport. It was the first time the game had ever been played in the Olympics, and it was my first big assignment. Here I was, this Rawlings rookie, and I couldn't believe this was actually happening to me.

What would be next? I had been living in San Diego since 1981, and along came the greatest moment in the city's sports history: The Padres made it to the postseason in 1984 for the first time since the team's inception in 1969. Their special moment came with the Padres down two games to one, in a best-of-five-games NL Championship Series against the Chicago Cubs, when Steve Garvey (a former Dodger) delivered a come-from-behind walk-off home run in the bottom of the ninth inning of Game Four. That swing provided the momentum the Padres needed to win the NL championship the next day and put the team in their first Fall Classic. Even though they lost the World Series to the dominating Detroit Tigers, the moment of Garvey's slam is still considered San Diego's best sports moment ever. And there I was, right in the middle of it, representing my new company and making lasting friendships with all the great players on both teams—including Garvey, my new hometown's hero. I was on top of the world thinking what a great job I had. Can it really be considered work when you are having so much fun? I soon found myself involved in some of baseball's most historic moments, some during my lifetime and some with ties to before my time.

Four years later, I was able to take my father—the man who inspired my love of baseball and who was a die-hard Dodgers fan from the team's days in Brooklyn—to Game One of the 1988 World Series between the Los Angeles Dodgers and Oakland Athletics. Together we saw a banged-up and limping Kirk Gibson come to the plate in the bottom of the ninth inning with two outs, a man on base, and the Dodgers trailing by one run. To quote radio announcer Vin Scully's words from that game, "In a year that has been so improbable, the impossible has happened." There was lightning in Gibson's bat as he put the ball into the right-field stands for a walk-off home run. It was a magical moment to witness, one that sparked a longtime friendship between me and the Dodgers' skipper, Tommy Lasorda. Across the field that day was the A's manager, Tony La Russa, with whom I later formed a friendship after he came to St. Louis to lead the Cardinals. More importantly, that game symbolized the meaning and memories created through a baseball moment, whether it was experiencing a game with my dad, watching a walk-off home run, or making new friends.

My journey with Rawlings continued placing me in the middle of exciting moment after exciting moment. I was in Camden Yards a few years later watching Cal Ripken Jr.'s countdown to 2,130 and 2,131 consecutive games with a special number eight ball we had created at Rawlings for the occasion. Soon after, I was on the field at Yankee Stadium for Mickey Mantle's monument celebration with a different piece of memorabilia—a Rawlings number seven ball made especially for that event. I was on the field to celebrate "The Mick" with many of the Yankees' current players, Mantle's teammates, and even Billy Crystal. The last man to walk onto the field was heralded over the stadium's public address system by the legendary voice of announcer Bobby Murcer as "the greatest living ballplayer, Joe DiMaggio." Here I was in the midst of one special moment in baseball history when I came side by side with another—"The Yankee Clipper." And guess what happened next? The following season, I got a call to do another special Rawlings memorabilia ball—number five—for DiMaggio. A couple of weeks later, I was in Chicago having breakfast with DiMaggio and discussing the details for launching the ball during Joe DiMaggio Day at Yankee Stadium. Soon, I was back out on the field as he entered Yankee Stadium in a 1956 Thunderbird (representing his 56-game hitting streak) to the lyric "Where have you gone, Joe DiMaggio?" from the song "Mrs. Robinson" by Simon & Garfunkel.

It has been an honor to spend more than four decades supporting the game I love, and I'm not telling these stories to brag about my experiences but rather to highlight baseball as an institution full of special and magical moments. And that is what this book is all about—the history of baseball and its many moments. Whether you're viewing from the stands, listening on a transistor radio in your youth, or watching on television, baseball creates moments that will live with you forever.

The focus of this book is the baseball glove and its ties to many of the game's most important moments. A baseball glove is the most personal part of each player's equipment. Unlike almost any other product in sporting goods, the glove evokes passion and emotion. When you get your glove (whether it's your first or not), you work to create the perfect pocket. You mold it, oil it, and then play catch with your dad, brother, or a friend to break it in. It becomes an extension of your hand—it's part of you! It's not like a pair of cleats or a bat that soon goes by the wayside. There are memories in every glove, and I am proud to say that Rawlings gloves continue to be used by more major leaguers than all other competitors' brands combined. In 2019, Rawlings became the official glove of Major League Baseball (MLB). And I am extremely proud to have played a role in making that happen.

Every year since creating the Rawlings Gold Glove Award in 1957, the company has recognized the game's finest defensive players. These annual awards became part of my responsibilities at Rawlings, and I have seen—to quote the iconic introduction to ABC's *Wide World of Sports*—"the thrill of victory and the agony of defeat" in the eyes of players as the award winners were announced. It's a reflection of just how much the Gold Gloves mean to the players and to baseball. This occasion feels even more meaningful when I represent Rawlings, standing side by side with each winner in their home stadium as they receive an ovation from their fans and accept the trophy for being the finest in the field. That recognition continues long after the ceremonies, as award winners take the field and play their games wearing the Gold Glove label and patch on their gloves.

In 2007, Rawlings celebrated the 50th anniversary of the award by announcing the all-time Gold Glove Team. It was an especially moving experience for me as I presented the award to some of the game's greatest, including Brooks Robinson, Ozzie Smith, Johnny Bench, Ken Griffey Jr., Joe Morgan, and—my boyhood hero—Willie Mays. It was a moment that showed the true meaning and longevity of this award. It also became the motivation to take this recognition to the next step.

A partnership was formed with ESPN to host the announcement of the Gold Glove winners shortly after the end of each season. Back in 1991 and 1992, Rawlings hosted a dinner in New York to recognize the players receiving the award. In 2011, the company turned the ceremony into a gala when we hosted the dinner at the historic Pierre Hotel in New York City (before moving to The Plaza Hotel the following year). For that dinner, we also decided to elevate the glove award experience even more. I collaborated with my good friend and partner Jamie Robinson, and we began laying out the process to develop the Platinum Glove Award. It was an award meant to answer the following question: Who is the best of the best among each league's Gold Glove Award winners each year? Initially, the selection was made by fans of the game. Two years later, we partnered with the Society for American Baseball Research (SABR) to add their new SABR Defensive Index™ as a complement to the fans' selection. Humbly, Jamie and I left our mark on baseball history with the creation of the Platinum Glove Award.

There is something special about hearing an MLB Network analyst commenting on a fielding play, "That was a platinum play right there, not gold. That was Platinum Glove worthy." This award that I was instrumental in helping create has now become an everyday piece of baseball lore. And so has the annual Gold Glove Award ceremony we created, which has risen to the likes of a red-carpet event at Hollywood's Oscars, but it's all about baseball, our national pastime.
I am humbled and awed to look back at the changes in the game over my 42-year career that has touched five different decades. It's a great game that's going to be around for decades to come, with many more moments and memories to be made—just as unforgettable as the ones celebrated in this book.

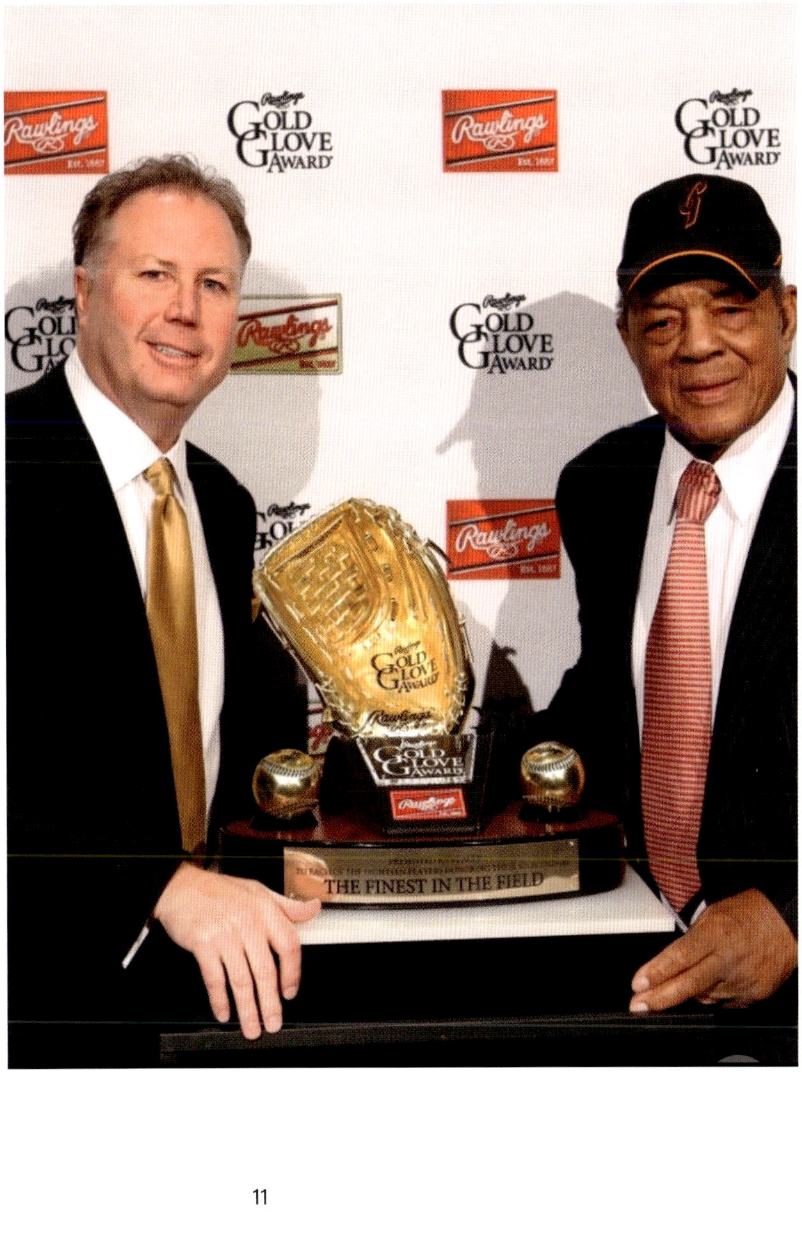

Thompson poses with Hall of Famer and 12-time Rawlings Gold Glove Award winner Willie Mays.

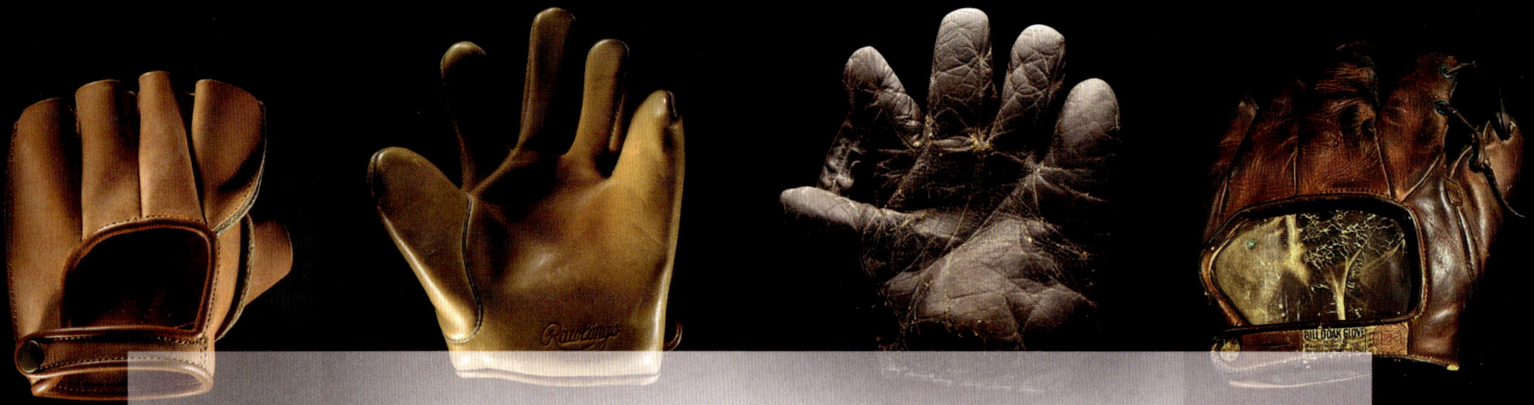

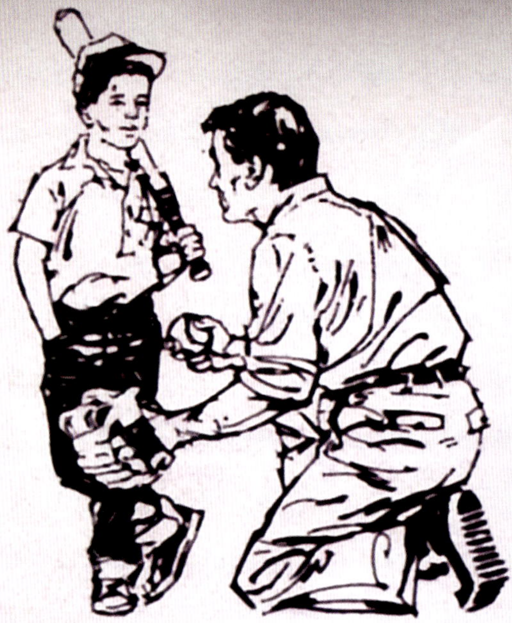

What Is A Baseball Glove?

A baseball glove is a beginning and an ending: a boy's first sure step towards manhood: a man's final, lingering hold on youth; it is promise . . . and memory.

A baseball glove is the dusty badge of belonging, the tanned and oiled mortar of team and camaraderie; in its creases and scuffs lodge sunburned afternoons freckled with thrills, the excited hum of competition, cheers that burst like skyrockets.

A baseball glove is Ty Cobb, Babe Ruth, Stan Musial, Mickey Mantle and a thousand-and-one names and moments strung like white and crimson banners in the vast stadium of memory.

A baseball glove is the leather of adventure, worthy successor to the cowboy's holster, the trooper's saddle and the buckskin laces of the frontier scout; it is combat, heroics, and victory . . . a place to smack a fist or snuff a rally.

Above all, a baseball glove is the union of father and son, boy and friends, man and men; it is union beyond language, creed or color.

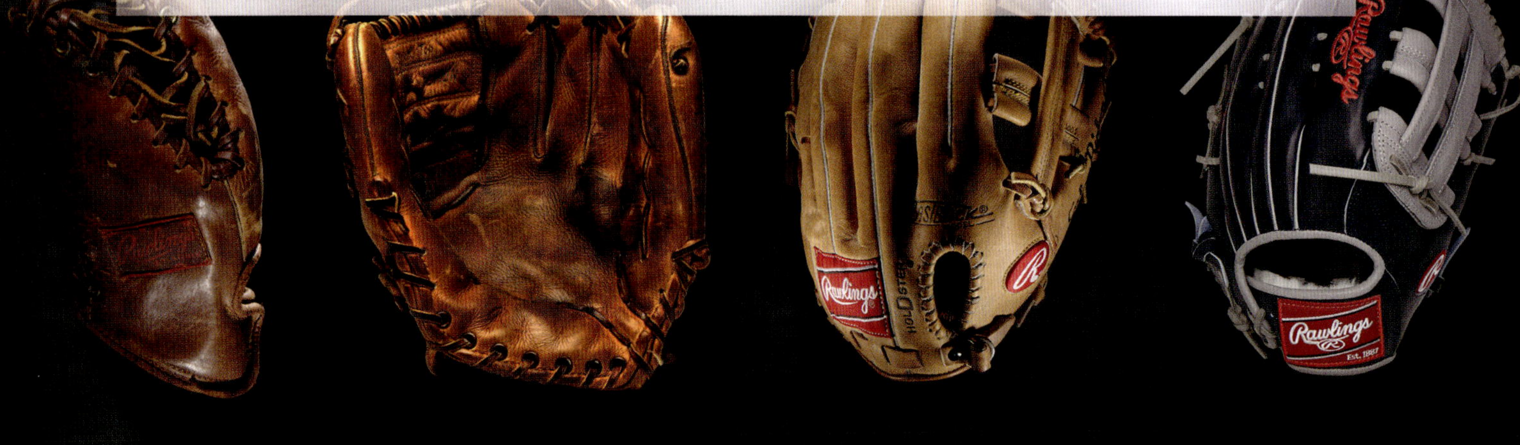

LOVE OF A GLOVE

In baseball, love can be found everywhere, especially in that one special piece of equipment—the glove. Of all the equipment used in the game, gloves have always been the most personal and most treasured. Your glove would go with you everywhere, hung on your bicycle's handlebars while you pedaled to and from the fields or strapped to your waist if you walked. The memory and love of that first baseball glove remain forever.

For many, that first glove is a cherished keepsake stored somewhere safe even years later. For others, it may have been handed down to a family member or, unfortunately, thrown out in the trash along with the baseball cards of their youth. But decades later, many adults can still rattle off their first glove's brand, model, and the player's signature printed across its palm as easily as reciting their social security number.

The love of a glove is not just the memory of owning a prized possession but also the memory of caring for it—keeping it clean, storing it safely, and even swaddling it like a baby. Over the years, young ballplayers have found many ways to work their glove to create the perfect pocket that would turn a dream catch into a reality. While some used shaving cream, Vaseline, saddle soap, or Rawlings Glovolium® to break it in and make it soft, others soaked their glove in water and pounded it by hand or with a mallet to form a pocket. Then they tied it up with a rubber band, rope, or tape. When all was done, many found a special place for their keepsake—whether in a box, a plastic bread wrapper, or even under their pillow. Then they lay their heads down to sleep to dream of the heroics their glove would bring in their next game.

These rituals were the same for players who eventually became Gold Glove winners or perhaps even Hall of Famers. Everyone who plays the game has a story. Sometimes that story doesn't even start with a leather glove. In the case of 13-time Gold Glove–winning Hall of Famer Ozzie Smith, his first glove was nothing more than a brown paper bag that he rolled down on his hand to catch tennis balls that he threw against a wall. Smith didn't have a real glove until he found an old, weathered one lying across from a local recreation center, looking like it had been left out in the rain. As mentioned in his foreword, Hall of Fame catcher Johnny Bench saved money from a paper route and picking cotton as a youngster to purchase his first glove—a six-finger fielder's glove, not a catcher's mitt, as one would surmise. In those early years, Bench was a pitcher and fielder before moving behind the plate. He then began using his dad's old catcher's mitt. (His dad had once dreamed of being a big-league player, too, and Johnny inherited his dream.)

As Smith began playing ball in school, he was loaned a six-finger Stan Musial model. It was really an outfielder's glove, but he liked it and kept using six-finger models throughout his professional career. Smith liked his gloves soft in the most sensitive part of his hand, where he would have more feel catching the ball. Along the way, he learned that the lanolin in shaving cream or baby oil gave the best results for creating the perfect softness. Bench got his glove in shape by soaking it in the hot clubhouse whirlpool and then wrapping it up around three balls and storing it in his locker for a few days. He then worked lanolin shaving cream into the glove and pounded the pocket with his baseball bat.

Another future Gold Glover, Steve Garvey, got his first glove at age six when he started to play Little League ball in Tampa, Florida. It was a top-of-the-line glove for a youngster, a Rawlings Heart of the Hide® model that his mom had spent between nine and twelve dollars on (big money in the mid-1950s). The glove came with a stern warning from his mom: "Don't lose this." To make sure he didn't, Garvey went everywhere with it strapped on his belt. The man with the most Platinum Glove Awards, Nolan Arenado, received a similar plea from his dad. Arenado still remembers that first glove. It was a Rawlings model with "Derek Jeter" embossed across the inside of it, and he remembers his dad's advice: "Put your telephone number on the glove so you don't lose it." That advice paid off about four times, he recalled, as the home phone rang with someone calling about his lost keepsake.

Even if they didn't grow up to be major leaguers, many young boys found their own love of a glove. Calling all those baseball games throughout his career always took Bob Costas back to the day when he was six years old and his dad took him to the local sporting goods store. After trying on many different gloves, he settled on a Harvey Kuenn model—it felt the best. He took it home, got some palm oil, rubbed it on the glove, put a baseball in, and stretched a rubber band around it to create the pocket. "That was the standard way to break in a glove back then," he said. "After which you just start playing catch with it until it loosened up and felt game ready. Let the memories begin."

And this passion was not limited to only young boys. Little girls found that same love of a glove as they grew up playing softball and sometimes baseball alongside their brothers and friends. That same special relationship created a lifetime of memories for young women who played in youth leagues, high school, college, and sometimes even the pros. College softball star pitcher Heidi Glaus had numerous gloves as she played tee ball through college. Her favorite was a Rawlings Trap-Eze® model that rarely left her side. "You would have thought it was 24-carat gold encrusted with diamonds," she said. "It was the glove that stayed with me through college, always with a softball in it and perfectly tied."

Vicki Schneider was one of the stars of the 1970s International Women's Professional Softball Association, playing for the St. Louis Hummers. She instantly recalled the moment she received a Rawlings Stan Musial Trap-Eze model glove for her eighth birthday. It was her first real glove—"the kind of treasure that feels bigger than a game," she said. She too undertook the ritual of breaking it in by rubbing oil in the leather and playing catch in the yard. "That glove became a part of me," she said. She still has it tucked away, along with all the memories it brought throughout her career—unforgettable catches, plays, and even triple plays in the pros.

No matter how many baseball gloves one has used over the years, that first glove remains a cherished memory. Whether they are destined to be a professional baseball or softball player, or just a sandlot player, a child's first glove becomes a prized possession. Over the nearly two centuries that baseball has been played in America, the glove remains the most personal piece of equipment for those who have played the game—something that everyone remembers.

BASEBALL BECOMES AMERICA'S GAME

The game of baseball that we know today traces its roots to pre–Civil War America. The exact genesis of the game has been the subject of debate and controversy by baseball historians for more than a century. Baseball and other similar games—like cricket or rounders, which were also played with a bat and a ball—date back to early folk games played centuries ago in Great Britain and Continental Europe. The long-heralded myth of the American game being invented in 1839 by Abner Doubleday in Cooperstown, New York, has been proven false in the last several decades, though the town is home to the crown jewel of baseball—the National Baseball Hall of Fame.

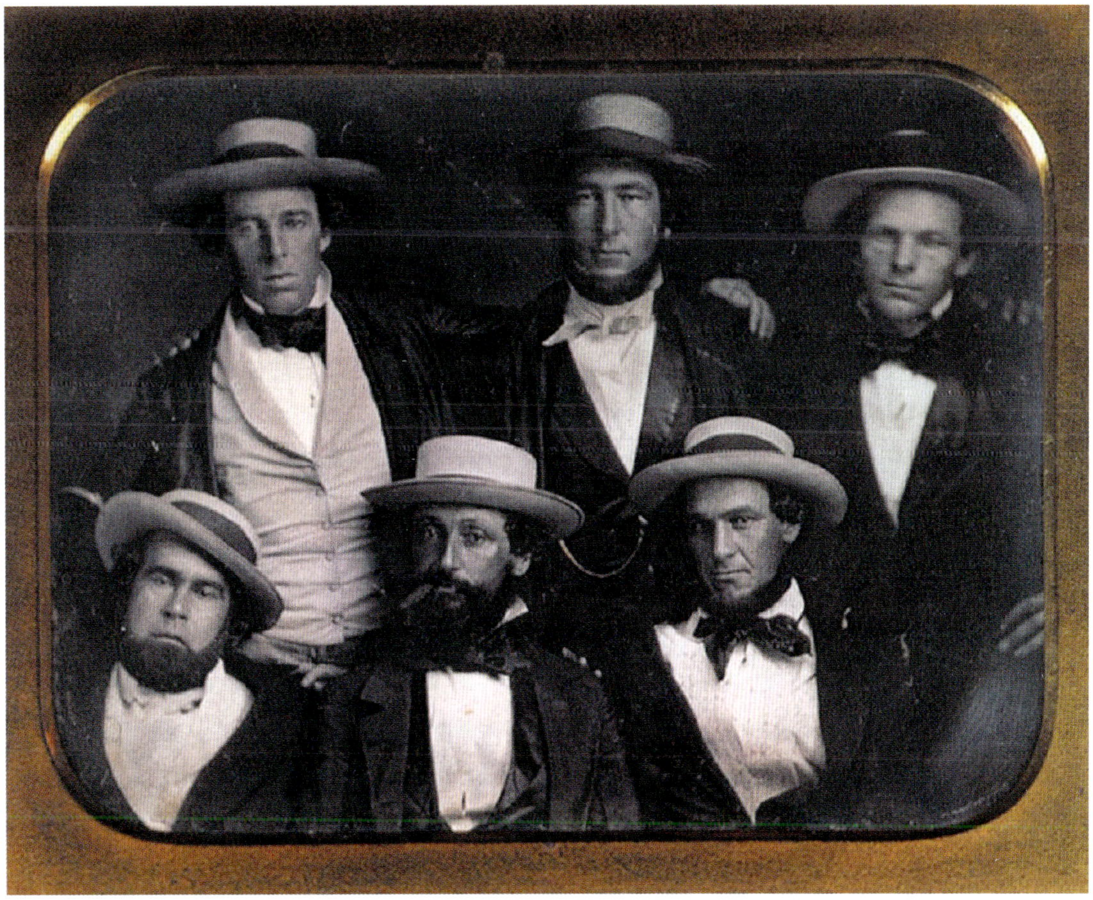

The father of baseball, Alexander Cartwright (top middle), is pictured with members of the New York Knickerbockers, including Alfred Cartwright (top left), William Wheaton (top right), Duncan Curry (bottom left), Daniel "Doc" Adams (bottom middle), and Henry Tiebout Anthony (bottom right), circa 1847.

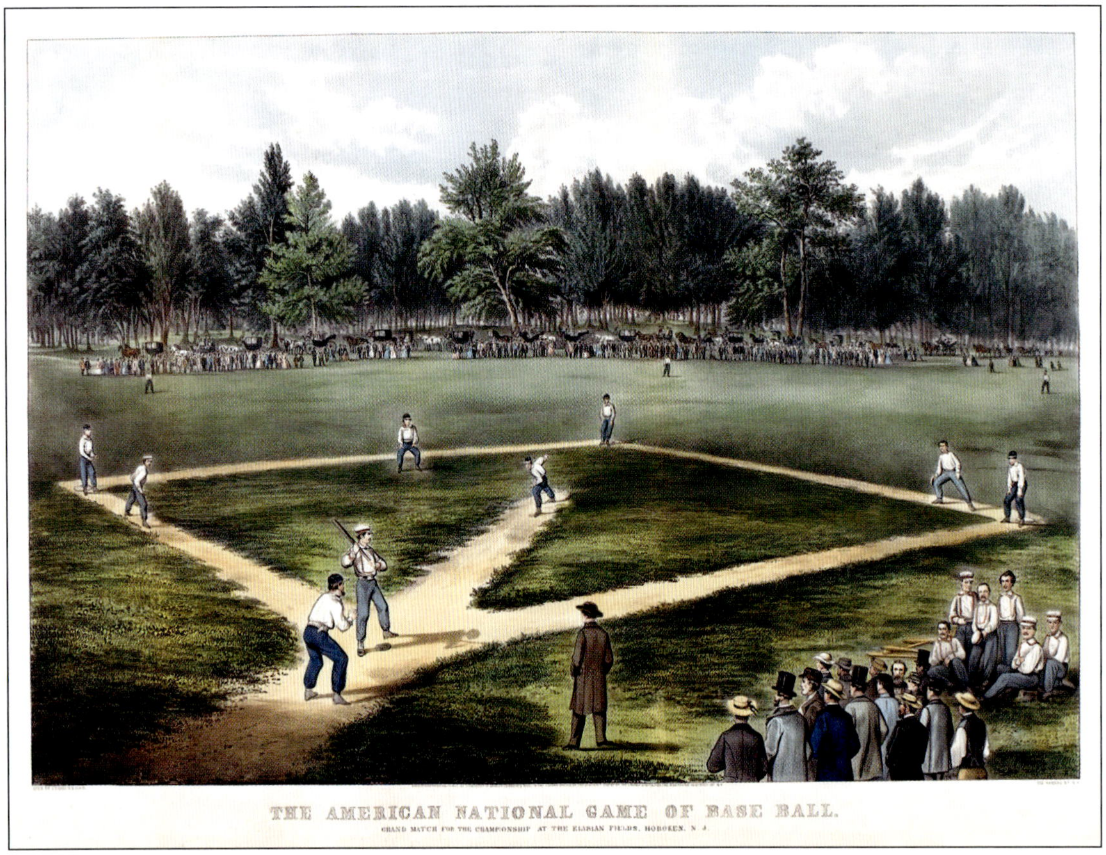

Elysian Fields in Hoboken, New Jersey, shown in 1866, was the site of modern baseball's first documented game two decades earlier.

Alexander Cartwright is now recognized as the father of modern baseball in America. In 1845, he drafted a set of 20 rules that became the foundation for today's game. The first documented game under such rules was played on June 19, 1846, at Elysian Fields in Hoboken, New Jersey, where Cartwright's New York Knickerbockers were defeated by the New York Nine, 23–1.

Soon, Cartwright's rules and format for baseball, along with a growing fascination with the game, spread across the heartland. During this initial period, baseball was an amateur sport. Organizational baseball spread with more fervor in the big cities of the northeastern United States due to their population density, and amateur club teams began popping up to play one another. Outside of those big cities, baseball was just a recreational sport or a social activity centered on town teams playing against other towns or factory teams playing against other factories. Recreational entertainment was extremely limited during this period of American history. There were no televisions, radios, motion pictures, or video games, so baseball became an instant hit in a world of hard labor. It was a game that could be played anywhere and enjoyed by anyone, a game that allowed a whole town to come together to root for their local nine and forget about the hardships and toils of daily life. It was this ability to bring people together with a joyful distraction that led to baseball becoming America's game.

As baseball's popularity continued its ascent during the decades immediately following the Civil War, American society was also undergoing an unprecedented economic transformation and manufacturing boom as the nation struggled to overcome the commercial and social damage inflicted by that war. The United States changed from an agriculture-based nation to a

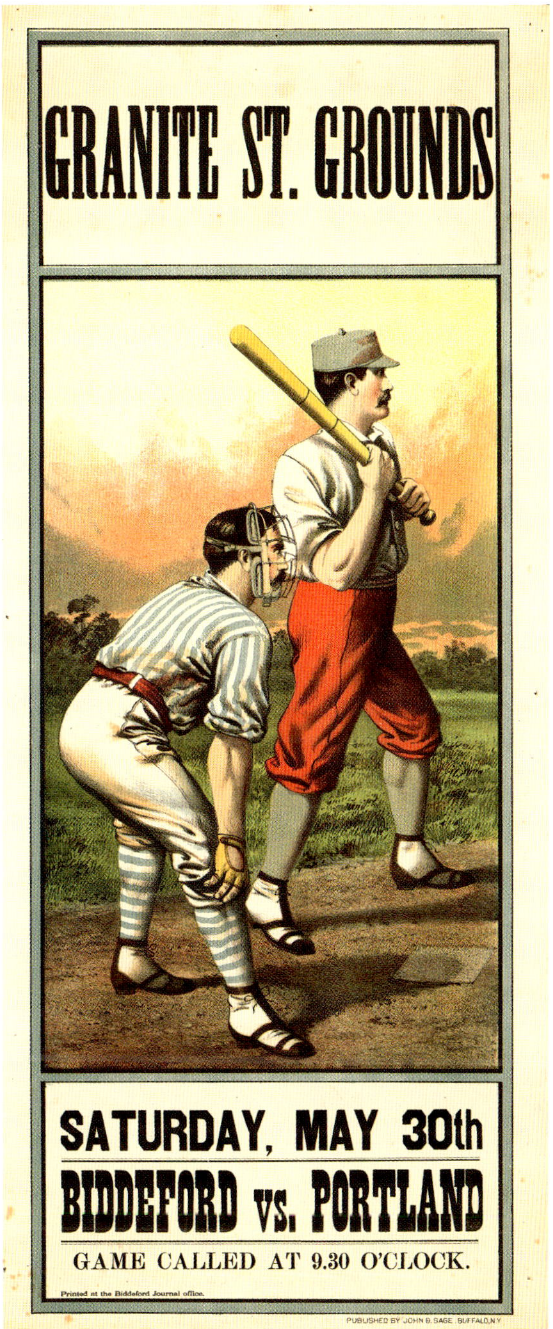

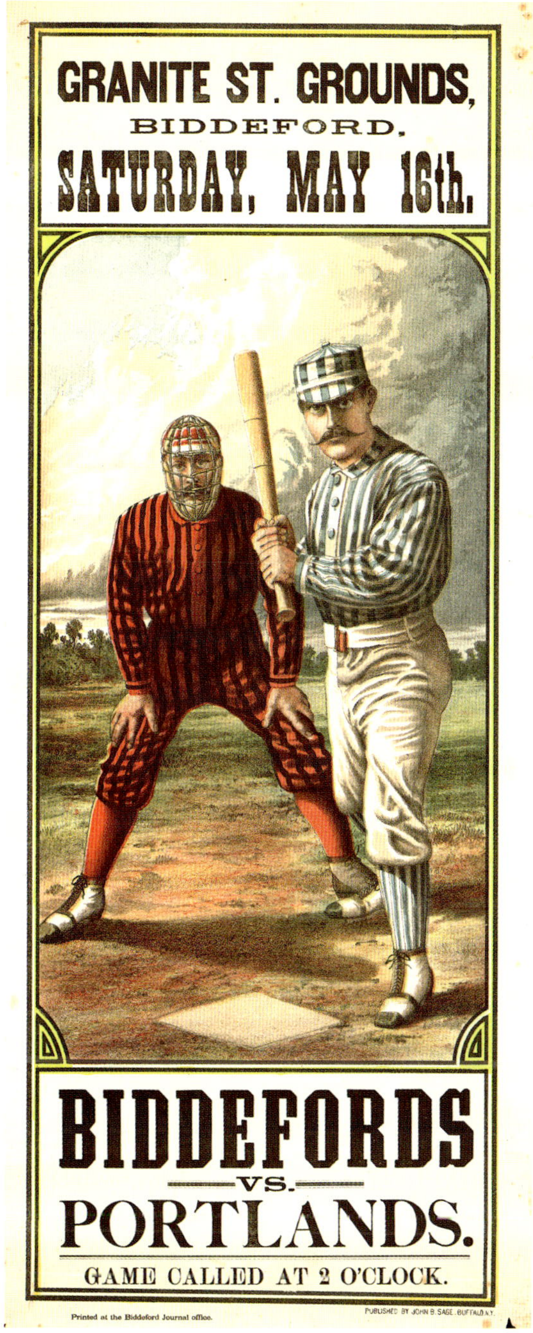

As baseball's popularity grew throughout the 1880s, amateur games were played across the country. These posters advertised games in Biddeford, Maine, circa 1886.

country of populous urban centers supported by the rapid expansion of technology and industries. Homeowners were introduced to running water, gas, electricity, and sewer systems. Public places such as schools, stores, restaurants, and government offices were lit by electricity for the first time. And public transportation enabled more people to live farther away from where they worked as suburbs sprouted up along newly laid metropolitan trolley lines. Lifestyles were changing, and many Americans were emerging with more leisure time and more disposable income.

Eager to spend their newfound time and money outside the workplace, Americans began turning to sports, either as spectators or participants. Across the nation, retailers began operating

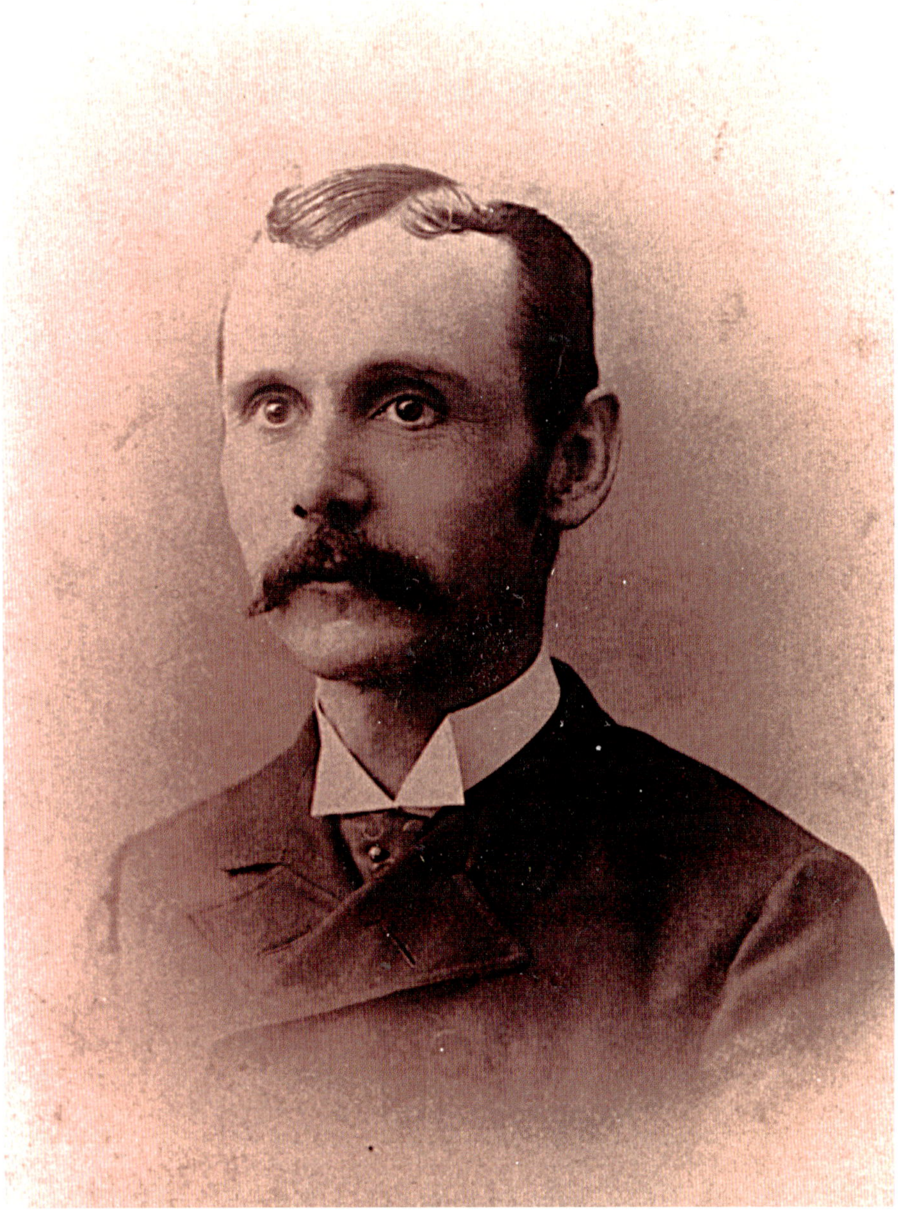

As American society began focusing more on sports, retailers began selling general sporting goods. George Rawlings (left) and his brother, Alfred, opened their first shop in 1887. The company's early catalogs and newspaper advertisements (opposite) highlighted the products Rawlings sold for a variety of sports.

as dealers in general sporting goods. The brothers George and Alfred Rawlings opened their first retail sporting goods shop in 1887. The store was located at the corner of Eighth and Chestnut Streets in downtown St. Louis, Missouri. The company's early catalogs and newspaper ads highlighted Rawlings as "dealers in fishing tackle, guns, baseball, football, golf, polo, tennis, athletic and general sporting goods."

A decade later, in January 1898, Charles Scudder joined the Rawlings brothers with an infusion of capital that turned the company into a manufacturer of athletic equipment in lieu of being only a retail seller of goods. The production line, led by visionary designer William Whitley, filled the Rawlings catalog with a diverse offering of sporting items, making it a one-stop shop for Americans and their changing lifestyles. But of all the sports, baseball became the Rawlings brothers' lasting legacy. And it was Scudder's vision, combined with America's evolving love of the game, that put the company on a path to becoming one of the most innovative baseball glove manufacturers in the world.

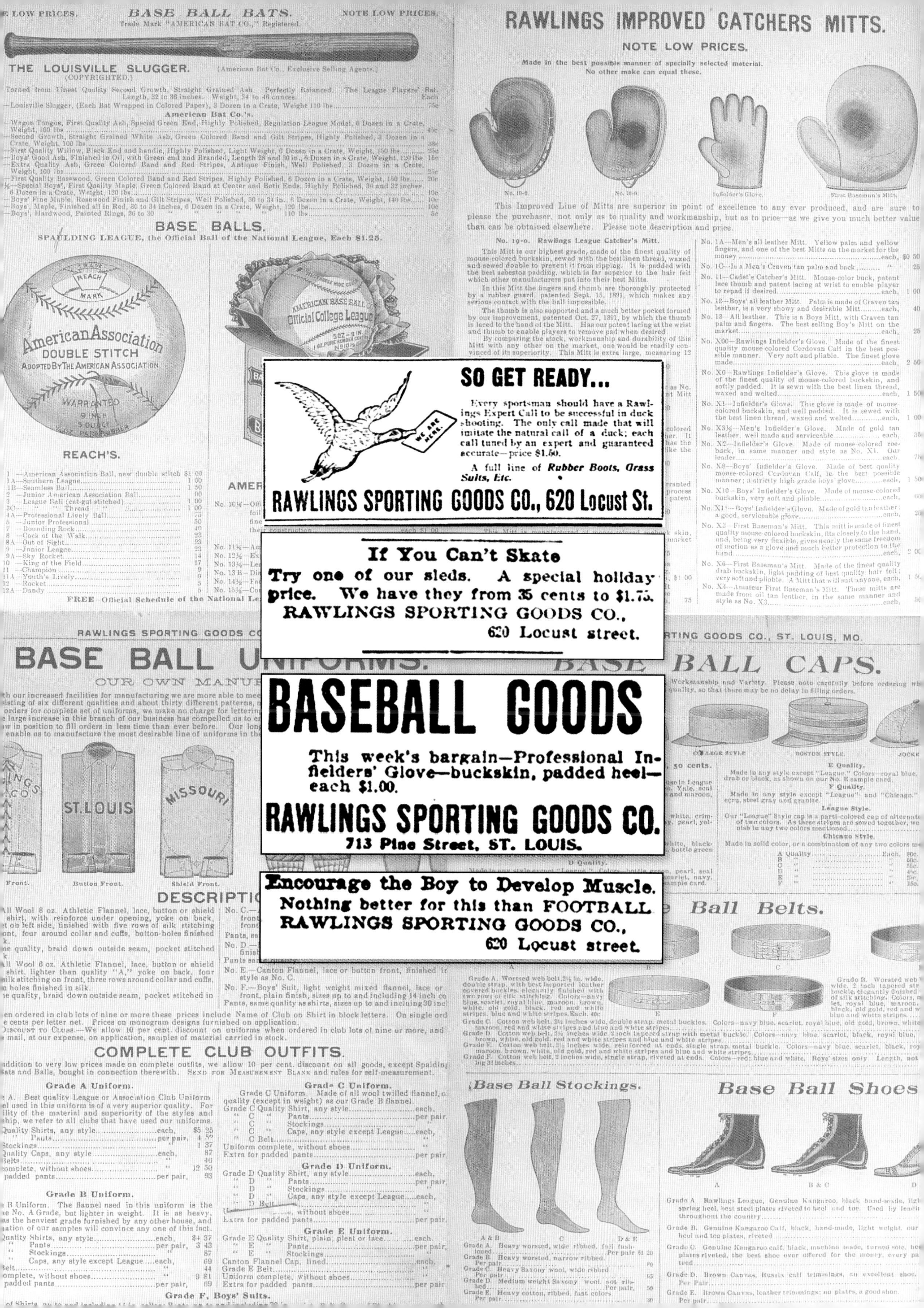
SO GET READY...
Every sportsman should have a Rawlings Expert Call to be successful in duck shooting. The only call made that will imitate the natural call of a duck; each call tuned by an expert and guaranteed accurate—price $1.50.
A full line of Rubber Boots, Grass Suits, Etc.
RAWLINGS SPORTING GOODS CO., 620 Locust St.
If You Can't Skate
Try one of our sleds. A special holiday price. We have they from 35 cents to $1.75.
RAWLINGS SPORTING GOODS CO.,
620 Locust street.
BASEBALL GOODS
This week's bargain—Professional Infielders' Glove—buckskin, padded heel—each $1.00.
RAWLINGS SPORTING GOODS CO.
713 Pine Street, ST. LOUIS.
Encourage the Boy to Develop Muscle.
Nothing better for this than FOOTBALL
RAWLINGS SPORTING GOODS CO.,
620 Locust street.
BASE BALL BATS.
THE LOUISVILLE SLUGGER.
RAWLINGS IMPROVED CATCHERS MITTS.
NOTE LOW PRICES.
BASE BALLS.
BASE BALL UNIFORMS.
BASE BALL CAPS.
COMPLETE CLUB OUTFITS.
Base Ball Belts.
Base Ball Stockings.
Base Ball Shoes

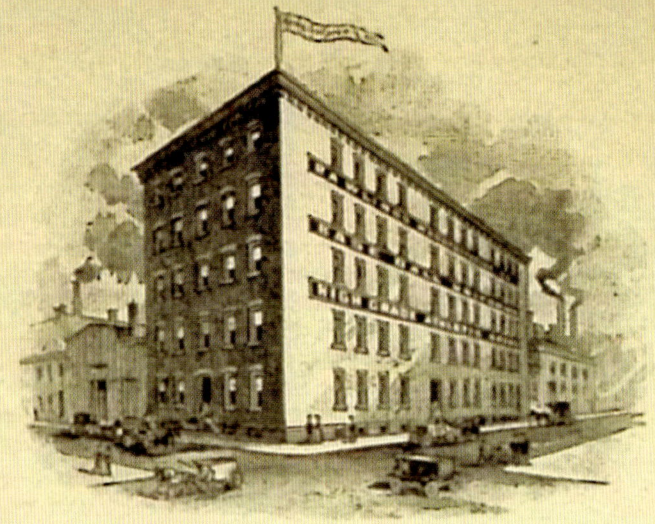

N. W. CORNER LUCAS AVE. AND TWENTY-THIRD ST.

IN presenting this catalogue of Base Ball and Athletic Goods, we desire to briefly summarize the reasons why our goods are above the ordinary and excel in the various particulars which determine quality.

Our many years of experience in the manufacture of these goods has impressed us with the idea that the best is none to good. Therefore, quality is absolutely the first consideration.

We use only the best materials obtainable, and employ only skilled labor of the highest class, and by keeping in close touch with the noted players and users, we are not only enabled to design our goods in an authentic manner, but also to interpret the trend of requirements, and give to our models an individuality not encountered in other makes. The result is quality, quality of design, of materials, of workmanship, and finish.

QUALITY IS OUR MOTTO

Rawlings Manufacturing Co.

SAINT LOUIS, MO., U. S. A.

Rawlings included its company mission statement in a 1908 catalog.

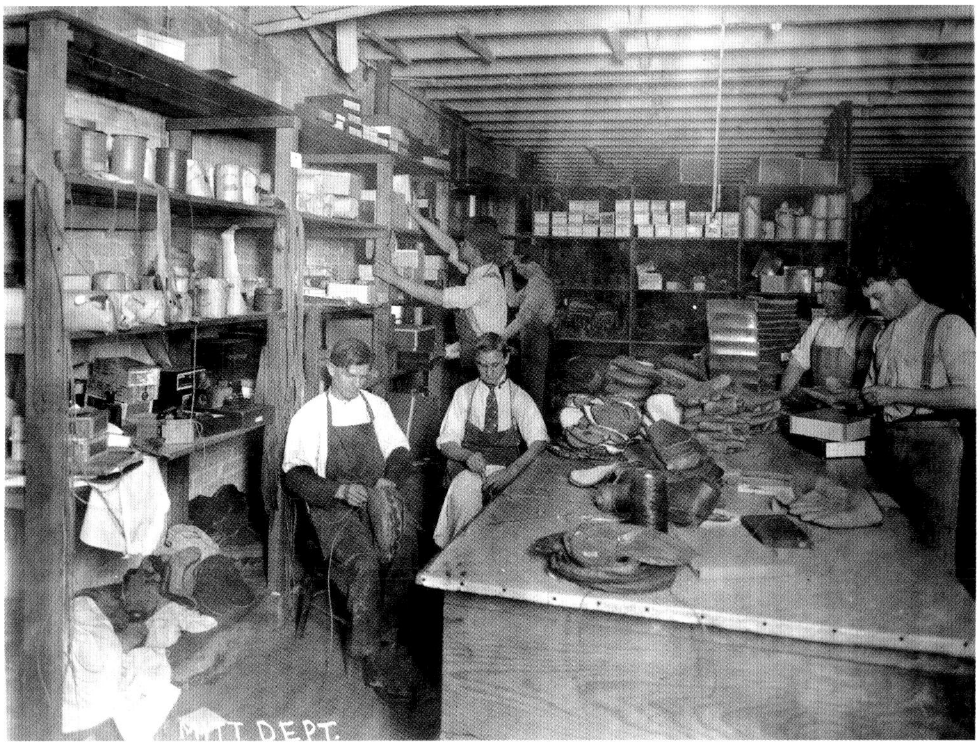

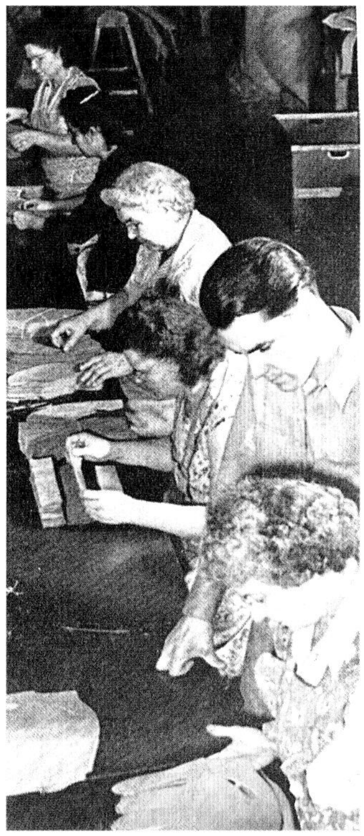

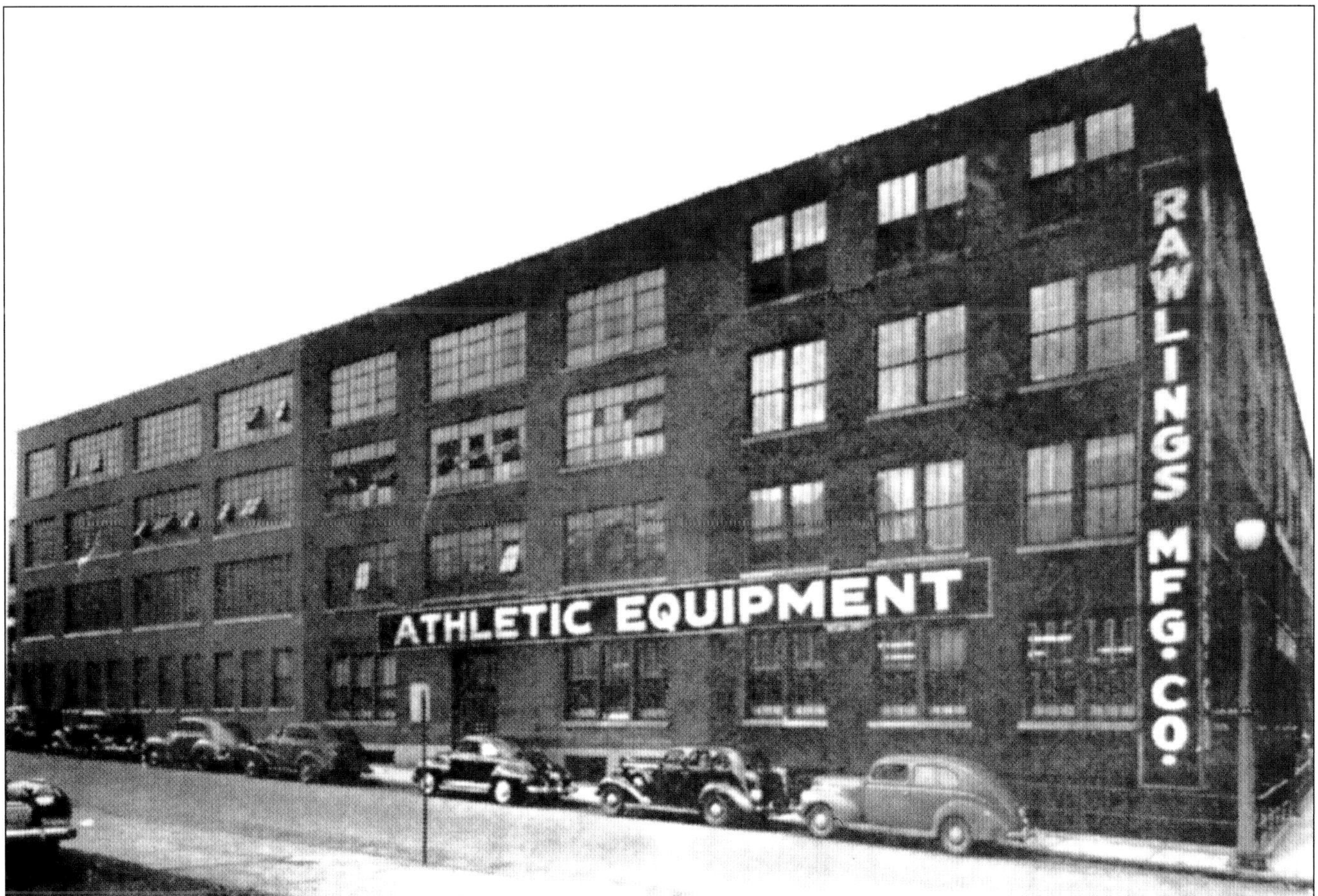

A Rawlings team is hard at work in the mitt department in the 1920s (top left). Inspectors carefully check all cuts of leather for bruises, scars, and uniform thickness before using them to make gloves (top right). The main Rawlings plant (above) was located at Lucas Avenue and 23rd Street in St. Louis for more than 50 years.

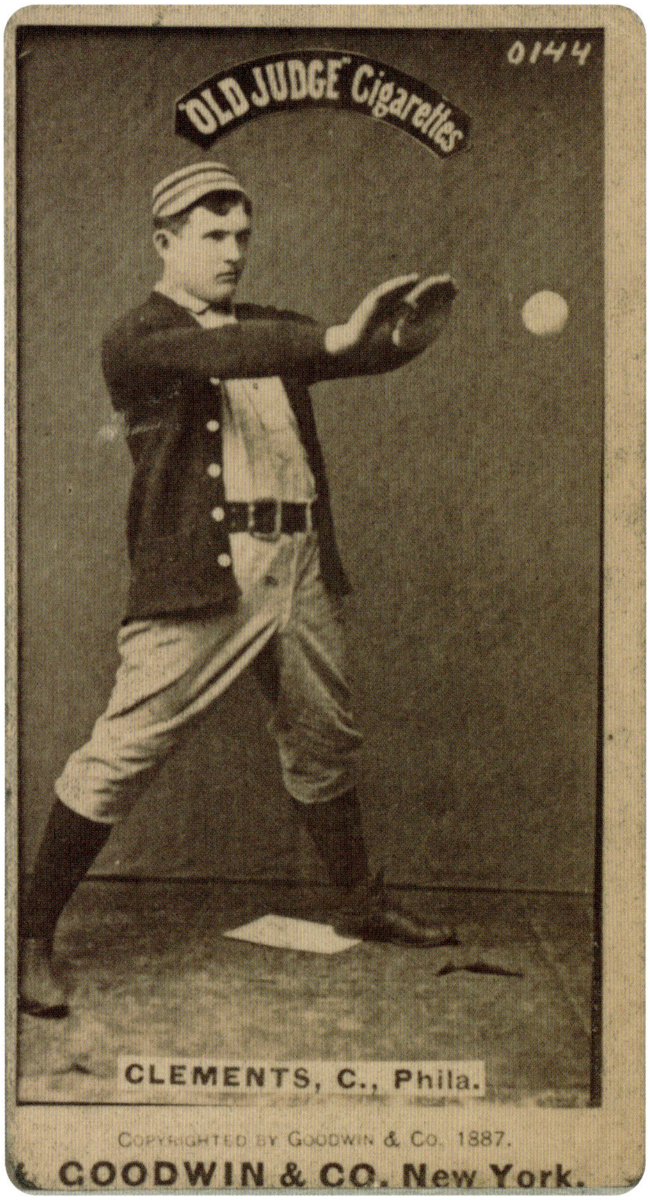

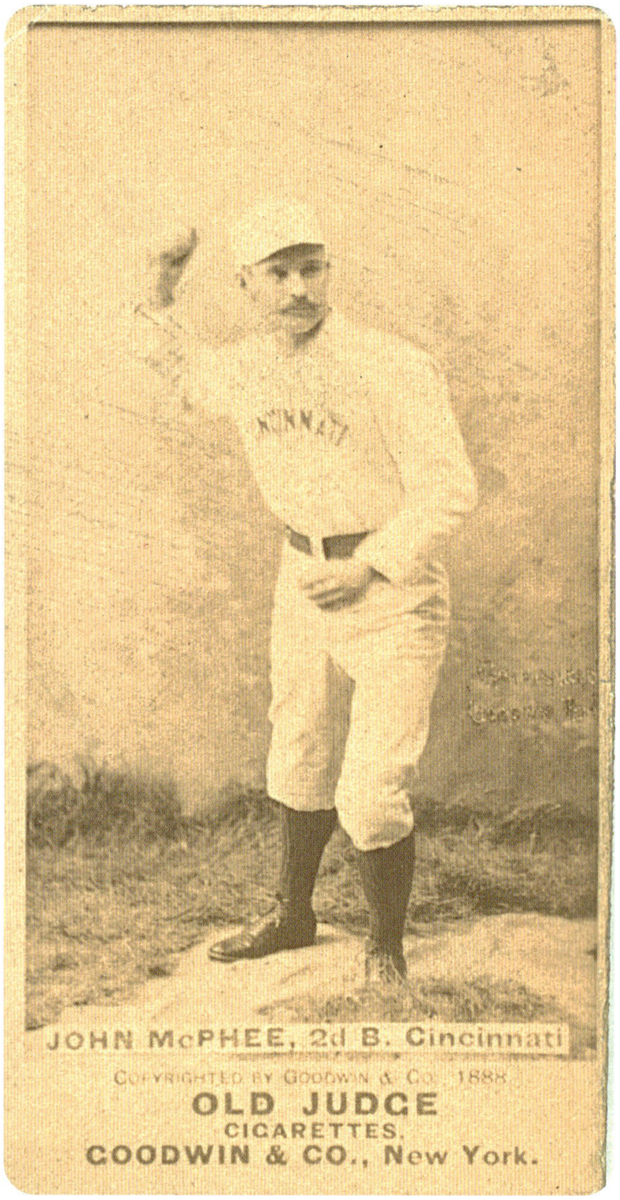

A baseball card featuring Philadelphia Quakers catcher Jack Clements (above, left), circa 1887, illustrates how catchers used to play standing up away from home plate, with no glove or equipment, waiting to catch the pitch on the bounce. Future Hall of Famer John "Bid" McPhee (above, right), second baseman for the Cincinnati Red Stockings, played most of his 18-year career without a glove.

BASEBALL GLOVES AND THE RAWLINGS LEGACY

Throughout its early history, baseball experienced several periods of change as it transformed into the game enjoyed by fans today. Although the basics of the game—throwing a ball, hitting a ball, catching a ball, and running the bases—remain the same, there were many innovations along the way. One was the development of the padded baseball glove. In the early years, baseball players were looked upon as tough "he-men." Swollen hands and knuckles, often wringing in pain, became a standard part of the game simply because players did not have any protection on their hands. Future Hall of Famer John "Bid" McPhee noted the impacts of gloveless play: "True, hot-hit balls do sting a little at the opening of the season, but after you get used to it there is no trouble on that score." That all changed on June 28, 1870, when Doug Allison—the catcher on baseball's first professional team, the Cincinnati Red Stockings—became the earliest known player to use an ad hoc baseball glove when he donned buckskin mittens to protect his hands during a game.

Despite the protection it offered, wearing a glove was not fully and immediately accepted. Players like Allison became a target for ridicule by fans and opposing teams. There is no record of a player other than Allison wearing a glove for another five years. That is, until the St. Louis Brown Stockings' Charlie Waitt began playing first base in the National Association in 1875. Waitt didn't want to feel the sting of the hard tosses across the infield, so he wore a thin, half-fingered, unpadded, flesh-colored glove. The glove's disguise didn't work and, like Allison, Waitt was teased and called a sissy. Two years later, the Chicago White Stockings' pitcher Albert Spalding moved over to first base and began wearing a glove to protect his hands. Others soon followed, and wearing a glove for protection became more popular. For the next several decades, the design of baseball gloves was for the protection of players'

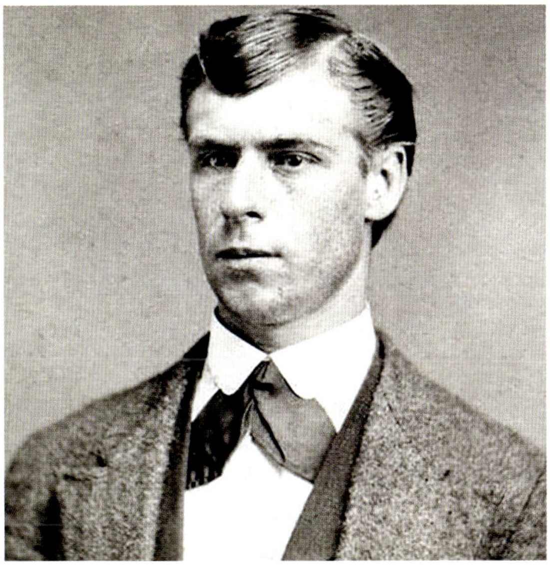

Doug Allison (right) was the earliest known player to try using a type of baseball glove when he donned buckskin mittens to protect his hands during a game in 1870.

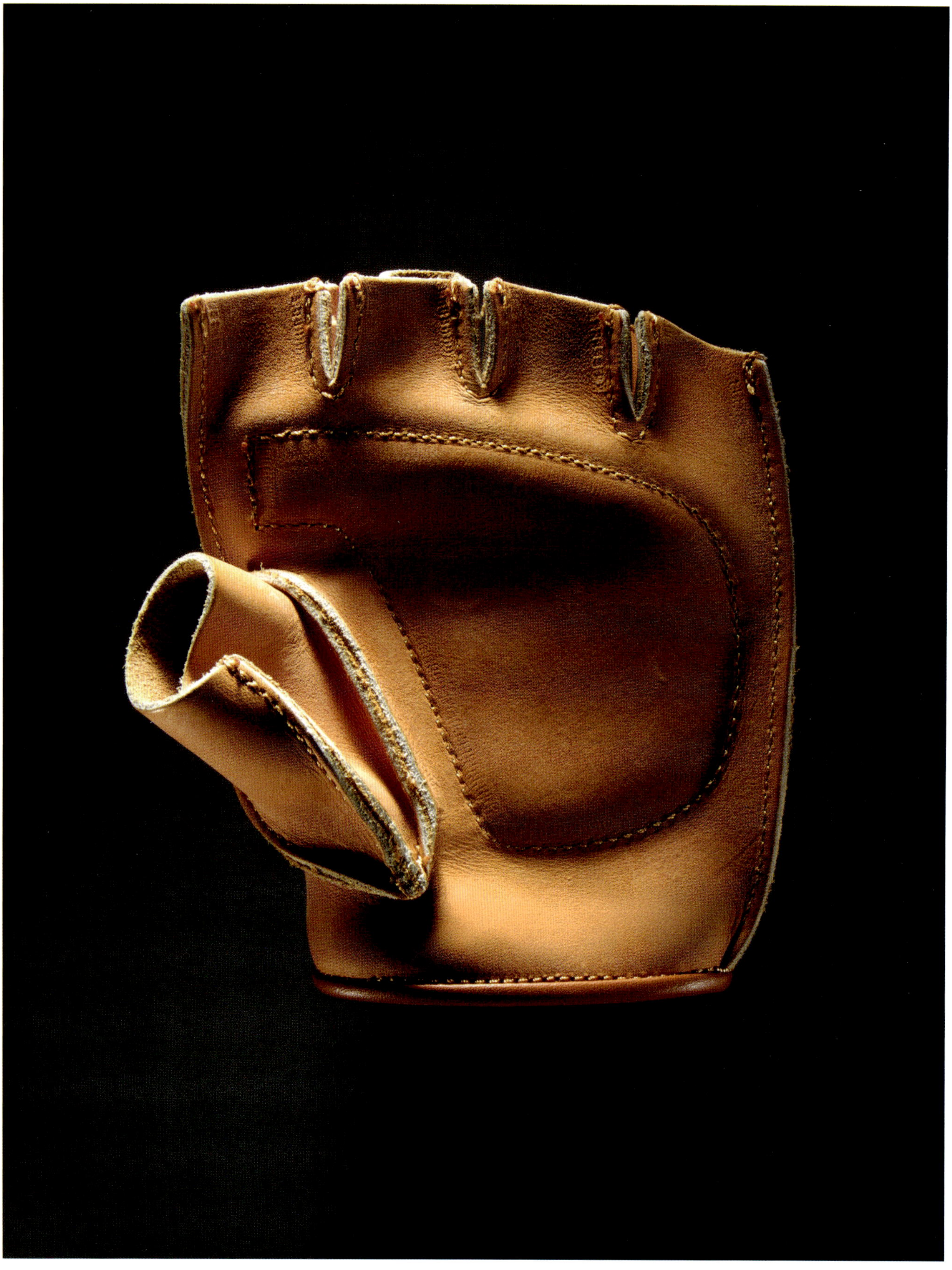

Baseball's first gloves were fingerless but offered padding for the palm of the hand. Rawlings submitted a patent for this glove in 1885.

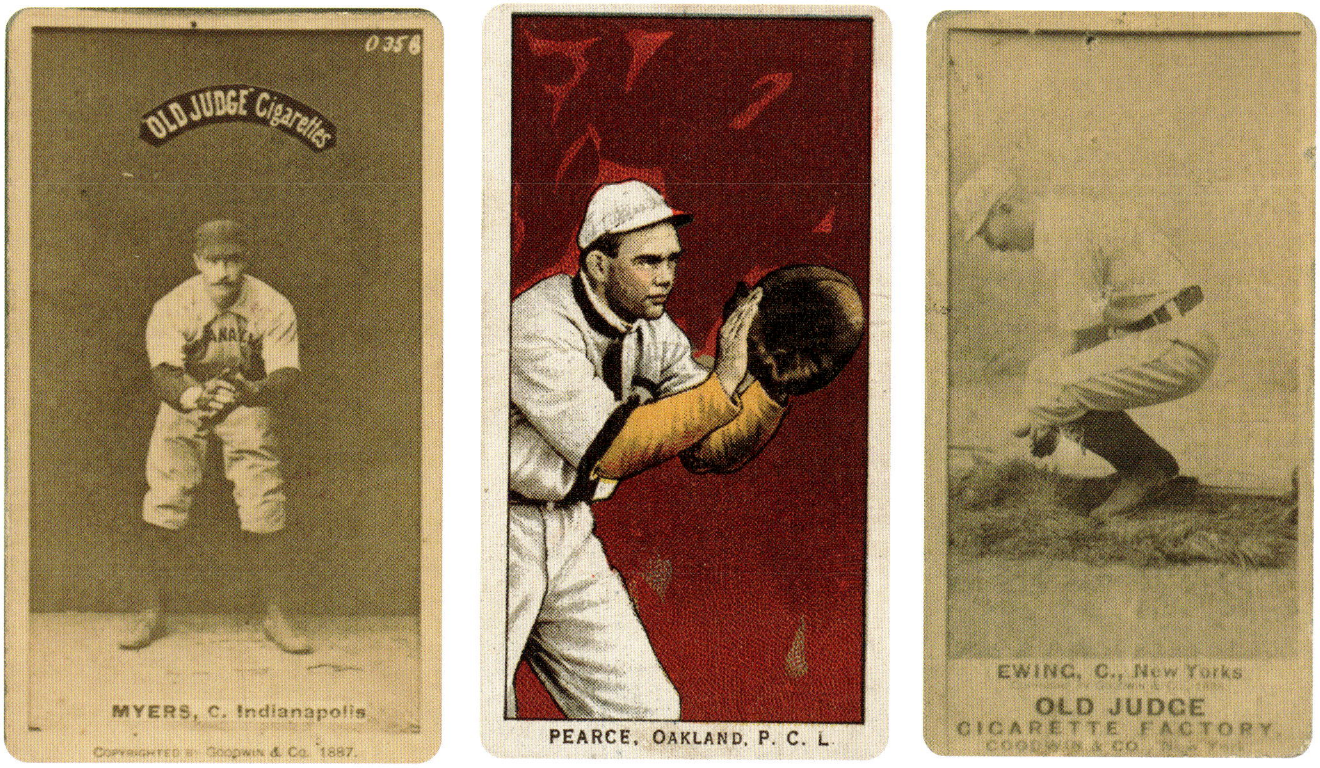

An 1887 Old Judge playing card featuring the Indianapolis Hoosiers' George Myers (above, left) shows the catcher with fingerless gloves on both hands. A 1911 Obak tobacco card featuring the Oakland Oaks' Bunny Pearce (above, middle) shows the catcher using a large, pillow-style mitt. Another 1887 Old Judge playing card features the New York Giants' Buck Ewing (above, right), who was one of the firsts to switch from an unpadded glove to a pillow-style mitt.

hands rather than improved catching. McPhee's Hall of Fame plaque recognizes him as "one of the 19th century's premier second basemen. He was a standout fielder despite playing barehanded for most of his 18-year career." He was one of the last players to start wearing a glove, and when he did in 1896, he set a record for fielding percentage at his position.

The introduction of gloves not only enhanced safety and deterred injuries but also helped revolutionize the game. With the glove's protection, catchers could position themselves directly behind the batter in lieu of standing 20 or more feet behind the plate. Closing that gap helped teams curtail base runners from stealing. In the early days, catchers often wore gloves on both hands to absorb the sting of pitches on their palms. But unlike modern gloves, the gloves of this era were fingerless to allow a better grip on the received ball and allow more accurate throws.

As the game continued to change, so did its rules. Beginning in 1880, catchers had to catch the pitch on the fly in order to register an out on a third strike. In 1891, the National League (NL) changed its official rules to allow large, padded mitts to be used by catchers. Buck Ewing—the first catcher inducted into the Hall of Fame, in 1939—was among the first to switch from an unpadded glove to the pillow-style mitt that would become the standard for decades to come.

And catching was not the only position that felt the impact of players wearing gloves. A catcher wearing a glove behind the plate allowed pitchers to begin throwing much harder

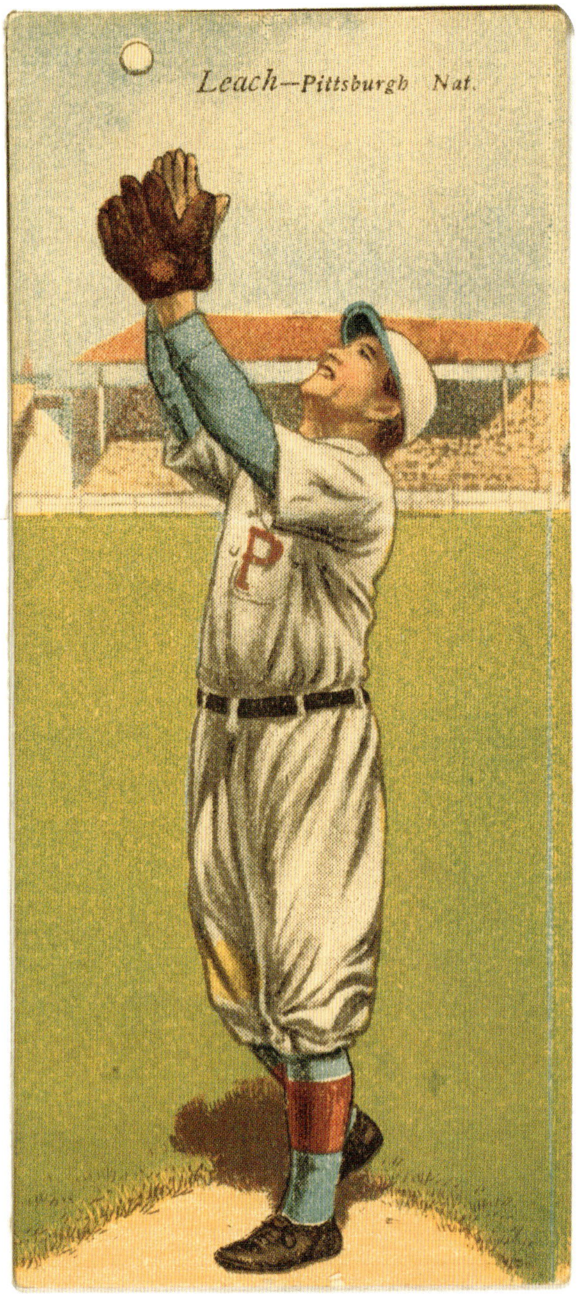

A 1911 T201 (Mecca Double Folders) tobacco card shows the Pittsburgh Pirates' Tommy Leach catching a fly ball.

once they could throw overhand. In the game's earliest years, pitching was exclusively underhanded. The rule had been officially formalized in 1845 in the Knickerbocker Rules, baseball's first standardized guidelines, which were written primarily by Cartwright. The rules mandated that pitchers "pitch" the ball from below their waist, with a stiff elbow and wrist, much like pitching horseshoes. There was no change to that rule until 1884, when the NL lifted the ban on overhand pitching.

In time, fielders also began using gloves, which subsequently led to better defensive play, lower-scoring games, and other rule changes. Prior to an 1864 rule change, baseball allowed a one-bounce out. Fielders (not yet wearing gloves) had a choice on how to catch a batted ball for an out. While running to catch batted balls in the air, a fielder could either attempt to catch the ball on the fly with their bare hands or wait for it to take a singular (and often safer to the hand) bounce first. Both counted as an out. The rule change that allowed only fly balls caught in the air to be an out further supported the adoption of the baseball glove in the field. And once players were wearing gloves, other rules soon followed. For example, the infield fly rule, introduced in 1895, assumed that infielders wearing gloves would make the catch and aimed to protect base runners from infielders purposely dropping balls to force a double play. Due to the use of gloves and many of these rule changes, the game of baseball had begun to lose some of its excitement.

To reinvent itself in 1920, baseball introduced a new set of rule changes to stimulate more offense. These actions led to what became known as the Live Ball Era. Cork-centered baseballs were introduced to allow balls to be hit harder and farther. This led to an increased number of hits in games. Balls were now replaced within games at the first sign of wear; new, clean balls were easier for hitters to see and thus hit. Another rule change eliminated the defacing, scuffing, and use of foreign substances by pitchers on the mound. (The new rule grandfathered in 17 pitchers who were still allowed to throw "doctored" pitches until they retired.) All these changes enhanced baseball's offensive productivity, leading to the evolution of new glove models to offset some of these changes and improve the game's defense.

Rules regulating the size and style of baseball gloves were introduced in 1895, limiting glove size for the first time—except for catchers and first basemen. The game was becoming more specialized by position, and the different positions soon demanded different glove models to define their defensive benefits. Catchers required significantly more padding to absorb the impact of harder throws, while infielders sought smaller gloves with a shallow pocket to allow faster transfers when making a quick throw for an out. Outfielders, on the other hand, sought larger gloves with a deeper pocket to extend their reach for fly-ball catches. Any new models introduced were required to fall within the size limitations set by MLB.

One of the most often asked questions about baseball rules involves players leaving their gloves on the field of play between innings. Prior to the rule change in 1954, corner infielders

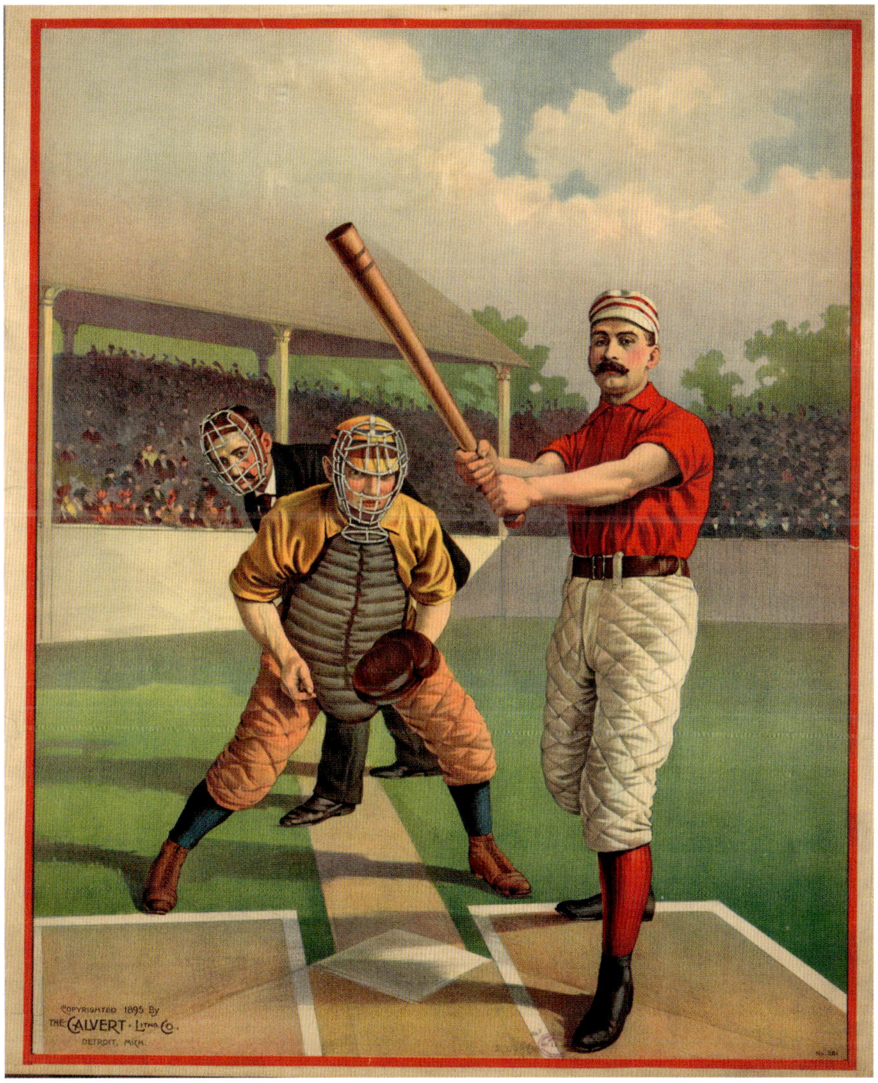

A sports poster from 1895 shows a batter standing at home plate, with the catcher and umpire awaiting the pitch. The grandstand is visible in the background.

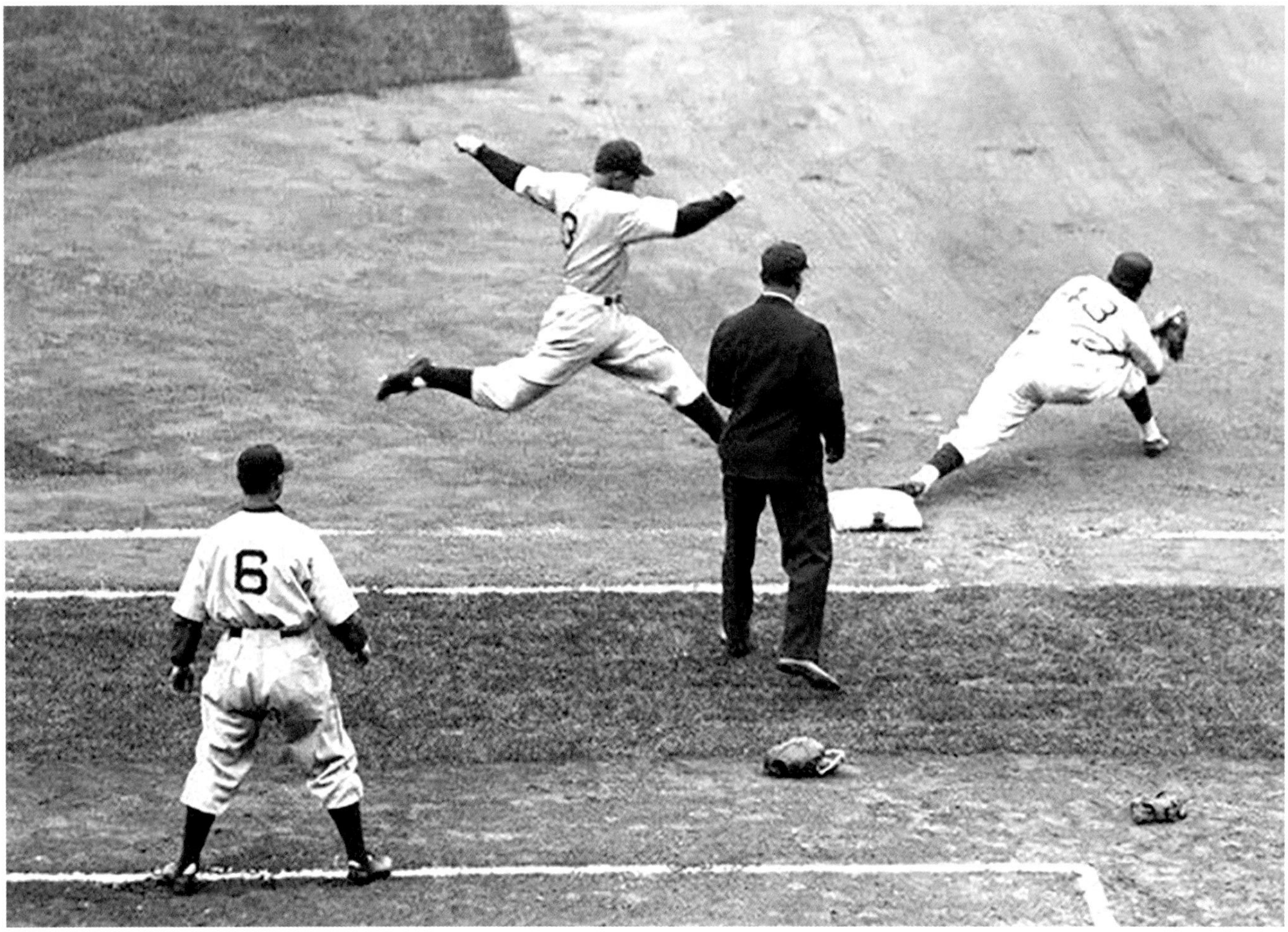

In the fourth game of the 1935 World Series at Wrigley Field, the Detroit Tigers' Mickey Cochrane runs to first base as the Chicago Cubs' Phil Cavarretta reaches out to catch the throw. Note that the Tigers' gloves were left on the field while they were at bat. Per a rule change in 1954, this practice is no longer allowed.

would toss their gloves in foul territory near the bases, while middle infielders would throw theirs in the middle of the diamond just off the infield dirt. Outfielders would toss their gloves on the outfield grass in fair play near the warning track. Catchers and pitchers were the only fielders who carried their gloves into the dugout. The newly adopted rule (3.10 Equipment on the Field) stated: "Members of the offensive team shall carry all gloves and other equipment off the field and to the dugout while their team is at bat. No equipment shall be left lying on the field, either in fair or foul territory."

To meet the growing need for protection, Rawlings came out with the original leather hand-wrap model glove that could be worn on either hand and was often worn on both hands. On September 8, 1885, George Rawlings was issued a patent for his company's padded glove. The patent document stated: "The glove is intended especially for the use of base-ball players and cricketers, the pads being for the prevention of the bruising of the hands when catching the ball."

While baseball was becoming a national sport, Rawlings began producing gloves and mitts to supply the local amateur and professional baseball organizations in its region long before expanding nationally. That explains why many of its first advertisements in newspapers and company catalogs featured gloves used by and designed for local players from the St. Louis Browns and Cardinals. Shortly after the calendar flipped to the 20th century, the Rawlings catalog was filled with glove models named after the game's best MLB players and also offered personal testimonials of the gloves' ease of play and excellence. George and Alfred Rawlings' sporting goods store had evolved into a national brand supporting baseball across the country. And as that brand evolved, so did the different types and models of gloves the company offered. Today, Rawlings

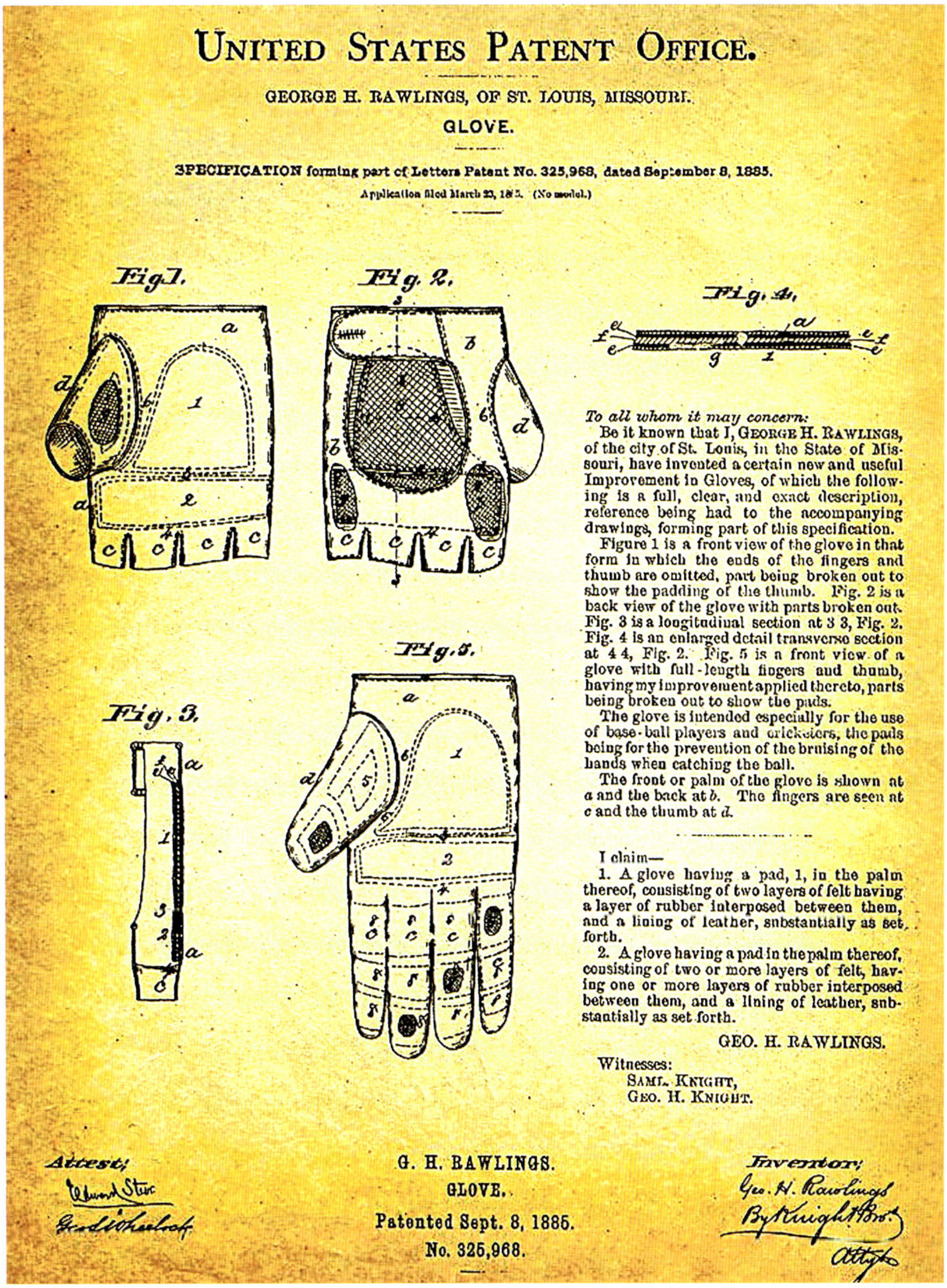

UNITED STATES PATENT OFFICE.

GEORGE H. RAWLINGS, OF ST. LOUIS, MISSOURI.

GLOVE.

SPECIFICATION forming part of Letters Patent No. 325,968, dated September 8, 1885.

Application filed March 23, 1885. (No model.)

To all whom it may concern:

Be it known that I, GEORGE H. RAWLINGS, of the city of St. Louis, in the State of Missouri, have invented a certain new and useful Improvement in Gloves, of which the following is a full, clear, and exact description, reference being had to the accompanying drawings, forming part of this specification.

Figure 1 is a front view of the glove in that form in which the ends of the fingers and thumb are omitted, part being broken out to show the padding of the thumb. Fig. 2 is a back view of the glove with parts broken out. Fig. 3 is a longitudinal section at 3 3, Fig. 2. Fig. 4 is an enlarged detail transverse section at 4 4, Fig. 2. Fig. 5 is a front view of a glove with full-length fingers and thumb, having my improvement applied thereto, parts being broken out to show the pads.

The glove is intended especially for the use of base-ball players and cricketers, the pads being for the prevention of the bruising of the hands when catching the ball.

The front or palm of the glove is shown at *a* and the back at *b*. The fingers are seen at *c* and the thumb at *d*.

I claim—

1. A glove having a pad, 1, in the palm thereof, consisting of two layers of felt having a layer of rubber interposed between them, and a lining of leather, substantially as set forth.

2. A glove having a pad in the palm thereof, consisting of two or more layers of felt, having one or more layers of rubber interposed between them, and a lining of leather, substantially as set forth.

GEO. H. RAWLINGS.

Witnesses:
SAML. KNIGHT,
GEO. H. KNIGHT.

G. H. RAWLINGS.
GLOVE.
Patented Sept. 8, 1885.
No. 325,968.

On September 8, 1885, George Rawlings was issued a patent for his company's padded glove, and the Rawlings legacy began.

gloves remain the most popular brand used among MLB players. They continue to be known for their high-quality leather, excellent craftsmanship, and a wide variety of models catering to different positions and playing styles.

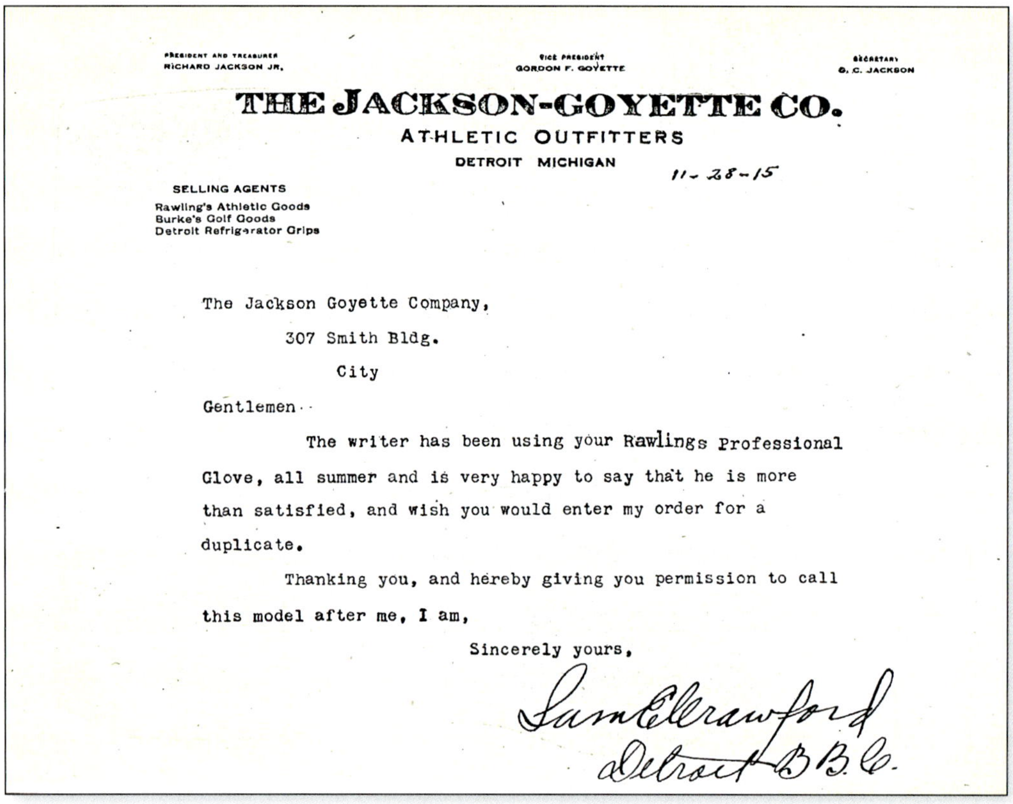

PRESIDENT AND TREASURER RICHARD JACKSON JR. — VICE PRESIDENT GORDON F. GOYETTE — SECRETARY G. C. JACKSON

THE JACKSON-GOYETTE CO.
ATHLETIC OUTFITTERS
DETROIT MICHIGAN

11-28-15

SELLING AGENTS
Rawling's Athletic Goods
Burke's Golf Goods
Detroit Refrigerator Grips

The Jackson Goyette Company,
307 Smith Bldg.
City

Gentlemen--

The writer has been using your Rawlings Professional Glove, all summer and is very happy to say that he is more than satisfied, and wish you would enter my order for a duplicate.

Thanking you, and hereby giving you permission to call this model after me, I am,

Sincerely yours,

Sam Crawford
Detroit B.B.C.

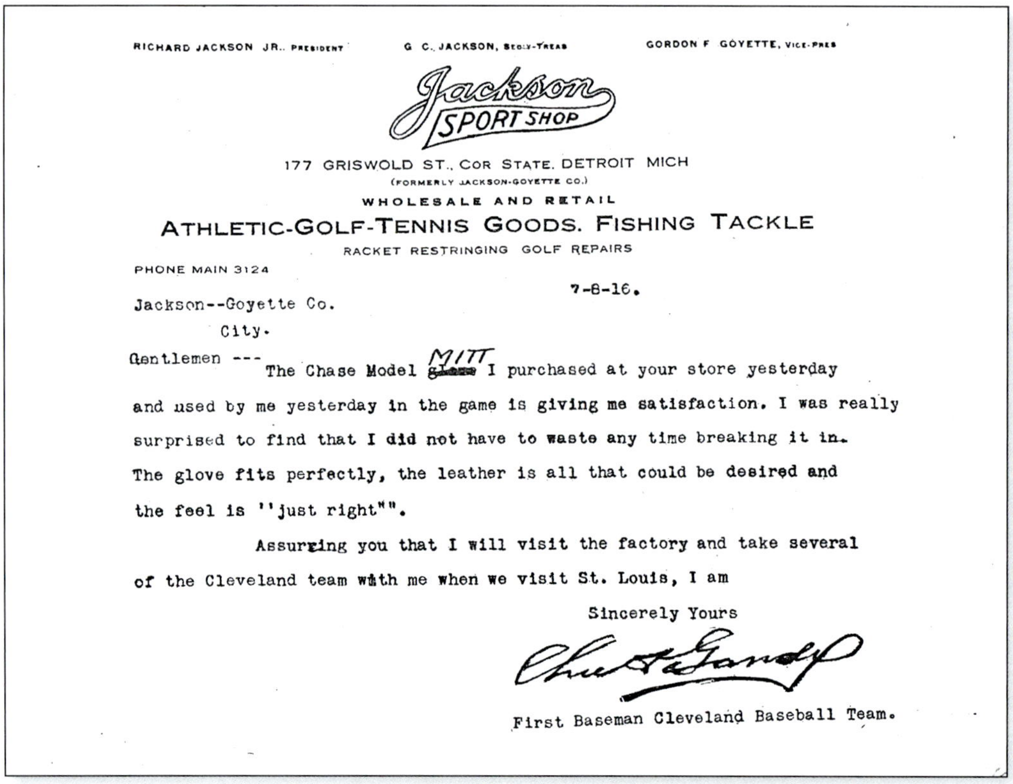

RICHARD JACKSON JR., PRESIDENT — G. C. JACKSON, SEC'Y-TREAS — GORDON F. GOYETTE, VICE-PRES

Jackson SPORT SHOP

177 GRISWOLD ST., COR STATE. DETROIT MICH
(FORMERLY JACKSON-GOYETTE CO.)
WHOLESALE AND RETAIL
ATHLETIC-GOLF-TENNIS GOODS. FISHING TACKLE
RACKET RESTRINGING GOLF REPAIRS
PHONE MAIN 3124

7-8-16.

Jackson--Goyette Co.
City.

Gentlemen --- The Chase Model ~~glove~~ MITT I purchased at your store yesterday and used by me yesterday in the game is giving me satisfaction. I was really surprised to find that I did not have to waste any time breaking it in. The glove fits perfectly, the leather is all that could be desired and the feel is ''just right"".

Assuring you that I will visit the factory and take several of the Cleveland team with me when we visit St. Louis, I am

Sincerely Yours

Chick Gandil

First Baseman Cleveland Baseball Team.

In 1915, the Detroit Tigers' Hall of Fame center fielder Sam Crawford wrote to indicate his satisfaction with his Rawlings glove and placed another order (left). In 1916, the Cleveland Indians' Chick Gandil wrote of his satisfaction with the Hal Chase model first baseman's mitt and promised to bring his teammates to the Rawlings factory on their next trip to St. Louis (bottom).

NEW DECADES AND NEW GLOVES

Over the years, there have been countless new models of gloves. Some were merely an enhancement of a previous model, while others were revolutionary in their design and purpose. But glove designs evolved slowly over the first century after they were introduced. Decades went by with gloves looking the same. The Rawlings Bill Doak glove, for example, was a standard favorite from 1919 until it was phased out in the mid-1940s. Was it because the players liked what they had? Or were they superstitious and avoided change for that reason?

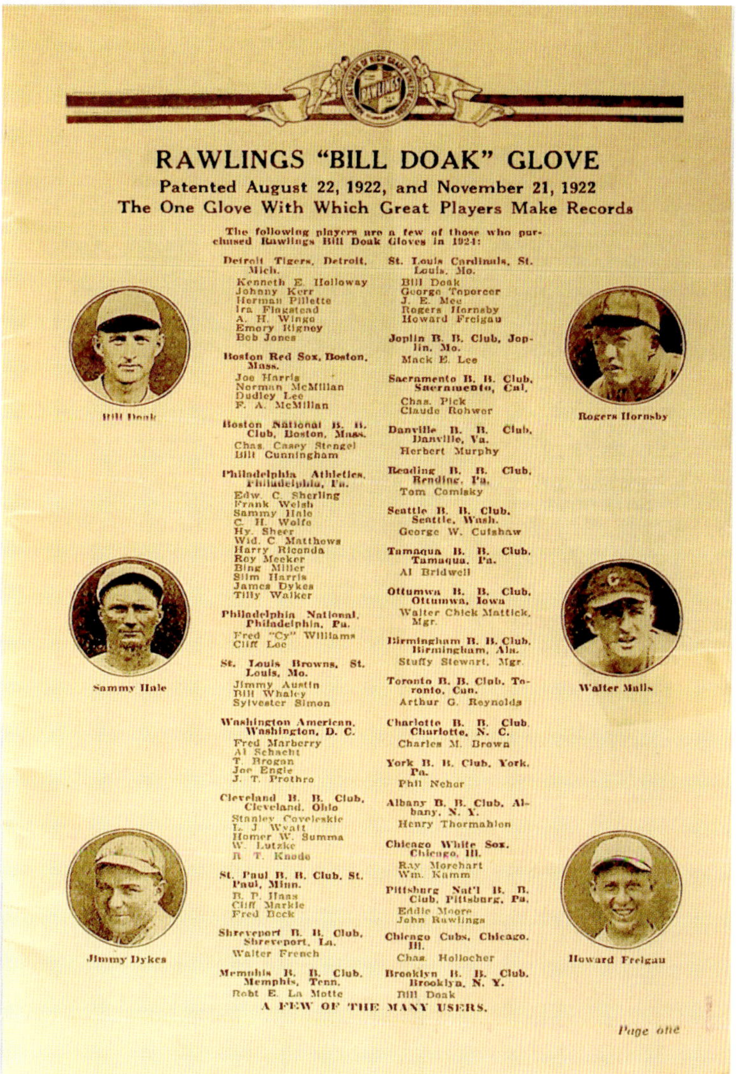

RAWLINGS "BILL DOAK" GLOVE

Patented August 22, 1922, and November 21, 1922

The One Glove With Which Great Players Make Records

The following players are a few of those who purchased Rawlings Bill Doak Gloves in 1924:

Detroit Tigers, Detroit, Mich.
Kenneth E. Holloway
Johnny Kerr
Herman Pillette
Ira Flagstead
A. H. Wingo
Emory Rigney
Bob Jones

Boston Red Sox, Boston, Mass.
Joe Harris
Norman McMillan
Dudley Lee
F. A. McMillan

Boston National B. B. Club, Boston, Mass.
Chas. Casey Stengel
Bill Cunningham

Philadelphia Athletics, Philadelphia, Pa.
Edw. C. Sherling
Frank Welsh
Sammy Hale
C. H. Wolfe
Hy. Sheer
Wid. C. Matthews
Harry Riconda
Roy Meeker
Bing Miller
Slim Harris
James Dykes
Tilly Walker

Philadelphia National, Philadelphia, Pa.
Fred "Cy" Williams
Cliff Lee

St. Louis Browns, St. Louis, Mo.
Jimmy Austin
Bill Whaley
Sylvester Simon

Washington American, Washington, D. C.
Fred Marberry
Al Schacht
T. Brogan
Joe Engle
J. T. Prothro

Cleveland B. B. Club, Cleveland, Ohio
Stanley Coveleskie
L. J. Wyatt
Homer W. Summa
W. Lutzke
R. T. Knode

St. Paul B. B. Club, St. Paul, Minn.
B. P. Haas
Cliff Markle
Fred Beck

Shreveport B. B. Club, Shreveport, La.
Walter French

Memphis B. B. Club, Memphis, Tenn.
Robt E. La Motte

St. Louis Cardinals, St. Louis, Mo.
Bill Doak
George Toporcer
J. E. Mee
Rogers Hornsby
Howard Freigau

Joplin B. B. Club, Joplin, Mo.
Mack E. Lee

Sacramento B. B. Club, Sacramento, Cal.
Chas. Pick
Claude Rohwer

Danville B. B. Club, Danville, Va.
Herbert Murphy

Reading B. B. Club, Reading, Pa.
Tom Comisky

Seattle B. B. Club, Seattle, Wash.
George W. Cutshaw

Tamaqua B. B. Club, Tamaqua, Pa.
Al Bridwell

Ottumwa B. B. Club, Ottumwa, Iowa
Walter Chick Mattick, Mgr.

Birmingham B. B. Club, Birmingham, Ala.
Stuffy Stewart, Mgr.

Toronto B. B. Club, Toronto, Can.
Arthur G. Reynolds

Charlotte B. B. Club, Charlotte, N. C.
Charles M. Brown

York B. B. Club, York, Pa.
Phil Nehor

Albany B. B. Club, Albany, N. Y.
Henry Thormahlen

Chicago White Sox, Chicago, Ill.
Ray Morehart
Wm. Kamm

Pittsburg Nat'l B. B. Club, Pittsburg, Pa.
Eddie Moore
John Rawlings

Chicago Cubs, Chicago, Ill.
Chas. Hollocher

Brooklyn B. B. Club, Brooklyn, N. Y.
Bill Doak

A FEW OF THE MANY USERS.

A mid-1920s Rawlings catalog listed major-league players by team, highlighting several who had purchased Bill Doak gloves in 1924.

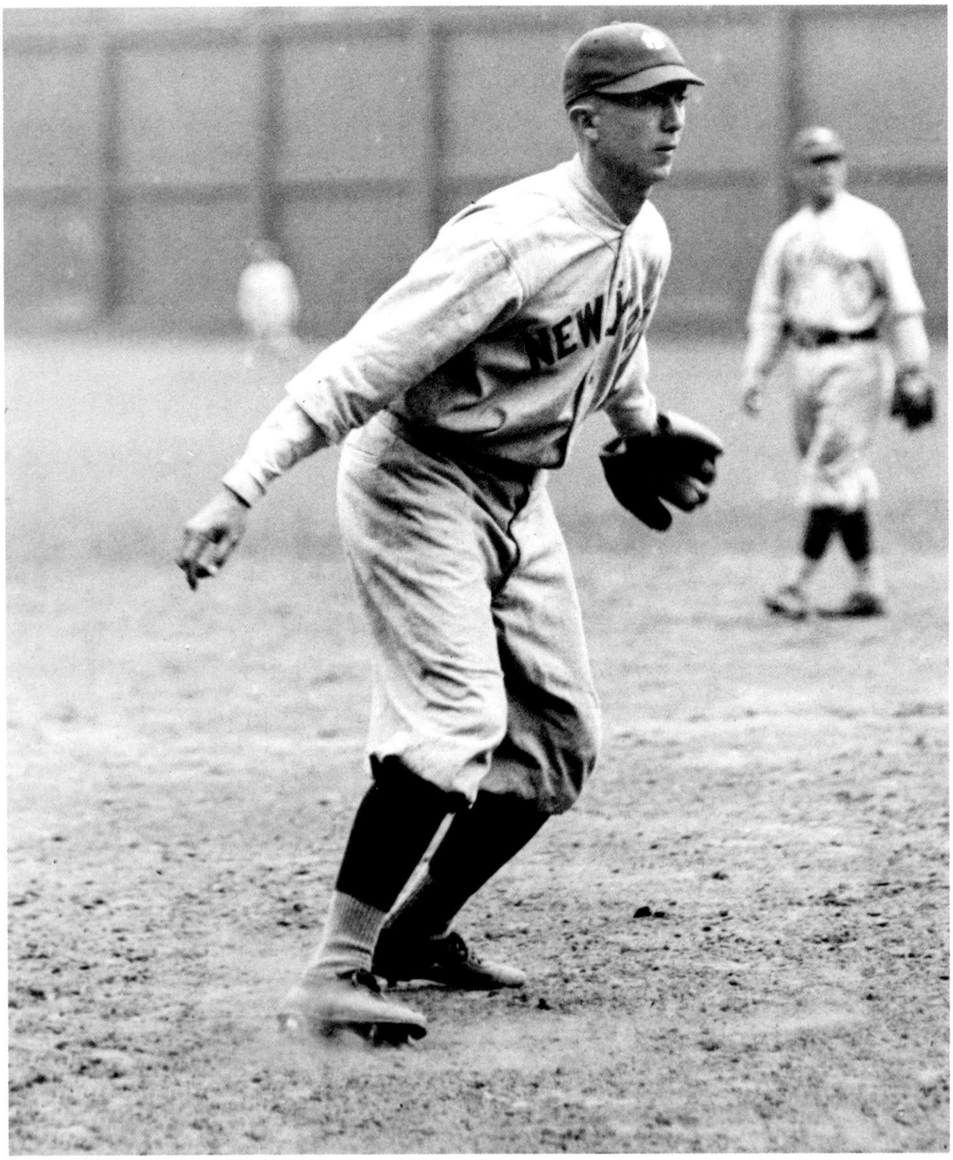

Third baseman and future Hall of Famer Frank Baker (left) of the New York Yankees was the top slugger of baseball's Deadball Era. He earned the moniker "Home Run Baker" from two clutch home runs that helped win Games Two and Three of the 1911 World Series. By 1910, the baseball glove had evolved to include padded fingers, as shown in this Rawlings glove of that era (opposite). It was another decade before lace was first used to connect the thumb and at least one finger to form a pocket to catch the ball.

Today's players and fans look back in amazement, wondering how anyone ever played the game with those early gloves—but they did and they were successful. Back in the 1950s, the great defensive third baseman Brooks Robinson met one of the game's earliest stars, Hall of Fame third baseman Frank Baker, at a stadium event. Baker was carrying one of the gloves he had used in his day. Robinson, the recipient of 16 Gold Glove Awards, said, "I don't know how the hell they caught anything with those gloves, honest to God. The fingers were separated, no lacing there, unbelievable." Like Robinson, it's easy to look back at those early gloves and wonder why they were made like that. For example, when the first lacing was introduced to connect the thumb to the first finger, why weren't all the fingers laced together to create an even better pocket?

By 1901, Rawlings had begun producing fielder's mitts covering all five fingers and padded in soft, pliable horsehide and calf leather. The glove was like an oversized winter mitten with no connectivity between the fingers and the thumb. It was soon enhanced with larger and heavier padding around the edges and on the wrist to increase durability and protection. There was, however, no defined pocket to capture the ball, which led to a saying that many kids constantly heard from their dads and coaches: "Use two hands when catching the ball." The purpose of these early

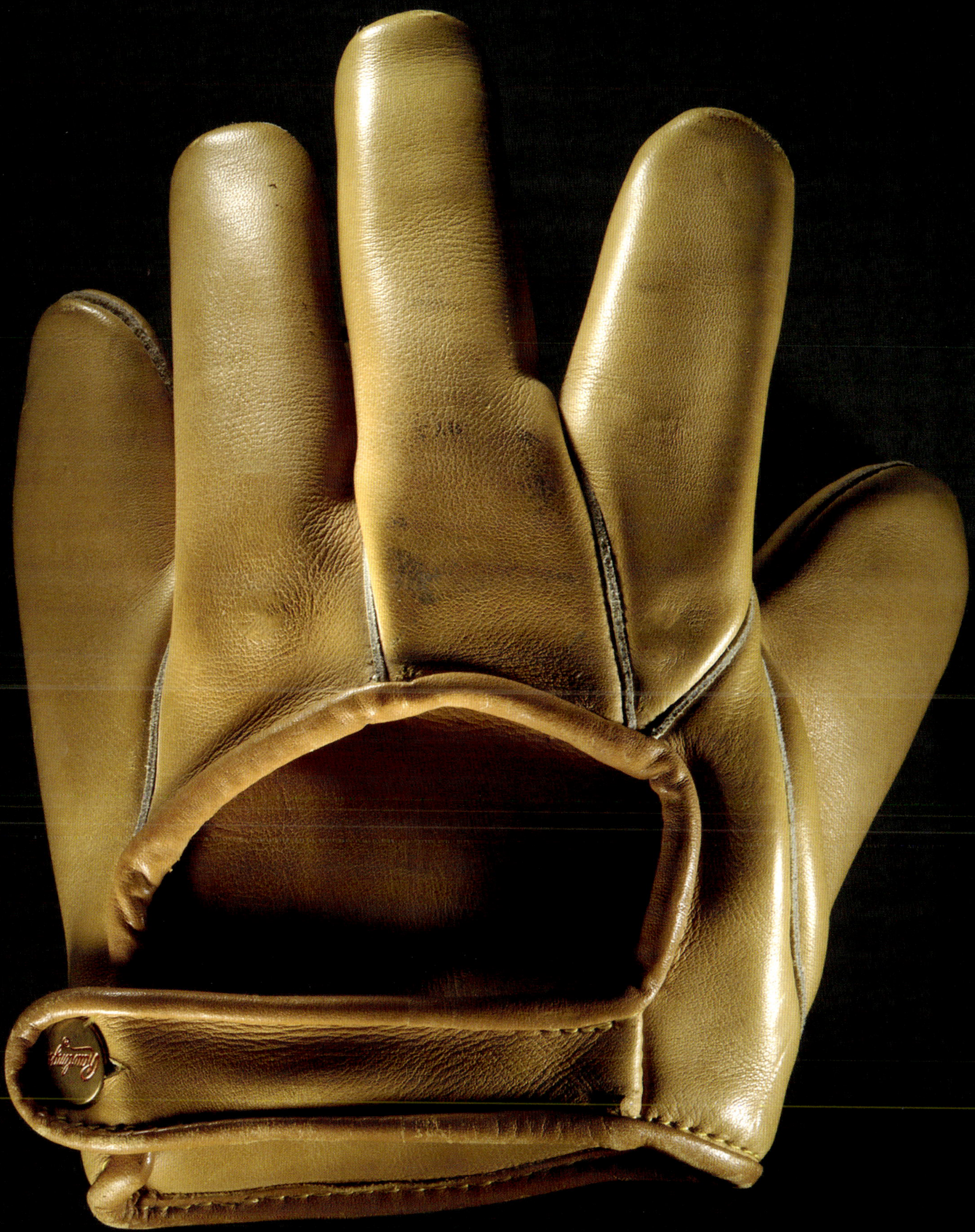

gloves was simply to stop the ball while the fielder's other hand would quickly grab and hold it. There were no one-handed catches with the gloves of this era.

In 1911, Rawlings introduced its newest glove, the Sure Catch. Also known as the Web-Fingered Glove, it offered a unique webbing made of a single piece of leather laced between the fingers, thumb, and palm. A decade later, the introduction of the Bill Doak glove revolutionized baseball with a built-in pocket created by attaching the thumb and forefinger together to form a web. The outside three fingers remained unattached and offered little assistance beyond stopping a ball and hopefully squeezing it into the pocket of the thumb and first finger. The glove became a popular standard for the next three decades. In 1933, Rawlings introduced a variation

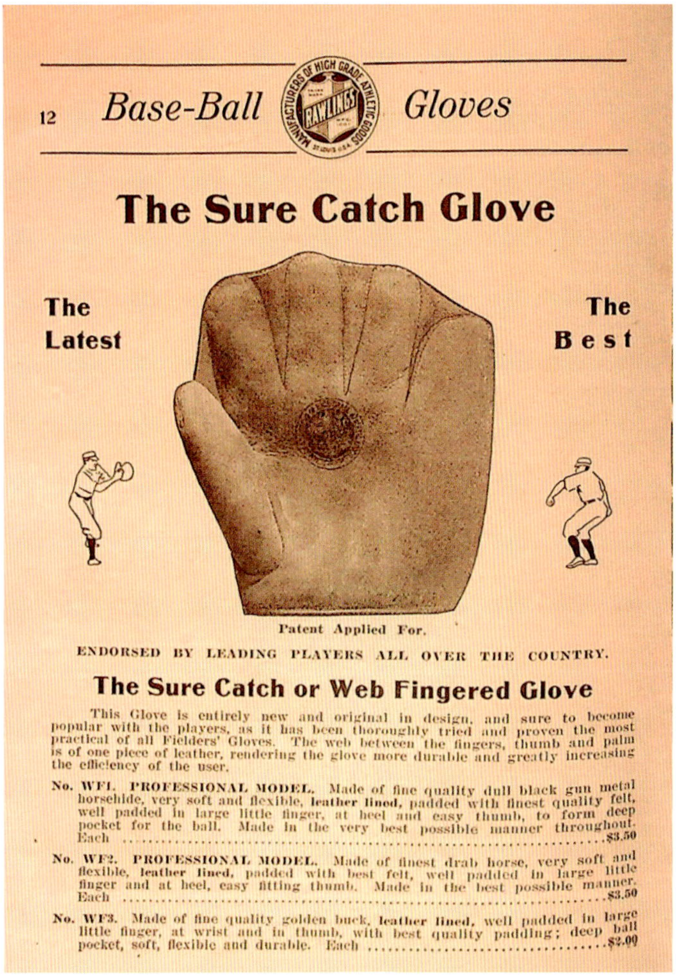

12 Base-Ball Gloves

The Sure Catch Glove

The Latest

The Best

Patent Applied For.

ENDORSED BY LEADING PLAYERS ALL OVER THE COUNTRY.

The Sure Catch or Web Fingered Glove

This Glove is entirely new and original in design, and sure to become popular with the players, as it has been thoroughly tried and proven the most practical of all Fielders' Gloves. The web between the fingers, thumb and palm is of one piece of leather, rendering the glove more durable and greatly increasing the efficiency of the user.

No. WF1. PROFESSIONAL MODEL. Made of fine quality dull black gun metal horsehide, very soft and flexible, **leather lined,** padded with finest quality felt, well padded in large little finger, at heel and easy thumb, to form deep pocket for the ball. Made in the very best possible manner throughout. Each $3.50

No. WF2. PROFESSIONAL MODEL. Made of finest drab horse, very soft and flexible, **leather lined,** padded with best felt, well padded in large little finger and at heel, easy fitting thumb. Made in the best possible manner. Each $3.50

No. WF3. Made of fine quality golden buck, **leather lined,** well padded in large little finger, at wrist and in thumb, with best quality padding; deep ball pocket, soft, flexible and durable. Each $2.00

The Rawlings Sure Catch or Web-Fingered Glove (above) was introduced in 1911. The web between the fingers, thumb, and palm was made of one piece of leather, rendering the glove more durable and greatly increasing the efficiency of the user. A decade later, a St. Louis Cardinals pitcher revolutionized baseball with the design of the Bill Doak glove (right).

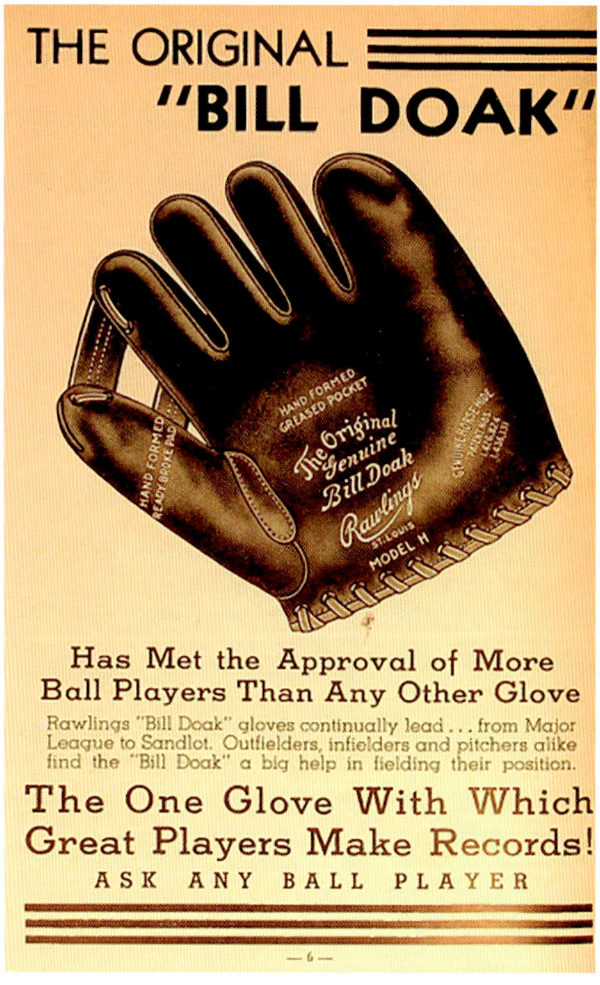

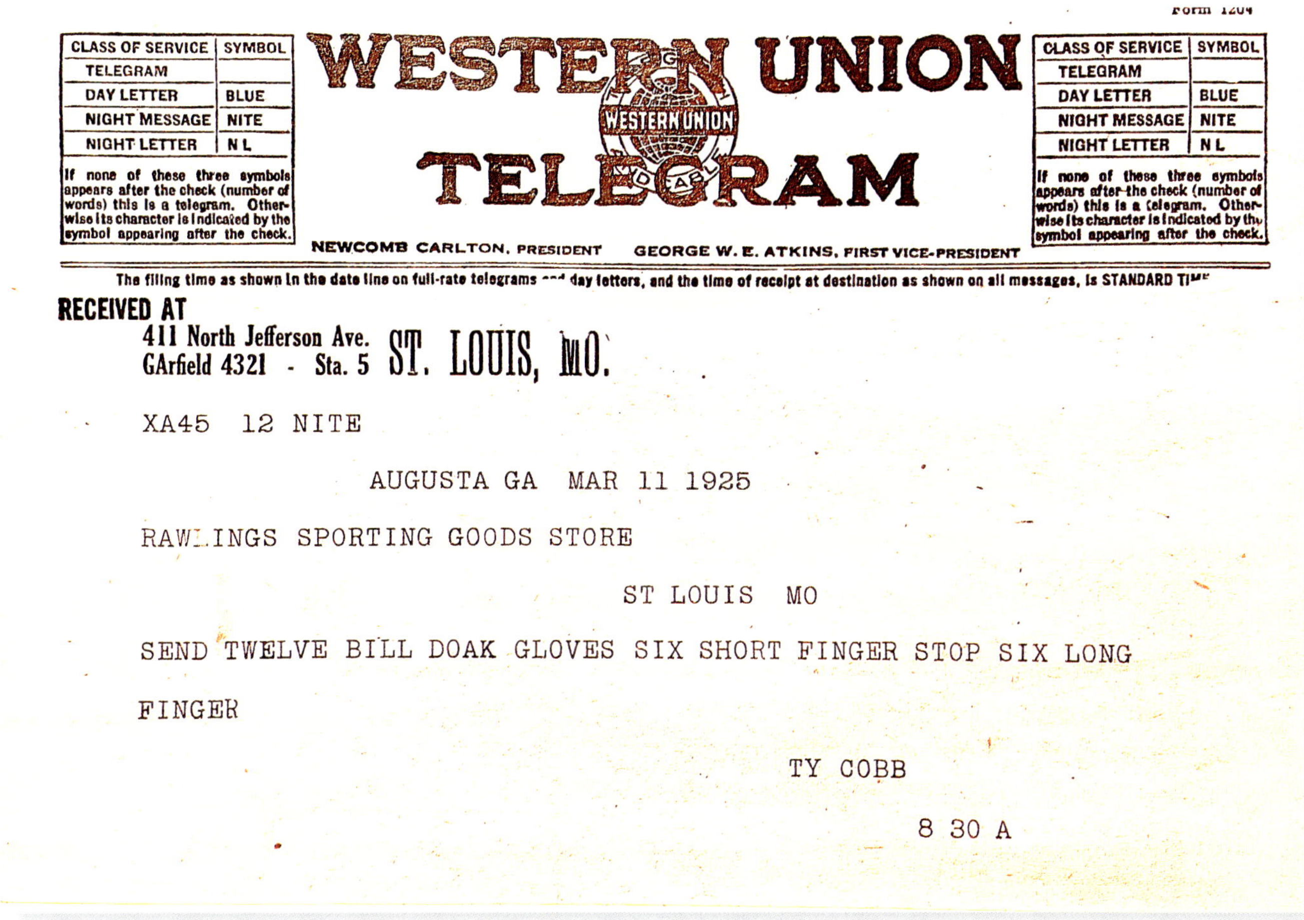

Form 1204

CLASS OF SERVICE	SYMBOL
TELEGRAM	
DAY LETTER	BLUE
NIGHT MESSAGE	NITE
NIGHT LETTER	N L

If none of these three symbols appears after the check (number of words) this is a telegram. Otherwise its character is indicated by the symbol appearing after the check.

WESTERN UNION TELEGRAM

NEWCOMB CARLTON, PRESIDENT GEORGE W. E. ATKINS, FIRST VICE-PRESIDENT

The filing time as shown in the date line on full-rate telegrams and day letters, and the time of receipt at destination as shown on all messages, is STANDARD TIME

RECEIVED AT
411 North Jefferson Ave.
GArfield 4321 - Sta. 5 ST. LOUIS, MO.

XA45 12 NITE

AUGUSTA GA MAR 11 1925

RAWLINGS SPORTING GOODS STORE

ST LOUIS MO

SEND TWELVE BILL DOAK GLOVES SIX SHORT FINGER STOP SIX LONG FINGER

TY COBB

8 30 A

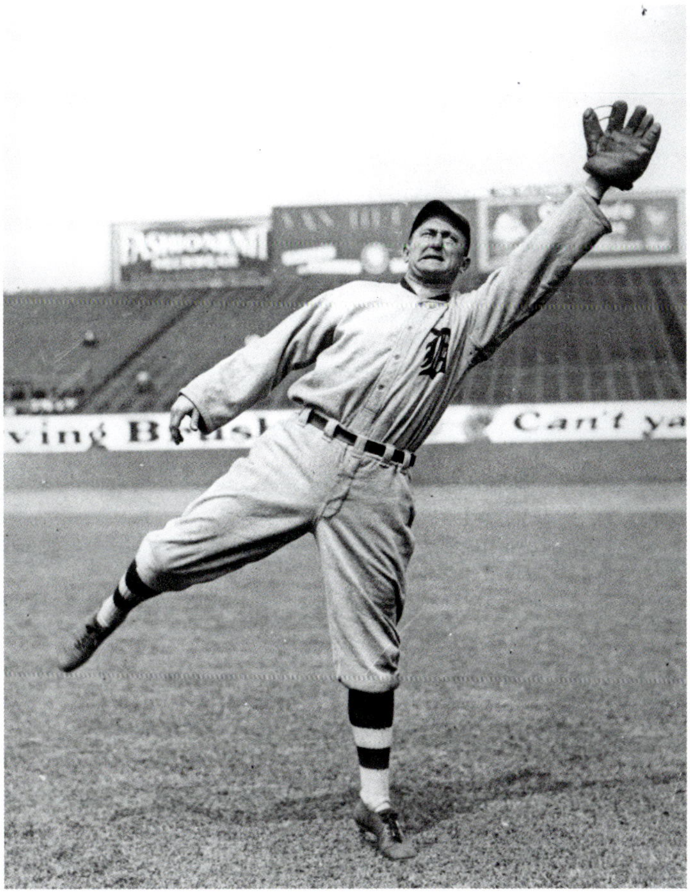

Hall of Famer Ty Cobb (left) was one of many players who approved of and used the Bill Doak glove. He ordered 12 of them from Rawlings via this 1925 telegram (above).

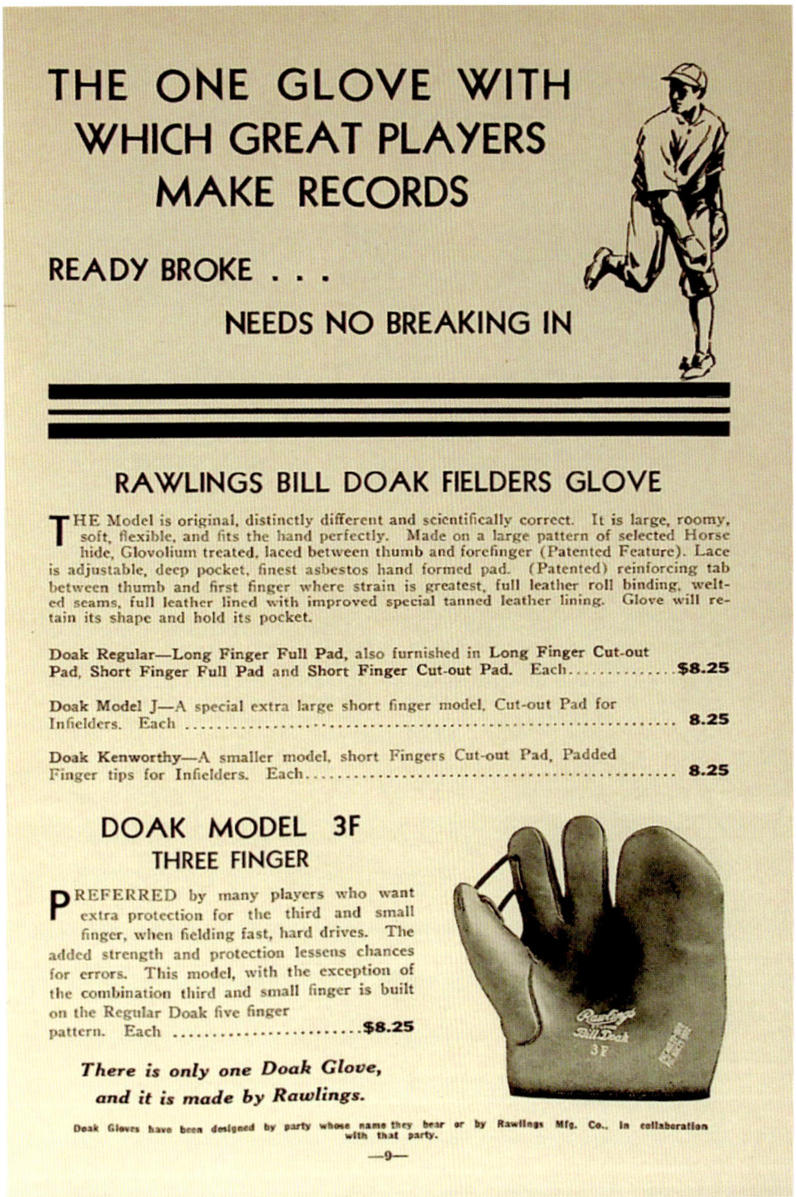

THE ONE GLOVE WITH WHICH GREAT PLAYERS MAKE RECORDS

READY BROKE . . .

NEEDS NO BREAKING IN

RAWLINGS BILL DOAK FIELDERS GLOVE

THE Model is original, distinctly different and scientifically correct. It is large, roomy, soft, flexible, and fits the hand perfectly. Made on a large pattern of selected Horse hide, Glovolium treated, laced between thumb and forefinger (Patented Feature). Lace is adjustable, deep pocket, finest asbestos hand formed pad. (Patented) reinforcing tab between thumb and first finger where strain is greatest, full leather roll binding, welted seams, full leather lined with improved special tanned leather lining. Glove will retain its shape and hold its pocket.

Doak Regular—Long Finger Full Pad, also furnished in **Long Finger Cut-out Pad, Short Finger Full Pad** and **Short Finger Cut-out Pad.** Each **$8.25**

Doak Model J—A special extra large short finger model, Cut-out Pad for Infielders. Each **8.25**

Doak Kenworthy—A smaller model, short Fingers Cut-out Pad, Padded Finger tips for Infielders. Each **8.25**

DOAK MODEL 3F

THREE FINGER

PREFERRED by many players who want extra protection for the third and small finger, when fielding fast, hard drives. The added strength and protection lessens chances for errors. This model, with the exception of the combination third and small finger is built on the Regular Doak five finger pattern. Each **$8.25**

There is only one Doak Glove, and it is made by Rawlings.

Doak Gloves have been designed by party whose name they bear or by Rawlings Mfg. Co., in collaboration with that party.

—9—

The Doak glove improved defensive play across the game of baseball, resulting in changes to both strategy and performance. The ancestor to all modern-day ball gloves, it was first sold by Rawlings in 1920 for nine dollars and remained available in the company's catalog until 1952. Rawlings introduced multiple variations of the Doak glove over the years, including the Doak Model 3F (left).

with the Doak Model 3F, a three-finger design that provided additional strength and extra protection. Every new model design enhanced the technology of catching and releasing the ball. Each enhancement improved the overall defensive play on the field.

The father-and-son team of Harry and Rollie Latina were the glove designers who were responsible for making Rawlings a continuing carousel of progress for 65 years. Harry, affectionately known as "The Glove Doctor," had started designing gloves for Rawlings in 1922. He eventually passed the title to Rollie when he retired in 1961, and Rollie remained the company's chief glove designer until his retirement in the 1980s. Their impact on baseball was immense. At one time, the two designers held about 90 percent of all baseball glove patents in the United States. Bob Clevenhagen became the company's lead designer in 1983. In 2011, *Smithsonian Magazine* labeled him "Baseball's Glove Man" after he followed the Latinas in the trade and produced the next generation of gloves for Rawlings.

Rawlings introduced the Deep-Well Pocket series of gloves just before the United States entered World War II in 1941. The Deep-Well Pocket model featured an area below the "crotch"

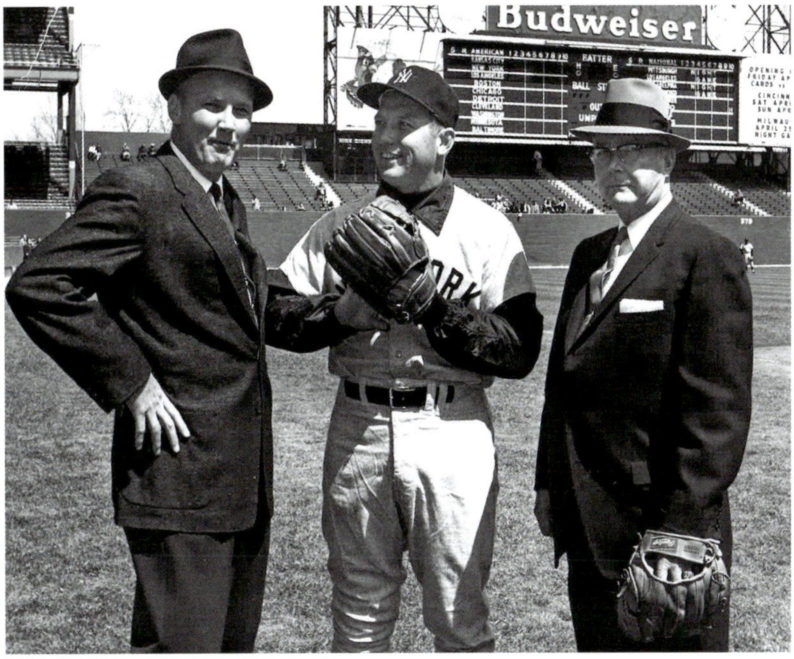

Rawlings glove designers Rollie Latina (left) and his father, Harry Latina (right), meet with Mickey Mantle in 1961 prior to an exhibition game at Busch Stadium in St. Louis.

Rawlings introduced the Deep-Well Pocket design in the summer of 1941.

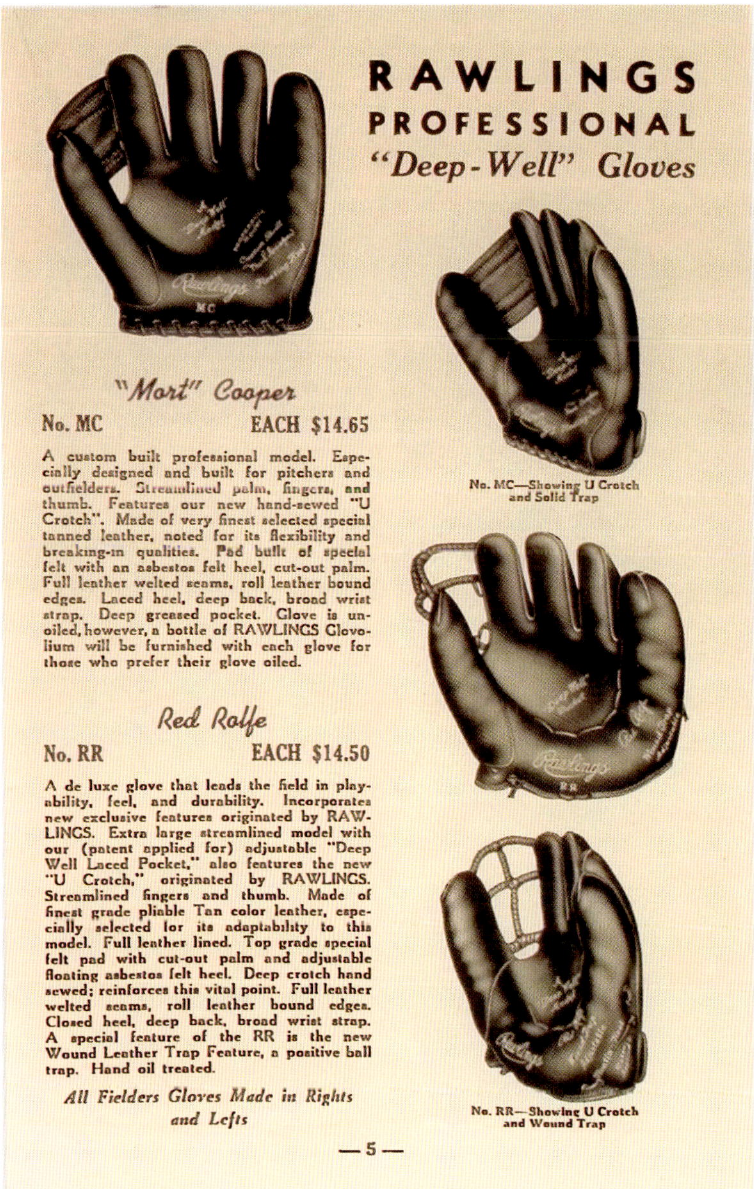

RAWLINGS
PROFESSIONAL
"Deep-Well" Gloves

"Mort" Cooper

No. MC **EACH $14.65**

A custom built professional model. Especially designed and built for pitchers and outfielders. Streamlined palm, fingers, and thumb. Features our new hand-sewed "U Crotch". Made of very finest selected special tanned leather, noted for its flexibility and breaking-in qualities. Pad built of special felt with an asbestos felt heel, cut-out palm. Full leather welted seams, roll leather bound edges. Laced heel, deep back, broad wrist strap. Deep greased pocket. Glove is unoiled, however, a bottle of RAWLINGS Glovolium will be furnished with each glove for those who prefer their glove oiled.

Red Rolfe

No. RR **EACH $14.50**

A de luxe glove that leads the field in playability, feel, and durability. Incorporates new exclusive features originated by RAWLINGS. Extra large streamlined model with our (patent applied for) adjustable "Deep Well Laced Pocket," also features the new "U Crotch," originated by RAWLINGS. Streamlined fingers and thumb. Made of finest grade pliable Tan color leather, especially selected for its adaptability to this model. Full leather lined. Top grade special felt pad with cut-out palm and adjustable floating asbestos felt heel. Deep crotch hand sewed; reinforces this vital point. Full leather welted seams, roll leather bound edges. Closed heel, deep back, broad wrist strap. A special feature of the RR is the new Wound Leather Trap Feature, a positive ball trap. Hand oil treated.

All Fielders Gloves Made in Rights and Lefts

No. MC—Showing U Crotch and Solid Trap

No. RR—Showing U Crotch and Wound Trap

—5—

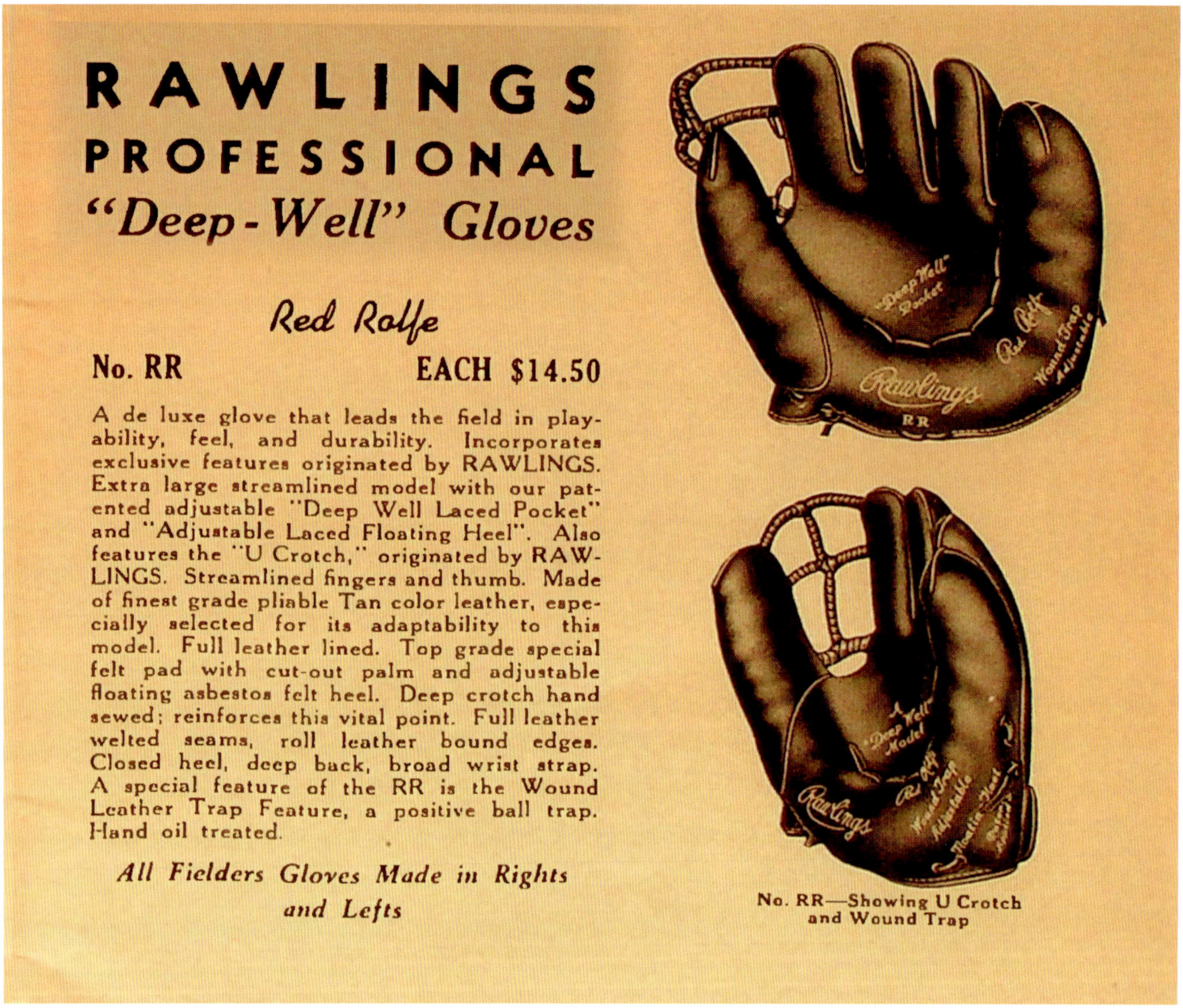

The Rawlings Red Rolfe (RR) model glove was one of the first to use the Deep-Well Pocket design and Wound Leather Trap. It was later discontinued partially due to controversy surrounding Al Gionfriddo's famous catch in the 1947 World Series.

of the glove, where padding, lacing, and webbing created an indentation or "well" to receive or trap the ball. The Rawlings Red Rolfe (RR) glove model was one of the first to use the design. It became an immediate sensation and was used by many future Hall of Famers and other players. But it soon came under scrutiny. One player who did not make it to Cooperstown—Al Gionfriddo, the Brooklyn Dodgers' reserve outfielder—had a dramatic World Series catch that led to a dispute. MLB eventually banned the use of the glove due to its rolled-lace web design that extended beyond the normal flat web area—though elements of that glove model have become common in today's game.

The Deep-Well Pocket was extended to all future Rawlings model gloves, from catcher positions to infielder and outfielder gloves. Whether aligned to players of the era or reengineered models of former players, the gloves remained large and stiff, with a thick, padded heel. The pocket, thumb, and fingers were also heavily padded. There was still no lacing between the first finger and the pinkie finger. The idea of a hinged glove to form a more complete pocket was not yet on the drawing board.

Often referred to as "The Claw," the Trapper model first baseman's glove was also introduced in the 1940s. As advertised, its design and construction "permitted [the] mitt to break as much on [the] little finger side as the thumb side [that] causes both sides of the mitt to close over [the] ball when [the] ball hits [the] center panel. [It] forms a positive trap." Baseball statistics clearly showed the Trapper was a direct cause of improved fielding percentages across MLB. Over the next decade, the George McQuinn T70 model became the premier glove of most big-league first basemen and a future president.

A 1948 Rawlings catalog declared its newest model line, the Playmaker, as "another Rawlings 1st," highlighting it as "the leader of a famous line of gloves." The Playmaker incorporated

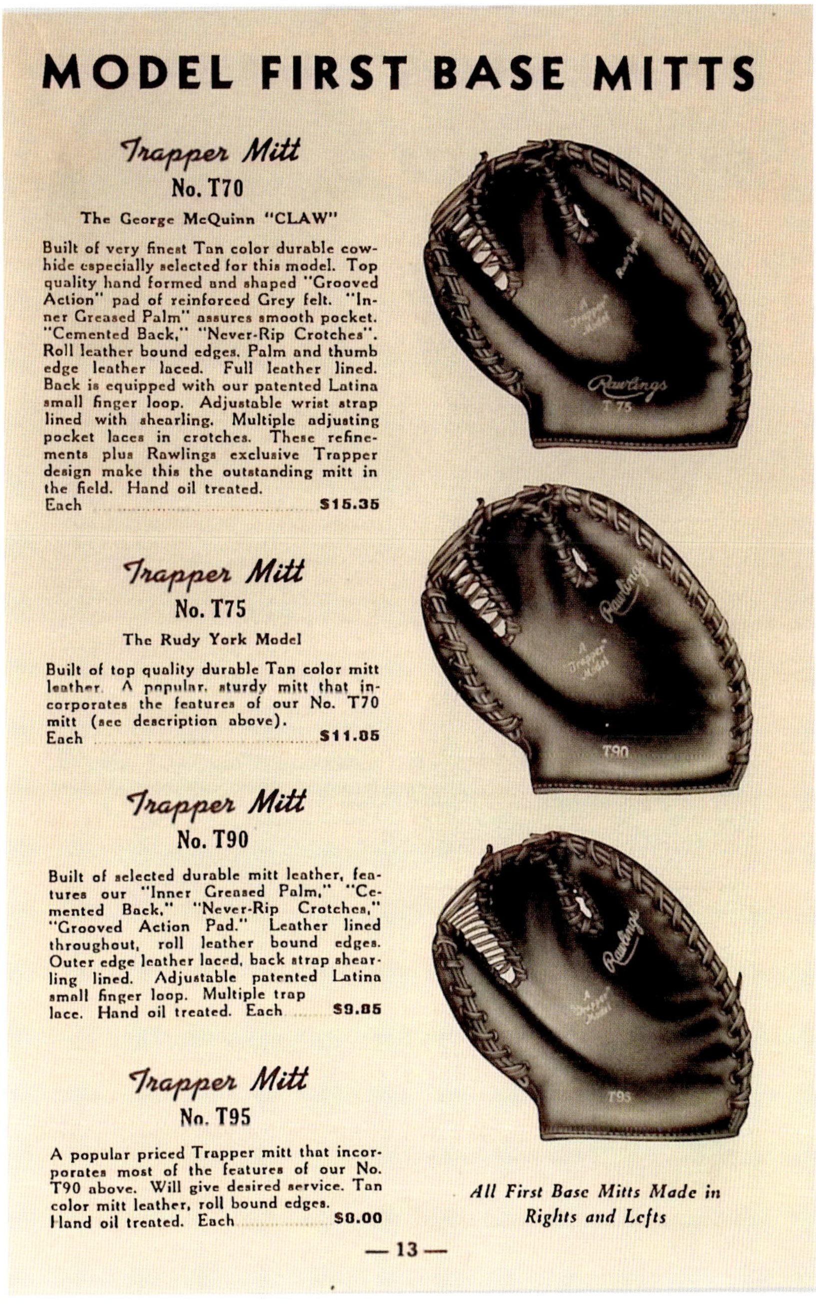

MODEL FIRST BASE MITTS

Trapper Mitt
No. T70
The George McQuinn "CLAW"

Built of very finest Tan color durable cowhide especially selected for this model. Top quality hand formed and shaped "Grooved Action" pad of reinforced Grey felt. "Inner Greased Palm" assures smooth pocket. "Cemented Back," "Never-Rip Crotches". Roll leather bound edges. Palm and thumb edge leather laced. Full leather lined. Back is equipped with our patented Latina small finger loop. Adjustable wrist strap lined with shearling. Multiple adjusting pocket laces in crotches. These refinements plus Rawlings exclusive Trapper design make this the outstanding mitt in the field. Hand oil treated.
Each $15.35

Trapper Mitt
No. T75
The Rudy York Model

Built of top quality durable Tan color mitt leather. A popular, sturdy mitt that incorporates the features of our No. T70 mitt (see description above).
Each $11.85

Trapper Mitt
No. T90

Built of selected durable mitt leather, features our "Inner Greased Palm," "Cemented Back," "Never-Rip Crotches," "Grooved Action Pad." Leather lined throughout, roll leather bound edges. Outer edge leather laced, back strap shearling lined. Adjustable patented Latina small finger loop. Multiple trap lace. Hand oil treated. Each $9.85

Trapper Mitt
No. T95

A popular priced Trapper mitt that incorporates most of the features of our No. T90 above. Will give desired service. Tan color mitt leather, roll bound edges. Hand oil treated. Each $8.00

All First Base Mitts Made in Rights and Lefts

— 13 —

The Deep-Well Pocket design was applied to a Trapper series of gloves for first basemen in 1942. These models also became known as "The Claw." The George McQuinn T70 model became one of the most popular gloves for Rawlings over the next two decades.

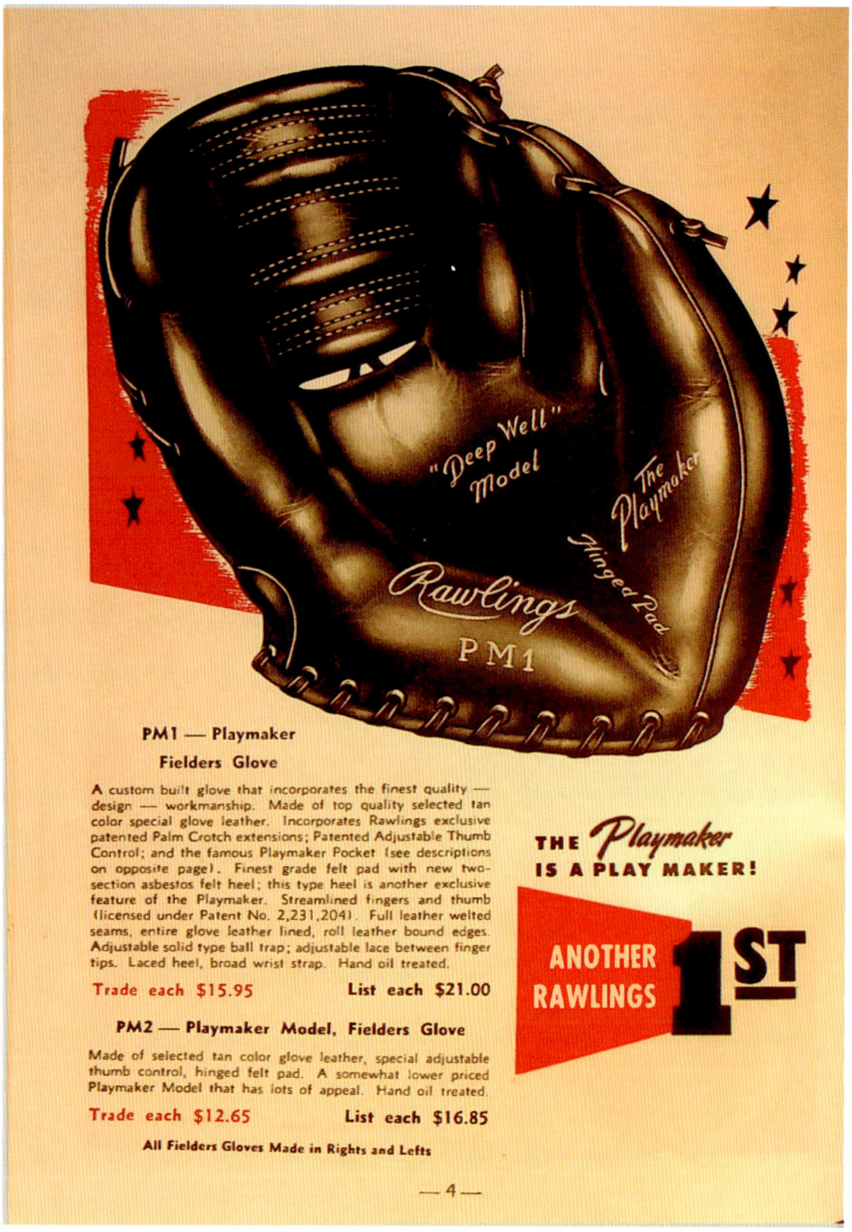

The next Rawlings glove innovation came in 1948 with its Playmaker line (left), a three-finger design that was one of the company's first models to connect all the fingers. By 1958, Mickey Mantle was a Triple Crown winner and an MVP. He was everyone's favorite baseball hero, and Rawlings heavily promoted a line of gloves with his inscription (opposite).

"Rawlings exclusive patented Palm Crotch extensions, Patented Adjustable Thumb Control, and the famous Playmaker Pocket." Its three-finger design made it one of the company's first models to connect all the glove's fingers. The catalog stated that the elimination of one finger allowed for a pocket of unusual spread and depth. The retention of three glove fingers ensured the feel of the fingers so important in ball handling.

The most popular gloves of the 1950s were the Mickey Mantle autographed personal model and the Duke Snider model, featuring the new Single Lazy "S" pocket lace, which attached the web to the palm of the glove. Mantle's model introduced extended finger stalls for better control while enticing young ballplayers to buy a glove bearing his autograph. Interestingly, Mantle changed his autograph from his early cursive up-and-down signature (the one he used to sign his Rawlings contract, which then appeared on his model gloves) to a signature with circular letters, causing many fans to question the authenticity of their Mantle autographs. Mantle has said he adapted his signature in order to more easily sign the round surface of a baseball. So, confused fans with a Mantle glove and an autographed baseball were often looking at two different signatures.

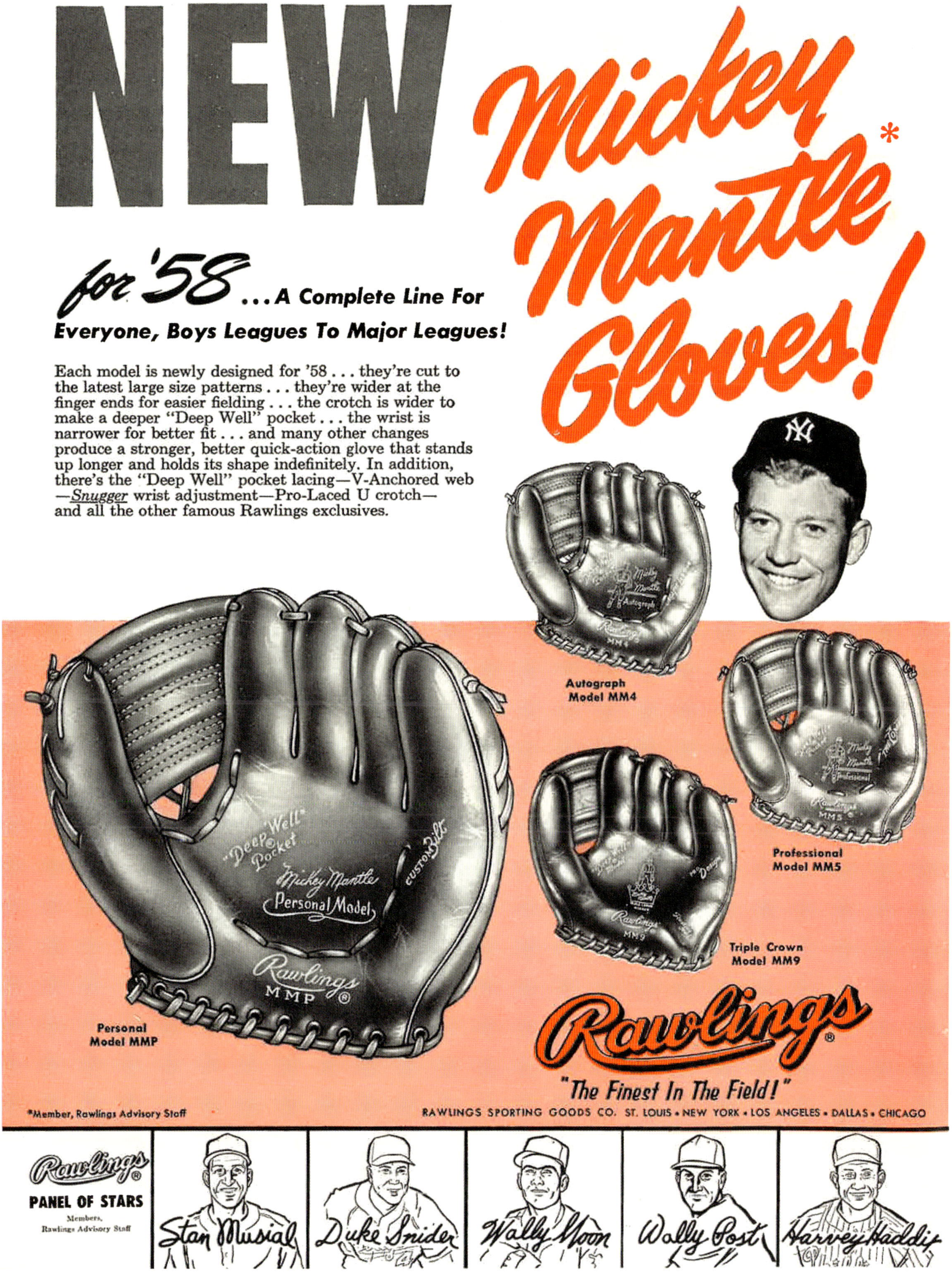
NEW
Mickey Mantle* Gloves!
for '58 ... A Complete Line For Everyone, Boys Leagues To Major Leagues!
Each model is newly designed for '58 . . . they're cut to the latest large size patterns . . . they're wider at the finger ends for easier fielding . . . the crotch is wider to make a deeper "Deep Well" pocket . . . the wrist is narrower for better fit . . . and many other changes produce a stronger, better quick-action glove that stands up longer and holds its shape indefinitely. In addition, there's the "Deep Well" pocket lacing—V-Anchored web—Snugger wrist adjustment—Pro-Laced U crotch—and all the other famous Rawlings exclusives.
"Deep Well" Pocket
Mickey Mantle Personal Model
Custom Bilt
Rawlings MMP
Personal Model MMP
Autograph Model MM4
Professional Model MM5
Triple Crown Model MM9
Rawlings
"The Finest In The Field!"
*Member, Rawlings Advisory Staff
RAWLINGS SPORTING GOODS CO. ST. LOUIS • NEW YORK • LOS ANGELES • DALLAS • CHICAGO
Rawlings PANEL OF STARS
Members, Rawlings Advisory Staff
Stan Musial
Duke Snider
Wally Moon
Wally Post
Harvey Haddix

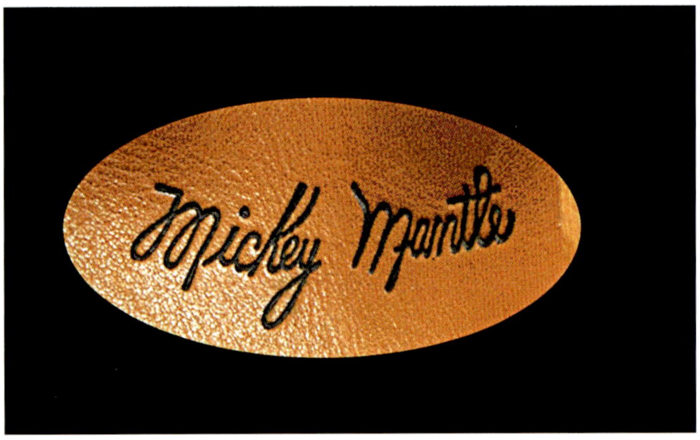

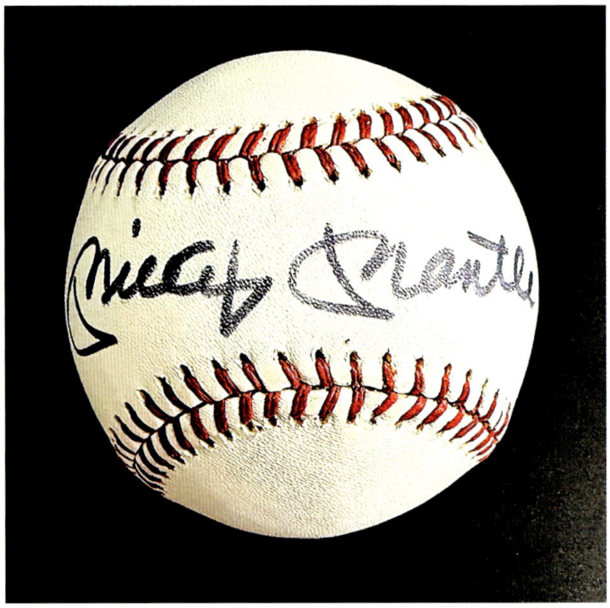

Note the change between Mickey Mantle's signature on a glove (above) and on a ball (right). While Mantle was earning acclaim on the field, Stan Musial was declared the Player of the Decade and graced the cover of a 1957 Rawlings catalog (bottom).

But the most heralded Rawlings glove during this period belonged to baseball's Player of the Decade, who was featured on the company's 1957 catalog cover—Stan Musial. The Stan Musial Personal Model (PM) glove was one of the first to highlight the company's new Heart of the Hide design. This glove was made from high-quality steer hide, which was known for its strength, excellent performance, and longevity. For more than 65 years, the Heart of the Hide logo has served as a guarantee of playing with only the finest, most durable leather. It has been used by multiple generations of players. It's a glove that players like today's Nolan Arenado and Marcus Semien continue to depend on for performance game after game.

In 1960, Musial became the first in a long line of MLB players using the new Trap-Eze model, heralded as "The First Really New Glove in 40 Years." It would continue to be used over the next 40 years by players like Ozzie

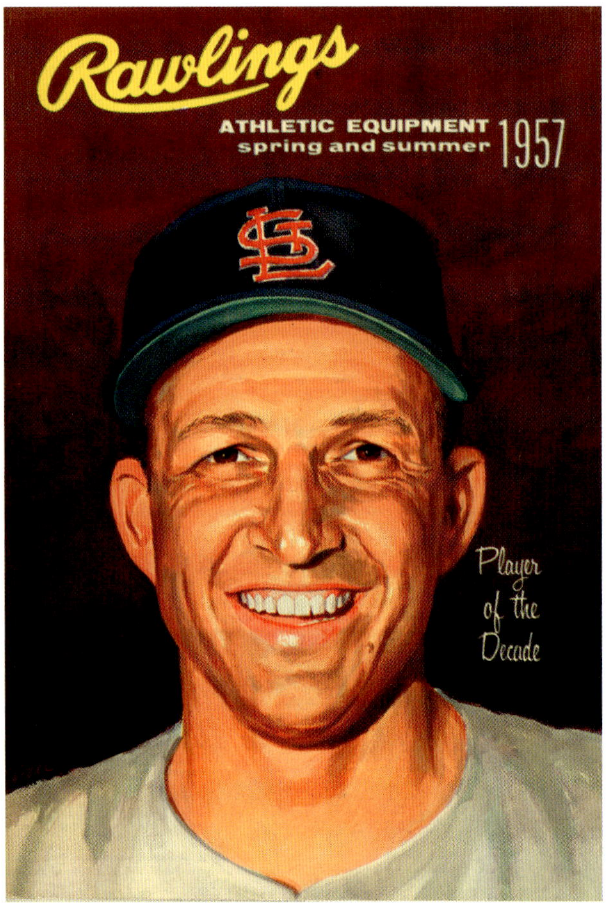

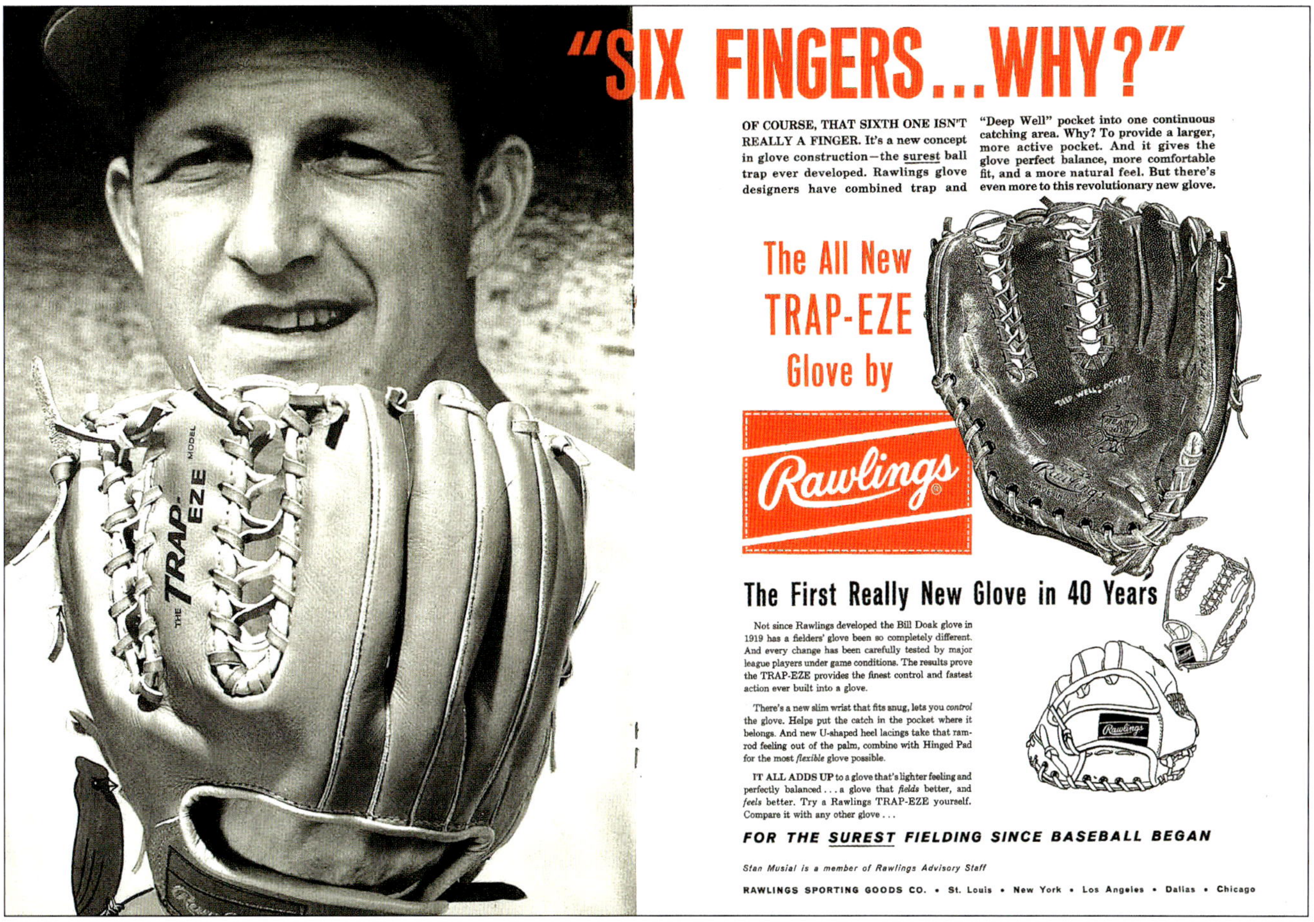

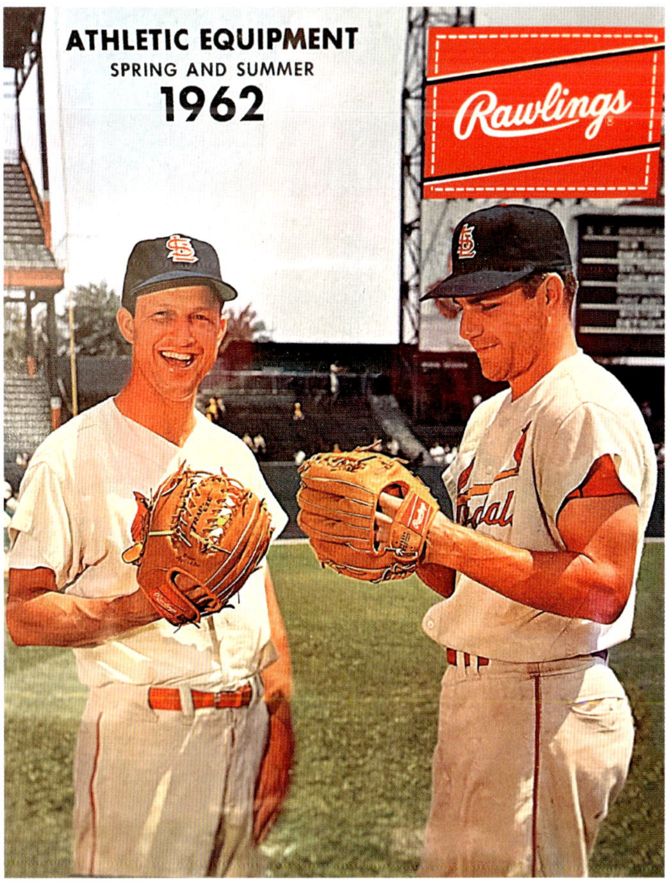

The next new Rawlings glove was the six-finger Trap-Eze model (above), the biggest redesign since the Bill Doak glove in 1920. While regularly using it in the field, Stan Musial and Ken Boyer became the company's leading spokesmen for the glove and were also featured on the cover of a 1962 Rawlings catalog (left).

Smith and Torii Hunter. While its radical design was often incorrectly called the six-finger glove, one wasn't a finger; it was a web. The glove was touted as "a completely new concept in glove construction—the surest ball trap ever developed . . . Rawlings glove designers have combined trap and the 'Deep Well' pocket into one continuous catching area" with the new design. It gave players confidence in extending their range in the field because they knew balls within reach would be trapped in their glove.

Eight years later, Rawlings developed the Fastback® model. Inspired by the fastback roofs of 1960s muscle cars and used in the field by Hall of Famers like Reggie Jackson and Willie Stargell, this revolutionary model was designed for increased

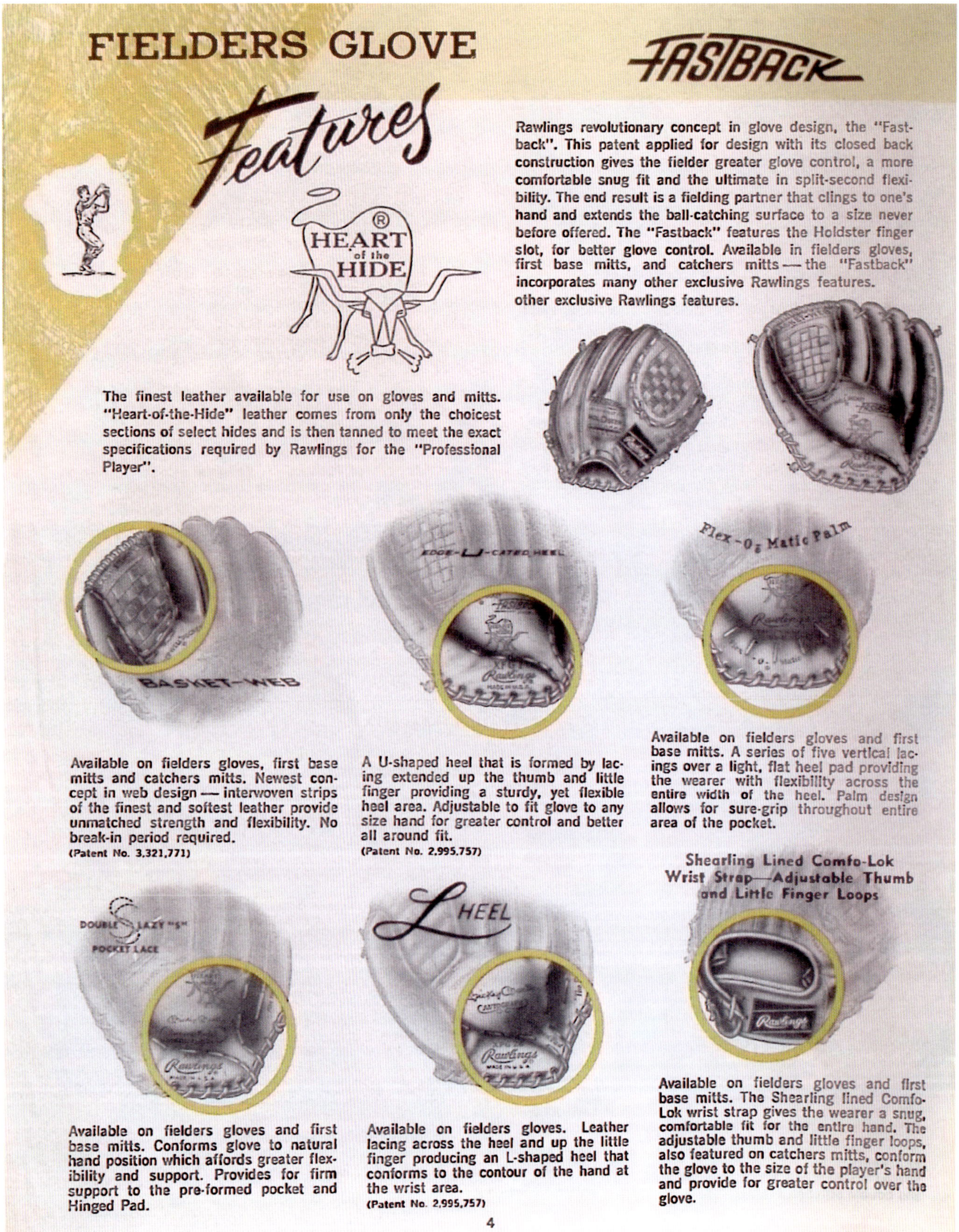
FIELDERS GLOVE

FASTBACK

Features

HEART of the HIDE

Rawlings revolutionary concept in glove design, the "Fastback". This patent applied for design with its closed back construction gives the fielder greater glove control, a more comfortable snug fit and the ultimate in split-second flexibility. The end result is a fielding partner that clings to one's hand and extends the ball-catching surface to a size never before offered. The "Fastback" features the Holdster finger slot, for better glove control. Available in fielders gloves, first base mitts, and catchers mitts — the "Fastback" incorporates many other exclusive Rawlings features.
other exclusive Rawlings features.

The finest leather available for use on gloves and mitts. "Heart-of-the-Hide" leather comes from only the choicest sections of select hides and is then tanned to meet the exact specifications required by Rawlings for the "Professional Player".

BASKET-WEB

Available on fielders gloves, first base mitts and catchers mitts. Newest concept in web design — interwoven strips of the finest and softest leather provide unmatched strength and flexibility. No break-in period required.
(Patent No. 3,321,771)

EDGE-U-CATED HEEL

A U-shaped heel that is formed by lacing extended up the thumb and little finger providing a sturdy, yet flexible heel area. Adjustable to fit glove to any size hand for greater control and better all around fit.
(Patent No. 2,995,757)

Flex-O-Matic Palm

Available on fielders gloves and first base mitts. A series of five vertical lacings over a light, flat heel pad providing the wearer with flexibility across the entire width of the heel. Palm design allows for sure-grip throughout entire area of the pocket.

DOUBLE LAZY "S" POCKET LACE

Available on fielders gloves and first base mitts. Conforms glove to natural hand position which affords greater flexibility and support. Provides for firm support to the pre-formed pocket and Hinged Pad.

L HEEL

Available on fielders gloves. Leather lacing across the heel and up the little finger producing an L-shaped heel that conforms to the contour of the hand at the wrist area.
(Patent No. 2,995,757)

Shearling Lined Comfo-Lok Wrist Strap—Adjustable Thumb and Little Finger Loops

Available on fielders gloves and first base mitts. The Shearling lined Comfo-Lok wrist strap gives the wearer a snug, comfortable fit for the entire hand. The adjustable thumb and little finger loops, also featured on catchers mitts, conform the glove to the size of the player's hand and provide for greater control over the glove.

4

During the 1960s and 1970s, Rawlings continued to come up with new innovations in baseball glove designs, as shown here in a 1969 catalog. Soon players of all ages were wearing gloves with unique Rawlings features, such as Basket-Web, Edge-U-Cated Heel, Flex-O-Matic Palm, Double S Lazy S Pocket Lace, L Heel, and Comfo-Lok Wrist Strap.

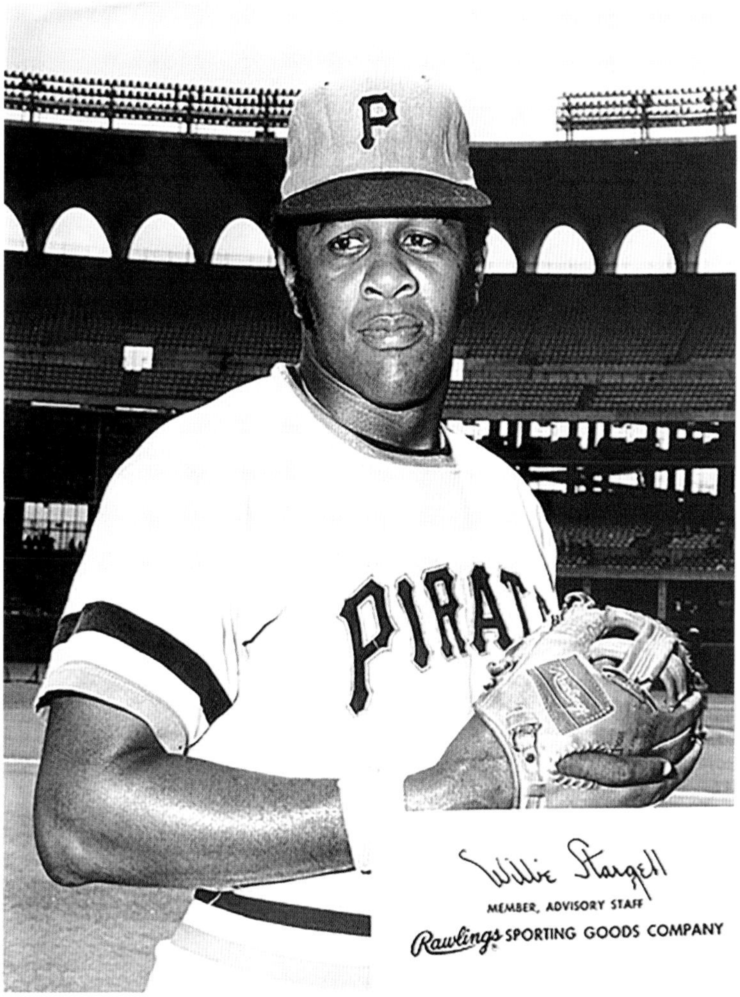

The Pittsburgh Pirates' Hall of Famer Willie Stargell wore the Rawlings Fastback model glove in games and advertisements.

glove control and extra protection for the back of the user's hand and knuckles. It broke from the traditional open back above the wrist strap and instead offered a closed-back pattern with a single hole for the player's finger. Coupled with the Rawlings Basket-Web® feature, it allowed gloves longer than 12 inches to begin being manufactured.

Glove enhancements continued over the next three decades, and Rawlings introduced the Pro Preferred® model in 2001. This glove featured the industry's first supple kip leather, deerskin linings, and 100-pound-tensile-strength laces to go along with an advanced 100 percent wool padding design. This glove breaks in to form the perfect pocket based on its owner's specific playing preference. The top pro-grade patterns and materials unite to deliver the quality and performance that the very best players in the game—like Mike Trout, Kris Bryant, and Anthony Rizzo—demand and rely on season after season.

The newest Rawlings model—the REV1X®—has rewritten history to become today's leading glove. This next-generation glove stands above all others due to its innovative construction and ultra-lightweight, form-fitting design, allowing for

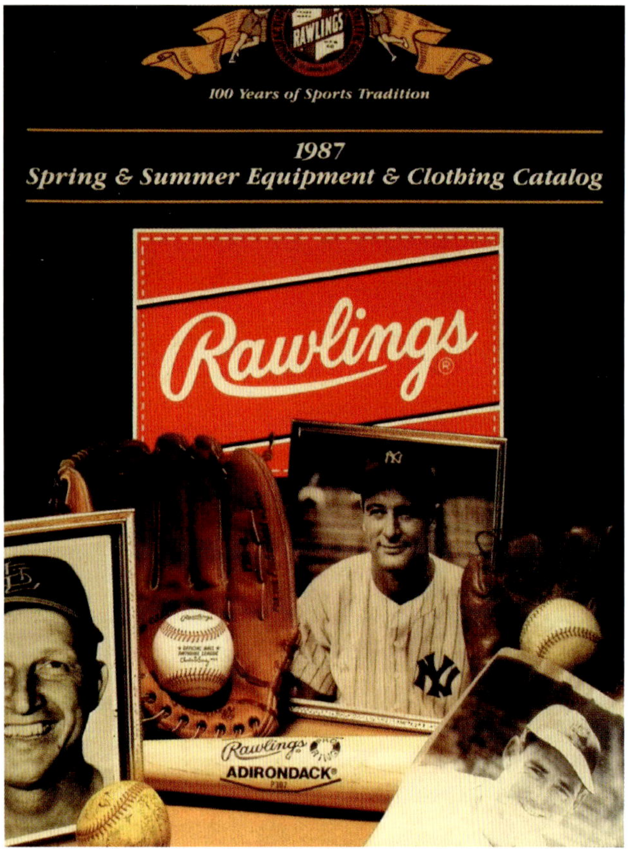

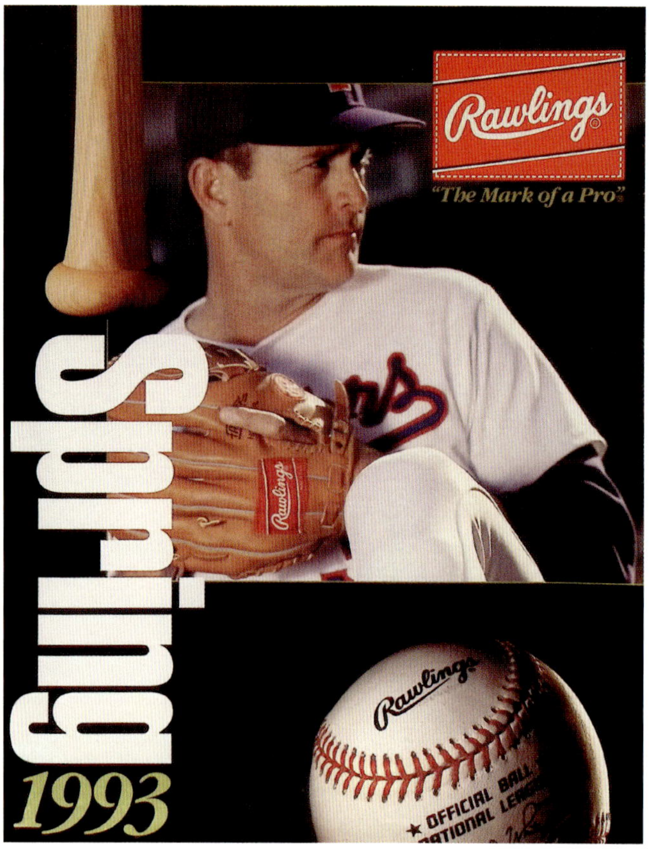

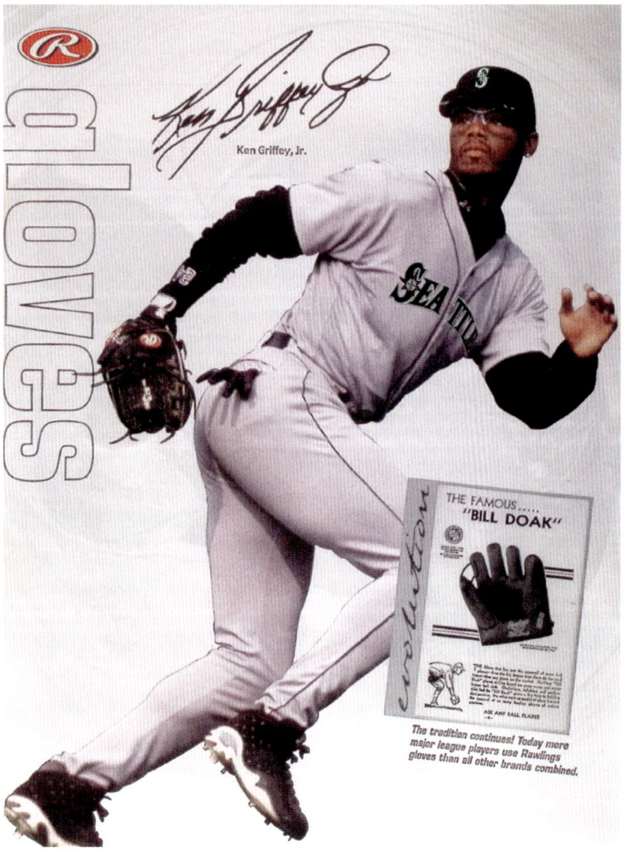

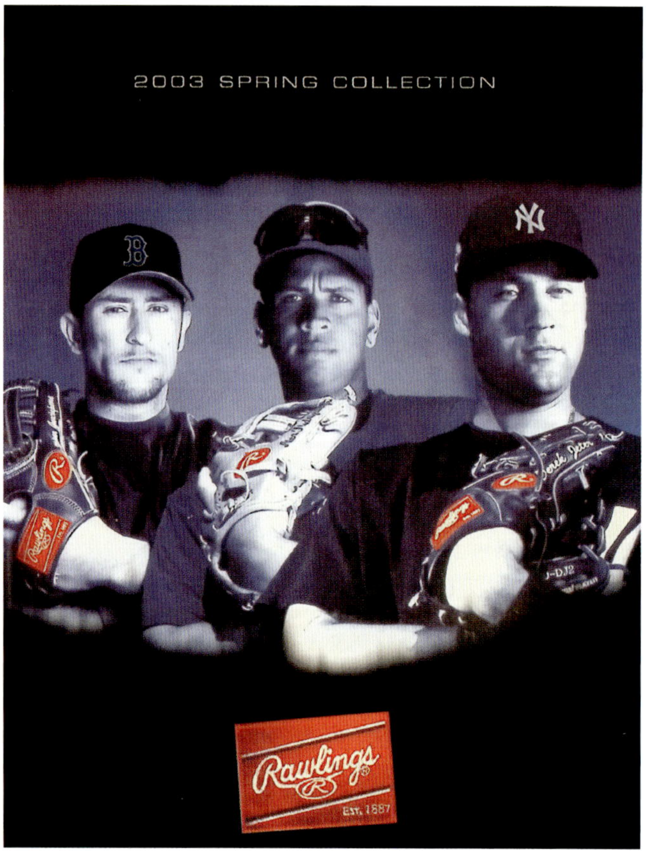

In the ensuing decades, Rawlings gloves could be found on the hands of many of baseball's greatest players, including Nolan Ryan, Ken Griffey Jr., Nomar Garciaparra, Alex Rodriguez, and Derek Jeter, as well as on the company's catalog covers.

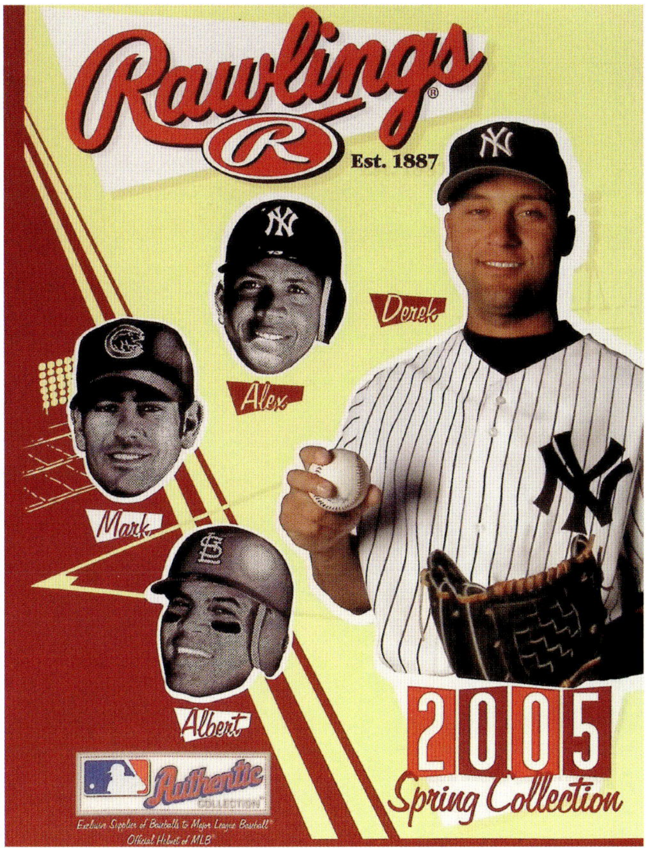

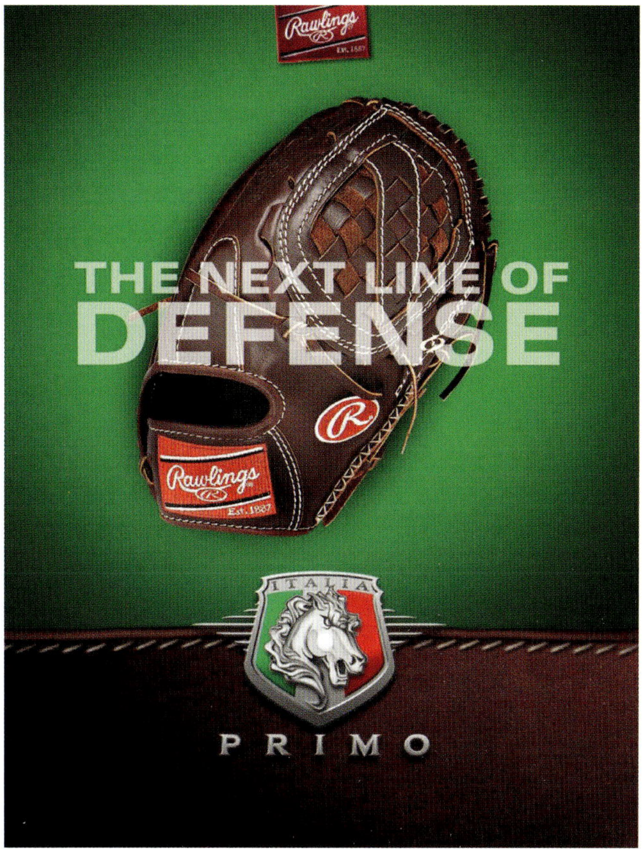

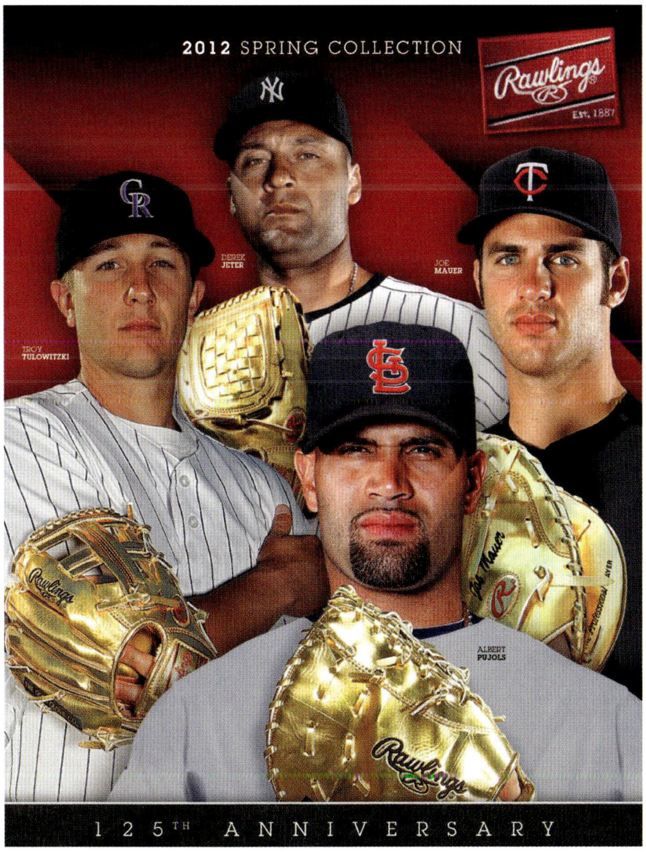

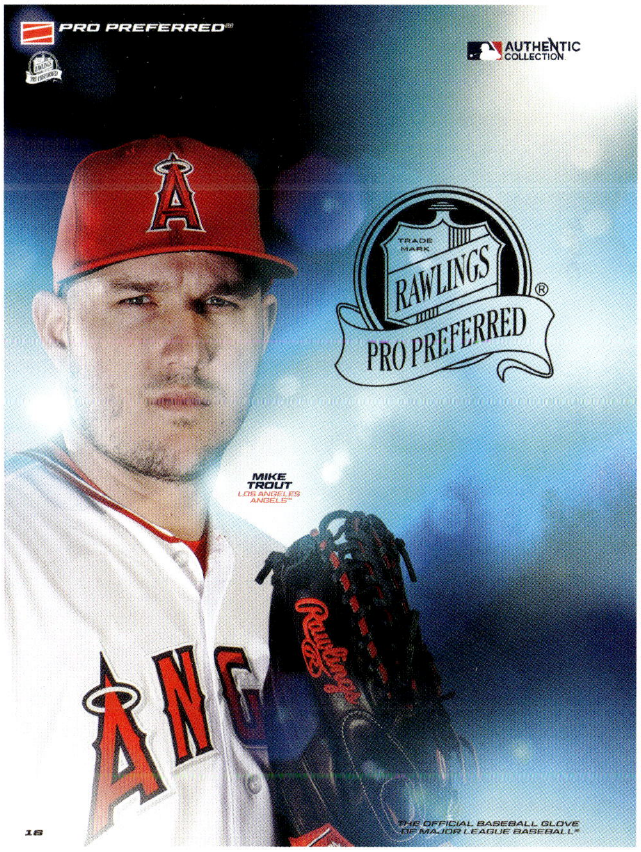

Many of these players were soon joined by a new generation of baseball greats—like Albert Pujols, Mark Prior, Troy Tulowitzki, Joe Mauer, and Mike Trout—on the field and on Rawlings catalog covers.

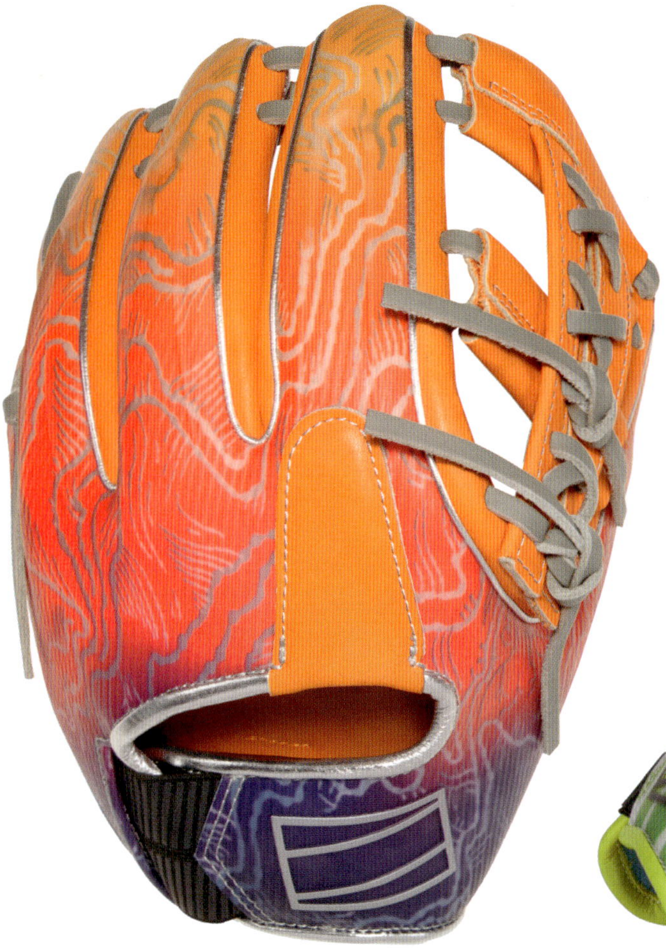

The REV1X model (left and below) has become today's leading glove due to its innovative construction and the fact that it gives players a chance to be creative and choose their own personal color and design. Gold Glove Award winner Francisco Lindor (bottom) was the first big user and promoter of the glove, often wearing different colors and designs during his team's home stands.

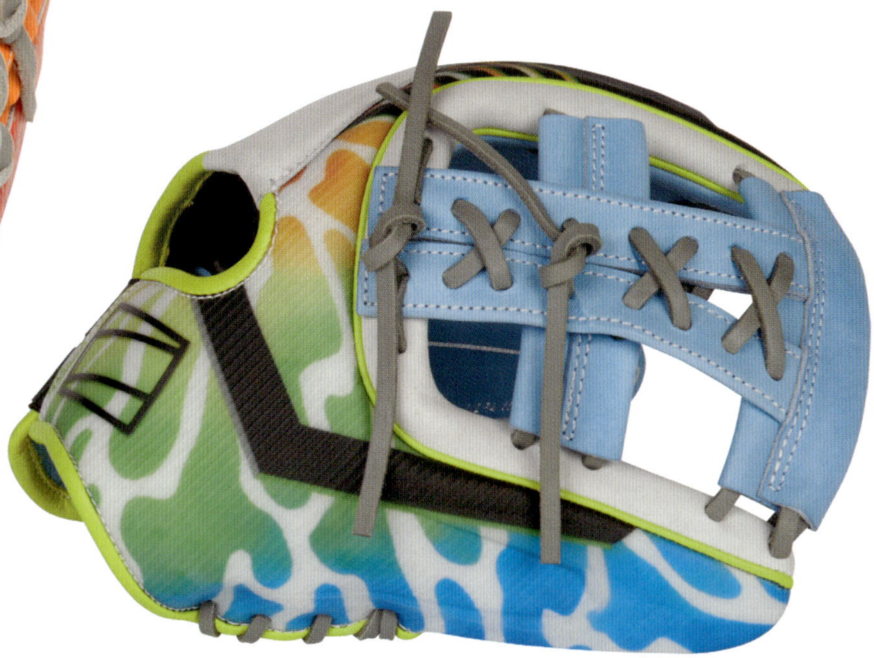

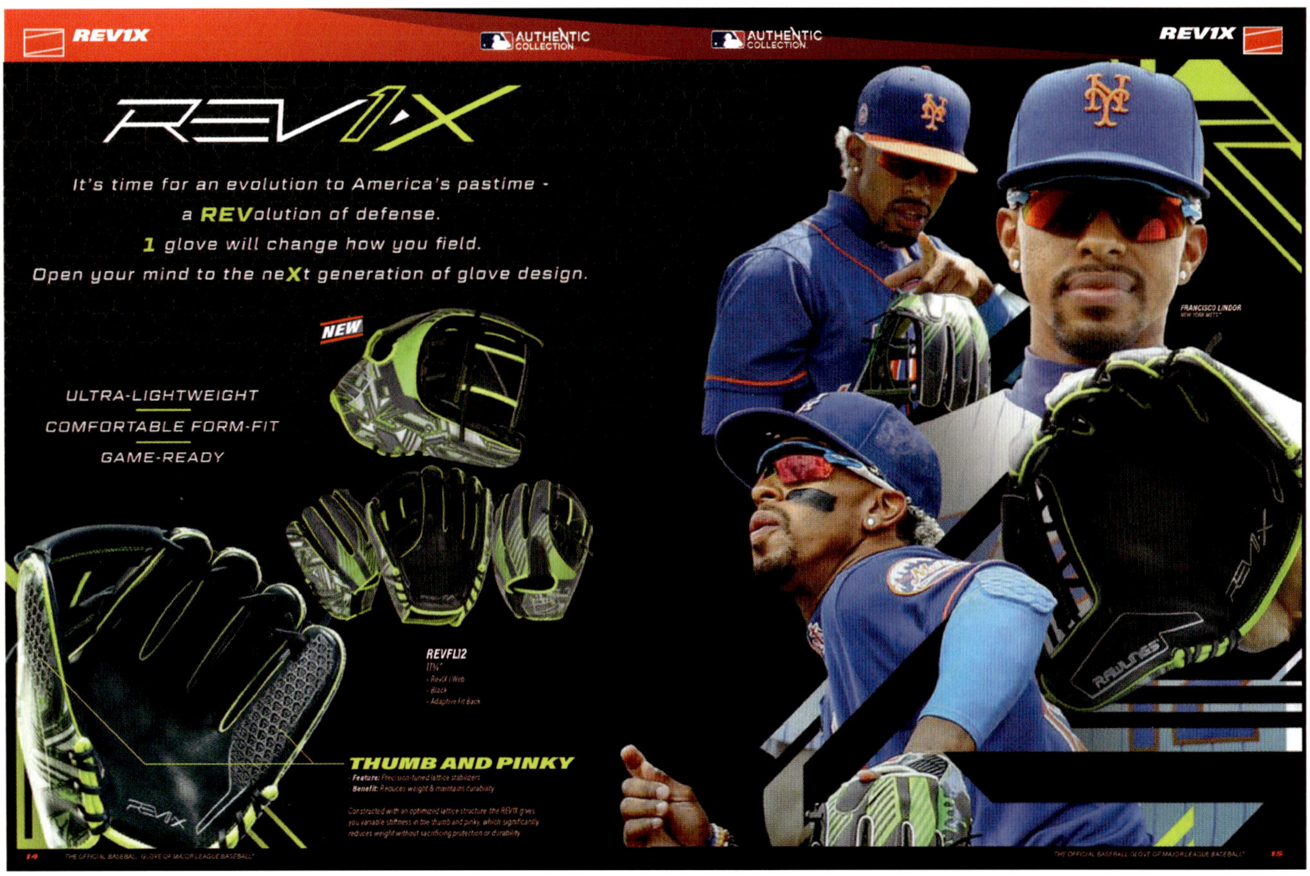

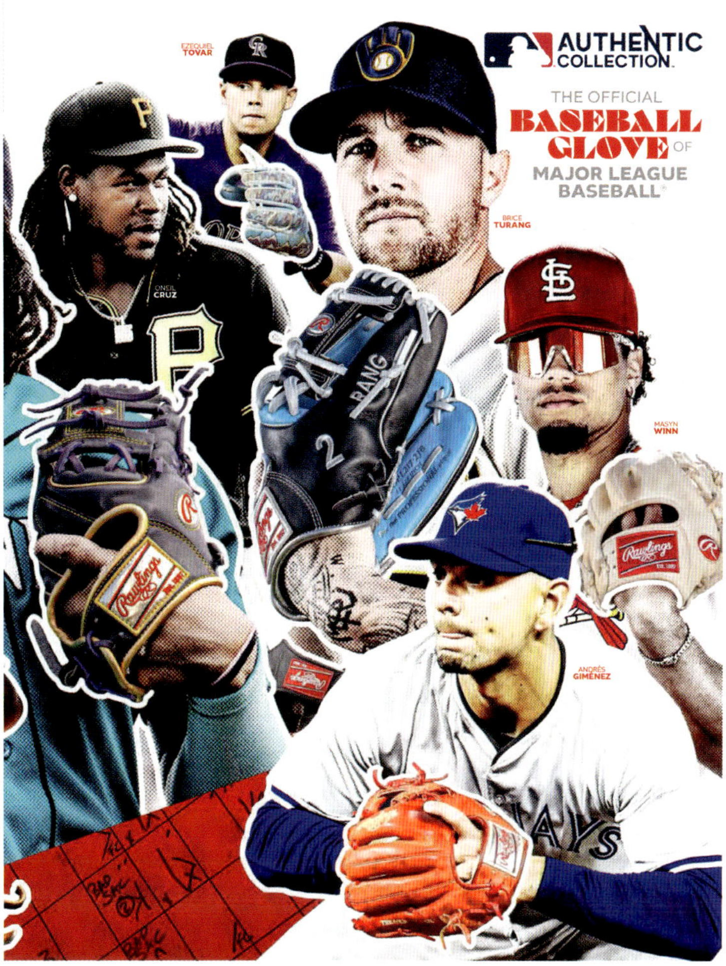

A 2026 Rawlings catalog (left) highlights a new generation of great defenders and their gloves: Oneil Cruz, Ezequiel Tovar, Brice Turang, Masyn Winn, and Andrés Giménez. The Baltimore Orioles' Cal Ripken Jr. (following spread) makes a diving catch against the Detroit Tigers at Camden Yards in 2000.

both speed and agility. The REV1X comes with a unique laceless web design to ensure excellent control and fielding durability. Formed around a Heart of the Hide leather palm, this futuristic glove is structured with a back side that uses synthetic technology, producing its lighter weight. In the past, gloves used stabilizers in the thumb and pinkie that broke down over time. REV1X's synthetic materials not only last longer but also provide the most comfortable glove for the hand. The synthetic materials also provide players with an infinite array of color and pattern choices to offer a style statement on the field. No single major-league player has promoted his personal style more than Francisco Lindor, and his ever-changing patterns and glove colors match his mood and uniform each day.

The evolution of baseball gloves has been an incredible journey—from the first fingerless designs to the bulky, loose-fitting, and heavily padded models from baseball's "golden years" to today's ultra-lightweight, form-fitting REV1X. While each new model sought an improvement in comfort and versatility, each new design was always driven to enhance players' performance. Throughout its long history of use in the game of baseball, the glove remains the most personal and irreplaceable piece of every player's equipment. Whether a player is young or old, amateur or professional, their glove will create moments that transform their days on the field into a lifetime of precious memories.

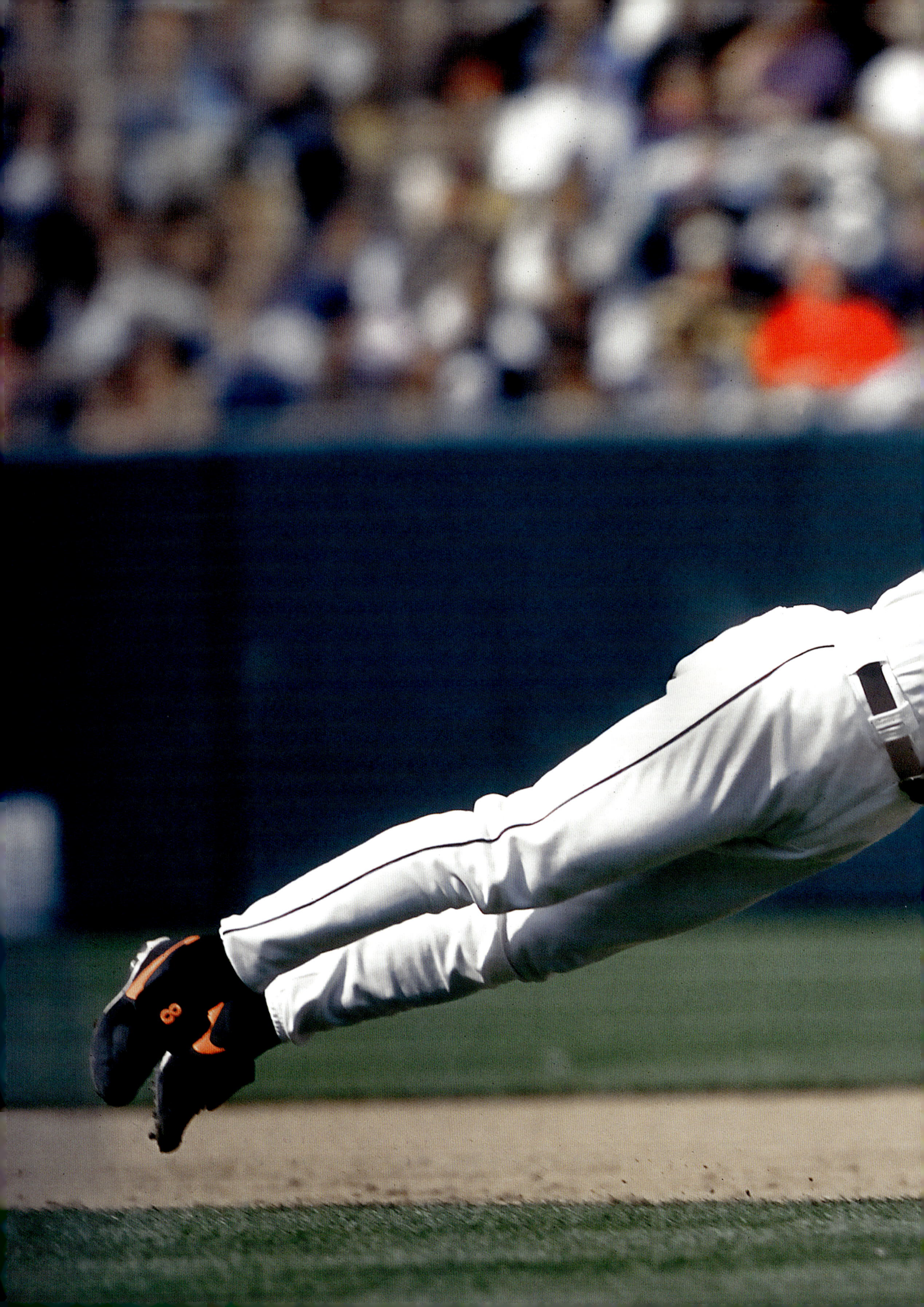

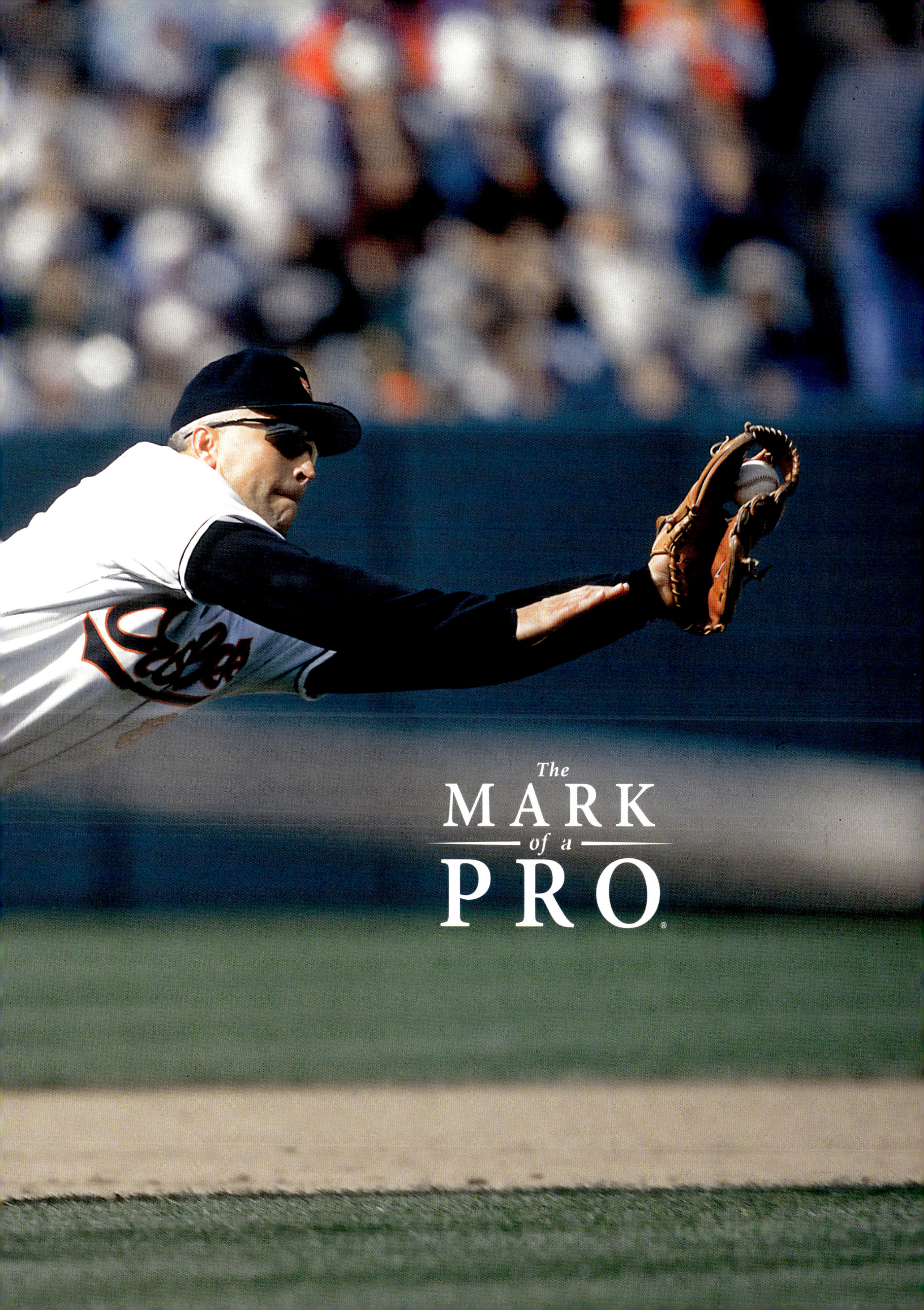

The MARK of a PRO®

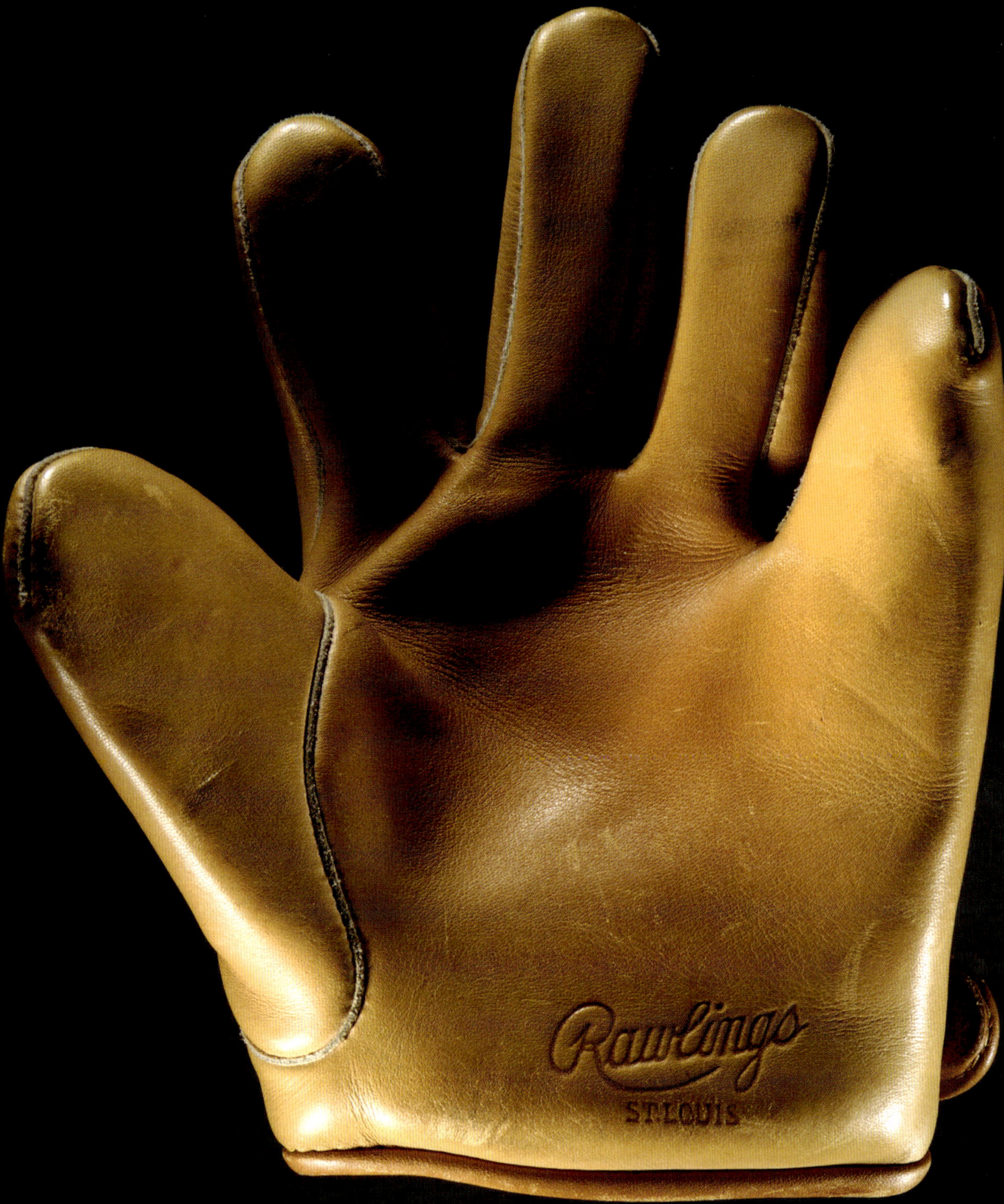
Rawlings
ST. LOUIS

JESSE BURKETT

The Hall of Fame Crab

As the calendar turned to the 20th century, professional baseball had already been played for over a quarter century. Future Hall of Famer Jesse Burkett was one of baseball's earliest stars endorsing the Rawlings brand despite his dubious nickname, "The Crab," which he had earned from his sarcastic taunts and complaints. Though he never played in a postseason during his 16 years in the big leagues, Burkett found himself a part of some of baseball's most interesting situations.

Burkett had been in the big leagues since 1890, playing one season with the New York Giants. He joined the New Yorkers as a pitcher and labored through an unimpressive 3–10 season. On the other side of the field, he batted .309 over 101 games to reposition himself as an everyday left fielder. Hitting became his forte after being purchased by the Cleveland Spiders prior to the 1891

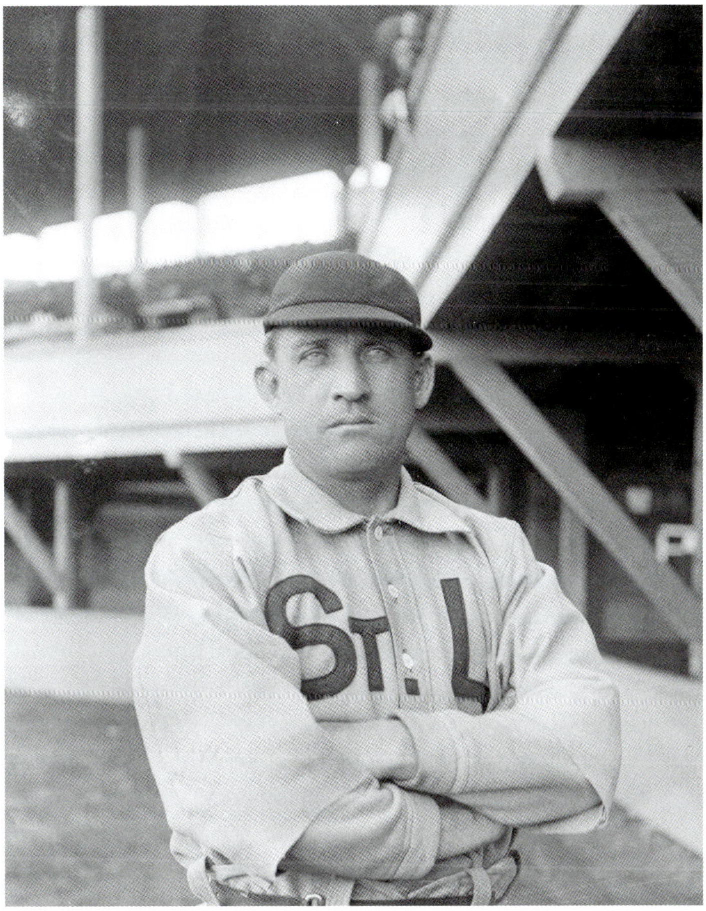

Jesse Burkett (left) appeared in Rawlings advertisements during the years when gloves were in transition from fingerless models to ones with padded fingers. This full-fingered fielder's mitt (opposite) was created with a softer, more pliable material made from horsehide and calf leather.

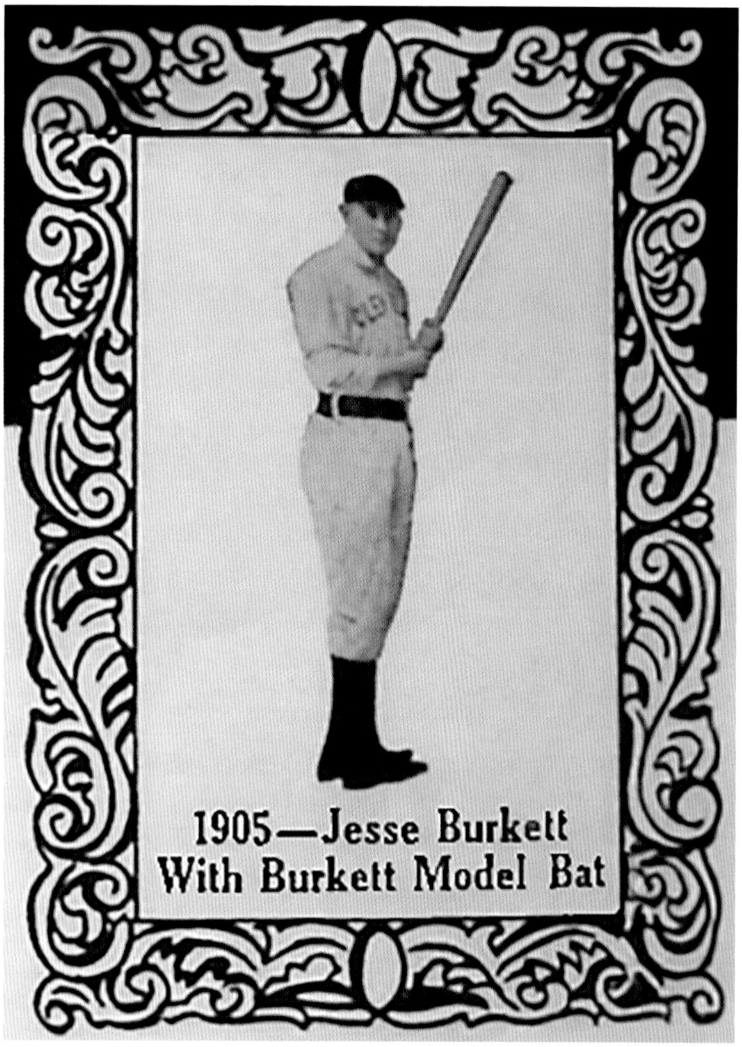

Burkett appeared in an early 20th-century Rawlings catalog promoting a bat.

season. Burkett soon topped all NL hitters in batting average and hits on two occasions—in 1895 (.405) and 1896 (.410). He also won the NL batting title in 1901 (.376). There was no American League (AL) until 1901. Burkett's Hall of Fame induction plaque from 1946 states that he "shares with Rogers Hornsby and Ty Cobb the record of hitting .400 or better the most times. Accomplishing this on three occasions." Research later revealed that Burkett's 1899 batting average was actually .396, but his plaque has never been changed. A related oddity of the game during this era was that prior to 1902 foul balls did not count as strikes, and Burkett was an expert in fouling off balls until he got the pitch he wanted to hit.

His time with the Spiders set up another interesting baseball moment. The Robison brothers, Frank and Stanley, owned the Spiders. In 1899 they purchased the NL's bankrupt St. Louis Browns (not to be confused with the 1902–1953 AL's St. Louis Browns) and changed the team's name to the St. Louis Perfectos (which they would change again in 1900 to the St. Louis Cardinals). Wanting to win the pennant, the brothers decided to move the best players from their Cleveland team, including future Hall of Famers Burkett, Cy Young, and Bobby Wallace, to St. Louis and put the worst of the group on the Spiders. The Spiders became the worst team in MLB history with a 20–134 record, but the St. Louis Perfectos did not win the coveted pennant; they finished in fifth place, 18.5 games behind the Brooklyn Superbas (later renamed the Dodgers).

Burkett's time with St. Louis's NL team was just three seasons, but his time in the city was six years. With the contraction of the NL in 1901 and the start of the AL that same year, the Milwaukee Brewers, one of the AL's original teams, was relocated to St. Louis in 1902 and renamed the Browns. In search of a higher salary, Burkett jumped to the Browns (which was allowed in those early years) and played there for three seasons before finishing his career with Boston's AL team in 1905. There were no Gold Gloves to be given out until 1957, but within the statistical record books of modern baseball (post-1901), Burkett remained a year-after-year leader in putouts. At five feet, eight inches, Burkett was not an overly powerful hitter. He only hit 75 home runs in his career. However, 55 of them were inside-the-park four-baggers—an MLB record that still stands today.

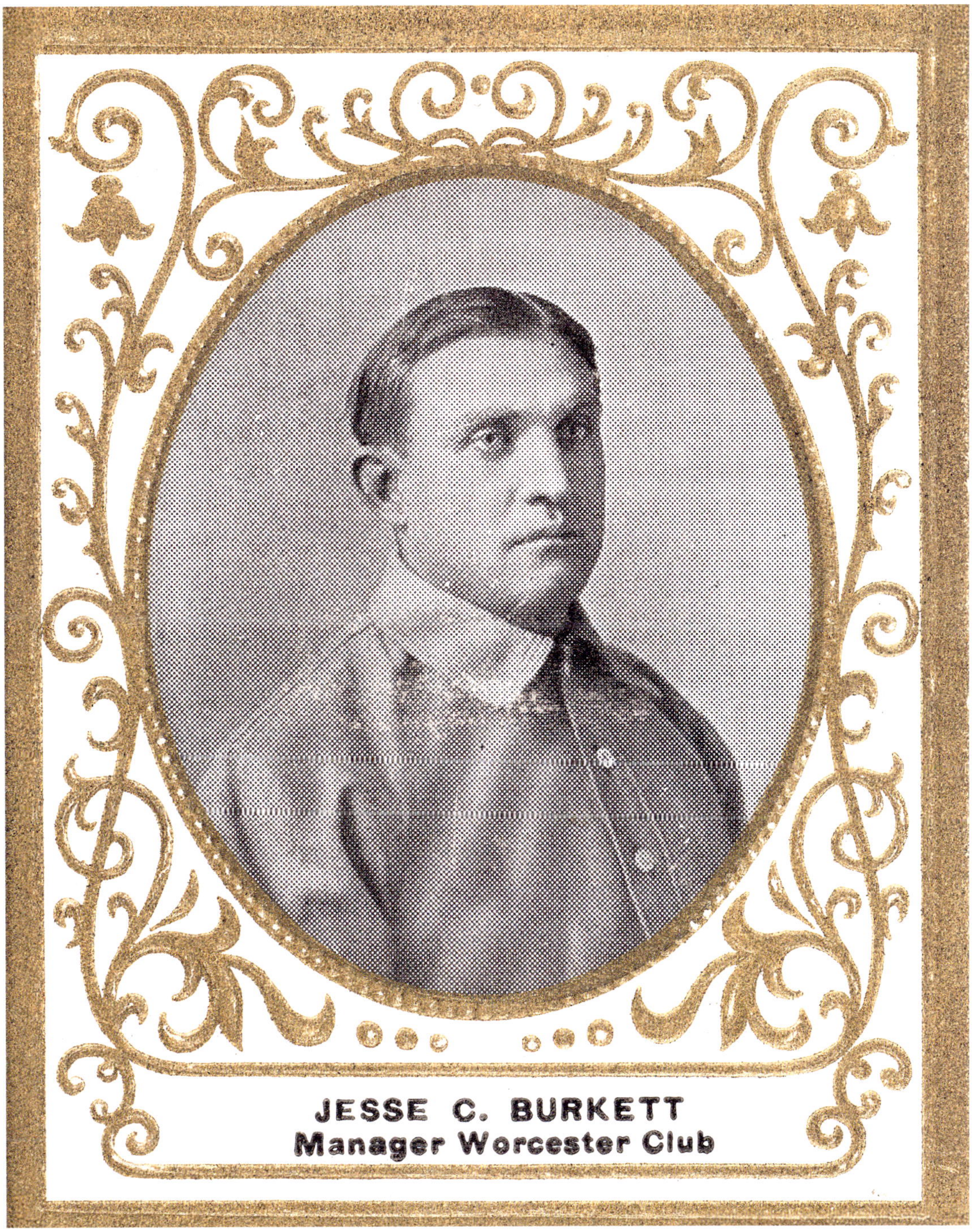

Burkett's image was also used on an American Tobacco Company playing card, circa 1909.

CHRISTY MATHEWSON

One for the Ages

There is a reason why, in January 1936, Christy Mathewson became one of the first five men ever elected to the Hall of Fame in Cooperstown, New York. Mathewson and the other four members of that first induction class—Ty Cobb, Babe Ruth, Honus Wagner, and Walter Johnson—were the biggest heroes in baseball, a game that had taken the nation by storm. Their induction into this new institution became a celebration to preserve the legacy of the game during the unfolding Great Depression and to cement baseball as America's pastime.

Mathewson, nicknamed "Matty," was the greatest pitcher of baseball's Deadball Era (1900–1920). Mathewson and Wagner were the only two of the first five Hall of Famers to have played their entire career during that period. Mathewson's career spanned 17 seasons between 1900 and

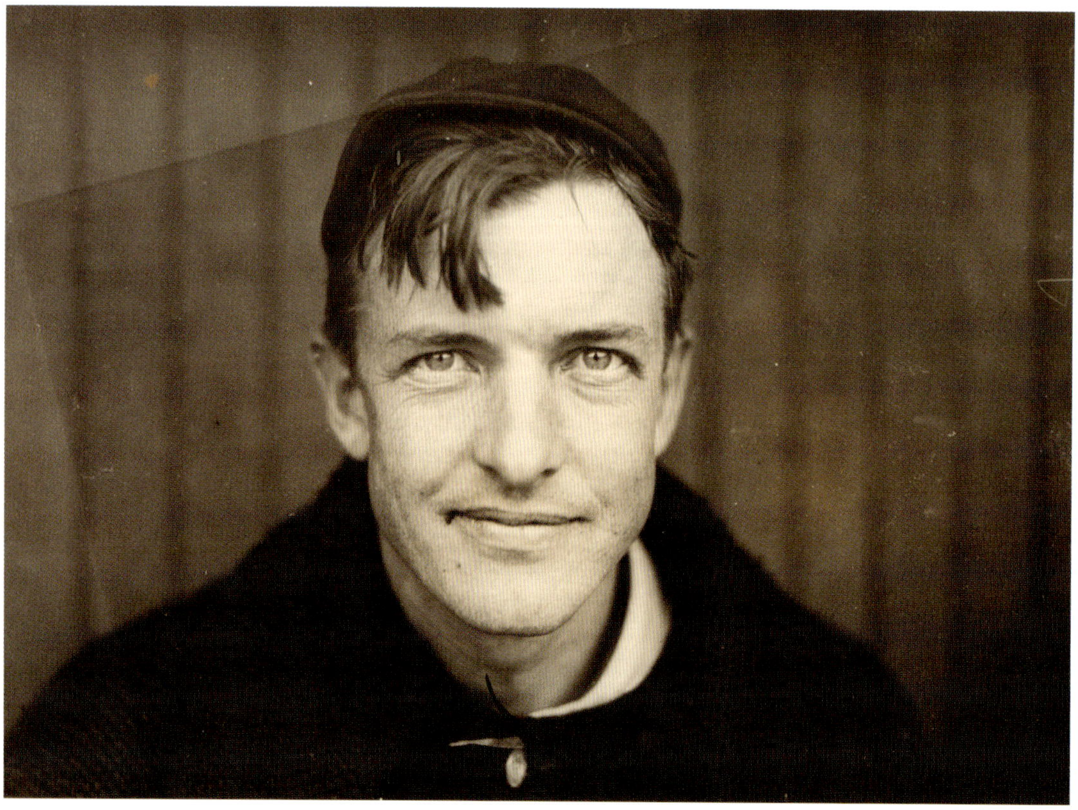

Christy Mathewson (above), shown circa 1910, used a Rawlings A-61 model glove (opposite) built with a leather piece placed between the thumb and first finger, which he later donated to the Hall of Fame.

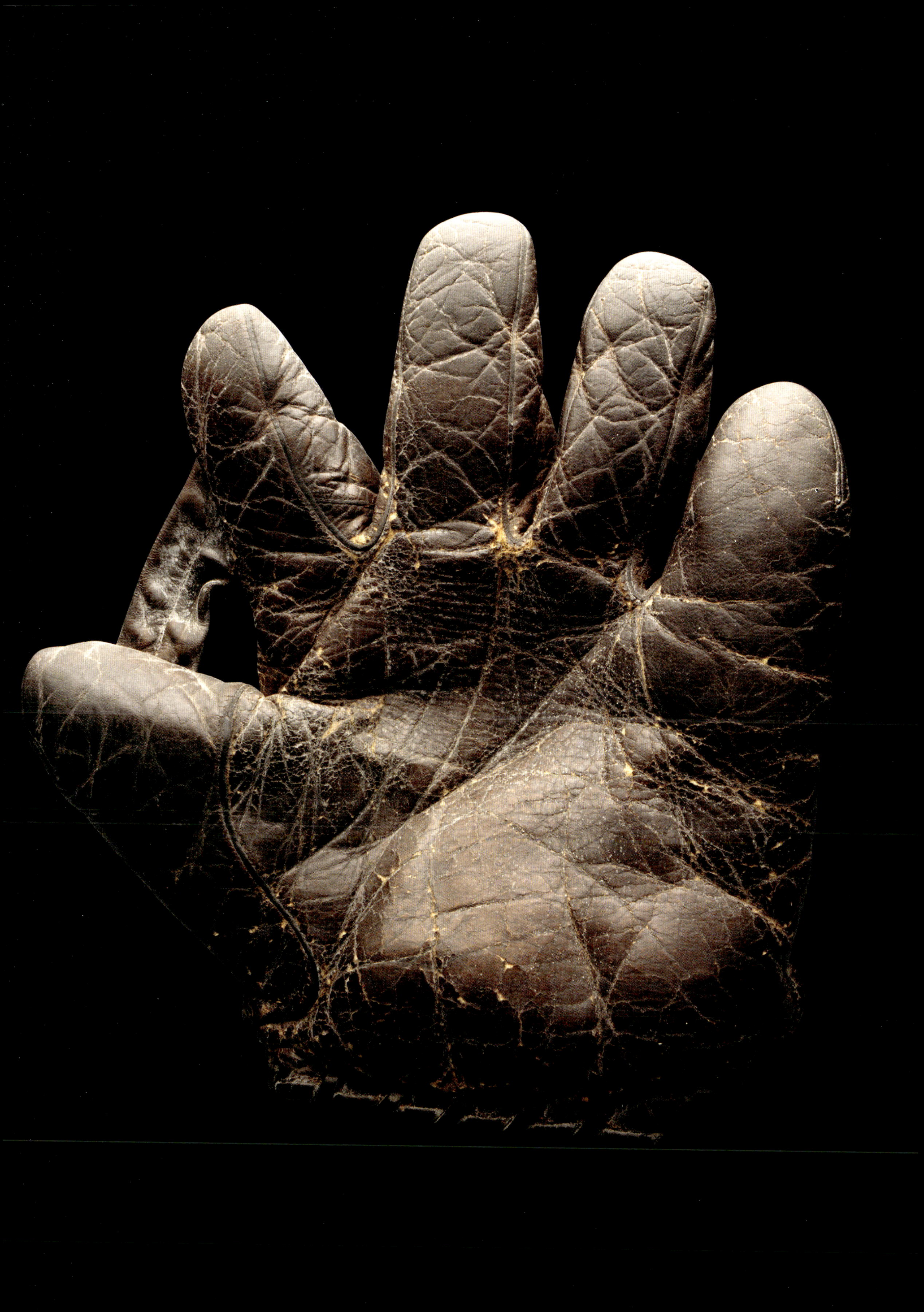

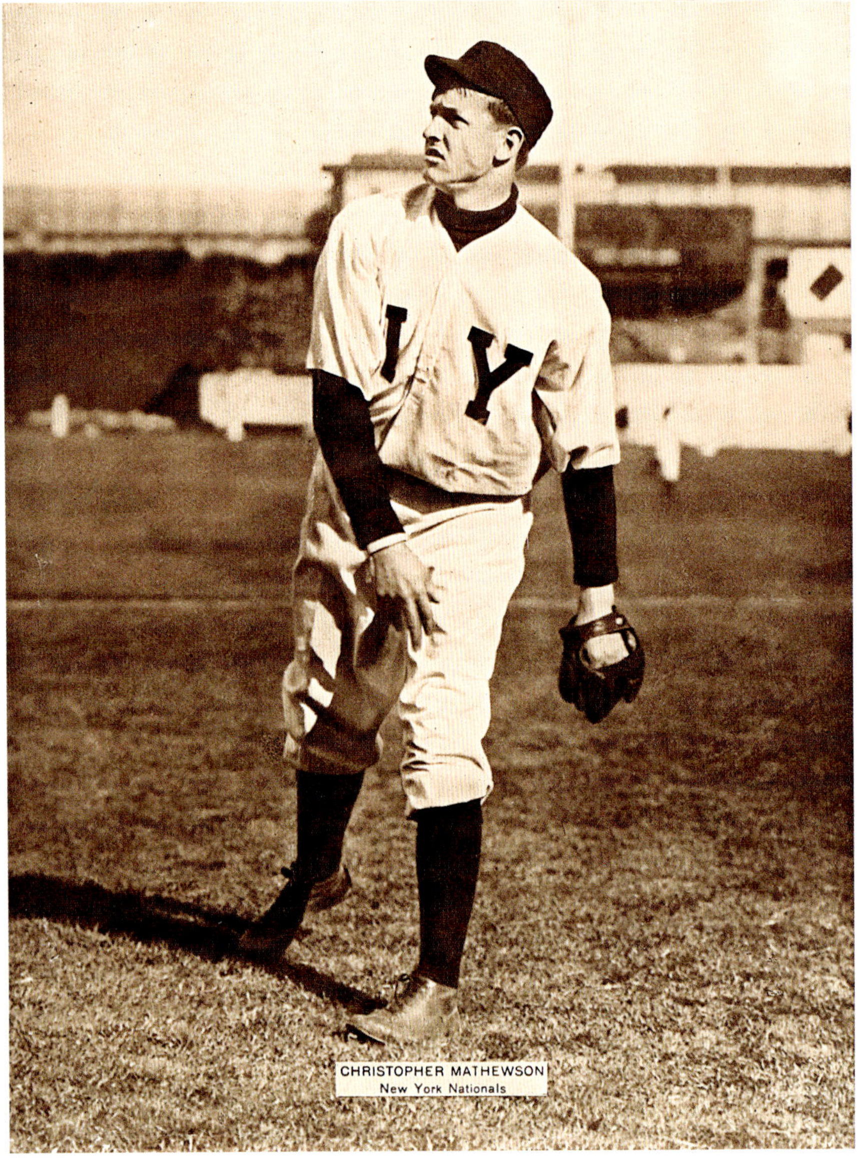

Mathewson, shown here circa 1912, was nicknamed "Big Six" after being compared to New York City's Big Six Fire Company, known for its speed in extinguishing fires.

1916. During that time, he posted a .655 winning percentage with 373 wins and only 188 losses. His career ERA was a remarkable 2.13 while posting a 106.7 WAR rating (the 27th best in baseball history). And that's after going 0–3 in his first season.

Between 1904 and 1914, Mathewson won at least 22 games every season and topped 30 wins four times. But the 1905 World Series cemented the legacy of his career. Even if he hadn't pitched in the Series that year, Mathewson's 1905 season was remarkable by itself. He posted his first of two pitching Triple Crowns by leading the league in wins (31), ERA (1.28), and strikeouts (206) to cap a truly dominating season-long performance. But it was that season's Fall Classic that is looked upon as the undisputed greatest pitching performance by anyone in the history of the World Series.

The year 1905 was the second occurrence of baseball's World Series, and it featured Mathewson's 105-game-winning New York Giants and Connie Mack's AL champion Philadelphia Athletics. Despite featuring the Athletics' three future Hall of Fame pitchers, the Series only lasted six days. Mathewson's Giants won the Fall Classic four games to one behind Mathewson's unequaled performance of winning three games in just six days. What made this

BASEBALL WRITERS ASSOCIATION OF AMERICA HALL OF FAME ELECTION

JANUARY 29, 1936

TOTAL BALLOTS CAST: 226. NECESSARY FOR ELECTION: 170.

ELECTED: Ty Cobb, 222; Babe Ruth, 215, Honus Wagner, 215;

Christy Mathewson, 205; Walter Johnson, 189.

TABULATION:

146 Larry Lajoie
133 Tris Speaker
111 Cy Young
105 Rogers Hornsby
80 Mickey Cochrane
77 George Sisler
60 Eddie Collins
58 Jimmy Collins
55 Grover Alexander
51 Lou Gehrig
47 Roger Bresnahan
21 Jimmy Foxx
9 Bill Terry

(Election conducted by Henry P. Edwards, Director American League Service Bureau)

feat so special was that Mathewson's three wins were each complete game shutouts. Over the course of 27 innings, Mathewson only allowed 14 hits and one walk and never allowed an Athletics player to touch home plate.

It was a performance and a career that secured Mathewson's stardom in those early days of baseball. And as one of the game's best, Mathewson was soon featured as a spokesperson for Rawlings. Mathewson was not only one of the Hall of Fame's first inductees but also the first to provide the museum with a glove for a 1937 exhibit. That glove became the foundation for the many historic gloves that would eventually be included in the museum's incredibly special collection of baseball memorabilia and artifacts.

The first Hall of Fame ballot from the Baseball Writers' Association of America (left) reveals the final count to elect the first five inductees—Ty Cobb, Babe Ruth, Honus Wagner, Christy Mathewson, and Walter Johnson. A 1915 Rawlings catalog spread (below) shows the Rawlings A-61 model glove on the left page and Mathewson and other baseball greats of the period endorsing the company's goods on the right.

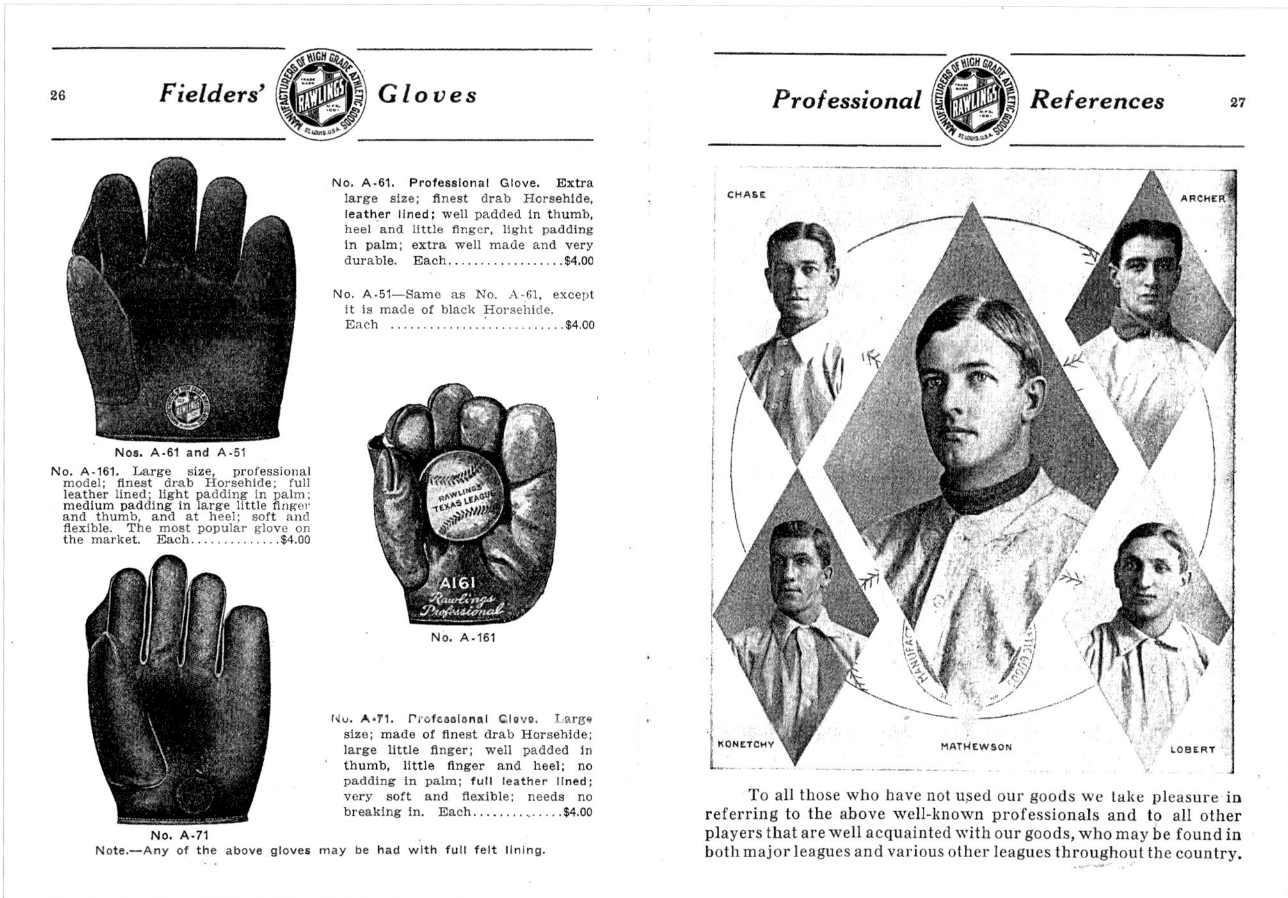
26 **Fielders' Gloves**

No. A-61. Professional Glove. Extra large size; finest drab Horsehide, leather lined; well padded in thumb, heel and little finger, light padding in palm; extra well made and very durable. Each.................$4.00

No. A-51—Same as No. A-61, except it is made of black Horsehide. Each $4.00

Nos. A-61 and A-51

No. A-161. Large size, professional model; finest drab Horsehide; full leather lined; light padding in palm; medium padding in large little finger and thumb, and at heel; soft and flexible. The most popular glove on the market. Each.............$4.00

No. A-161

No. A-71. Professional Glove. Large size; made of finest drab Horsehide; large little finger; well padded in thumb, little finger and heel; no padding in palm; full leather lined; very soft and flexible; needs no breaking in. Each..............$4.00

No. A-71

Note.—Any of the above gloves may be had with full felt lining.

Professional References 27

CHASE

ARCHER

KONETCHY

MATHEWSON

LOBERT

To all those who have not used our goods we take pleasure in referring to the above well-known professionals and to all other players that are well acquainted with our goods, who may be found in both major leagues and various other leagues throughout the country.

BILL DOAK

The Revolutionary

For most ballplayers, their career's heroics take place on the field of play. Some will become All-Stars, and some will become Hall of Famers. Many will fortify their career as everyday players, while others will enjoy spending their big-league time as bench jockeys. But some will impact the game beyond their time on the field.

With the spitball still a legal pitch when he first took to the mound for the Cincinnati Reds in 1912, "Spittin' Bill" Doak's big-league career as a starting pitcher lasted 17 seasons. He became one of only 17 players after the 1919 season to be grandfathered in and excluded from baseball's ban against throwing the substance-aided pitch. Although he spent 13 of those years with the St. Louis Cardinals, Doak wasn't with the team when they played in the 1926 and 1928 World Series. At his best, Doak won 19 and 20 games during the 1914 and 1920 seasons, respectively, on his way to a 169–157 career record supported by a 2.98 ERA and a 23.2 WAR.

While 1919 ushered in Doak's continued legal use of the "spitter," the year also cast him in one of baseball's most impactful off-field moments that would soon forever change the game. Six years after the Cardinals purchased his contract in 1913, Doak was still toeing the mound in St. Louis, which was also the headquarters of Rawlings Sporting Goods. Rawlings had been the designer of many forms of baseball gloves since the late 1880s. For Doak and all players before him, a baseball glove's purpose was more for hand protection than functional fielding. That, however, was about to change due to Doak's foresight.

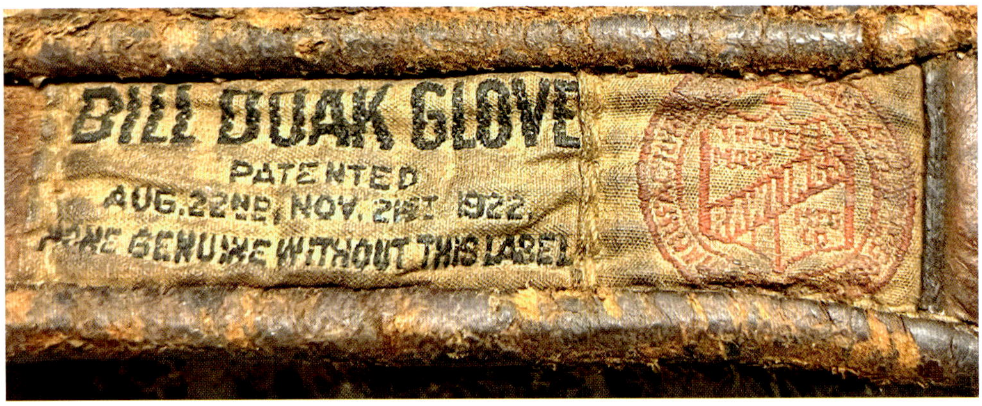

The Rawlings Bill Doak model glove (opposite) revolutionized baseball by inserting adjustable laced webbing between the glove's thumb and first finger. A Bill Doak model label (above) appeared on the gloves in 1922.

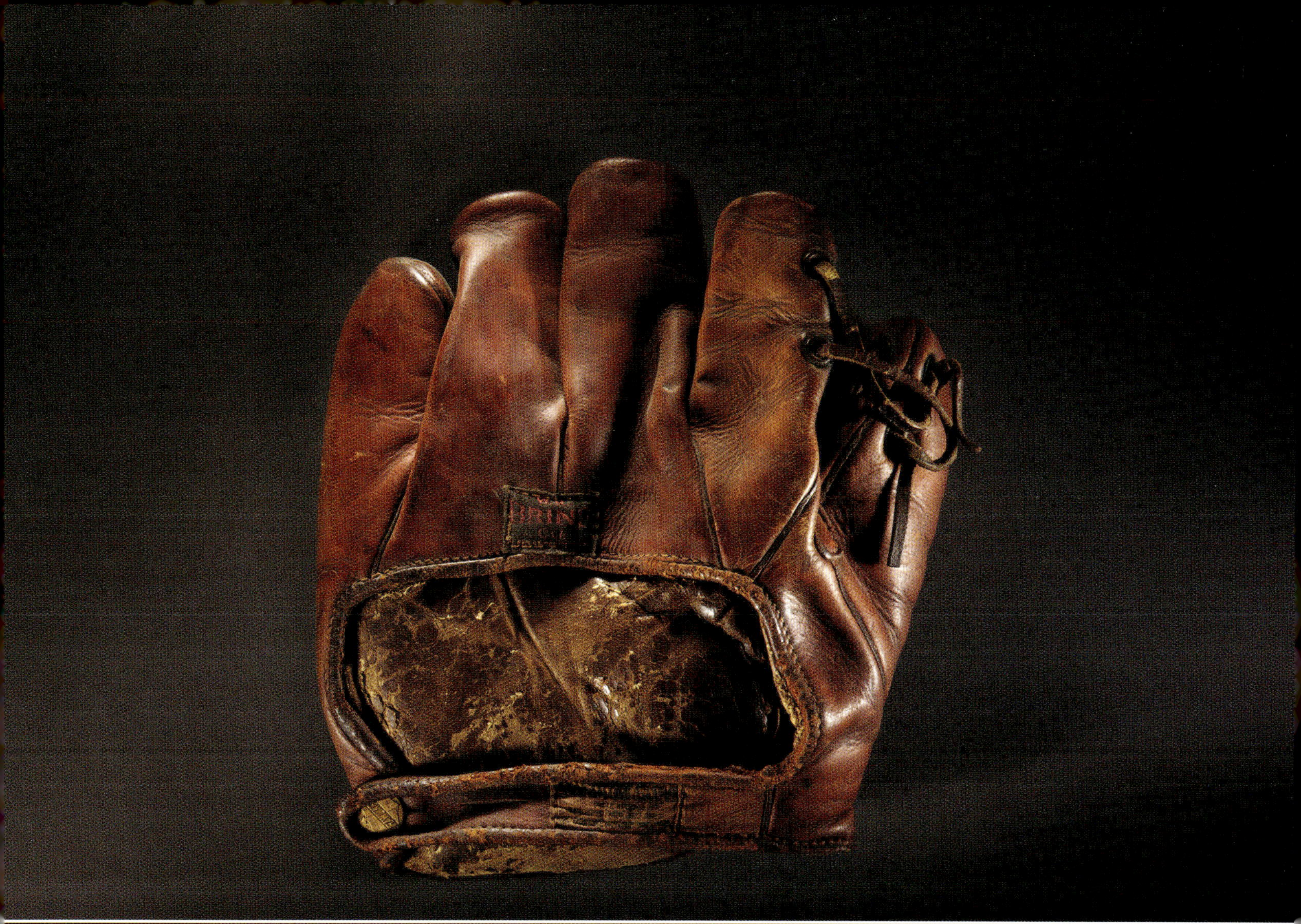

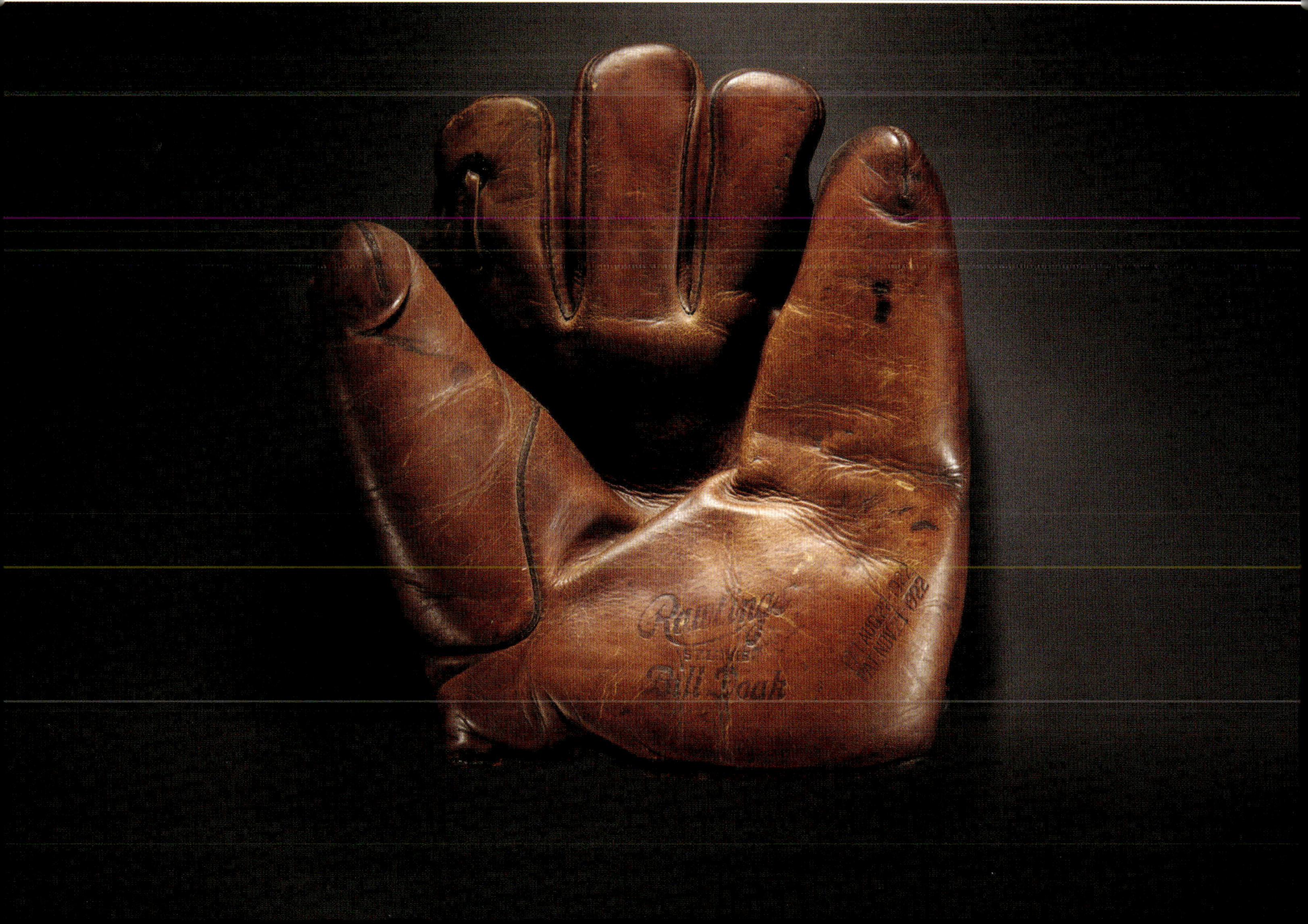

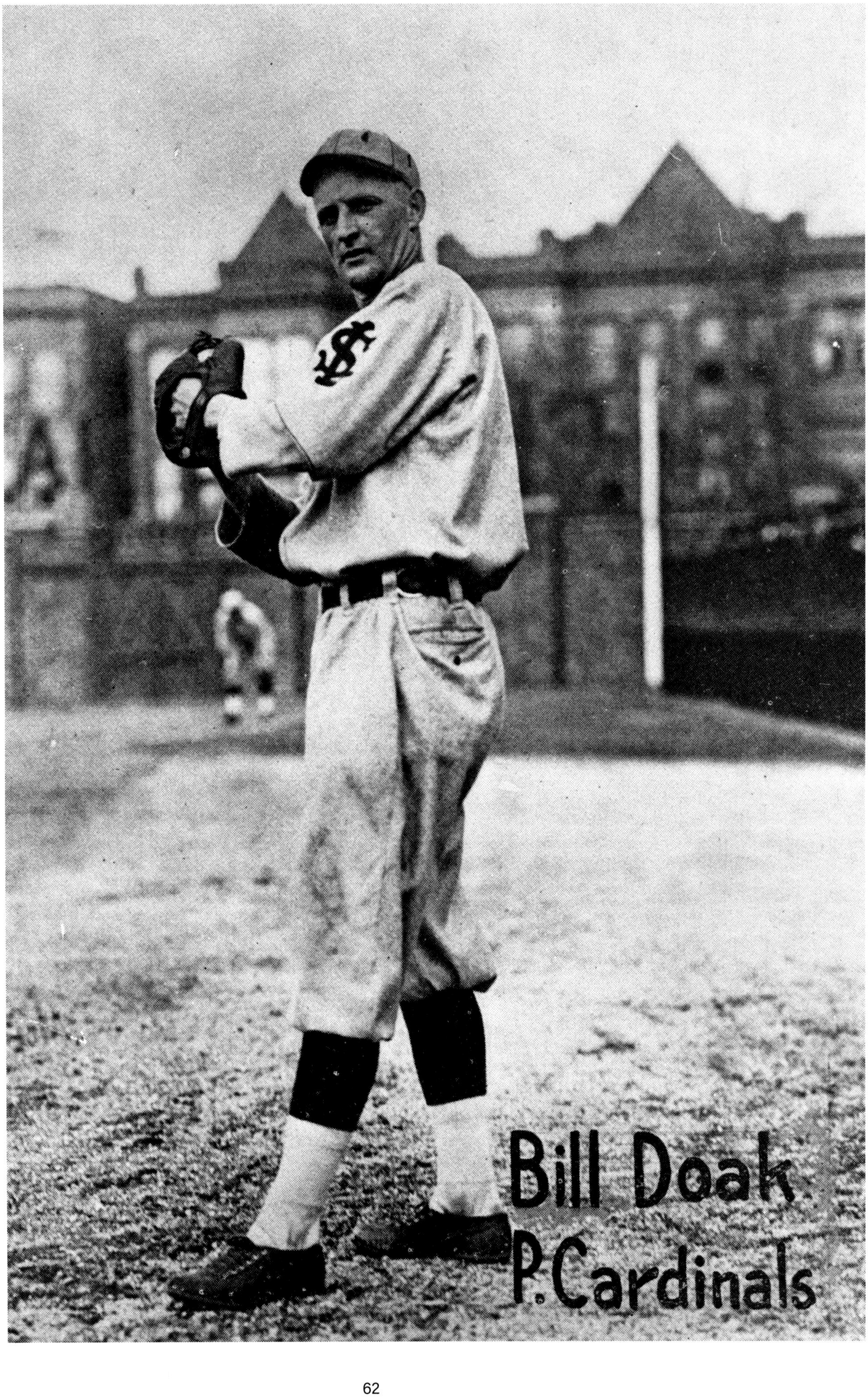
Bill Doak
P. Cardinals

Doak began working with the Rawlings production chief, William Whitley, to develop a revolutionary new baseball glove design that would quickly become the standard for decades to come. The unique element of the new glove design was the webbing between the glove's thumb and first finger. The glove's design used a large leather piece laced between thumb and forefinger, forming a deep pocket to catch the ball. This pocket could snare balls as well as catch those on the very tips of the thumb and first finger—something earlier gloves could not do. In advertising, it was heralded as "The One Glove With Which Great Players Make Great Records."

The company's 1922 patent of the design ensured that "there is only one Doak glove, and it is made by Rawlings." More importantly, the Doak glove improved defensive play across the game of baseball, resulting in changes in both strategy and performance. This ancestor to all modern-day ball gloves was first sold by Rawlings in 1920 for nine dollars and remained available in the company's catalog for over three decades until 1952. Though he barely won more games than he lost, Doak left a memorable impact on the game of baseball while earning up to $25,000 in annual royalties for the rest of his life.

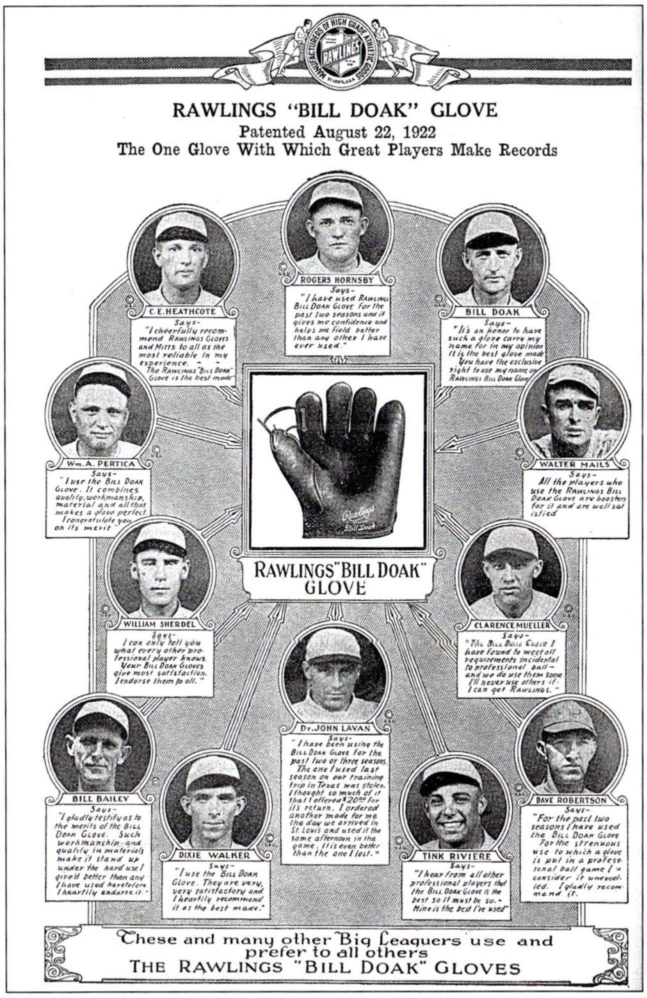

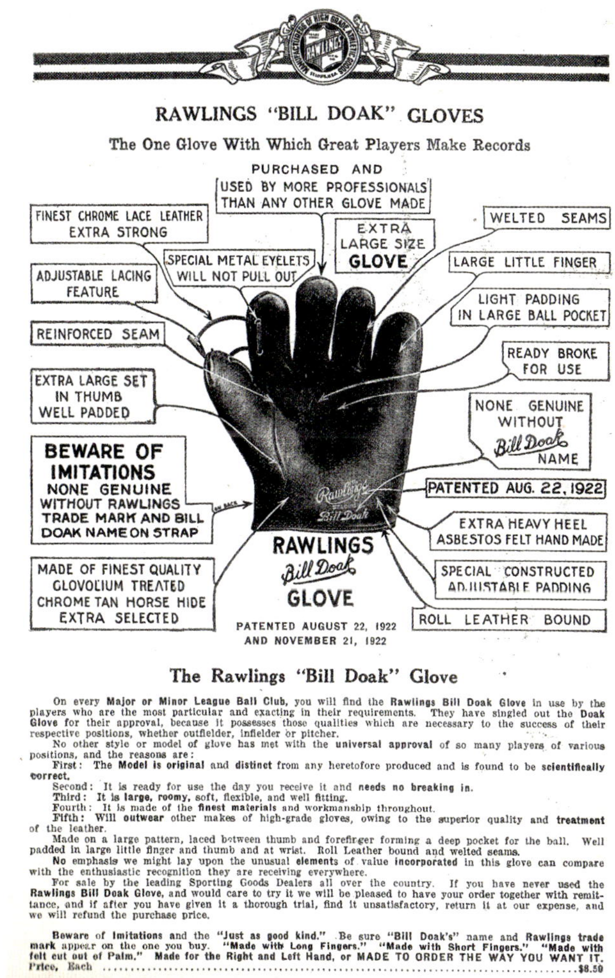

Doak (opposite), pictured here circa 1919, was a pitcher who spent most of his career with the St. Louis Cardinals. These 1920s Rawlings advertisements and testimonials (above) feature the Bill Doak model glove.

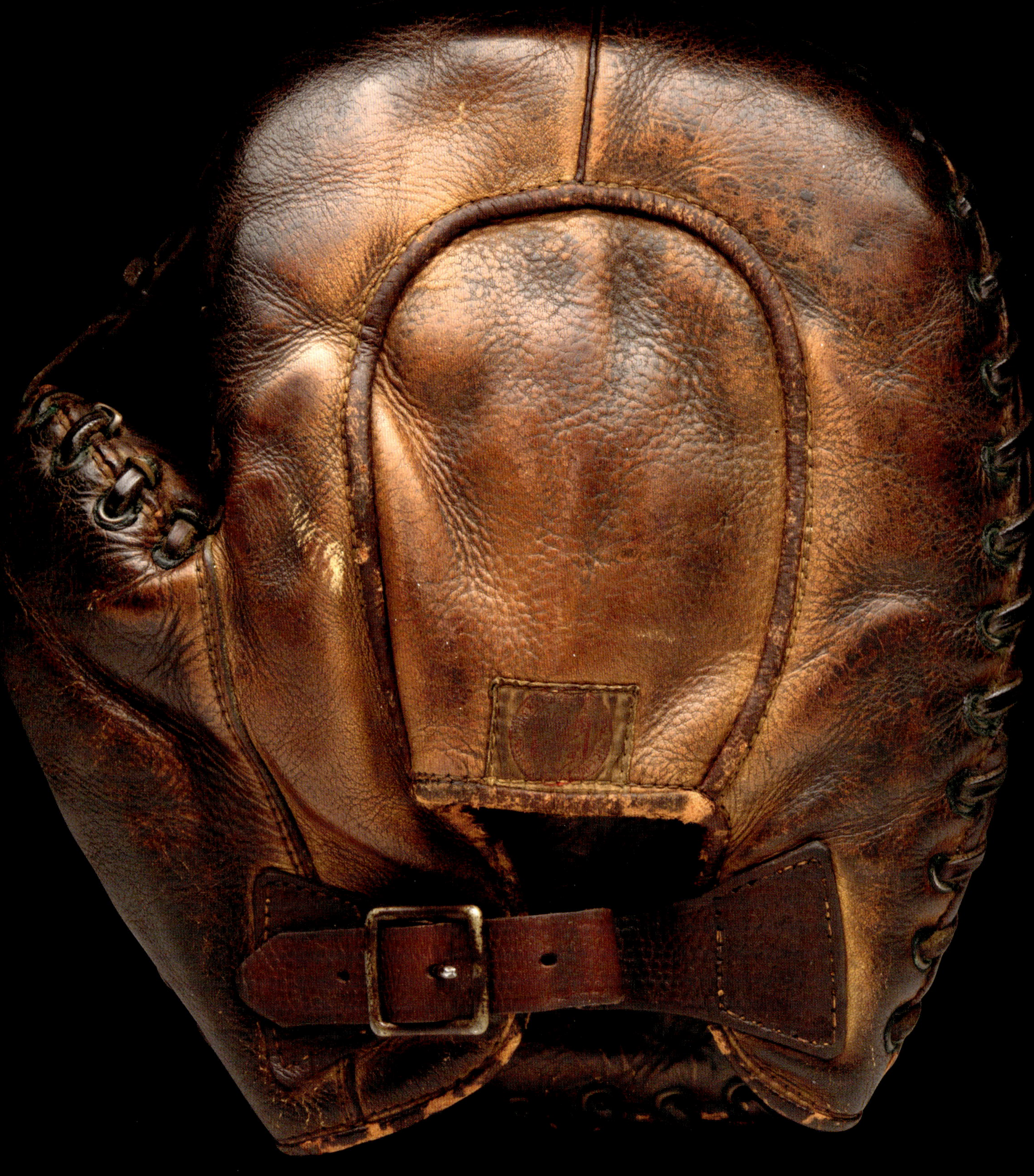

GEORGE SISLER

Use It and Have the Best

The slogan for the Rawlings George Sisler model first baseman's mitt was "use it and have the best." It was announced in 1924 as "the superior of all basemen's mitts . . . built under the personal supervision and direction of George Sisler, premier first baseman of the AL and used by him in all games." Advertisements declared that it was "guaranteed to meet the most exacting requirements of professional players."

Sisler's guidance meant a lot in 1924. Two seasons earlier, Sisler had batted .420; led the AL with 51 stolen bases, 18 triples, and 134 runs scored; and won the league award, which became baseball's first MVP Award. Sisler's offensive kudos included hits in 41 straight games (a record that stood until Joe DiMaggio broke it with 56 straight in 1941). As amazing as the 1922 season was, Sisler didn't think it was his best. In 1920, he hit .407 and collected 257 hits (another record set by the man nicknamed "Gorgeous George" that stood for 84 years until broken by Ichiro Suzuki in 2004). While Sisler and Ty Cobb are the only two AL hitters with two .400 seasons, Sisler's combined three-year stats (1920–1922) calculate to a .400 batting average over that span.

Sisler played for the St. Louis Browns, a forgotten team. The Browns changed cities in 1953, when Bill Veeck sold his team to interests in Baltimore that immediately changed its moniker to the Orioles. And like his team, Sisler is often overlooked because the Orioles do not regularly honor the Browns heroes within the franchise. During his playing days, Sisler was clearly one of the game's top offensive players, but his exploits at the plate were often overshadowed by the prowess of Babe Ruth's record-setting home runs, which were happening at the same time that Sisler was topping the .400 mark.

In the field, Sisler began his career as a pitcher, twice beating his hero, Walter Johnson. But his contributions at the plate demanded that Sisler play every day, and he

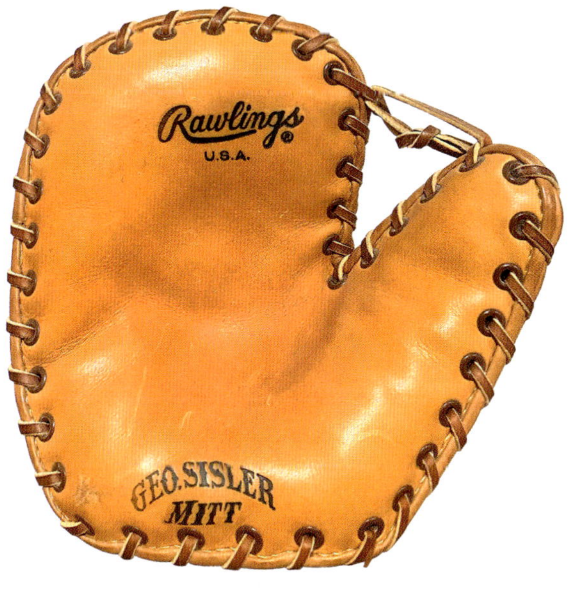

The George Sisler model first baseman's mitt (opposite and left) became the standard glove for players for the next two decades.

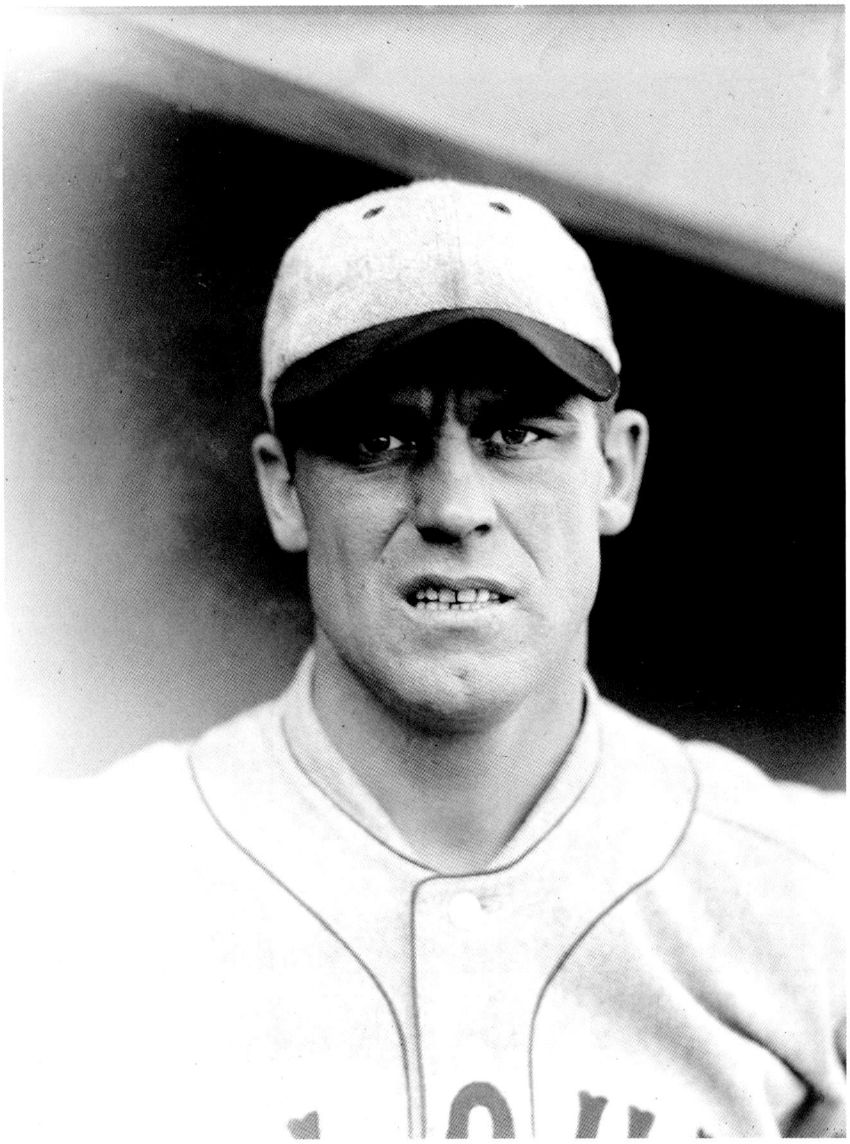

Sisler—future Hall of Famer and one of baseball's best all-around first basemen—played for the St. Louis Browns (1915–1927), the Washington Senators (1928), and the Boston Braves (1928–1930).

became a regular first baseman. Sisler quickly adapted to his new position, covering more ground than most first basemen of his era, and he was soon recognized as baseball's first great first baseman of the Live Ball Era (post-1920). But like his offensive play, Sisler's sterling defensive play was overshadowed by another Yankee—Lou Gehrig. Interestingly, each player's career batting average was .340, and Sisler's 164 triples exceeded Gehrig's career total by just one instance. On the bases, Sisler had three times more stolen bases (375) than the man known as "The Iron Horse." While Sisler was the better pure hitter, Gehrig was a better power hitter. Over on defense, Sisler was known as one of baseball's best all-around first basemen and considered a better defender than Gehrig. Sisler led his league in assists seven times, and his career assist record as a first baseman (1,529) was the best in baseball for 58 years until it was broken in 1987 by Keith Hernandez. Both Sisler and Gehrig were great players, but Gehrig played in the glory of America's biggest city on a team regularly winning the World Series, while Sisler never played on a pennant winner.

Even though Sisler may have been overshadowed by Ruth and Gehrig, his true abilities were summed up by one of the best in the game when Cobb described Sisler as "the nearest thing to a perfect ballplayer." And that perfection lived on for decades with the legacy of the George Sisler model glove.

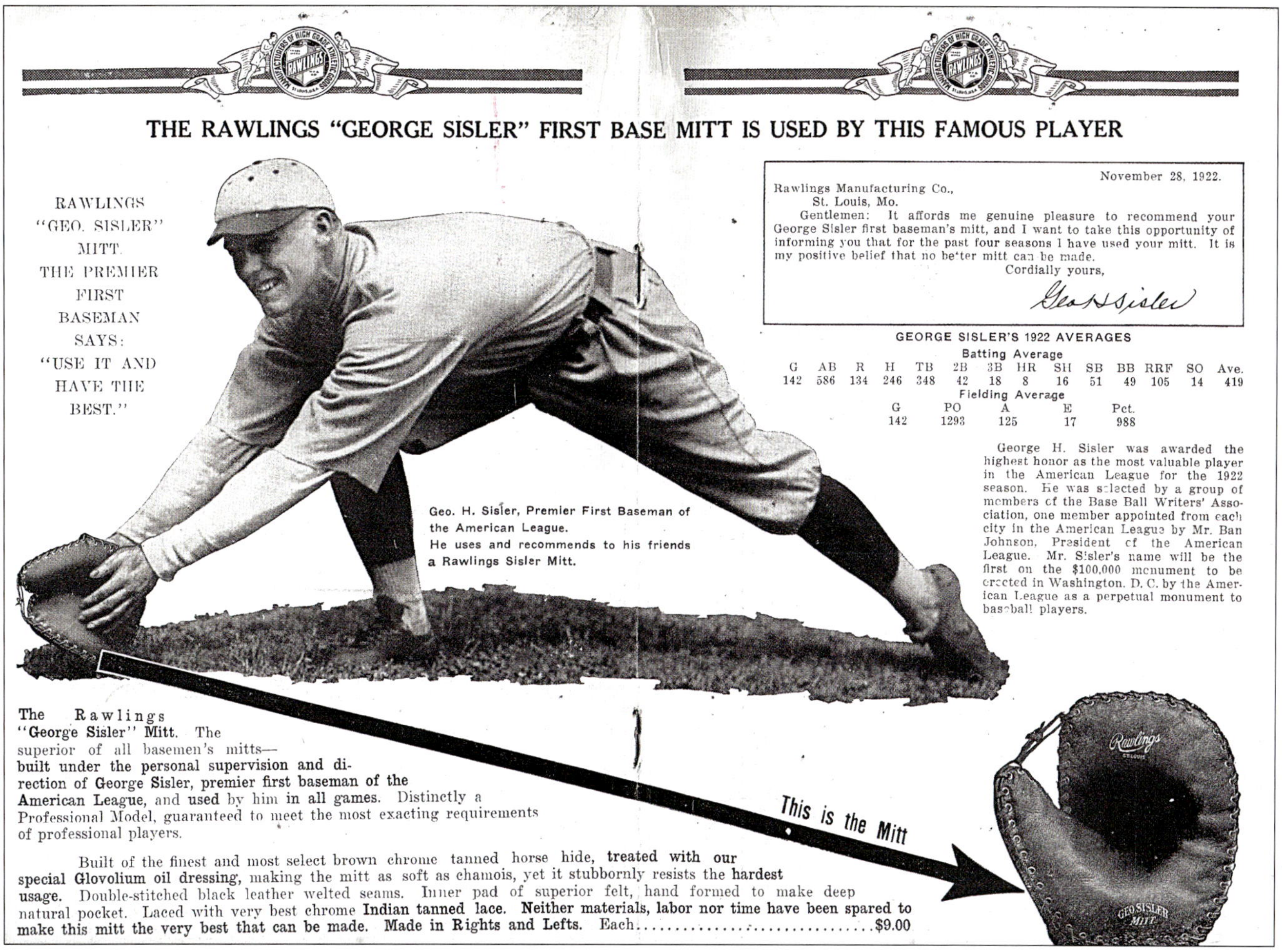

Sisler appeared in a 1923 Rawlings catalog promoting the George Sisler first baseman's mitt (above), on a 1927 York Caramels baseball card (right), and in another 1923 Rawlings catalog advertisement (far right).

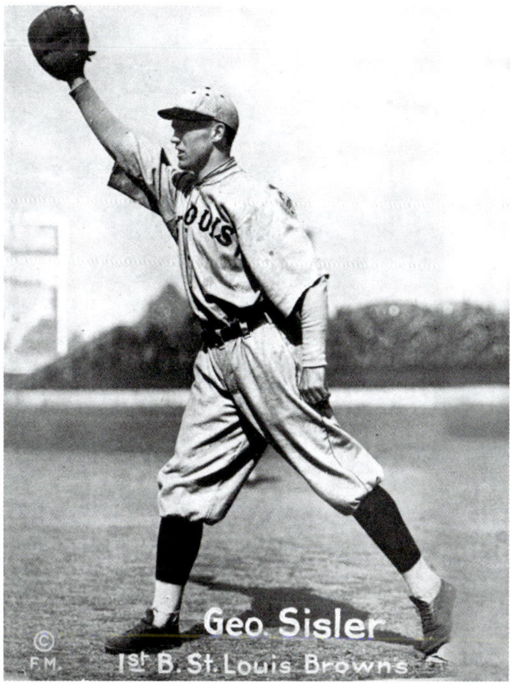

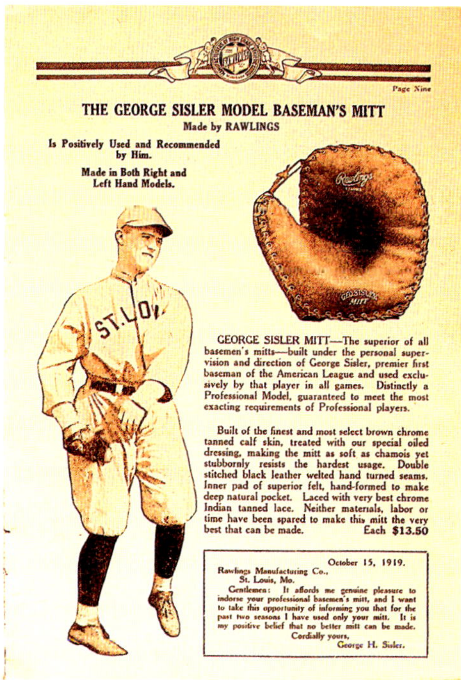

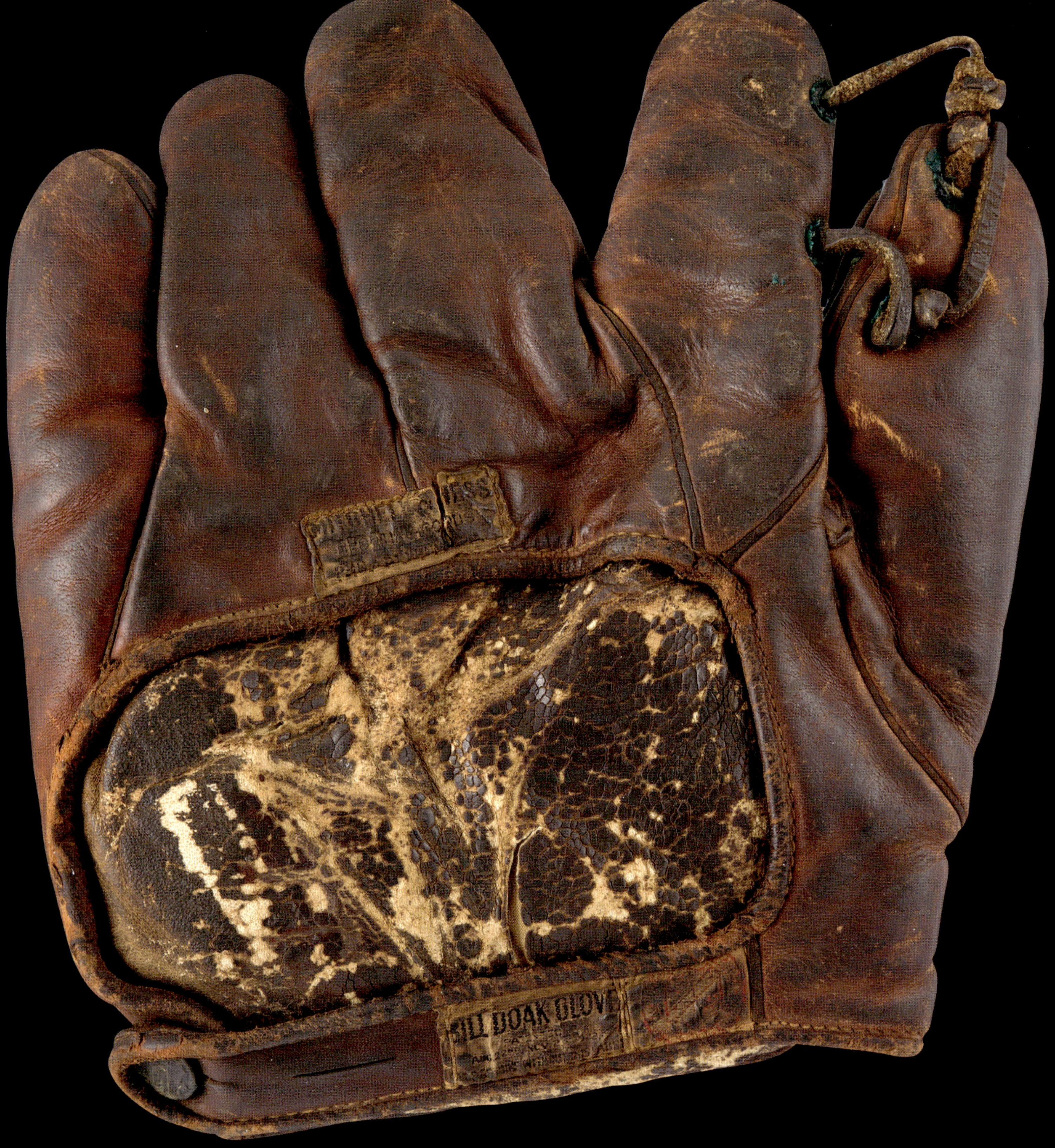
BILL DOAK GLOVE

ROGERS HORNSBY

A Catch, a Tag, and a Championship

In October 1926, two of baseball's greatest players were involved in one of the most surprising and impactful plays in MLB history. It was a moment that set the pace for baseball's two winningest World Series teams—the New York Yankees and the St. Louis Cardinals. Babe Ruth and Rogers Hornsby led their teams to league pennants that year and found themselves in the middle of the game-ending play of the World Series.

It was the Yankees' fourth pennant in six years (previous wins were in 1921, 1922, and 1923), having won their first world championship in 1923. In time their success led them to 41 pennants and 27 world championships. Their World Series wins remain 16 more than baseball's next winningest team—the Cardinals.

The Cardinals were under the leadership of player-manager Rogers Hornsby, who remains baseball's greatest right-handed batter to ever play the game. That year was the Redbirds' first trip to the Fall Classic. It was not, however, their last. They went on to play in 18 more World Series. With their 11 wins, they remain the only other team with double-digit world championships. The two teams met each other again in four future World Series (1928, 1942, 1943, and 1964).

There were 12 future Hall of Famers playing in the 1926 World Series. The Cardinals and the Yankees each had six players, and the Yankees had a seventh—their manager, Miller Huggins. The dynasty-building Yankees were led by the combo of Ruth's and Lou Gehrig's offensive prowess. The Cardinals were led by Hornsby and pitchers Jesse "Pop" Haines and Grover Cleveland Alexander. The first five games of the Series were full of excitement. The New Yorkers

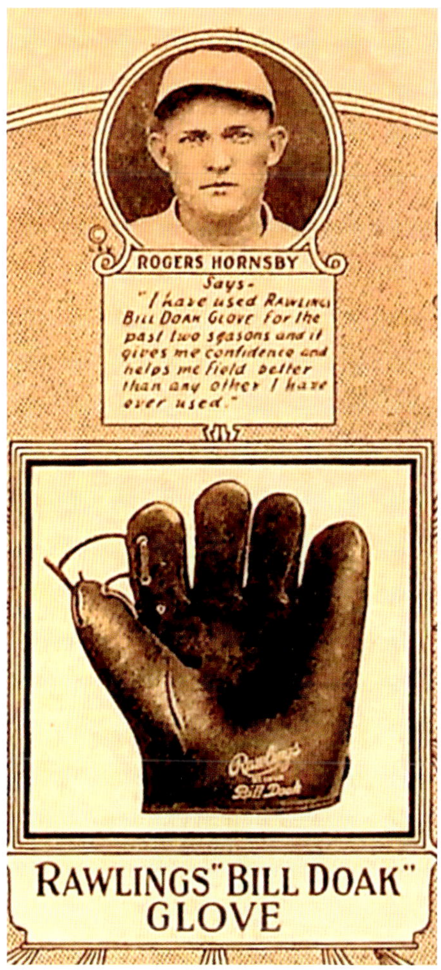

Rogers Hornsby not only used the Bill Doak model glove (opposite) but also appeared in a 1924 Rawlings catalog advertisement for the mitt (right).

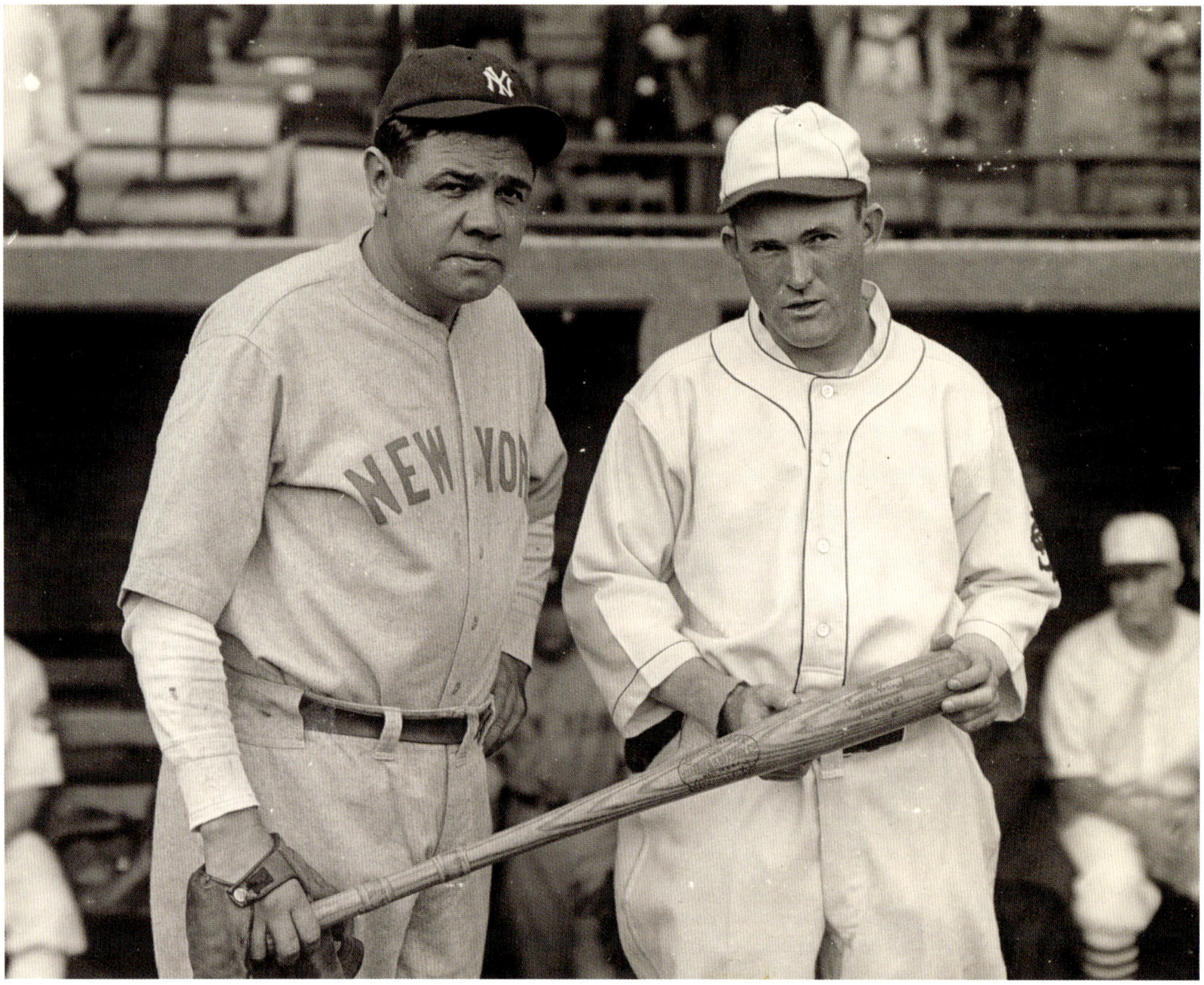

Two of baseball's greatest players, Babe Ruth and Rogers Hornsby, meet in the 1926 World Series (above). Hornsby appeared on the cover of a 1924 Rawlings catalog (right).

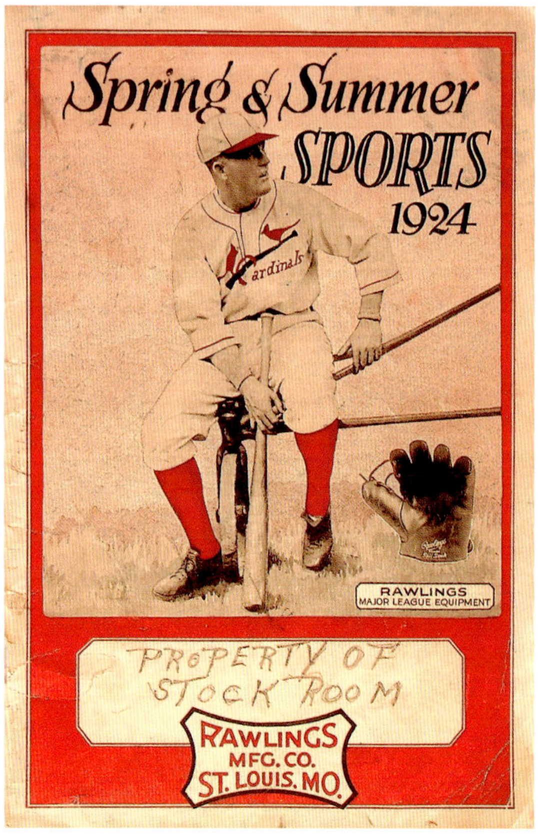

won the opener, but the Cardinals came back to win the next two games. Of Ruth's four homers in the series, three came in Game Four on October 6, the day "The Bambino" famously promised in a note to young Johnny Sylvester, who was suffering a life-threatening illness, "I'll knock a homer for you in Wednesday's game." Instead, Ruth hit three that day to tie the World Series at two games apiece. The teams split the next two games to set up the Series winner at Yankee Stadium.

Alexander's aging arm had pitched a complete game victory in Game Six the day before for his second World Series win. Haines had the other Redbirds win in Game Three and was back on the mound for the deciding Game Seven. Ruth scored the Yankees' first run with a homer in the third inning. But in the top of the fourth the Cardinals rolled back, aided by timely

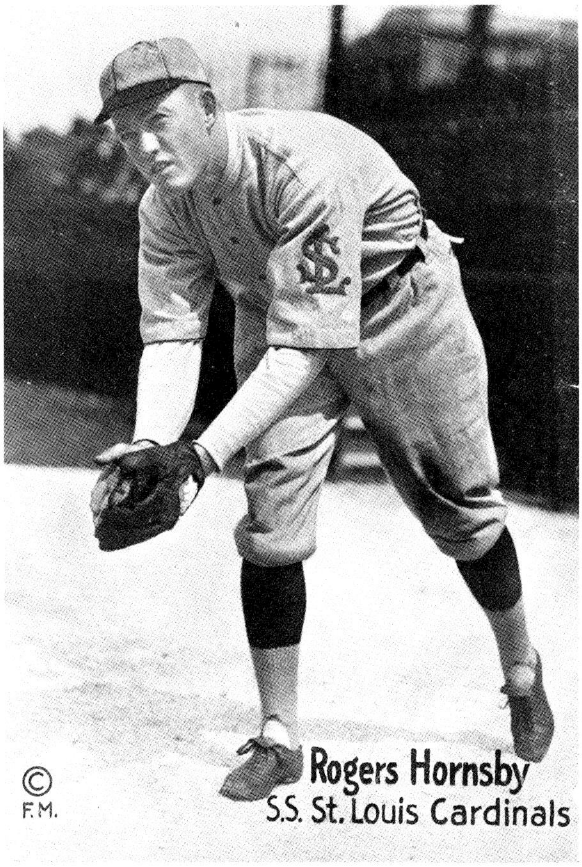

singles and a few Yankee errors, to take a 3–1 lead. New York got a run back in the sixth, and then in the seventh, after loading the bases with two outs and the dangerous Tony Lazzeri coming to the plate, Haines noticed his knuckleball had torn a blister on his finger. That led to a call to the bullpen to bring in Alexander, a man the team had picked up on waivers, to figure out how to hold the lead. In a dramatic showdown, he struck out Lazzeri on four pitches. Alexander then held the Yankees in check into the bottom of the ninth and got the first two outs before allowing a walk to Ruth.

To the surprise of everyone in the stands, on the first pitch to the next batter, Bob Meusel, Ruth broke for second base. The Cardinals' catcher Bob O'Farrell made a clean catch on the called strike and threw a laser into the outstretched glove of the waiting Hornsby at second base to tag the sliding Ruth out to end the game and win the World Series for the Cardinals. Later, Ruth was quoted as saying he tried to steal because "the way Alex[ander] was pitching, they'd never get two hits in a row off him, so I better get in position to score if they got one."

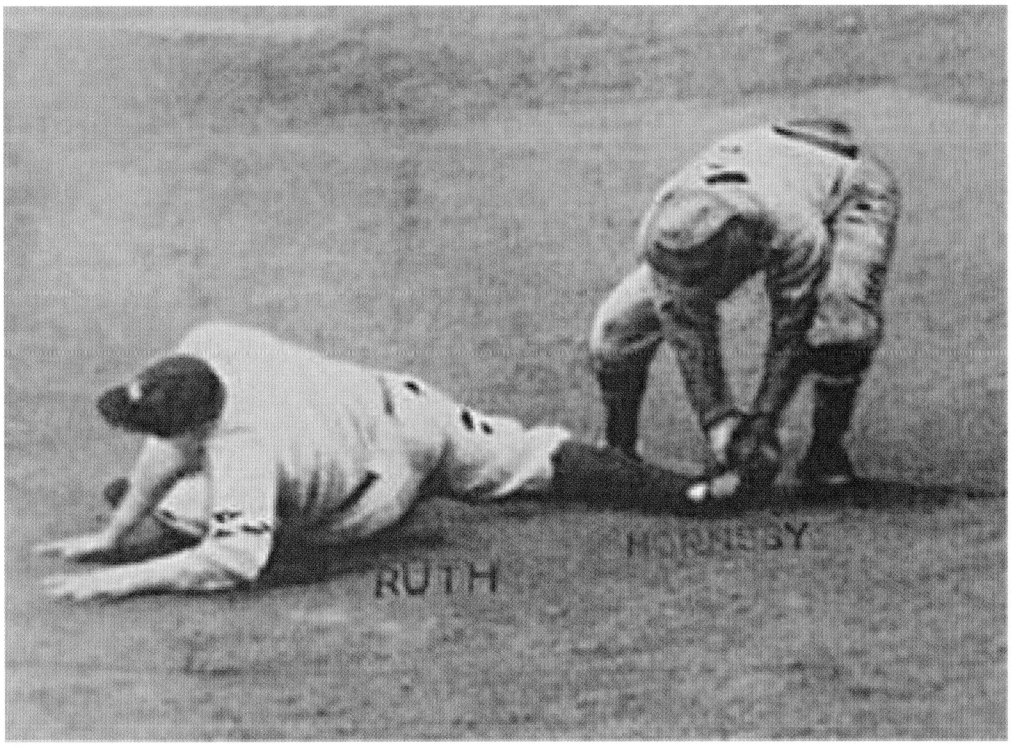

A 1917 tobacco card shows Hornsby in action (above). Babe Ruth is tagged out while trying to steal second base with two outs in the bottom of the ninth inning of Game Seven of the 1926 World Series, giving the St. Louis Cardinals their first World Series win (left).

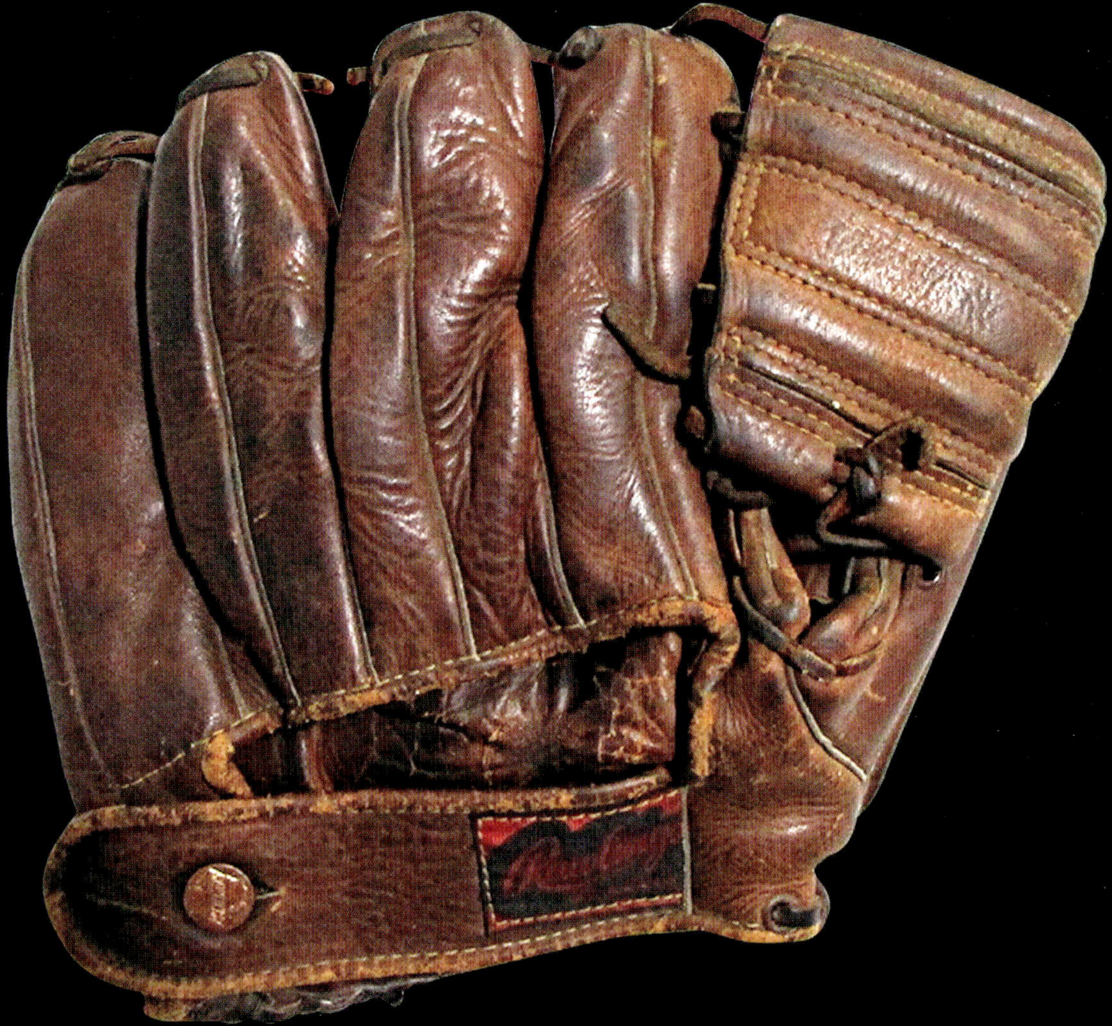

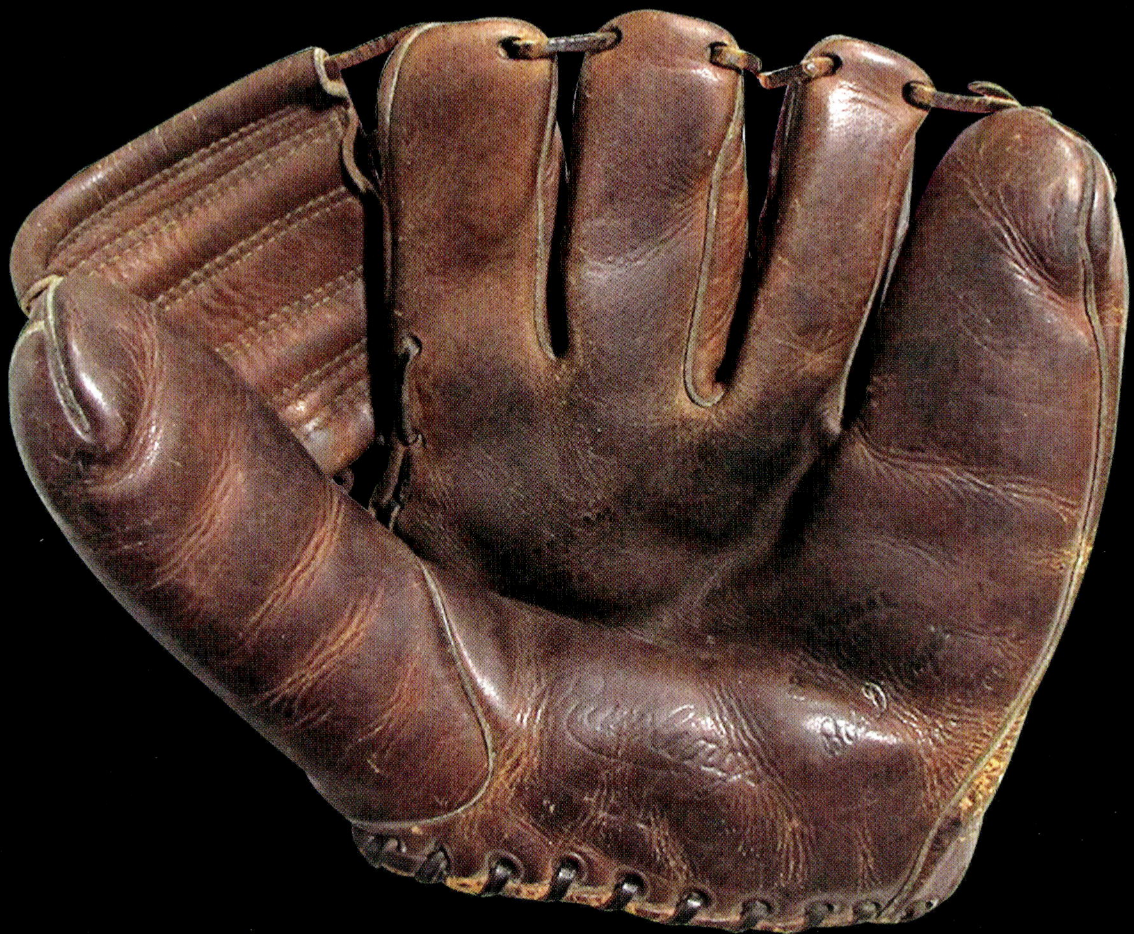

JACKIE ROBINSON

The Perfect First

Twenty-two years before Neil Armstrong stepped off the lunar lander onto the surface of the moon, declaring "That's one small step for [a] man, one giant leap for mankind," the Dodgers' Jackie Robinson had already taken one small step in baseball that became one giant leap for America. By stepping over the white chalk line in Brooklyn's Ebbets Field on April 15, 1947, to take his position at first base against the visiting Boston Braves, Robinson reshaped the game of baseball and American society.

It had been nearly 71 years since the Boston Red Caps beat the Philadelphia Athletics 6–5 in the first game played in NL history on April 22, 1876. From that day on, MLB's history was written and its record books established. Yet, until Robinson took the field in Brooklyn that day in 1947, there had been no Black players within its history.

Today the story is well-known: Dodgers' executive Branch Rickey chose and guided Robinson to be the pioneer, trusting him to carry the weight of that historic moment upon his shoulders and not fail. The seeds of the growing American civil rights movement had already been planted within the past decade as Americans of all races and backgrounds came together to fight the evils of World War II. They fought and died side by side on the battlefields and worked side by side in the factories on the home front to support the war effort. Now it was time to play the game of baseball side by side on the same diamond.

But it was not going to be easy or openly accepted. Rickey knew there would be hostilities—death threats, racial slurs repeatedly hollered out, and objects thrown from fans in the stadium seats. And he wanted a player with the ability to resist fighting back. Robinson was that player. From that first game in Brooklyn, the 28-year-old Robinson spoke to the world through his performance on the field. By the

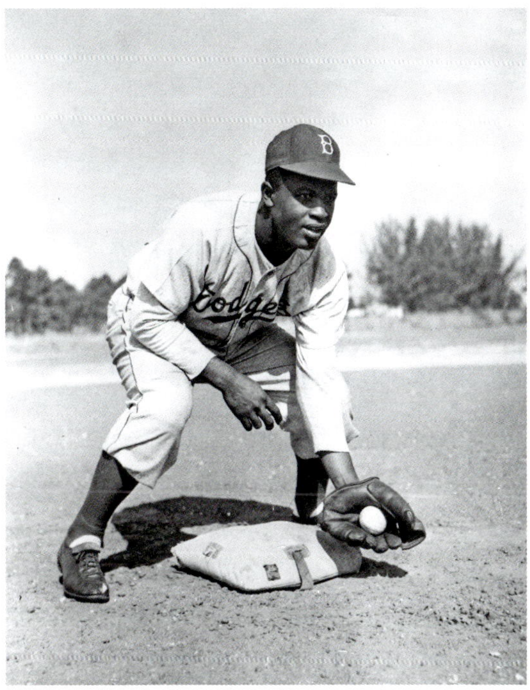

Jackie Robinson used this Rawlings Bob Dillinger model glove (opposite) while playing for the Brooklyn Dodgers. A young Robinson (right), shown here during spring training, is ready to show off his skills in the major leagues.

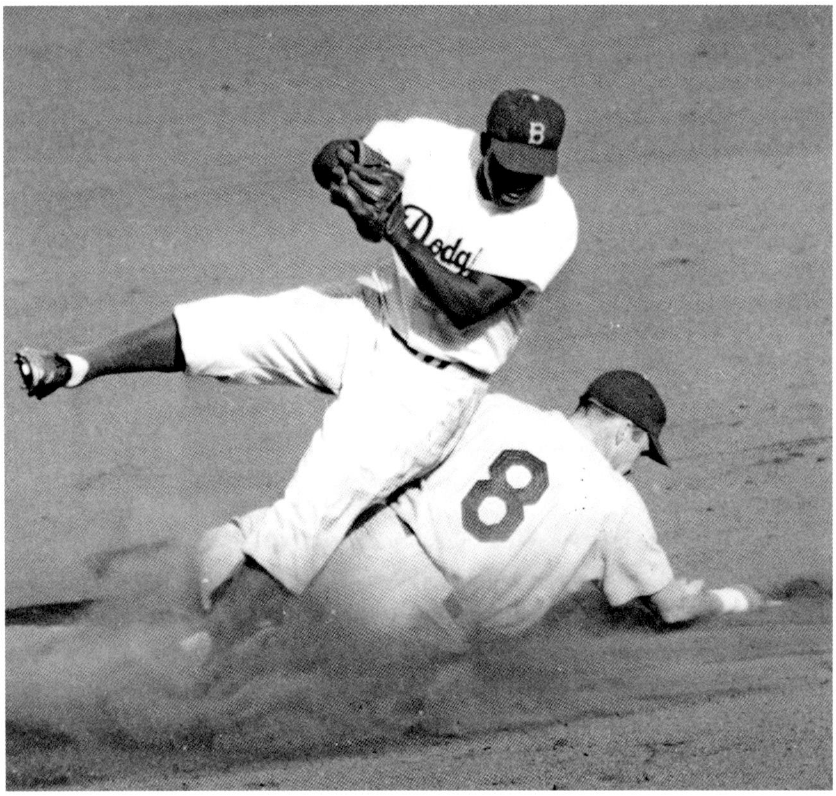

Robinson proves his toughness as he stands his ground on a double play.

season's end, his play had earned him the 1947 MLB Rookie of the Year Award (there weren't separate AL and NL awards until 1949). Two seasons later, Robinson led the league in hitting and was chosen as the NL MVP winner. In 1955, after playing in four previous World Series (1947, 1949, 1952, and 1953), Robinson helped lead the Dodgers to their first and only world championship in Brooklyn. The six-time All-Star would play in one more Series in 1956 before retiring at age 37. He was inducted into the Hall of Fame in 1962 and passed away much too early—at the age of 53—in 1972.

As described by Roger Kahn in his book *The Boys of Summer*, "Robinson could hit and bunt and steal and run. He had intimidating skills, and he burned with a dark fire. He wanted passionately to win. . . . He bore the burden of a pioneer, and the weight made him more strong. If one can be certain of anything in baseball, it is that we shall not look upon his like again."

Most fans remember seeing footage of a muscular Robinson—a career .311 hitter—on the basepaths, taunting pitchers before taking off to steal the next base or aggressively stealing home to beat a protesting Yogi Berra in the 1955 World Series. His offense and dominance of the game are highlights of his 10 years wearing the Dodger Blue, but his defensive skills and play are often overlooked. His athleticism became a critical part of his team's success. His ability to play multiple positions throughout his career continued to enhance the Dodgers' lineup and winning ways.

He began his professional career playing shortshop for the Negro Leagues' Kansas City Monarchs in 1945. After being signed by Rickey the following year, he joined the Dodgers' top minor-league club in Montréal, where he led the team to the Little World Series title playing second base. With Pee Wee Reese and Eddie Stanky in place up the middle for the Dodgers in Robinson's 1947 rookie season, he continued his defensive travels around the infield, playing all 151 of his games at first base. The following season, Robinson began a five-year run as the

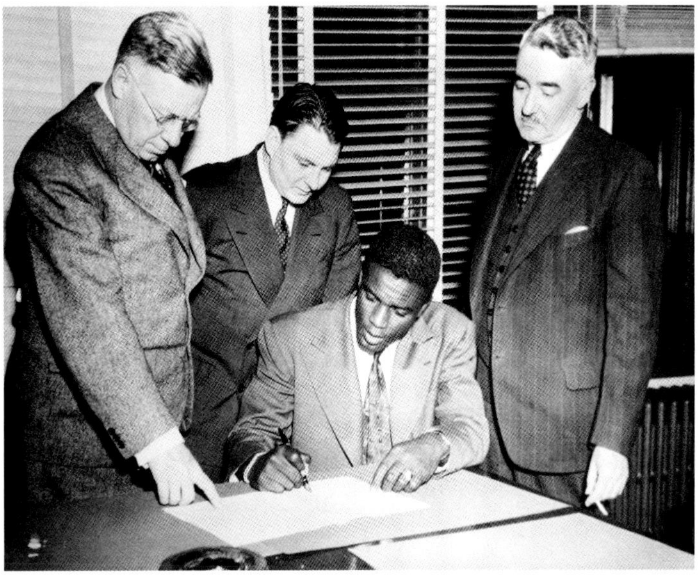

Robinson signs his contract to play for the Dodgers' minor-league team, the Montréal Royals, in 1946 (right). A description of the Bob Dillinger model glove like the one Robinson used appeared in a 1940s Rawlings catalog (below).

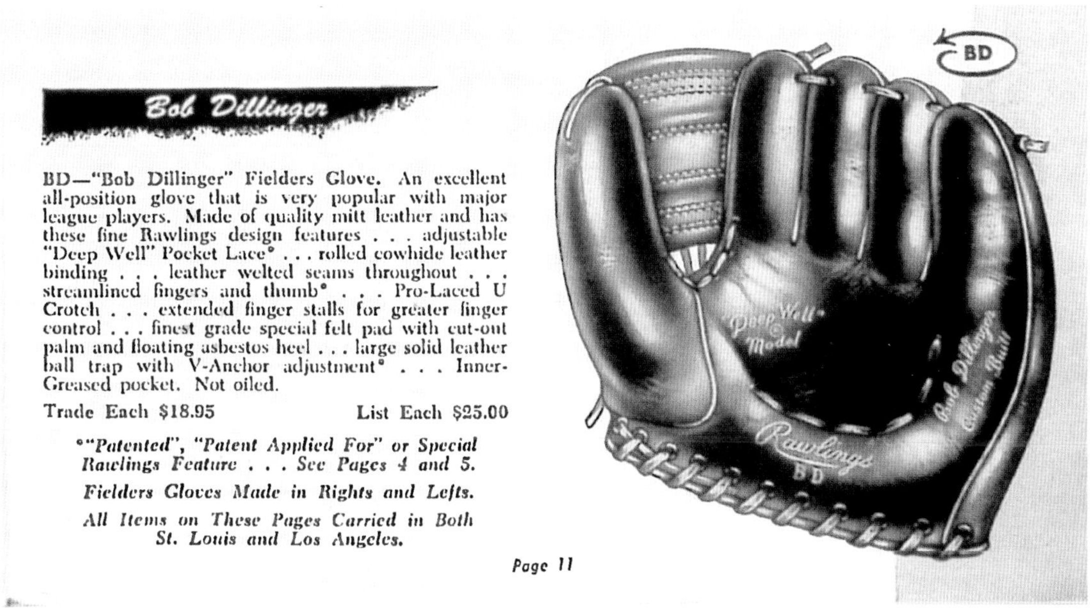

Bob Dillinger

BD—"Bob Dillinger" Fielders Glove. An excellent all-position glove that is very popular with major league players. Made of quality mitt leather and has these fine Rawlings design features . . . adjustable "Deep Well" Pocket Lace* . . . rolled cowhide leather binding . . . leather welted seams throughout . . . streamlined fingers and thumb* . . . Pro-Laced U Crotch . . . extended finger stalls for greater finger control . . . finest grade special felt pad with cut-out palm and floating asbestos heel . . . large solid leather ball trap with V-Anchor adjustment* . . . Inner-Greased pocket. Not oiled.

Trade Each $18.95 List Each $25.00

*"*Patented*", "*Patent Applied For*" *or Special Rawlings Feature . . . See Pages 4 and 5.*

Fielders Gloves Made in Rights and Lefts.

All Items on These Pages Carried in Both St. Louis and Los Angeles.

Page 11

Dodgers' starting second baseman. He was not as smooth as other infielders of the day, but his sure-handed play was enhanced by good instincts, allowing him to expand his range and make the needed plays. Robinson's toughness was quickly put on display when standing his ground on double plays, as sliding players often tried to make a statement by taking him out of the play.

While there were no Gold Gloves to be handed out during Robinson's years in the majors, a 1987 "Player's Choice" survey selected Robinson as the greatest second baseman of his era, despite his limited seasons at the position. Beginning in 1953 and for the rest of his career, Robinson's athleticism allowed him to strengthen the Dodgers' defense by splitting his time on the field between third base and the outfield. It was a move that allowed Jim Gilliam to play second base and win that year's NL Rookie of the Year Award.

Robinson was the perfect first. He was the man and the player that Rickey needed to break baseball's color barrier. Robinson had both the mental and physical toughness and the ability to make that first step over a major-league chalk line and set in motion a defining moment for Black and white players to come together—not just on a baseball field but across all of American society.

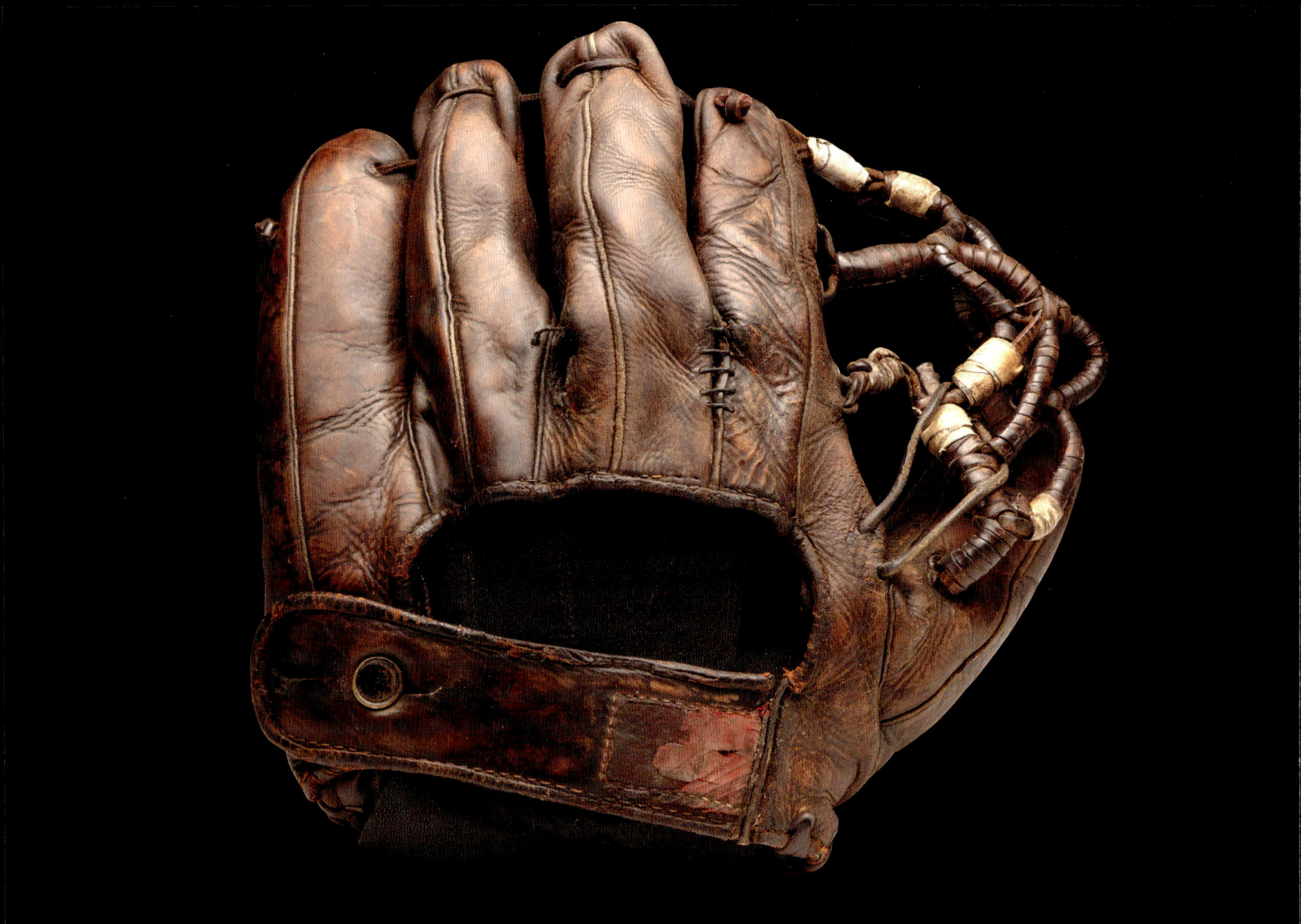

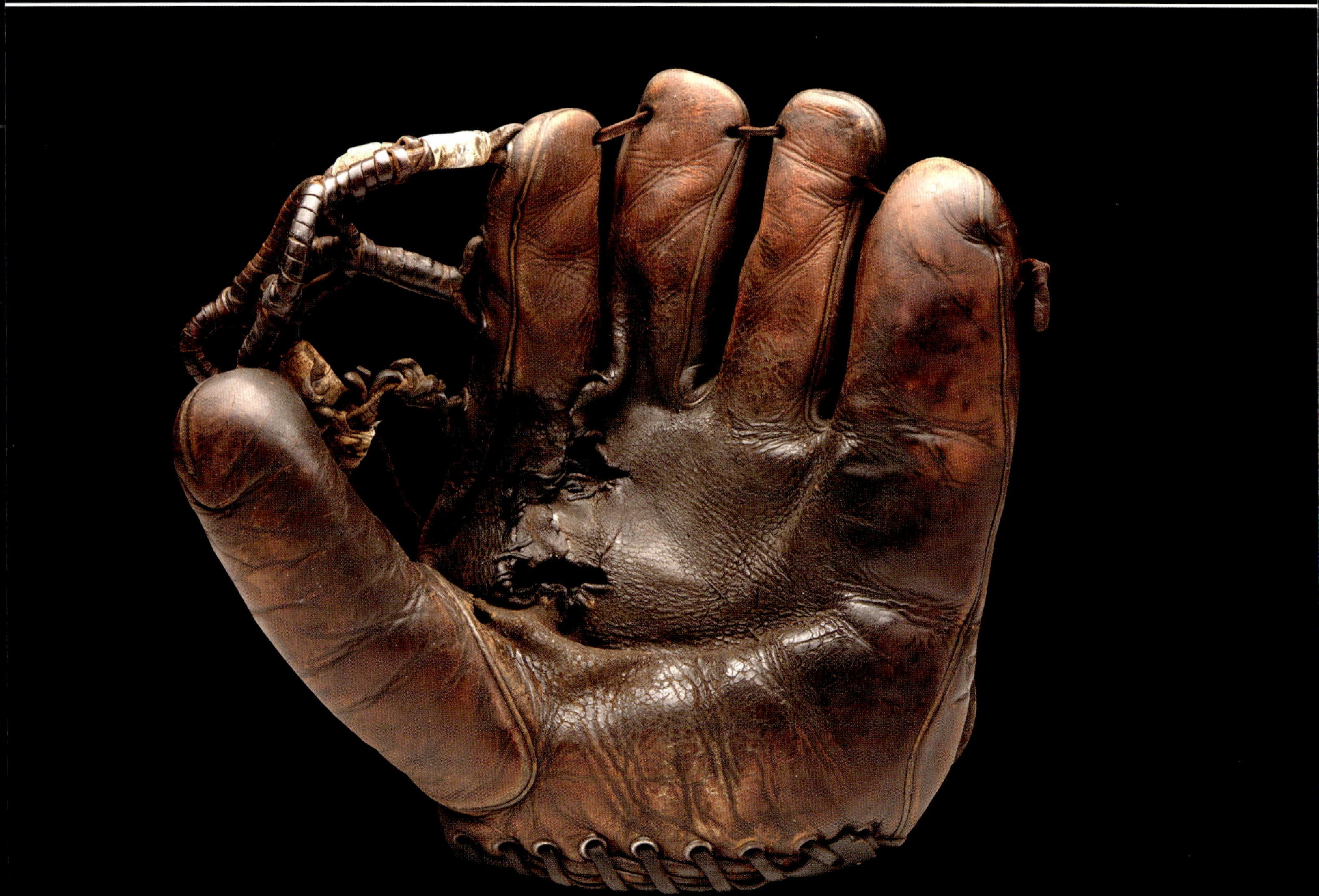

JOE DIMAGGIO

He Was Human After All

The day was Friday, October 5, 1947. The place was Yankee Stadium in the Bronx, New York, where 74,065 fans were settled in, hoping to see the Yankees clinch their 11th world championship. The moment happened in the sixth inning of Game Six of that year's World Series. The cast of characters included Joe DiMaggio and the Brooklyn Dodgers' five-foot, six-inch journeyman outfielder Al Gionfriddo, who had been brought into the game as a defensive replacement that inning. The Dodgers were trying to hold onto their lead and send the Series to a championship-deciding Game Seven.

Yankees play-by-play announcer Arch McDonald had given DiMaggio the moniker "The Yankee Clipper" in 1939, during his third season in the big leagues, when comparing his speed and range in getting to baseballs in center field to the new Pan American Clipper airplanes, which were extending travel to farther distances in quicker times. Two years later, in 1941, he was labeled "Joltin' Joe DiMaggio" as one of baseball's greatest all-around players. This nickname came from a song by Les Brown and His Orchestra, featuring vocalist Betty Bonney. It was the same year that DiMaggio put his amazing 56-game hitting streak into MLB's record book.

DiMaggio played in the World Series in 1936, 1937, 1938, 1939, 1941, and 1942. All became world championships except for the 1942 loss to the St. Louis Cardinals. DiMaggio lost the next three years to military service during World War II (1943–1945), but he and the Yankees were back in the Fall Classic in 1947 and DiMaggio won his third MVP Award.

Gionfriddo had come to the Dodgers in a trade from the Pittsburgh Pirates earlier that season and had only played in 37 games. As DiMaggio came to bat in the bottom of the sixth inning of that 1947 World Series game, the Dodgers were hanging on to an 8–5 lead. There were two outs, with two Yankee runners on base. What happened next was described by legendary broadcaster Red Barber's call: "Belted. It's a long one, deep into left center. Back goes Gionfriddo, back, back, back, back . . . he makes a one-handed catch in front of the bullpen! Oh, doctor!" Gionfriddo had been playing DiMaggio close to the left-field foul line when DiMaggio launched the ball toward the left-center wall in front of the Dodgers' bullpen. The Dodgers' left fielder was off and running, chasing the flight of the ball as it headed for the outfield fence for a potential four-bagger. The fence stood just under four feet in height. With his hat flying off and his body twisting and turning at the fence, Gionfriddo made the catch with his right-gloved hand at the

A Rawlings Red Rolfe (RR) model glove, with the patented Deep-Well Pocket, was used by Al Gionfriddo to make a catch and prevent Joe DiMaggio's home run in the 1947 World Series.

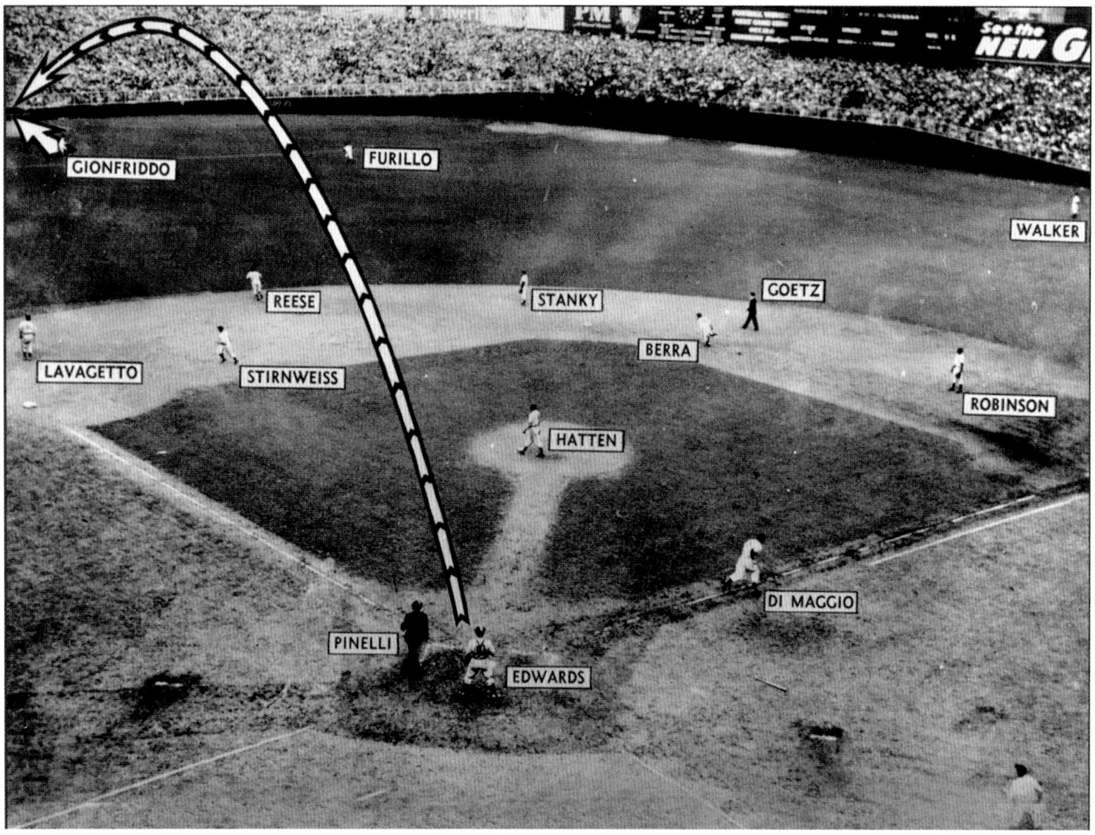

An arrow shows the path of DiMaggio's sixth-inning drive in Game Six of the 1947 World Series—the one Gionfriddo caught to save the game.

wall next to the 415-foot sign. The catch shattered the dream of a DiMaggio comeback home run that could lead to the championship that day.

More than anything else, Gionfriddo's catch proved that DiMaggio was human after all. The man who never, ever showed emotion, no matter the moment or the game, rounded first base and headed to second base, thinking he had tied the game, then stopped and kicked up a cloud of dirt in frustration. The fans in the stadium saw what many in baseball have called the greatest catch in World Series history. Baseball's future great historian David Halberstam was a 13-year-old sitting in the stands and watching the catch in disbelief, a catch he later called his "favorite sports memory." In contrast to Willie Mays's great World Series catch in 1954—where Mays had what seemed like acres of Polo Grounds field to run to make his overhead catch—Gionfriddo was quickly running out of real estate and into a wall when he made his historic grab.

The moment has been immortalized in baseball history by the film and photo of Gionfriddo making the catch as he hugs the wall, as well as the companion photo of the iconic moment of DiMaggio showing his humanity. The moment was also used in the 1989 star-studded film *Dad*, where a dying character played by Jack Lemmon told his son, played by Ted Danson, "This man [DiMaggio], who never showed any emotion, he was human after all. It took Al Gionfriddo to bring it out. Do you know what that means to me?" His son said, "What?" And the father replied, "In America, anything is possible if you show up for work."

Gionfriddo showed up for work that day and, like the biblical David, took down the giant superstar. It was the last MLB game that "Little Al" played. After that catch, his career ended. DiMaggio and the Yankees won Game Seven the next day. DiMaggio went on to play in and win

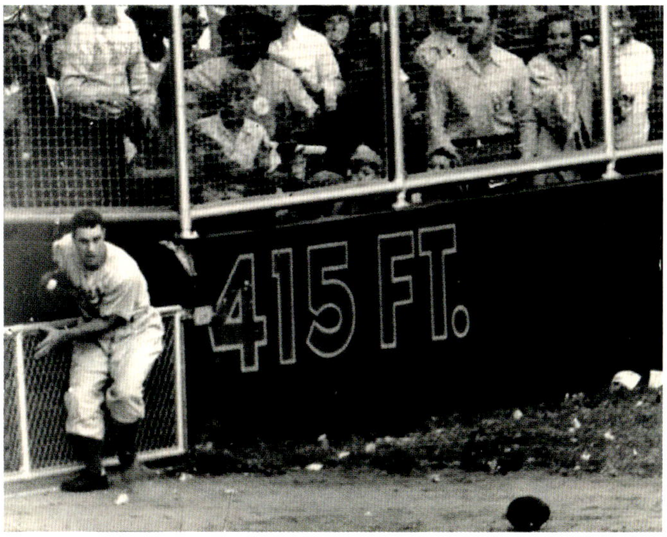

The Brooklyn Dodgers' left fielder, Gionfriddo, catches DiMaggio's blast at the Yankee Stadium bullpen wall to stop the New York Yankees' rally.

three more World Series titles (1949, 1950, and 1951). His nine championships remain the second-most won, trailing only teammate Yogi Berra's 10.

But that is not the end of the story. Even though the Yankees won the World Series the next day, DiMaggio was still haunted by the catch, and he started a campaign to disallow the glove model Gionfriddo had used to make the catch. The Rawlings Red Rolfe (RR) model was introduced in 1941 with the endorsement of the Yankees' four-time All-Star third baseman. The glove's unique design had been created by the company's lead glove designer, Harry "Doc" (short for "Glove Doctor") Latina. The RR model first introduced the company's famed Deep-Well Pocket, along with an extended rolled-lace web or net type of trap. Latina said his design would "give them [players] an extra step in the outfield by the increased length of the web." It became an immediate sensation and was being used by many future Hall of Famers and other players.

While Gionfriddo did not make it to Cooperstown as a player, his glove did to highlight the moment and the man who made one of the greatest catches in World Series history. DiMaggio was so upset by the catch that his frustration lingered, as he believed the diminutive Dodger would not have caught the ball with an ordinary, smaller glove. DiMaggio's assertions eventually led MLB officials to ban the rolled-lace glove. And yet—hypocritically—it turns out the Yankee Clipper had also been using the rolled-lace glove during parts of his career.

DiMaggio kicks the dirt in disgust after seeing Gionfriddo's outstanding catch of what could have been a game-changing home run.

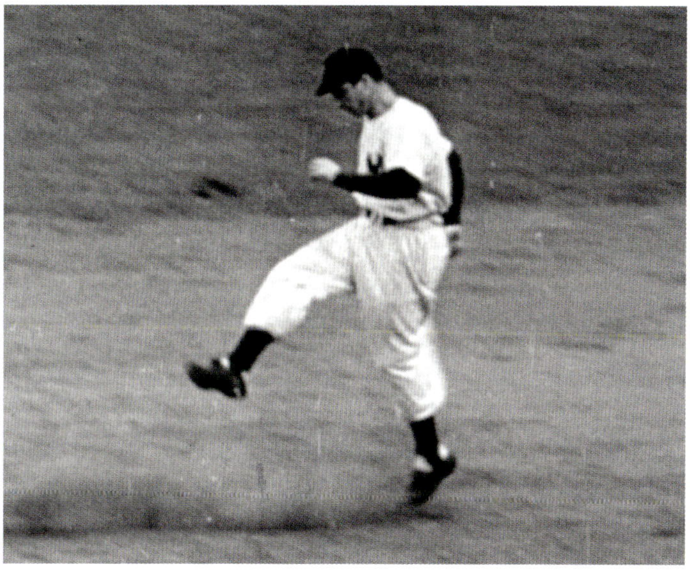

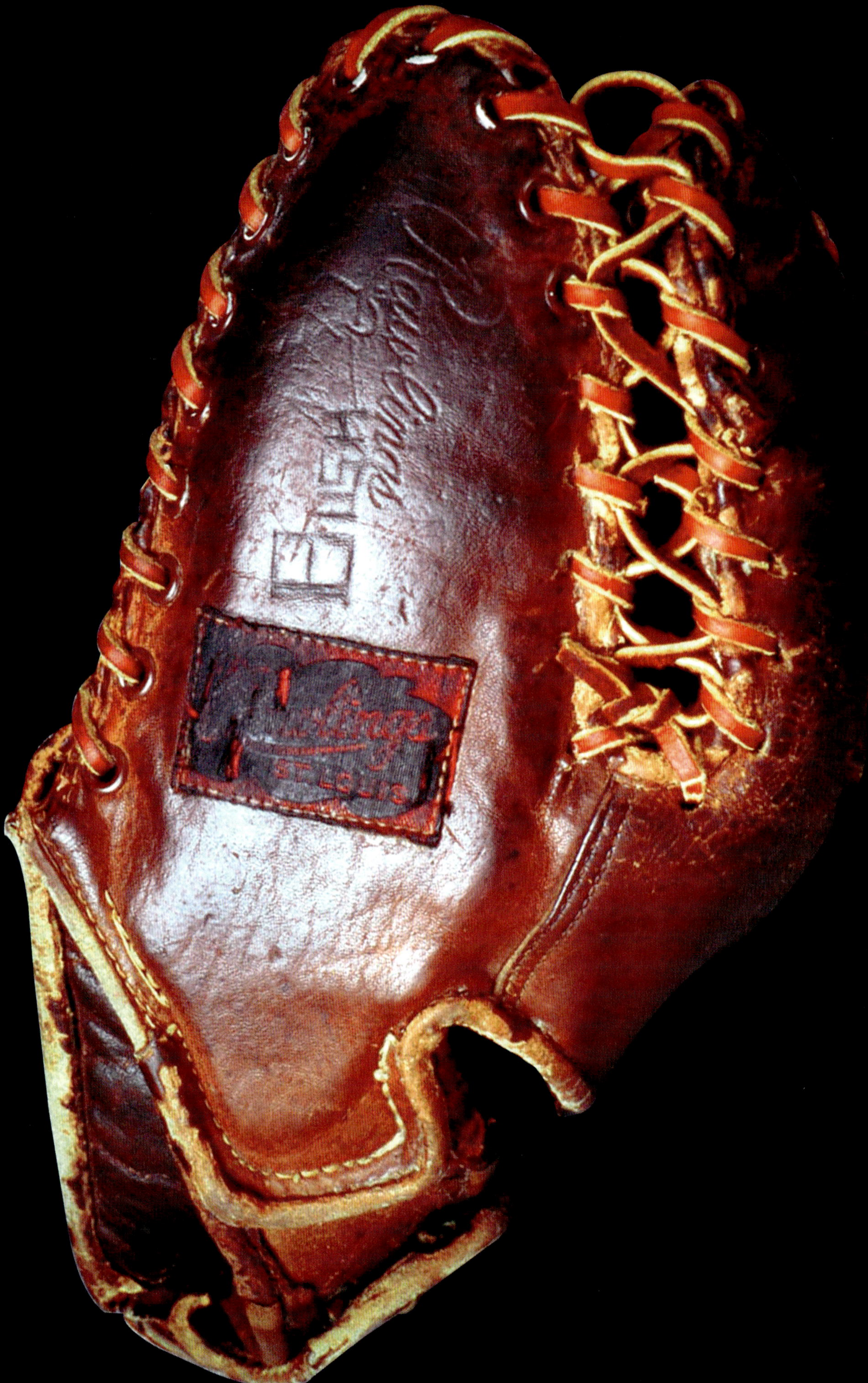

GEORGE H. W. BUSH

A Presidential Keeper

America's 41st president, George H. W. Bush, had a lifelong love of sports. He was a fisherman and played golf, soccer, and tennis. He even had a horseshoe pit installed on the White House lawn. His maternal grandfather founded golf's Walker Cup, and his father served as president of the United States Golf Association. But it was baseball that captured the future president's fancy. It became his lifelong passion, and his Rawlings 1940s George McQuinn Trapper model glove was always close by. Nicknamed "The Claw," it was the premier first baseman's mitt of the period, and it served Bush well, from his days playing for the Yale Bulldogs to his days in the White House's Oval Office.

After returning from service in World War II in 1945, Bush enrolled at Yale University. It was too late to play baseball that year, but he was able to play on the school's undefeated soccer team. The next season, in 1946, he got his shot at playing college baseball and became the team's starting first baseman. Like his idol Lou Gehrig, he never missed a game in his three-season career, and like the Yankee great, he became the team's captain.

The left-handed-throwing and right-handed-hitting Bush turned out to be an exceptionally good fielder (.983 fielding average), but only an average hitter (.224 batting average with one home run). Nonetheless, in 1947, Bush's Yale Bulldogs won the Eastern Intercollegiate Baseball League for the second year in a row and were awarded an invitation to the NCAA Tournament, where they lost to the University of California, Berkeley, in the NCAA's first College World Series. Bush's 1948 Yale team once more won their way into the College World Series before losing in the best-of-three-games final against the University of Southern California. Even though Yale never won a national championship during Bush's time there, Bush and his McQuinn Trapper did win three league titles. And there was one more special moment on Yale's baseball field that final season: On June 5, 1948, Babe Ruth came to Yale to donate the original manuscript of his autobiography to the university. On the ceremonial receiving end of that manuscript was the captain of the uniformed Yale baseball team—Bush. Ruth passed away just a couple of months later.

Out of all Bush's experiences and accomplishments at Yale, his most important takeaway was his George McQuinn Trapper, with its big web and deep pocket that established a new era in defense at first base. Bush kept his treasured glove with him throughout his political career. In the summer of 1984, while serving as vice president, 60-year-old Bush played in an old-timers'

President George H. W. Bush used this Rawlings George McQuinn Trapper model glove throughout his playing days at Yale and in numerous All-Star events and later kept it in his Oval Office desk at the White House.

Rawlings

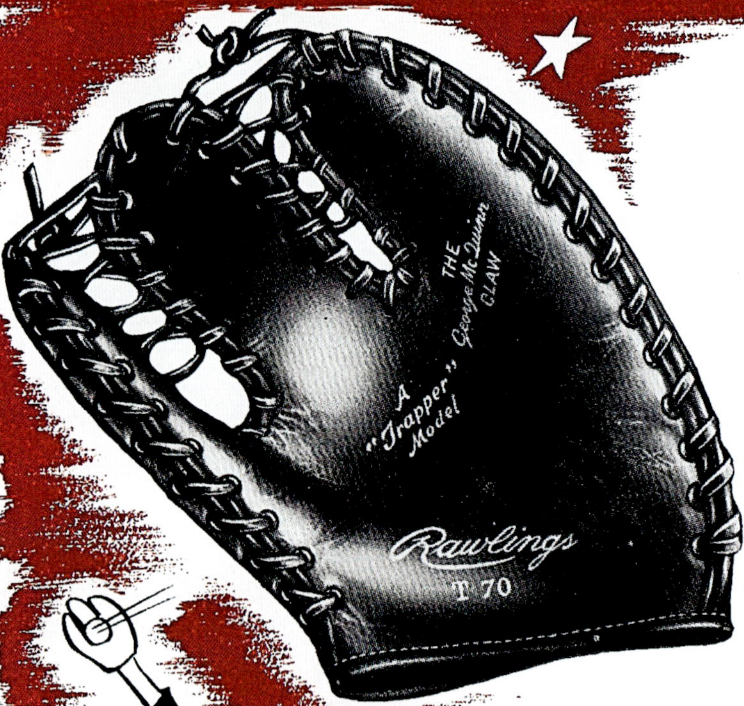

T70

GEORGE McQUINN
THE Original CLAW!

Built of very finest Tan color durable cowhide especially selected for this model. Top quality, hand-formed, "Grooved Action" pad of Grey felt. Finger section has impregnated reinforcement between layers of felt padding. Inner-Greased palm. Cemented back. Never Rip crotches. Thumb is also reinforced with full flexible impregnated reinforcement under back, this feature prevents thumb from falling into pocket. Roll leather bound edges. Palm and thumb edges leather laced. Full leather lined, adjustable small finger loop. Adjustable wrist strap lined with shearling. Multiple adjusting pocket laces and crotches. Hand oil treated. These refinements plus Rawlings patented trapper design and construction make the T70 **first** on first base.

Trade each $15.95
List each $21.50

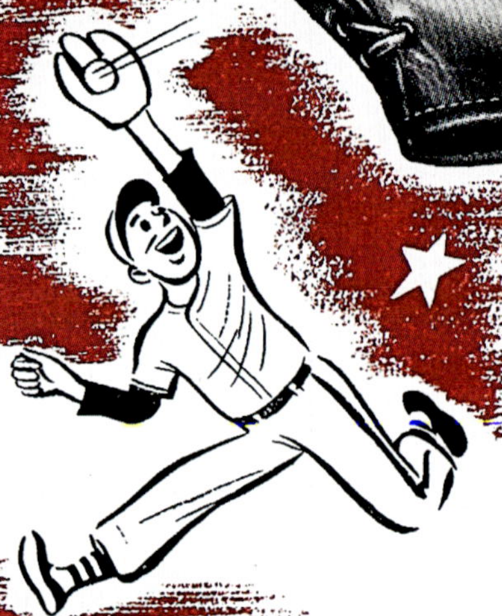

ORIGINATED BY RAWLINGS
and Covered By These Patents
Patent No. 2,281,315
and
Design Patent No. 132,636

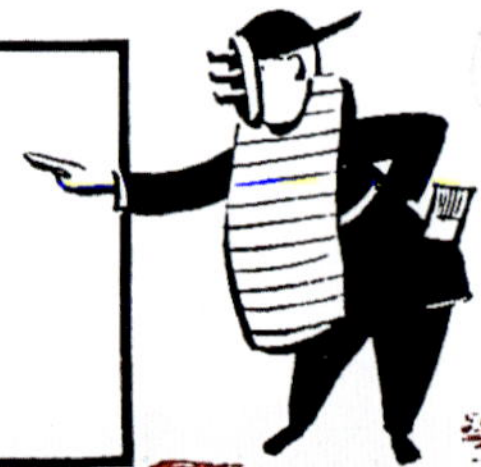

Often called "The Claw." Trapper design permits mitt to break as much on little finger side as on thumb side. Both sides of mitt close over ball when ball hits center panel, forming a positive trap.

RUDY YORK

T75 — Rudy York "Claw" Trapper Mitt.

Built of top quality durable Tan color mitt leather. Popular, sturdy mitt that incorporates the features of the T70.

Trade each $13.85 **List each $18.50**

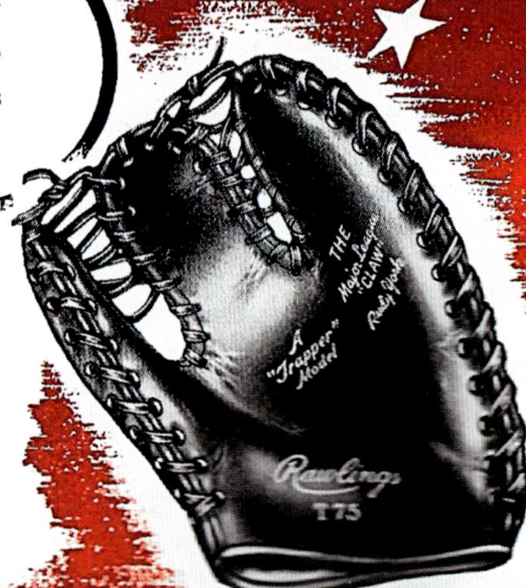

game with former MLB stars. The former expert-fielding and average-hitting Bulldog singled into left-center field off Milt Pappas, but his more impressive feat came on defense. Future Hall of Famer Orlando Cepeda hit a hard groundball down the first-base line. Bush dove to his left, knocked the ball down, picked it up, and threw out Cepeda. His glove helped make the play.

Once he moved into the White House four years later, Bush kept his Trapper in a drawer in the Oval Office desk. The president was known to regularly take the glove out to keep it oiled and give it a few fist bumps while thinking through his historic decisions. He even wore the mitt on April 3, 1989, when he threw out the ceremonial first pitch at the home opener at the old Memorial Stadium in Baltimore, becoming the first president to throw a game's first pitch from the pitcher's mound. Today that George McQuinn Trapper glove resides in the George H. W. Bush Presidential Library in Texas. Since 2025, Rawlings has partnered with the College Baseball Foundation as the presenting sponsor of the George H. W. Bush Distinguished Alumnus Award to honor the accomplishments of college baseball players who achieve greatness off the diamond.

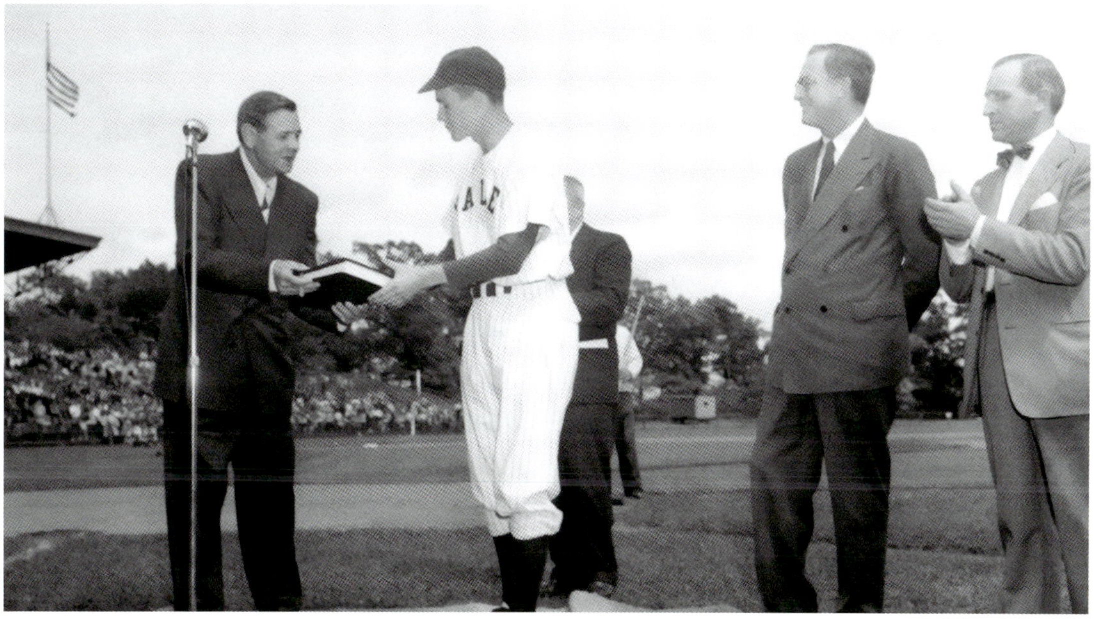

The George McQuinn Trapper model glove is highlighted in a 1940s Rawlings catalog (opposite). Often called "The Claw," it was the leading first baseman's mitt for decades. Bush—Yale's team captain—receives a copy of Babe Ruth's autobiography manuscript at a ceremony on the campus prior to a baseball game in 1948 (above).

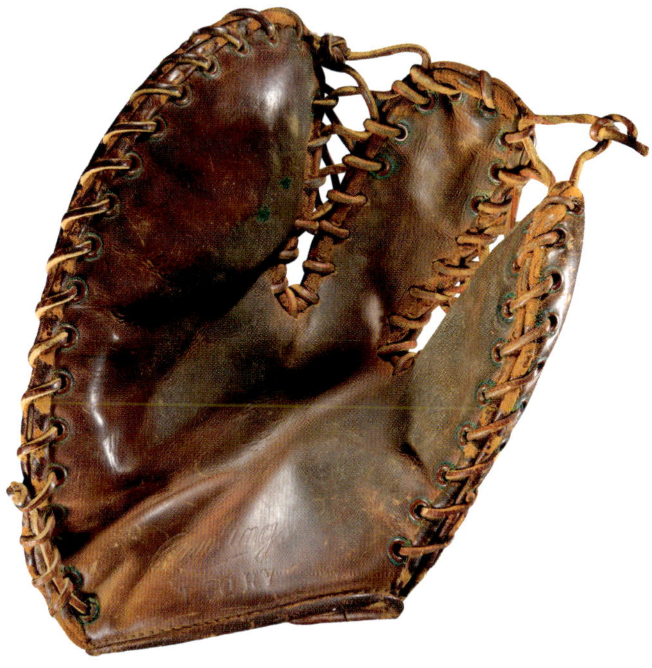

SATCHEL PAIGE

Ole Satch

There isn't any question whether Leroy "Satchel" Paige was one of baseball's all-time greats. He began pitching for the Negro Leagues' Birmingham Black Barons in 1927 at age 20. Until Jackie Robinson broke baseball's color barrier in 1947, Black players could not play alongside white players in MLB games even though they often barnstormed with each other during the offseason. Paige played for six Negro Leagues teams before he became the seventh African American player to cross the white line on an MLB field in July 1948 as a 42-year-old rookie with Bill Veeck's Cleveland Indians.

While playing in the Negro Leagues, Paige chalked up eight All-Star selections and recorded a pitching Triple Crown in 1944. He led the Negro Leagues multiple times in games, innings, wins, winning percentage, shutouts, strikeouts, saves, and ERA. He even won a Negro Leagues World Series with the Kansas City Monarchs in 1942 and would later win one in the major leagues. On October 10, 1948, Paige entered Game Five of that year's World Series in relief of Bob Feller. It marked the first time an African American played and pitched in a Fall Classic. Paige got his outs, and the Indians got a championship the next day.

When Veeck took over ownership of the St. Louis Browns in 1951, he again signed Paige, who had been dropped from the Indians after Veeck sold the team in 1949. Paige stayed with Veeck until he sold the Browns at the end of the 1953 season.

Throughout his career, age meant nothing to Paige, as he noted in one of his most insightful quotations: "Age is a question of mind over matter. If you don't mind age, it don't matter." It didn't seem to matter to the rest of baseball either. His stats told the story.

He remained an effective pitcher in his years on a not-very-good Browns team and was even selected to two All-Star Games at ages 45 and 46 in 1952 and 1953. Released by the Orioles after the Browns were sold and moved to Baltimore, Paige continued pitching for three more years with the Phillies' AAA minor-league team before making one more appearance back in the big leagues.

Playing in the Negro Leagues never brought a player an MLB pension, and Paige's limited years with the Indians and Browns did not qualify him for one either. But then Kansas City Athletics owner Charlie Finley had the idea of engaging the great pitcher, who lived a few blocks up the street from the Athletics' Municipal Stadium, in order to draw more fans. Paige was already a local hero due to his eight seasons with the Monarchs. It was also a way to add time to Paige's tenure and get him closer to a pension. Finley brought Paige onto the Athletics' coaching staff to guide his young pitchers and electrify the crowd.

This Rawlings G500 model glove was one of many that Satchel Paige used during his career, from 1927 to 1965.

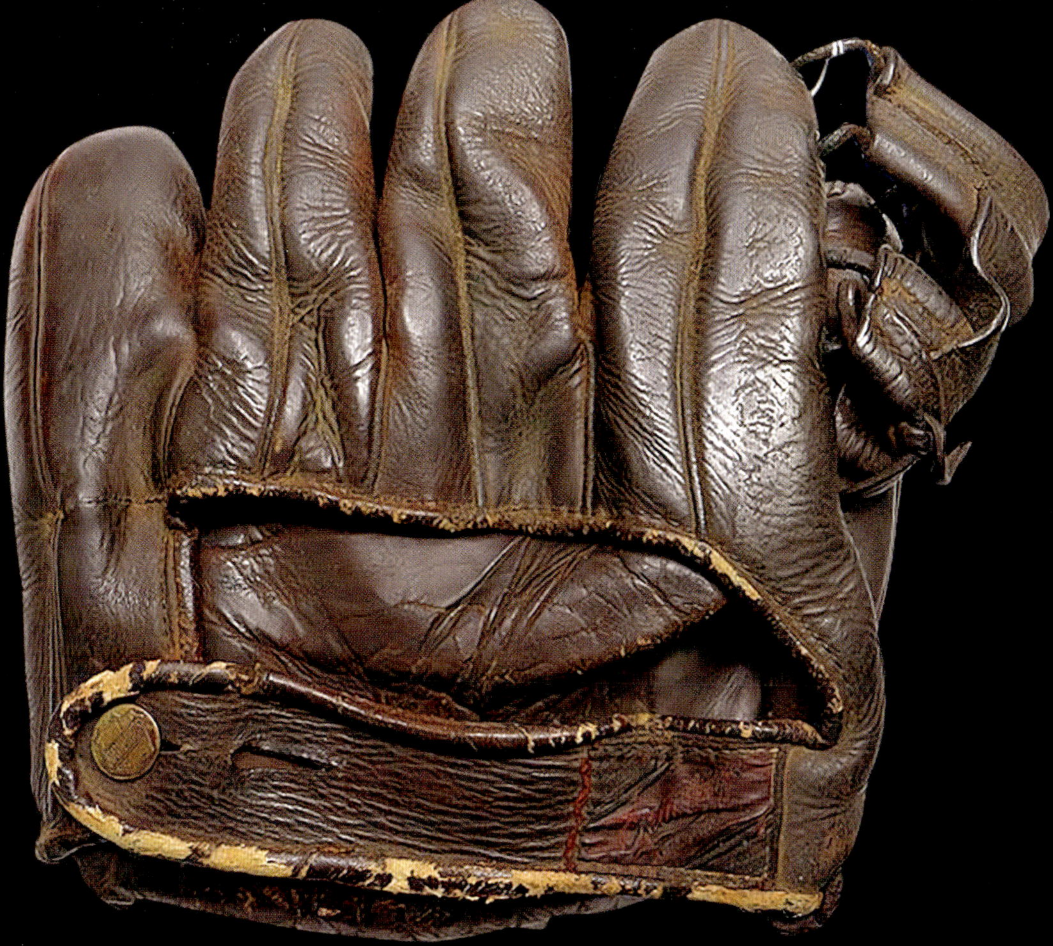

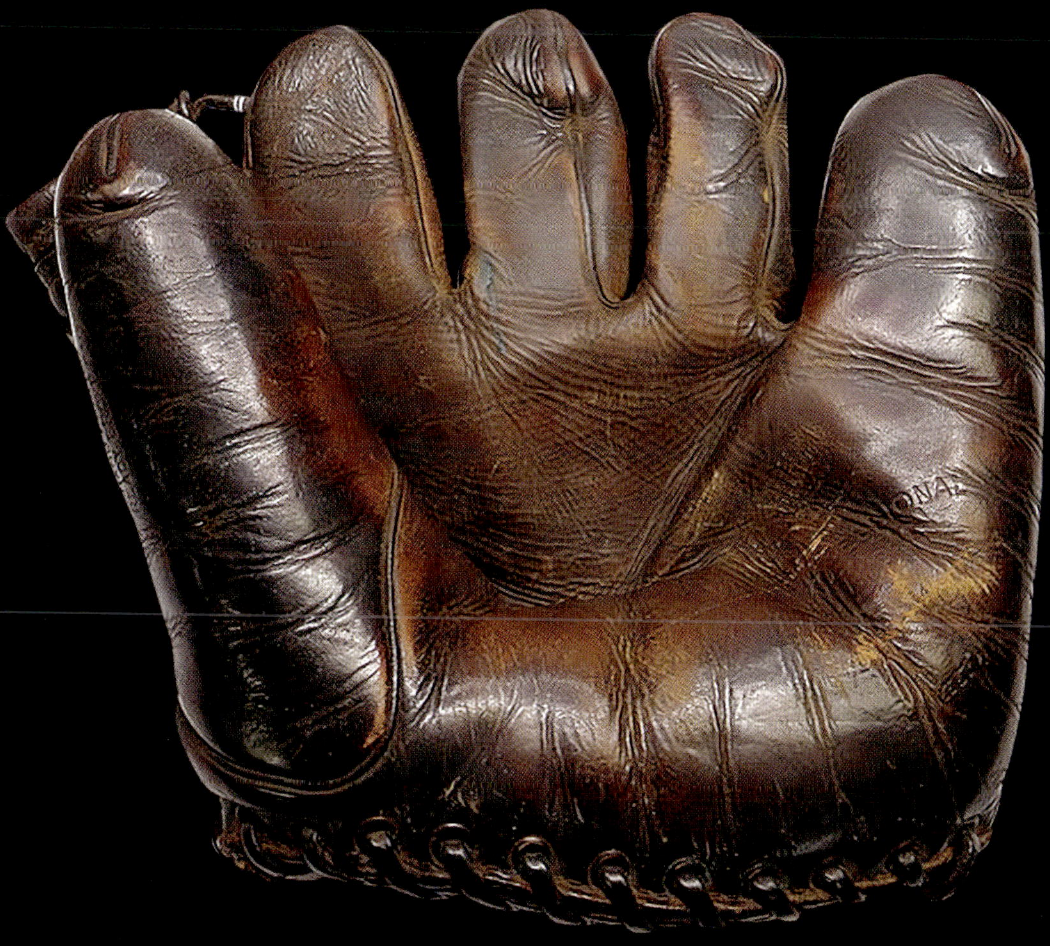

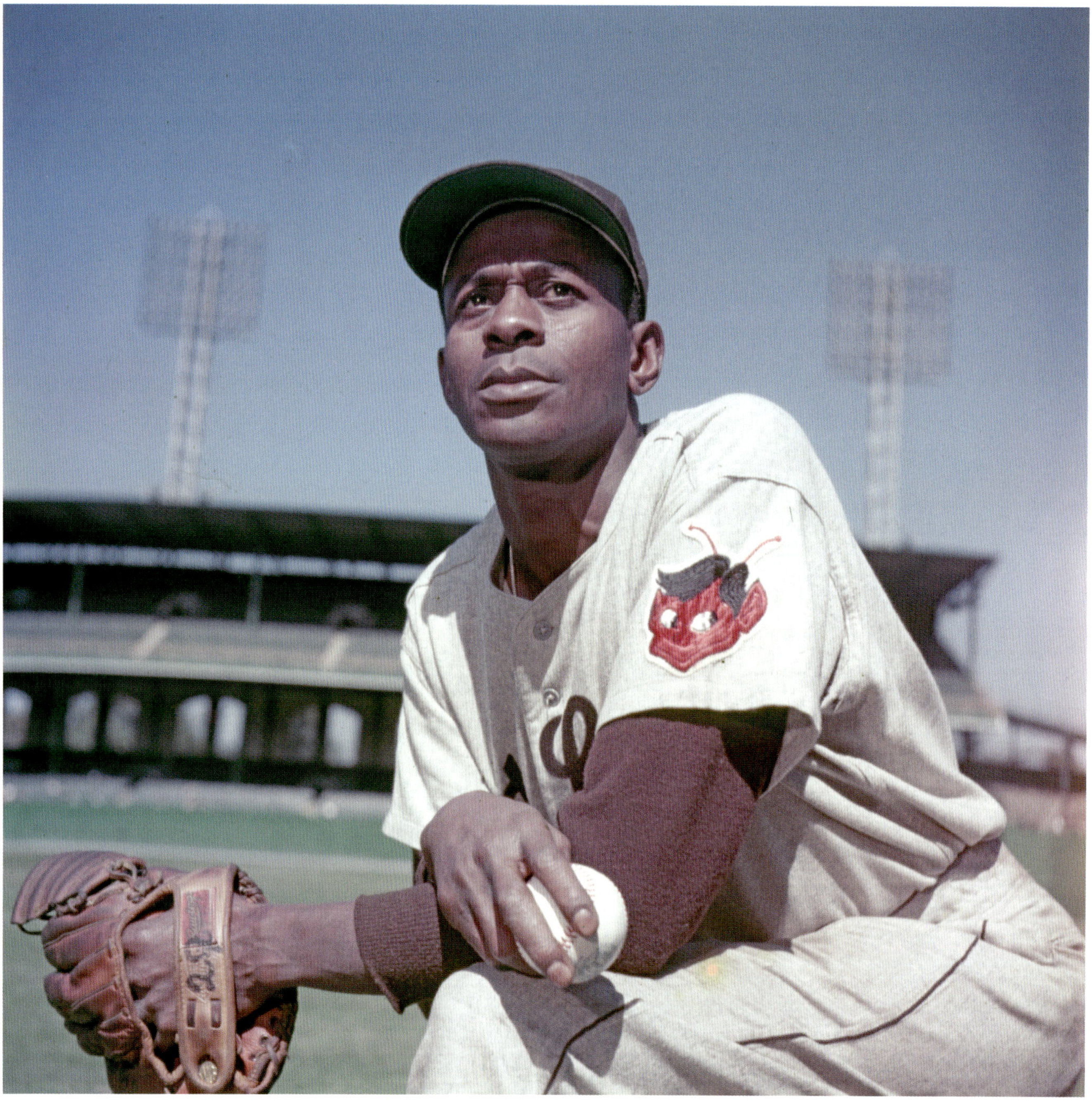

In 1951, Paige used a Rawlings G500 model glove while playing for the St. Louis Browns.

On September 25, 1965, in an evening promoted as "Satchel Paige Appreciation Night," the crowds came to honor one of the greatest pitchers of both the Negro Leagues and major leagues. Finley positioned Paige sitting in a rocker down in the Athletics' bullpen with a nurse rubbing liniment on his pitching arm. Soon, Paige was warming up to make a start against the visiting Boston Red Sox. It was all business that night, just as it had been for the last 40 years. The 58-year-old Paige took the mound in the first inning. After the first two batters were retired, Carl Yastrzemski came to the plate. As a child decades earlier, Yastrzemski had watched his dad face Paige. The 1963 (and 1967 and 1968) batting champion doubled off the outfield wall. It was the only hit that Paige gave up in his three innings of pitching that night. His start was recorded as a one-hit shutout with one strikeout over three innings. That outing was Paige's final curtain call in the big leagues before being called for induction into the Hall of Fame in 1971.

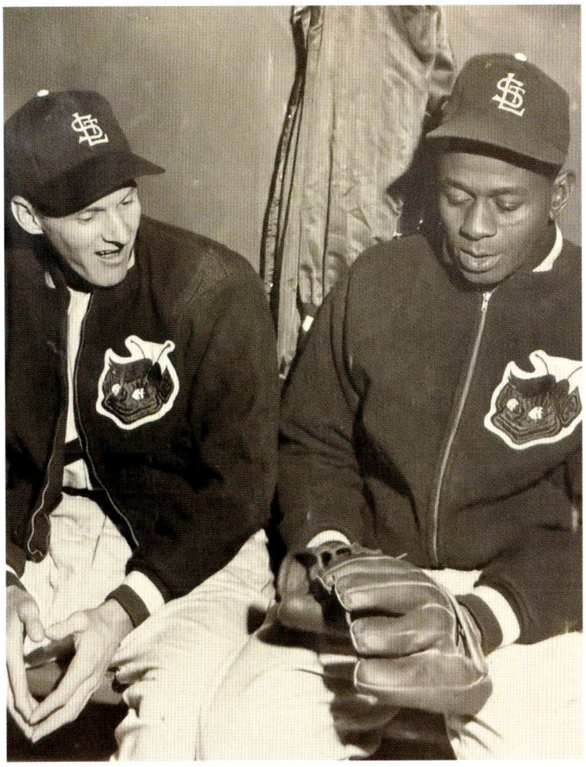

Paige discusses his G500 glove with his manager, Marty Marion, whose own Rawlings glove was embossed with the phrase "Mr. Shortstop" in the 1940s.

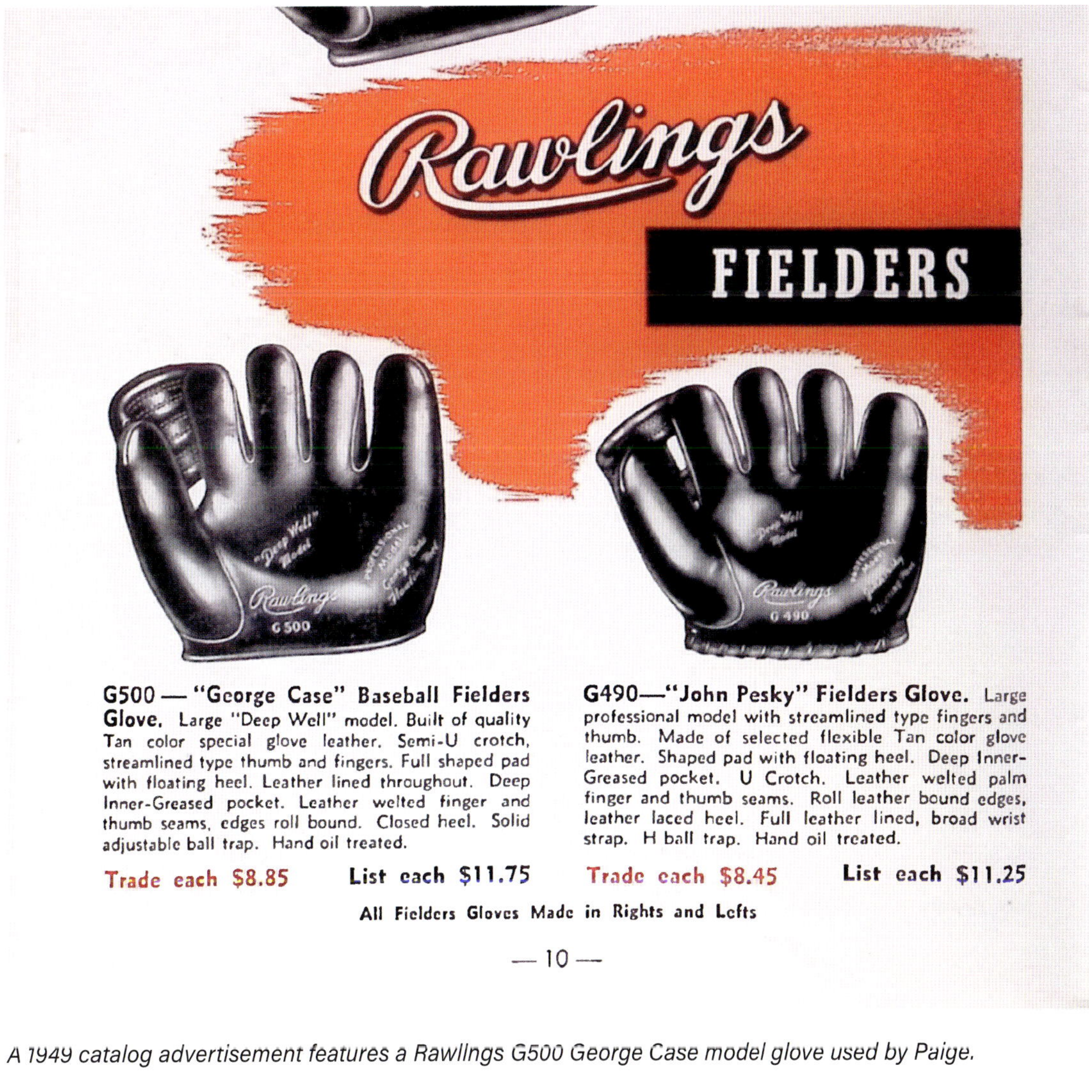

A 1949 catalog advertisement features a Rawlings G500 George Case model glove used by Paige.

WILLIE MAYS

The Catch

After playing several seasons for the Birmingham Black Barons in the Negro Leagues and within the New York Giants' minor-league teams, Willie Mays made a giant splash on the big-league scene after his late May call-up in 1951. That season, the 20-year-old hit 20 home runs and batted .274 on the way to winning the NL's Rookie of the Year Award and playing in his first World Series. His career was put on hold in 1952 and the following year after being drafted into military service. Back in the big leagues in 1954, the player nicknamed "The Say Hey Kid" was ready to relaunch his Hall of Fame career. And he did it by winning the first of his three MVP Awards. Although he led the majors in batting average (.345) and slugging percentage (.667) in 1954, his career-defining moment happened during that year's Fall Classic.

Mays's offensive production in the 1951 World Series was limited to a .182 batting average and only one run driven in. In the 1954 World Series, his offense was a little better; he hit .286 while driving in three runs. He never hit a home run in any of the four Fall Classics he played in. Baseball fans don't remember his offense from the 1954 World Series (or any other Series), but they do remember his one remarkable defensive moment.

On September 29, 1954, Mays made one of the greatest and most famous catches in World Series and baseball history. It happened during the eighth inning of Game One against the Cleveland Indians, played in the Giants' spacious Polo Grounds in Upper

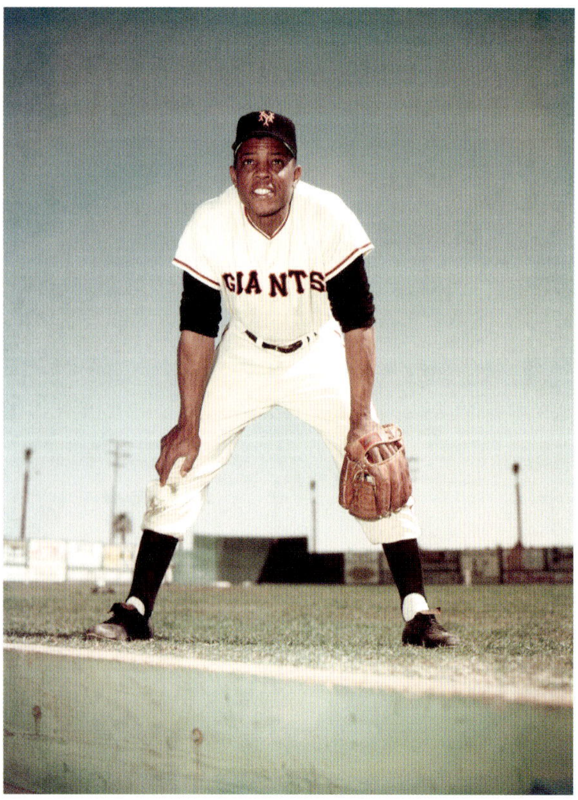

Willie Mays (left), shown here in the 1950s, was the recipient of 12 Gold Glove Awards. Mays was not under contract with Rawlings at the time of the 1954 World Series, but he used this Harvey Haddix model glove (opposite, top) to make what has been called the greatest catch in baseball history (following spread). Later in his career, he used this Rawlings XPG3 Flex-O-Matic Warren Spahn model glove (opposite, bottom).

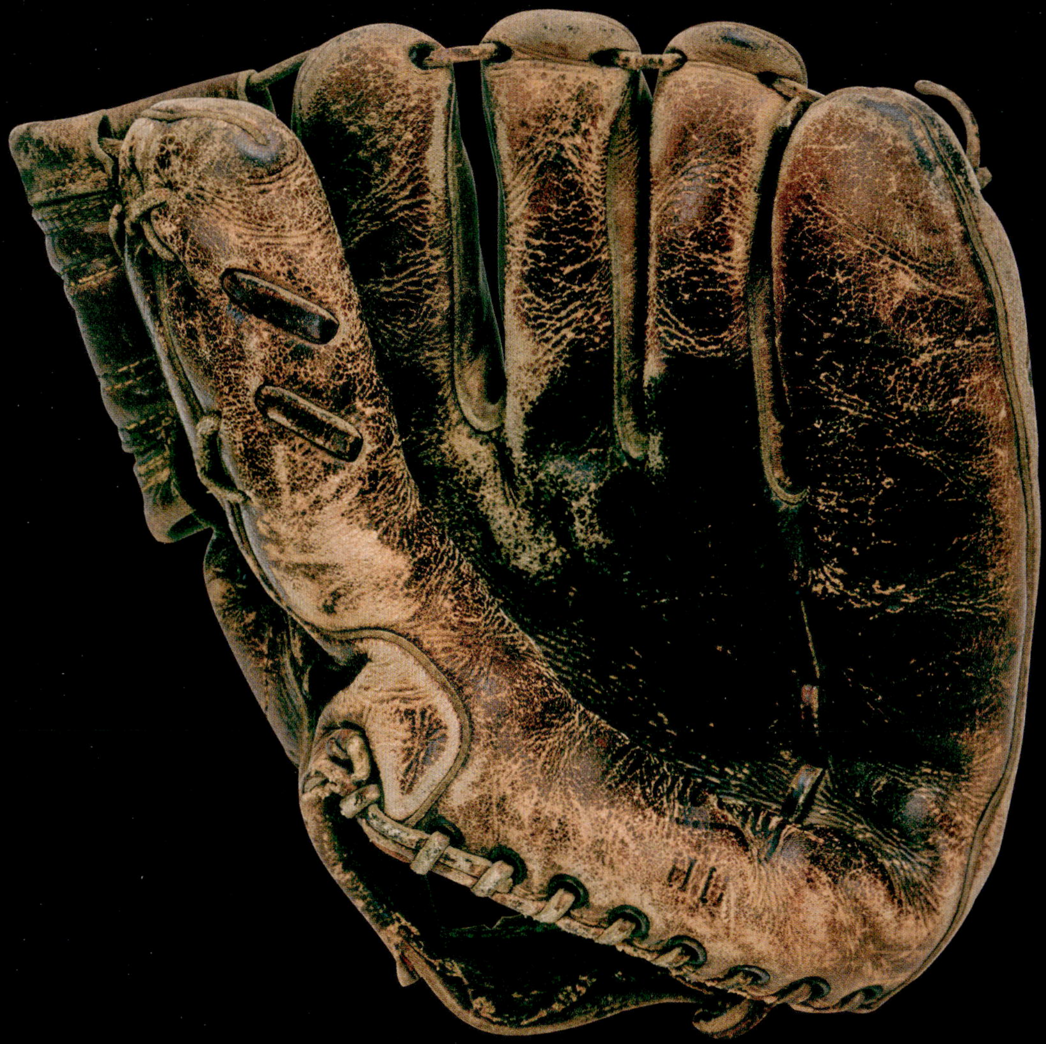

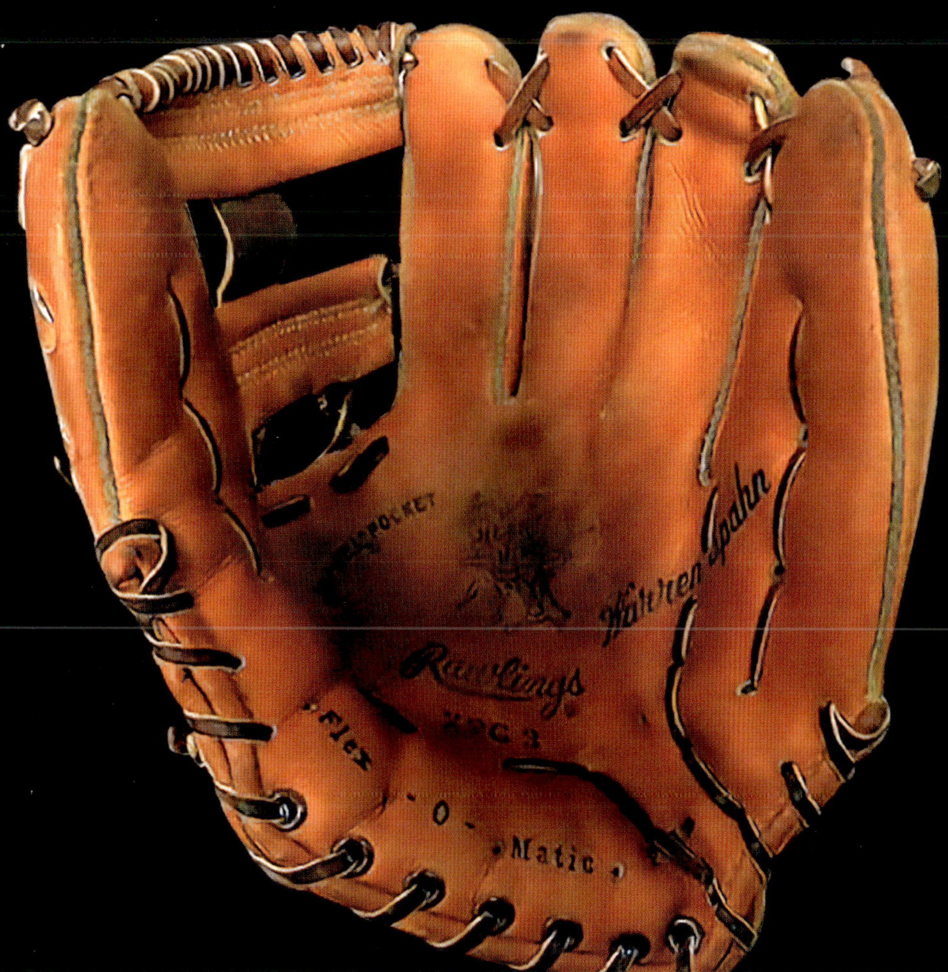
Warren Spahn
Rawlings

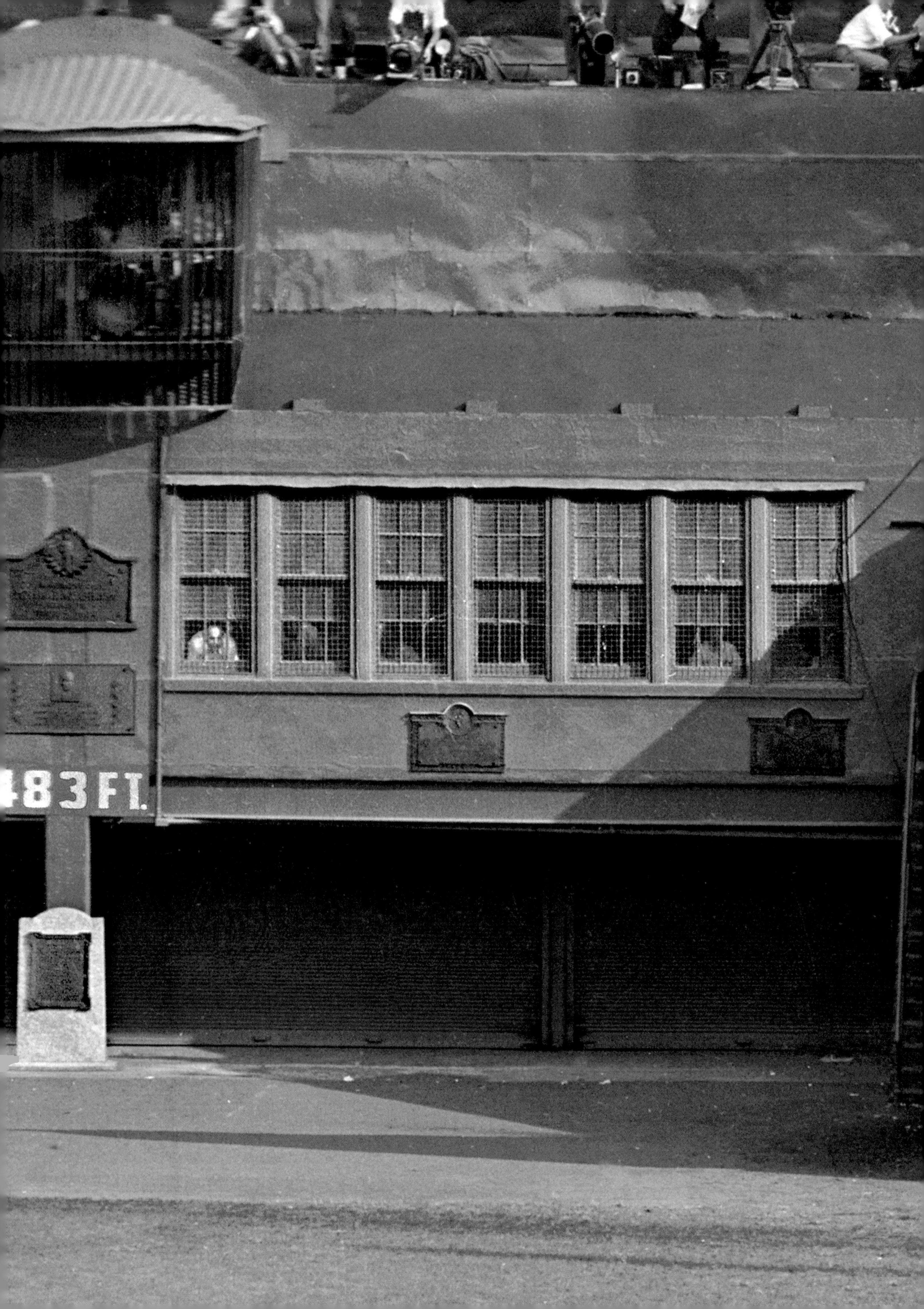
483 FT.

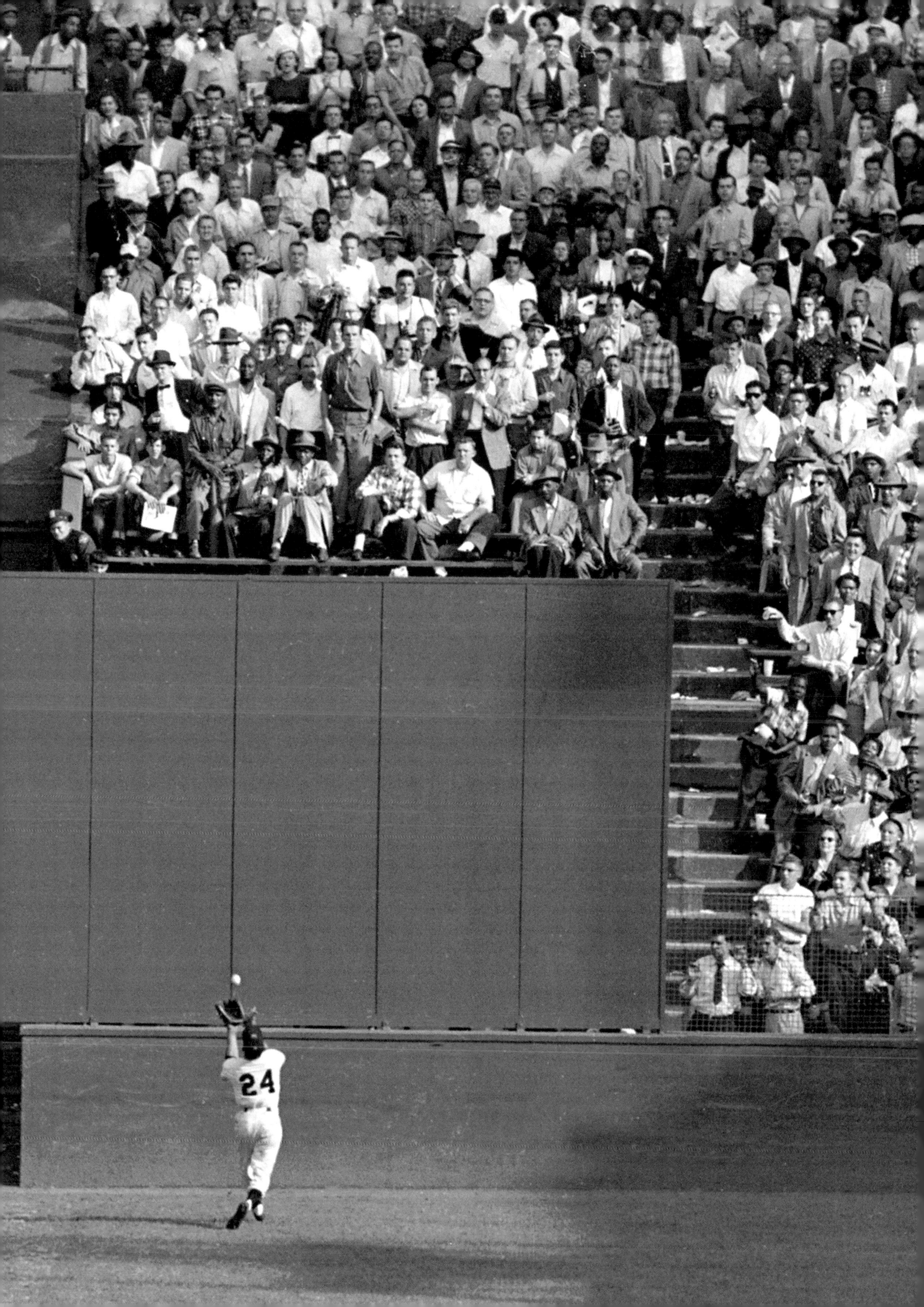
24

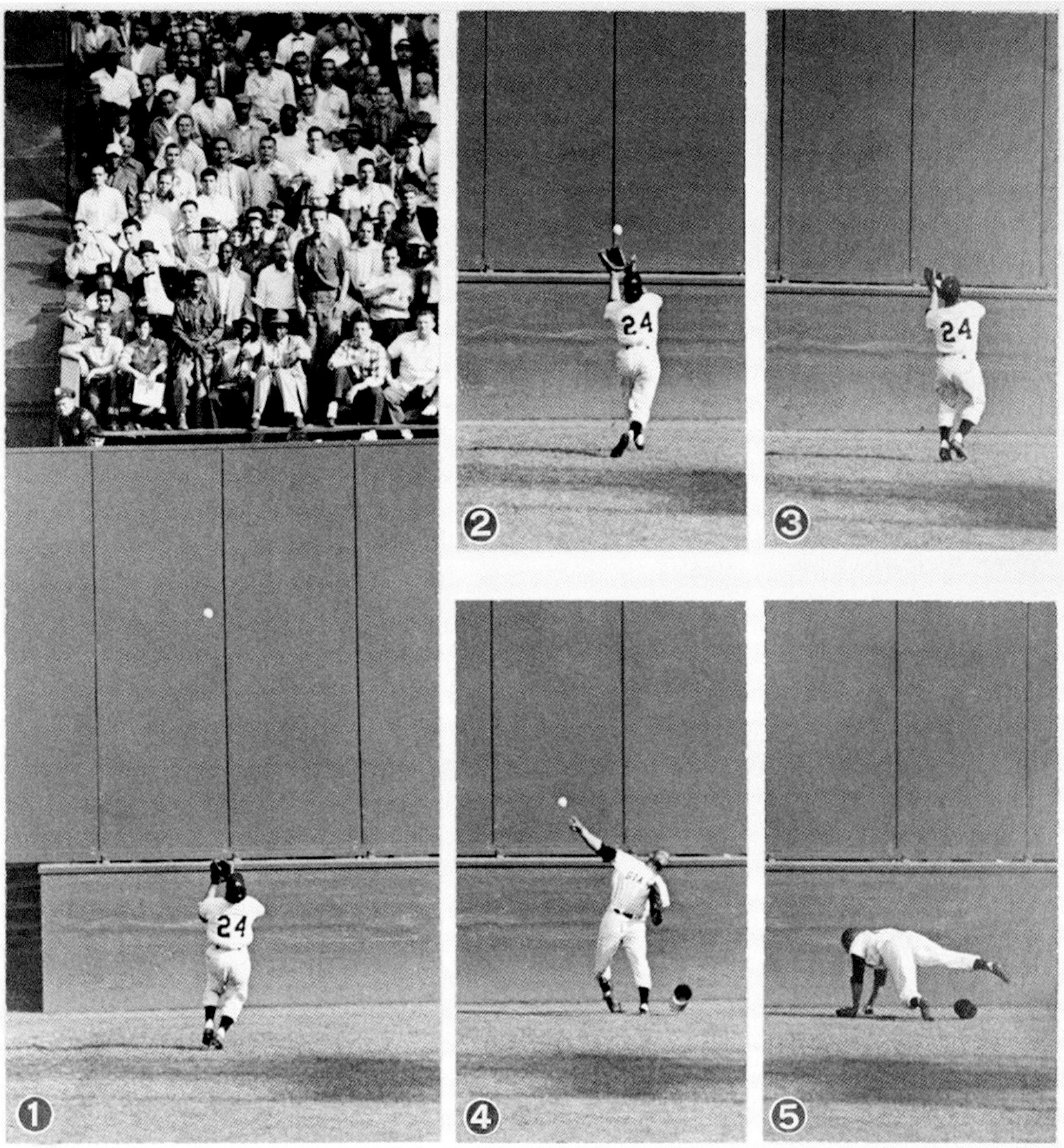

A numbered sequence shows Mays making the famous catch off the bat of Vic Wertz in Game One of the 1954 World Series at the Polo Grounds in New York.

Manhattan. The center-field wall stood 483 feet from home plate (brought in from the days when it was at 505 feet). With the score tied 2–2 in the top of the eighth, it looked like the Indians were about to break the tie when their first two batters reached base on a walk and a single. The Giants brought in a southpaw to face the left-handed-hitting, three-time All-Star Vic Wertz, who earlier had driven in the Indians' only two runs with a triple. On the fourth pitch of his at-bat, Wertz crushed a pitch to deep center field that would easily have been a home run in every other MLB stadium. Mays was playing a shallow center field to prevent a runner from scoring on a ball hit on the ground his way. When the ball was hit, Mays turned and was off chasing the ball into the deep part of the ballpark with his back to the infield.

The next moment was etched into baseball history, with NBC television broadcaster Jack Brickhouse's call of the play off the bat of Wertz: "There's a long drive . . . way back at center field . . . way back, back, it is a . . . Oh my! Caught by Mays! The runner on second, Doby, is able to go to third. Willie Mays just brought this crowd to its feet with a catch which must have been an optical illusion to a lot of people! Boy! . . . Notice where that 483-foot mark is in center field? The ball itself—Russ [directed to Russ Hodges, Brickhouse's color commentator], you know this ballpark better than anyone else I know—had to go about 460, didn't it?"

Upon making the over-the-shoulder catch at full speed with his hat flying off, Mays immediately spun around and threw the ball to second base to prevent the lead runner, Larry Doby, from scoring the go-ahead run. Doby could not go beyond third base due to the quickness of Mays's throw. The next batter walked to load the bases with one out, but the Giants got out of the inning with a strikeout and a fly out. No runs scored.

Wertz never got a home run or even a hit. The Indians never took the lead, and the Giants ended the 10th inning with a three-run walk-off pinch-hit home run by Dusty Rhodes for a win, leading to a sweep of the Series in four games for a world championship. Was Mays's catch the difference in the Series? The unimaginable catch kept the Indians from taking the lead, possibly winning Game One, and building momentum. The fans in the stands gasped at the catch, and so did the national audience watching the televised game at home and listening to Brickhouse's call. Mays went on to play 23 seasons in the big leagues and participate in 24 All-Star Games. During that period, he won 12 consecutive Gold Glove Awards (1957–1968). The five-tool first-ballot Hall of Famer did it all, and in one game of the 1954 World Series, he showed it all to the world of baseball.

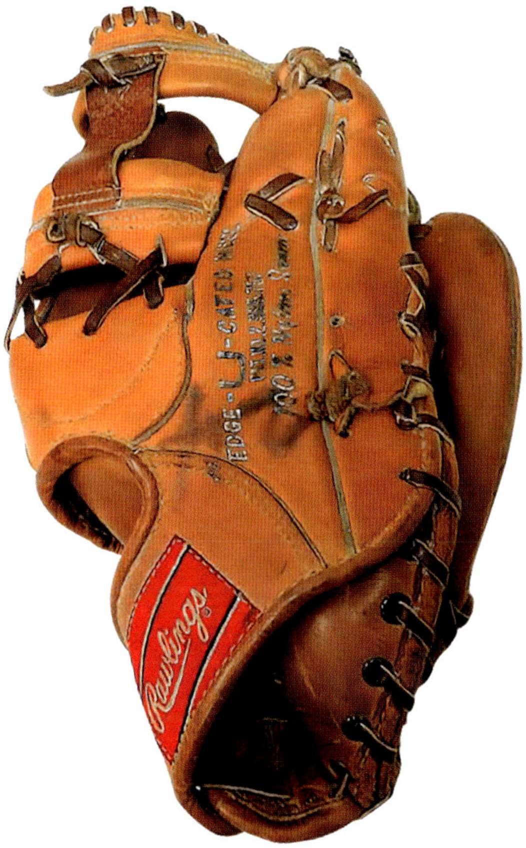

This view shows the backside of Mays's Rawlings XPG3 Flex-O-Matic Warren Spahn model glove.

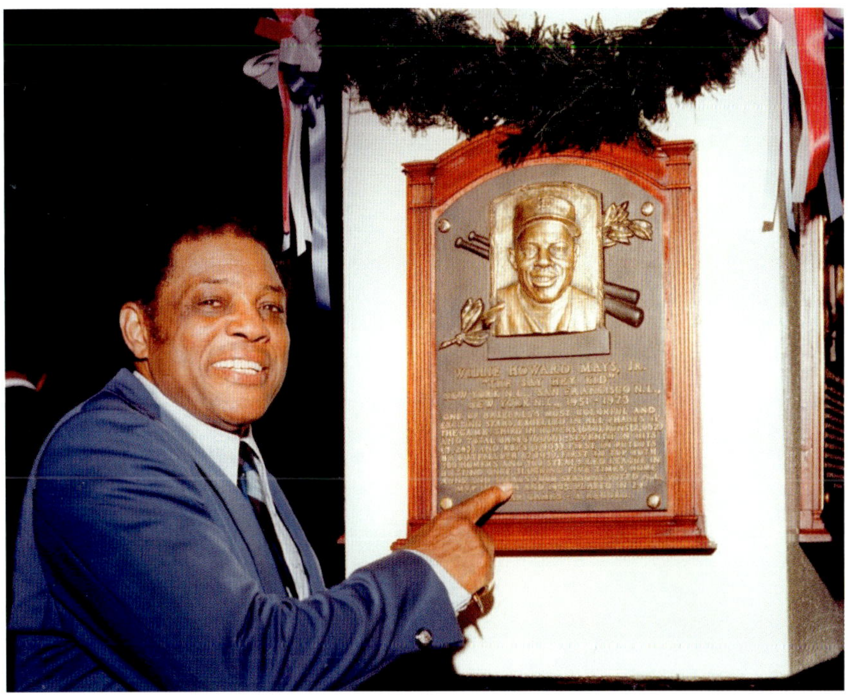

Mays poses in front of his Hall of Fame plaque in 1979.

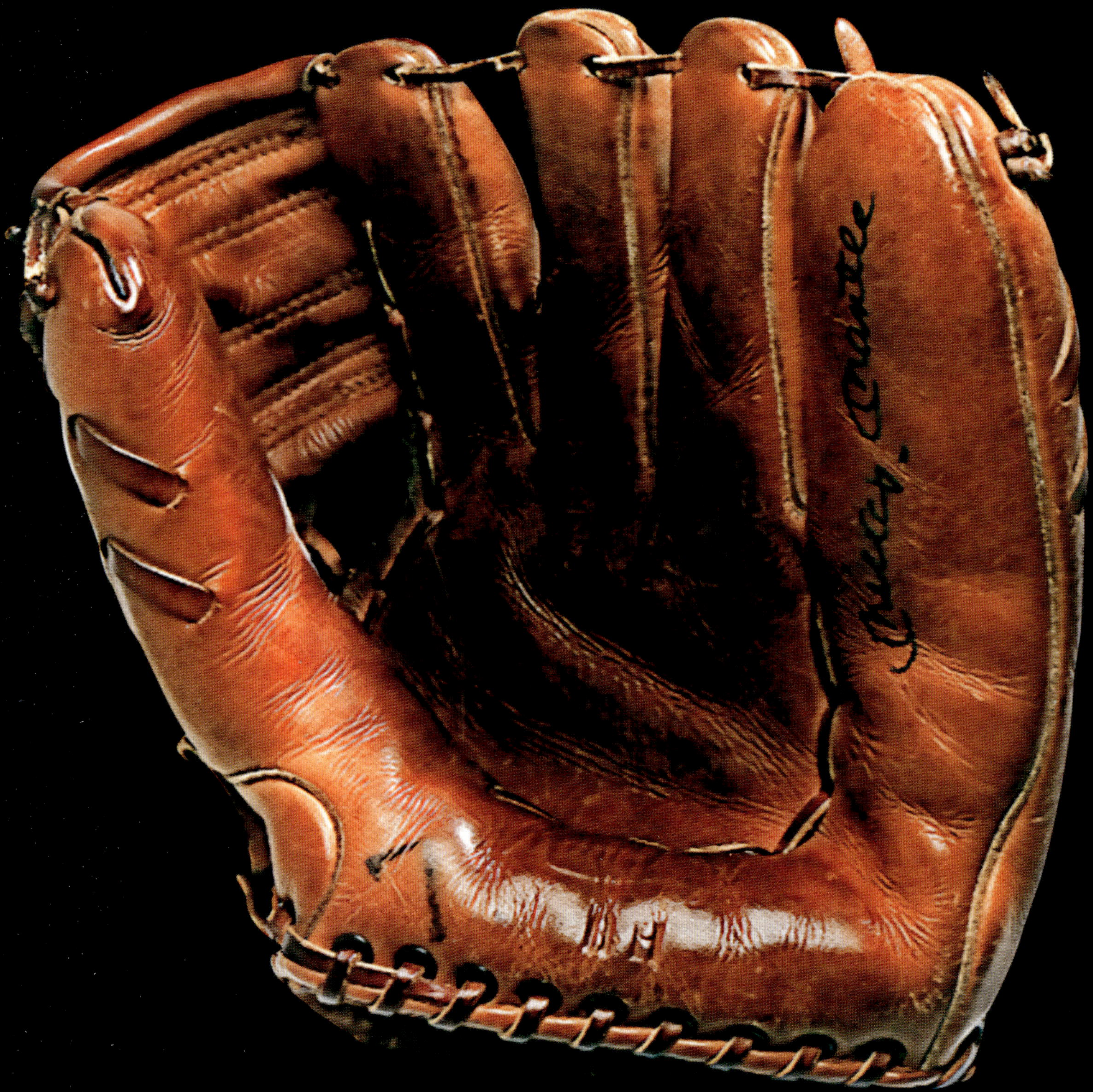

MICKEY MANTLE

The Perfect Save

Mickey Mantle began his Hall of Fame career in 1951 with a call-up to the big-league New York Yankees. He arrived as a five-tool prospect. He had it all. He hit for average, and he hit with power. He had speed as well. He could get down to first base from home plate faster than anyone else, and he could use that speed to chase down balls in the field and get them quickly back into the infield with his strong arm. Upon his arrival in camp, Mantle was immediately heralded as the next recipient in the passing of the torch of generational Yankee greats that began with Babe Ruth, transferred to Lou Gehrig, and was followed by Joe DiMaggio. DiMaggio had made it known that 1951 would be his last season, and "The Mick," as Mantle would soon be nicknamed, was the next in line. His uniform number was even chosen to signify this progression: Ruth (3) to Gehrig (4) to DiMaggio (5) to Mantle (6).

That was a lot of pressure to put on a 19-year-old playing in New York, and Mantle almost folded under it. His career didn't get off to a great start, and Mantle was sent down to the minors at midseason. He didn't do well there either, and he was ready to pack his bags to head back home to Commerce, Oklahoma, when his dad showed up with a tough-love talk that quickly turned his son

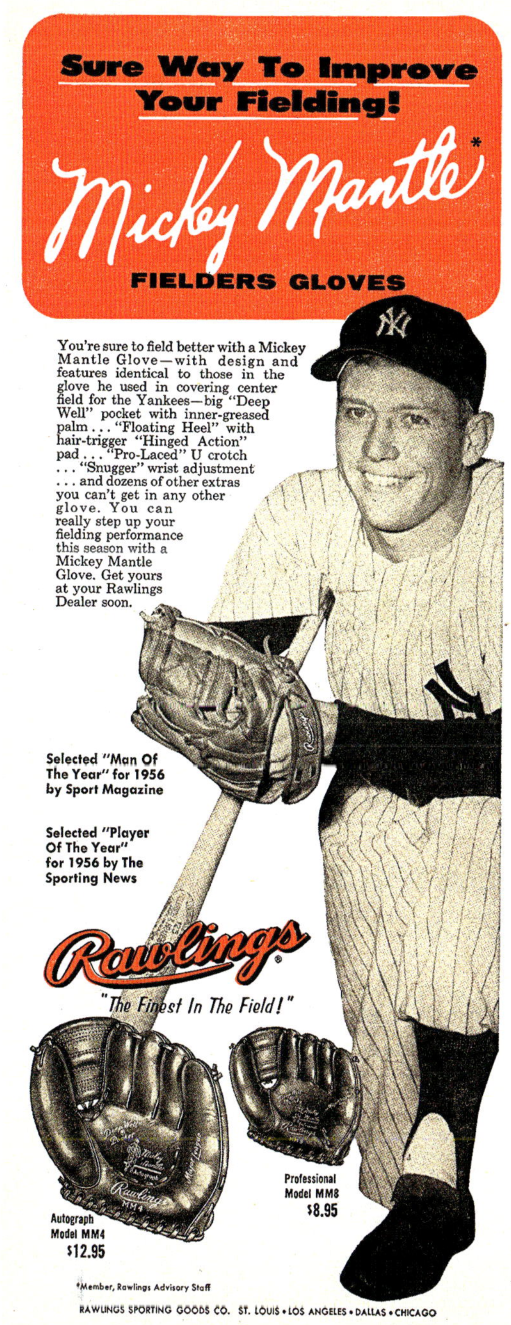

In the 1956 World Series, Mickey Mantle used a Rawlings Harvey Haddix (HH) model glove (opposite) to make the perfect catch. Soon Mantle's own model glove appeared in Rawlings advertisements (right) across the country.

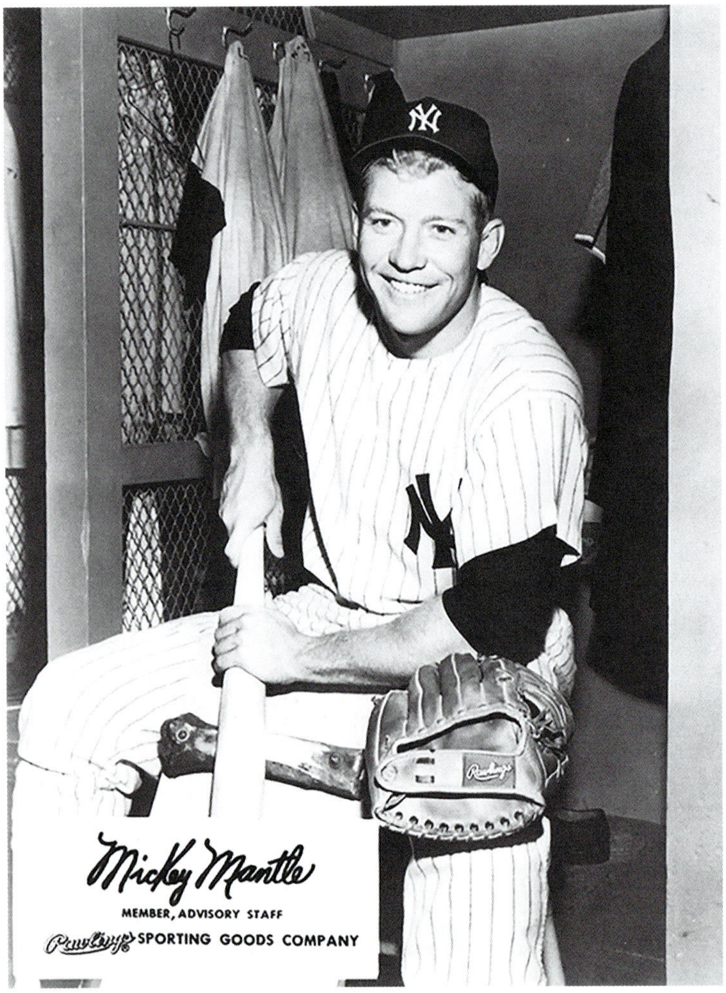

Mantle appears in a 1950s Rawlings advertisement (left), on a 1959 Rawlings catalog cover (below, left), and on a Rawlings autographed advertising poster (below, right). Notice the change in Mantle's signature from the earlier ad to the later poster. Mantle is about to make the catch that saves Don Larsen's perfect game in Game Five of the 1956 World Series at Yankee Stadium (opposite).

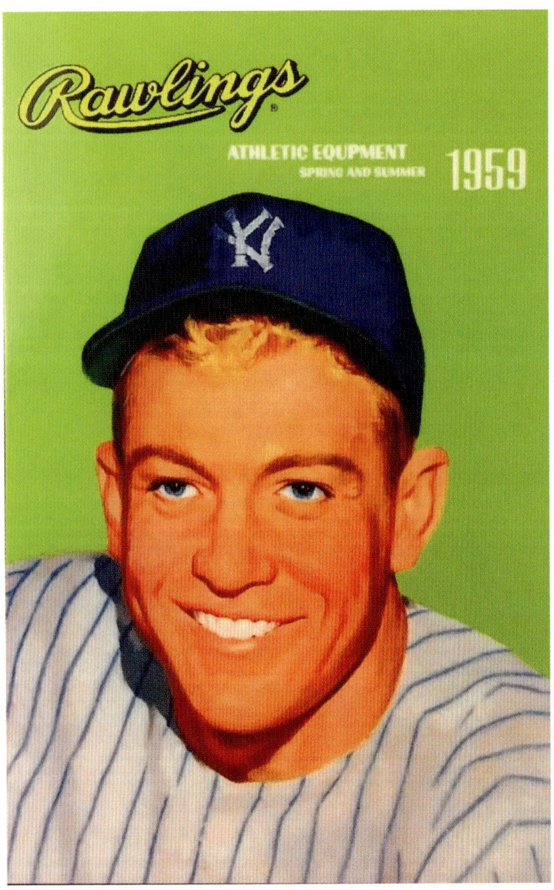

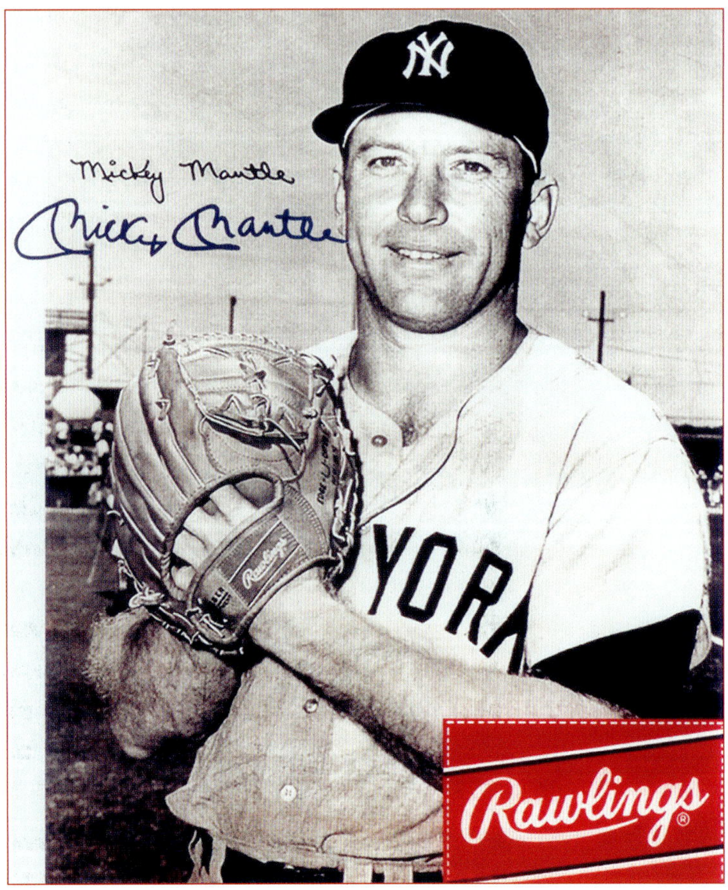

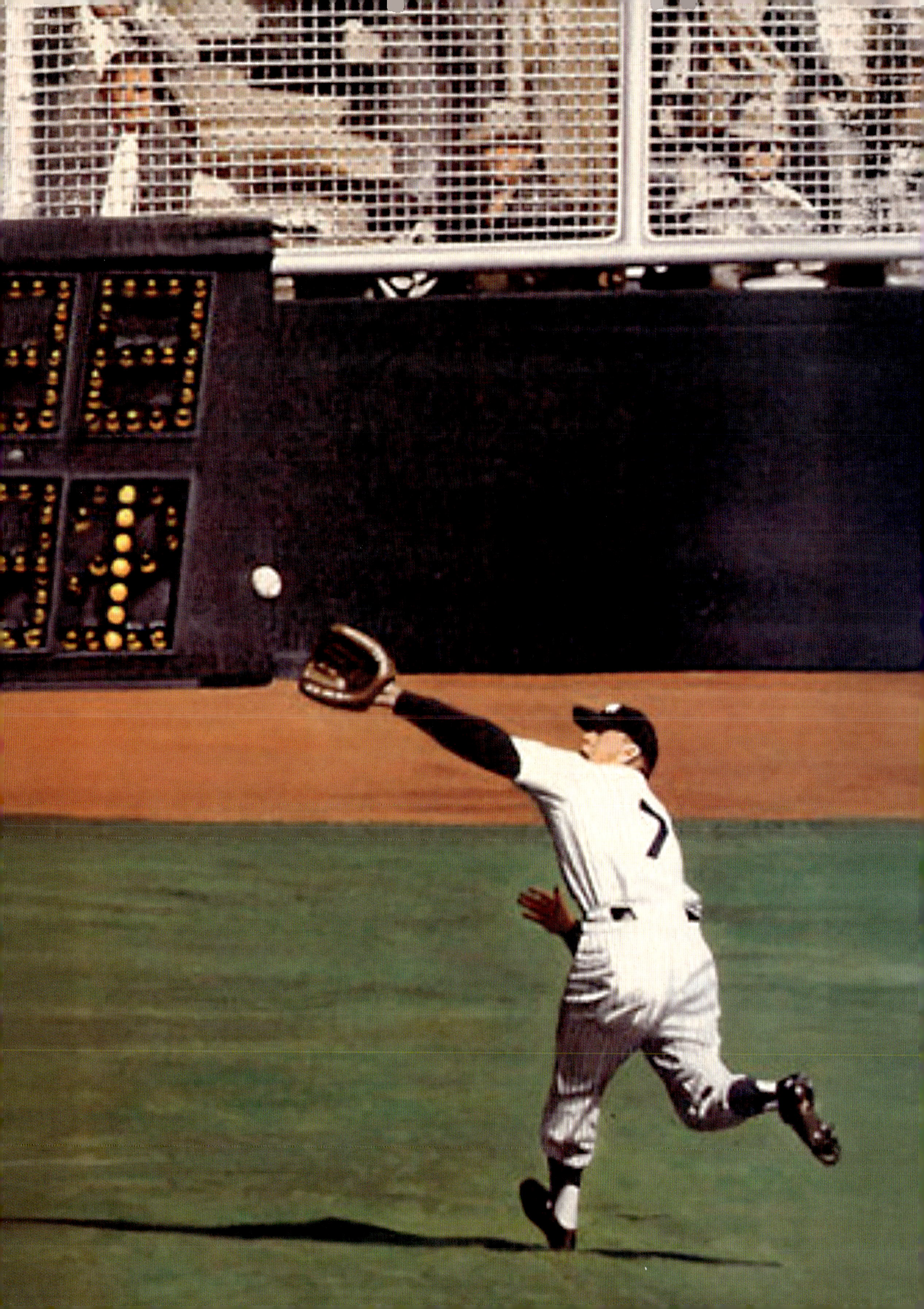

Mantle runs into Yankee Stadium's deep left-center field to make the catch (right), allowing Larsen to pitch the best game ever thrown in a Fall Classic. Mantle claimed this was the best catch he ever made. The Mickey Mantle Deep-Well Pocket model (below), introduced in 1960, became one of the most demanded gloves of the decade.

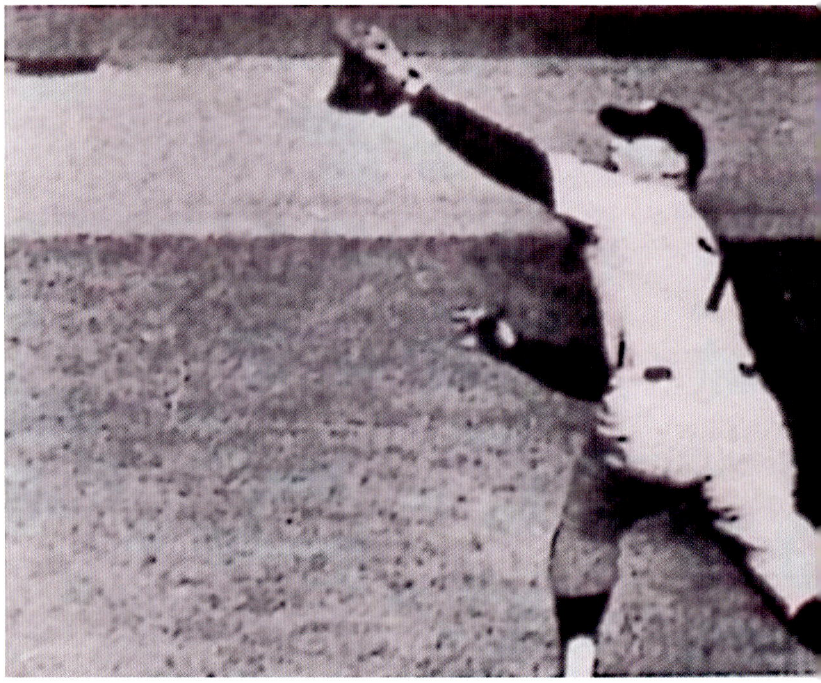

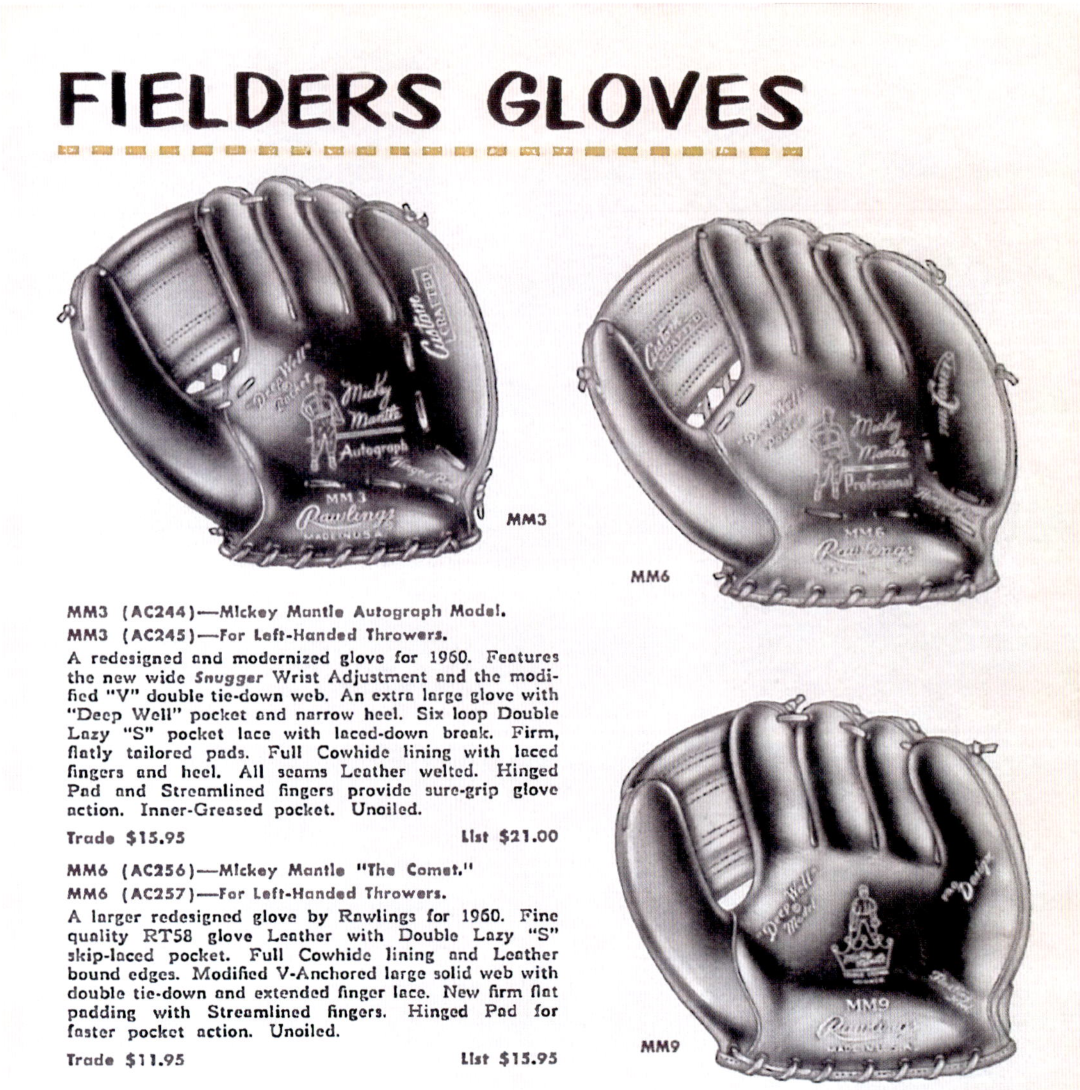

FIELDERS GLOVES

MM3

MM6

MM3 (AC244)—Mickey Mantle Autograph Model.
MM3 (AC245)—For Left-Handed Throwers.

A redesigned and modernized glove for 1960. Features the new wide *Snugger* Wrist Adjustment and the modified "V" double tie-down web. An extra large glove with "Deep Well" pocket and narrow heel. Six loop Double Lazy "S" pocket lace with laced-down break. Firm, flatly tailored pads. Full Cowhide lining with laced fingers and heel. All seams Leather welted. Hinged Pad and Streamlined fingers provide sure-grip glove action. Inner-Greased pocket. Unoiled.

Trade $15.95 **List $21.00**

MM6 (AC256)—Mickey Mantle "The Comet."
MM6 (AC257)—For Left-Handed Throwers.

A larger redesigned glove by Rawlings for 1960. Fine quality RT58 glove Leather with Double Lazy "S" skip-laced pocket. Full Cowhide lining and Leather bound edges. Modified V-Anchored large solid web with double tie-down and extended finger lace. New firm flat padding with Streamlined fingers. Hinged Pad for faster pocket action. Unoiled.

Trade $11.95 **List $15.95**

MM9

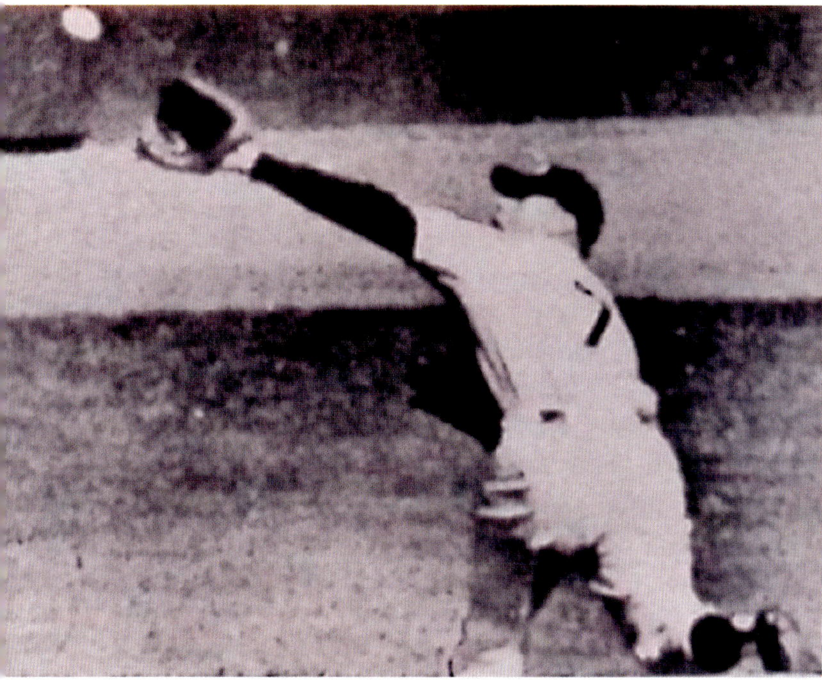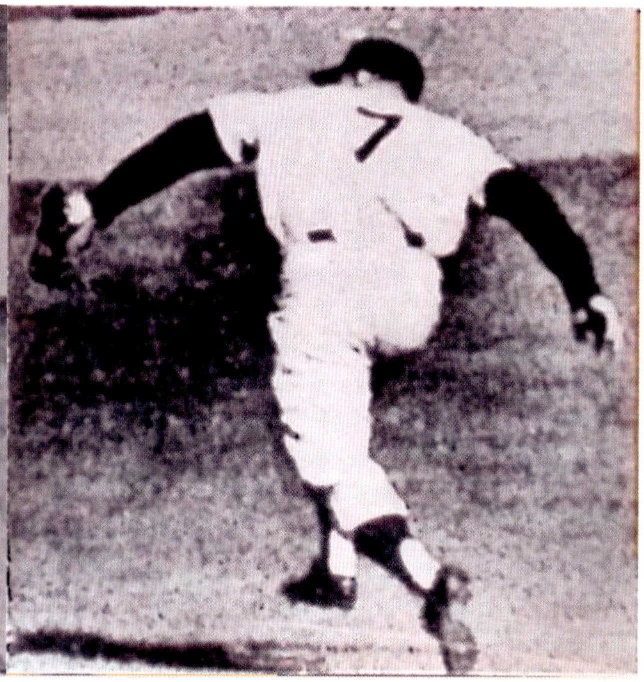

around both physically and mentally. He became a phenom again in the minors, and by late August was back in the Bronx to stay for the rest of his career—this time changing to uniform number 7.

The fire that was lit by Mantle's father led the future Hall of Famer to 12 pennants and seven World Series titles. He became a 20-time All-Star and a Gold Glove winner once (in 1962). But his best season was 1956, when he won the AL Triple Crown and made the most memorable catch of his career—known as "the perfect save."

It happened on October 8 in Game Five of the 1956 World Series between the Brooklyn Dodgers and the New York Yankees. With the Series tied two games apiece, Yankee pitcher Don Larsen took his career 30–40 record (at the time) to the mound for the Yankees. The game would become one of baseball's most memorable because Larsen threw the first and only World Series perfect game. No hits, no runs, no one safe at first, and much of that was due to Mantle, who had put the Yankees' first run on the scoreboard with a homer in the fourth inning.

In the very next inning, Mantle and his glove made the difference in the top of the fifth when future Hall of Famer Gil Hodges hit a long fly ball deep into the spacious left-center field (457 feet) of Yankee Stadium, where—after a long, long run and a final lunge—Mantle made a spectacular backhanded catch on what would surely have been an extra-base hit. In another ballpark, it very well could have been a home run. With most other players in center field, it would have been a double or a triple. But with Mantle and his speed in center, it was an incredible catch that wound up being an out and kept Larsen's perfect game in place. Mantle considered that game and that play the most significant of his career. It was a catch typical of Mantle's early career defensive heroics. It was certainly a catch worthy of the Gold Glove, but that award wouldn't be presented for another season. However, the Harvey Haddix (HH) model glove that Mantle used to make the perfect catch would soon be modified to become the Mickey Mantle (MM) model, a favorite glove of players of all ages over the next two decades.

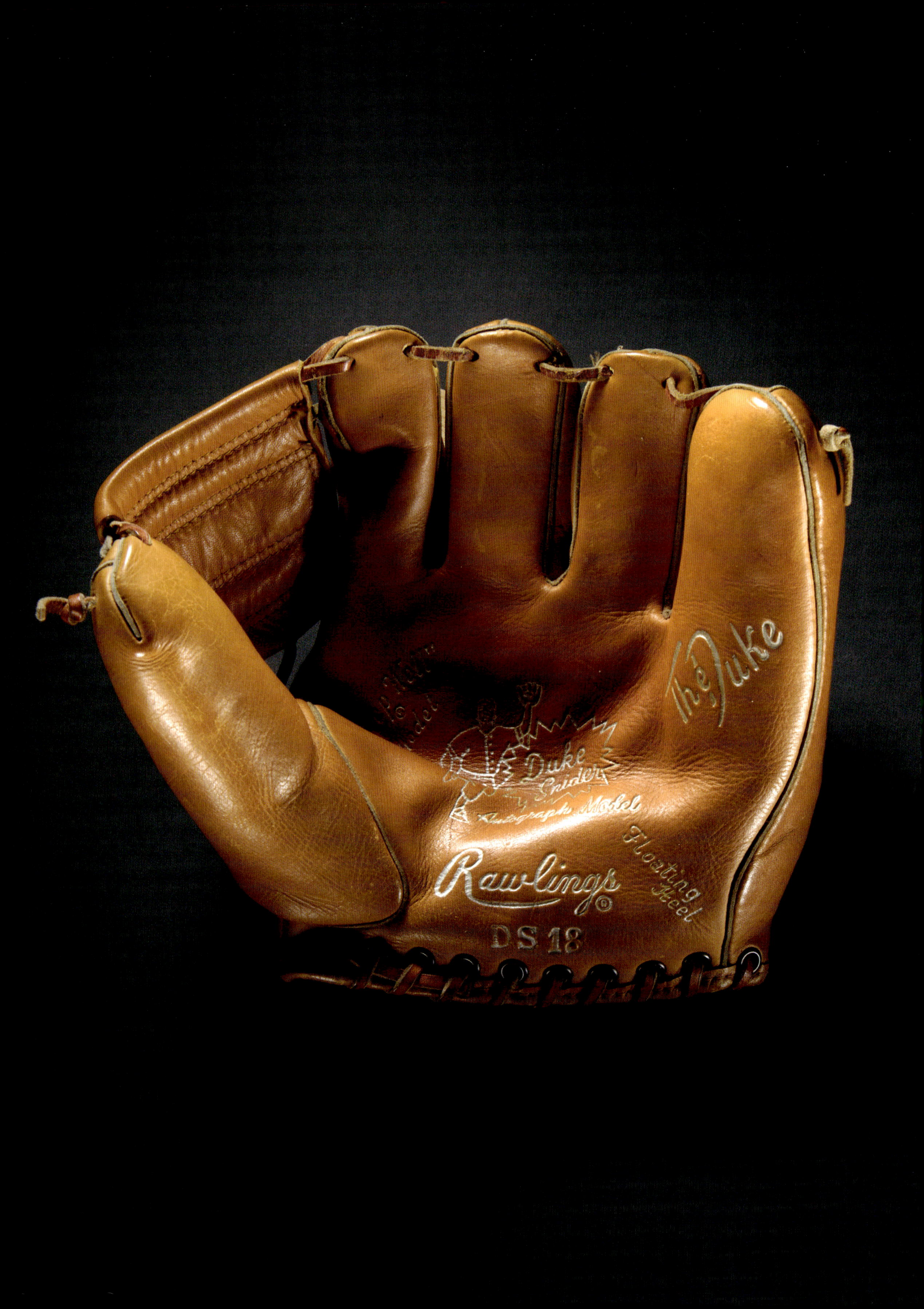
The Duke
Duke Snider
Autograph Model
Rawlings
Floating Heel
DS 18

DUKE SNIDER

And the Duke

In Brooklyn, Edwin Donald Snider was simply known as "The Duke," a name given by his parents when he was a youngster due to the way he strutted around like he was royalty. Across baseball in the 1950s, Snider was known as the third leg of the famous "Willie, Mickey, and The Duke" maxim that highlighted the three cornerstone future Hall of Fame center fielders from New York's three major-league clubs. Their play sparked a three-team fan debate over which player was the best. The 1981 Terry Cashman song "Talkin' Baseball" was inspired by these three heroes of the outfield and introduced new generations of fans to this iconic debate from the golden years of baseball.

When fans think of home-run hitters and superstars of the 1950s, Willie Mays and Mickey Mantle immediately come to mind. Only a few fans would name eight-time All-Star Snider if asked who hit the most home runs during that decade. Snider had made his major-league debut with the Brooklyn Dodgers in 1947. Five years older than Mays and Mantle, who each played

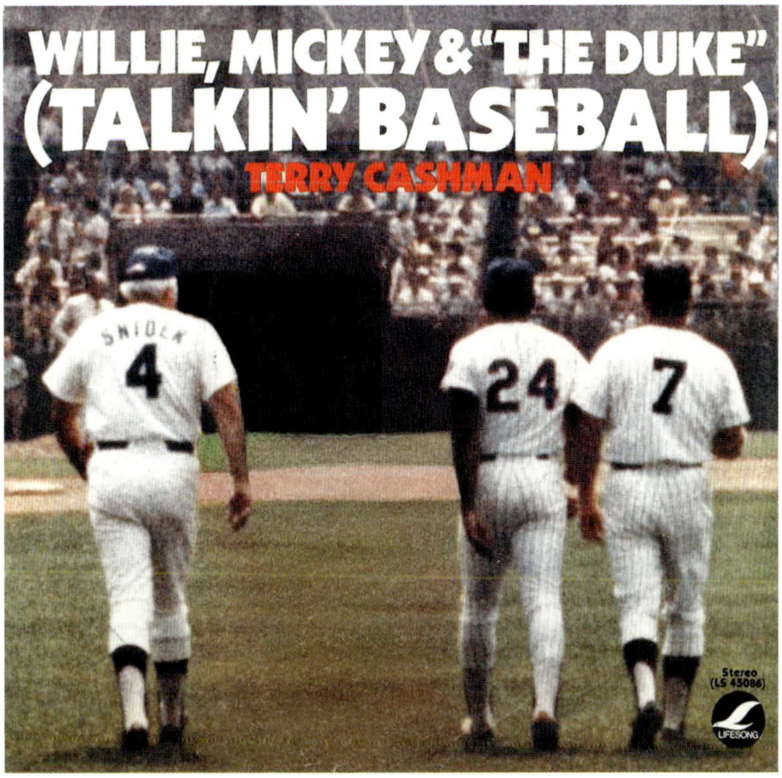

This retail Duke Snider DS18 glove (opposite) was offered in Rawlings catalogs in the 1940s and 1950s. Terry Cashman's 1981 song "Talkin' Baseball" (left) highlighted the debate over which New York major-league team had the best center fielder.

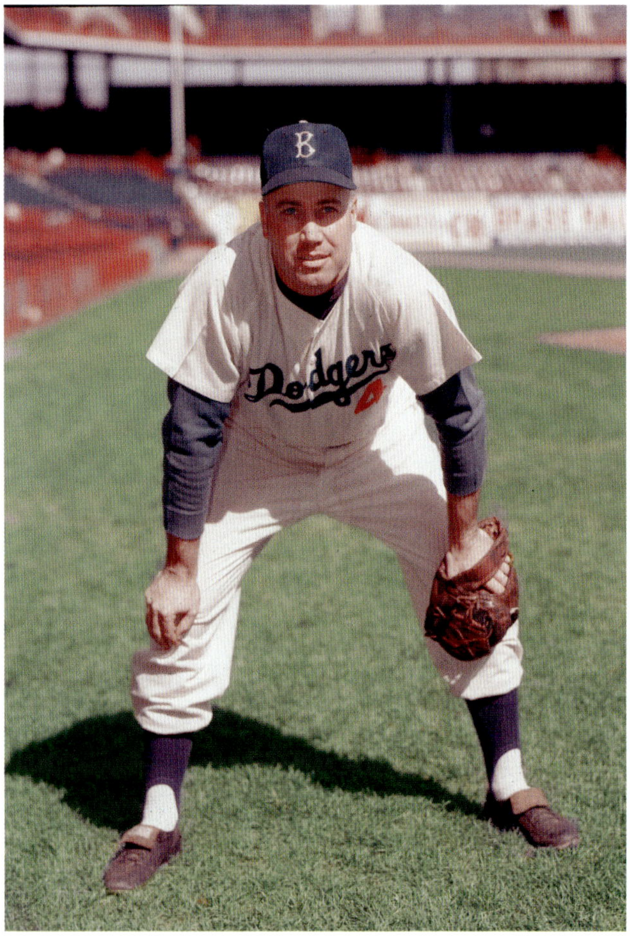

Snider, shown here in the 1950s, was the center fielder for the Brooklyn Dodgers.

their first game in 1951, Snider went yard 326 times during the 1950s. Mantle only homered 280 times and came in fourth on the list behind the Dodgers' Gil Hodges and the Braves' Eddie Mathews. Mays's 250 dingers were only good for seventh place on MLB's 1950s home-run leaderboard. By the end of his career, Snider had hit 407 homers compared to Mantle's 536 and Mays's 660.

Even though he never won a Gold Glove or received an MVP Award, Snider was truly baseball's best slugger during the 1950s. He also did something that no one else would do during that decade, including Mantle and Mays. He put together five consecutive seasons of 40 or more home runs (1953–1957). In fact, only seven other players in MLB history have accomplished that feat: Ralph Kiner, Adam Dunn, Barry Bonds, Ken Griffey Jr., Alex Rodriguez, Sammy Sosa, and Babe Ruth. Paralleling his home-run exploits of the 1950s, Snider plated the most RBIs of the decade as well.

Within Snider's record-setting five seasons, 1955 was his best. His 42 home runs and 136 RBIs powered the Dodgers to their fourth World Series in seven seasons (1949, 1952, 1953, and 1955). More importantly, his postseason's four home runs, seven RBIs, and .320 batting average against the Yankees guided the Dodgers to Brooklyn's first and only World Series championship. Snider's efforts became the catalyst for the storied Brooklyn team chronicled in Roger Kahn's *The Boys of Summer*. Snider played in another losing cause in the 1956 Series and was also on the Dodgers' first pennant and world championship in 1959—the year after the team relocated to Los Angeles. Snider's 11 World Series home runs remain the most by an NL player. Only Mickey Mantle (18), Babe Ruth (15), and Yogi Berra (12), who were all AL players, have more.

Throughout the 1950s, the competition between Mays and Snider stoked the debate over who was the NL's better center fielder. Snider was a dead pull hitter whose explosive swing was made for the short right-field wall (297 feet) of Ebbets Field. His blazing speed and grace in the outfield regularly found him within the top five of the NL's leaderboard for assists and putouts. Between 1949 and 1955, Snider led the league in center-field fielding percentage in 1951, 1952, and 1955, while finishing second during the other four seasons. Unfortunately, Snider's best defensive seasons came before the advent of baseball's Gold Glove in 1957. Six times in the 1950s, Snider placed within the top 10 of votes for the NL's MVP, including 1955, when he was runner-up to teammate Roy Campanella by just five votes. He was, however, selected as that season's MLB Player of the Year by *The Sporting News*.

Age takes its toll on all baseball warriors, and an ailing knee plagued Snider in his later years and limited his playing time on a rebuilding Dodgers team. In his 17th season in the majors, Snider went back to New York in 1963. He was sold to the Mets to continue his pursuit of 2,000 hits and 400 home runs, something only six players in the big leagues had accomplished. Snider played his final season in 1964 with the San Francisco Giants as a part-time player alongside Mays, his former rival from New York. When the season was over so was Snider's storied career. His .295 batting average, 407 home runs, 2,226 hits, and 1,333 RBIs ensured his election into Cooperstown in 1980 and a continued legacy with Cashman's hit song the following year.

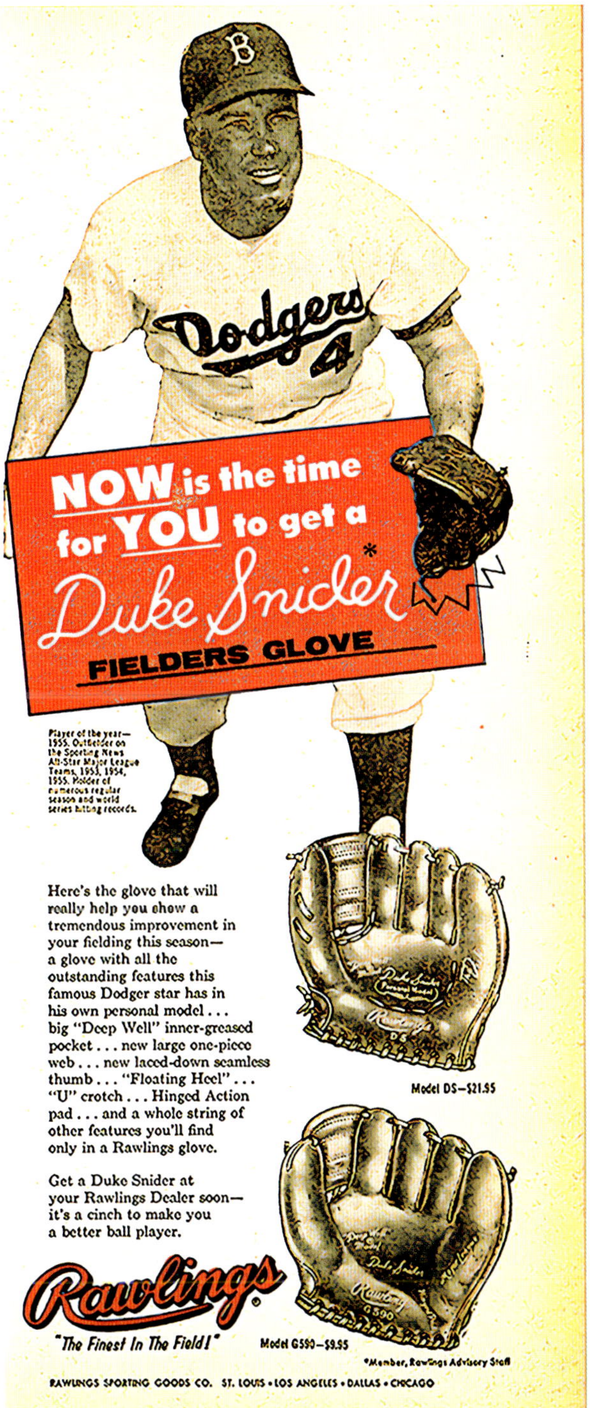

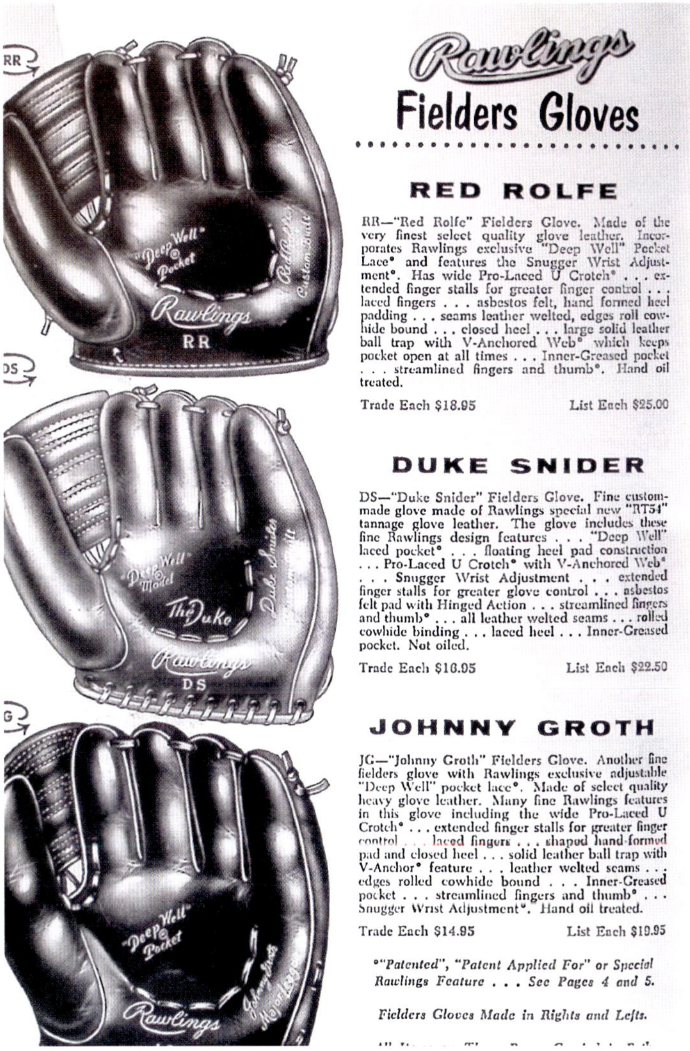

These two Rawlings advertisements from the 1950s feature the Duke Snider model glove.

BOBBY SHANTZ

The Little Man Who Played Big

Bobby Shantz grew up outside Philadelphia, dreaming of playing for Connie Mack's Philadelphia Athletics. It seemed like a long stretch for a boy who was exceedingly small. As a teenager he measured only four feet, four inches. When he graduated from high school in 1943, he was still less than five feet tall. A year later, when Shantz received his draft notice during the height of World War II, he was turned down because he was still below the 60-inch mark. He eventually topped out at five feet, six inches.

His love of baseball began with his father teaching him the game and how to pitch. The young Shantz developed a snappy curveball paired with remarkable control, a combination that should elevate anyone's career. What held Shantz back was his size. He was looked upon as too small to play the game professionally. But he kept playing locally, and his pitching efforts always stood out wherever he played. Eventually MLB scouts took notice, and he was soon taking part in some of baseball's most memorable moments with acclaim and awards.

In November 1947, the little boy who could, did. He signed a contract with the Athletics and posted an 18–7 record while striking out 212 batters in 214 innings during his first season in the minors in 1948. The next year, he was in the majors, and he stayed for the next 16 years (with seven teams) before retiring with a 119–99 record and a 3.38 ERA. His baseball dreams had come true.

Shantz had the uncanny ability to succeed as both a starter and a reliever. Sixty-eight percent of his appearances were in relief. Despite playing on a poor A's team in 1951 that finished in sixth place, Shantz posted an 18–10 record and was selected to his first of three All-Star Games (1951, 1952, and 1957). A year later, he was the best pitcher in baseball. He led the majors in WAR (8.8) and wins while going 24–7 with a 2.48 ERA. The little man became the big man when he was awarded the AL's MVP Award. In that year's All-Star Game, Shantz entered in the fifth inning and struck out Whitey Lockman, Jackie Robinson, and Stan Musial all in a row. There were thoughts of whether he could carry it into the eighth and repeat Carl Hubbell's 1934 feat of striking out five straight stars, but rain started falling and put a halt to what may have been.

Shantz suffered severe shoulder issues that limited his playing time during the next several seasons. He moved with the A's to Kansas City in 1955 and found success again. Two years later, Shantz was traded to the Yankees, where he put together a league-leading ERA season and appeared in his first of two World Series with the New Yorkers. He also won the first of his eight

Bobby Shantz used this Rawlings Eddie Mathews model glove during his 1955 and 1956 seasons with the Kansas City Athletics.

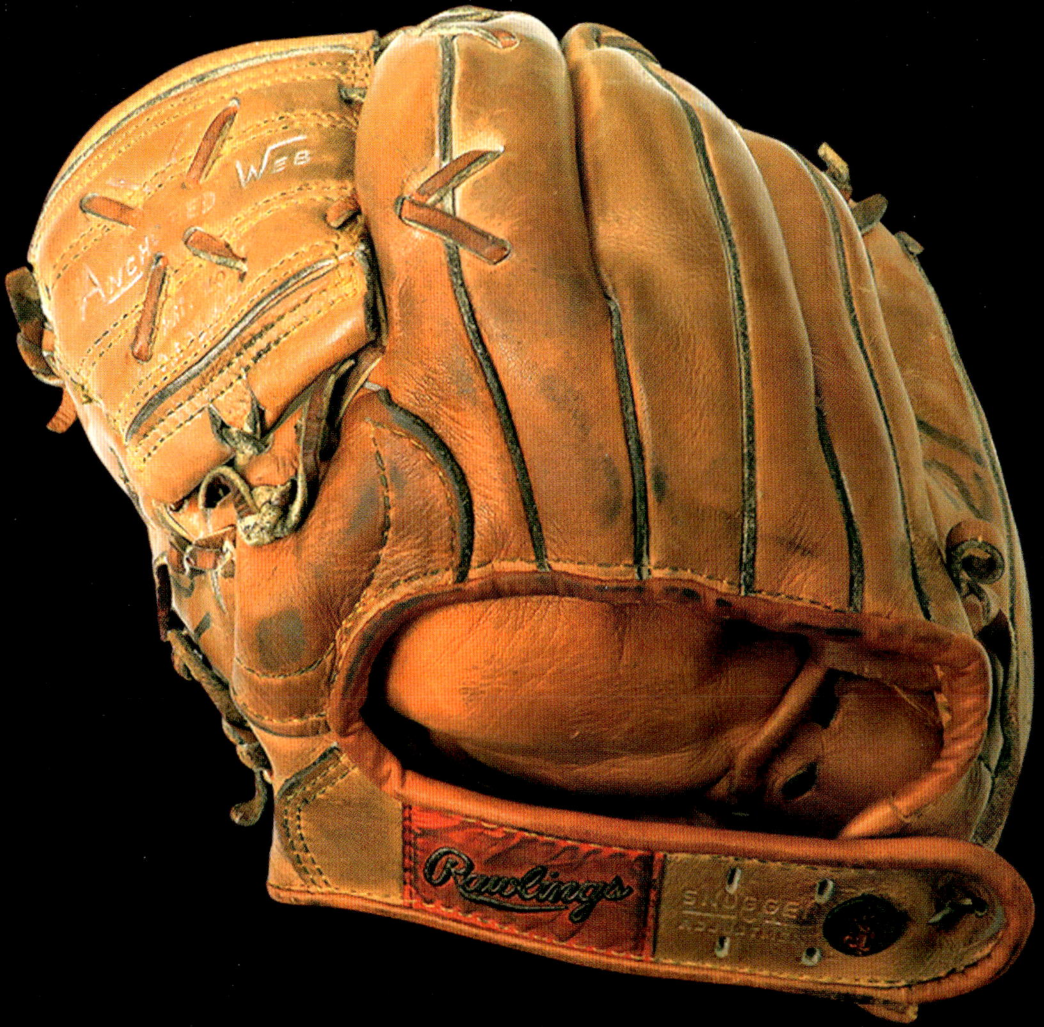
Rawlings

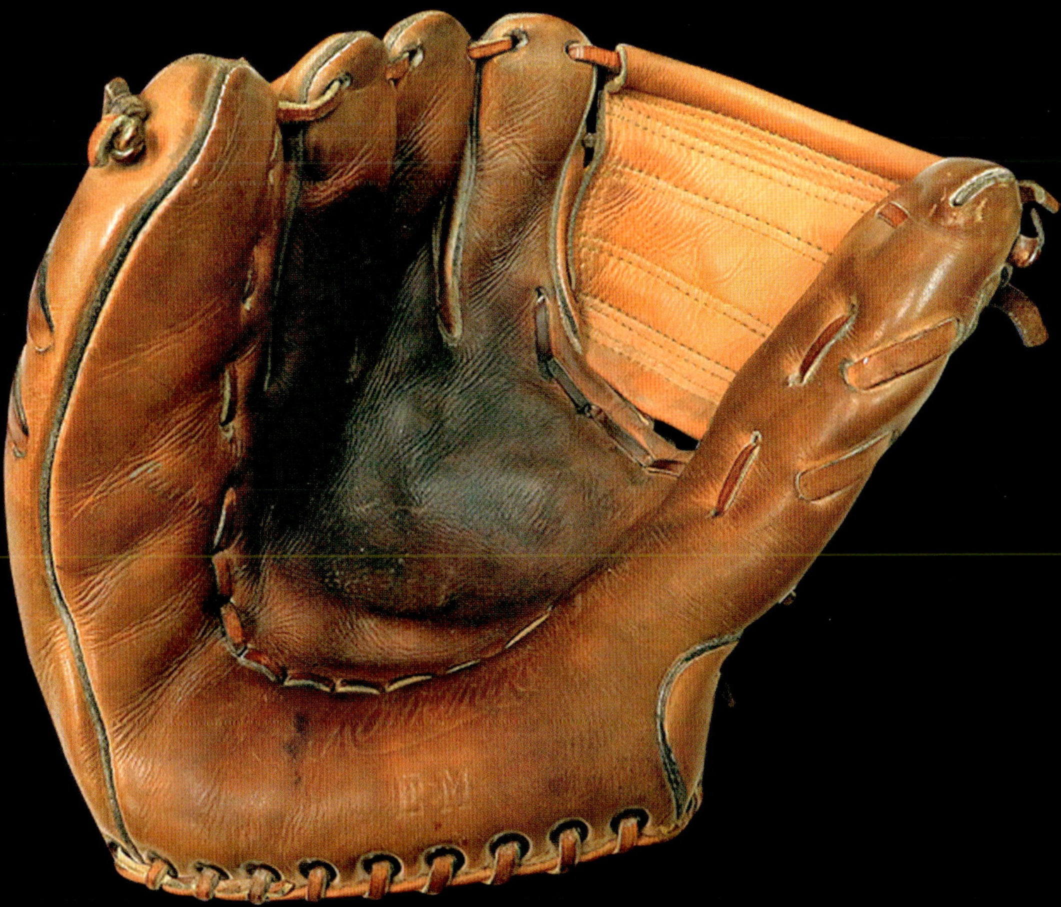

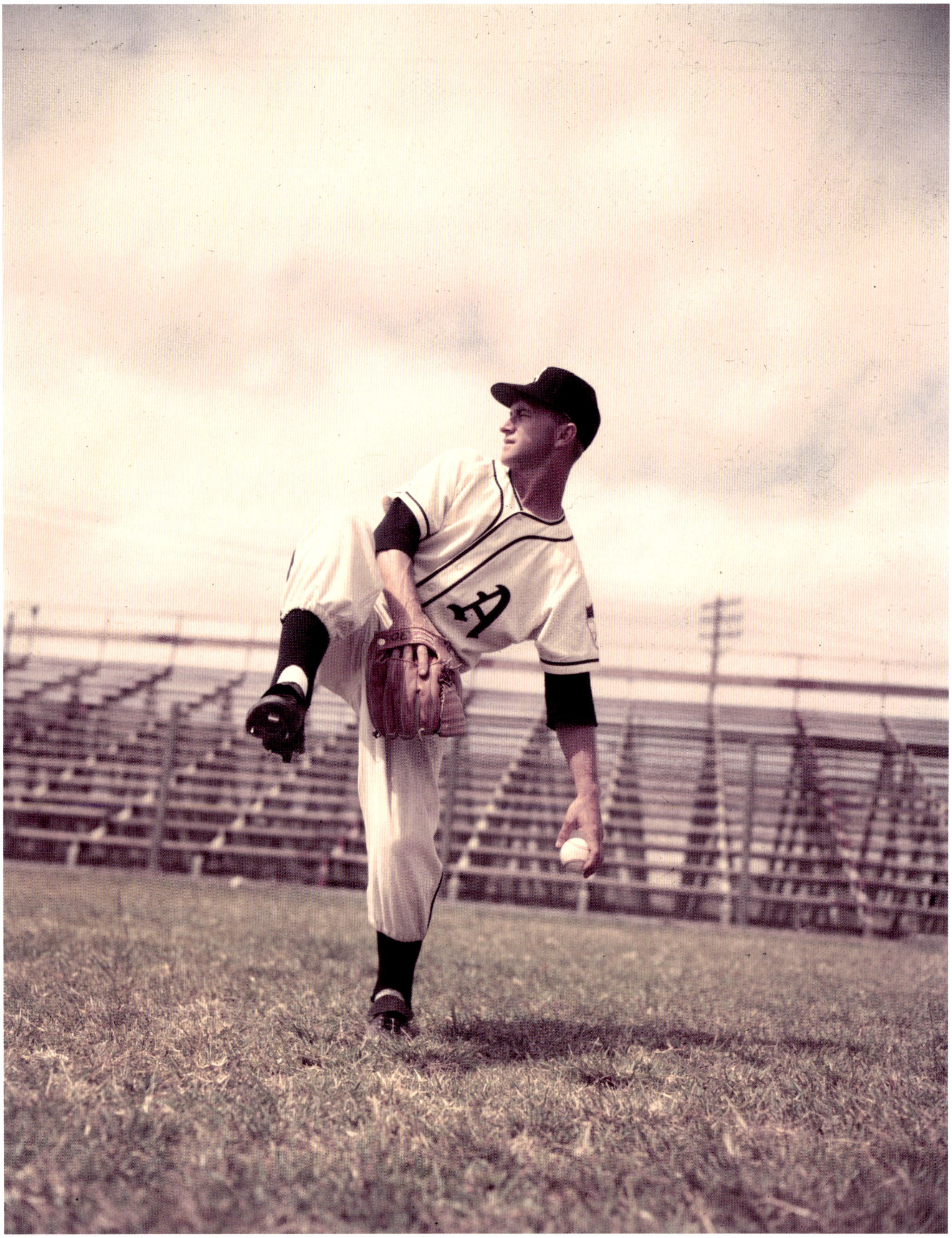

Shantz practices during spring training for the Philadelphia Athletics in the 1950s.

consecutive Gold Gloves (1957–1964). What made the recognition so special was that it was the award's inaugural year and only nine were given across MLB.

He was the first pitcher to win a Gold Glove, causing fans to wonder how many more he would have won if the award had been available earlier in his career. Interestingly, another southpaw, Jim Kaat—the recipient of 16 Gold Gloves (1962–1977), the longest consecutive streak by a pitcher—emulated Shantz's mechanics. While growing up, Kaat listened to broadcasters call Shantz "the best fielding pitcher in baseball." They described Shantz's motion: "He finishes on the balls of his feet. He is being square to the hitter. He is ready to go—left or right." Then Kaat would go to his backyard with a tennis ball and practice like Shantz for hours. "When I got to spring training in my first year with the Senators," Kaat said, "I was going through pitching drills and the coach said, 'Kid, you look like Bobby Shantz,' and I said, 'Thank you very much.'"

Shantz never won a championship in New York. The Yankees lost in 1957, and he was injured in 1958. Shantz was then part of one of baseball's most memorable games—Game Seven of the 1960 World Series. In the eighth inning, with a runner on first, the Yankees were leading 7–4 and ready to taste the champagne. Shantz had entered the game in the third inning and faced the minimum of 15 batters for five innings. The Pirates got a hit to start the eighth, then Shantz's pitch to the next batter appeared to be a sure double play before taking a bad bounce into shortstop Tony Kubek's Adam's apple. The Pirates went on to tie the game after Shantz was relieved and won the game with Bill Mazeroski's walk-off home run.

Over the next four years, Shantz was traded to five different teams. He was part of the Cardinals' trade to the Cubs with Ernie Broglio for Lou Brock in 1964, and later that season he was traded back home to Philadelphia, where he couldn't help prevent the historic Phillies collapse. Despite all the trades and changing teams, Shantz continued to be recognized as the best defensive pitcher in the game as he continued to win Gold Gloves and prove that a little man can play the game.

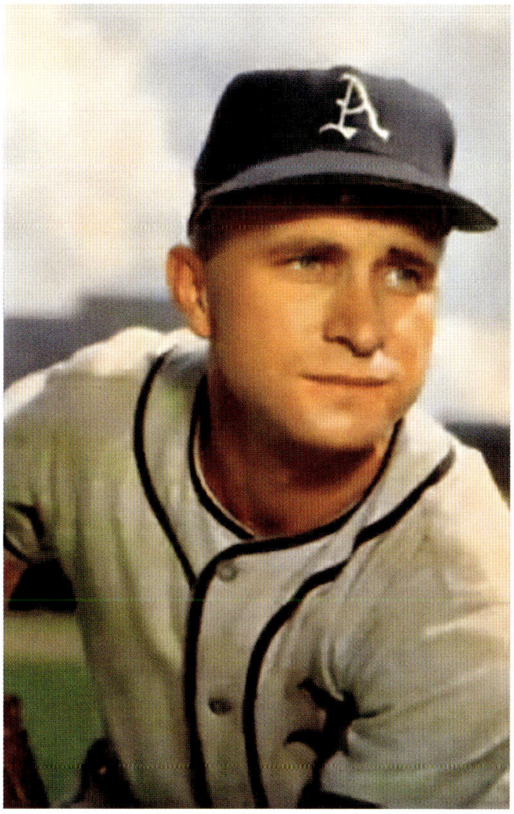

Shantz, shown here in 1953, was part of the original Gold Glove Award class of 1957. He went on to win the award in eight consecutive seasons.

MINNIE MIÑOSO

The Latin Jackie Robinson

Saturnino Orestes Miñoso was affectionately known as "Minnie." His rise in baseball—from Cuba to America's Negro Leagues to MLB's Hall of Fame—became an inspiration for all young Latino boys playing the game. He was MLB's first Latin superstar. "Minnie Miñoso is to Latin ballplayers what Jackie Robinson is to Black ballplayers," wrote Orlando Cepeda in his autobiography.

Miñoso's story is a tale of a young boy growing up playing baseball in his native Cuba before making it to the major leagues in 1950 and playing 1,948 big-league games during 20 seasons spread across five decades. Miñoso began his professional career by playing multiple positions for multiple teams in the Cuban Leagues before heading to America in 1946 and signing with the Negro National League's New York Cubans—a team he would play with through 1948. While with the Cubans, Miñoso was twice selected as a Negro Leagues All-Star third baseman (1947–1948) and helped guide them to the Negro World Series title in 1947. Miñoso's electrifying speed on the field soon led to his nickname "The Cuban Comet."

While Jackie Robinson was breaking MLB's color barrier in 1947—the same year as the Cubans' Negro World Series title—Miñoso was being scouted by Abe Saperstein, the legendary owner and coach of the Harlem Globetrotters. Saperstein guided Bill Veeck to sign Miñoso. Veeck had enabled the breaking of the AL color barrier in 1947 with his signing of Larry Doby for the Cleveland Indians. Veeck signed Miñoso in late 1948. He was assigned to play the last two weeks (11 games) of the season with the team's single-A club in Dayton, where he batted .525.

The next spring, the 25-year-old Miñoso made the Indians opening day lineup against the St. Louis Browns and walked in his lone pinch-hit appearance. Unable to crack the starting lineup of the Indians' reigning world championship team in 1949, Miñoso spent the remainder of that season and the following one with the Indians' AAA team in San Diego before being traded to the White Sox on May 1, 1951. After homering in his first game, Miñoso helped put the Sox on a winning path. He soon became a fan favorite in Chicago, and he made his first of nine appearances in the All-Star Game. Miñoso became a regular AL leader in hit-by-pitches, triples, and stolen bases. He exceeded the 100-mark multiple times for runs scored and RBIs. In his first 11 seasons in the majors, Miñoso hit over .300 eight times, and in the other three seasons, he never hit below .280.

As good as he was at the plate, Miñoso was equally as good in the field, whether playing third base or the outfield. Every year between 1953 and 1961, Miñoso was ranked in the AL top

Minnie Miñoso used this Rawlings H-Web model glove during his later playing days.

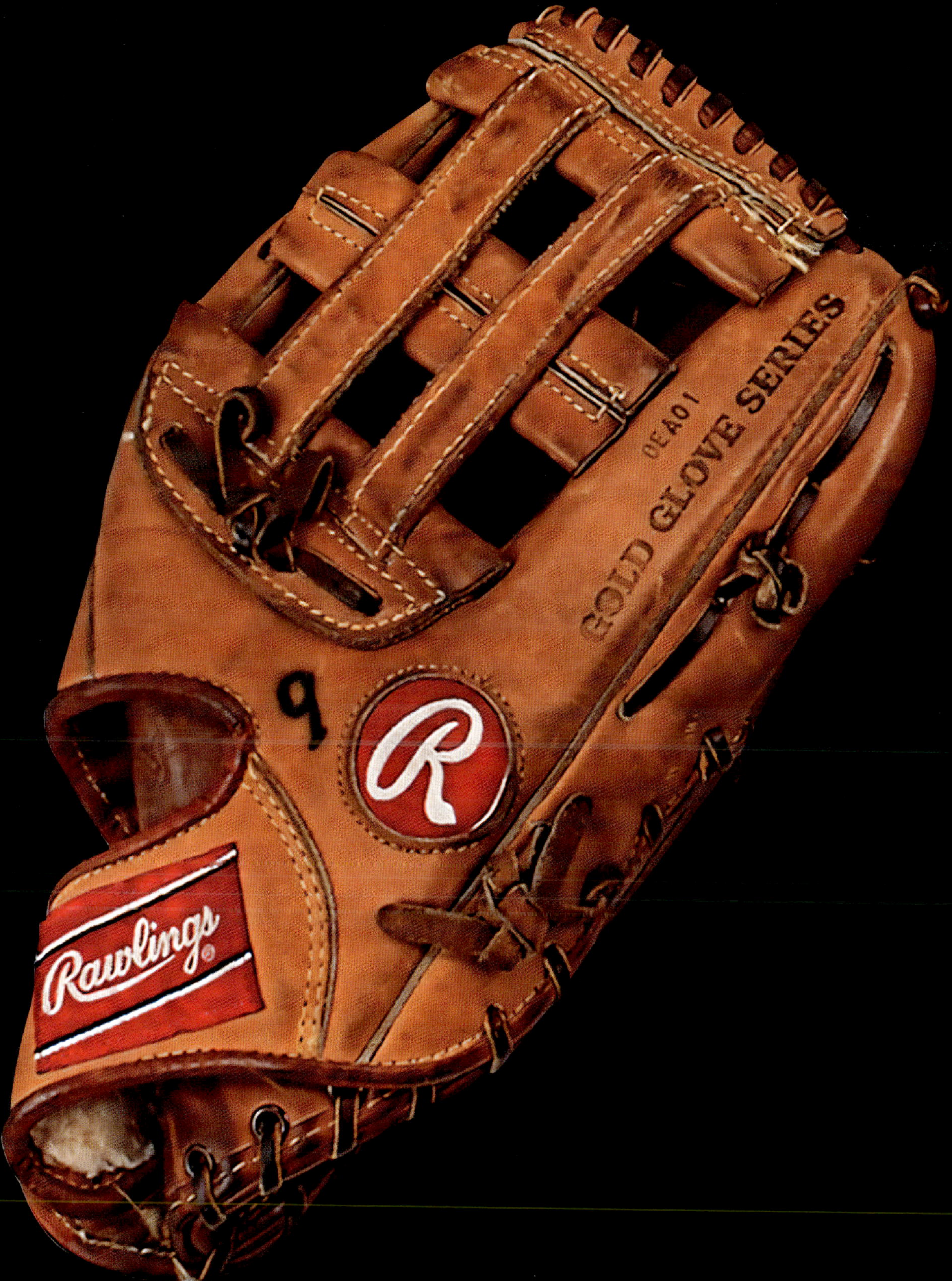
GOLD GLOVE SERIES
Rawlings

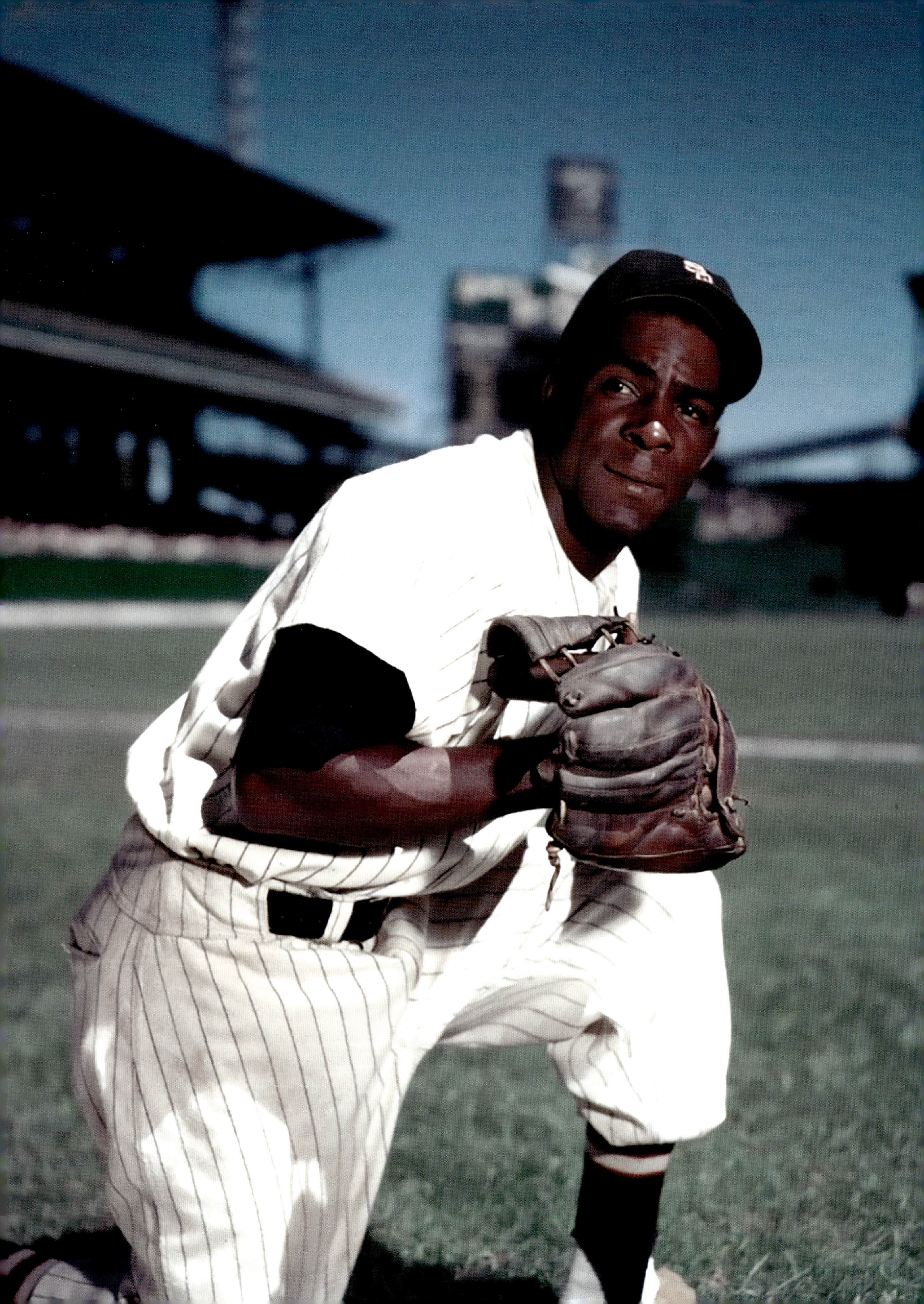

five in fielding percentage. Six times between 1953 and 1960, he ranked in the top five in outfielder's assists, and he ranked in the top five in double plays by an outfielder three times during the same period. That level of play deservedly led to Miñoso's selection in 1957 as one of the nine winners of MLB's inaugural Gold Glove Award. He went on to win two other Gold Gloves in the AL in 1959 and 1960 after the award was expanded to recognize nine players from each league in 1958.

Miñoso missed the White Sox' 1959 World Series appearance due to a trade back to Cleveland that year; Veeck quickly brought him back to the Sox the next year, but he was eventually traded to the Cardinals in 1962 as they sought a veteran outfielder who would help them contend for a pennant—something Miñoso would never be a part of in the major leagues. Miñoso only played 39 games with the Redbirds after running into the Sportsman's Park wall, fracturing his skull and breaking his wrist. Sold to the Senators after that season, he eventually retired after playing the 1964 season once more with the White Sox. In 1976, while coaching the Sox, Veeck reactivated him for three games, and Miñoso got a hit playing in his fourth decade. In 1980, at the age of 56, he was reactivated once again with the Sox for two games and two at-bats (no hits) for his fifth decade in the big leagues.

His was a career that broke barriers. As a very dark-skinned man, he faced the dual prejudices against Black and Latino players during America's segregated 1950s and 1960s. And through it all, the man known as "Minnie" played the game he loved and became an inspiration to all baseball lovers.

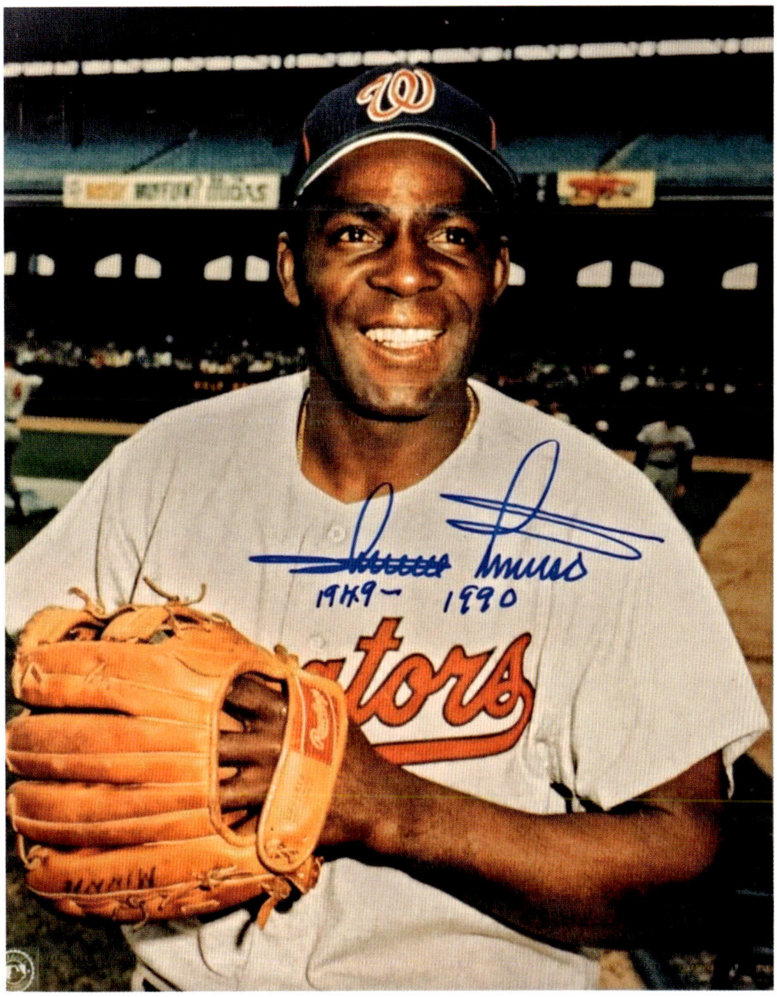

The three-time Rawlings Gold Glove recipient (opposite) was part of the inaugural class of award winners in 1957. Miñoso (left) played for four teams—the Cleveland Indians, Chicago White Sox, St. Louis Cardinals, and Washington Senators—during a career that lasted more than 30 years.

STAN MUSIAL

The Man

One word fully describes the baseball player known simply as "The Man." That word is *consistency*, and his name was Stan Musial. He spent 22 seasons with the St. Louis Cardinals, and while he is considered the best player in their franchise history, he is also remembered as one of the greatest and most consistent hitters to ever play the game. This first-ballot Hall of Famer recorded a lifetime batting average of .331—against 3,630 career hits. Interestingly, 1,815 were hit at home and 1,815 were hit on the road.

Musial made his MLB debut in late September 1941, hitting .426 in just 12 games. The following year, in his first full season, he started a streak of 16 consecutive seasons hitting greater than .310. His best year at the plate was 1948, when he hit .376 and put together one of the greatest seasons by an MLB ballplayer ever. Musial led the NL in hits, runs, doubles, triples, RBIs, batting average, on-base percentage, slugging percentage, and on-base plus slugging percentage.

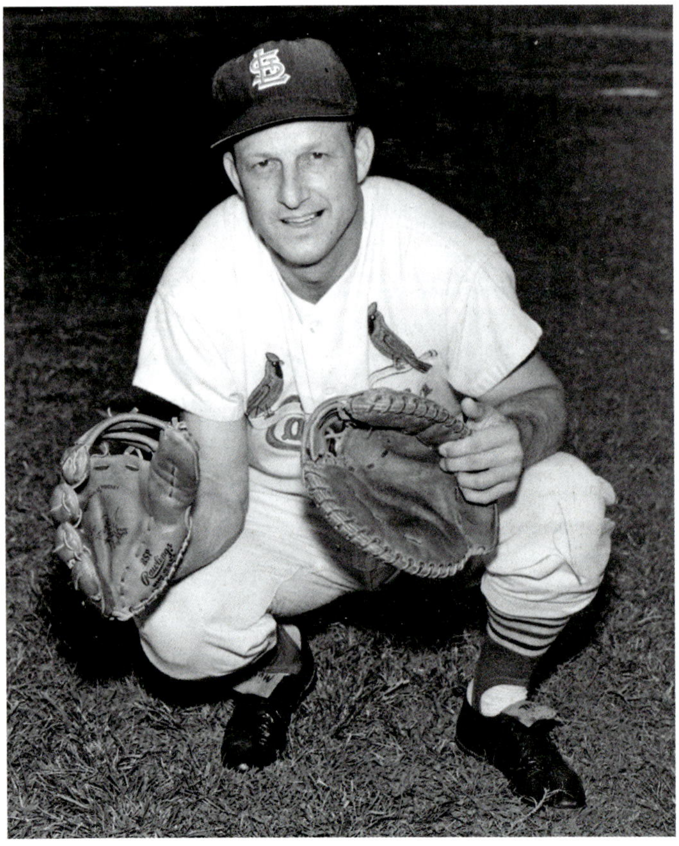

Stan Musial (left) was the first to play at least 1,000 games in both the infield and outfield. Musial used this Rawlings Trapper-style first baseman's mitt (opposite, top) in a 1940s game. He used this Rawlings H-Web model glove (opposite, bottom) in the outfield circa 1946.

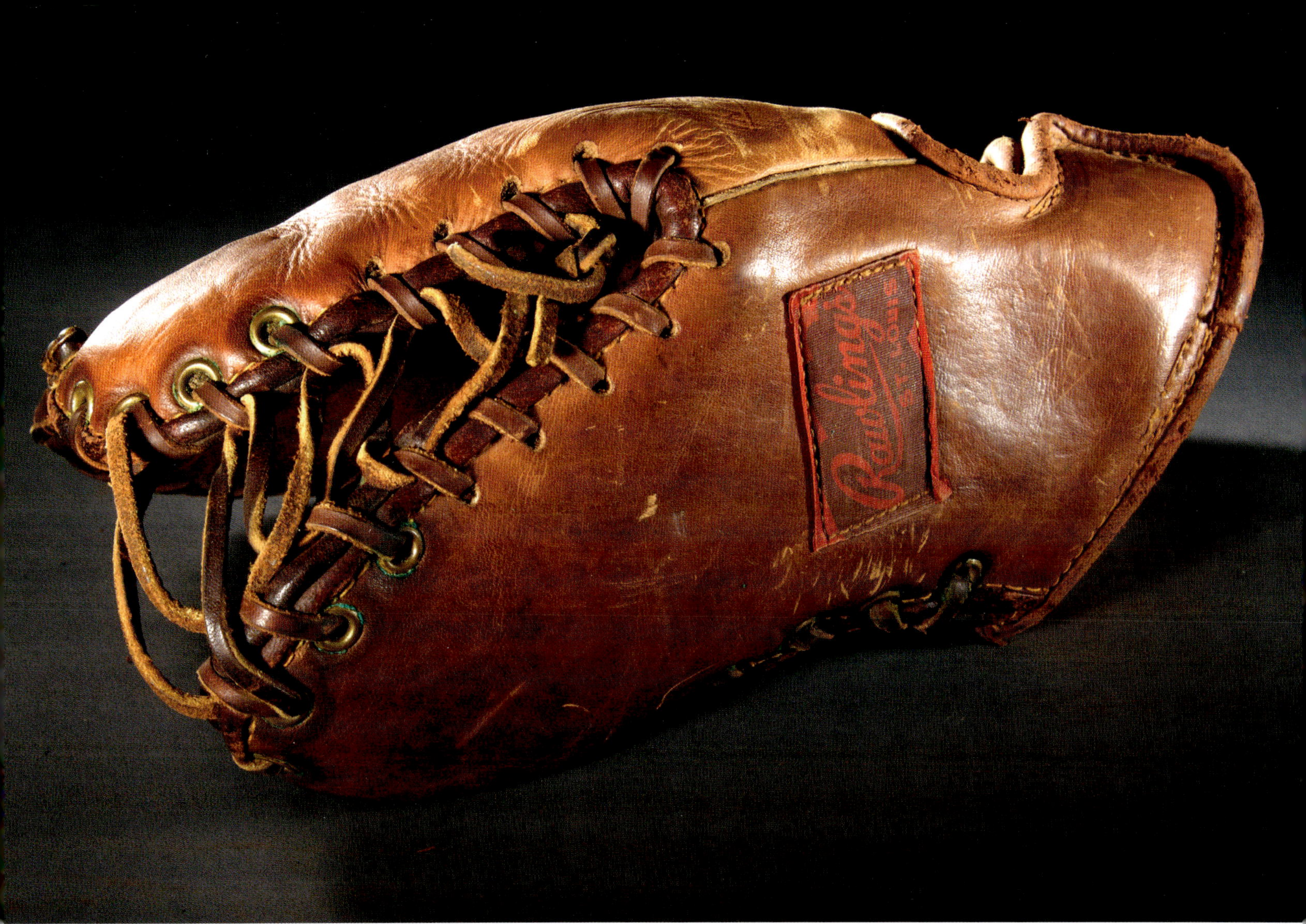
Rawlings
ST. LOUIS

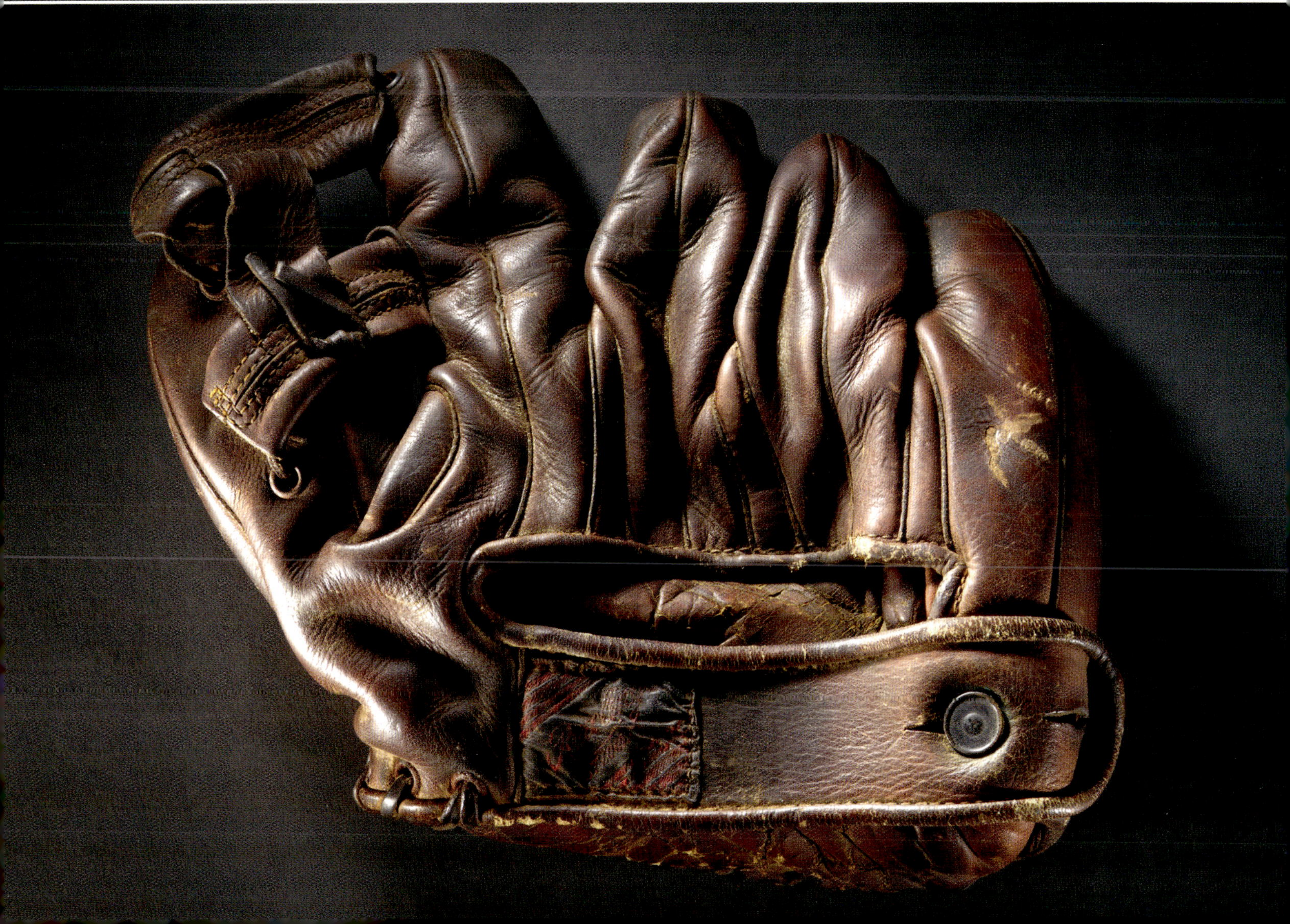

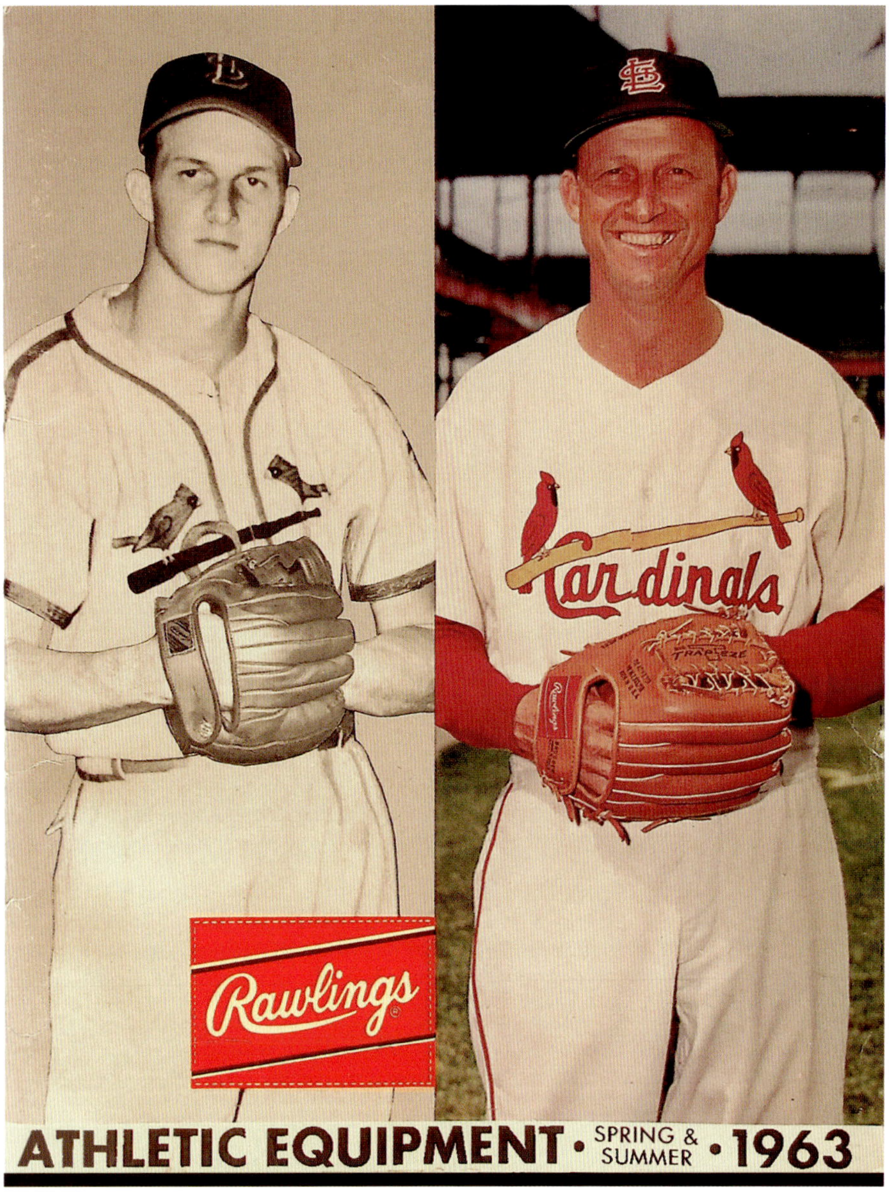

Musial appeared on the cover of a 1963 Rawlings catalog.

The only category he did not lead was home runs, where he fell one short—but perhaps not. Musial had one home run rained out and a second drive in Philadelphia's Shibe Park that hit the speaker of the PA system above the fence and was ruled a ground rule double by the umpire. If it had counted, Musial would have won the Triple Crown.

In the 10 seasons following that near Triple Crown year, there was little change in his season averages: .335 batting average, .426 on-base percentage, .582 slugging percentage, 189 hits, 38 doubles, 7 triples, 29 home runs, 104 runs, and 105 RBIs. When Musial retired at the end of the 1963 season, the three-time MVP and seven-time NL batting champion held or shared 17 MLB, 29 NL, and 9 All-Star Game records. Most significantly, at his retirement, he was the MLB career leader in extra-base hits (1,377) and total bases (6,134). He was the NL leader for career hits (3,630), RBIs (1,951), games played (3,026), at-bats (10,972), runs scored (1,949), and doubles (725). His 475 home runs ranked second in NL history when he retired, leaving fans to wonder how many more homers Musial would have hit if the Cardinals' Sportsman's Park did not have a screen running across right field from the top of the wall to the roof of the pavilion, or if he hadn't missed the 1945 season due to serving in the U.S. Navy in World War II.

How fearful were his opponents and their fans of his hitting prowess? In June 1946, Brooklyn fans were so weary of the Dodgers' inability to get Musial out, they began chanting during a game, "O-h-h, here comes the man again." As legendary sportswriter Bob Broeg wrote, it was not "*that* man" but "*the* man" out of respect, and thus Musial was forever branded with that nickname. Sixty-two seasons after Musial's last game, only Pete Rose, Ty Cobb, and Hank Aaron have more hits in MLB history than him. To further highlight his impact on the game, only Aaron, Barry Bonds, and Albert Pujols have more career extra-base hits than him.

While a model of consistency on offense, Musial was just as consistent on defense. He began his career in the minors as a pitcher until he hurt his shoulder while diving for a ball in the outfield. (He played in the outfield on the days he wasn't pitching.) The injury ended his pitching career. During his first four seasons in the big leagues, Musial played exclusively in the outfield. He then showed his versatility in the field when he came back in 1946 after a year in the U.S. Navy and began playing the majority of his games at first base as a temporary fill-in that lasted until 1960. Musial played 1,890 games in the outfield and 1,016 games at first base and became the first major leaguer to play more than 1,000 games at two different positions. Had the Gold Glove been awarded during this period, Musial may very well have been a recipient at either position, or perhaps a recipient of baseball's first Gold Glove for utility players.

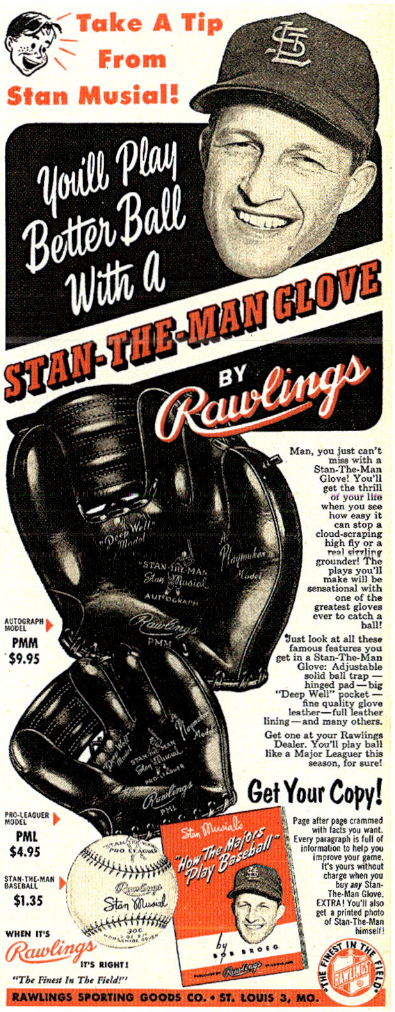

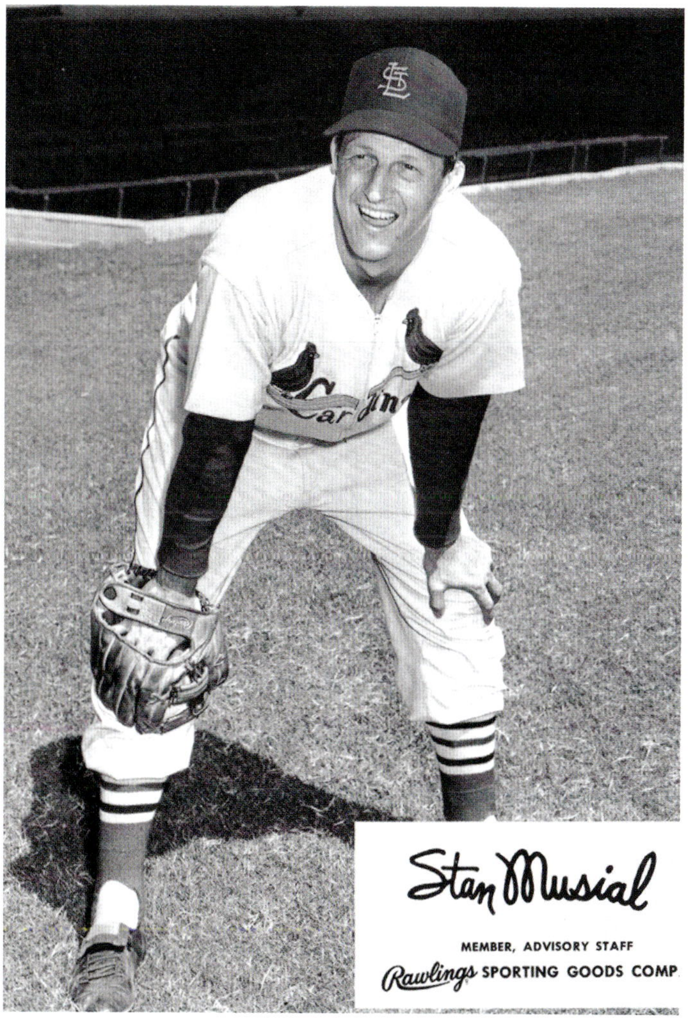

Musial also lent his image to two 1950s Rawlings advertisements.

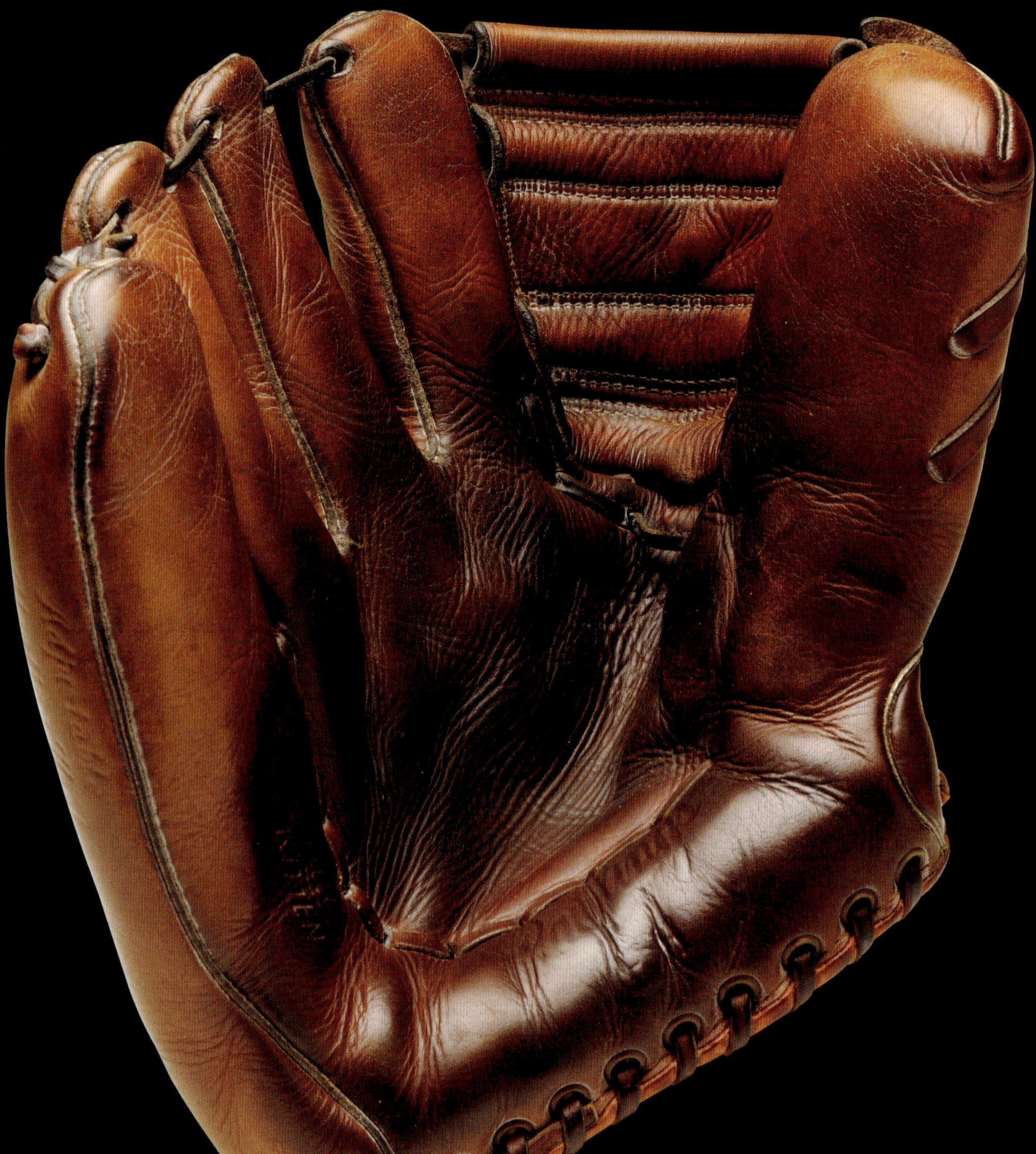

HARVEY HADDIX

Was This the Greatest Game Ever Pitched?

Even though his name was etched in the palm of one of the most popular Rawlings gloves of the 1950s, Harvey Haddix is never mentioned or included on any list of baseball's greatest pitchers. However, for one evening in 1959, there was no one better than the man nicknamed "The Kitten." His evening on the mound on May 26 has been described as the greatest game ever pitched in MLB history. The one regretful stain on Haddix's special moment was that he wasn't the winner. He was the game's losing pitcher.

So, if the 36-year-old Haddix and his Pirates teammates lost, what made the game that night so special? The Pirates were in Milwaukee playing the Braves in County Stadium. The Braves were sending the 1957 World Series MVP, Lew Burdette, to the mound against Haddix. Haddix had spent the day in bed with the flu, but like a trooper he came to the ballpark ready to take the start on a cold, windy, and drizzly night. How many innings would he last in those conditions?

The answer was 13, and 12 of them were perfect. Haddix became the first man in MLB history to pitch 12 innings without giving up a hit or allowing a runner on base. It was 36 men up and 36 men down, a feat never accomplished by anyone else—not even the great Cy Young, Walter Johnson, or Christy Mathewson.

With a performance like that, why wasn't the game over in nine innings? Burdette had surgically worked around the 12 Pirate hits that

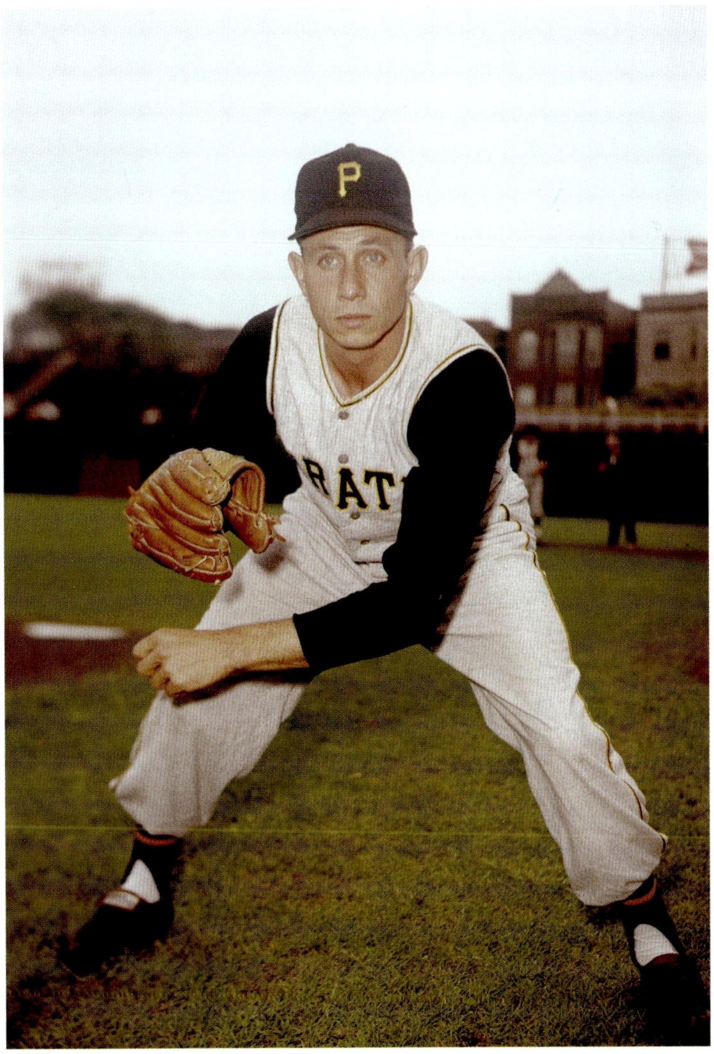

Harvey Haddix used this Rawlings HH model glove (opposite) during his career. The three-time Gold Glove Award winner (left) for the Pittsburgh Pirates poses before a game against the Chicago Cubs circa 1963 at Wrigley Field.

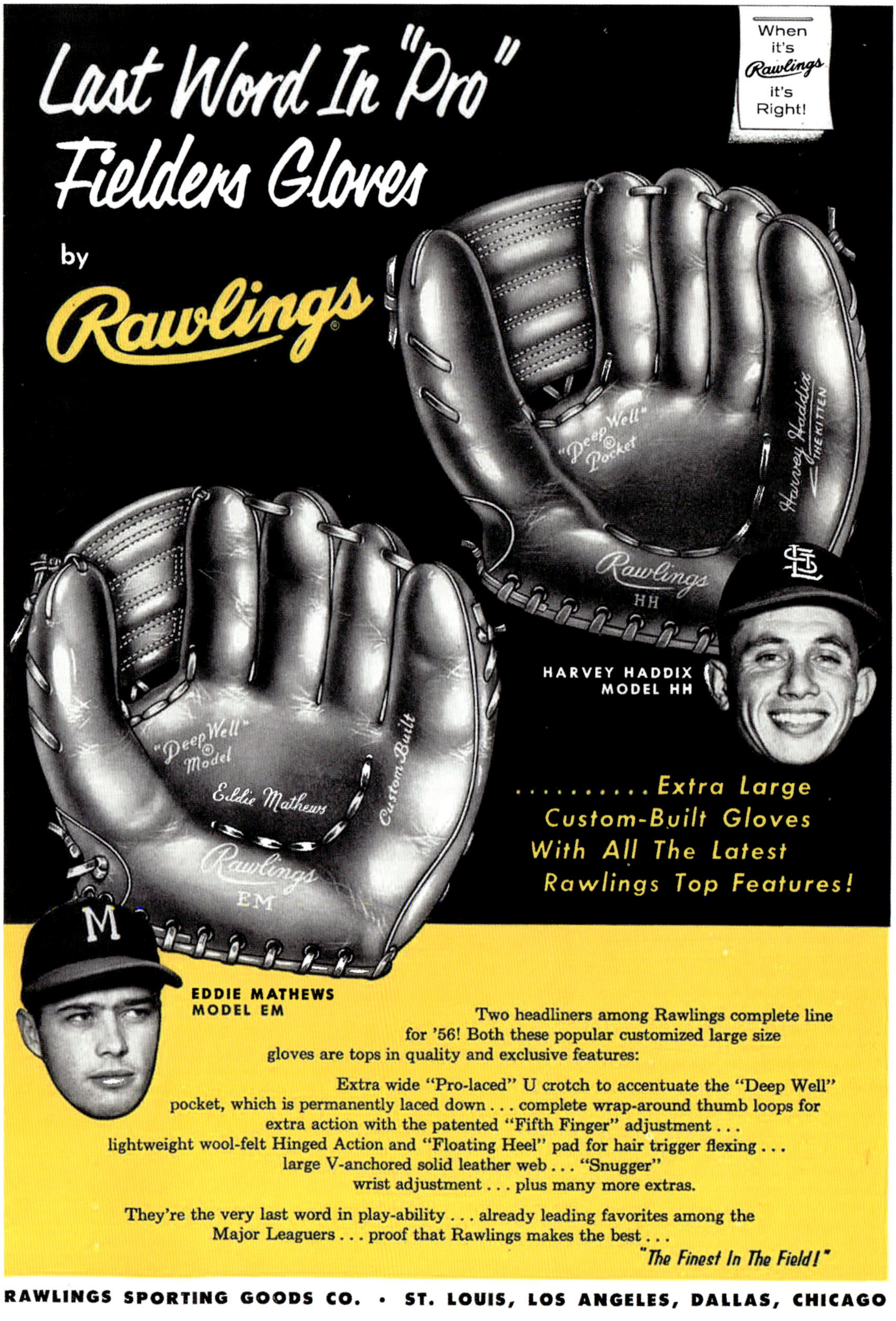

This late 1950s Rawlings advertisement features the Harvey Haddix (HH) model glove.

he had given up without allowing a runner to score. That included the top of the 13th inning, when Haddix stayed in the game to bat for himself and flied out to center for the second out. The Pirates did follow with a hit but left the runner on base for the eighth time.

In the bottom of the inning, Haddix was still on the mound to face the Braves' first batter, Félix Mantilla, who hit a ball to third baseman Don Hoak, whose hurried throw skipped into the dirt for an error at first base. The "perfecto" was over on the 37th batter, but Haddix's no-hitter remained intact. The next batter, Eddie Mathews, offered a sacrifice bunt to move Mantilla to second to bring up Hank Aaron, who was intentionally walked. Slugger Joe Adcock was up next and sent Haddix's second pitch over the outfield wall for what was initially declared a three-run home run, but after Aaron touched third base and turned to go to the dugout, thinking the ball had stayed in the park and the game was over, he was passed on the basepaths by Adcock and called out, meaning Adcock's home run turned into a double and only one run was scored to end this remarkable game with a 1–0 win by the Braves.

Haddix's performance has been called an immortal moment. But what made it even more amazing was the fact that Braves pitcher Bob Buhl was telegraphing the Pirates' catcher's signs from the bullpen to each hitter except for Aaron, who did not want the distraction. And despite knowing what was coming, the Braves could not touch Haddix's nasty slider and wicked fastball for 12 complete and perfect innings.

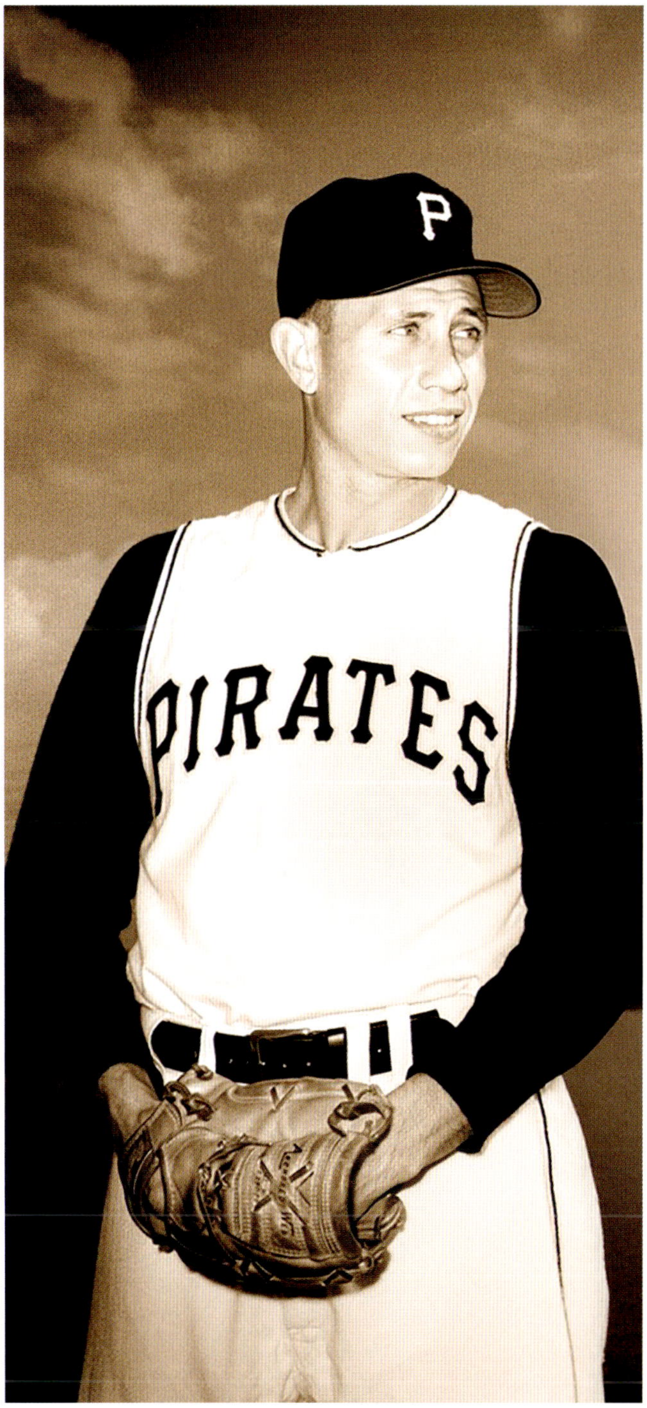

Haddix's defense helped the Pirates get to the Fall Classic in 1960, and his 2–0 record helped his team win the world championship. He won his final Gold Glove that year.

ROBERTO CLEMENTE

The Complete Ballplayer

Roberto Clemente's journey into baseball began on the ball fields of his native Puerto Rico. He became one of the best Latin American players to ever play in the majors and is remembered as one of the most complete players the game has ever seen. Over his 18-year career in the big leagues, Clemente was the face of the Pittsburgh Pirates right up until his untimely death on New Year's Eve in 1972.

Clemente's days in baseball mirrored the racism within American society, except he felt additional pressure as a double minority—Latino and Black. He thus used his position in baseball to advocate for the better treatment of minorities—especially Latin Americans. Clemente sadly passed away during a humanitarian effort that he had initiated to help victims of a devastating earthquake that had taken place a week earlier in Managua, Nicaragua. The cargo plane carrying Clemente and other relief workers developed trouble soon after takeoff from Puerto Rico, and all aboard were lost at sea. It was a loss for baseball and all mankind.

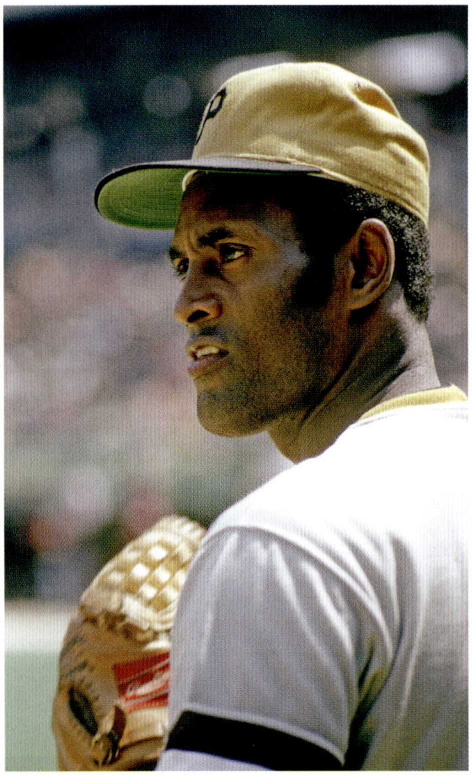

Clemente had become a superstar in the early 1960s with his flash of speed and his powerful throws from right field. At bat, he swung at almost everything thrown his way, while winning four NL batting titles (1961, 1964, 1965, and 1967) and being named the league's MVP in 1966. Clemente hit over .300 in 13 of his 18 seasons and hit over .290 in two others. He played on two World Series championship teams with the Pirates (1960 and 1971) and won the Series MVP in the latter. He even had a hit in each of the 14 games of those two Series. Clemente was the first Latin American ballplayer to win a league MVP, a World Series championship (as a starting position player), and a World Series MVP. These

Outfielder Roberto Clemente warms up for the Pittsburgh Pirates before a game in the early 1970s (left). He played for the Pirates from 1955 to 1972. Clemente used this Rawlings Fastback Basket-Web model glove (opposite) during his career.

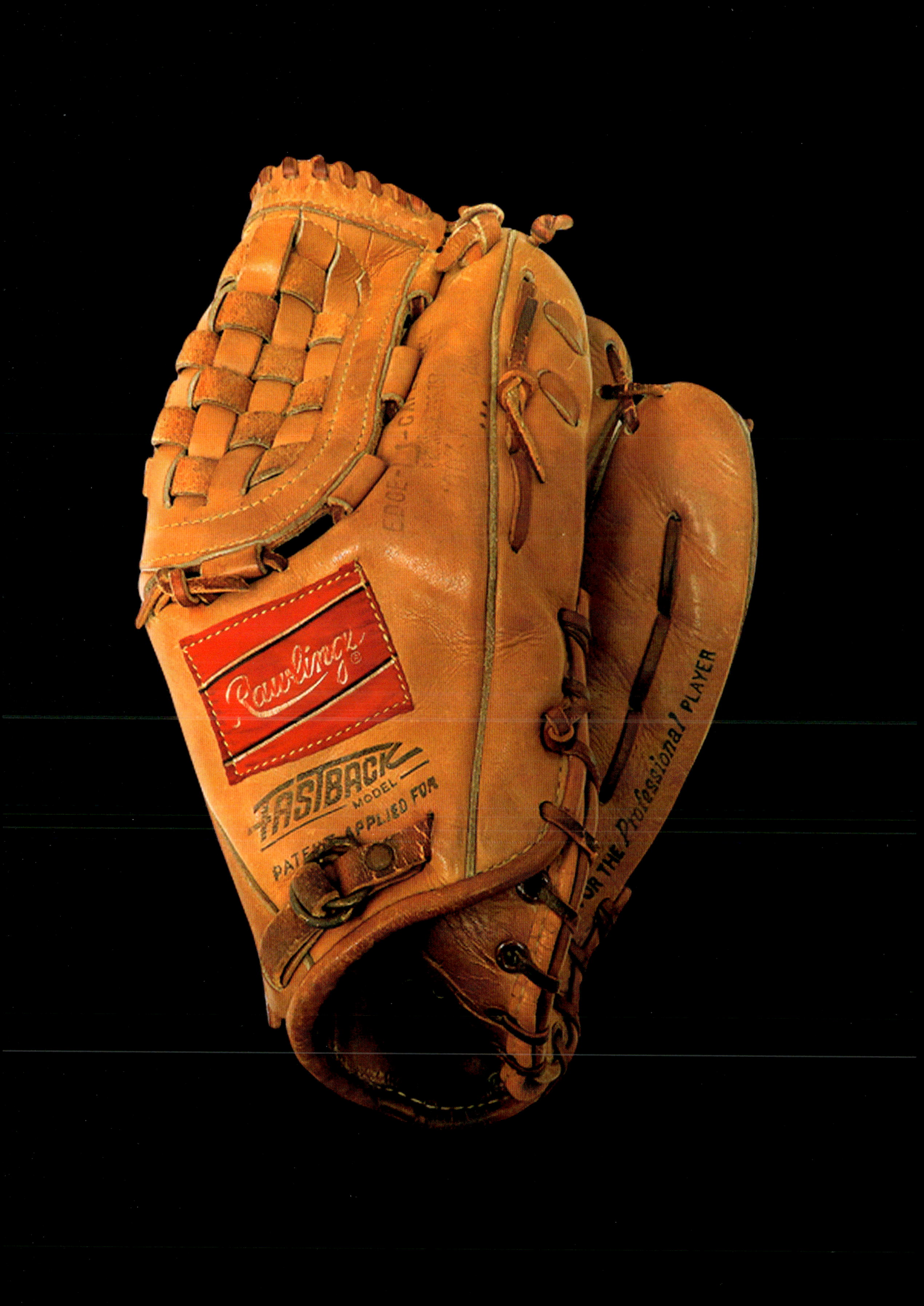
Rawlings
FASTBACK
MODEL
APPLIED FOR
FOR THE Professional PLAYER

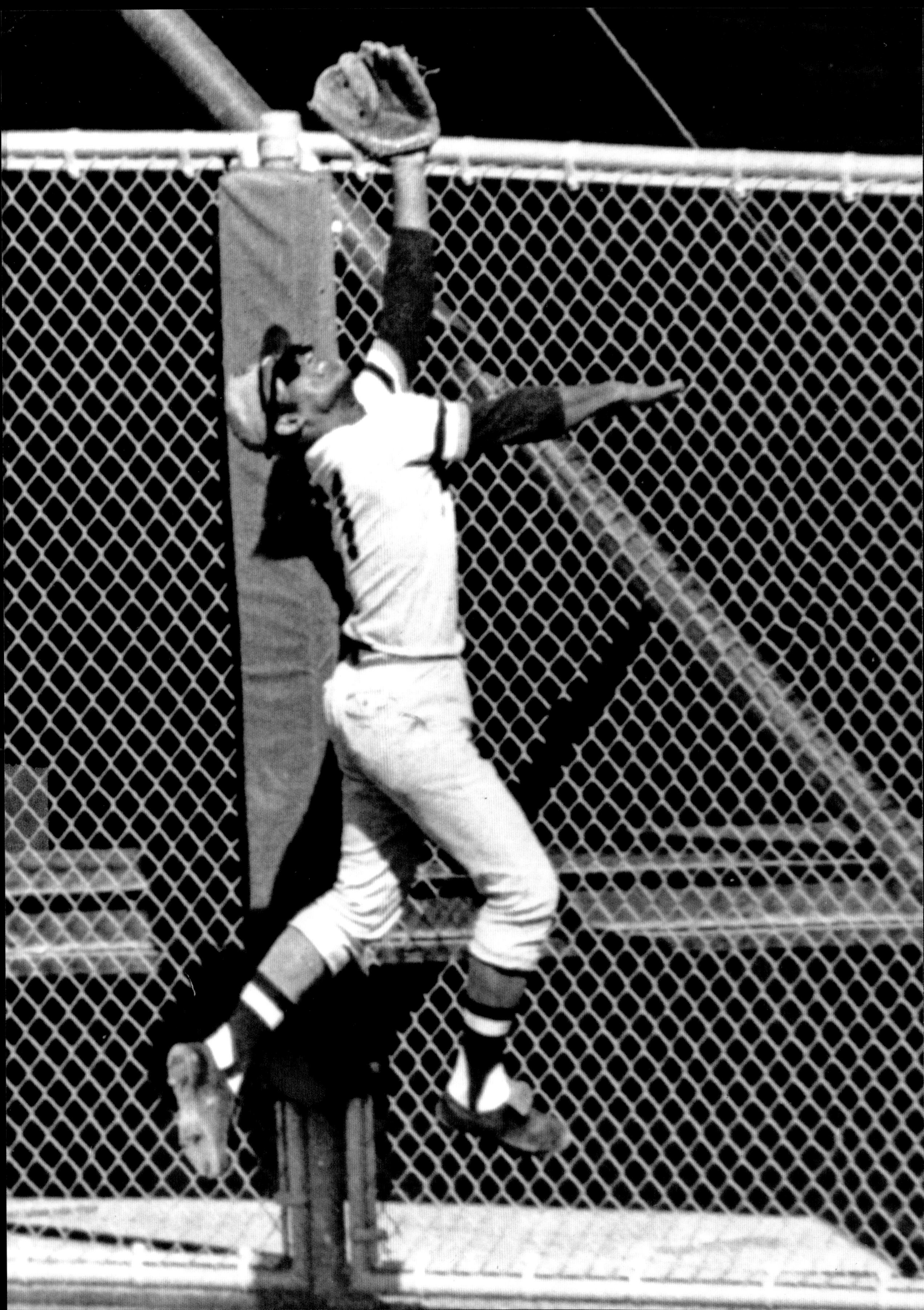

accomplishments elevated his fame in the Latino community.

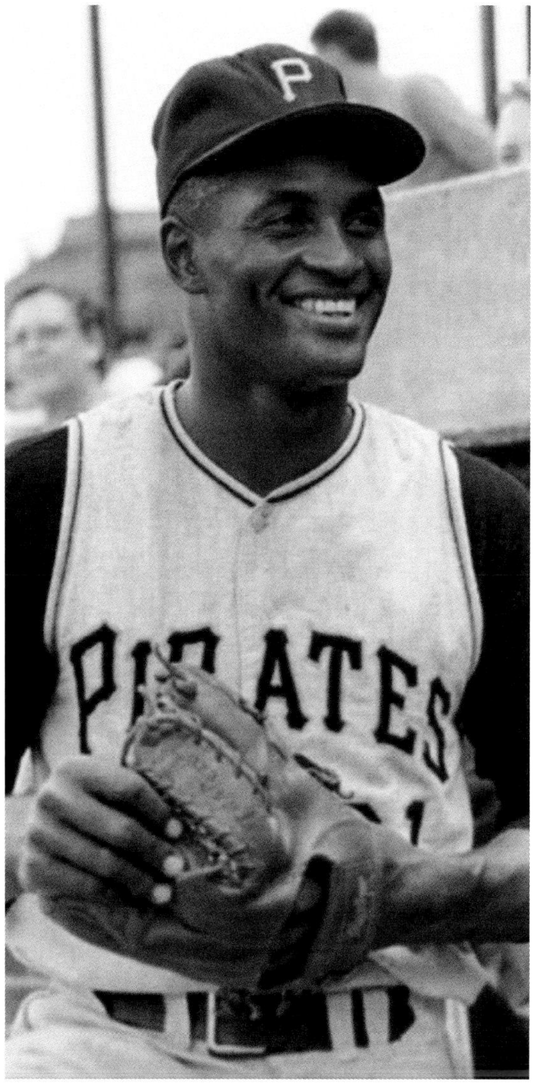

While his offensive skills were at the top of baseball's charts during his playing days, there are those who believe his defensive skills were far better—a fact supported by 12 consecutive Gold Gloves (1961–1972), which ties Willie Mays as the most by an outfielder. Blessed with a powerful throwing arm and tremendous speed to run down balls, Clemente led the NL in outfield assists five times and became the league's all-time leader. Today, only AL player Harry Hooper's 335 career assists (1909–1925) in right field exceed Clemente's 256. Twice he led the NL in putouts by a right fielder, including one season when he led the majors. He still ranks second for the most putouts by a right fielder in the game, trailing only former Pirate Paul Waner.

The 15-time NL All-Star had many highlight-reel moments across his 18 seasons with the Pirates. But his most memorable moment may have happened in his second-to-last game of the 1972 season. It was the final hit of his career—a double to left field at Three Rivers Stadium off Mets lefty Jon Matlack. The hit was Clemente's 3,000th career hit, making him just the 11th player to reach that number in MLB history and the first Latin American player to record the honor. In the five decades since his sudden passing, Clemente's actions on and off the field have remained an inspiration for the Latin American community and the world of baseball.

Clemente makes a leaping attempt for a ball at the right-field wall circa 1971 (opposite). During the early 1960s, Clemente used a Rawlings Trap-Eze model glove (above).

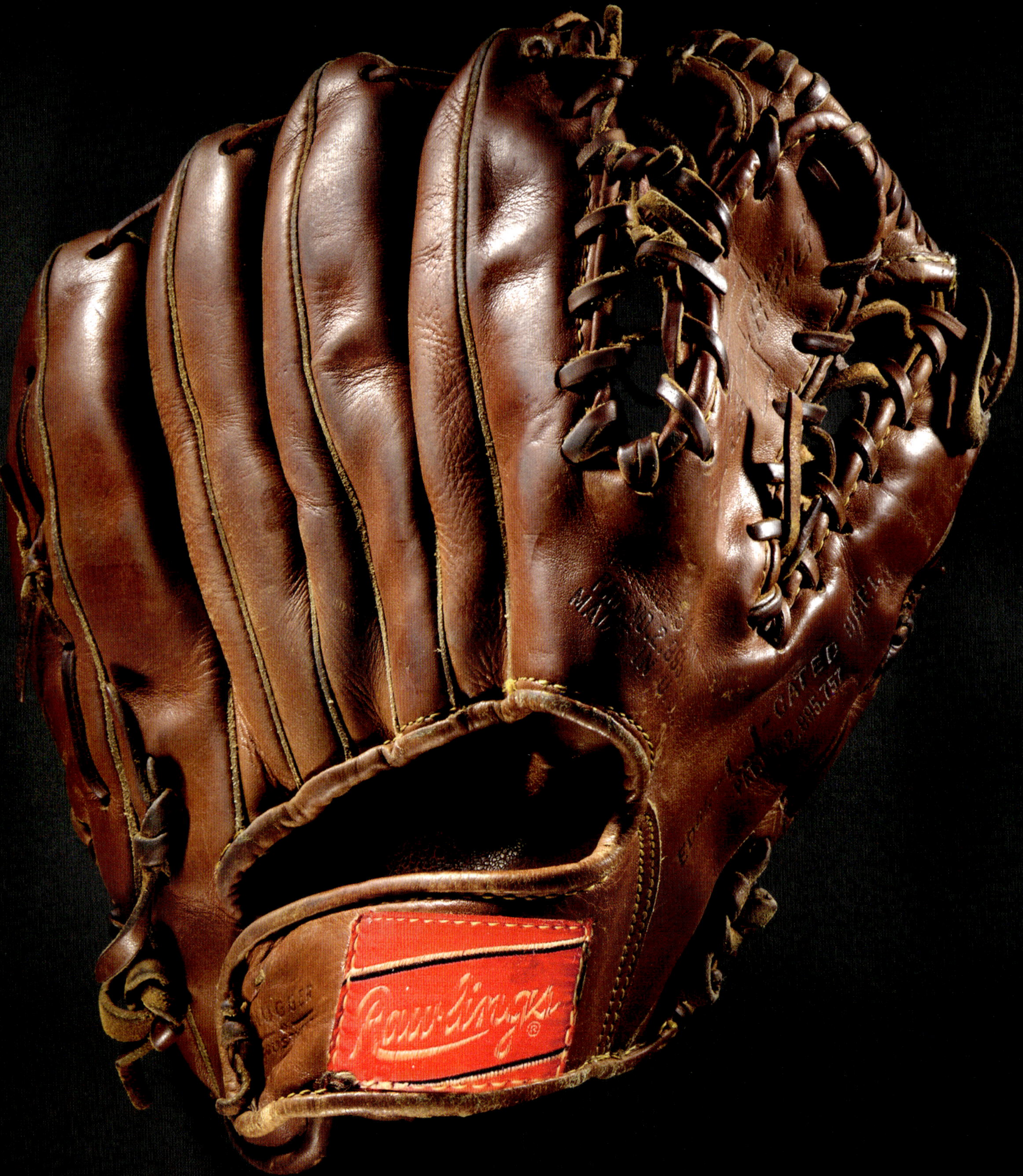
Rawlings

KEN BOYER

He's a Good One

Ken Boyer grew up in a baseball family. Seven of his 14 siblings signed professional baseball contracts. Three made it to the majors. Ken and his brother Cloyd played for the St. Louis Cardinals (different years), while his brother Clete played for the New York Yankees.

Boyer joined the Redbirds out of high school in 1949 as a pitcher who played a little third base. As his pitching stats faltered in his second season, his hitting kept him with the organization. In 1951, he was moved to the Cardinals Class A team managed by George Kissell, the man who defined the "Cardinal Way" by emphasizing defensive play. Boyer continued hitting over .300 before losing the next two seasons to military service.

He hadn't lost a step when he returned to the Cardinals AA team in 1954 under the tutelage of former NL batting champion Dixie Walker, who continued honing Boyer's hitting skills. The guidance from two of the organization's best had the student ready for his MLB debut in 1955 alongside future Hall of Famers Stan Musial and Red Schoendienst. In his rookie season, Boyer batted .264 while launching 18 home runs and slugging .425. Any chance Boyer had for the NL Rookie of the Year was eclipsed by his teammate and eventual award winner Bill Virdon.

There was no sophomore slump for Boyer in 1956. Playing third base, Boyer hit .306 and was selected to his first of 11 All-Star teams. The next season featured a twist. To make room for standout Eddie Kasko at third base, the athletic Boyer moved to center field and led all NL defenders in fielding percentage. But with Kasko hurt and the Cardinals acquiring Curt Flood for center field, it was back to third in 1958. Even though he had been away from the hot corner, Boyer showed

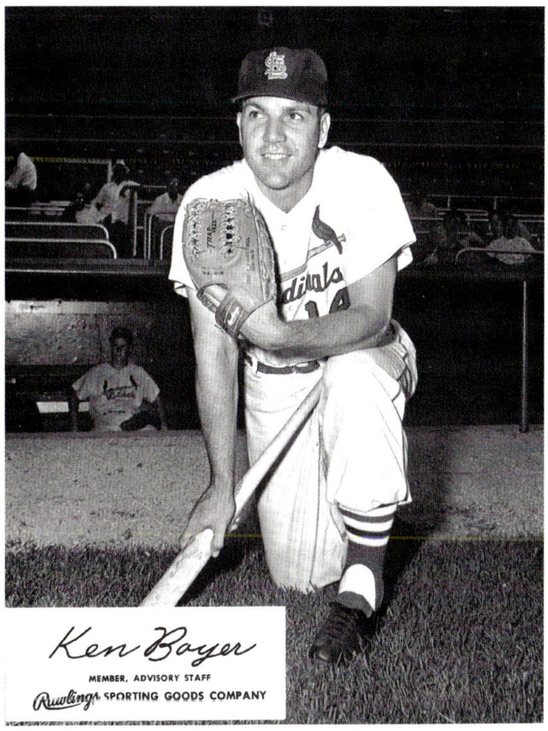

Ken Boyer used a Rawlings TT20 Trap-Eze model glove (opposite). This glove style was the first to feature the Big T Trap-Eze, a T-shaped webbing with laces meant to secure the baseball in the pocket when caught. An early 1960s Rawlings advertisement features the 1964 NL MVP (right).

his defensive agility and walked away with the NL's first Gold Glove at third base. Boyer won four more golden trophies with his glove work between 1959 and 1963 while hitting over .300 and averaging 27 home runs each season. (His brother Clete's Gold Glove win in 1969 made them the first brothers to win the award.)

Providing leadership on the field and at the plate, Boyer was named team captain in 1961. His 1964 MVP performance helped the Cardinals overcome an 11-game deficit to win their first pennant and world championship in 18 years. The World Series matched Ken against Clete, who

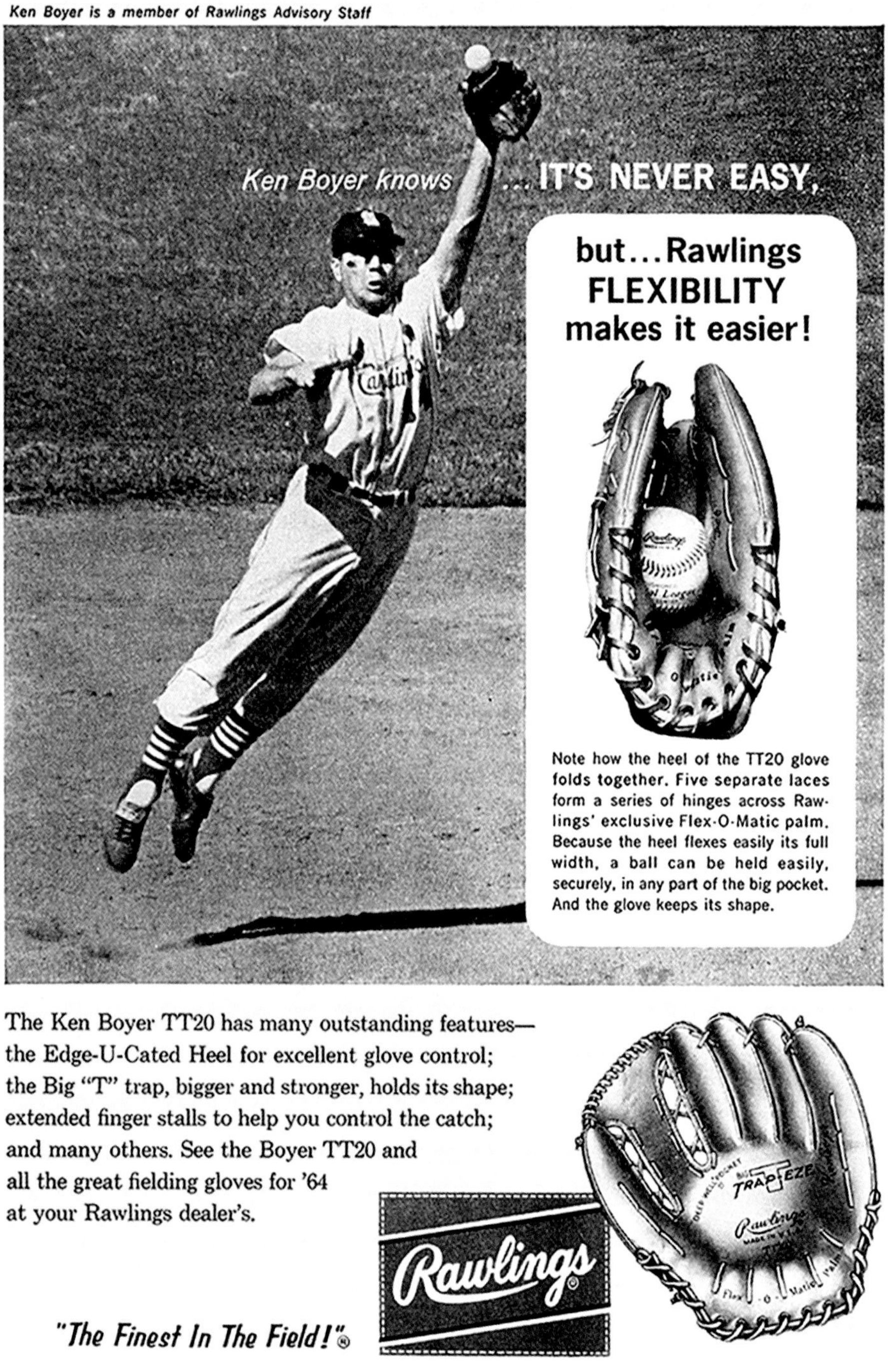

A 1964 Rawlings advertisement features the Ken Boyer TT20 Trap-Eze model glove.

Boyer's excellent fielding and defense using a Rawlings TG 15 Trap-Eze model glove, shown here in a 1960s advertisement, led to five Gold Glove Awards.

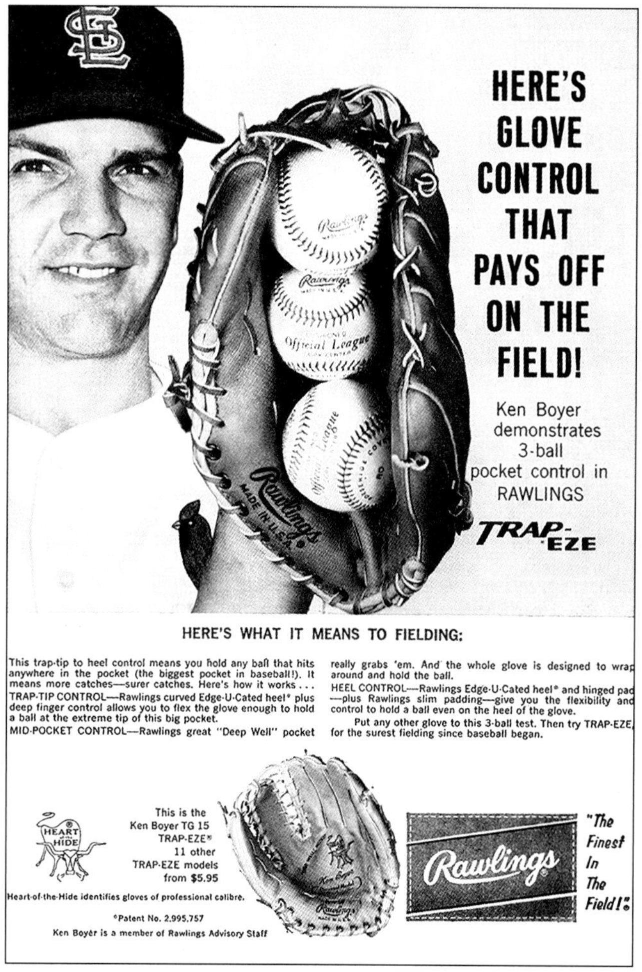

was playing in his fifth postseason with the Yankees. While Bob Gibson provided the Cardinals' punch from the mound, Boyer did the same from the plate. With the Redbirds down two games to one going into Game Four, the Yankees jumped out to a 3–0 lead in the first inning and were on their way to what looked like a 3–1 edge in the Series. That is, until Boyer came to the plate with the bases loaded in the sixth inning and put Al Downing's pitch over the boards for a 4–3 win to even the Series.

The teams traded wins in the next two games to set up the deciding battle for the championship with Game Seven. Which Boyer brother would become a world champion? With the Cardinals leading 6–0 at the end of the fifth inning, Mickey Mantle cut the lead in half with a three-run homer, but Ken, who already had two hits, homered in the seventh to make it a 7–3 game. After a scoreless eighth, the Yankees pushed two across the plate with two home runs but couldn't take the lead. One of those two homers came from Clete, marking the only time in World Series history that brothers homered in the same game.

Despite his contributions to the game on both offense and defense, Boyer's name has never been called at Cooperstown. He played the game with his head down every day while producing year after year. The final epitaph for Boyer's career can be summarized by a statement from Musial: "The ballplayers know he's a good one, but nobody else does." Will that change one day and will Boyer's name finally be called at the Hall of Fame?

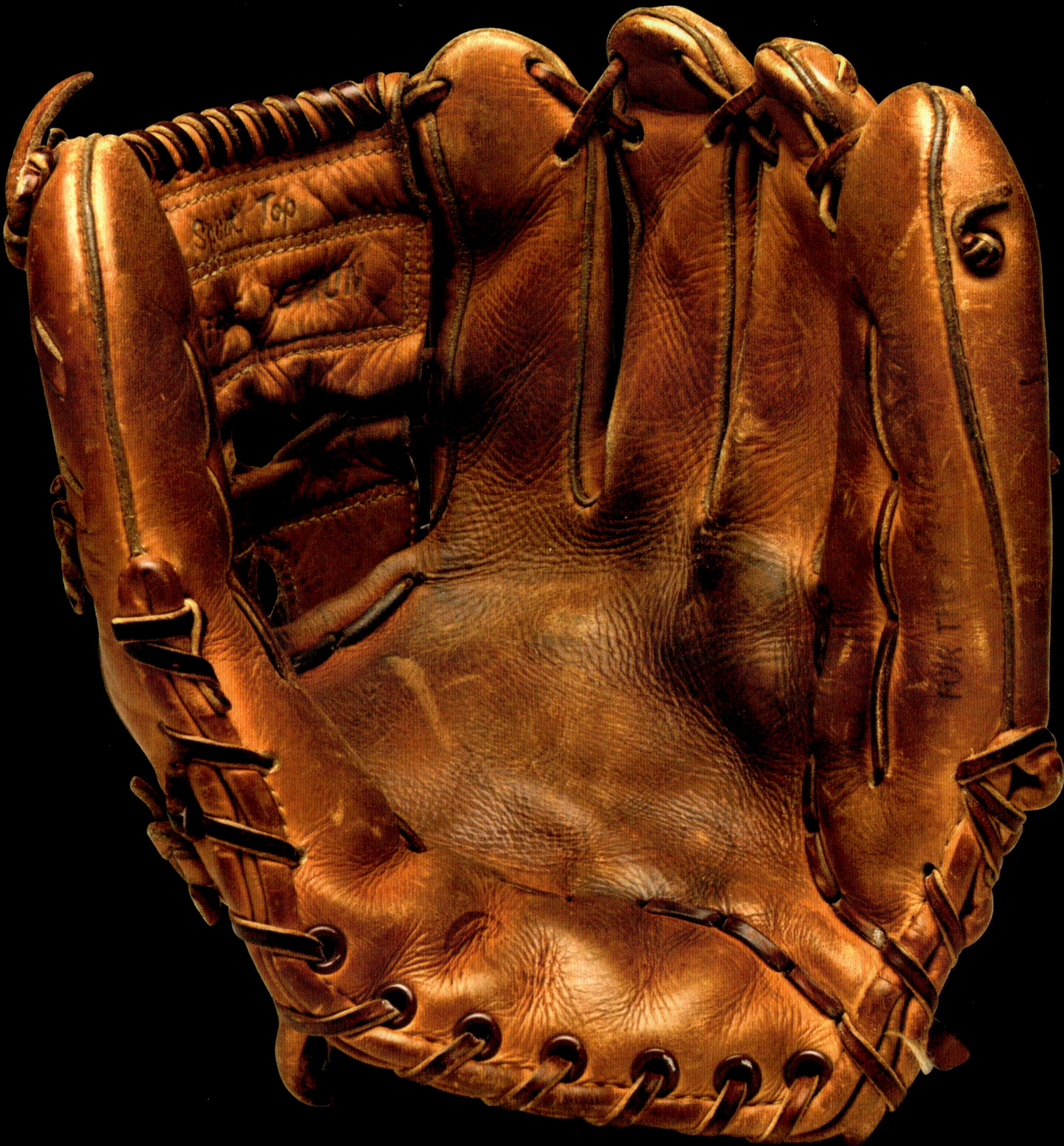

BROOKS ROBINSON

The Human Vacuum Cleaner

How does an MLB ballplayer wind up with "The Human Vacuum Cleaner" as his nickname? In the case of the man to whom it was given, it was because he seemed to sweep up everything hit his way. That man was Brooks Robinson, and he played third base for the Baltimore Orioles for 23 seasons (1955–1977). His career résumé labeled him as arguably the best defensive third baseman to ever play the game.

MLB's record books support that claim and fully recognize Robinson's unparalleled defensive skills. At his retirement he held the records at third base for seasons played (23), fielding percentage (.971), games played (2,870), putouts (2,697), assists (6,205), and double plays (618). His dominance at the hot corner was recognized with 16 consecutive Gold Glove Awards (1960–1975). That's the most of all the winning position players. He also represented the Orioles and the AL in the All-Star Game 18 consecutive times.

Robinson won the AL MVP in 1964 and was the 1966 All-Star Game MVP in a losing cause, but it was his 1970 World Series MVP performance that displayed his skills to the world. With that Series award, Robinson became the first player to win baseball's MVP hat trick.

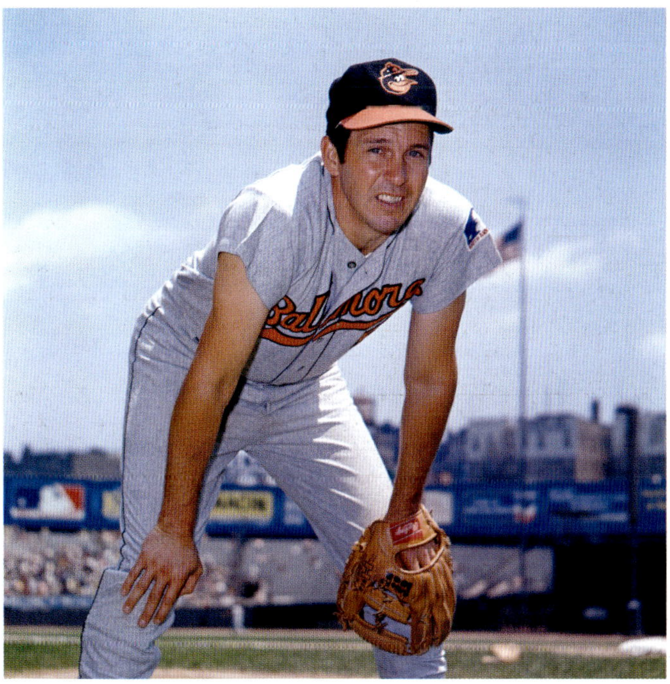

Brooks Robinson used this Rawlings glove (opposite) at the hot corner for the Baltimore Orioles during the late 1950s. Robinson (left), the Orioles' third baseman, is the owner of 16 Gold Glove Awards—the most won by a position player.

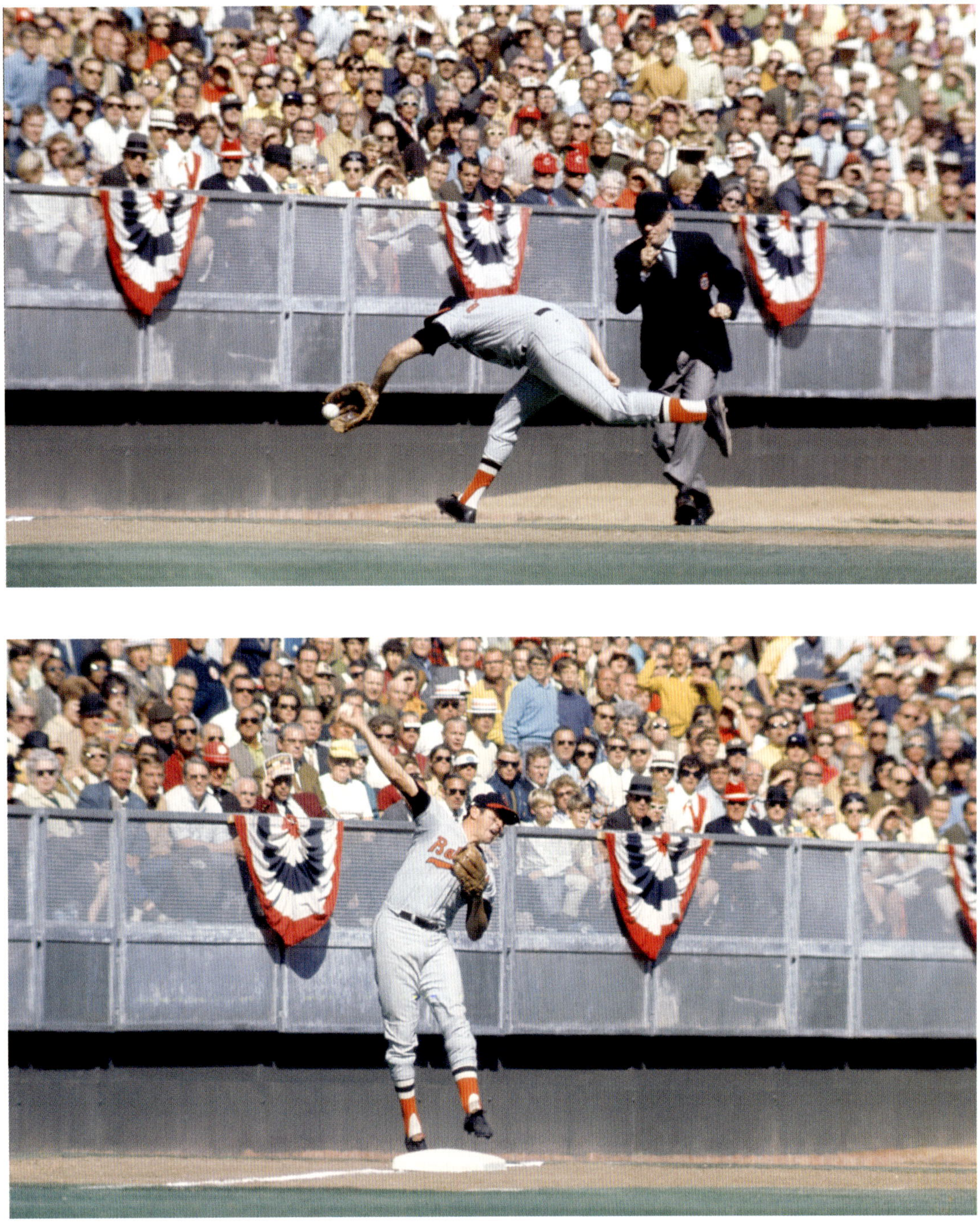

This play in Game One of the 1970 World Series led to Robinson earning the nickname "The Human Vacuum Cleaner."

Baseball fans already knew he was good going into Game One of the 1970 World Series between the Baltimore Orioles and the Cincinnati Reds. He had already won 10 straight Gold Gloves, but his performance that fall let fans know why he was the master of the hot corner.

For a Series that would be remembered for Robinson's defensive highlight reel, it began with an error on the first ball hit to him during Game One's second inning. But from that moment on, Robinson stole the show, the game, and the Series. It wasn't about stealing bases; it was about Robinson robbing hits with his Rawlings glove. Some have called his backhanded grab of a sure extra-base hit destined for the left-field corner a game changer. Others have called it a Series changer, and still others have called it a Hall of Fame play.

The play came with the score tied 3–3 and the Cincinnati Reds' Lee May leading off the sixth inning. May scorched a one-hopper past third base that looked like it would surely be a lead-off double. That is, until Robinson ranged to his right to glove the ball. With his momentum carrying him far into foul territory, he wheeled 180 degrees and made a perfect one-hop throw—on Riverfront Stadium's artificial grass surface—that a stretched-out Boog Powell at first base grabbed to beat May by a half step. This was the first Fall Classic played on artificial turf, and Robinson made the most of it. His defensive gem pushed the momentum to the Orioles, who won the game 4–3 on a subsequent Robinson solo home run in the next inning. After the loss, in a postgame interview, May talked about the sixth-inning robbery of his for-sure double and christened Robinson with the nickname "The Human Vacuum Cleaner"—a moniker Robinson would carry for the rest of his career. Robinson's response was a continued assault on the Big Red Machine over the next four games to win the world championship.

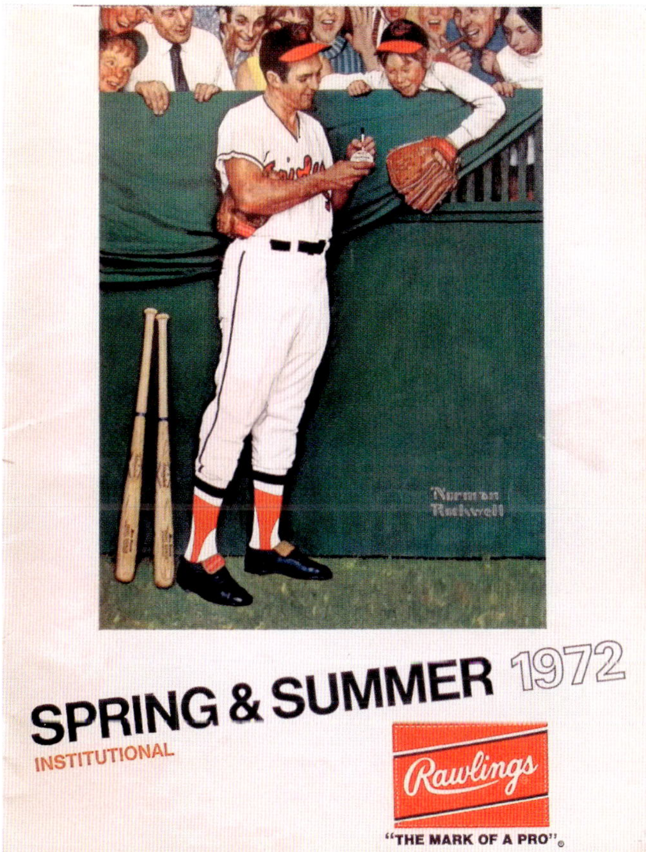

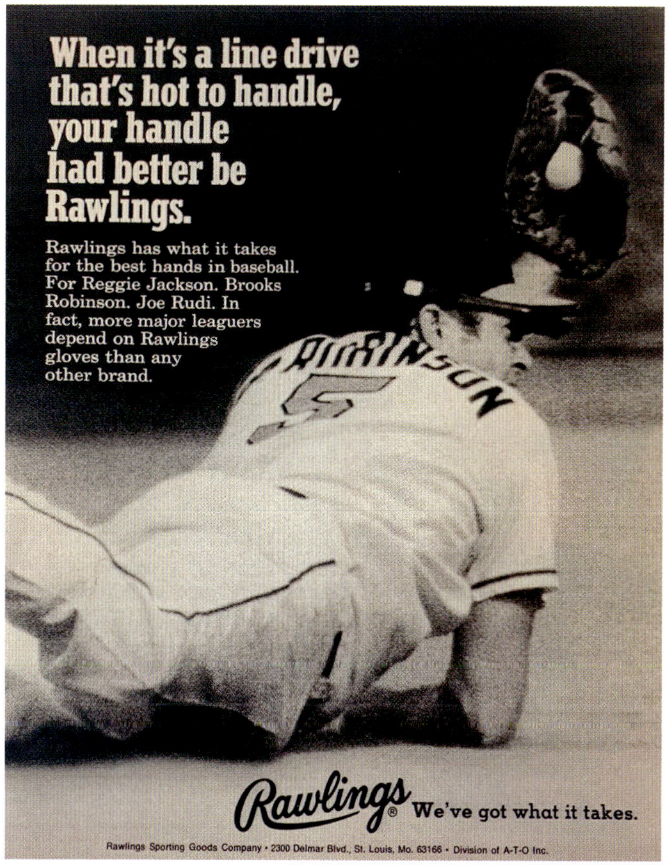

A Norman Rockwell print of Robinson signing autographs for fans appeared on a 1972 Rawlings catalog cover (above, left). Robinson was also featured in a 1970s Rawlings advertisement (above, right).

SADAHARU OH AND MASANORI MURAKAMI

The First from Afar

Many fans have grown up believing baseball was first introduced to the Japanese population by American occupation forces following the end of World War II. However, Babe Ruth and his fellow major-league All-Stars had already played a barnstorming series of games against local teams across the island nation in 1934, followed by a game against the Japanese All-Stars. This tour happened seven years before the start of the war. But baseball's roots in Japan go back another half century before this tour. It started with an American professor named Horace Wilson, who began teaching the game to his students at Tokyo's Kaisei Academy in 1872. By 1920 professional leagues were forming across the country, just as they had in America.

Baseball soon became Japan's most popular sport. The All-Star team that faced Ruth's squad stayed together and became the Yomiuri Giants. The Giants and Japan's other professional teams eventually formed a two-league entity known as the Japanese Baseball League, which was reorganized in 1950 as Nippon Professional Baseball—the equivalent of America's major leagues. Like the New York Yankees, the Yomiuri Giants became the league's powerhouse, winning championships bolstered by a star home-run hitter like Ruth. The Giants' standout Japanese player of Chinese descent was Sadaharu Oh (王貞).

Oh played 22 seasons (1959–1980) at first base with the Giants, and his 868 homers make him, to this day, baseball's all-time career home-run leader. While MLB's home-run king Hank Aaron was passing Ruth's record of 714 home runs in April 1974, the six-years-younger Oh was hitting his 600th home run that same season. While Aaron never hit 50 home runs in a season, Oh did it three times (55 in 1964, 51 in 1973, and 50 in 1977). After Aaron retired in 1976, Oh kept hitting the ball over the fences and passed Aaron's 755 homers for the career title on September 3, 1977. Six years after Oh's retirement, Barry Bonds hit the first of his 762 home runs over 22 seasons to become MLB's career home-run leader. Although Bonds played in 155 more games than Oh's 2,831, he remained 106 homers shy of Oh's record.

The left-handed-hitting Oh led his league in home runs 15 times and was an All-Star 18 times. The five-time batting champion hit .301 for his career and recorded 2,786 hits to go along with 2,170 RBIs. After his first three seasons, in which he did not hit more than 17 home runs, Oh changed his batting approach. He incorporated Zen and samurai training, along with a new

Masanori Murakami used this Ken Boyer Trap-Eze Heart of the Hide model glove during his playing days. Note the number 10 on the glove, which was Murakami's uniform number in 1964. The following season, he wore number 37. The handwritten Kanji characters read "Murakami."

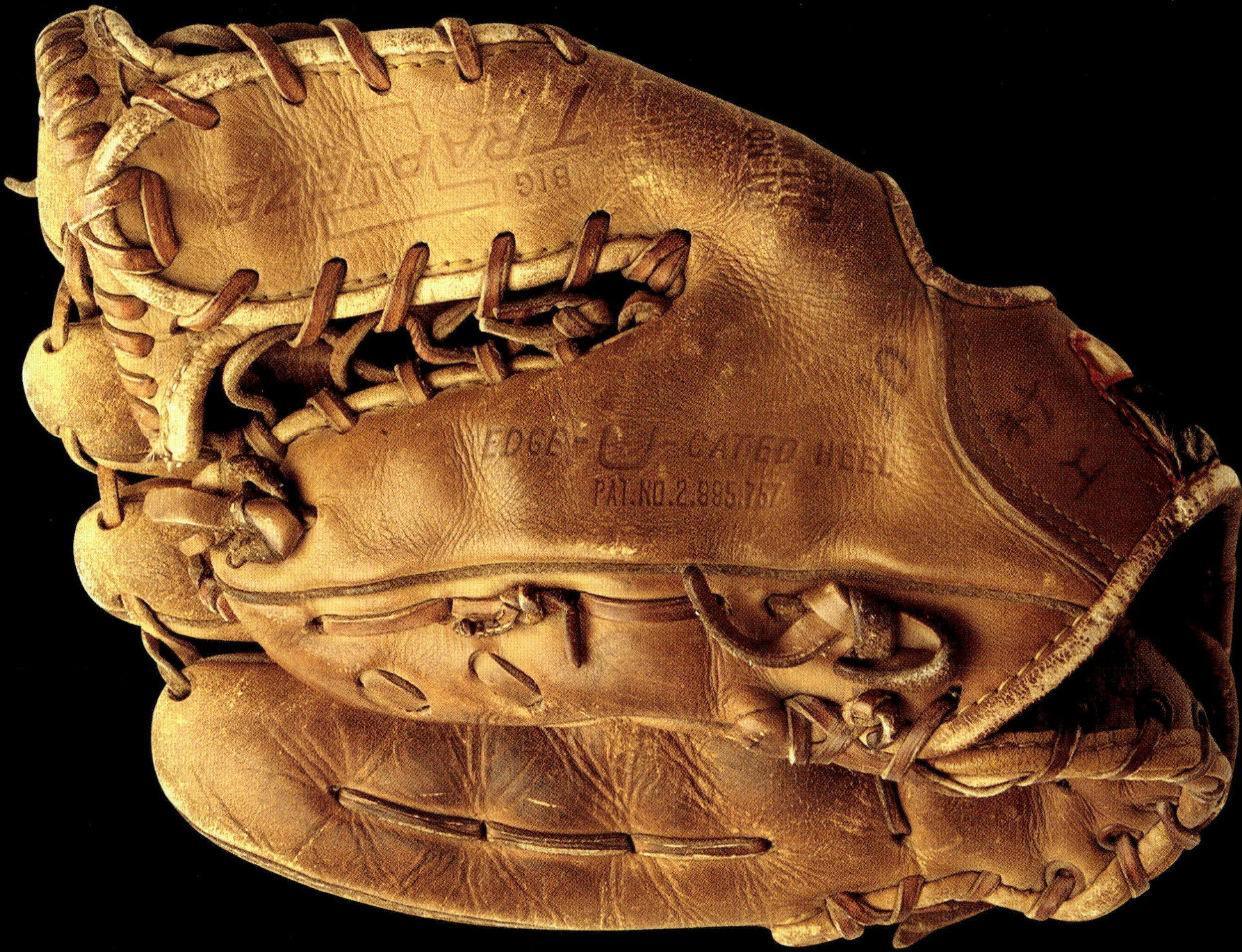
EDGE-U-CATED HEEL
PAT.NO.2,885,757

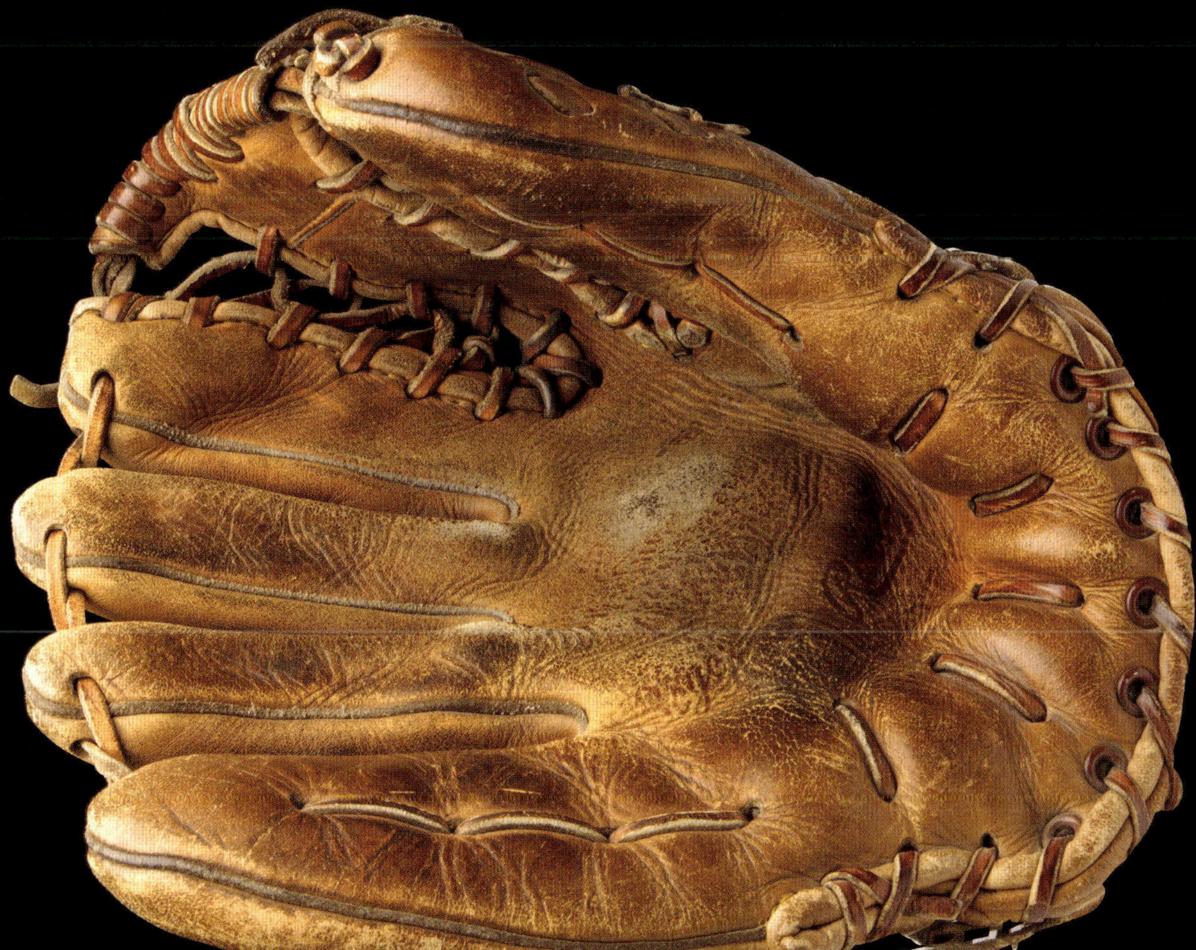

stance in which he raised his right leg like a flamingo while balancing on his left foot before swinging at the pitch to provide his home run power.

Today MLB is filled with players from Japan and other Asian countries. Yet despite his stats and all-time records, Oh never received the chance to play in America due to the constraints of the Immigration Act of 1924, which effectively barred Japanese immigration to the United States. The act cast a period of isolation between the two countries that lasted until the years after World War II. Following the war, an agreement was reached between Japanese baseball and the major leagues to keep Japanese players out of America's big leagues to ensure that the integrity of baseball's reserve clause remained intact. (Prior to free agency, the reserve clause stated that players could not switch teams or break their contracts.) There was, however, one player who made it through the cracks of this structure and made it to the major leagues in 1964. His name was Masanori Murakami (村上 雅則).

Murakami, also known as "Mashi," was a left-handed relief pitcher who, along with two other players from Japan's Nankai Hawks in Osaka, joined the San Francisco Giants' single-A club in Fresno as part of an exchange student program. After going 11–7 in 49 games (all but one in relief), Murakami was called up on September 1, 1964, to become the first Japanese player in the major leagues. In his nine games for the Giants that season, he recorded one win in 15 innings while finishing five of the contests.

As soon as the season ended, international drama started, as the Hawks and Giants battled over Murakami's future. The teams and legal systems argued over which team the pitcher would play for in 1965. For MLB, letting Murakami go back to Japan, where he had a three-year contract, would be an affront to its sacred reserve clause. The resolution allowed Murakami to play one more year for the Giants before returning to Japan, where he would play for 17 more seasons.

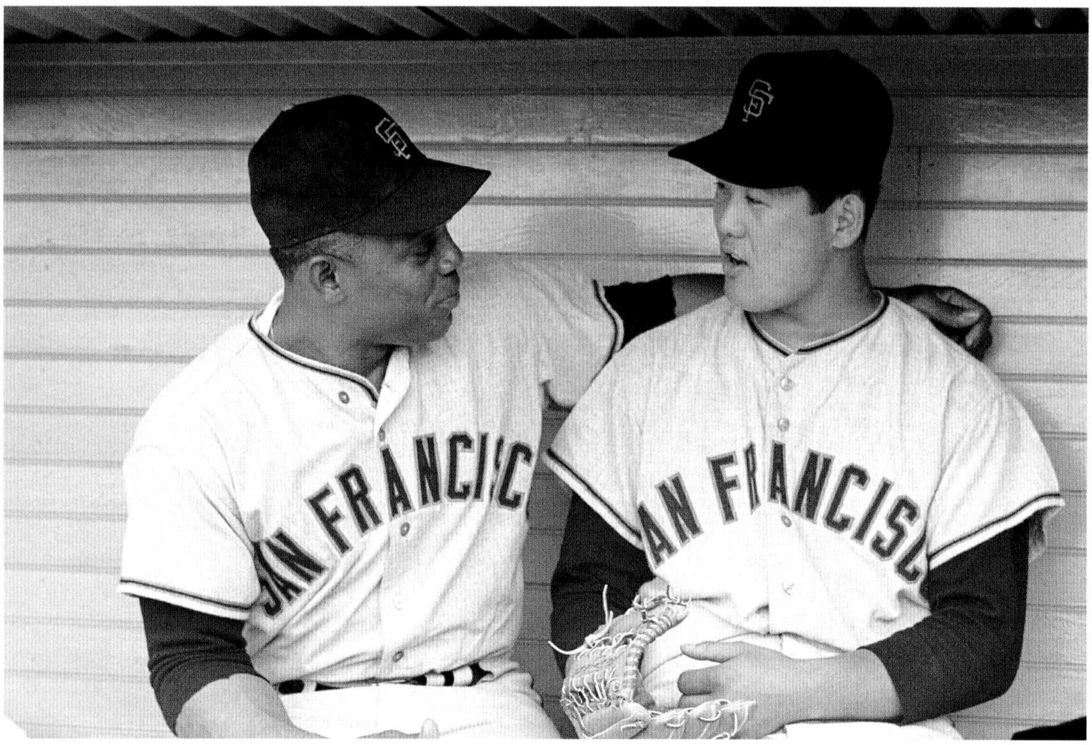

Murakami and Willie Mays have a good laugh in the dugout prior to a twi-night doubleheader in Philadelphia. Murakami had won the second victory of his rookie season with the San Francisco Giants over the St. Louis Cardinals the night before.

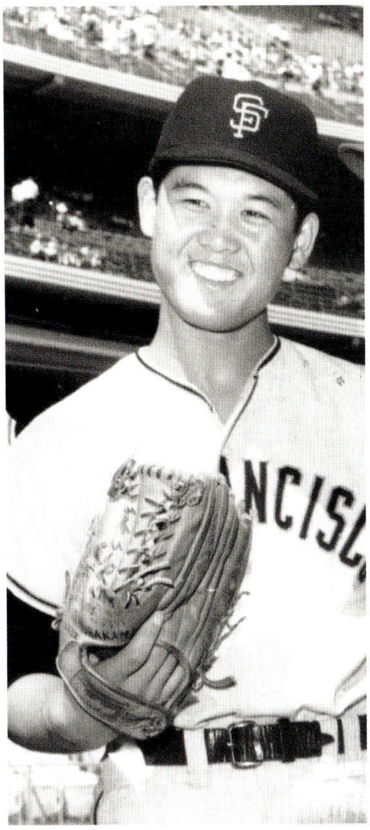

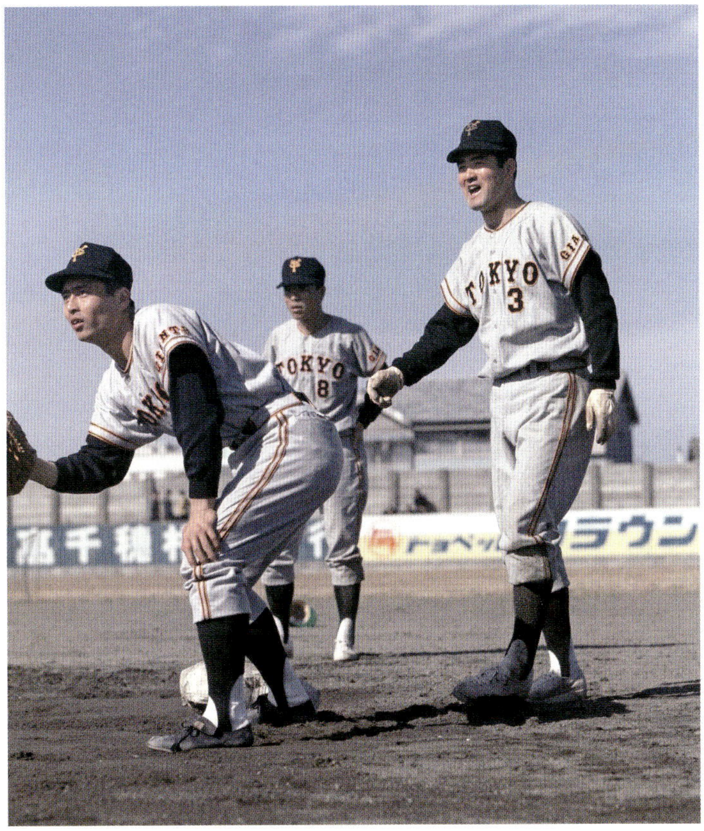

Left-handed pitcher Murakami (above, left), shown circa 1964, was the first Japanese player in the major leagues. Sadaharu Oh, Katsutoyo Yoshida, and Shigeo Nagashima of the Yomiuri Giants practice during spring training in Miyazaki, Japan, in 1965 (above, right). While at the plate for the Giants at Korakuen Stadium in Tokyo, circa 1964, Oh shows off his unique batting stance (below).

During his two major-league seasons, Murakami's pitching line read 5–1, with an ERA of 3.43 and nine recorded saves in 54 games. Murakami proved that Japanese players could play at the major-league level, but his legal battle opened issues with the reserve clause. The two countries' professional leagues signed an agreement to honor each other's contracts, effectively stopping Japanese players from playing in America's big leagues for the next 30 years, until Hideo Nomo signed with the Los Angeles Dodgers in 1995.

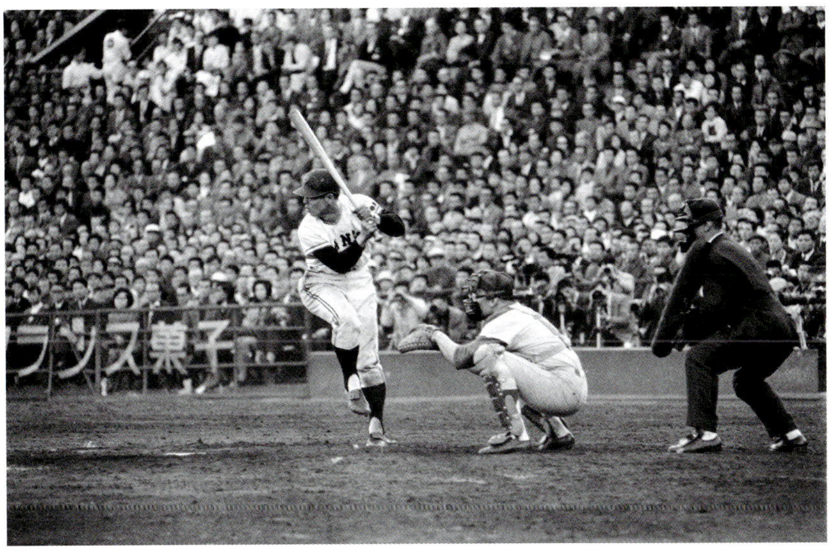

BOB GIBSON

The Game Changer

It is unlikely that there has ever been a better all-around athlete who pitched in the big leagues than Bob Gibson. An all-state high school basketball player, Gibson initially paused his baseball career to spend a year playing for the Harlem Globetrotters before becoming a St. Louis Cardinal. His athleticism was just one measure of his success. On the field he was a fierce and determined competitor, which made him a legend of the game. How good was Gibson? He once told the Associated Press, "I was good. That was the attitude I had. All of the writers thought I was tough, and so did the players. Well, that's the way I was. I grew up fighting a lot of things."

It was an attitude that made him a winner and a Hall of Famer. Gibson's displays of toughness are part of the legend. In the 1964 World Series, he took the mound with just two days' rest following a complete Game Five win to throw another complete game victory in Game Seven. In July 1967, Roberto Clemente slashed a line drive directly off Gibson's shin. Gibson then got up and pitched to three more batters before his leg gave out. But he healed quickly and was able to finish the season and win three complete games in that year's Fall Classic.

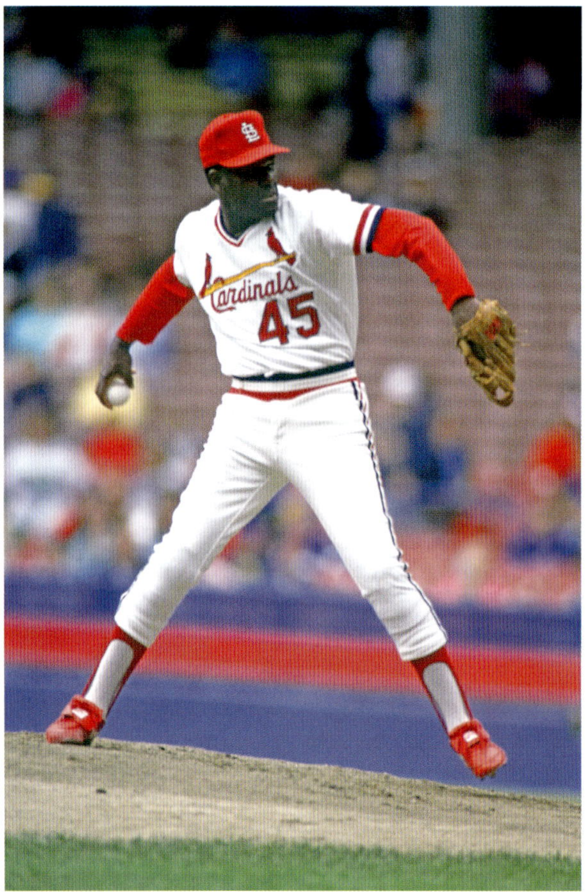

St. Louis Cardinals Hall of Famer Bob Gibson (left) used a Rawlings professional XFG6-H Fastback model (opposite). Gibson preferred the Rawlings glove, but since he was under contract with a different glove vendor, he had to be sure the logo of the competing maker wasn't visible. Gibson took care to comply with this requirement. The marked-out Rawlings logos are a distinguishing feature of this bona fide game-used glove.

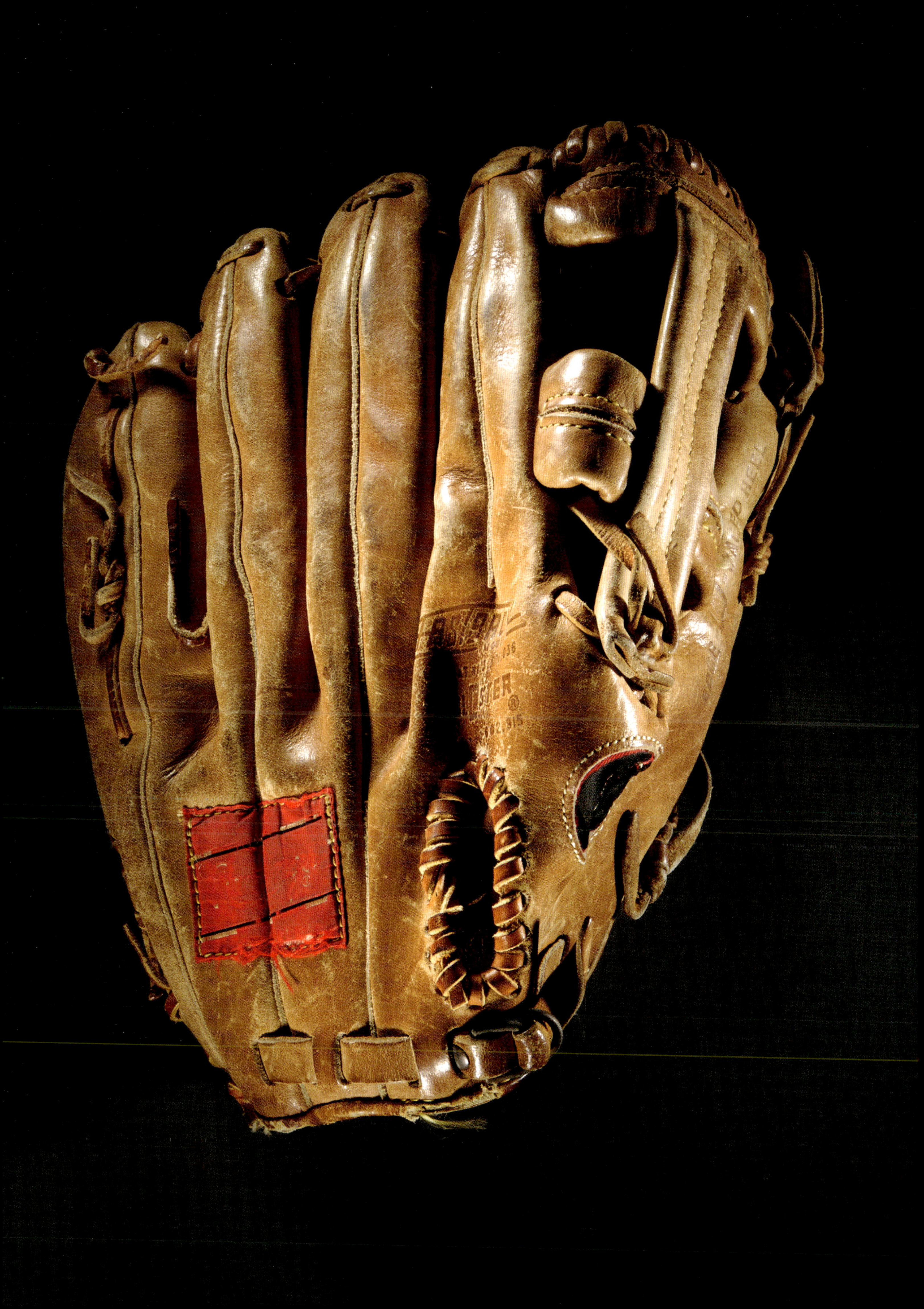

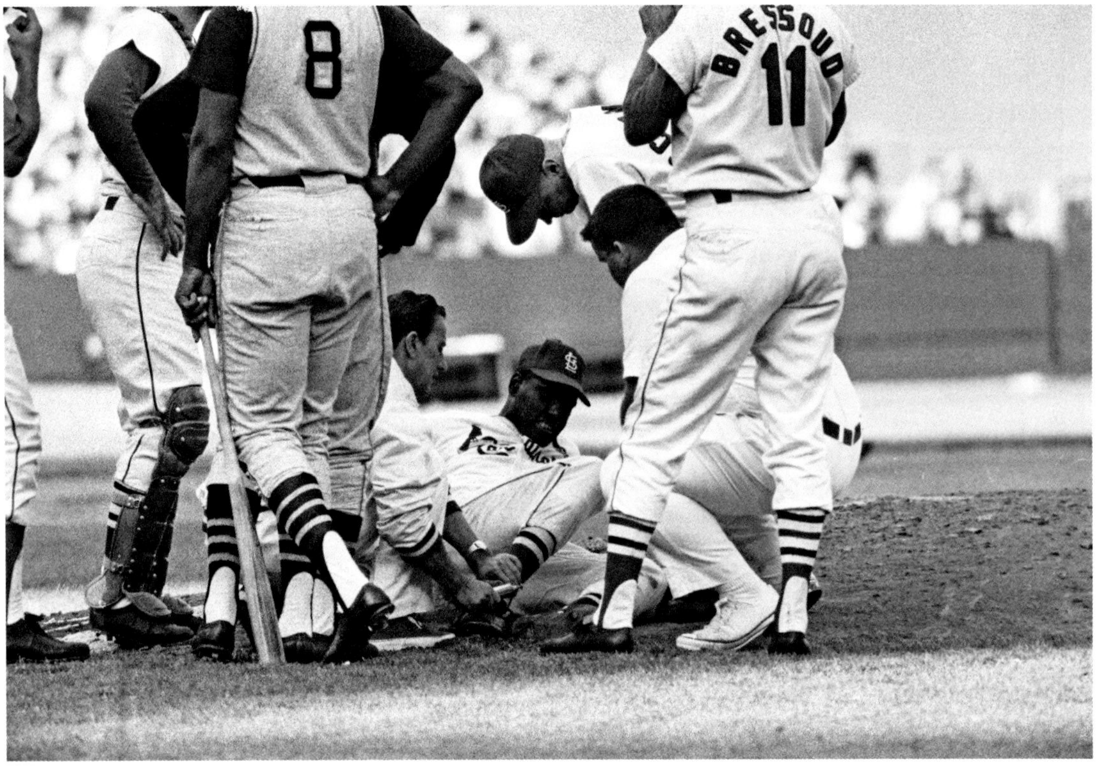

As trainer Bob Bauman works on his right leg, Gibson grimaces in pain after being hit by a line drive from the Pittsburgh Pirates' Roberto Clemente in the fourth inning of a Cardinals-Pirates game in 1967. Gibson suffered a fracture to his right fibula on the play, but he pitched to three more batters before collapsing.

In the history of baseball there have only been a handful of players whose actions triggered changes to the game. Gibson set the tone for 1968 becoming "the year of the pitcher." His 22–9 record paired with a 1.12 ERA led to the "Gibson Rule," when MLB lowered the height of the pitcher's mound to offset his pitching dominance. His 1968 ERA is the lowest in modern MLB history (post-1920). That year, Gibson started 34 games and completed 28 with 13 shutouts. During the months of June and July, he never lost a game, and eight of his 12 wins were shutouts. He won both the NL MVP and Cy Young Awards in recognition of his domination from the mound.

But Gibson was not just a one-season wonder. He did it for 17 seasons as a St. Louis Cardinal. His Hall of Fame plaque summarizes his pitching: "Five-time twenty-game winner. His 3,117 strikeouts made him only 2nd pitcher to reach 3,000" (after Walter Johnson). In 1962, he became the first pitcher to strike out more than 200 batters in a season, a feat he would accomplish eight more times. In two of the three World Series Gibson pitched in, he was selected as the Series MVP. In his three Fall Classics, he won seven consecutive games while throwing eight complete games.

In a career filled with many signature moments, his iconic Game One outing against the Detroit Tigers in the 1968 World Series fully illustrated the essence of Gibson's dominance and determination. That year's Fall Classic opener pitted Gibson against Denny McLain, baseball's first 30-game winner since Dizzy Dean in 1934. Gibson struck out seven of the first nine hitters he faced that day. Every batter in the Tigers' lineup struck out at least once. By the time the game reached the top of the ninth inning, Gibson had struck out 14 hitters and the Cardinals were leading 4–0.

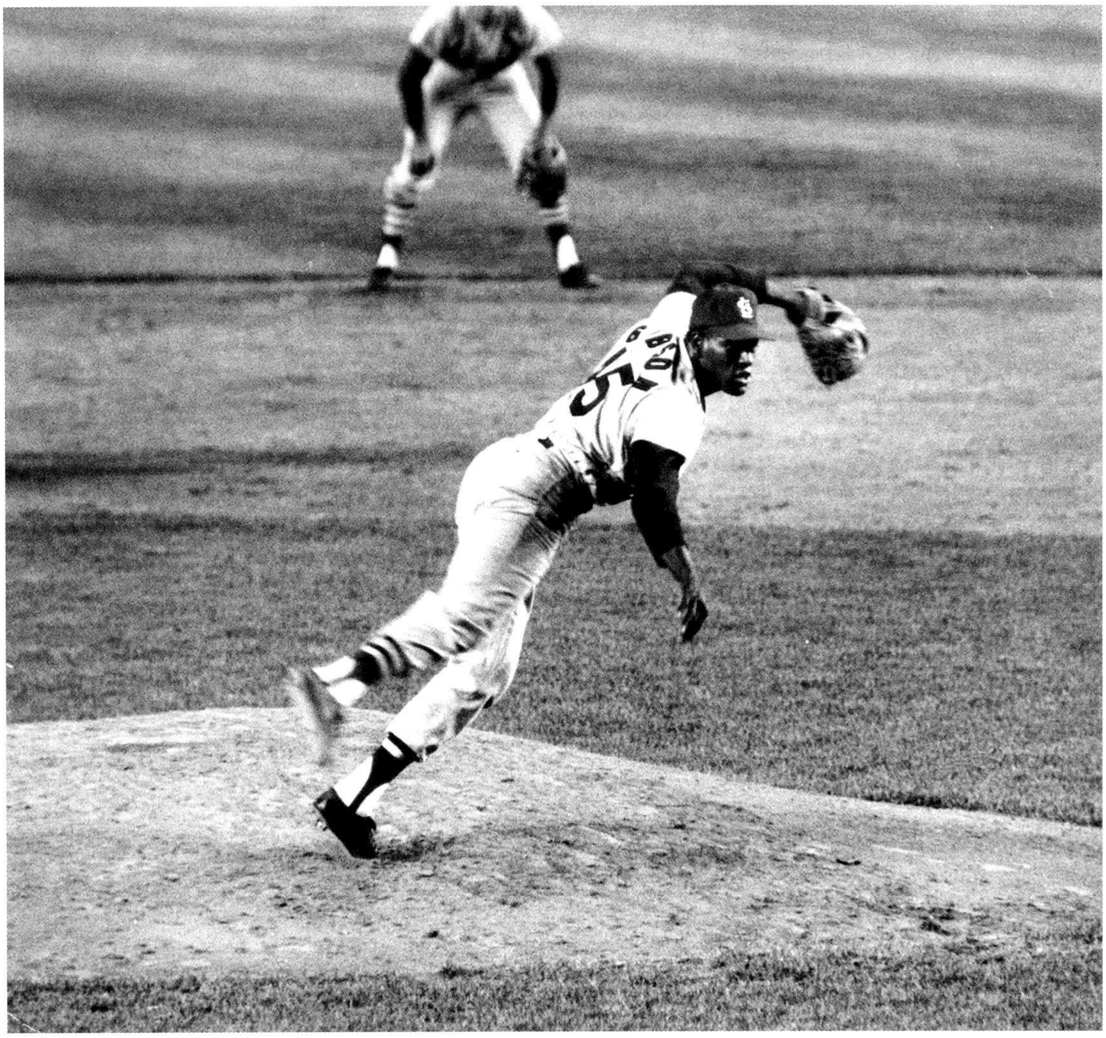

The ever-intense Gibson was not only a skilled pitcher but also a winner of nine Rawlings Gold Glove Awards during his career.

Future Hall of Famer Al Kaline came to bat with no outs and a runner on first. He went down swinging. The Busch Stadium scoreboard behind the pitcher typed out, "Bob Gibson just tied Sandy Koufax's World Series record of 15 strikeouts in a game." The standing-room-only crowd rose in applause. Catcher Tim McCarver started walking to the mound and pointing toward the scoreboard to let Gibson know what he had done. But Gibson waved him away and shouted, "Give me the ball!"—not to retrieve as a keepsake but to deliver the next pitch. Was there ever any doubt he wouldn't get the record?

From the on-deck circle, sluggers Norm Cash and Willie Horton watched and waited like two death row prisoners on their way to the executioner. Cash was first. He went down swinging at a 2–2 slider before it was Horton's turn. Horton battled to a 2–2 count before freezing as he stared down an unhittable slider that punched him out and sealed Gibson's new record at 17 strikeouts and a world championship. It also tied a Series record with his sixth consecutive win, which Gibson would break a few days later in another matchup win against McLain. At the Series end, Gibson had broken his own 1964 record (31) of most strikeouts in a World Series with 35. Baseball's great competitor had dominated the Tigers and showed why he was one of the best there ever was.

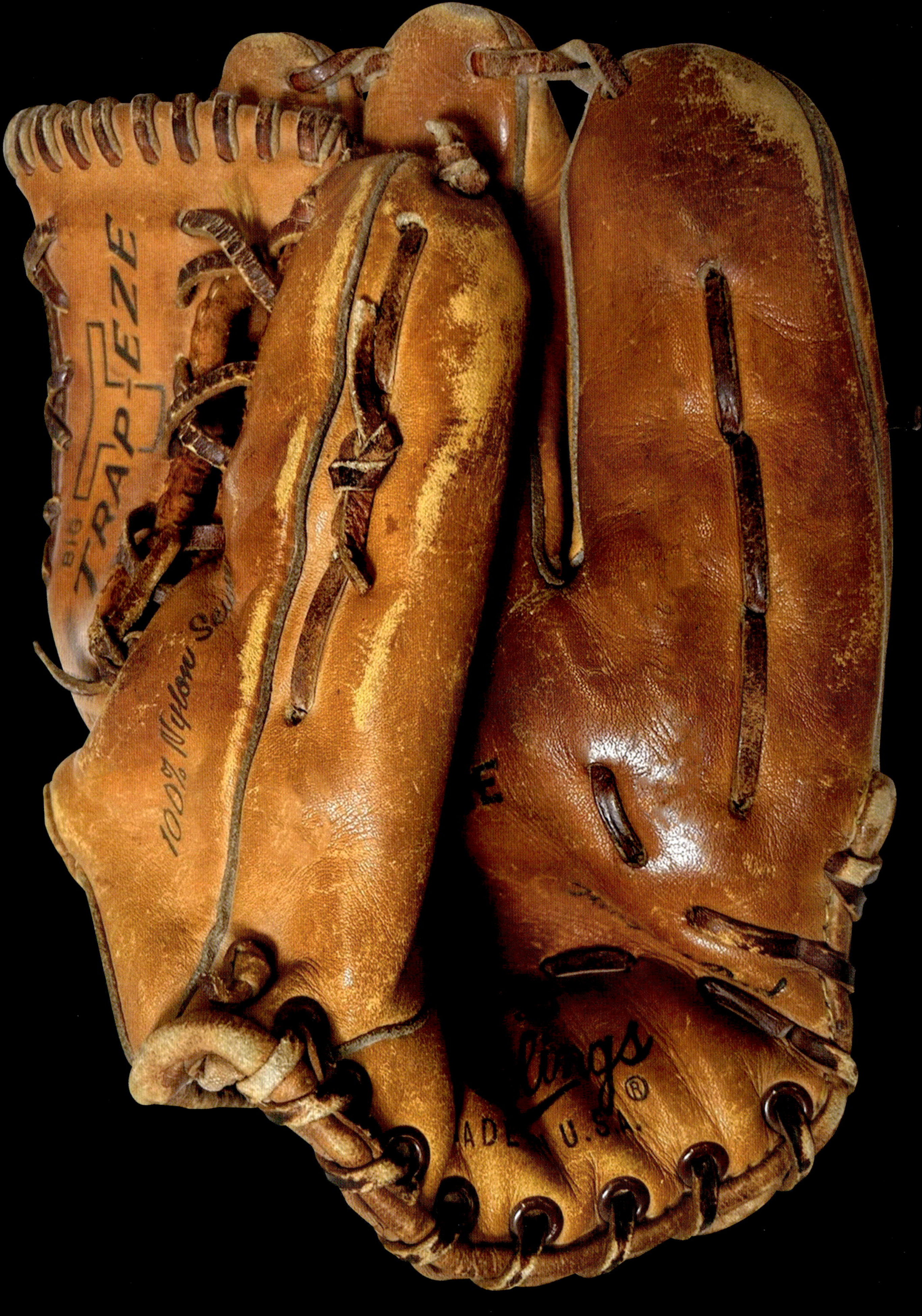
BIG
TRAPEZE
100% Nylon

CURT FLOOD

One Man's Stand

The memories of how good Curt Flood was as a player have often been eclipsed by his plays off the field. Flood was the Cardinals' center fielder and co-captain during the 1960s, when the team won three NL pennants and two world championships.

With Flood in center field, the speedy Lou Brock in left field, and the strong-armed Roger Maris in right field, the St. Louis outfield was one of baseball's best. Flood alone captured seven consecutive NL Gold Glove Awards between 1963 and 1969. In the 10 consecutive seasons between 1960 and 1969, the steady Flood led NL center fielders in fielding percentage three times, rank second four times, and rank third another two. In 1966, Flood handled 396 chances without an error and even appeared on the cover of the August 19, 1968, issue of *Sports Illustrated*, along with the caption "Baseball's Best Centerfielder." And this was all accomplished at a time when the NL had many great center fielders—Willie Mays, Vada Pinson, and Jim Wynn, among others.

Paralleling his outfield acclaim, Flood would turn in a career batting average of .293 over his 15 seasons in the big leagues (in three of those years, he played in fewer than 13 games). In seven of the 12 full seasons, he hit over .300, topping out at .335 in 1967. In the outfield and at the plate, Flood delivered and was selected as an NL All-Star three times (1964, 1966, and 1968). He seemed to have it all in St. Louis. He was loved by the city's fans and had earned recognition

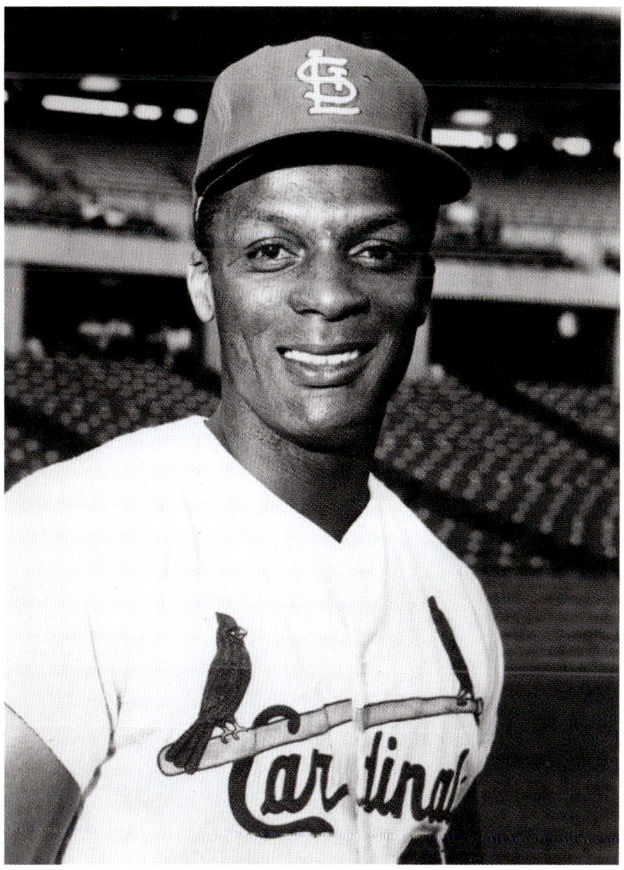

Curt Flood (right), a seven-time Gold Glove winner, used this Rawlings Stan Musial Trap-Eze Heart of the Hide model glove (opposite) early in his career with the St. Louis Cardinals.

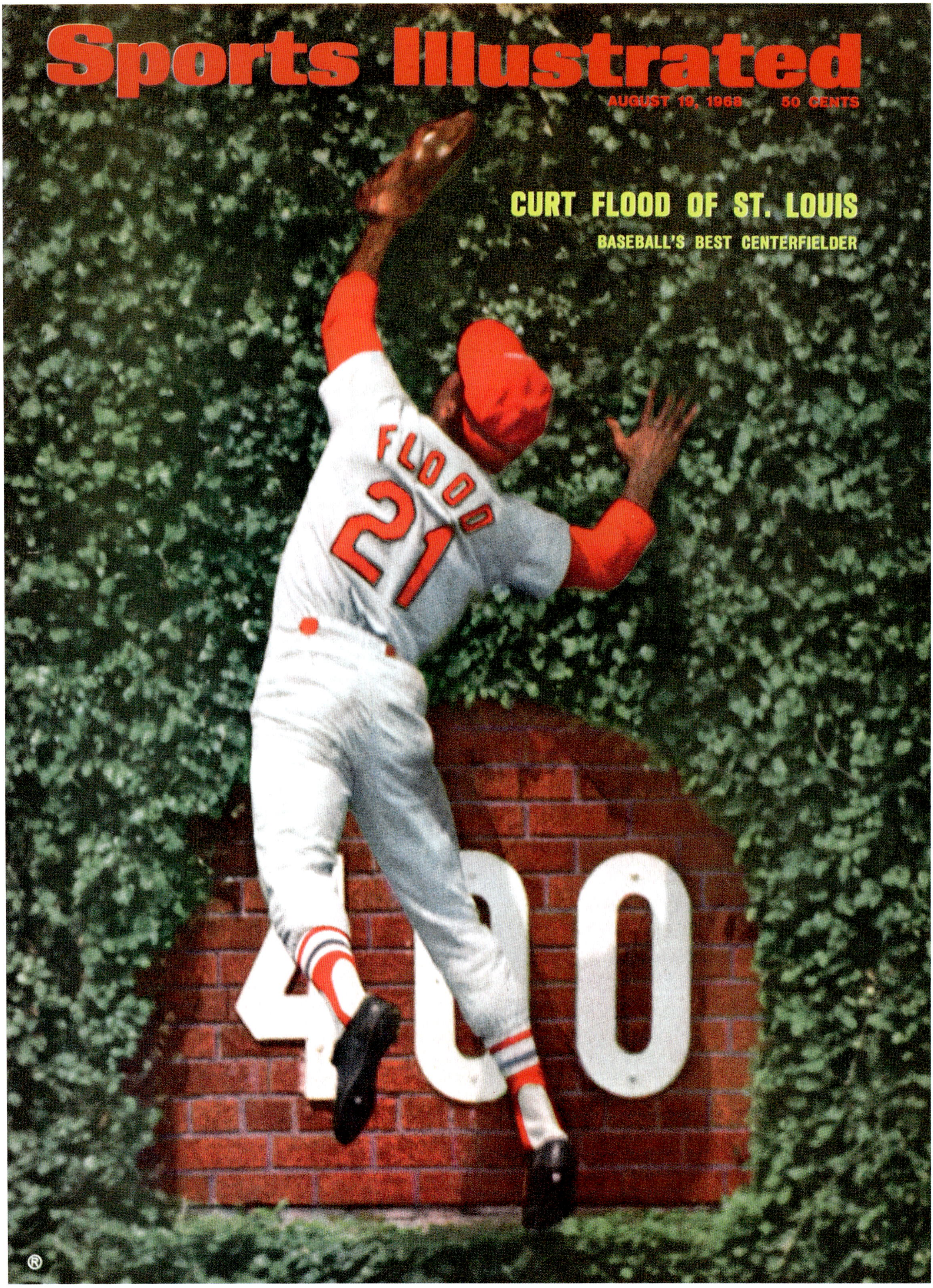

Sports Illustrated
AUGUST 19, 1968
50 CENTS
CURT FLOOD OF ST. LOUIS
BASEBALL'S BEST CENTERFIELDER
FLOOD
21
400
®

across the world of baseball. Then suddenly everything seemed to change after Game Seven of the 1968 World Series.

Frustration seemed to boil after the Cardinals had taken a three-games-to-one lead in the Series against the Detroit Tigers, then lost the next two games. Game Seven became a pitcher's duel between Bob Gibson and the Tigers' Mickey Lolich. It was a scoreless game in the top of the seventh inning. The Tigers had two men on base, and what appeared to be the third out on a fly ball to center field off the bat of Jim Northrup turned out to be misjudged and misplayed by Flood after he slipped trying to reverse his direction to get to the ball. Northrup ended up on third, and the Tigers went up by two runs. They won the game 4–1, and Flood became the fall guy for fans' frustration over a disappointing loss and a missed third world championship in five years.

But the biggest headline from Flood came after the following season when the Cardinals included him in a seven-player trade to the Philadelphia Phillies. Flood and Tim McCarver, along with two others, headed to the Phillies in exchange for three players, including Dick Allen. The outspoken Flood refused to go. He believed baseball's reserve clause was unfair and kept players beholden for life to the team with which they had last played, even after satisfying the terms and conditions of their contracts. The legal debate went all the way to the Supreme Court, which rejected Flood's bid to be a free agent in 1972. Although he did not win, his actions set the stage for eventual free agency in 1975.

Flood was only 31 years old and making $90,000 in his final 1969 season with the Cardinals (over four times what he made in his first World Series championship season of 1964), but he gave up the game to pursue his litigation. He tried a brief 13-game comeback with the Washington Senators two years later before leaving baseball for good. In looking back, Flood was in the prime years of his career when he decided to stand his ground and attempt to break the shackles of baseball's reserve clause. One can only wonder how many more Gold Gloves he would have won and what contributions he would have made to a team. Would it have culminated in a career that on its own would have opened a door to Cooperstown? Some fans believe his stand against the reserve clause has prevented his induction into the venerable institution. Whether it has or not, there is no debate over what Flood accomplished while playing on a baseball diamond during the 1960s.

Flood played for the Cardinals from 1958 to 1969. In 1968, baseball's best center fielder appeared on the cover of Sports Illustrated.

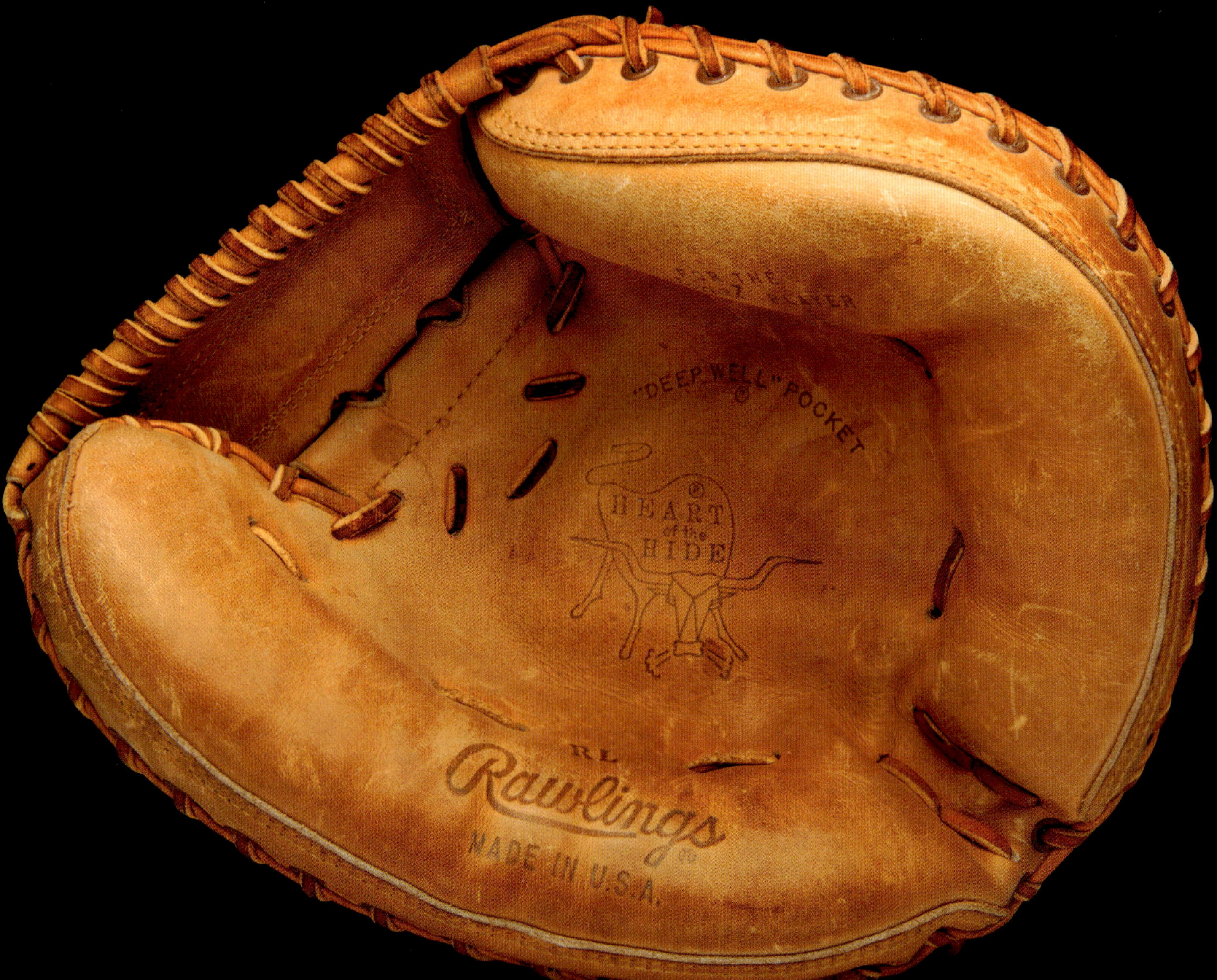
"DEEP WELL" POCKET
HEART of the HIDE
RL
Rawlings
MADE IN U.S.A.

JOHNNY BENCH

Simply the Best

One of baseball's most beautiful off-the-field attributes is that it inspires debates about numerous aspects of the game. Which is the best city in baseball? Which stadium was/is the best ever? Which team was the best in history? Which player was the best at their position? So many questions and so many differing answers to ponder. However, there is one position that few people disagree on. Who is the all-around greatest catcher to play the game? The near-unanimous response is Johnny Bench.

Over the century and a half that MLB has been played, there have been great defensive catchers who possessed strong arms or the ability to block balls in the dirt. There have been catchers who excelled as the quarterback on the field with their ability to call a game's pitches. There have also been great catchers who provided a team with an offensive punch at the plate. Put all those things together and you have Bench—the gold standard of catching who could do it all.

When ranking the greatest catchers in the history of baseball, Bench always rises to the top, as noted by sportswriter Roger Kahn on an episode of ESPN Classic's *SportsCentury* series. To quote Kahn: "I remember I said to Red Smith, 'I've seen Campy and Berra, this fellow's better than that.' And Red said to me, 'I've seen Dickey and Mickey Cochrane, and this fellow is better than them also. Ergo, Johnny Bench is the best catcher who ever lived."

Bench played his entire 17-year career with the Cincinnati Reds. It was a career

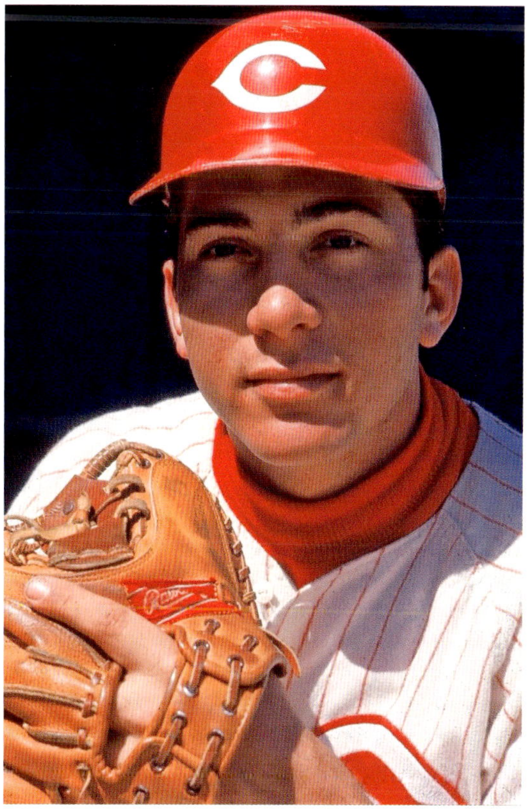

Johnny Bench's game-used Rawlings RL 10 model glove (opposite), with the revolutionary hinge on the bottom of the palm, allowed him to easily grab balls with just one hand. Bench (right) was a 14-time All-Star who played in four World Series and won the Rawlings Gold Glove Award in 10 consecutive years between 1968 and 1977.

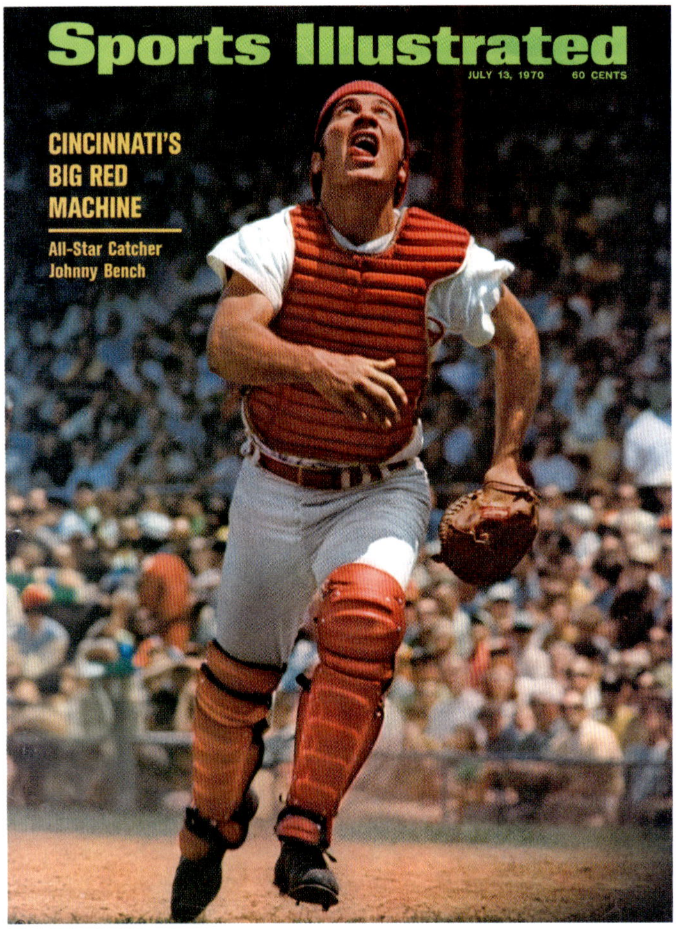

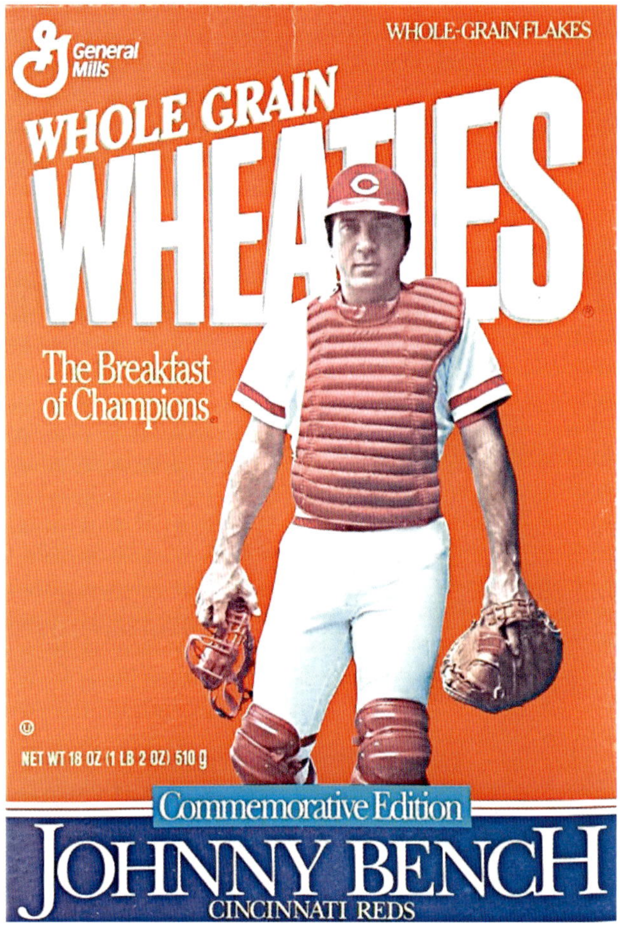

Bench, shown on the cover of Sports Illustrated *in 1970 (above, left), was the heart of the Cincinnati Reds' Big Red Machine. He was also the first major leaguer to grace the front of a Wheaties cereal box (above, right).*

that began with a Rookie of the Year Award in his first full season (1968) and culminated as a first-ballot Hall of Famer at age 41. Bench won two MVP Awards (1970 and 1972) and 10 consecutive Gold Glove Awards (1968–1977). Nicknamed "The Little General," Bench appeared in 14 All-Star Games while helping lead Cincinnati's Big Red Machine to six NL Championship Series that led to four World Series appearances and two world championships (1975 and 1976).

While at the plate swinging a bat, Bench twice led the major leagues in home runs (1970 and 1972) and three times in RBIs (1970, 1972, and 1974). Behind the plate, he redefined how the catcher's position was played. Bench became a catcher as a youngster playing in Oklahoma because his dad told him that catching was the quickest way to get to the major leagues. That advice and hard work made the young Bench baseball's first Rookie of the Year to win a Gold Glove in the same season. And he did it before he was 21 years old.

After experiencing a broken thumb in the minors, he became one of the first one-handed catchers in the game to avoid further injuries to his unprotected hand. Bench would position his right hand behind his back to protect against foul tips and quickly whip it around to garner the ball out of his mitt to hold runners on base. His mitt established a new trend as well. Whereas the circular pillow-style catcher's glove had been the standard since the turn of the century, Bench began using a hinged catcher's mitt to ensure a better grip on the ball when fielding bunts and throws at the plate. Bench retired from the game in 1983, holding the MLB record for home

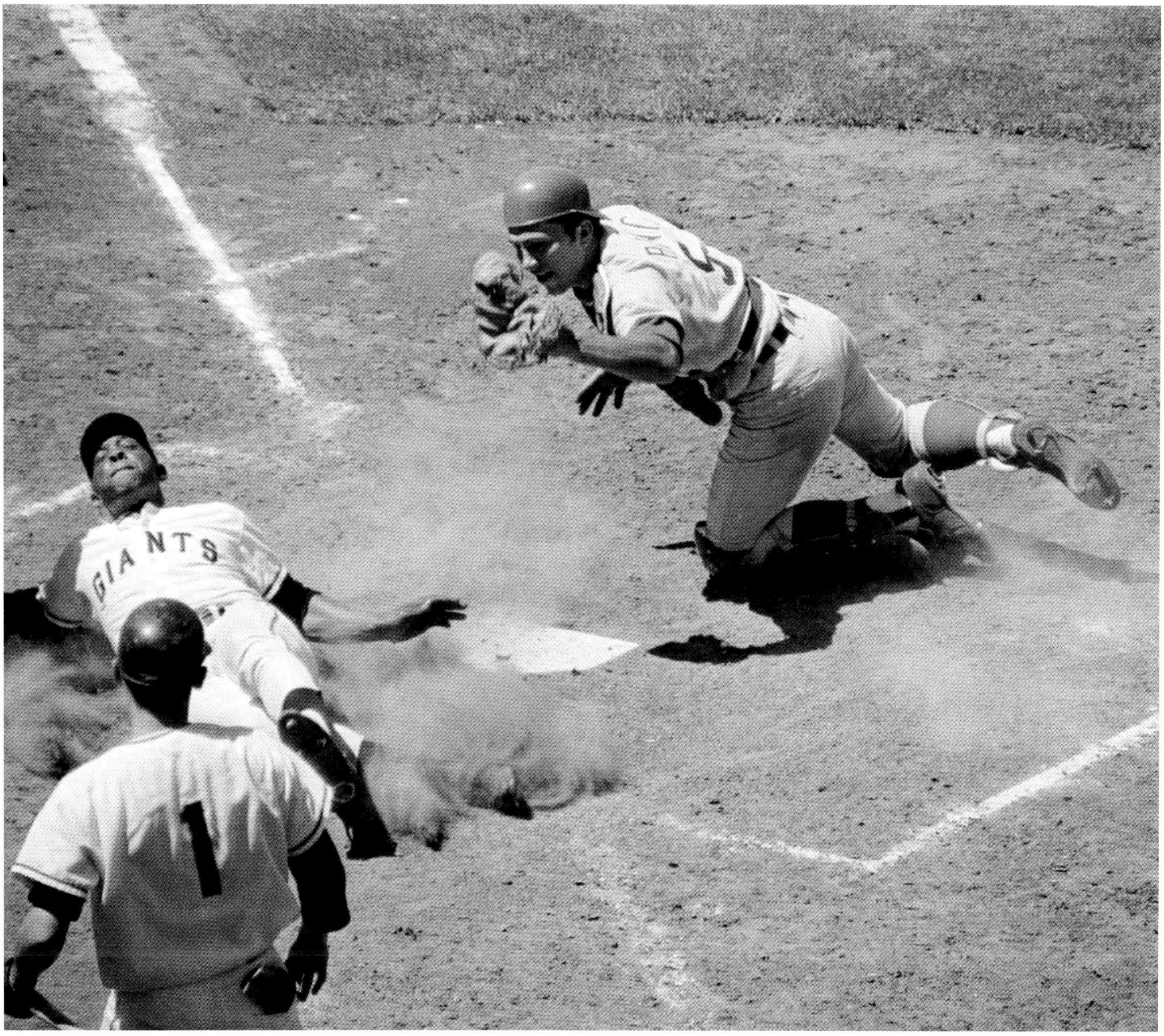

In a 1968 game, the San Francisco Giants' center fielder, Willie Mays, is tagged out at home plate in the eighth inning by Bench.

runs by a catcher (389). Five years later, he got a plaque on the wall in Cooperstown, and in 1989, Bench also became the first individual baseball player pictured on the front of a Wheaties cereal box—wearing his catching equipment and holding his Rawlings glove.

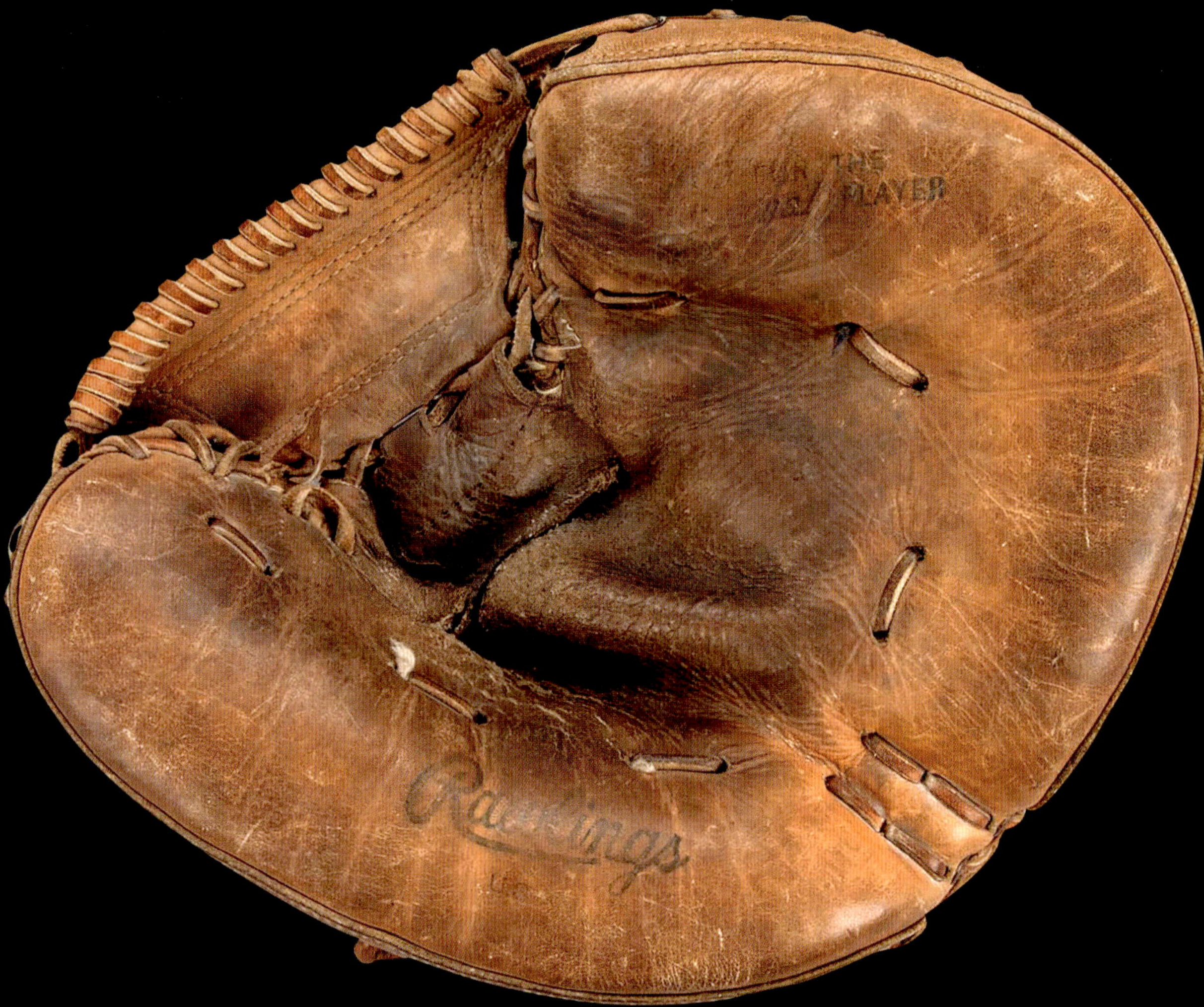
Rawlings

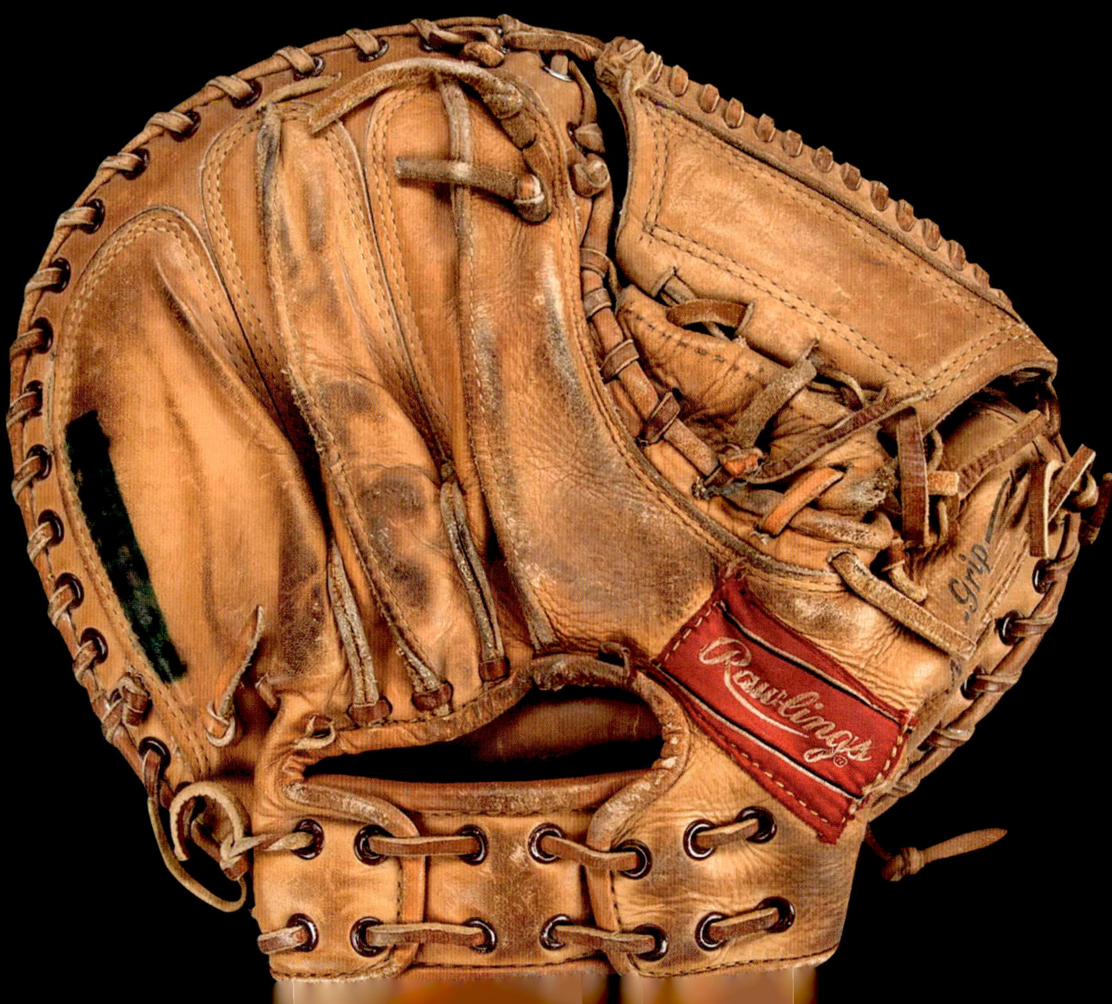
Rawlings
Grip

THURMAN MUNSON

The Walrus

Thurman Munson's 11 seasons in the big leagues became a lifetime of memories for not just Yankees fans but all fans watching baseball during the 1970s. With his bushy mustache and ragged hair hanging out from under his hat, Munson was the scruffy leader of the Bronx Zoo—the nickname given to the mismatched and often controversial collection of Yankees players during the later years of the 1970s. His legacy was not the result of his sudden death in July 1979, but something he had earned years earlier within the confines of the House That Ruth Built.

Munson's nicknames—"The Tugboat," "Squatty Body," and "The Walrus"—were reinforced by his wrinkled pinstriped flannels draped in the dirt from his catcher's position. To many, he looked more like a softball player than one of the best in the game he played. And play he did. Drafted as the fourth player taken in the first round of the 1968 draft, Munson turned a late-season call-up to the Yankees squad in 1969 into an AL Rookie of the Year Award a year later. And he only got better. He went to the All-Star Game seven times and won three consecutive Gold Gloves (1973–1975). In five of his 11 seasons, he hit over .300—a task accomplished by only three MLB catchers before him and six since. During three of those seasons hitting over .300, Munson drove in 100 runs or more. He had become an offensive catalyst for another Yankees dynasty in the making that would win three consecutive AL pennants (1976–1978). The latter two pennants became world championships, with Munson batting .373 with one home run and 12 hits in 16 World Series games. On the defensive side, Munson became the only catcher in MLB postseason history to record at least a .300 batting average (.357) and 20 RBIs (22), and to throw out 20 would-be base stealers (24).

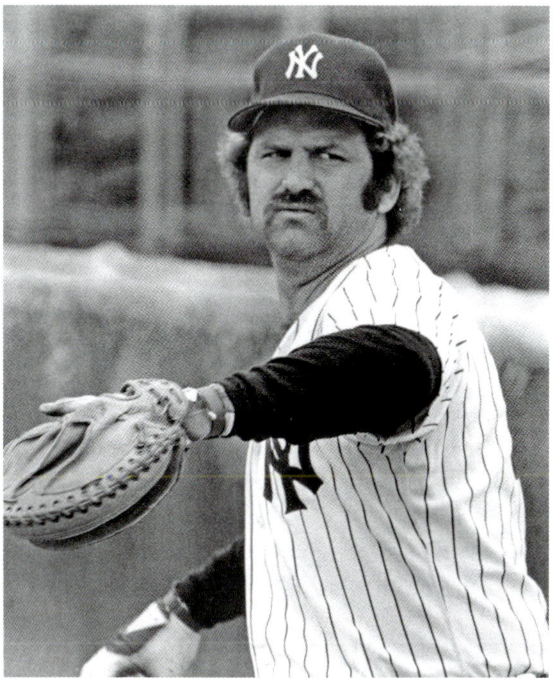

Thurman Munson used this Rawlings catcher's mitt (opposite) in a 1971 game. The New York Yankees' captain (right) won three consecutive Gold Glove Awards between 1973 and 1975 and also appeared in seven All-Star Games in his shortened 11-year career.

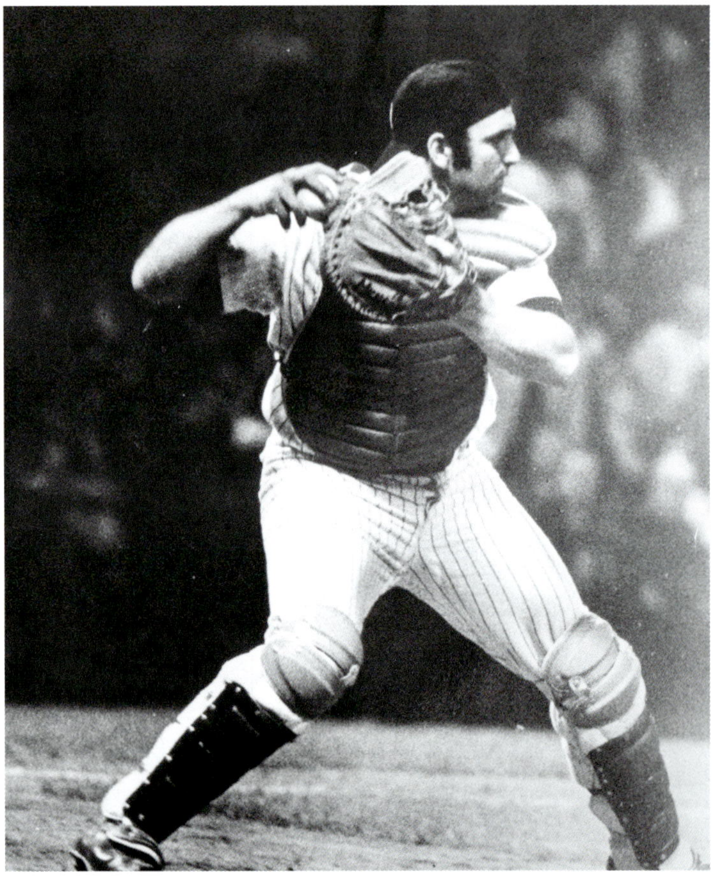

Munson was the leader of the team known as the Bronx Zoo.

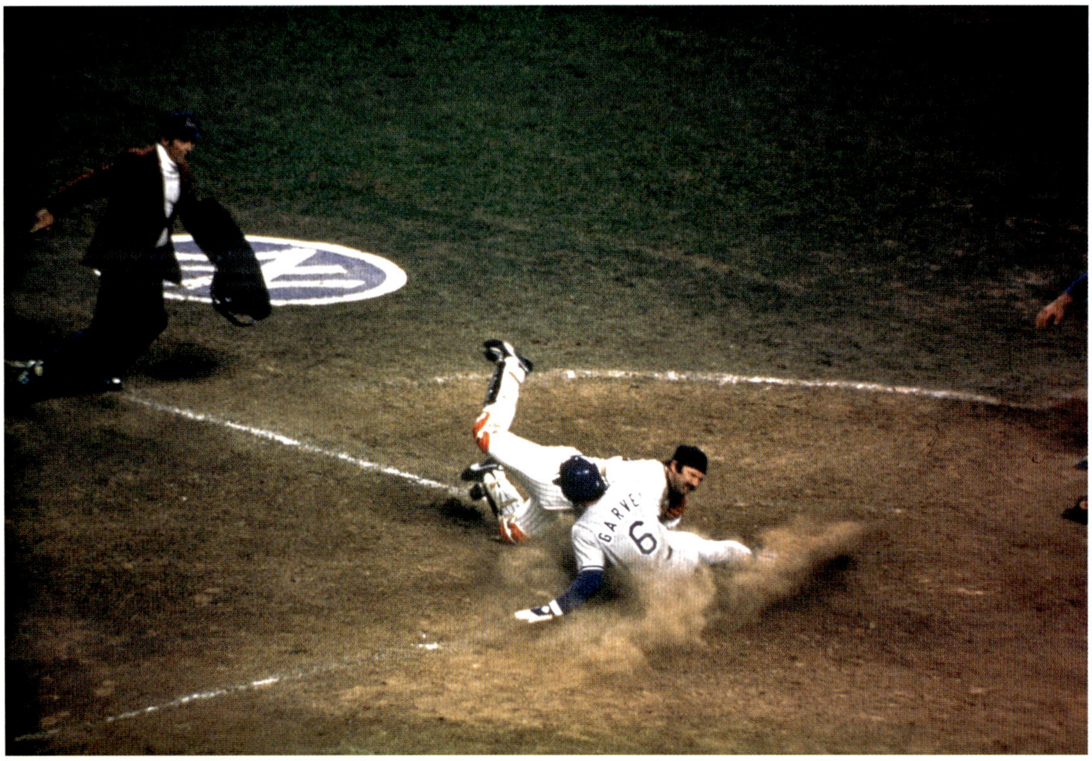

Munson tags the Los Angeles Dodgers' Steve Garvey at the plate in the sixth inning of the 1977 World Series opener in New York.

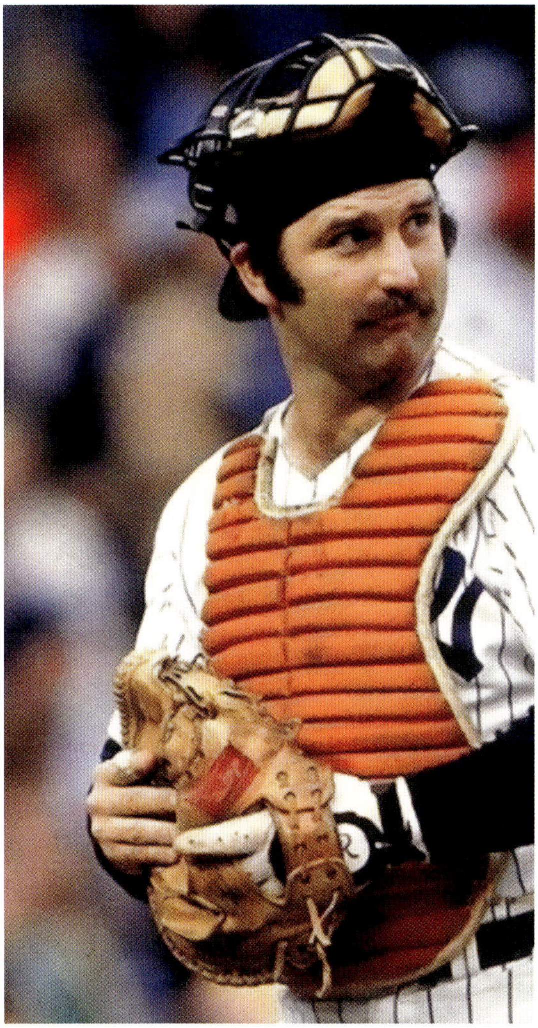

Munson was named the AL MVP in 1976.

Munson's career became a pinstriped legacy in 1976 when Yankees manager Billy Martin named him the team's first captain since Lou Gehrig—another Yankee who died before his career was complete. In his announcement, Martin highlighted his rationale for Munson's selection by telling the New York media, "He has just the right cockiness; he's a born leader." And a leader he was. With the team winning the first of their three pennants, Munson was named the 1976 AL MVP after posting a slash line of .302/.337/.432. In the New Yorkers' unparalleled history, Munson and Aaron Judge are the only Yankees to win both the Rookie of the Year and MVP Awards. Like Munson, Judge was subsequently named the Yankees' captain in 2023.

As one of the most dominant players of this era, Munson was named by *The Sporting News* as the AL catcher of the decade after leading all catchers in the league in hits, runs, doubles, RBIs, and batting average. It's unfortunate that his playing time was cut short by the tragic crash of a plane he was piloting. What more could he have accomplished in an extended career? Are his statistics worthy of the Hall of Fame as is or would a few more years have iced his path to Cooperstown—a place that has yet to call his name for induction? There were those across the world of baseball who called for his Hall of Fame selection shortly after his passing, much like Roberto Clemente's expedited induction after his death in an airplane crash in 1972. But it did not happen, nor did it ring out in Munson's years of voting eligibility. Even though there is no plaque hanging on Cooperstown's iconic walls for Munson, his legacy lives on in the memories he gave us as one of the best players of the 1970s.

DAVE CONCEPCIÓN

El Rey David

Dave Concepción was a key member of the Cincinnati Reds dynasty known as the Big Red Machine that won four NL pennants and two world championships in the seven seasons between 1970 and 1976. Concepción was affectionally nicknamed "El Rey David" (The King David) by Cincinnati's baseball-loving fans as a form of respect for his unparalleled defensive abilities. He was recognized with five Gold Glove Awards (1974, 1975, 1976, 1977, and 1979), but he was more than just a good glove man. Concepción's 19-year career, spent entirely with the Reds, was filled with many key moments at the plate, where he delivered to keep the Reds' machine rolling. The adulation and recognition led to nine All-Star Game selections.

Concepción's ascent into the majors in 1970 followed a string of great Venezuelan imports who had preceded him at shortstop. He had grown up idolizing two of his fellow countrymen who were playing in the big leagues during his youth: Chico Carrasquel and Luis Aparicio. Carrasquel was a four-time All-Star with the Chicago White Sox, and future Hall of Famer Aparicio was a 13-time All-Star who succeeded Carrasquel as the Sox' shortstop. Aparicio became a model of defensive excellence, winning nine Gold Gloves. In time, Concepción's stardom would become the inspiration for a new generation of Venezuelan Gold Glove–winning shortstops like Ozzie Guillén (1) and Omar Vizquel (11). Both players' uniforms blazoned the number 13 throughout their careers in honor of their childhood hero, Concepción.

Batting down in the order, Concepción batted over .280 eight times while exceeding the .300 mark three times. Twice Concepción's season ended with double-digit home-run numbers. He also added an edge that helped the Reds' offensive numbers with his speed. He had seven seasons exceeding 20 steals, with a career high 41 in 1974.

But in the end, Concepción's career is remembered as a cornerstone of defense for a Big Red Machine team made up of All-Stars and future Hall of Famers including Johnny Bench, George Foster, Ken Griffey Sr., Joe Morgan, Tony Pérez, and Pete Rose. Concepción and Morgan are remembered as one of baseball's best double-play combinations of all time, and they appeared beside each other in four All-Star Games. Eight times Concepción ranked in the top 10 in double plays turned at shortstop, and eight times he ranked in the top 10 in fielding percentage at the position.

During a time when more big-league parks—like his home field at Cincinnati's Riverfront Stadium—were using artificial turf, Concepción became a pioneer at shortstop. He began

Dave Concepción used a Rawlings RBG50 H-Web Fastback model glove at times during his career with the Cincinnati Reds.

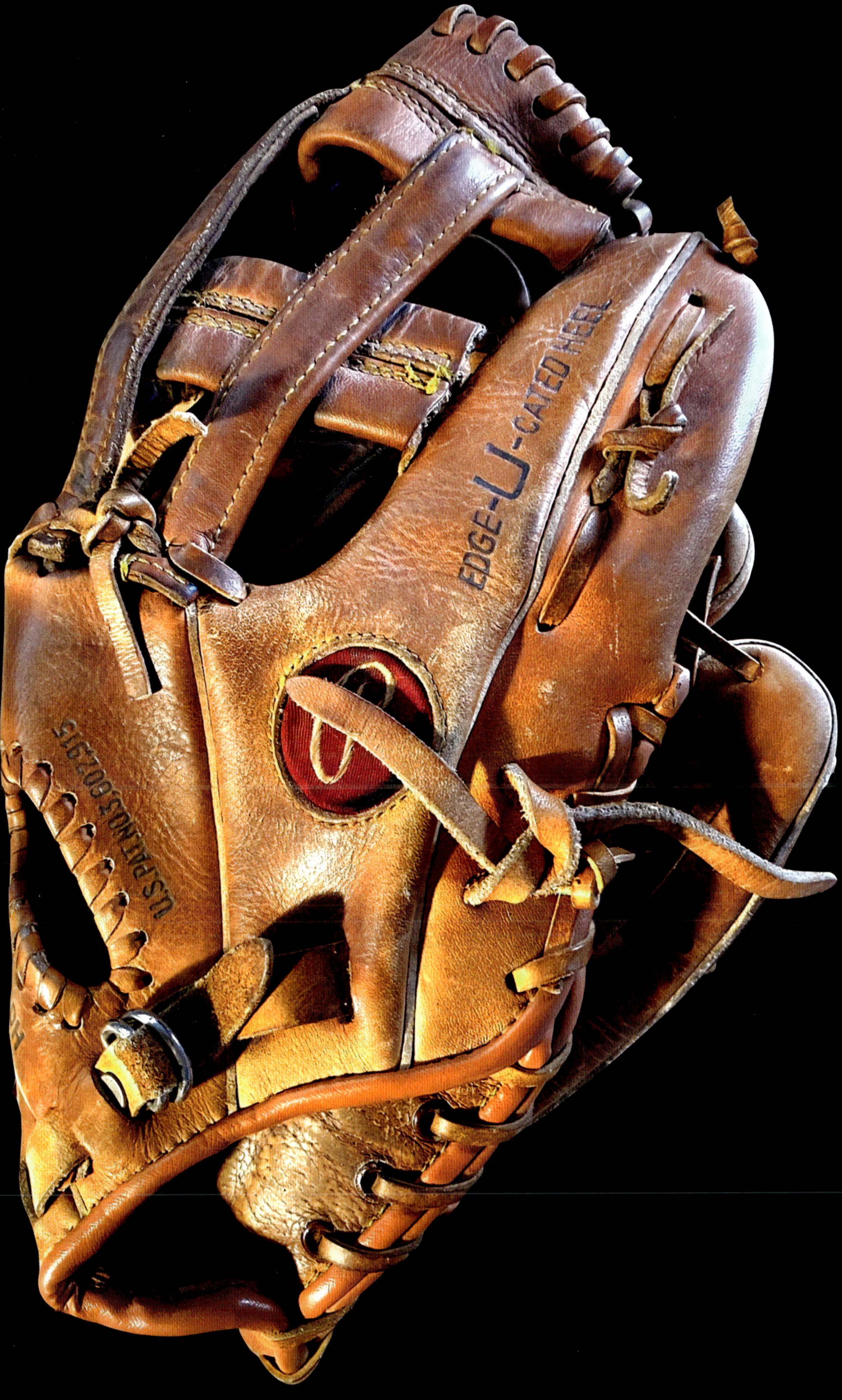
EDGE-U-CATED HEEL
U.S. PAT. NO. 3,602,915

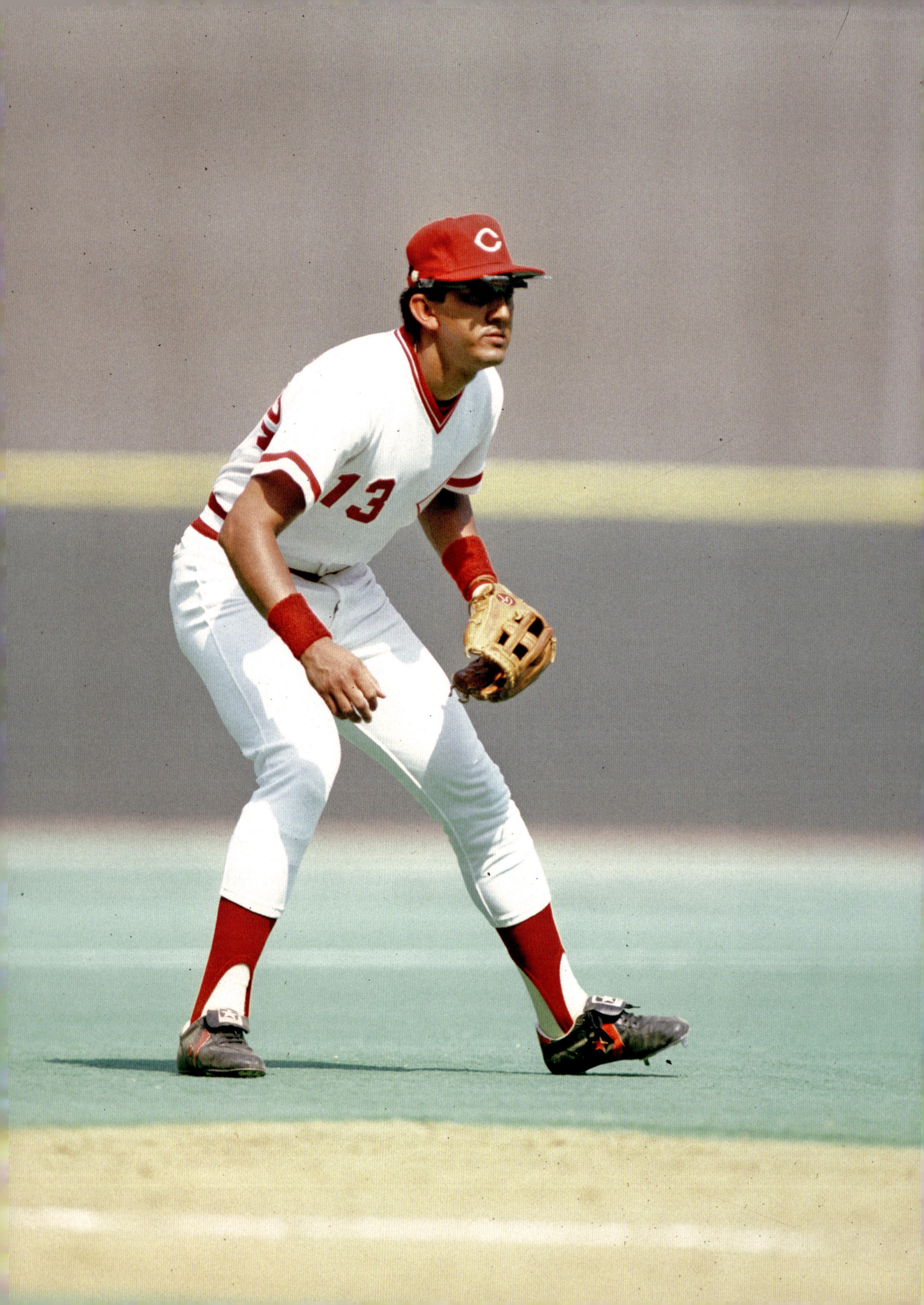
13

one-hopping his fielded throws off the turf to first base to create a more accurate throw that was easier for first baseman Pérez to catch. Knowing that the turf's bounce ensured that accuracy allowed Concepción to better position himself on the field and expand his range in the hole to either side of his play. Concepción's defense was the mortar that cemented the offense from his teammates that made this Reds dynasty one of the greatest in baseball history.

As the game moved past Concepción's days on the field, great shortstops like Cal Ripken Jr. and Ozzie Smith revolutionized the position in their own way. However, in the era of the Big Red Machine, nobody did it as well as Concepción, as Hall of Fame shortstop Pee Wee Reese pronounced when comparing Concepción to his peers at the time: "Mark Belanger may be a little smoother than Concepción. Larry Bowa is very quick. Rick Burleson is a leader type. Bill Russell has an accurate arm. But no one does everything as well as Concepción. It's possible that no one ever has."

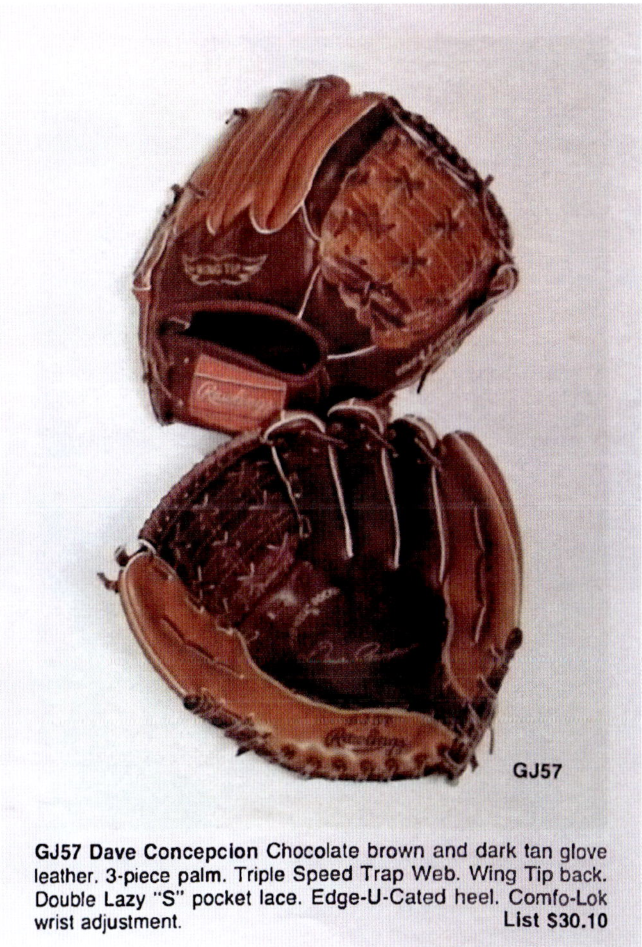

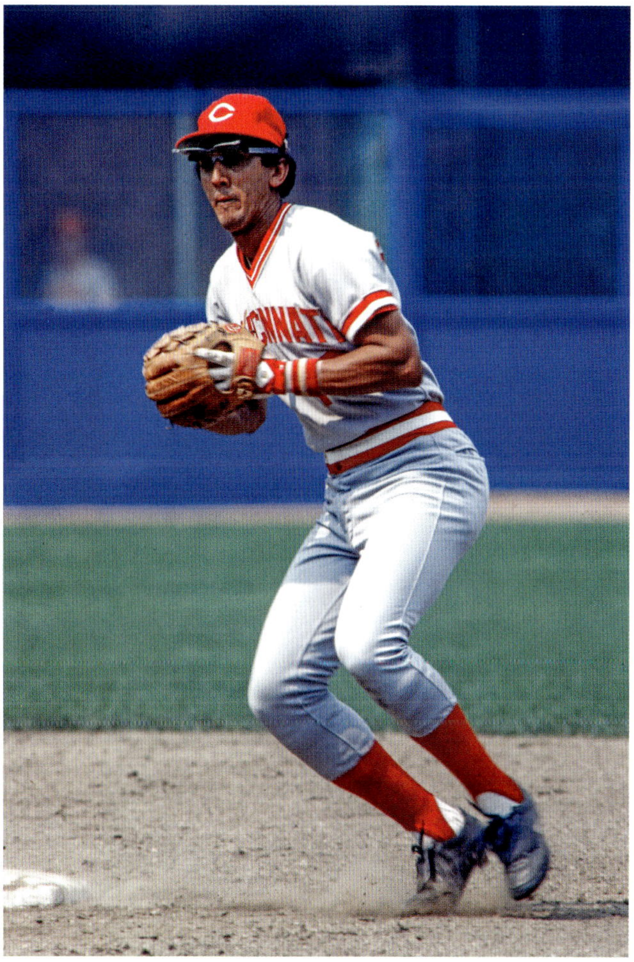

Concepción (opposite), a five-time Gold Glove Award winner, was a staple at shortstop for the Cincinnati Reds' Big Red Machine in the 1970s. A Rawlings advertisement from that decade featured the Dave Concepción GJ57 model glove (above, left). Concepción mans the shortstop position for the Reds (above, right).

STEVE GARVEY

The Boys of Summer's Son

Whether Steve Garvey lived up to his baseball-playing nicknames of "Mr. Clean" and "Captain America" remains debatable. There is, however, one description that is undeniable. Garvey was truly a child of *The Boys of Summer*. His dad, Joe, was a Greyhound bus driver and devoted Brooklyn Dodgers fan from Long Island, New York, who moved to Tampa, Florida, where Steve was born. As fate would have it, in March 1956, Garvey's father was given the job of busing the reigning world champion Dodgers across the Sunshine State during spring training. But there's more to the story. His dad talked the team into letting his son be one of their batboys in the spring—a job the seven-year-old would hold for the next six seasons (1956–1961).

Later, Garvey also served as a batboy for the Detroit Tigers and New York Yankees, but his days with the Dodgers were truly a dream come true for the father and son. It was the time of Roy Campanella, Gil Hodges, Pee Wee Reese, Jackie Robinson, and Duke Snider. Young Garvey joined the club in the spring after the Dodgers' impossible dream season of 1955, when they won the team's first and only world championship and the last of their 12 pennants in Brooklyn.

As a youthful batboy, Garvey got to know all these players, but there was one player he was particularly drawn to over and over. That player was Hodges, the Dodgers' right-handed-hitting, future Hall of Fame first

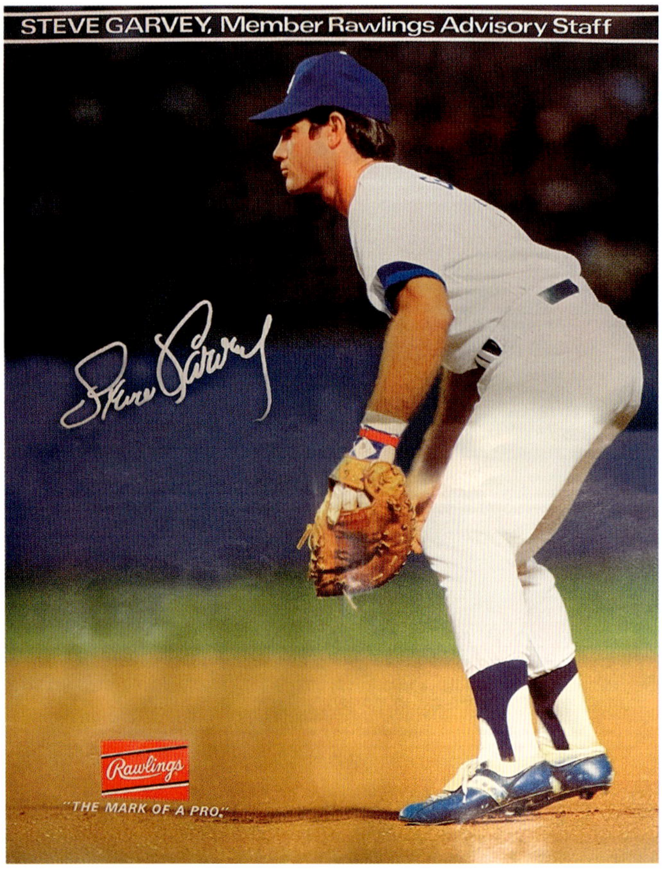

A 1970s Rawlings advertising poster features four-time Gold Glove Award winner Steve Garvey (left). Garvey sometimes used a Rawlings DCT professional model first baseman's mitt (opposite) during his 19 seasons in the big leagues.

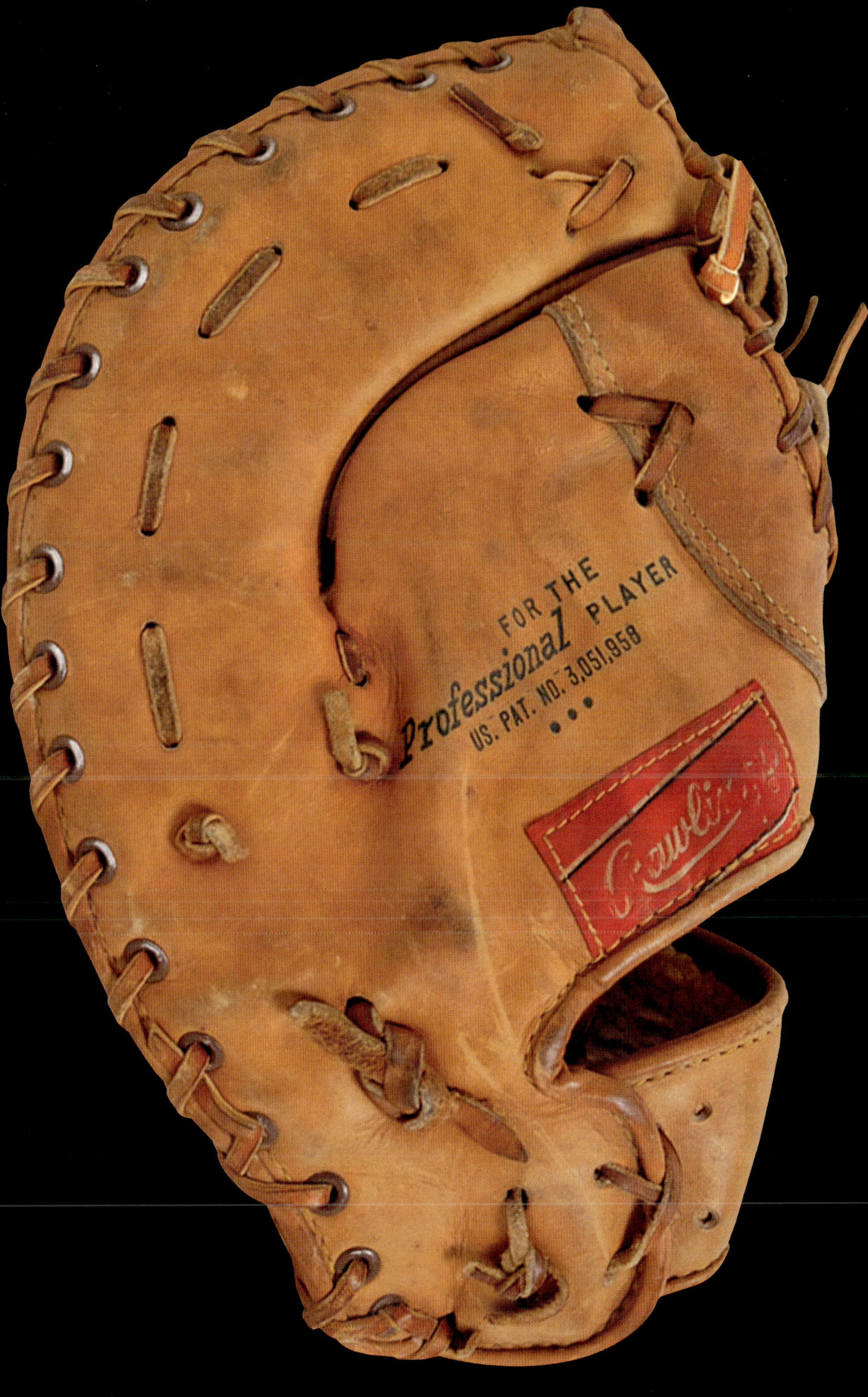
FOR THE
Professional PLAYER
U.S. PAT. NO. 3,051,958
Rawlings

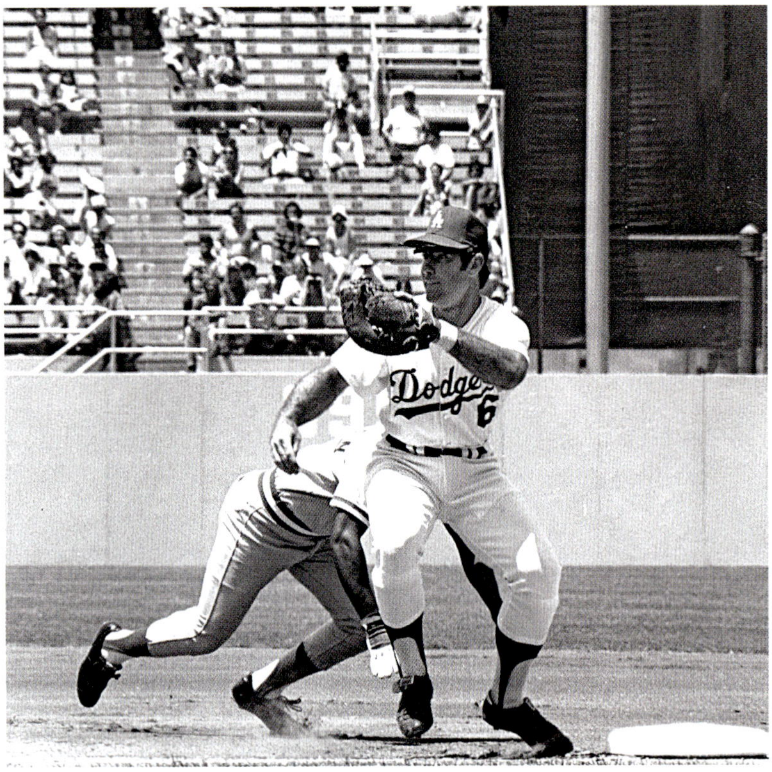

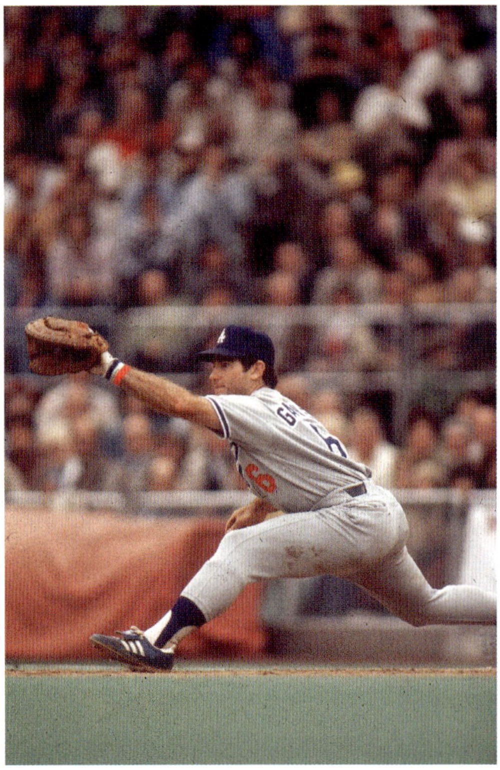

The Los Angeles Dodgers' Garvey attempts to pick off a runner at first base (above, left). Garvey stretches out to make the play at first base against the Philadelphia Phillies in Game Two of the 1978 NL Championship Series (above, right).

baseman. Hodges always took the time to talk and play catch with Garvey. Interestingly, it would be Hodges's first-base position that Garvey would man 16 years later, in a career that included 10 All-Star Game appearances (1974–1981, 1984, and 1985), an NL MVP Award (1974), five NL pennants (1974, 1977, 1978, 1981, and 1984), and a World Series championship (1981). Garvey became the first player to win two All-Star Game MVP Awards (1974 and 1978) while also winning two more in the NL Championship Series (1978 and 1984).

With his photogenic looks and powerful bat, Garvey became a baseball star in Los Angeles and across baseball. His first selection to an All-Star Game in 1974 came in a year when he wasn't even listed on the ballot. Fans noticed his July .338 batting average and impressive home-run and RBI counts and voted him in with a lead that exceeded 20,000 votes over the next contender. He rewarded those fans with an MVP performance in that year's Midsummer Classic. Playing every day, he became the Dodgers' most dependable hitter. In 1975, he began a 1,107-consecutive-game streak with the Dodgers, and that streak extended to 1,207 games (the NL record and fourth longest in MLB history) after he signed as a free agent with the San Diego Padres in 1983, following a contract dispute. In his 14 seasons in Los Angeles, Garvey batted .301 with 211 home runs in Dodger blue. He continued to deliver as a Padre, hitting .294 in 1983 and .284 in the following season to help the team win its first NL pennant. His consecutive-game streak ended on July 29, 1983, after he broke his thumb in a collision at home plate.

What became a storied and productive career at the plate did not start out as a pretty picture in the field. Garvey was not blessed with an arm strong enough for the outfield, and he was positioned at third base during his minor-league years and the first three seasons of his big-league career. During that period, Garvey was always high on the leaderboard for errors and was even the MLB leader at third base in 1972. The following season saw him move over to first base, where he replaced the Dodgers' Wes Parker, the winner of six consecutive Gold Gloves at the position. Within a year (1974), Garvey became the cornerstone of the Dodgers' vaunted defense of Ron Cey, Bill Russell, and Davey Lopes. He won his first Gold Glove for the Dodgers at first base, just as his hero Hodges had done 17 seasons earlier. Garvey went on to win three more consecutive golden trophies for his defense. Always a very good hitter, Garvey also turned into one of the NL's top defensemen on his way to becoming one of the game's most complete players of the 1970s and early 1980s.

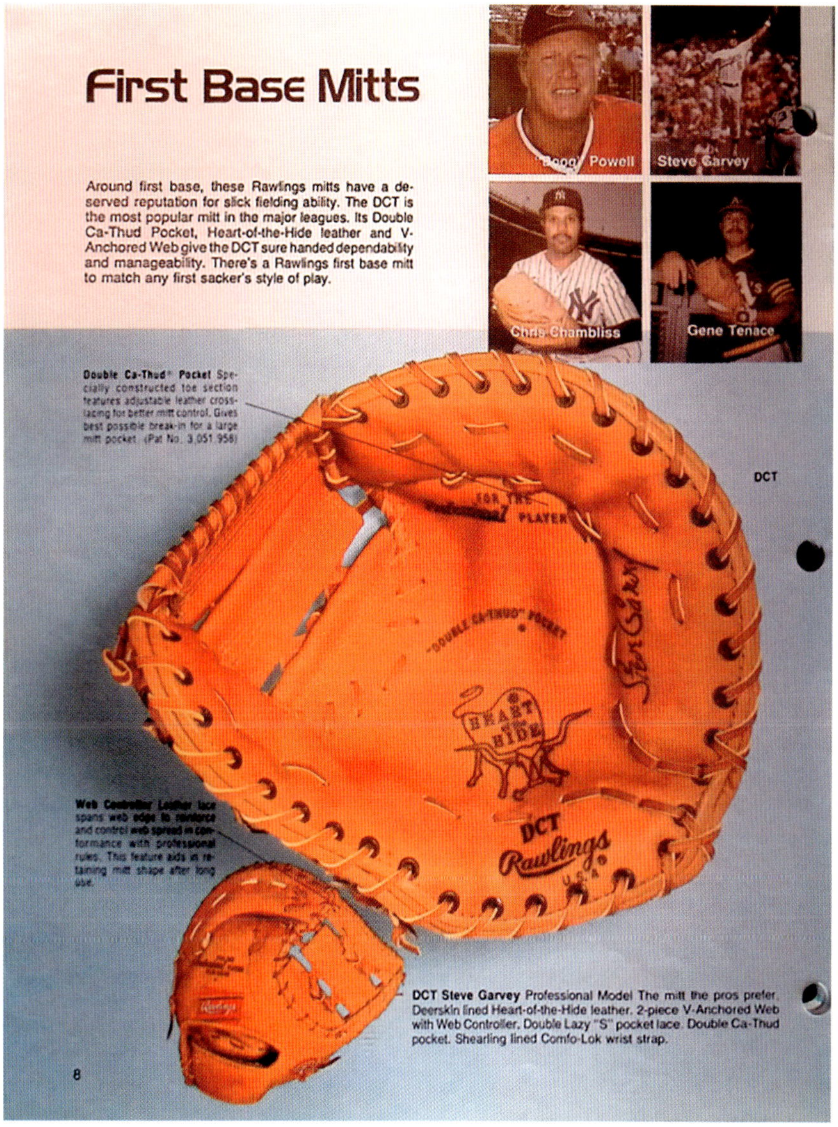

A 1976 Rawlings catalog advertisement features the Steve Garvey DCT professional model first baseman's mitt.

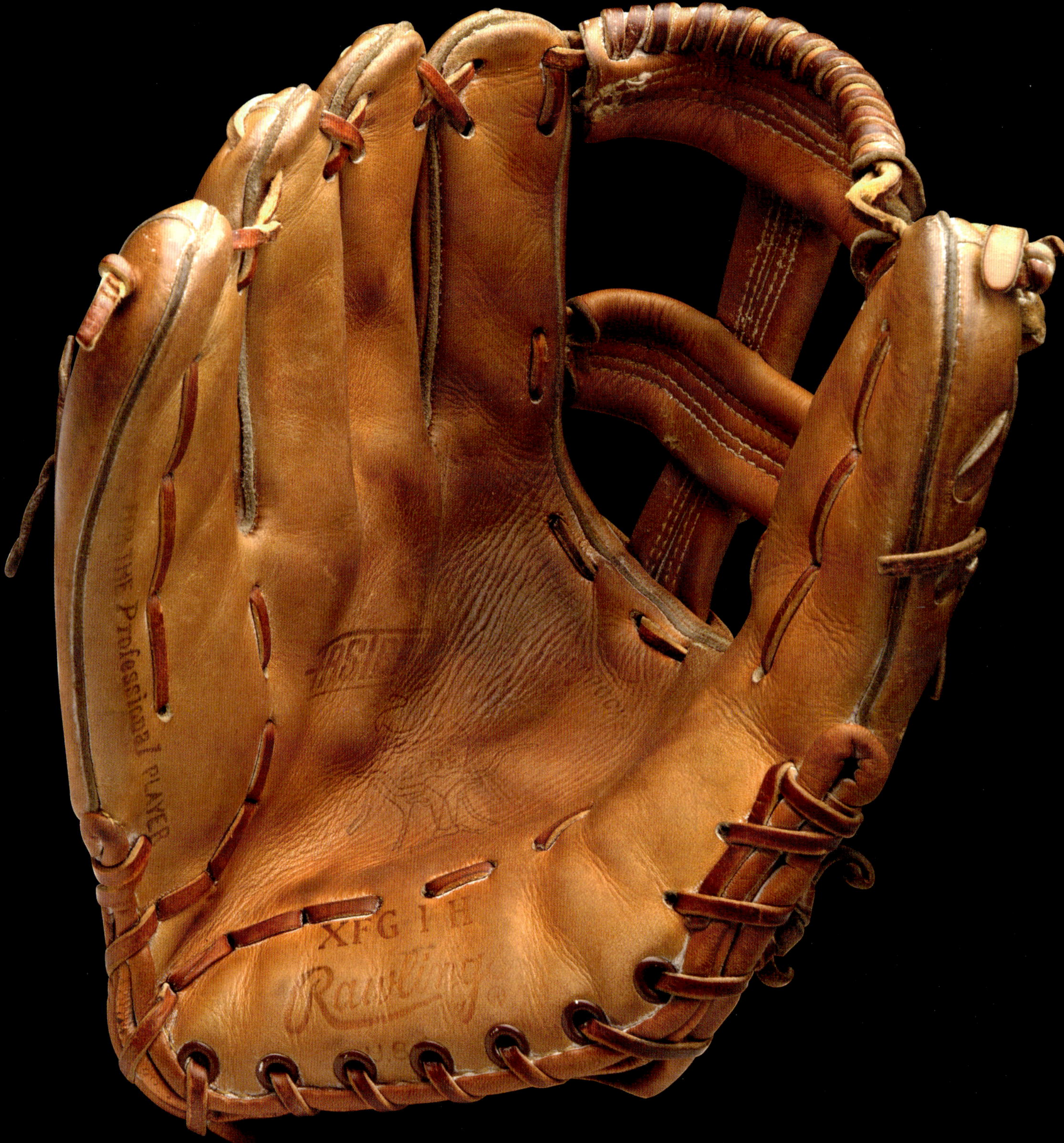
Professional PLAYER
XFG 1 H

REGGIE JACKSON

Mr. October

Reggie Jackson was a star who shined brightly across many of baseball's greatest moments of the 1970s—in regular-season games, All-Star Games, postseason games, and especially across five World Series (four championships). But the outspoken Jackson didn't just leave his charisma on the field. After moving to the Big Apple in 1977, he let the world know where he stood: "I didn't come to New York to be a star. I brought my star with me." And in June of that year, he was quoted in an issue of *Sport* magazine, bragging and referring to himself as "the straw that stirs the drink."

There was a time when it seemed like Jackson's words were making headlines everywhere. Yet throughout the ensuing controversy, there was always one clear fact: Jackson delivered, and he was a winner. Across his 21 years in the big leagues, only twice did he play on a team with a losing season. He contributed to his team's first-place finishes 11 times. Following his 1977 World Series heroics as a Yankee, there was even a candied delicacy named after him (the Reggie! Bar)—something Jackson had prophesied would happen if he ever got to play in New York.

Jackson's career had taken off in his second full season in the big leagues with the Oakland Athletics in 1969. The previous season, he had hit 29 "dingers," as he described his shots over the outfield fence. But in that second season, Jackson's swings were followed in the sports pages of daily newspapers nationwide as he began chasing the home-run records of Babe Ruth and

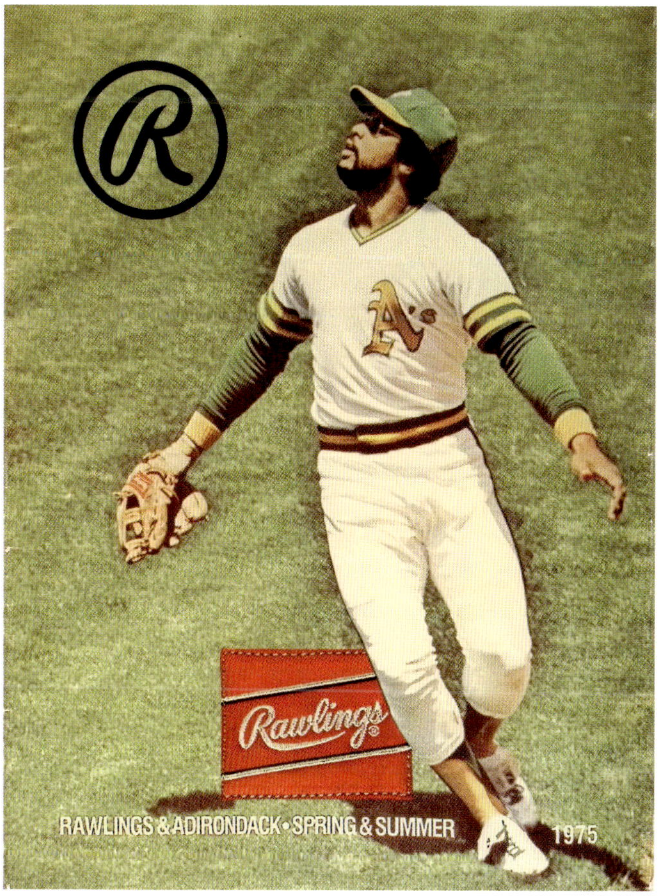

The Rawlings XFG Fastback model (opposite) was one of the gloves Reggie Jackson used during his career. The 14-time All-Star was on the cover of a 1975 Rawlings catalog (right).

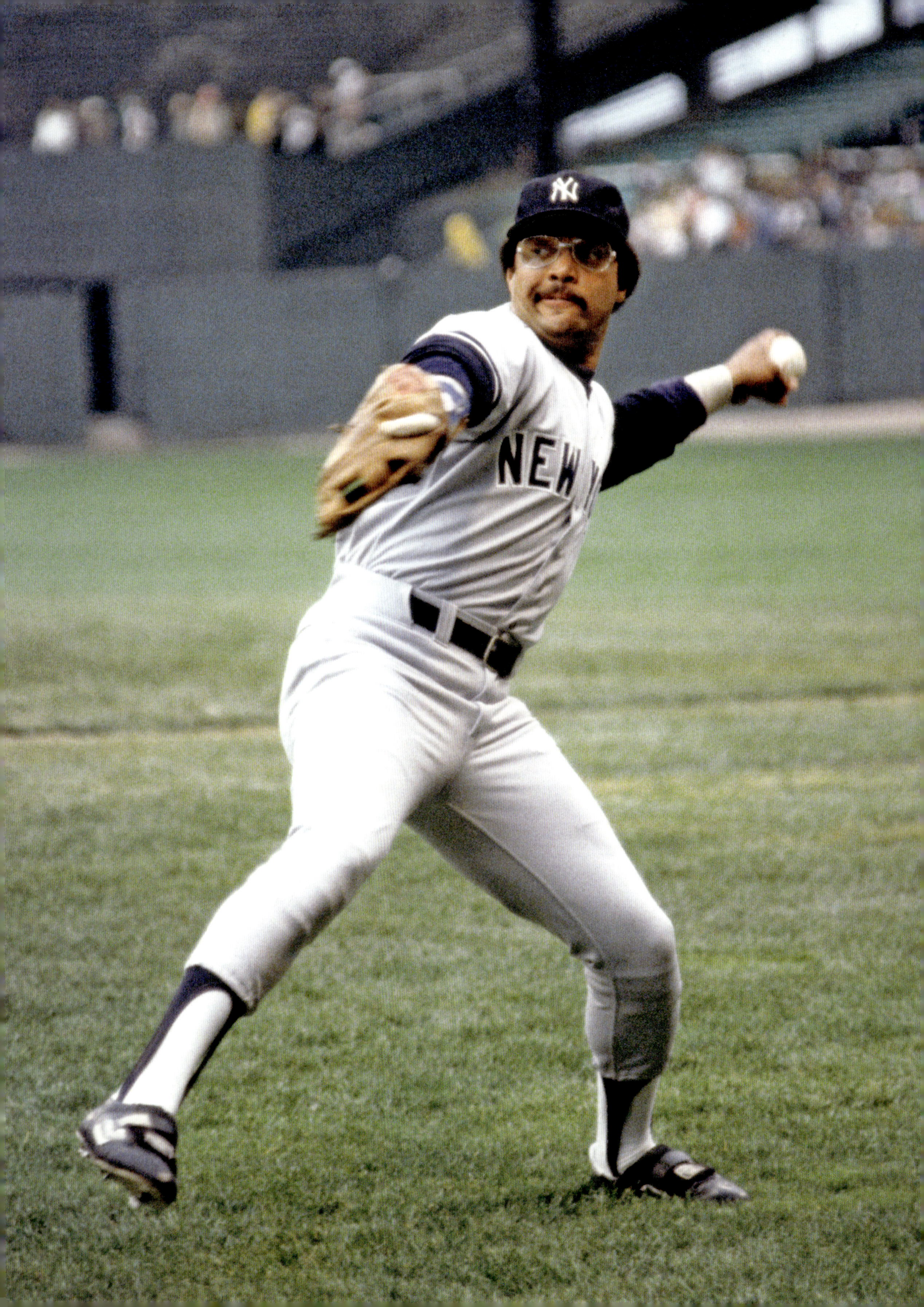
NEW Y

Roger Maris. On July 29, Jackson hit his 40th dinger, and all bets were that he would top their records—he was 27 games ahead of Ruth's run to 60 and 14 ahead of Maris's march to 61. But it was not to be. Despite having a game with two home runs and 10 RBIs that season, Jackson finished the season with only 47 homers.

His reputation continued to grow as the A's built an unparalleled dynasty during the 1970s, winning three consecutive world championships with a team composed of many of baseball's best. As one would expect, Jackson's play stood out. His monstrous home run off Tiger Stadium's rooftop transformer in the 1971 All-Star Game only added to the brilliance of his star power.

Jackson missed the 1972 World Series due to a hamstring injury that happened while scoring the tying run in a come-from-behind victory in the AL championship's final game. But he made sure he was in the World Series the following year. His dominating performance leading the AL in home runs, runs, and RBIs led to his unanimous selection as the league's MVP—only the sixth unanimous vote at that time in league history. He also walked away with his first of two World Series MVP Awards.

Despite a growing agitation within the A's clubhouse, the team pulled off a three-peat in 1974 and bested the Dodgers in five games during the Fall Classic, with Jackson demonstrating his defensive skills and clinching Game Five. He had always shown speed on the field, and his rifle arm helped cut down Bill Buckner at third base in the eighth inning to erase the Dodgers' last chance at winning.

Jackson had hit only two dingers in his first two World Series, but that was about to change when he got to New York in 1977. Once more facing the Dodgers in another tight postseason Series, Jackson homered in Game Four and then again in his final swing in Game Five to tie his output in his previous two Fall Classics with two dingers. In his first at-bat of Game Six, he never swung his bat, walking on four pitches. Then, in each of his next three attempts at bat, he homered on the first pitch. In just four consecutive swings of the bat, Jackson hit four home runs against four different players, leading to his third world championship. It became one of World Series history's greatest moments and christened Jackson forever as "Mr. October."

Jackson added two more homers when the Yankees beat the Dodgers in the 1978 World Series rematch and another when the same two teams met again in the 1981 Series. While his 10 home runs fall short of Mickey Mantle's record of 18 Series homers, his .755 Series slugging percentage remains the highest in MLB history. But fans often remember Jackson for his achievements at bat in October and forget his all around play on the bases and in the outfield, which stirred baseball headlines in the 1970s and 1980s.

Jackson, an outfielder for the New York Yankees, warms up prior to a game against the Chicago White Sox at Comiskey Park in 1979 (opposite). The Reggie! Bar (right) was named after Mr. October.

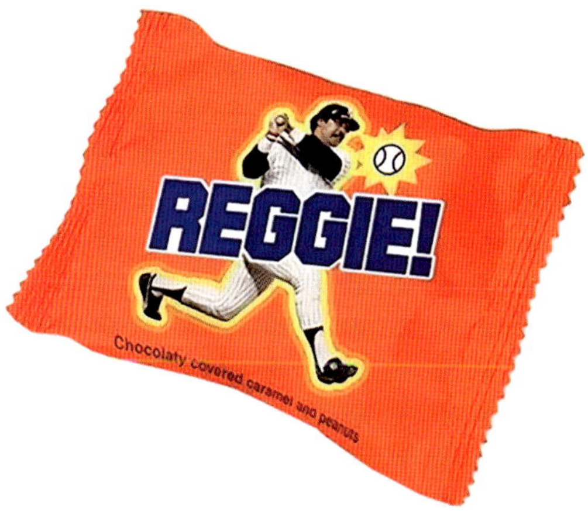

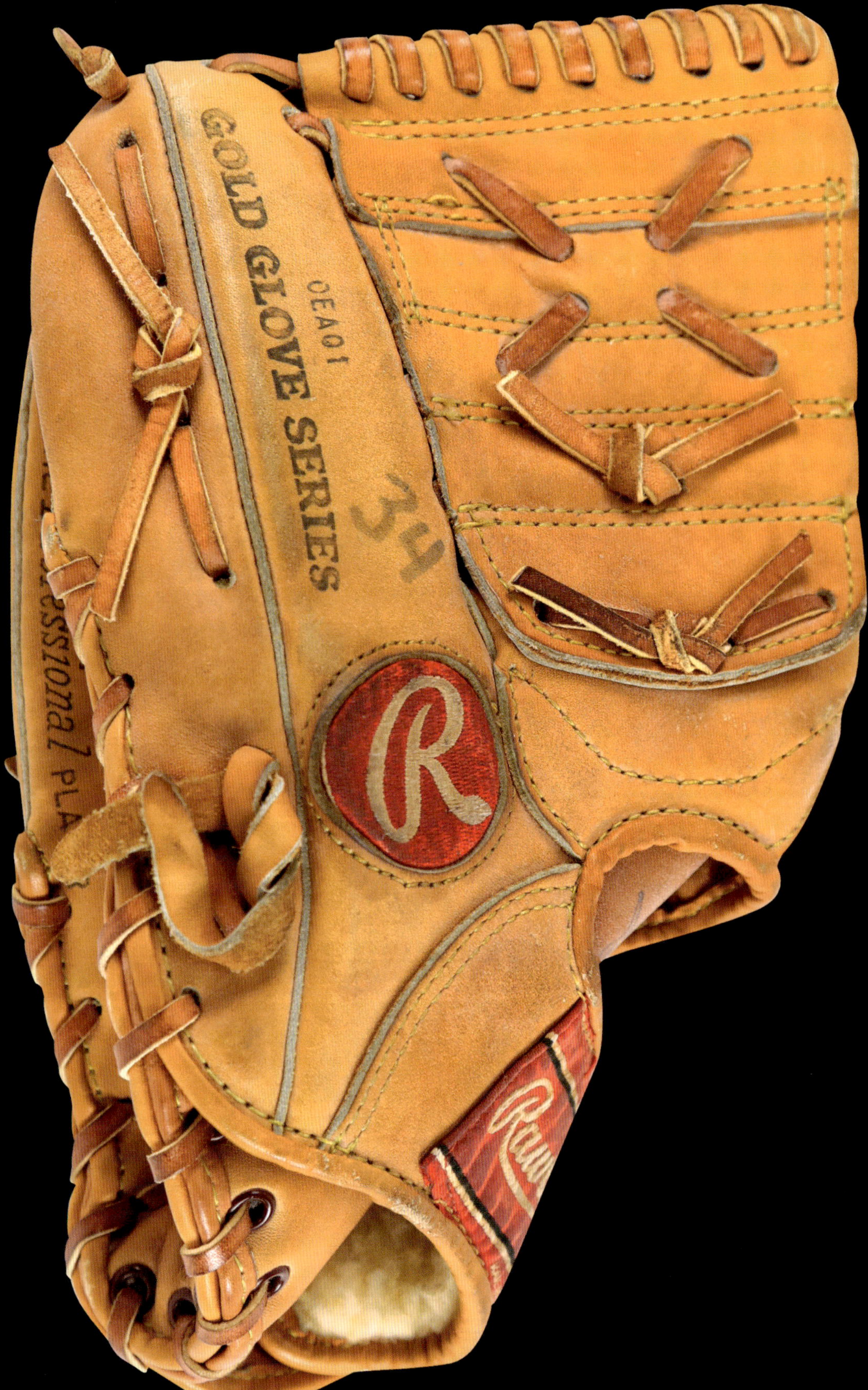
GOLD GLOVE SERIES
OEA01
34

FERNANDO VALENZUELA

Fernandomania

Nineteen-year-old Fernando Valenzuela made his big-league debut on September 15, 1980, with the Los Angeles Dodgers. He was just like many other young rookies who have been called up in September to provide innings while their teams were in the midst of a pennant race. Such was the situation for the Dodgers that year. They were neck and neck with the Houston Astros for MLB's West Division title. In fact, they were tied on the night of Valenzuela's debut with just 20 games left to play.

His first trip to the mound had none of the hoopla that in time would become known as Fernandomania. On that September evening, Valenzuela was simply a chubby young former Mexican League prospect who had done well but not spectacular (14–11) in the Dodgers' minor-league system. Valenzuela pitched in eight of the next 17 games, leading up to a three-game showdown between the Astros and Dodgers on the last three days of the season. Those appearances were all in relief, and in each instance, the lefty did not give up a single run. In game 157 of the season, Valenzuela picked up his first big-league win while closing out a victory over the Giants to keep the Dodgers two games behind the Astros.

The Dodgers had fallen three games behind the Astros as the teams headed into a showdown weekend three days later. Los Angeles needed to win three straight games over Houston to force a playoff and then a fourth win for the division title. With the Dodgers trailing 2–1 going into the ninth inning of the first game, Valenzuela blanked the Astros for the next two innings. The Dodgers tied it in the ninth and won it in the tenth, giving Valenzuela his second career win. After winning again the next day, the Dodgers needed a victory in the season finale to keep playing. With his team trailing 3–1, Valenzuela came in at the top of the sixth to pitch two innings of no-hit ball to hold Houston at bay while the Dodgers pushed the winning run across the plate in the eighth inning to force a playoff game.

It was a winner-take-all game 163. The Astros pounced on the Dodgers early and had a 7–1 lead when Valenzuela came in to pitch a scoreless two frames in the sixth inning. But the damage had already been done. While the season was over for the Dodgers, Valenzuela's career was just taking off. He had just pitched in 10 of his team's final 21 games and had not given up a single run.

Heading into the 1981 season, Valenzuela was ready for prime time and baseball was in for a treat. On the season's opening day, Valenzuela shut out the Astros with a five-hit complete game. Fans were not only amazed at his success but also captivated by his pitching delivery and his dominating screwball. While in his windup, he would lift his arms up over his head and, with a

Fernando Valenzuela used a Rawlings RBG4 model glove during his 17 seasons in the big leagues.

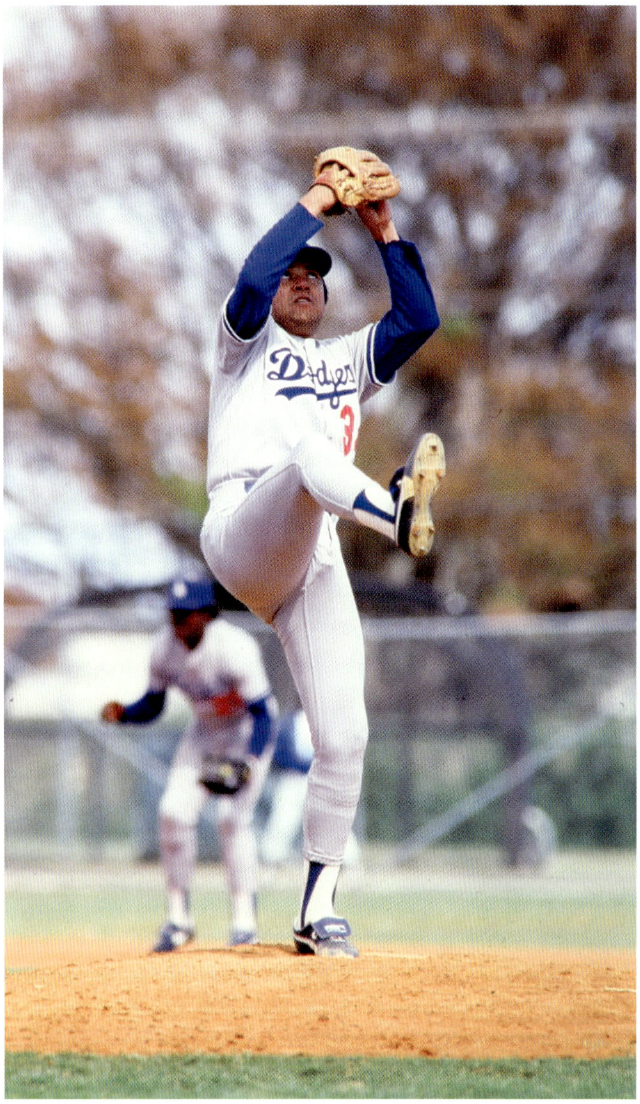

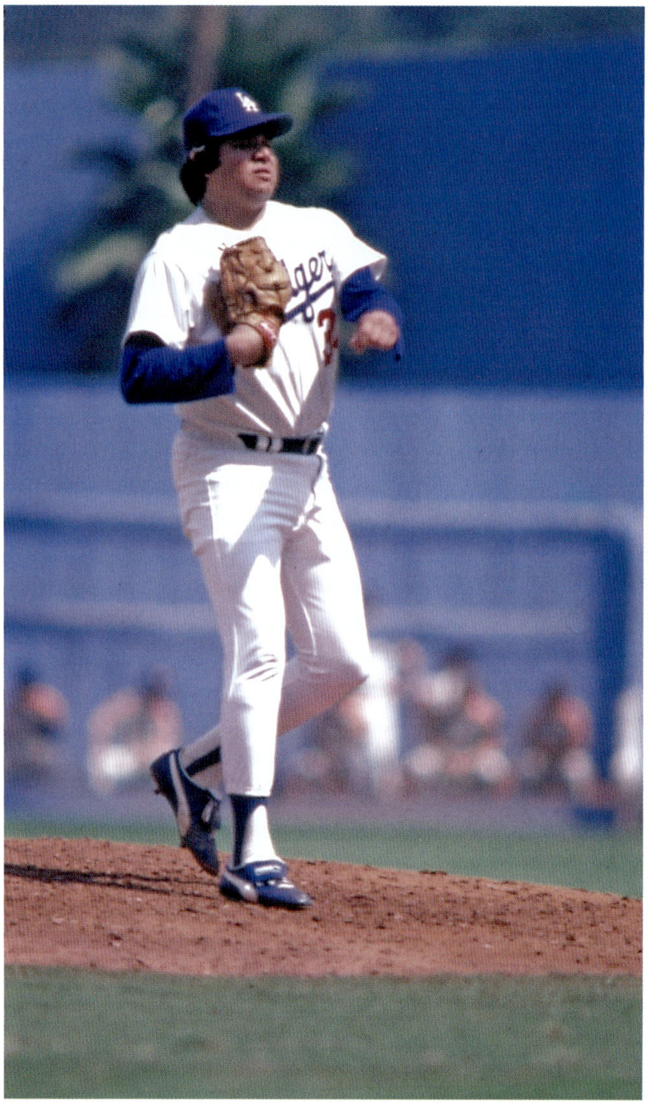

With his eyes straight up to the sky, Valenzuela turns to throw his next pitch (above, left). Valenzuela (above, right) was the 1981 Rookie of the Year and Cy Young Award winner.

high kick of his right leg and his head tilted slightly backward, he would roll his eyes straight up to the sky before turning to throw his next pitch. As the pitches kept coming, so did the wins. Valenzuela won seven more games to start the season 8–0. Seven of the wins were complete games and five were shutouts. He only allowed four earned runs in 72 innings. At the season's end, his record stood at 13–7 with 11 complete games and eight shutouts. His 180 strikeouts led the majors, and Valenzuela was ready to cash in. He took home the NL Rookie of the Year and the Cy Young Award—the only player in the game to have ever won both in the same year.

And yet there was still more to win that season. Valenzuela won the decisive game in the NL Championship Series against the Montréal Expos to send the Dodgers to the World Series against the New York Yankees. He got a complete-game win in Game Three in his only appearance, but it was enough to help his team win a world championship in the only World Series he would play in. Valenzuela was selected to six consecutive All-Star Games (1981–1986) and even pitched a no-hitter against the Cardinals in June 1990. While not necessarily having the physique of an athlete, he was a decent hitter for a pitcher, winning two Silver Slugger Awards, and his agility on the mound was rewarded with a Gold Glove Award in 1986.

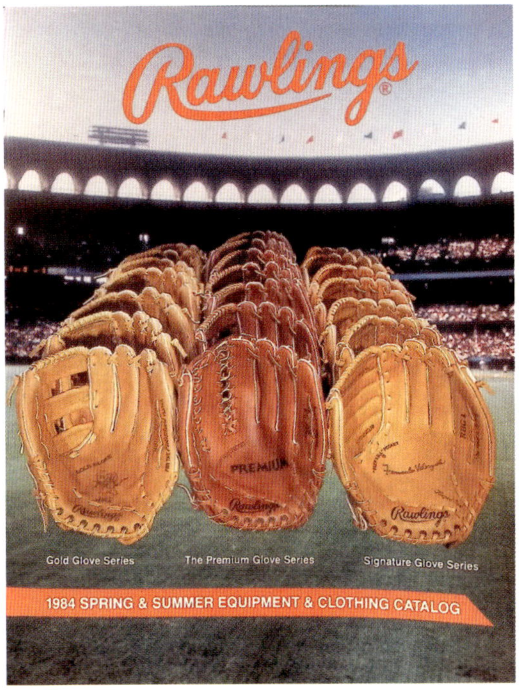

The Fernando Valenzuela RBG4 model glove was highlighted on the cover of a 1984 Rawlings catalog (left). A close-up shows the autographed pocket of the RBG4 model glove (below).

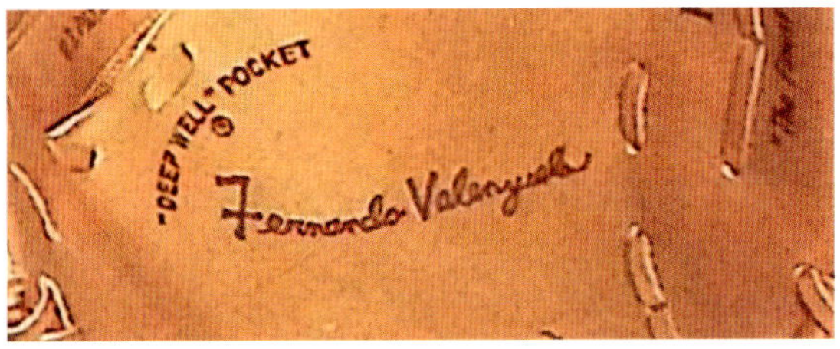

Throwing more than 250 innings per season for six consecutive years (1982–1987) left a strain on Valenzuela's fabled arm that limited his success in his later years. However, nothing will ever take away the excitement and intrigue he brought to baseball in the 1980s. His sheer dominance led him to become the game's first great player of Mexican descent and an inspiration to baseball fans throughout the world.

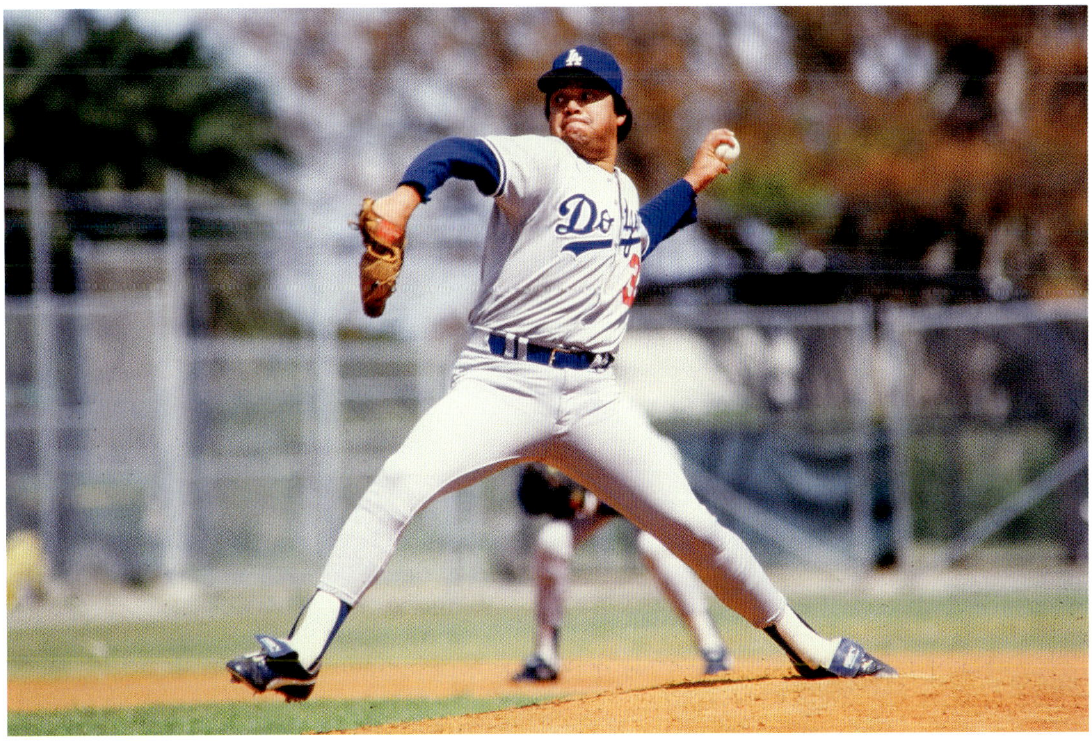

Starting in 1981, Valenzuela stirred the nation with Fernandomania. In 1986, he won a Rawlings Gold Glove Award.

KEITH HERNANDEZ

A First at First

Throughout the history of baseball, first base has been the position of many of the game's mightiest power hitters. Among Hall of Fame inductees, first base (28 inductees) ranks just behind right field (29) as the most common position played (excluding pitchers). It's also perceived as an easier position that often becomes the final position for many aging superstars.

Despite that perception, first basemen must field the hot shots down the line that seem destined for the right-field corner. Or the pendulum can swing to those soft bunts that must be covered and grabbed while also chasing pop flies with the uncertain trajectory of the field or the stands. And it's the first baseman's responsibility to grab over half of each game's putouts—from those thrown right to the glove to those skipping wildly off the infield turf. If Gold Glove Award winners represent the best of the best at each position defensively, one would have to classify Keith Hernandez as the best covering first base. Between 1978 and 1988, Hernandez won the award 11 straight years while playing for the St. Louis Cardinals and the New York Mets. That is the most Gold Glove wins in the majors at first base, with Don Mattingly in second place after winning nine gold trophies of his own in the AL. In 1987, Hernandez became the career leader in assists at first base when he surpassed another St. Louis player—George Sisler.

Hernandez's play revolutionized the position as he evolved a new way of coverage. His athleticism offered a keen ability to aggressively charge bunts and make quick tags. Hernandez could be

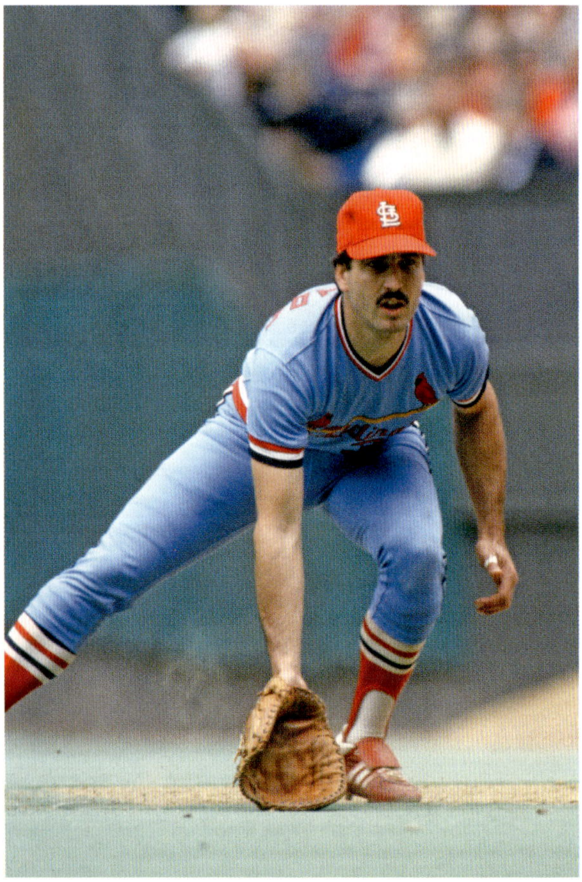

In 1979, Keith Hernandez (left) won an NL batting title and was named co-MVP with Willie Stargell. Hernandez's glove of choice was a Rawlings Fastback model first baseman's mitt (opposite).

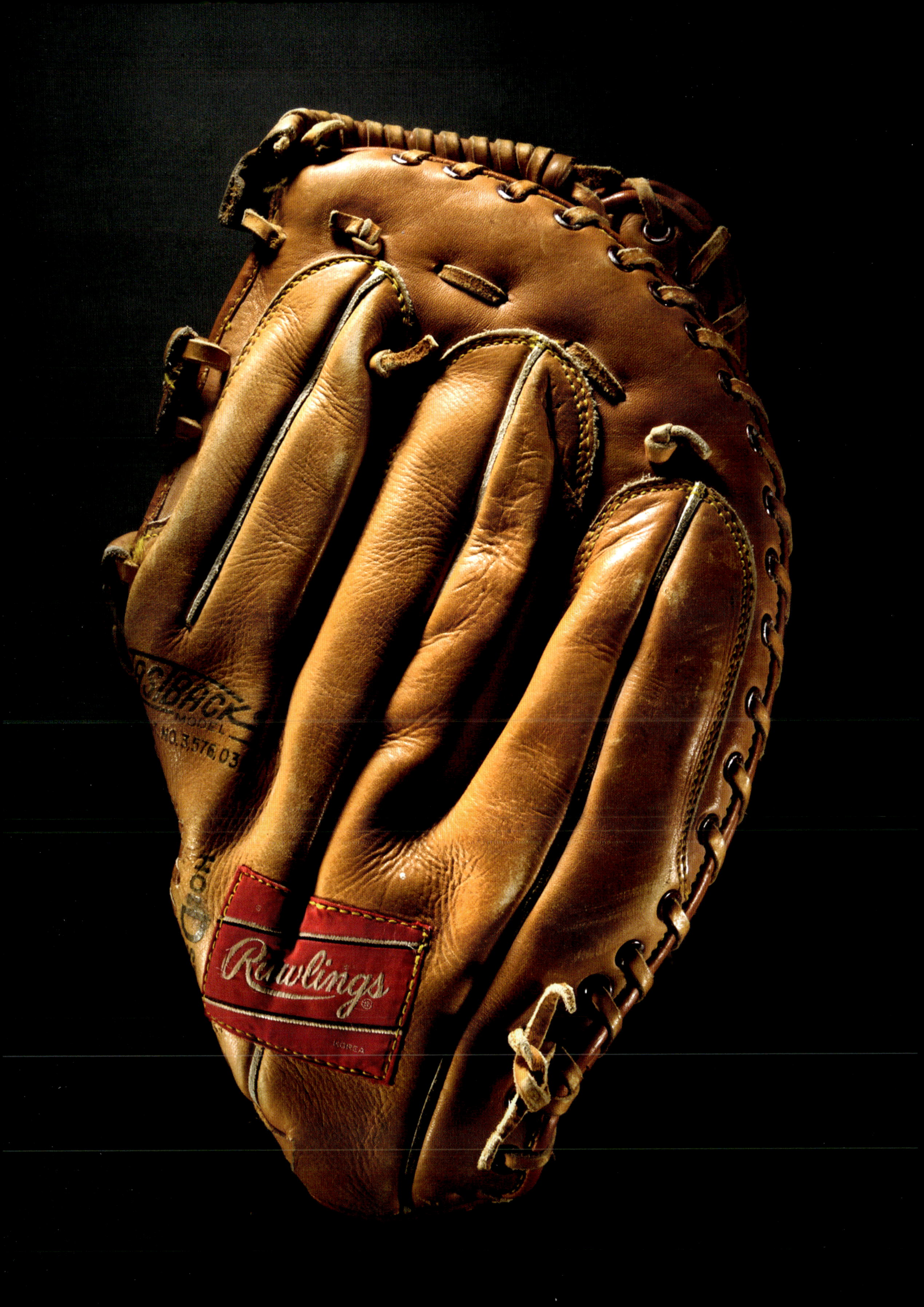
Rawlings

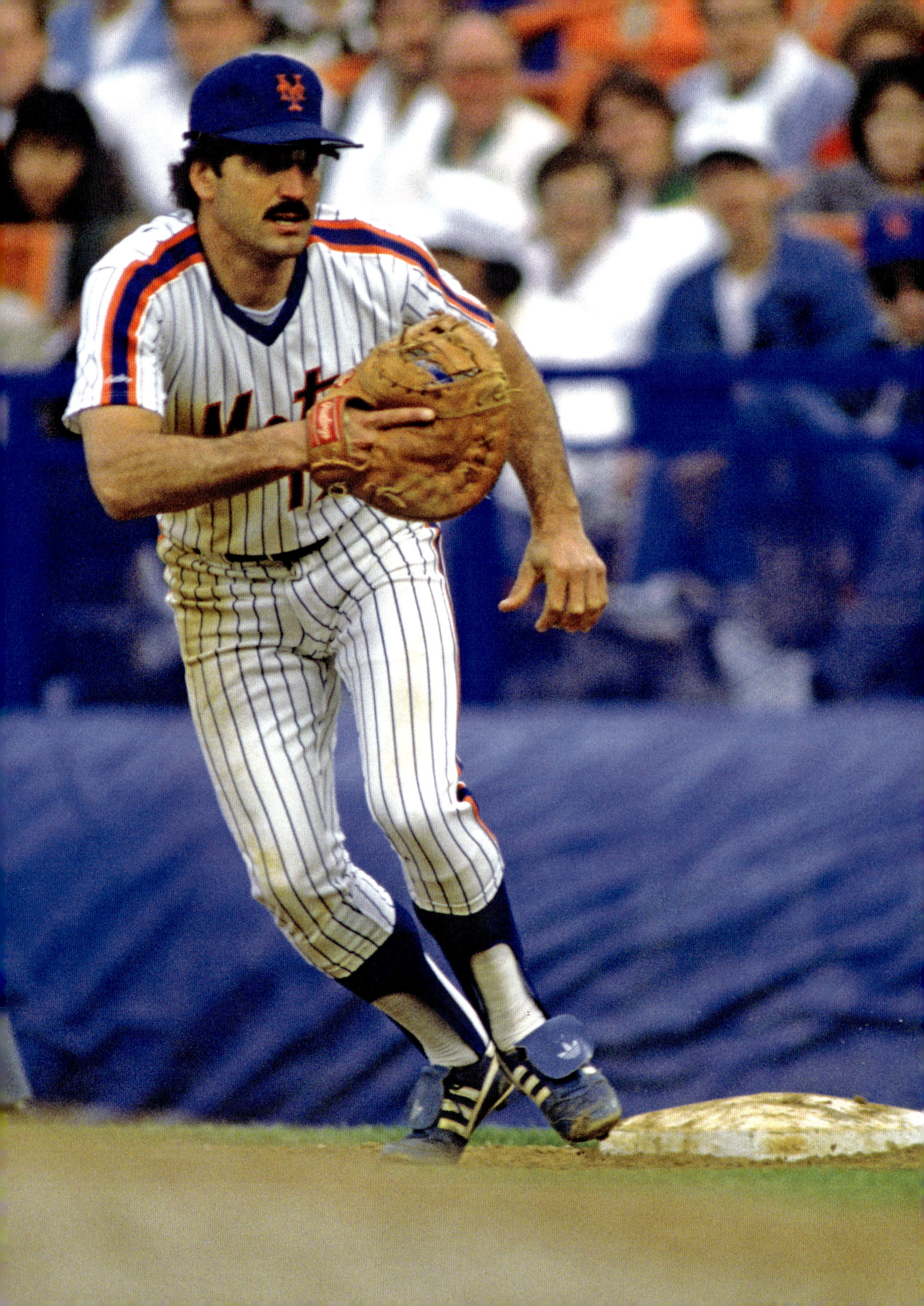

seen playing deep on the infield dirt while not sacrificing range covering his position. His presence on the field was almost the equivalent of a southpaw shortstop on the right side. His astonishing reflexes and superb footwork allowed him to quickly field balls dropped in front of him on the bunt or drives slashed into the hole to his right. Hernandez could quickly pivot to turn a double play or, with his strong arm, cut down a runner trying to get to third base. For Cardinals and Mets fans, these were not one-time highlight-reel plays; they were consistent game-in and game-out moments that marked Hernandez's elevated level of play and led to World Series championships for both franchises.

Joining the ranks of great hitters who covered first base in the past, Hernandez won an NL batting title in 1979 and was selected as co-MVP that year with Willie Stargell. He led the league twice in runs scored and once in doubles and walks. His skills on the field and at the plate once posed an ongoing question among fans about whether Hernandez knocked in more runs with his bat or saved more runs with his glove. His ability to lead in offense and defense has made him one of the best first basemen to ever play the game.

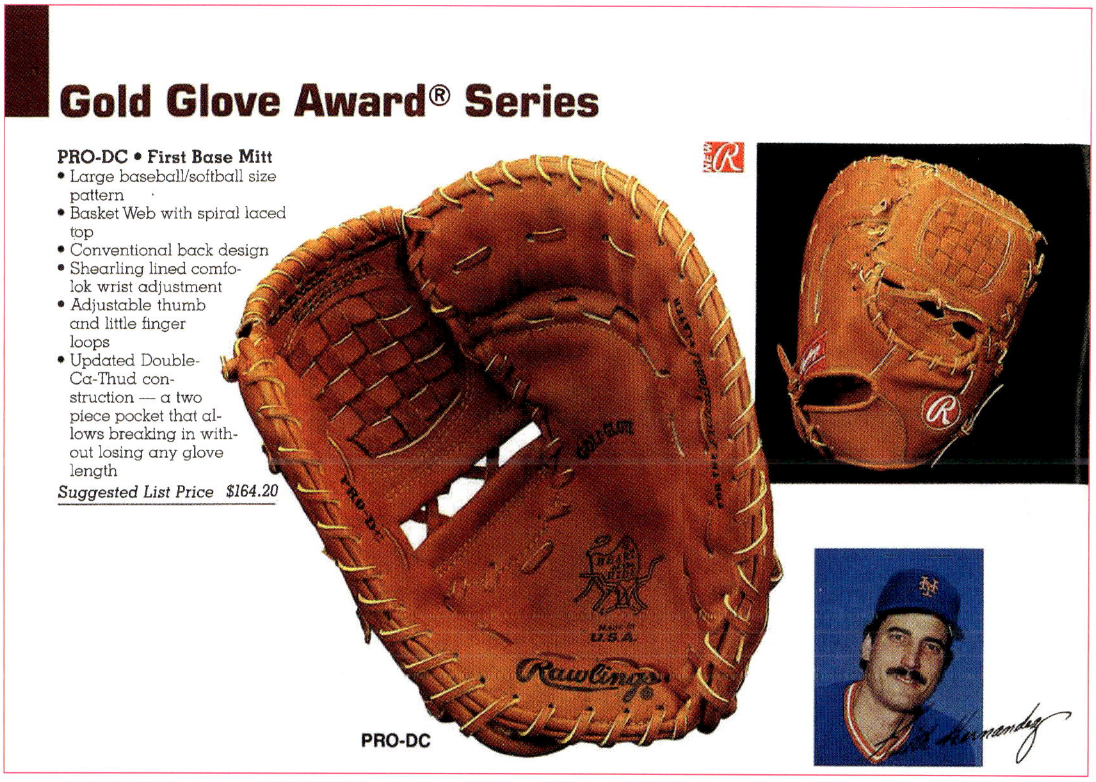

Hernandez (opposite) was an 11-time Gold Glove Award recipient who also won two World Series championships. A mid-1980s Rawlings catalog features the Keith Hernandez PRO-DC model glove (above).

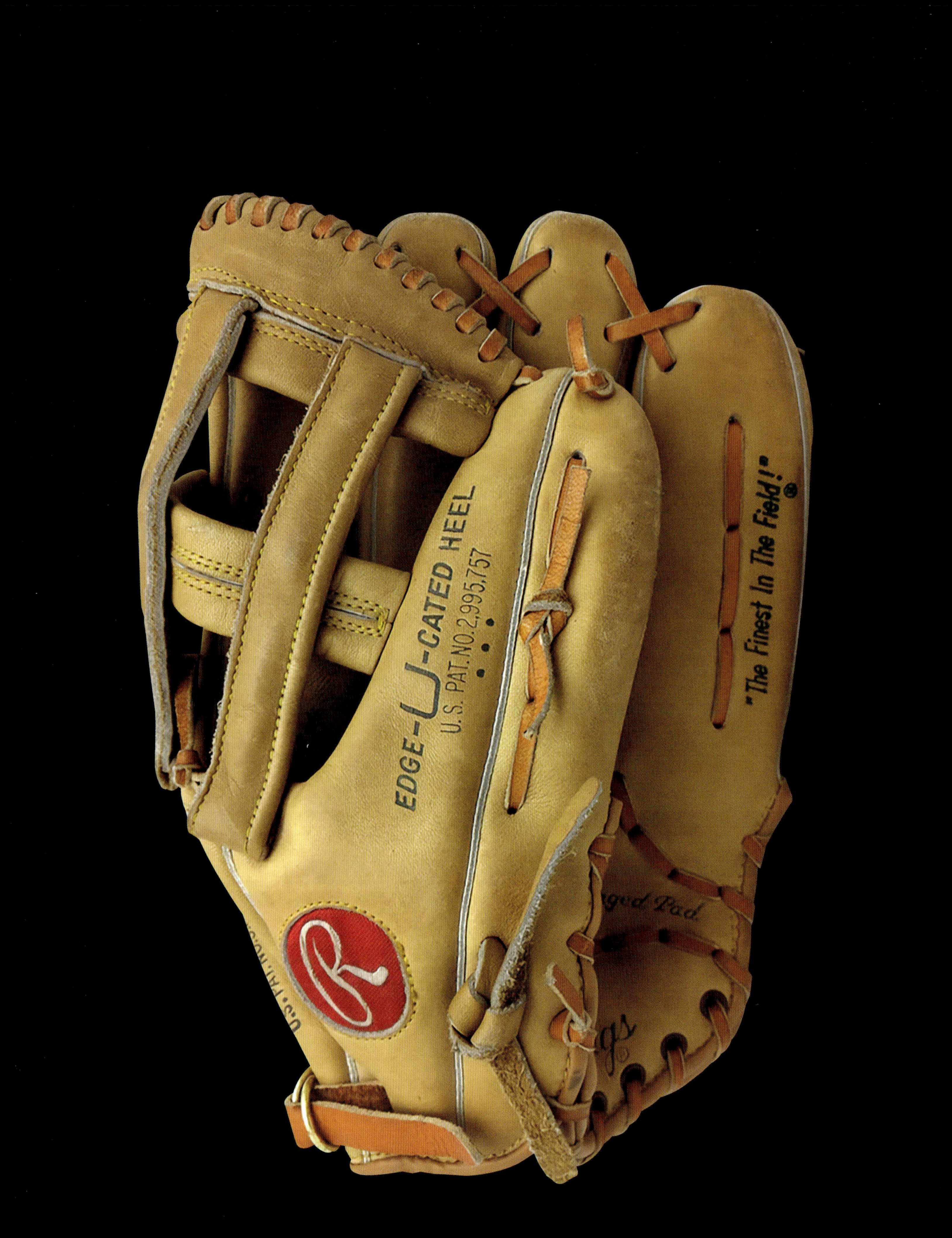
EDGE-U-CATED HEEL
U.S. PAT. NO. 2,995,757
"The Finest In The Field!"

MIKE SCHMIDT

The Total Package

Although the careers of Brooks Robinson and Mike Schmidt overlapped for only six seasons (1972–1977), baseball fans still debate who was the better third baseman from each end of the 100-mile stretch of Interstate 95 between Baltimore and Philadelphia. Both made it into Cooperstown's Hall of Fame at the hot corner. But which player was better?

There is no doubt that Schmidt was the greatest ballplayer to ever put on a Philadelphia Phillies uniform during the 18 years he spent playing in the City of Brotherly Love. But was he better than Brooks, the man known as "The Human Vacuum Cleaner"? Was Schmidt the game's best all-around third baseman? Robinson won 16 Gold Glove Awards and an MVP Award during his 23 seasons wearing a Baltimore Orioles uniform, but he only hit half the number of homers that Schmidt walloped. Was Schmidt more the total package at third base?

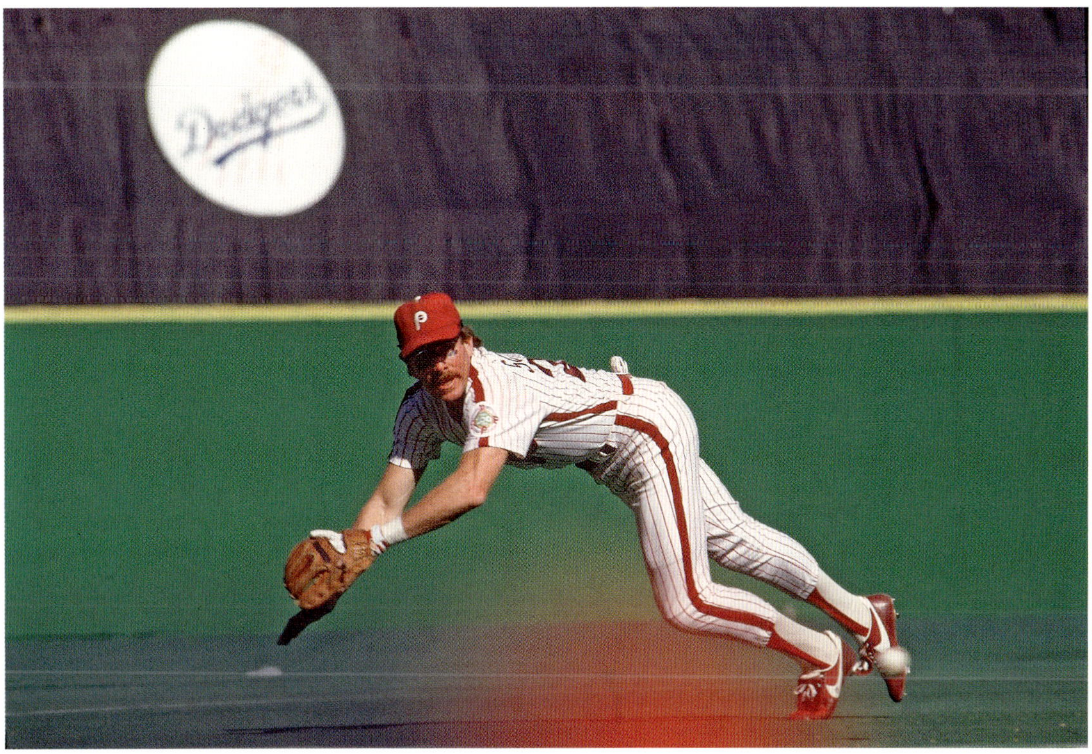

Many of Mike Schmidt's 10 Gold Gloves were won using a Rawlings 1061 model glove (opposite) with an H-Web design and Edge-U-Cated Heel feature. Schmidt, the Philadelphia Phillies' third baseman, makes a diving and fielding catch against the Baltimore Orioles in Game Four of the 1983 World Series (above).

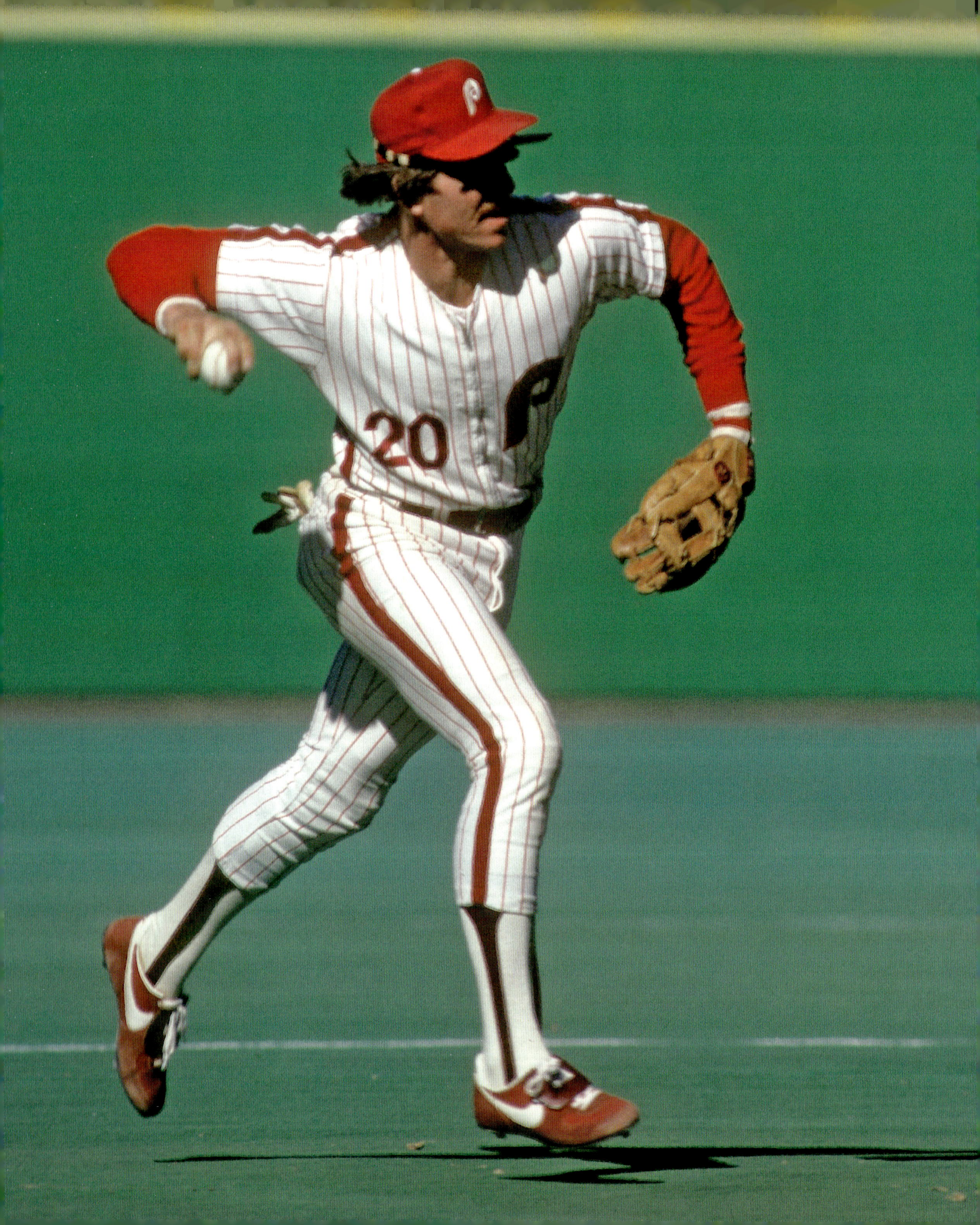
20

Perhaps a hint of why he may have been considered the best lies in the words inscribed on Schmidt's 1995 Hall of Fame plaque: "unprecedented combination of power and defense with unusual mixture of strength, coordination, and speed made him one of the game's greatest third basemen." Schmidt's physicality created a defensive wall at third base while he clubbed home runs year after year until he became the 14th player—and the youngest in MLB history—to exceed the 500-home-run mark, before finishing his career with 548 four-baggers. Eight times he was the NL home-run leader (six of those seasons as the MLB leader). Only Babe Ruth had more home-run titles (12).

Consistency was a cornerstone of Schmidt's career. Three times he hit at least 40 balls over the wall to go along with 10 seasons of 30 or more home runs. His 1980 total of 48 homers was the most in a season by a third baseman until it was later passed by Alex Rodriguez in 2007. (Rodriguez's record, 54, still holds today.) Schmidt hit 509 of his 548 home runs while playing third base, which today remains the career record at the position.

The year 1980 was Schmidt's ninth season in the big leagues. He had already led the NL in home runs three times and proven his worth in the field with outstanding defense. But things were about to change for Schmidt (who had been named the team captain) and the Philadelphia Phillies. It would become one of the most epic seasons in the history of the franchise, and Schmidt would make history on his own as he guided the Phillies to the NL pennant. Since the Fall Classic's inception in 1903, the Phillies had only been to the World Series twice (1915 and 1950). Each time they came up short of a world championship. Their third time to the postseason finale in 1980 was the charm.

Powered by Schmidt's major-league home-run title and his NL RBI crown, the Phillies won the pennant and then the World Series over the Kansas City Royals in six games. Schmidt received the first of his three NL MVP Awards and was also selected as the World Series MVP after batting .381 (8 for 21) with two homers and seven RBIs. Schmidt had found his potential and became the backbone of a team that went on to win another NL pennant three years later. They lost the 1983 Series to the Orioles in five games, but Schmidt continued to pad his Hall of Fame career. His 313 home runs during the 1980s were the most in the majors. He was the NL's MVP again in 1981 and 1986, and he continued playing stellar defense throughout his years in the big leagues.

Schmidt was selected to 12 All-Star Games during his career. His continued fielding excellence brought home 10 Gold Glove Awards—including nine consecutively between 1976 and 1984. He is one of only three players in MLB history (along with Willie Mays and Ken Griffey Jr.) to win 10 Gold Gloves and hit at least 500 home runs and the only infielder ever to do so. Blessed with outstanding range and a strong arm, Schmidt finished in the top 10 in defensive WAR eight times during his career, while also leading NL third basemen six times in participating in double plays and seven times in assists.

By the end of his career, Schmidt was the all-time Phillies leader in over a dozen categories on offense, including career home runs, RBIs, and walks. In 1983, when the Phillies celebrated their 100th anniversary, the Philadelphia fans voted Schmidt the greatest player in the history of the franchise. With his powerful offense and exceptional defense, Schmidt was the total package, helping transform the Phillies into perennial contenders.

Schmidt makes a play at third base during a game in the 1980s.

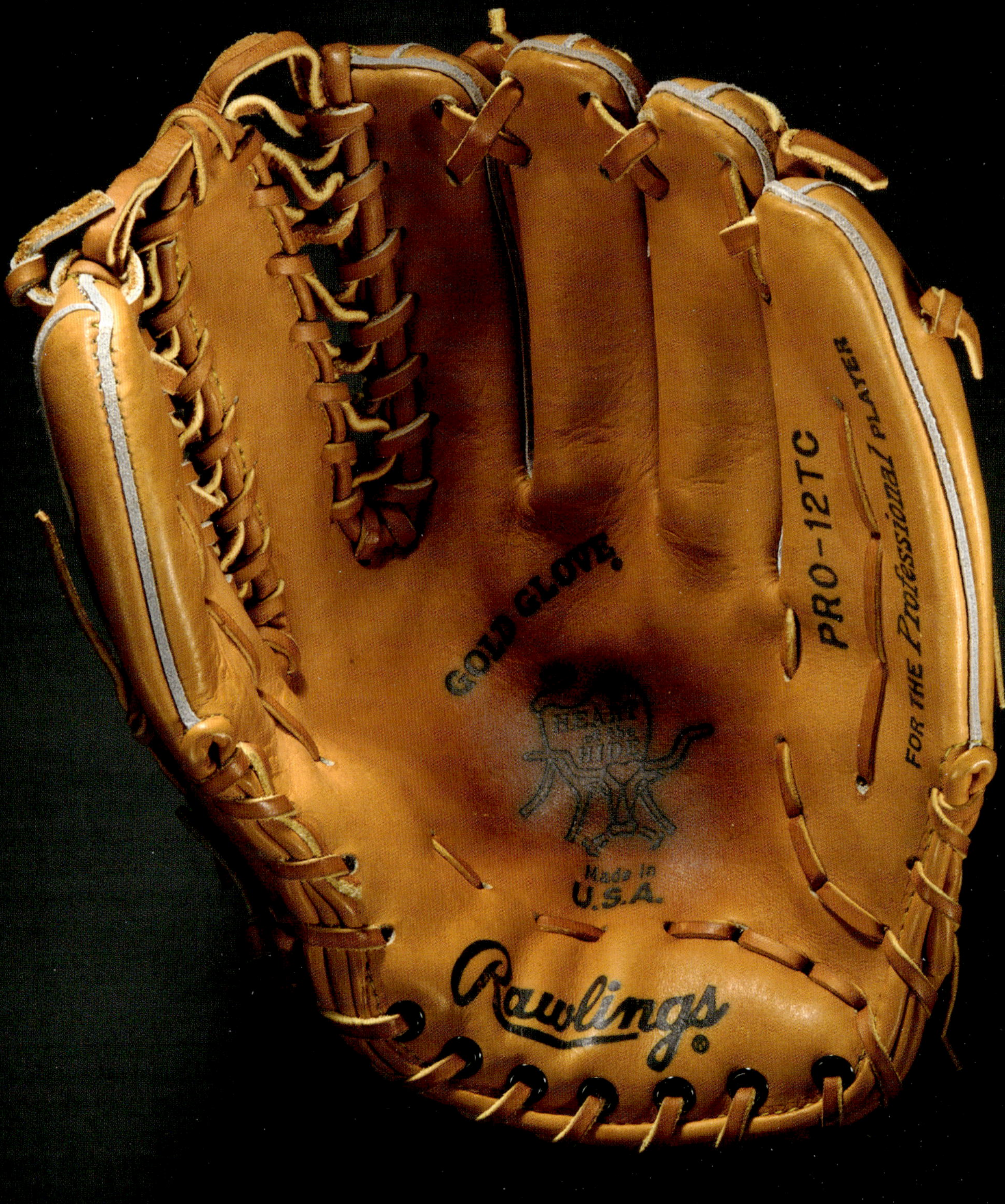
GOLD GLOVE
PRO-12TC
FOR THE Professional PLAYER
Made in
U.S.A.
Rawlings

OZZIE SMITH

The Wizard of Oz

Throughout the 20th century, the St. Louis Cardinals have had three generations of great shortstops. It began with the original "Mr. Shortstop," Bobby Wallace, in the early 1900s and was followed by Marty Marion, the next player to be awarded the moniker in the 1940s. Marion's Rawlings glove of that era was even etched "Mr. Shortstop." The player known as "The Wizard of Oz" then inherited the title in the 1980s. While each player transformed the position, none had a more profound impact on the game than Ozzie Smith.

Smith's career began as a no-hit, all-glove trip through the San Diego Padres' system that turned into a journey down a yellow brick road paved with 13 consecutive Gold Glove Awards. Along the way he evolved into an offensive contributor to be reckoned with while becoming one of the greatest—if not *the* greatest—defensive shortstops of all time.

His nickname became more than just a play on his first name and an old Judy Garland movie. There was magic within the athleticism of his acrobatic style of play at shortstop. Few balls could ever go beyond his reach. Was it sorcery that guided every ball hit his way into his glove? And how was it always followed by a quick, on-time throw that beat each runner at first base or turned into a double play? By the end of his career, "The Wizard" had set six MLB fielding records among shortstops, including most assists, double plays, and chances accepted. He also led

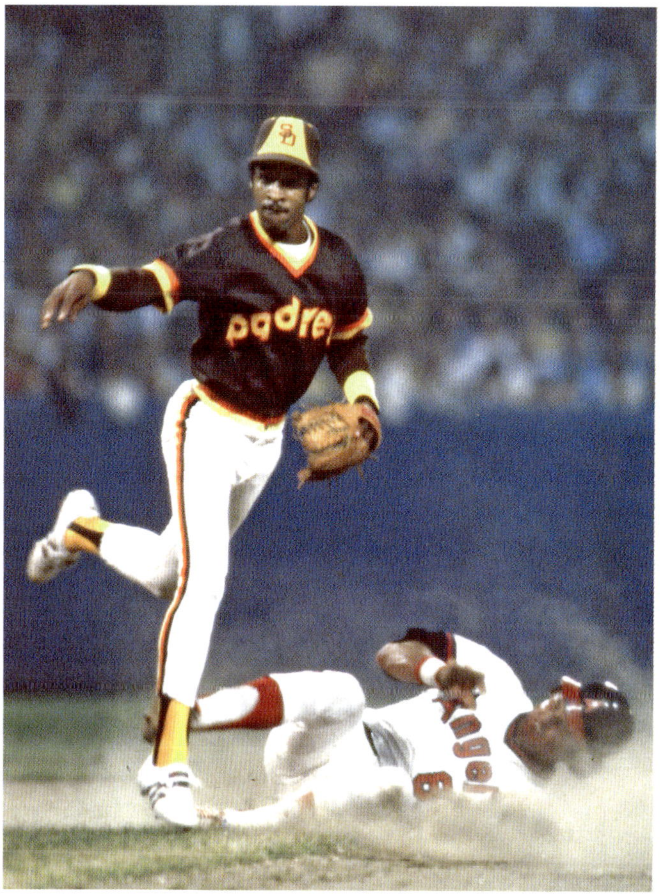

Ozzie Smith used what has been nicknamed a six-finger glove throughout his career, including this PRO-12TC model (opposite). Smith makes a play on the California Angels' Fred Lynn in the 1981 All-Star Game at Cleveland Municipal Stadium in Ohio (right).

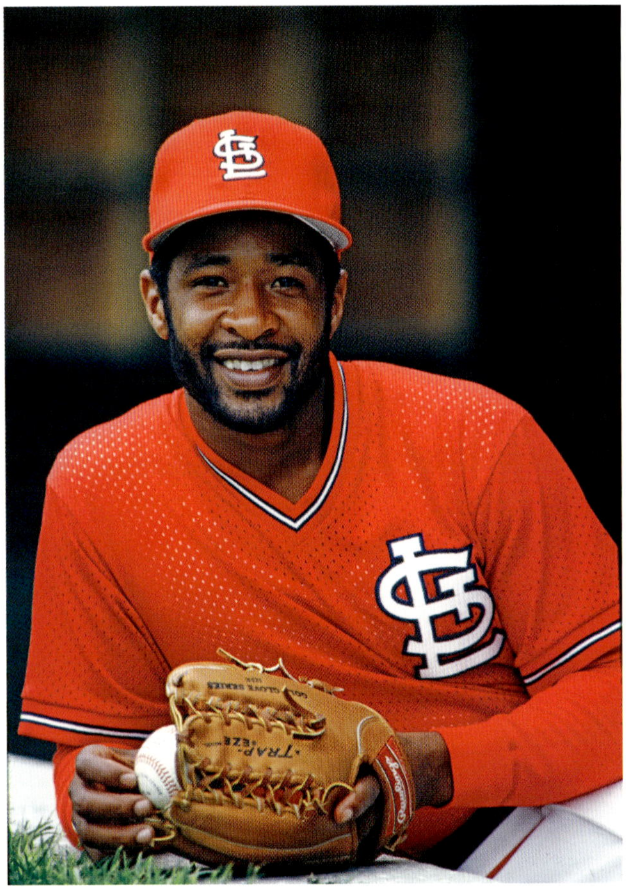

Smith spent his first four seasons with the San Diego Padres, winning two of his 13 Gold Glove Awards with the team. Then he spent the next 15 seasons with the St. Louis Cardinals and earned an additional 11 Gold Glove Awards.

the NL in fielding percentage eight times. What was the defensive perception of Smith? In a 1987 *Sports Illustrated* interview, former Mets shortstop Bud Harrelson said, "The thing about Ozzie is, if he misses a ball, you assume it's uncatchable. If any other shortstop misses a ball, your first thought is, 'Would Ozzie have had it?'"

With his revolutionary style of defense, Smith garnered the full attention of the baseball world while helping the Cardinals reach three World Series in the 1980s and win a championship in 1982. Throughout his career, he turned unimaginable plays into easy outs. One time in San Diego, in 1978, he did it without a glove. A groundball up the middle was thought a sure hit by all except the shortstop, who had a radar lock on the ball. After a few steps to his left, he dove to snare the ball with his extended glove hand when it took a strange bounce back in the other direction toward his hip. No problem for Smith. He merely reached back with his bare hand, caught the ball, hopped to his knees, and easily threw the batter out at first.

Even when he used his glove to make the catch, there was magic. While playing in St. Louis in a tied game in the ninth inning, the visitors had runners on first and second base. Their batter blooped a ball over the shortstop's head toward an indefensible spot in left-center field that looked like it would surely produce the tie-breaking run. With the Cardinals' left and center fielders charging in for the ball and the shortstop also in pursuit, a three-way player crash seemed imminent. But one of the players was Smith, who—with his back to the infield and his acrobatic ways—quickly redirected himself away from his teammates and snared the ball without a run scoring. The Phillies manager, John Felske, called it "one of the best, if not the best play, I've ever seen." To add to the magic and mystique of the day, Smith then scored the winning run for the Cardinals in the bottom of the ninth.

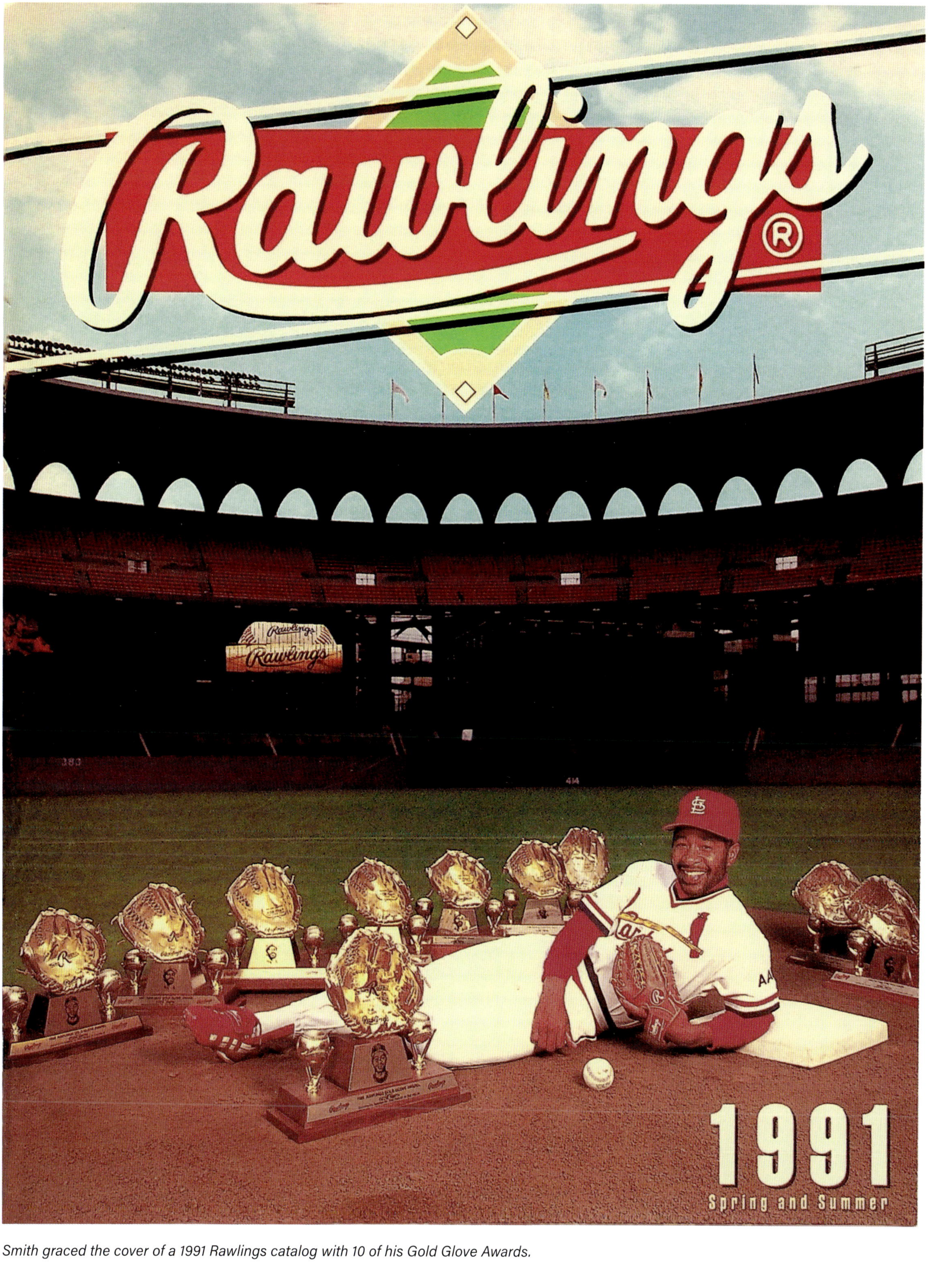

Smith graced the cover of a 1991 Rawlings catalog with 10 of his Gold Glove Awards.

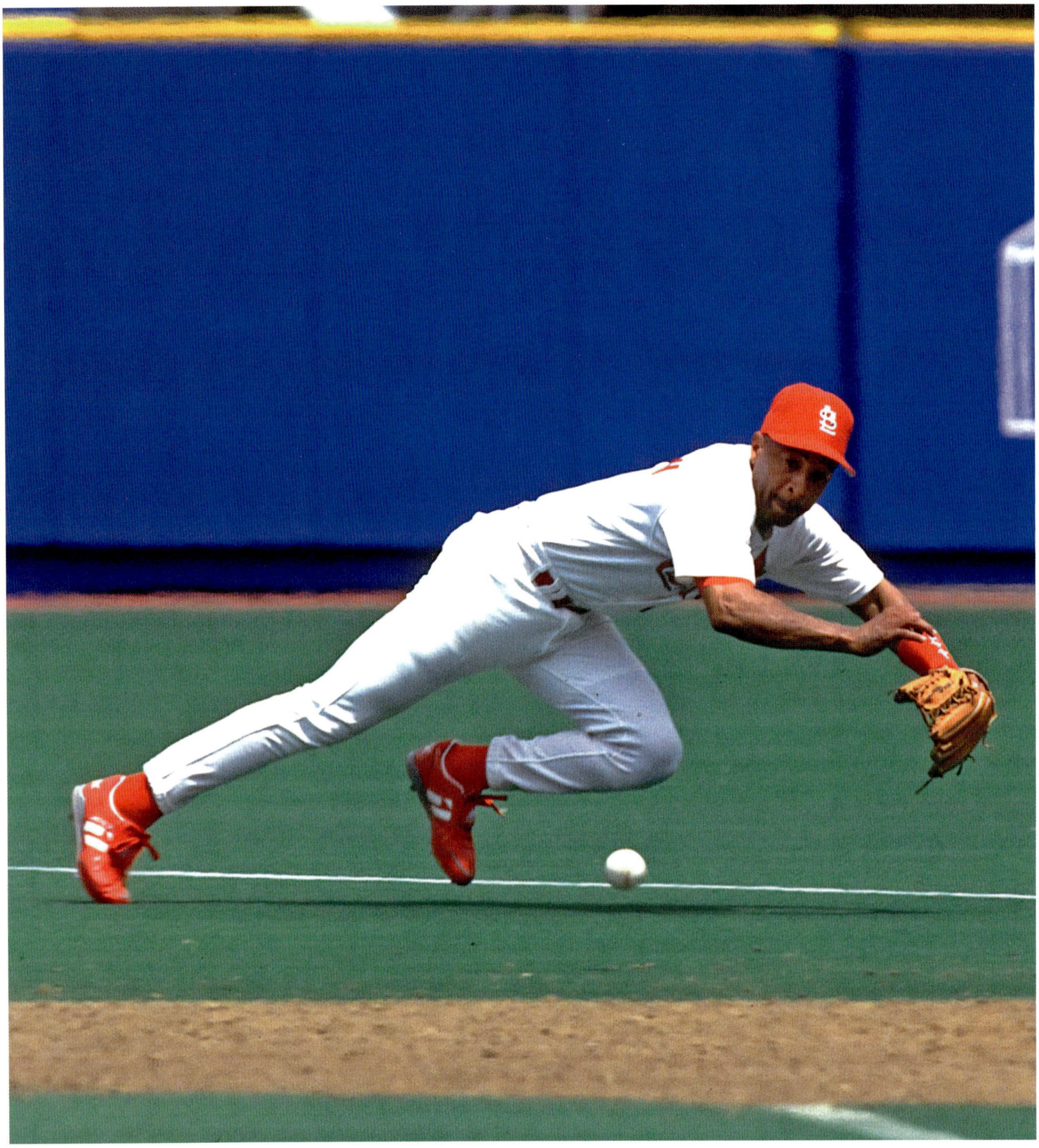

Smith's incredible range made him one of the greatest shortstops in the history of baseball.

Of the 276 former players inducted into baseball's Hall of Fame, only 62 were first-ballot selections. Four of them, including Smith, were shortstops. The others—Honus Wagner, Cal Ripken Jr., and Derek Jeter—were all talented players, but none of them could equal the defensive play of "The Wizard."

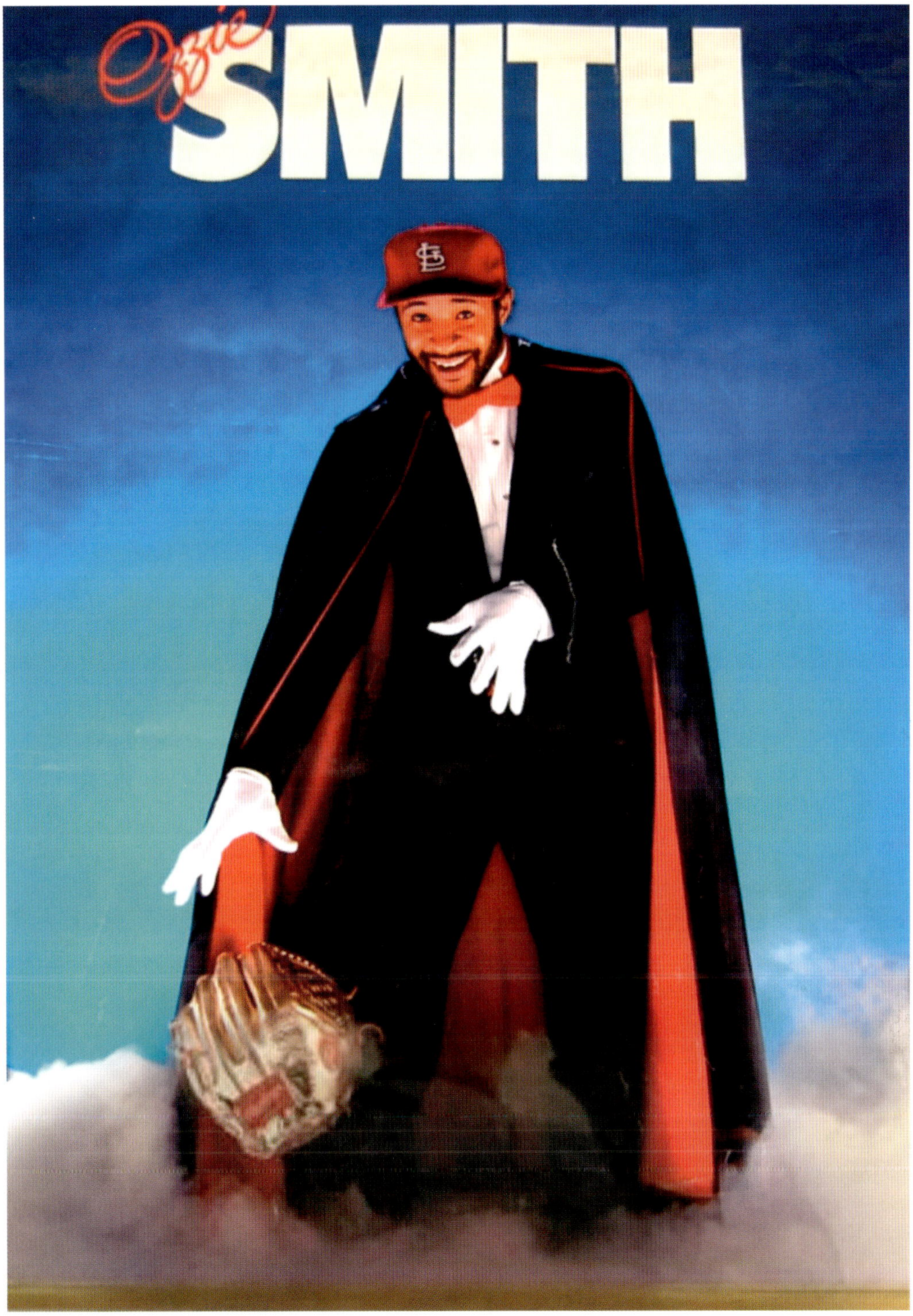

This early 1980s poster underscores Smith's nickname—"The Wizard"—and the magic within his glove.

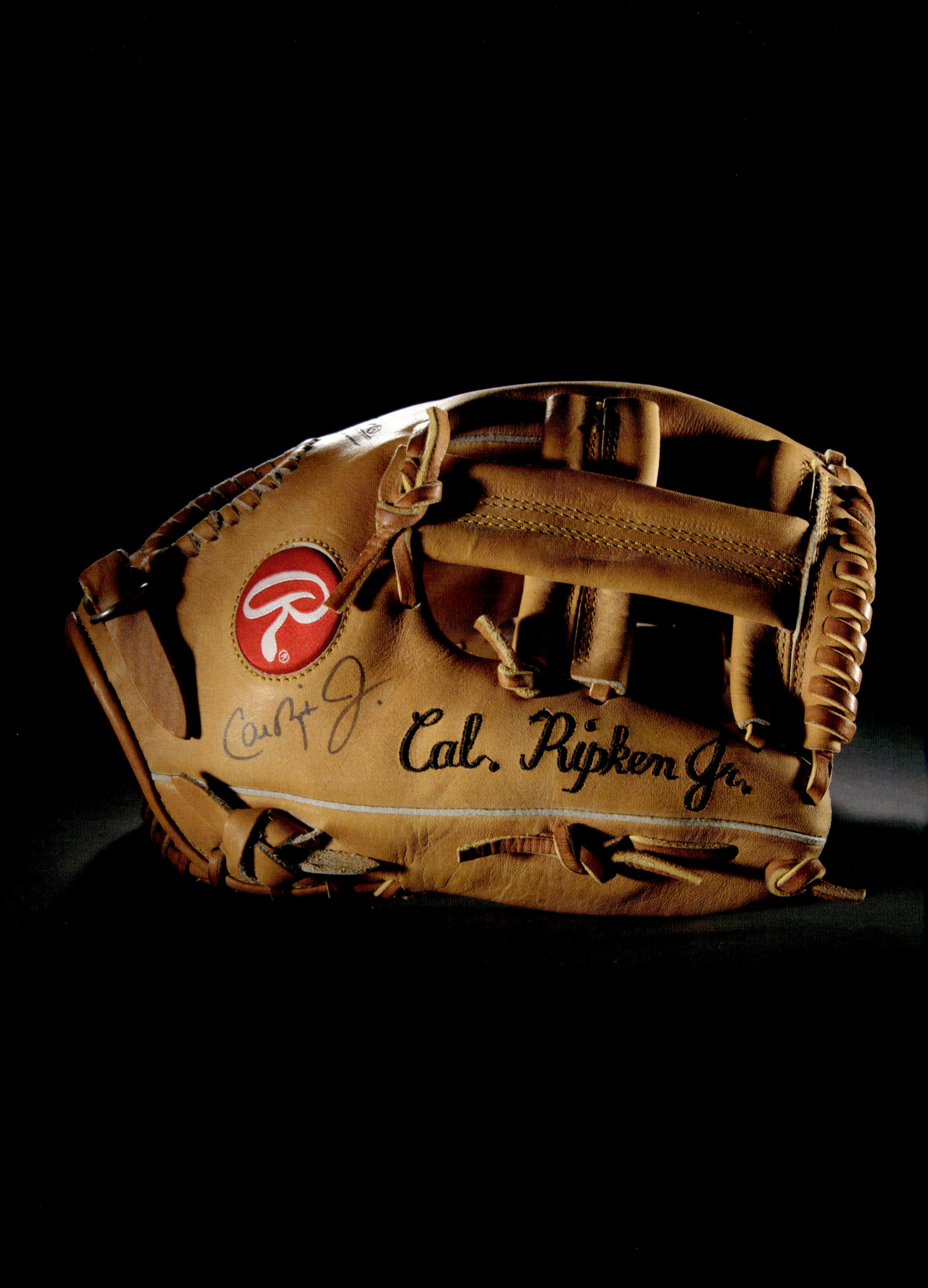
Cal. Ripken Jr.

CAL RIPKEN JR.

The Iron Man

It is easy to say that the Baltimore Orioles' Cal Ripken Jr. was an everyday player. Between May 30, 1982, and September 19, 1998, he played in every scheduled game—a total of 2,632 games over more than 16 years of his 21-year career—without taking a single day off. Of Ripken's 3,001 career games played, 88 percent were played back-to-back, earning him the nickname "The Iron Man." Only one other player in MLB history has played in more than 2,000 consecutive games—the New York Yankees' Lou Gehrig, who was affectionately labeled "The Iron Horse" a half century earlier. Ripken's streak was nearly three seasons longer than Gehrig's, whose record mark of 2,160 games ended on April 30, 1939, when he began feeling the awful effects of the amyotrophic lateral sclerosis (ALS) disease that would soon take his life.

But Ripken's streak also had a more important purpose. It was exactly what the sport needed following a contentious players' strike that shut down baseball on August 12, 1994. MLB cancelled not only the remaining regular-season games but also the playoffs and World Series. The conflict between the players and owners continued into the start of the next year's spring training, with the owners planning to play the season with "replacement players"—an action that only further stirred the pot of discontent. When a settlement was finally reached, the new season was postponed for three weeks and an abbreviated 144-game season was scheduled.

The work stoppage left a bad taste in the mouths of baseball fans, who

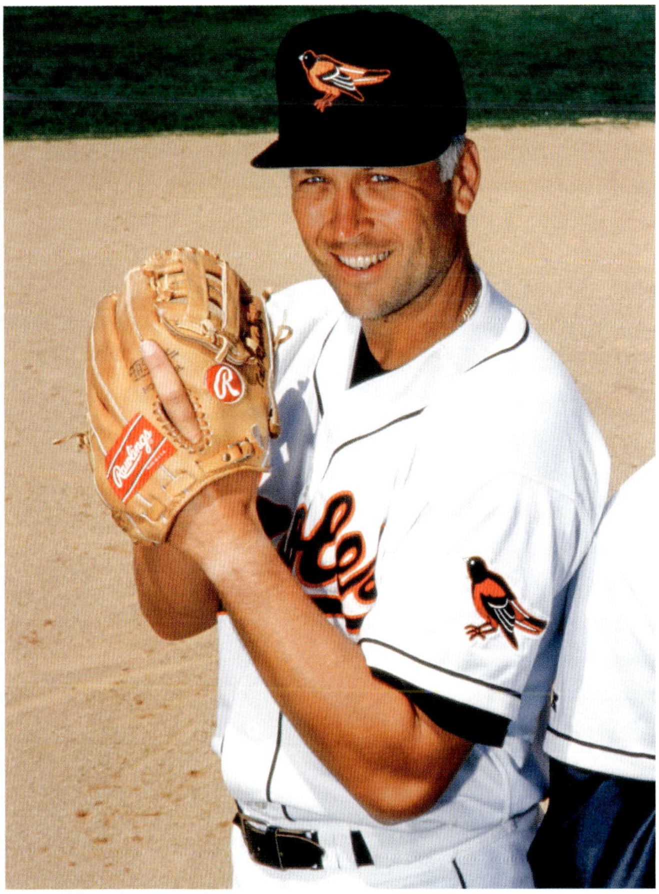

Cal Ripken Jr. used this Rawlings PRO-6BFB-SO model glove (opposite) during his career. Ripken (right) stands ready to take the field with a Rawlings Fastback glove.

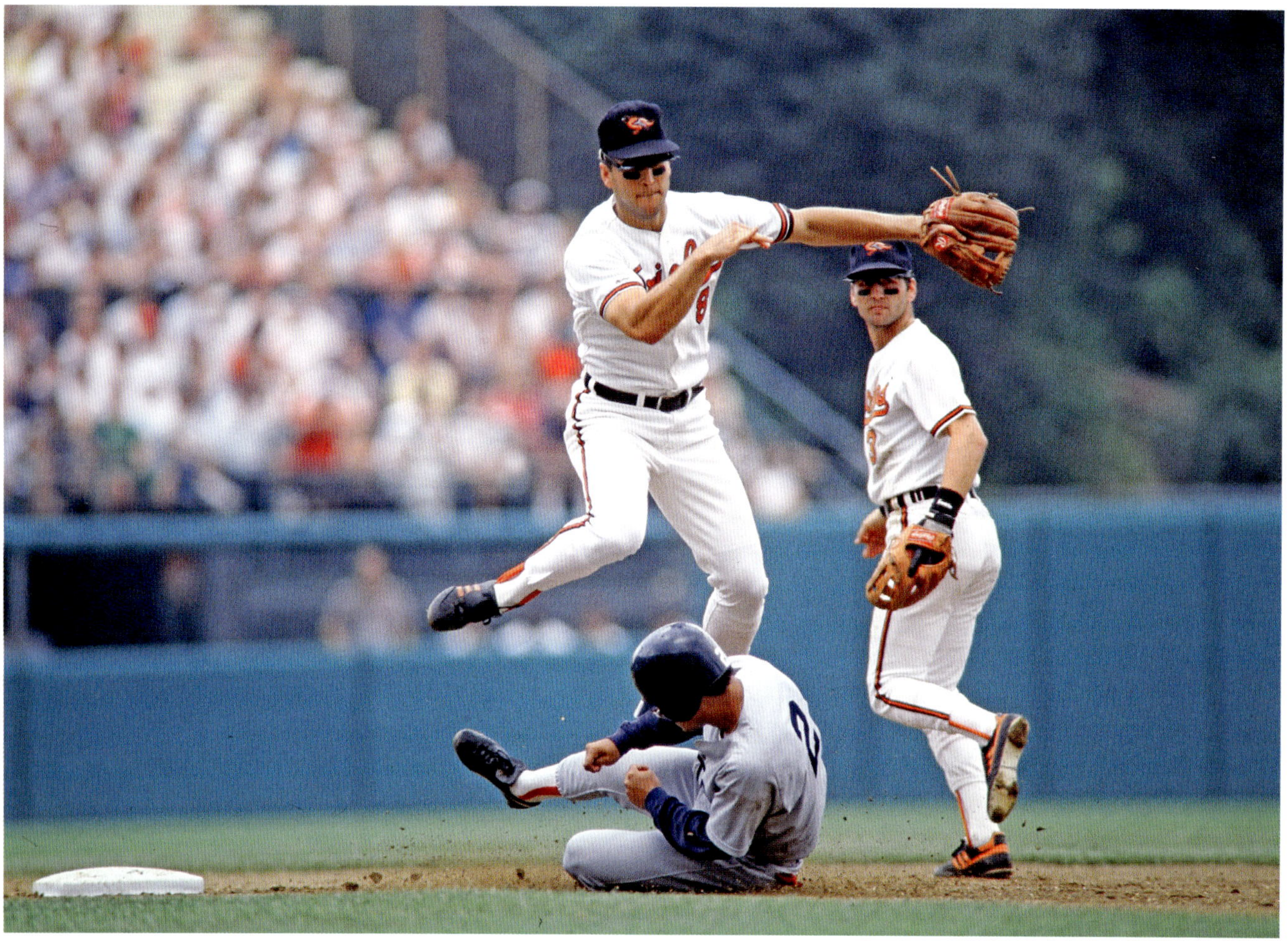

Ripken turns a double play alongside his brother, Billy, the Baltimore Orioles' second baseman.

wondered what the future held for the game. But that sour taste soon turned sweet as the fan base rallied around Ripken's countdown toward Gehrig's 2,160-game record, one deemed by many as unbreakable. On the night of September 5, 1995, Ripken took the field and tied Gehrig's milestone with a bang, collecting three hits, including a home run, to set the stage for the next evening, when he homered again in the bottom of the fourth inning. Over five million fans were glued to their television sets, waiting for the bottom of the fifth inning, when the game would become official and Ripken's streak would reach 2,161. With the Orioles leading and the third out made in the top of the fifth, the stage was set for one of baseball's greatest moments—a Camden Yards celebration that included a 20-plus-minute delay as Ripken took a victory lap around the stadium for the congratulatory fans, who had by now forgotten the upheaval of baseball's labor dispute. The tonic that was Ripken became the salve that healed MLB's ills.

There is, however, more to Ripken than just this streak. A player must be good to be in the lineup day in and day out, and Ripken was exceptionally good. He made his big-league debut late in the season on August 10, 1981, to maintain his rookie eligibility and walk away with the 1982 AL Rookie of the Year Award. The following year, in the Orioles' 1983 World Series championship season, Ripken took home the first of his two AL MVP Awards after leading the league in hits, doubles, and runs scored. He won the award again in 1991, when he became the first AL player to claim the award while playing on a losing team. Despite Ripken batting .323 with 34 home runs and 114 runs scored, the 1991 Orioles finished in sixth place in the AL East Division with a 67–95 record.

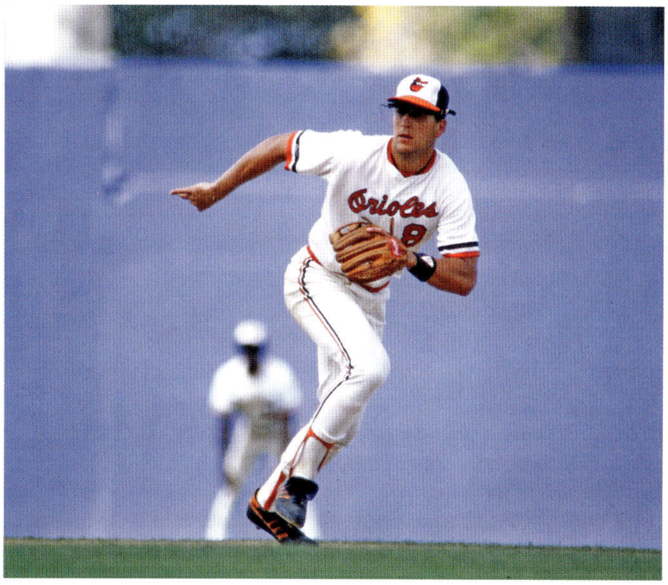

Ripken was a model of consistency for 2,632 straight games.

Ripken only played in that one Fall Classic in 1983, but he was selected to 19 consecutive Midsummer Classics (1983–2001)—missing the All-Star Game only in his first two big-league seasons. During the first 15 years of his career, Ripken played exclusively at shortstop before transitioning to third base for his final five seasons. His size and power transformed the shortstop position across MLB. At six feet, four inches, the future Hall of Famer (inducted in 2007) "ripped" 353 of his 431 career home runs at shortstop, the most in the history of the game played at that position. Ripken and Alex Rodriguez are the only shortstops to have hit over 300 home runs (Rodriguez hit 345). The combination of power to go along with his 3,184 career hits made Ripken one of baseball's more formidable and consistent forces in the game.

But Ripken was not just about offense. He was a complete player. Defensively, Ripken's two Gold Gloves at shortstop reflect his mastery of that position. Four times he led the AL in fielding percentage at shortstop and another time at third base. He was regularly atop the league's leaderboard for assists, putouts, and double plays. Ripken proved he could do it all, and he did so with a streak that brought back fans' belief in and love of the game.

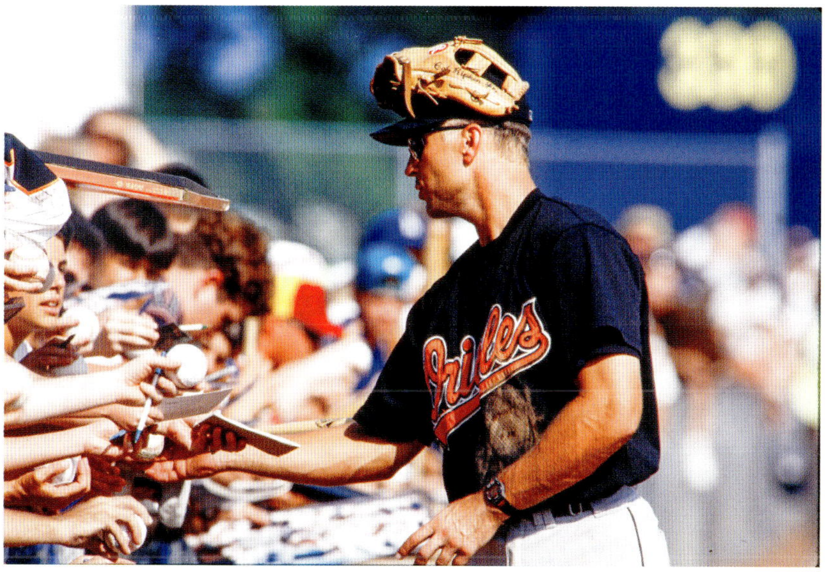

Ripken, shown here signing autographs, was also consistent in supporting his fans.

RYNE SANDBERG

Ryno

Described as a "sure-handed second baseman with power and speed" on his Hall of Fame plaque, Ryne Sandberg spent 16 seasons in the big leagues as a poster child for dignity and professionalism within the game. At the same time, he set records at the plate and in the field. By the end of his career, he was looked upon as one of the best to ever play his second-base position.

Sandberg's big-league debut began with a 13-game stint for the Philadelphia Phillies in September 1981. After the season, when the Phillies and the Chicago Cubs traded shortstops (Larry Bowa for Iván DeJesús), the Cubs general manager and former Phillies field manager insisted that Sandberg be a part of the trade coming to Chicago. In his first season in the Windy City, Sandberg found himself at third base for 133 games. Despite not being his natural position, he fared well, batting .271 and stealing 32 bases while coming in sixth in the NL Rookie of the Year voting.

The next season, Sandberg was moved back to second base and won the first of nine consecutive Gold Glove Awards (1983–1991). He was the first NL player to receive a Gold Glove in his first season after changing positions. In 1984, Sandberg was chosen for the first of 10 consecutive All-Star Game selections, and his play took the Cubs to the postseason for the first time since 1945. Sandberg scored 114 runs that year, the first of three seasons in which he led the league in that category as well as topping the leaderboard in triples (19). His .314 batting average, 19 home runs, and 32 stolen bases cemented Sandberg's selection as the 1984 NL MVP—which had last been won by a Cub in 1959, when Ernie Banks took the award for the second consecutive year.

The career .285 hitter remained a steady offensive threat who began adding power to his swing each season; in 1990, he led the NL with 40 home runs after hitting 30 the year before. Sandberg also led the league in runs and total bases that year while reaching the 100-RBI mark for the first time, something he would do again the following season. When he won the home-run title in 1990, Sandberg moved into Hall of Fame territory as the first second baseman to ever hit more than 30 home runs in consecutive seasons and to lead the league in home runs since Rogers Hornsby's efforts in 1925. When the 10-time All-Star retired from the game in 1997, at the age of 38, he had hit more home runs (277) playing second base than any other second baseman in the majors. (In subsequent decades, both Jeff Kent and Robinson Canó would surpass his home-run mark.)

Ryne Sandberg used this Rawlings PRO SP-B model glove, with a Gold Glove Award patch partially visible across the back, during part of his 16-year career.

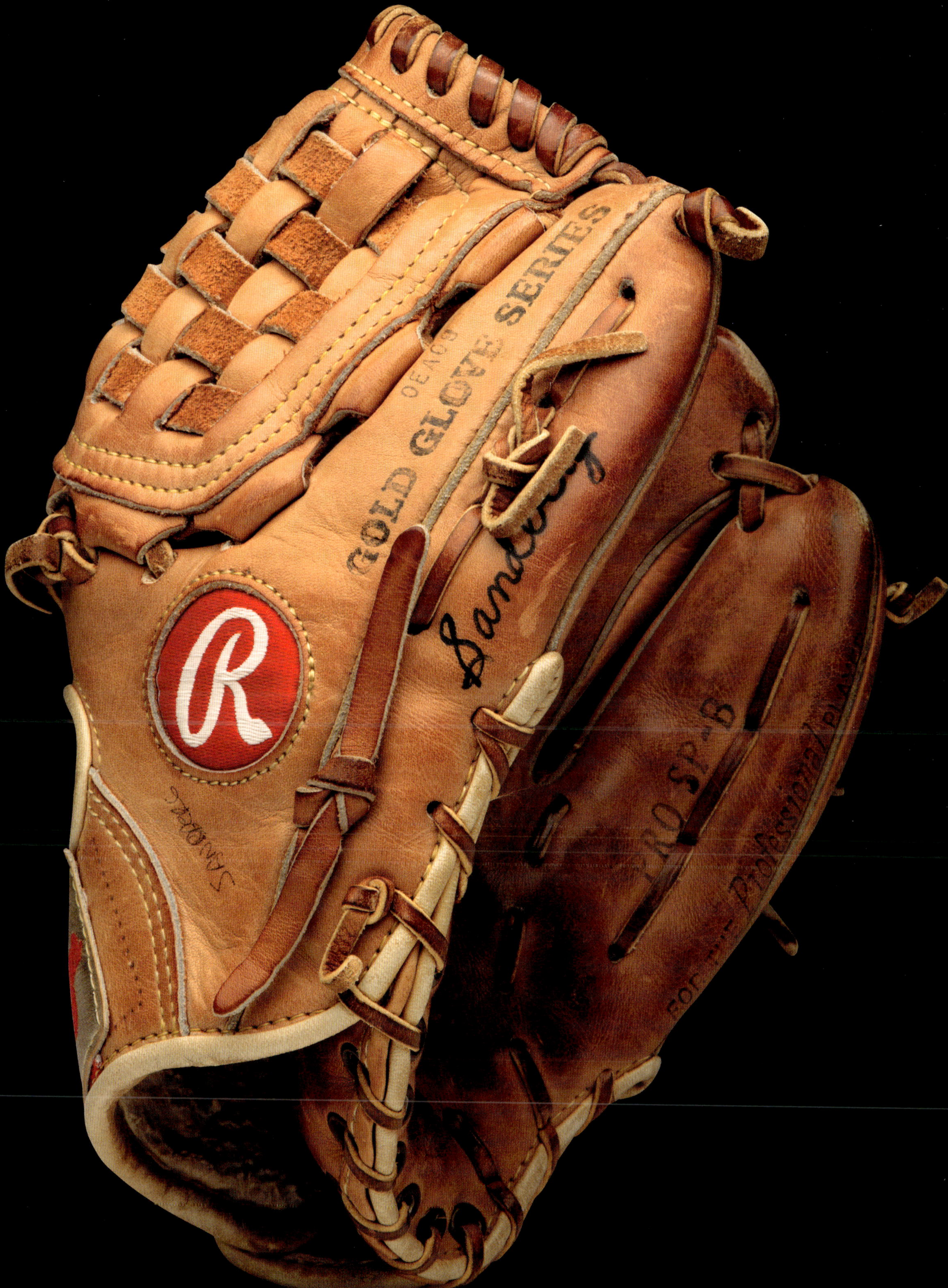
GOLD GLOVE SERIES
PRO SP-B

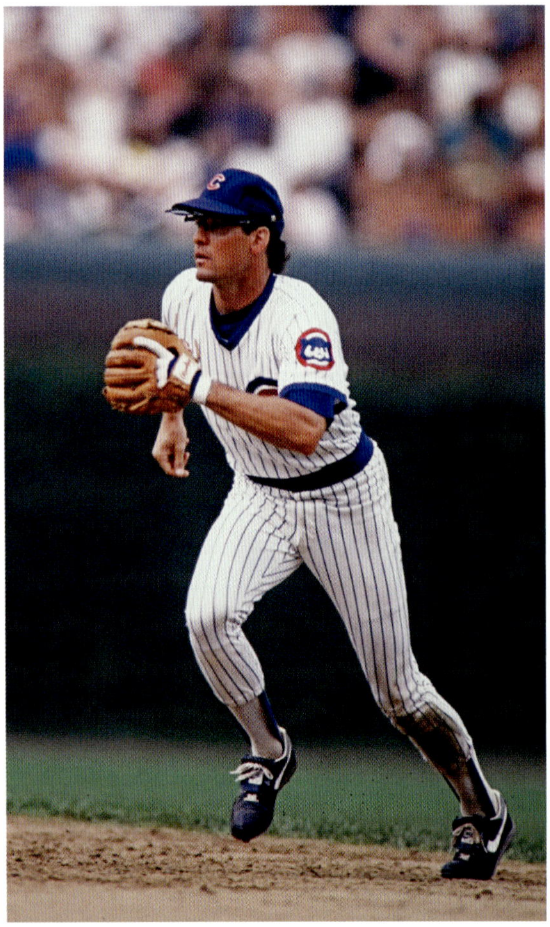

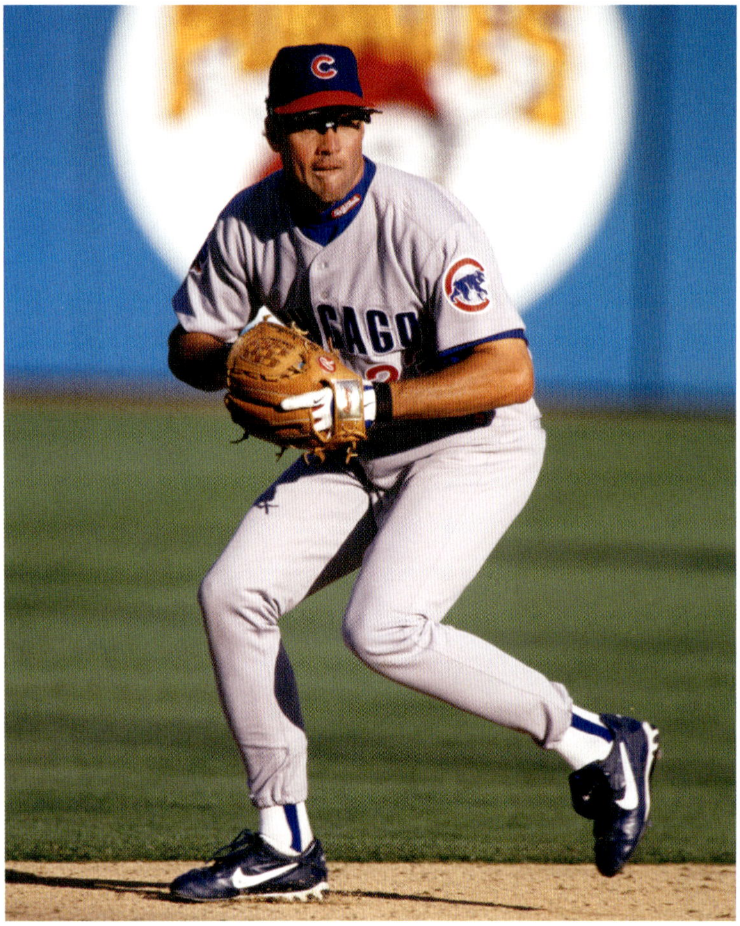

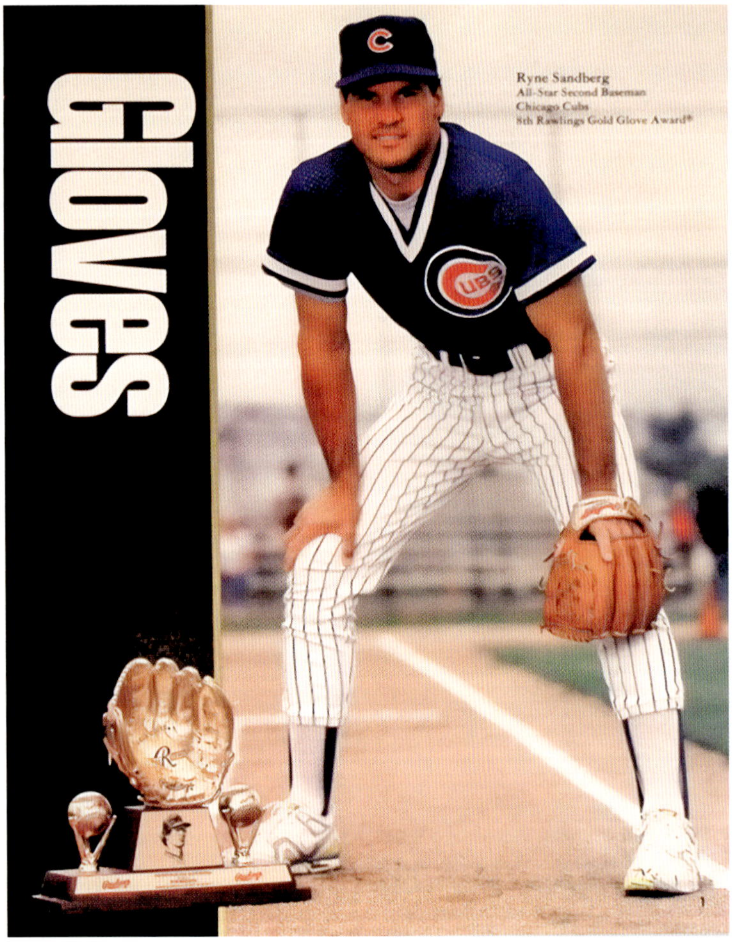

In 15 seasons playing second base, Sandberg (above and left) was a 10-time All-Star who won nine Gold Glove Awards. In 1992, the future Hall of Famer (opposite) signed a contract to become the highest-paid major leaguer at that time.

In 1992, Sandberg had signed a new $7.2 million annual contract to become the highest-paid major leaguer ever to play the game at that time, and that big salary was not just for batting. His MLB records weren't just being set at the plate. In the field, he set career records at second base for fielding percentage (.989) and consecutive errorless games in a season (90) and over two seasons (123). His nine Gold Gloves were the most by a second baseman until Roberto Alomar surpassed him with 10. Sandberg also led NL second basemen in assists seven times and fielding percentage four times. His 571 assists in 1983 were the most among Gold Glove–winning second basemen in the majors. With these supporting stats at the plate and in the field, it is easy to summarize Sandberg as a complete player worthy of his 2005 Hall of Fame induction.

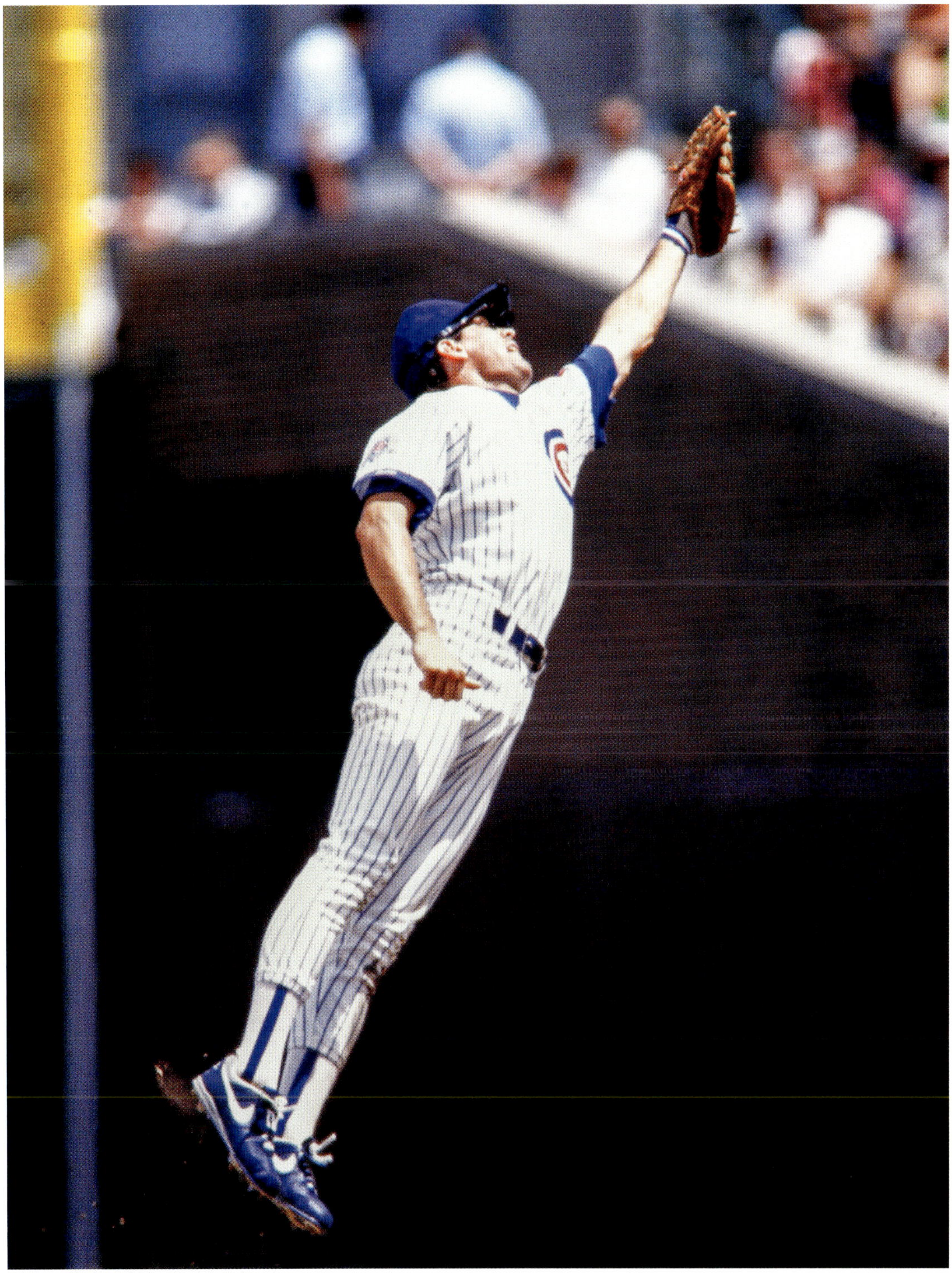

TONY GWYNN

Hitting Is Easy, Defense Is Hard

Tony Gwynn's Hall of Fame plaque describes baseball's hitting star as "an artisan with a bat." With MLB stadiums as his canvas and his bat as his brush, Gwynn stroked 3,131 hits en route to a career batting average of .338, the highest since Ted Williams retired in 1960 with a .344 career average. Gwynn's .338 remains the 22nd-highest recorded average in big-league history following the recent inclusion of six players from the Negro Leagues with higher averages. In 19 of his 20 MLB seasons, he batted over .300. The lone season he missed the mark was his first in the big leagues, when he played in only 54 games.

It was a career in which the accolades came quickly and elevated Gwynn into comparison to some of the best who ever played the game. In his first full season, in 1984, the player who would become known as "Mr. Padre" was selected to his first of 15 All-Star Games while batting .351 and winning the first of his eight NL batting titles, which tied the great Honus Wagner for the most wins in the NL. Gwynn's offense helped create two other firsts—the San Diego Padres' first NL West title and first NL pennant. Gwynn was continuously trying to improve his game. He was one of the first to study video of his at-bats, as well as pitchers and even umpire tendencies. In 1987, Gwynn hit .370, the highest batting average posted in the NL since Stan Musial hit .376 in 1948. And Gwynn exceeded his mark in 1994 and 1997, with averages of .394 and .372, respectively. His three consecutive NL batting titles (1987–1989) marked the first triple win since Musial's (1950–1952). Gwynn's batting kudos continued within the annals of baseball history.

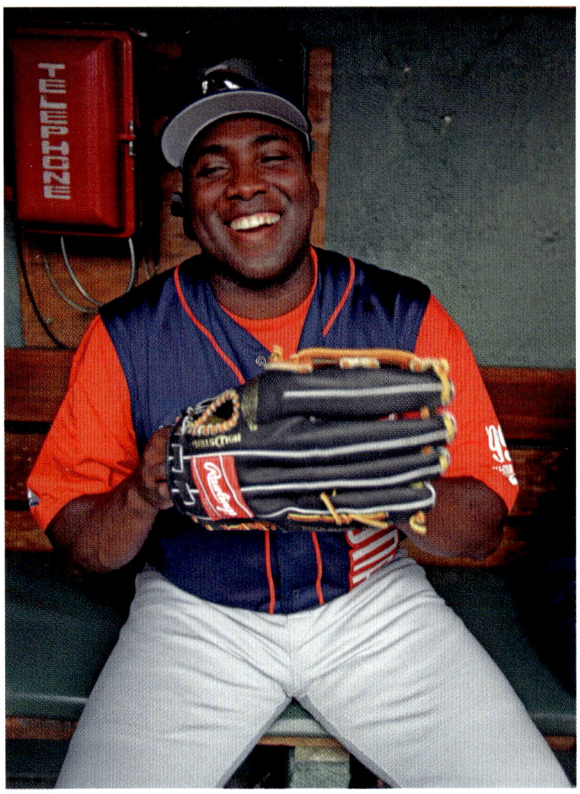

The defensive prowess of Tony Gwynn (left) was the result of hard work and led to five Gold Glove Awards. This black-and-tan PRO-HFB Fastback model (opposite) was one of Gwynn's gloves.

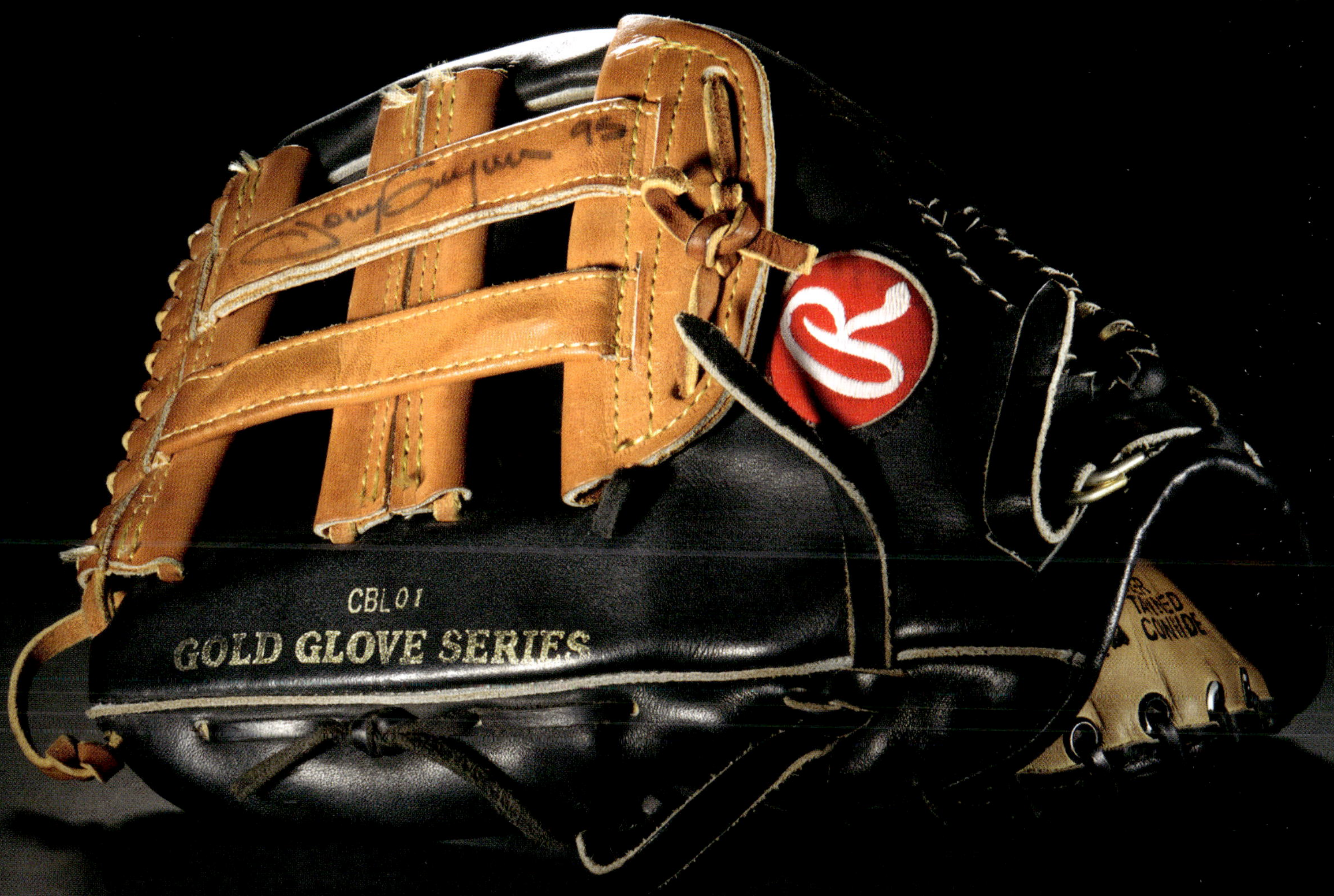
CBL01
GOLD GLOVE SERIES

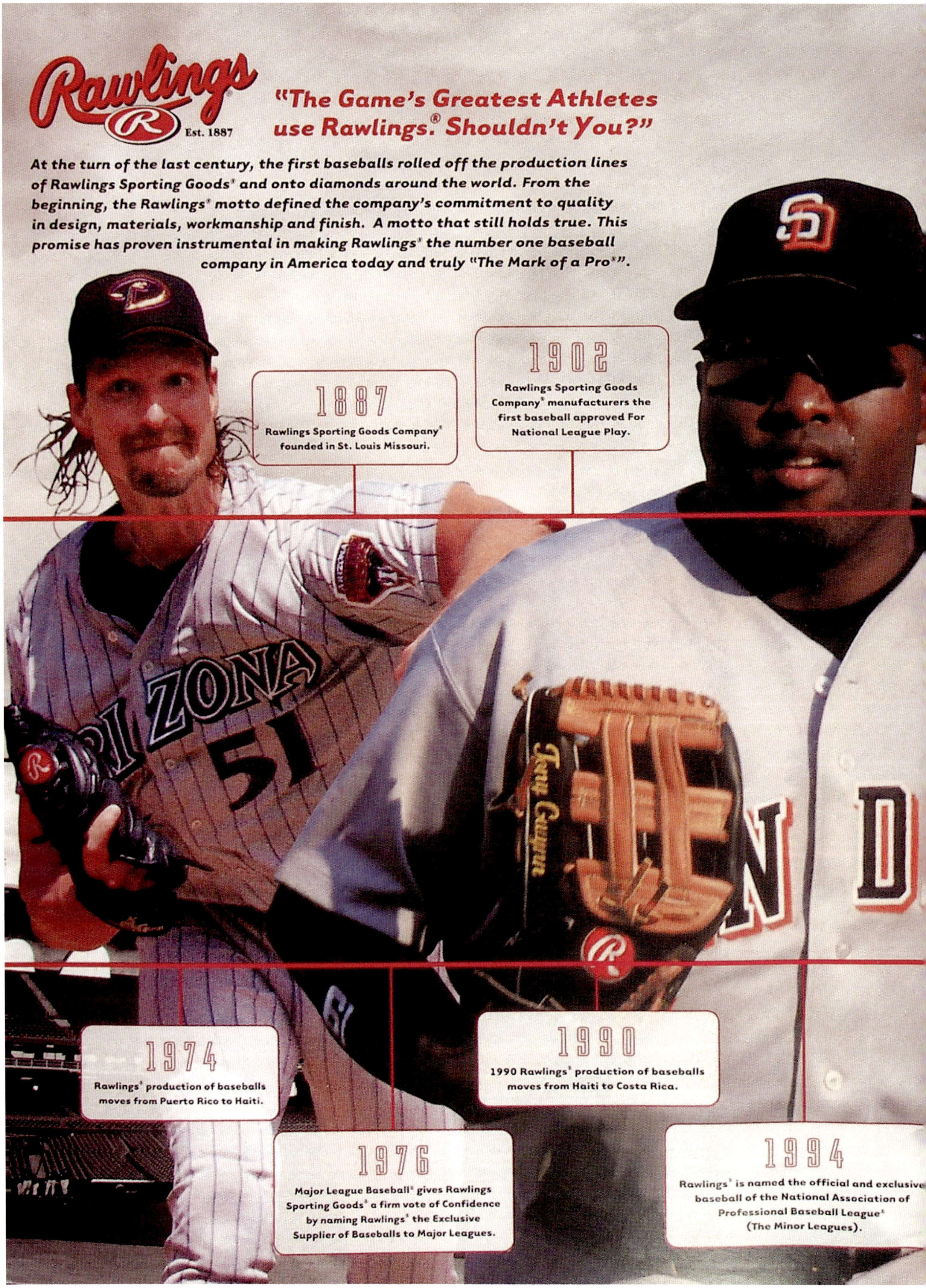
Rawlings
Est. 1887
"The Game's Greatest Athletes use Rawlings.® Shouldn't You?"
At the turn of the last century, the first baseballs rolled off the production lines of Rawlings Sporting Goods® and onto diamonds around the world. From the beginning, the Rawlings® motto defined the company's commitment to quality in design, materials, workmanship and finish. A motto that still holds true. This promise has proven instrumental in making Rawlings® the number one baseball company in America today and truly "The Mark of a Pro®".
1887
Rawlings Sporting Goods Company® founded in St. Louis Missouri.
1902
Rawlings Sporting Goods Company® manufacturers the first baseball approved For National League Play.
ARIZONA
51
Tony Gwynn
1974
Rawlings® production of baseballs moves from Puerto Rico to Haiti.
1976
Major League Baseball® gives Rawlings Sporting Goods® a firm vote of Confidence by naming Rawlings® the Exclusive Supplier of Baseballs to Major Leagues.
1990
1990 Rawlings® production of baseballs moves from Haiti to Costa Rica.
1994
Rawlings® is named the official and exclusive baseball of the National Association of Professional Baseball League® (The Minor Leagues).

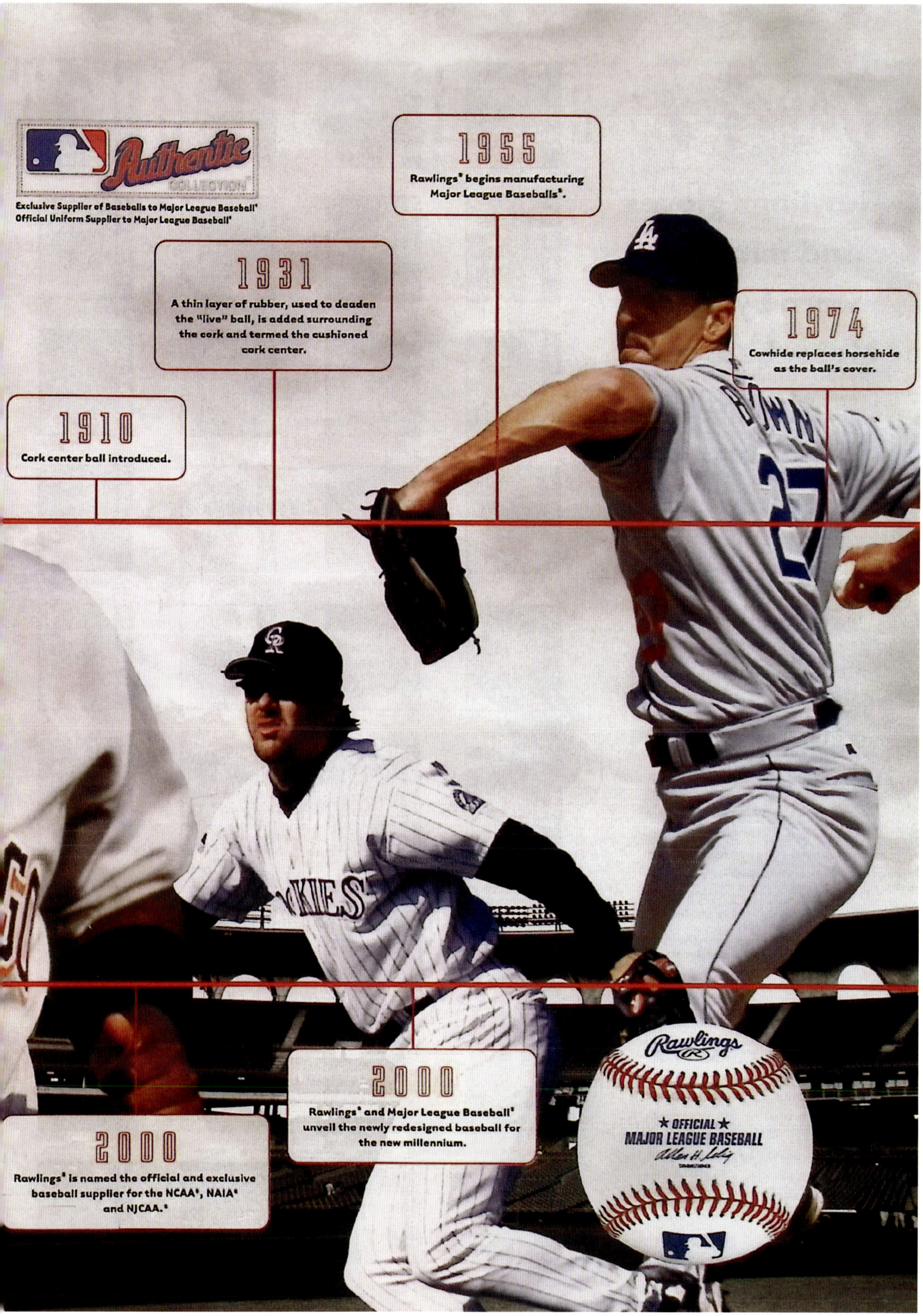

1910
Cork center ball introduced.

1931
A thin layer of rubber, used to deaden the "live" ball, is added surrounding the cork and termed the cushioned cork center.

1955
Rawlings® begins manufacturing Major League Baseballs®.

1974
Cowhide replaces horsehide as the ball's cover.

2000
Rawlings® is named the official and exclusive baseball supplier for the NCAA®, NAIA® and NJCAA.®

2000
Rawlings® and Major League Baseball® unveil the newly redesigned baseball for the new millennium.

Gwynn was front and center among many of baseball's best players in an early 2000s Rawlings advertisement (previous spread). In addition to his Gold Gloves, Gwynn (opposite) won eight batting titles and was selected to 15 All-Star Games.

His .394 average in 1994 was the NL's highest since the Giants' Hall of Famer Bill Terry hit .401 in 1930. Throughout that season, the question of whether Gwynn would become baseball's first .400 hitter since Ted Williams hit .406 in 1941 arose. The question was never answered. The players' strike began that year on August 12, which ended the season and Gwynn's chances at the plate. Baseball fans never got to see if Gwynn could close that .006 batting gap to get to the .400 mark. Despite the missed mark, Gwynn remained a model of hitting consistency. Thanks to this consistency, Gwynn recorded both his 2,000th and 3,000th hits on August 6—his mother's birthday—exactly six years apart.

During the later years of Gwynn's career, when home runs were becoming the novelty of nightly highlight reels, many fans thought he should have won an MVP Award or two. They thought his stats were being overshadowed by home-run stars—Gwynn only hit 135 home runs during his career. His style was to drive the ball to get on base. You can't touch home plate until you are safe at first, and that's what he did throughout his career. Gwynn once told a *Chicago Tribune* writer, "People put a premium on the home-run hitters. I know what I am. I'm a contact hitter and not a home-run hitter. I'm not an Andre Dawson, a Dale Murphy, an Eric Davis, or a Jeffrey Leonard. I'm a Tony Gwynn, and I'm not going to try to be something I'm not."

But one thing Gwynn did change and improve was his defense. In 1986, he won the first of his five Gold Glove Awards, telling reporters, "I was as proud of winning that Gold Glove as anything. I always felt I could hit. But when I came to the NL, I wasn't a real good fielder. I worked at that harder than my hitting for a long time. But people don't know that. I'd take hundreds of balls and work on my throwing." Gwynn worked on his routes to use his speed to chase down balls (he had stolen 56 bases in 1987), and he worked to strengthen his arm. Twice he led the NL in assists in right field, including once (in 1986) when he was the MLB leader, a season during which, in an August game, he threw out three Mets runners. His most important defensive play occurred during Game Three of the 1998 NL Division Series against the Houston Astros. Gwynn made a perfect throw to third base to nail Moisés Alou for a key out in the fifth inning, preserving the 2–1 win that helped Gwynn and the Padres get to their second World Series.

Gwynn struggled with health issues after his retirement due to his longtime use of chewing tobacco. Despite his early passing at the age of 54, the first-ballot Hall of Famer (inducted in 2007) continues to be remembered as one of the most consistent pure hitters of his generation, who also just happened to be one of the top right fielders in the game.

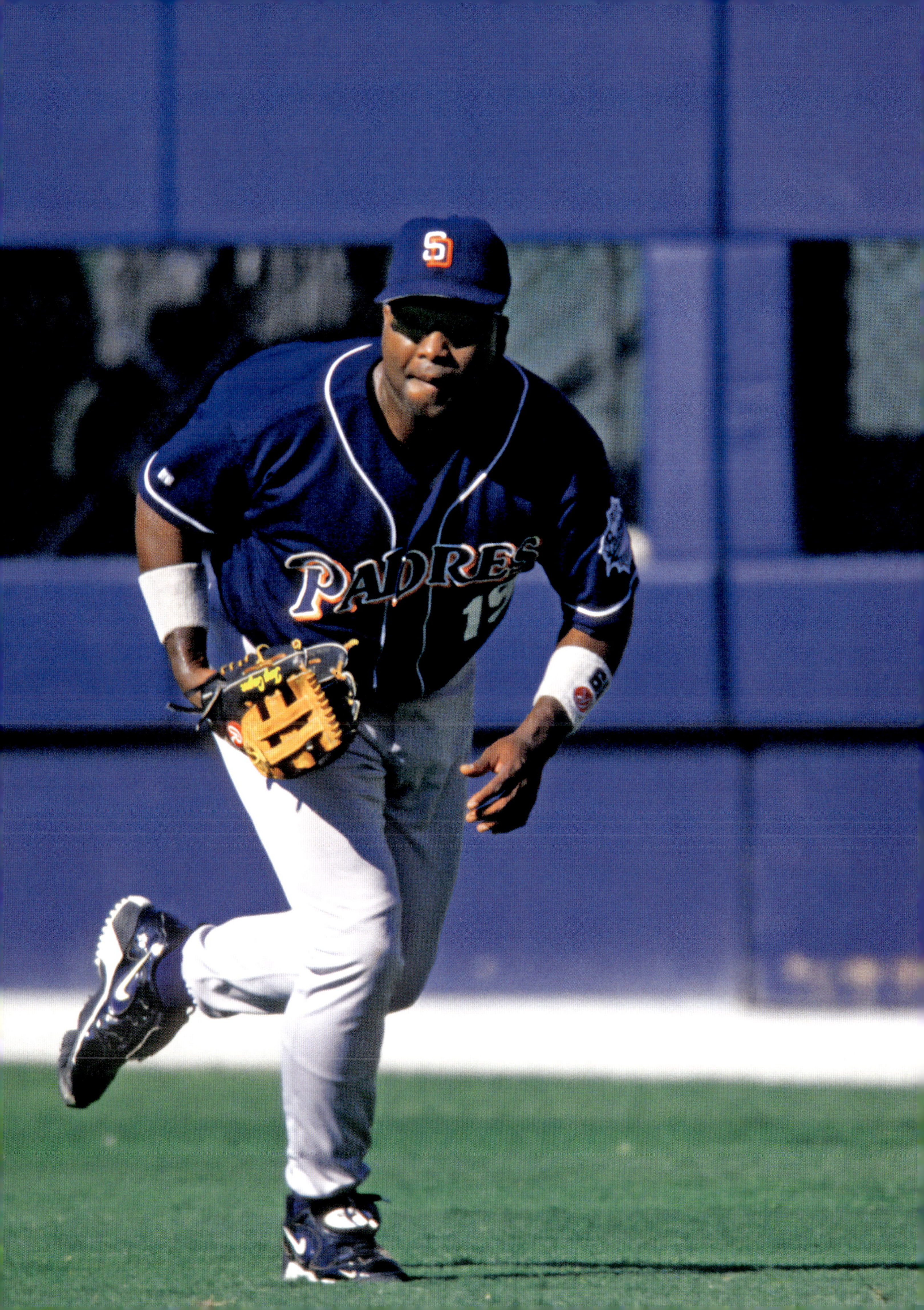
PADRES

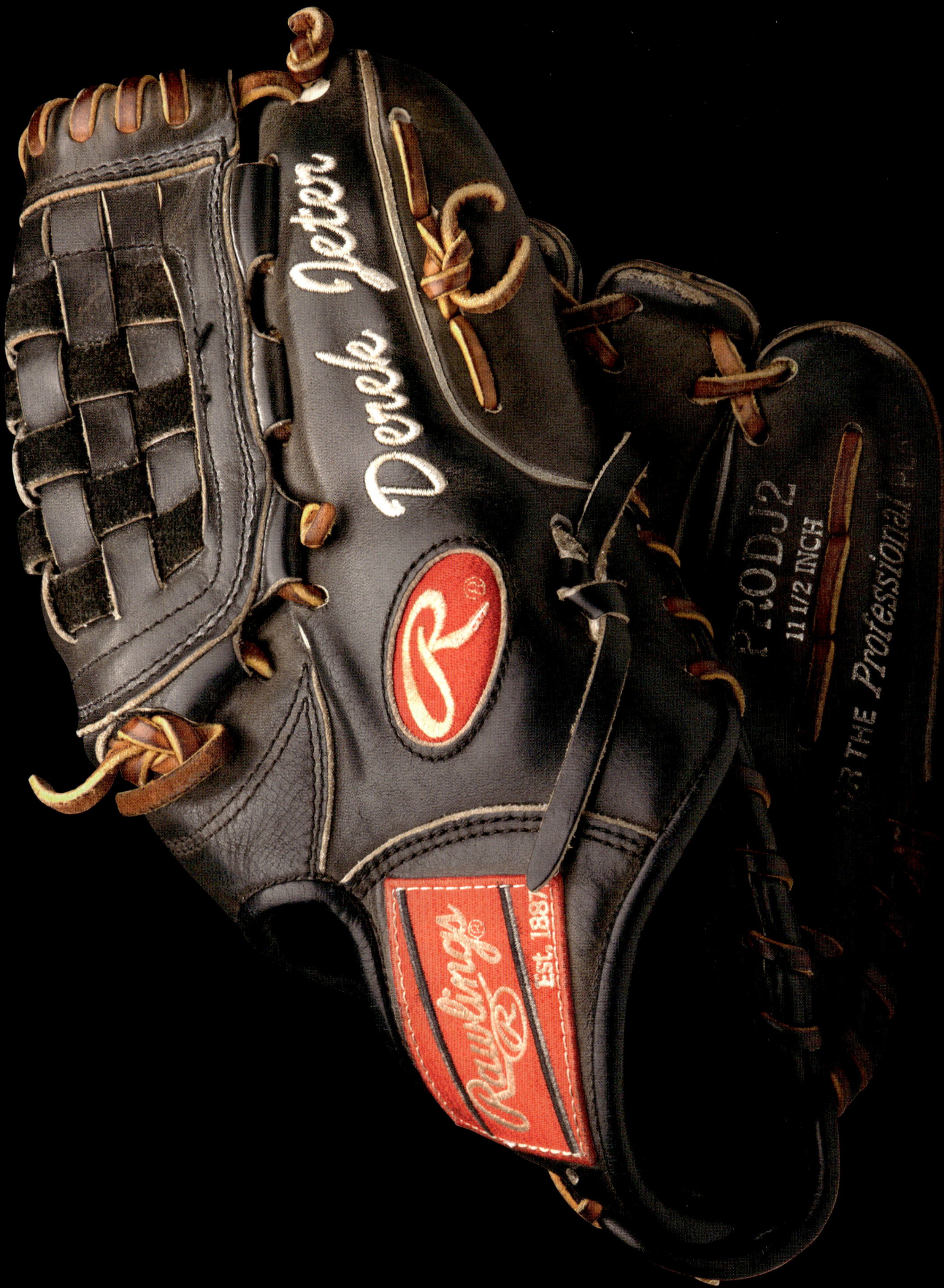

Derek Jeter
Rawlings
Est. 1887
PRODJ2
11 1/2 INCH

DEREK JETER

Captain Clutch

In the era of nightly highlight reels on television, so many of them came from the Bronx, where Derek Jeter showed the world how he hustled to become the best and smartest player on the field. Jeter would admit that he might not be the most talented player in a given game, but he always believed and showed that no one would work harder than him. It was a trait that stood out, helping the Yankees win ballgames, and it eventually sent Jeter to baseball's Hall of Fame at the end of a 20-year career in the big leagues. It was also an attribute that led to him being named the 15th captain in Yankee history in 2003—a post he held until his retirement in 2014.

Fellow Yankee teammate Jason Giambi summarized Jeter's leadership the best when he said, "His leadership style was his work ethic." And it was an infectious work ethic that led the Yankees to seven pennants and five World Series championships (1996, 1998, 1999, 2000, and 2009) during Jeter's playing days. To put that contribution into perspective, the greatest Yankee of them all—Babe Ruth—also helped guide the New Yorkers to seven pennants, but the team only won four World Series championships.

Jeter joined the Yankees' big-league club as a 20-year-old in 1995 and immediately showed his worth as that year's unanimous AL Rookie of the Year. Over the next 20 years, the career .310 hitter was selected to baseball's annual All-Star Game 14 times. He won five Gold Glove Awards on the defensive side of the field and stroked 3,465 hits at the plate (sixth most ever). In 2000, Jeter was both the All-Star Game MVP and the World Series MVP. His 200 postseason hits remain the best in baseball history.

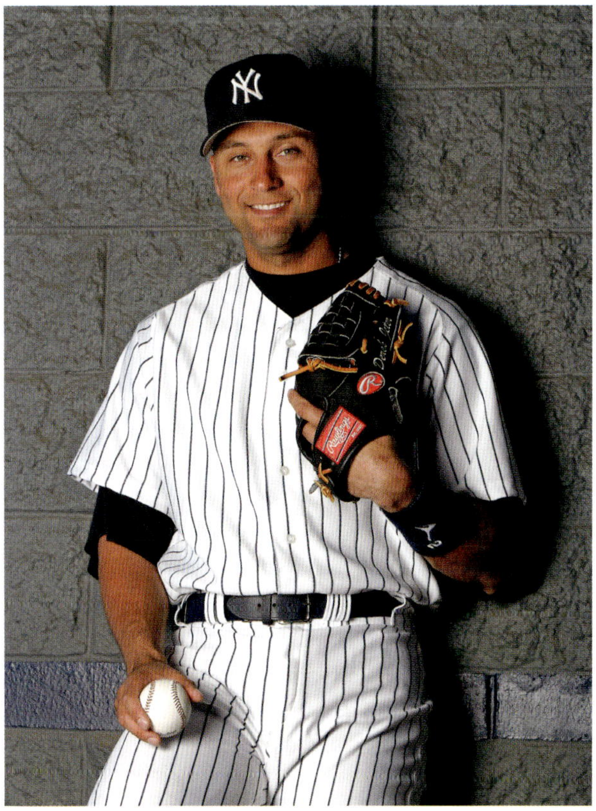

A five-time Gold Glove Award winner at the shortstop position, Derek Jeter used this Rawlings PRODJ2 model glove (opposite) during his career with the New York Yankees. Jeter (right) was a 14-time All-Star during his 20 seasons in the major leagues.

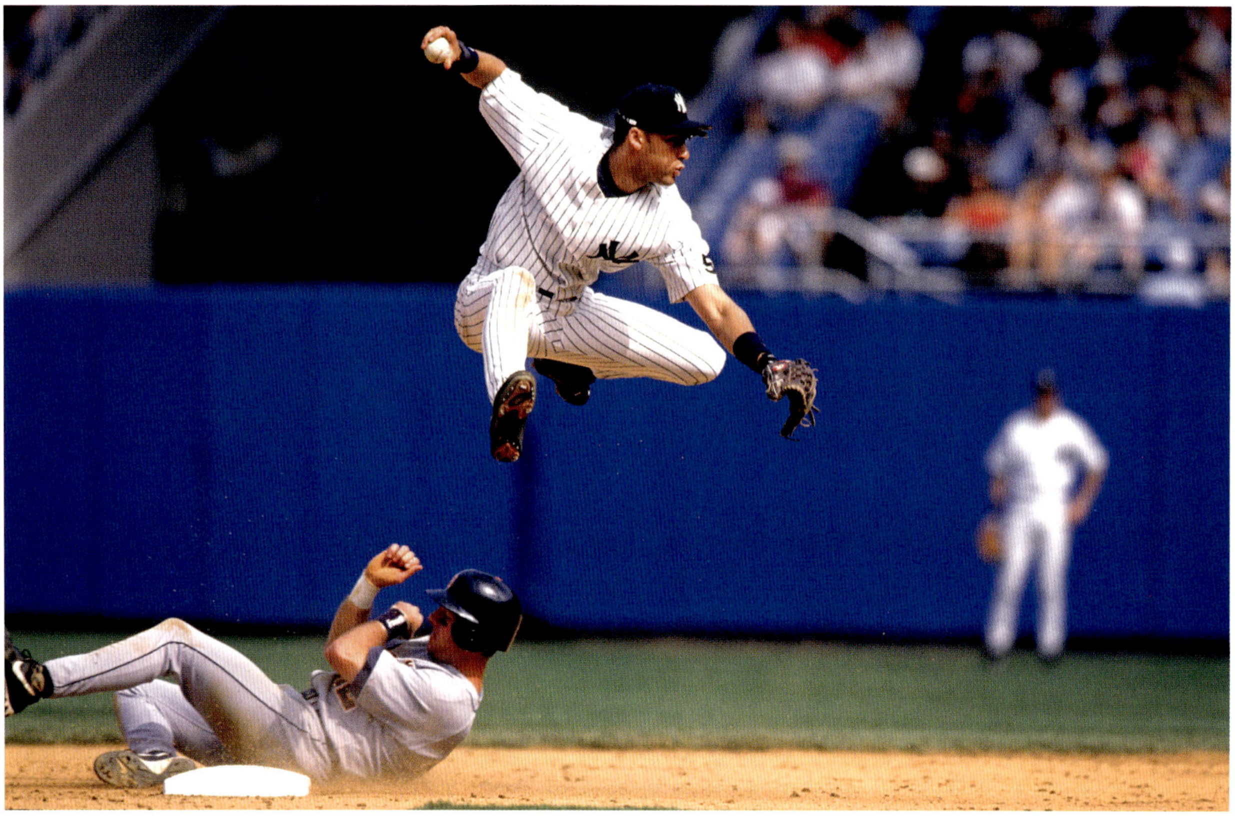

Jeter's defensive artistry is on full display as he turns a double play at second base.

When it was time for Jeter's election to Cooperstown in 2020, he became a first-ballot inductee after being named on 396 of the 397 ballots. His 99.7 percent tally was the second-highest total in Hall of Fame voting; it was replicated in 2025 with Ichiro Suzuki's election (393 of 394 ballots). Only Jeter's teammate Mariano Rivera received a higher voting percentage when he was unanimously selected to the Hall of Fame in 2019 (425 of 425 ballots).

Jeter's career honored his offensive prowess as well as his defensive play. What was the best play that the shortstop ever made? Two immediately come to mind. The first occurred in July 2003, when the Yankees were at home trying to stave off a Red Sox rally in the 12th inning of a critical series. It was a play in which the always hustling Jeter emerged from the seats along the third-base line with a bloody nose. He had chased down the third out by grabbing a fouled popup and plunging into the seats with all his momentum. The catch prevented Boston's two men on base from scoring and allowed the Yankees to eventually win the game.

But the defensive play that best highlights his nickname, "Captain Clutch," didn't happen in the confines of Yankee Stadium. It happened on the nation's other coast, during Game Three of the 2001 AL Division Series in the Oakland Coliseum. The Athletics had already won the first two games of the best-of-five series, and the New Yorkers needed a win to avoid elimination. The Yankees were leading 1–0 in the seventh inning, and the Athletics were batting with two outs and a man on first base. Oakland's Terrence Long hit a liner down the right-field line; Yankee outfielder Shane Spencer finally caught the ball on a hop in the right-field corner but then overthrew two cutoff men trying to return the ball to the infield. Jeter had the wherewithal to run from his shortstop position and grab the errant throw in foul territory along the first-base line near the first-base on-deck circle. Jeter quickly snared the ball and, in a single motion, backhanded a flip to catcher Jorge Posada, who was able to tag the running Jeremy Giambi out by an eyelash at home plate to preserve the win and continue the Yankees' march to the World Series. Jeter's instincts had put him in a position to make a play that few others would have and because of that—and his many other plays—the Yankees were winners.

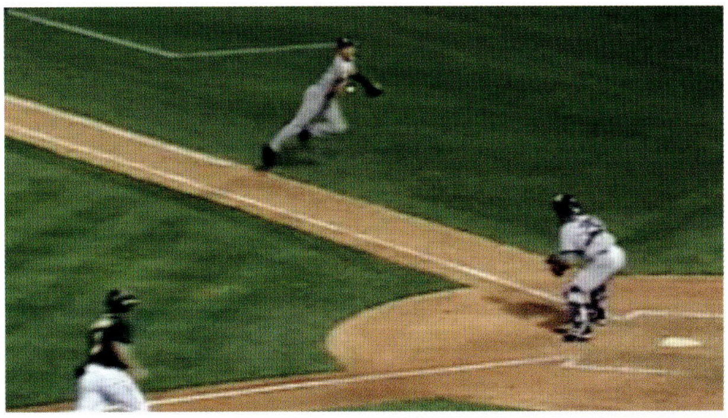

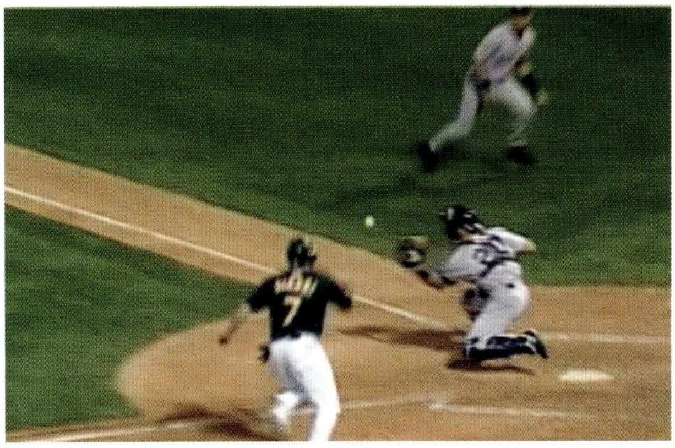

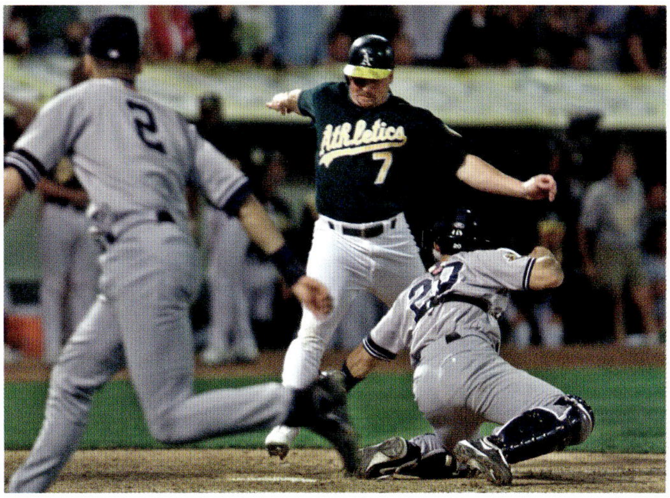

Jeter runs from his shortstop position into foul territory on the first-base side to catch the ball (top left). He then spins (left) to flip the ball back to catcher Jorge Posada to tag the running Jeremy Giambi out at home plate (above) to preserve the win and continue the Yankees' march to the World Series. The play became known as "The Flip." Jeter was regularly featured in Rawlings catalogs (below).

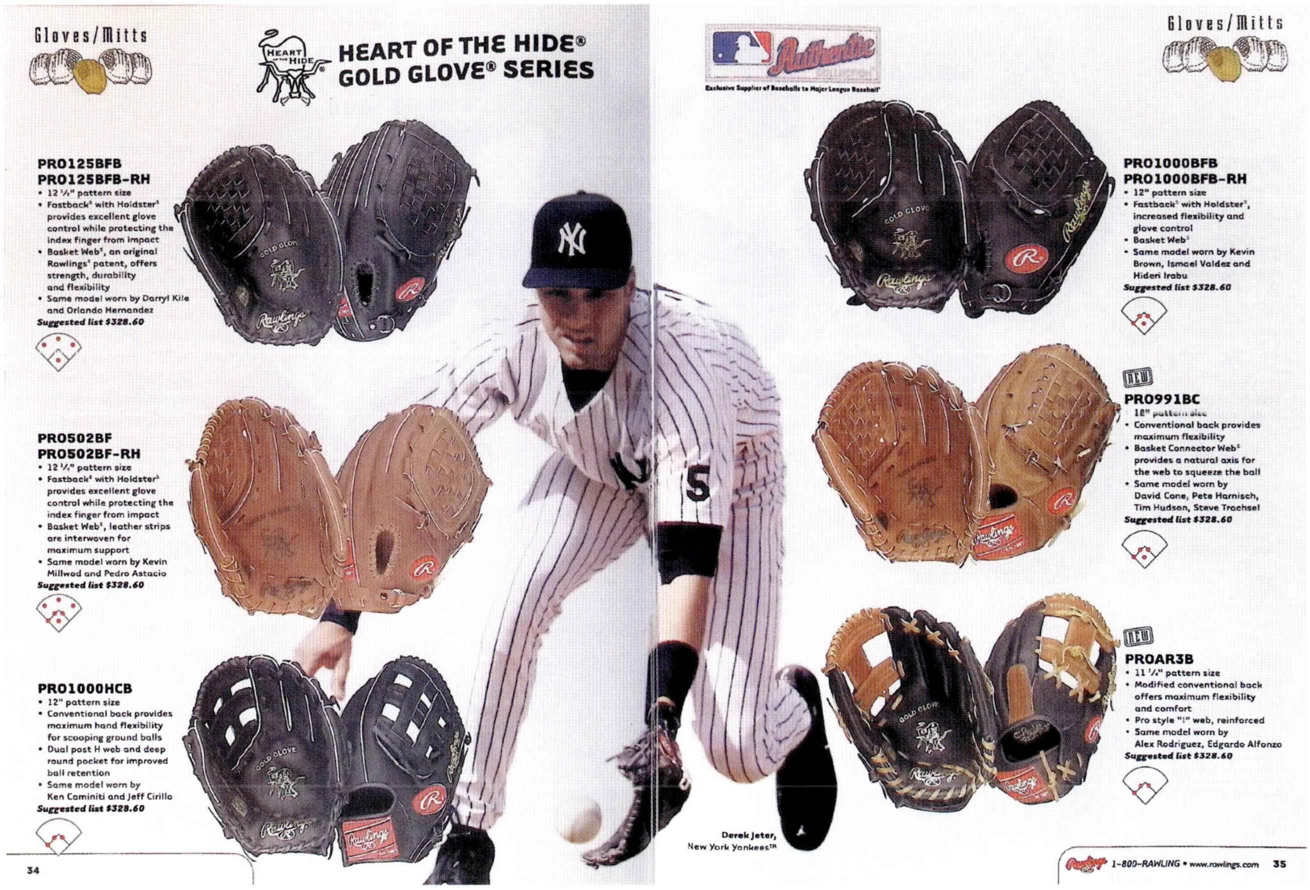

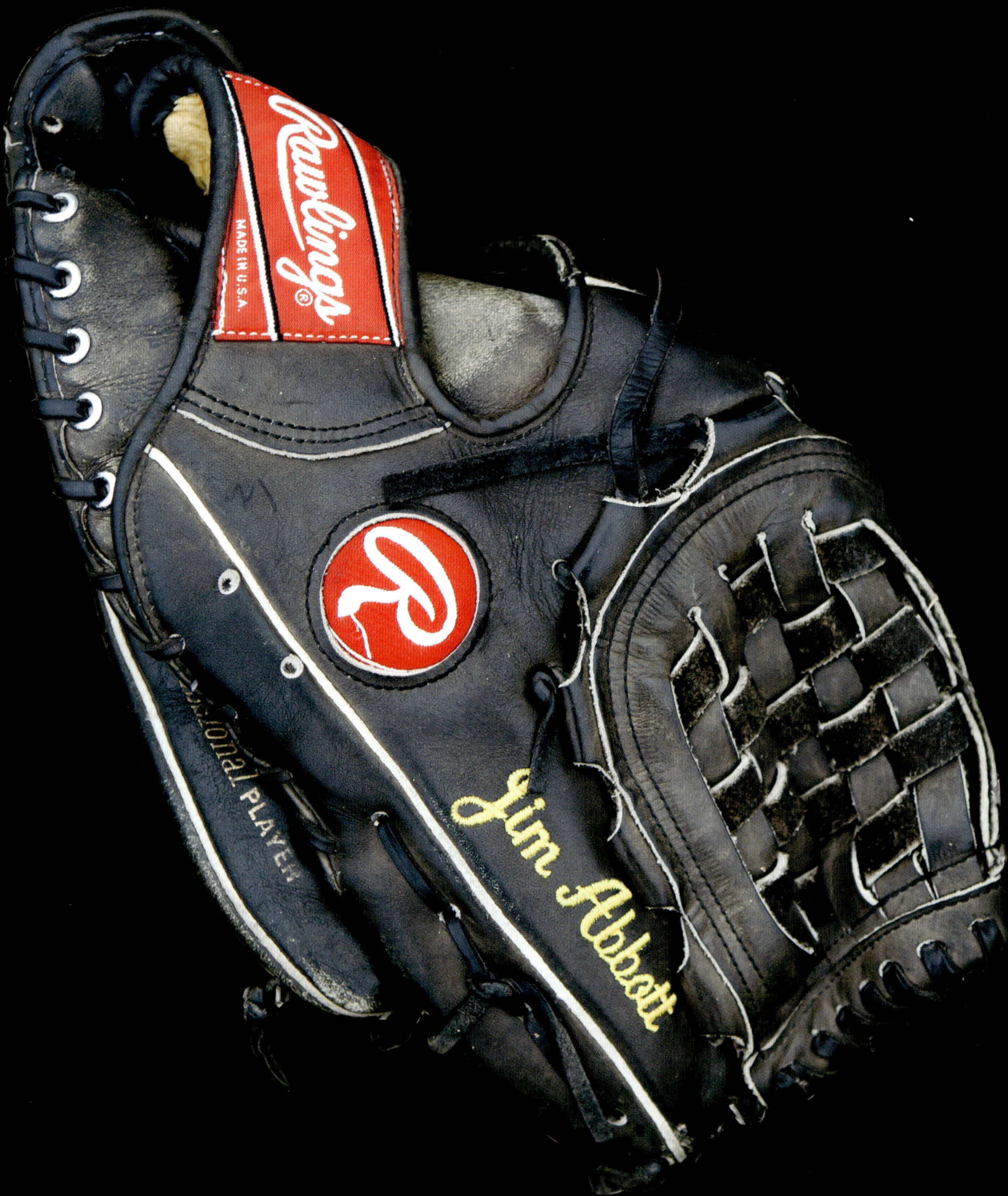

Rawlings
MADE IN U.S.A.
Jim Abbott
PLAYER

JIM ABBOTT

Determined

Over the course of MLB's 150-year history, there have been several players who played the game with a disability. Mordecai "Three Fingers" Brown chalked up 239 big-league wins while missing two digits on his pitching hand in the early 1900s. Chad Bentz pitched 40 MLB games with a deformed right hand. Freddy Sanchez was a three-time All-Star who won the 2006 NL batting title with a clubbed right foot and a severely pigeon-toed left foot. The St. Louis Browns fielded the one-armed outfielder Pete Gray during their 1945 season.

When reading through Jim Abbott's list of baseball accomplishments, one would never suspect that the star pitcher was born with a deformed right arm. Anatomically, his arm ends at the wrist. His 11–3 record at the University of Michigan helped the Wolverines win the 1987 Big Ten Conference championship. He then became the first American pitcher to beat the Cuban national team in 25 years, with a three-hit complete-game performance. That was followed by two wins in the Pan American Games that year without giving up a run. In recognition of these amateur performances, Abbott was selected as the 1987 recipient of the Sullivan Award, given to the nation's outstanding amateur athlete, and the Golden Spikes Award, presented to the country's top amateur baseball player—a prize he won over future Hall of Famers Ken Griffey Jr. and Jack Morris. The next year, he won an Olympic Gold Medal by beating the Japanese team in a complete-game win in the tournament's final game.

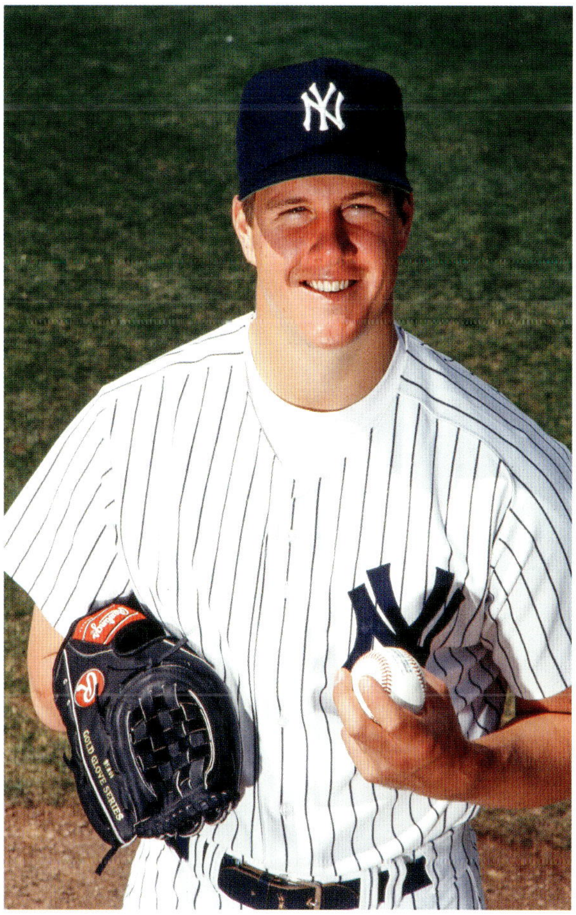

Though he was born without a right hand, Jim Abbott (right) used a standard Rawlings fielder's glove (opposite) that he adapted himself. Despite his disability, Abbott pitched in 263 games over 10 seasons in the major leagues.

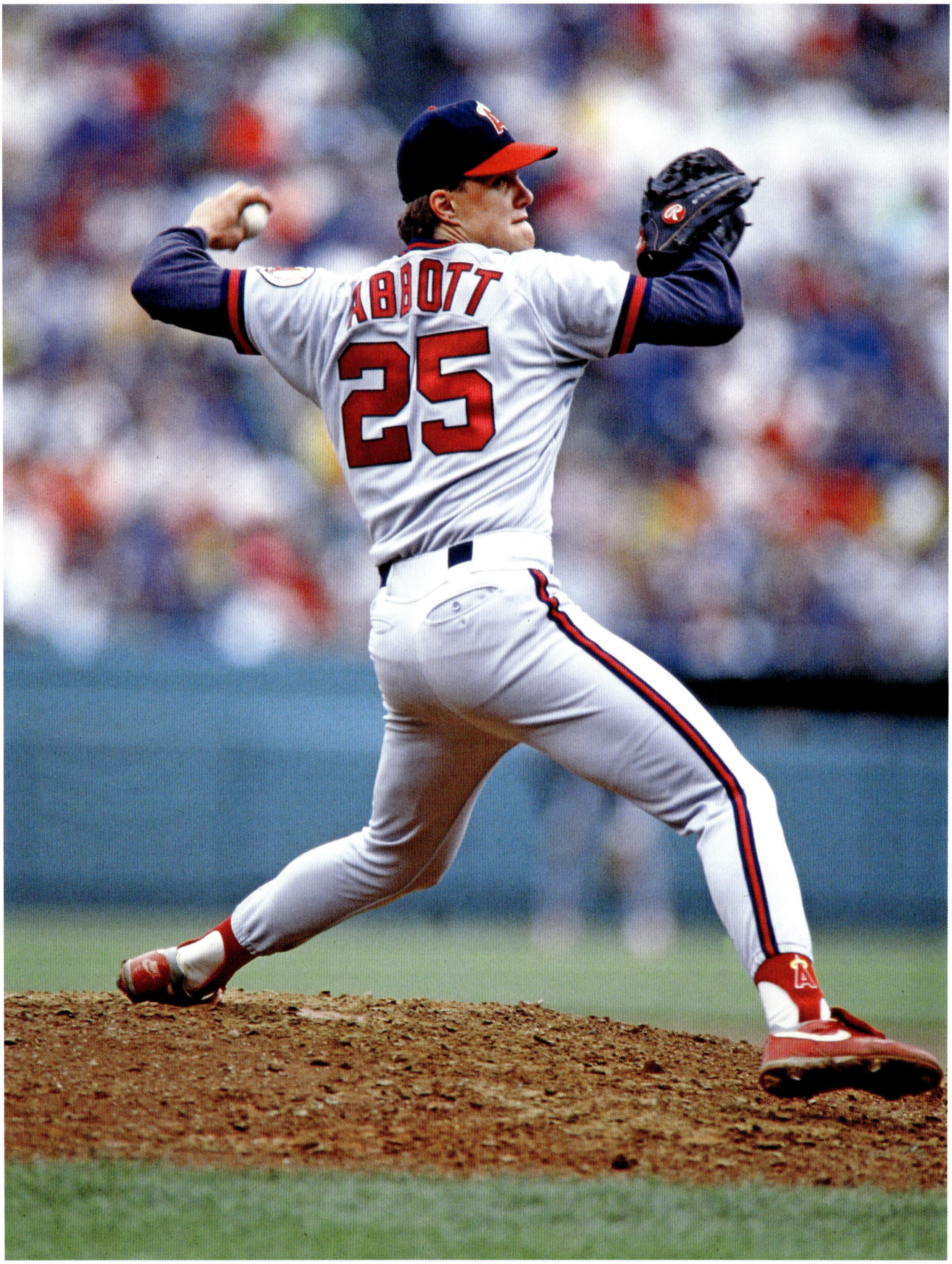

The California Angels picked Abbott in the first round of the 1988 amateur draft.

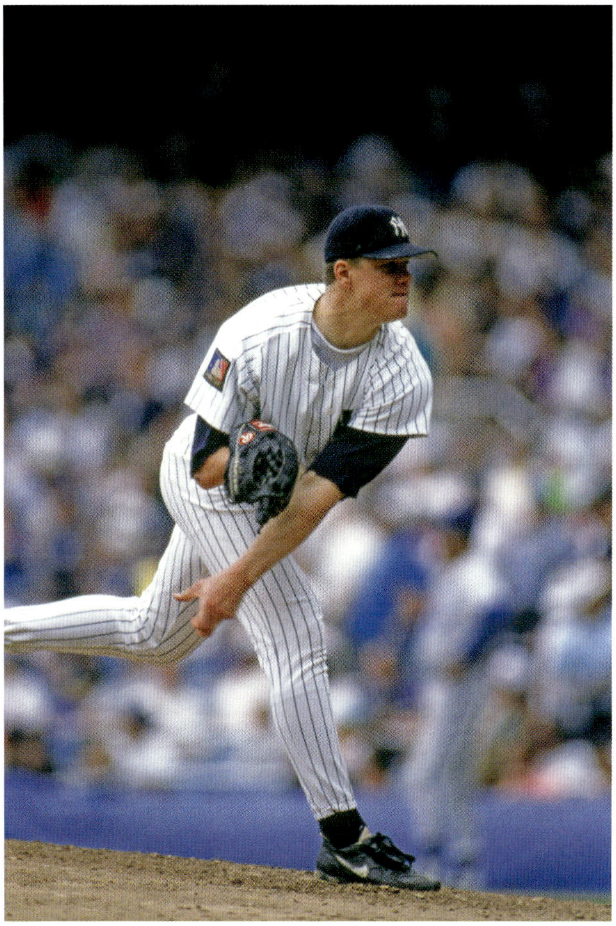

On September 4, 1993, Abbott pulled off an incredible feat: He no-hit the Cleveland Indians.

Besides having the ability to impressively pitch with his good arm, Abbott had become adept at fielding his position from the mound. While pitching, he used a Rawlings right-hander's fielding glove that, before each pitch, he perched over the end of his right arm. With the follow-through of his delivery, he would slide his left hand into the glove and be ready to field any ball hit his way. Once a ball was fielded, he would cradle the glove between his chest and right arm, grab the ball with his left hand, and make the necessary throw. On the occasions when a batter bunted the ball or the swinging hit came as a slow roller, Abbott often didn't have time to go through the motions of the glove transfer, so he would toss his glove aside and field the ball with his bare hand.

Abbott turned down his first chance to play pro ball after high school when the Toronto Blue Jays chose him in the 35th round of MLB's 1985 amateur draft. He instead went to college, proved his ability to pitch and field with the best in the country, and was selected in the first round (eighth pick overall) in the 1988 amateur draft by the California Angels. The six-foot, three-inch, left-handed pitcher wasn't sent to the minors to hone his skills after signing. His résumé said he was ready for the big leagues, and he wouldn't appear in a minor-league game until he had already played seven seasons in the major leagues.

Abbott made the pennant-favored Angels' roster during spring training in 1989, right after his Olympic performance. His team didn't make it to the postseason that year or in any other year of Abbott's 10 seasons in the majors. After four seasons and a 47–52 record, the Angels—fearing they could not meet his salary demands—sent the pitcher to the Yankees at the end of the 1992 season. While the New Yorkers were stocking their team with high-profile players for a hoped-for pennant, Abbott's 20–22 record over his two seasons in pinstripes didn't help them get into the playoffs. But on September 4, 1993, Abbott delivered a moment that few thought a one-armed pitcher could ever do. He pitched a no-hitter against the Cleveland Indians in the latter stages of the season's tight pennant race. To date, 322 no-hitters have been thrown in the history of the major leagues. Only one was thrown by a one-armed pitcher.

The adulation of the no-hitter pushed aside the ridicule that Abbott often experienced throughout his days in baseball. While his athleticism lifted him through each game, he managed the off-field pressures with composure and determination. He left the Yankees after the 1994 season, pitching for four different teams over the next four years and compiling an 87–108 pitching record over 10 seasons. Making it to the big leagues is hard for most players with two arms. A determined Abbott made it with just one arm, and his pitching talent allowed him to play in the major leagues for a decade.

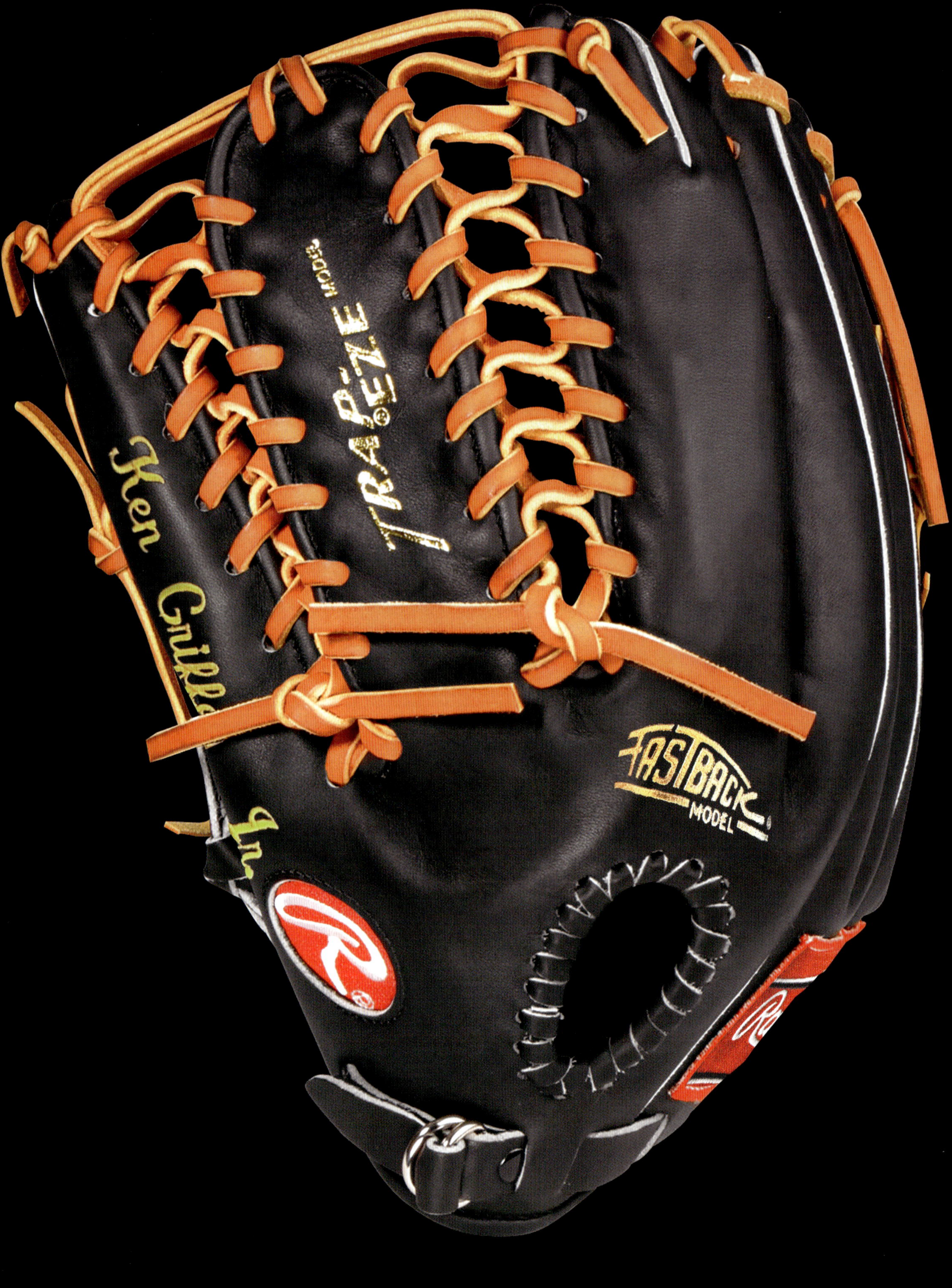
TRAP-EZE MODEL
FASTBACK MODEL

KEN GRIFFEY JR.

The Kid

Sitting within the rolling hills of America's Rust Belt alongside the Monongahela River, on a bend south of Pittsburgh, is the town of Donora, Pennsylvania. It was from this mining and manufacturing city that "The Kid," Ken Griffey Jr., would one day follow "The Man," Stan Musial, all the way to Cooperstown. Each would play 22 seasons in the big leagues, and each was born in Donora on November 21—but 49 years apart. In fact, "The Kid" was born the very year that "The Man" was inducted into baseball's Hall of Fame in 1969.

Coincidences aside, each man became one of the premier players of their respective generations. Griffey's 22 seasons patrolling center field were split among the Seattle Mariners (1989–1999 and 2009–2010), the Cincinnati Reds (2000–2008), and the Chicago White Sox (2008). He became one of the leading faces of baseball with his 13 selections to the annual All-Star Game (1990–2000, 2004, and 2007), where he won the Midsummer Classic's MVP Award in 1992. And that win was not his only one; he unanimously won the AL MVP Award in 1997.

Griffey was known as "Junior" while growing up and playing in the shadows of his father's outstanding MLB career with Cincinnati's Big Red Machine. Ken Griffey Sr. batted .296 over a 19-year career that included back-to-back World Series championships (1975 and 1976), and his career lasted long enough for the duo to become the first father and son to play in the majors at the same time, during the 1989 season. The following year, he joined the Seattle

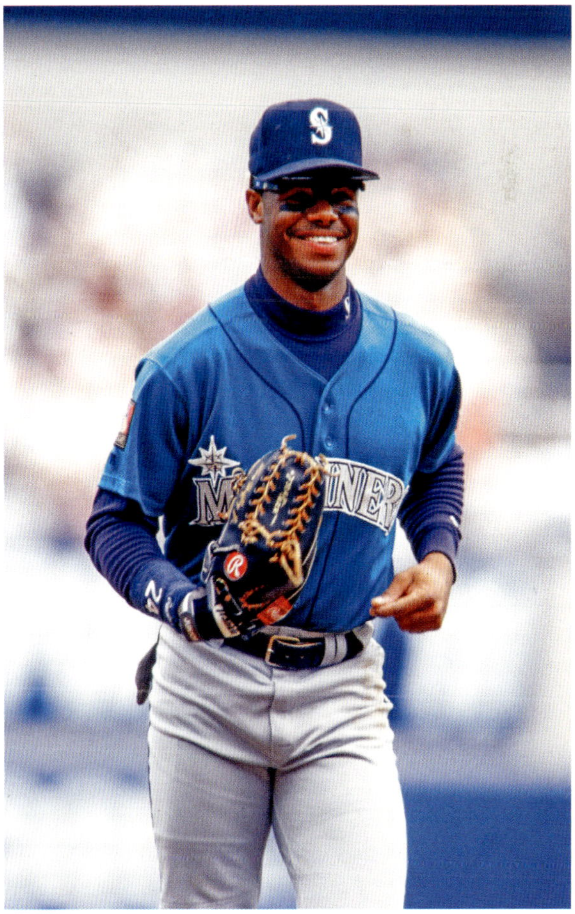

Ken Griffey Jr. used a PROTB24 Trap-Eze Fastback model glove (opposite). Nicknamed "The Kid," Griffey (right) always had a smile on his face when out on the field.

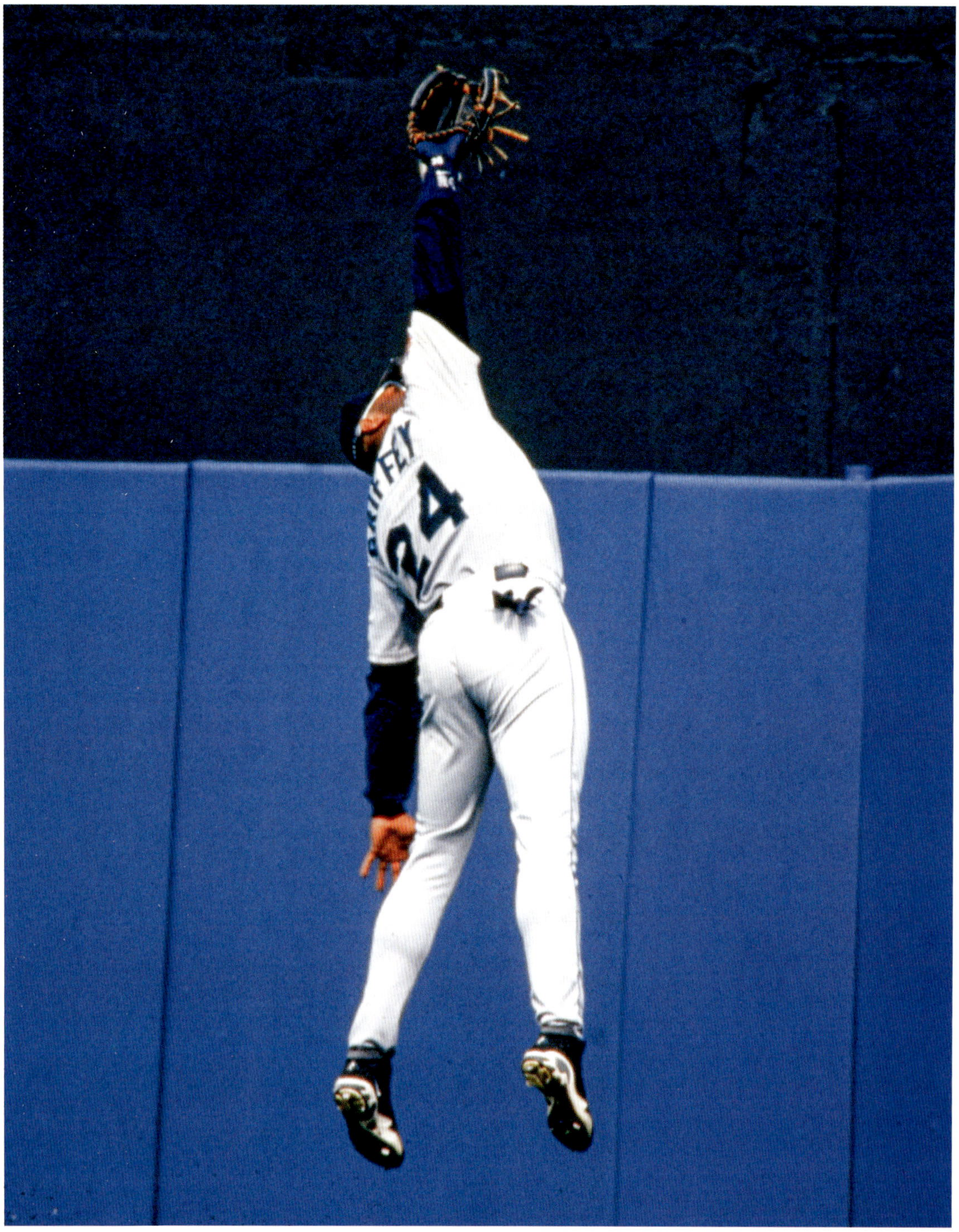

Many of baseball's best highlight-reel clips of the 1990s showed the 10-time Gold Glove Award winner crashing high on the outfield wall to make a catch.

Mariners for his son's sophomore season, making them the first father and son to play on the same team. That fall, on September 14, they also became the first—and only—father and son to hit back-to-back home runs in a game against the California Angels.

During the season he played with his dad, Griffey was selected to the first of his 13 All-Star Games. That year also marked the first of his 10 consecutive Gold Glove Award wins in center field, as well as his first time hitting .300 and tallying 22 homers and 80 RBIs. His offense continued to improve as he rattled off five consecutive seasons hitting over .300, and he went on to hit 40 or more home runs in seven of the next eight seasons. He reached the 56-home-run mark twice, and he was viewed as a potential candidate to top Roger Maris's record (61) the year prior to Mark McGwire's record-setting 1998 season.

Griffey had been the real deal ever since his name was called out as the first pick in MLB's 1987 amateur draft. His heroics at the plate for the Mariners helped reignite a love of baseball for a city that had lost its expansion team (the Pilots) after just one season nearly two decades earlier. He had become the complete player, adding one dazzling play after another to save a Mariners' win. Early in his sophomore season, Griffey made a show of what was to come by going up over the Yankee Stadium wall to catch a would-be home run off Jesse Barfield's bat to snuff out a New York rally. Plays of that nature became regular highlight-reel hype that focused on Griffey's trademark happy smile during his sprint back to the dugout.

During the early 1990s, it seemed as though no one could do it better on defense. There was nothing that could stop Griffey, including the outfield wall. In May 1995, he challenged the Kingdome wall for another out-of-this-world catch of a deep drive by Baltimore's Kevin Bass. Climbing the wall at full speed, Griffey made a backhanded catch that became known as "The "Spider-Man Catch." His encounter with the wall shattered his right wrist and cost him 73 games that season. He did, however, make it back in time to help the Mariners overcome a 13½-game deficit to secure the team's first AL West title and first playoff appearance.

Griffey's stellar defense made another playoff statement during his time with the White Sox in 2008. In the fifth inning of game 163's tiebreaker, Griffey threw a bullet from center field that cut down a runner at the plate to preserve his team's 1–0 victory and send the Sox to the playoffs. But time and injuries were taking a toll on his body and performance. He spent his last two seasons back in Seattle before heading into retirement, and he was called to Cooperstown in his first season of eligibility in 2016. He ended his career with 630 home runs, a feat accomplished by only eight other players. During his 22 seasons, Griffey played 111 or fewer games eight times, which raises the question of how many more balls he could have hit over the wall if the wear and tear of his all-out defensive play hadn't cost him time in the game.

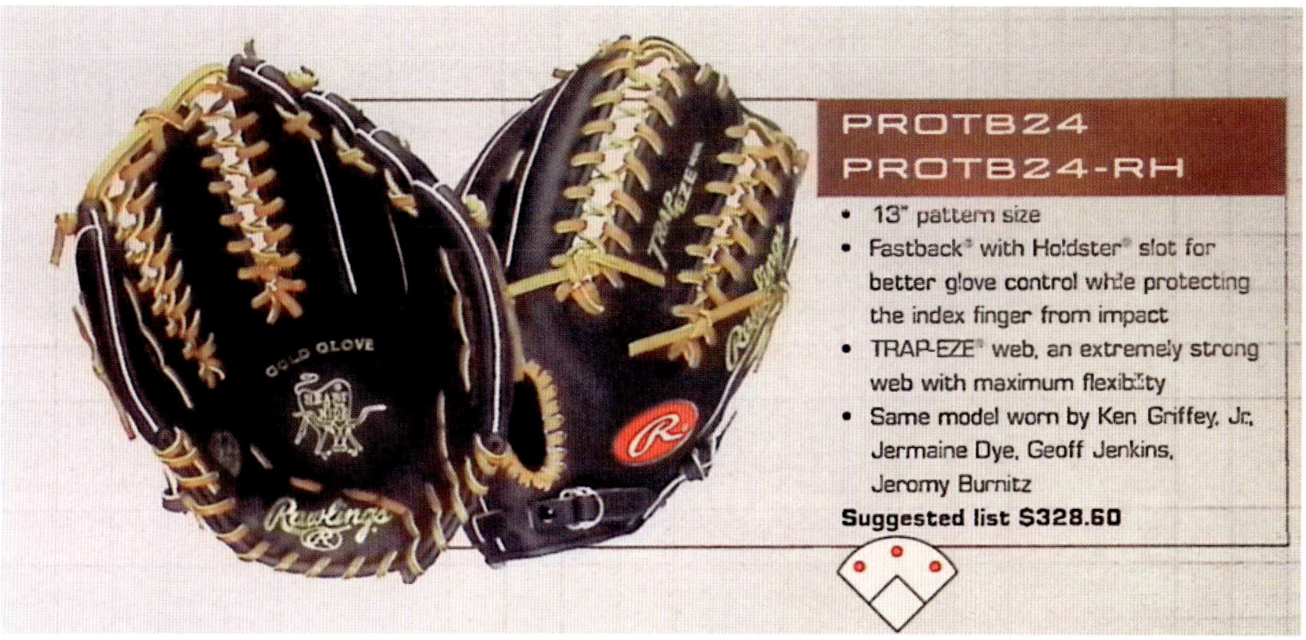

A 1990s Rawlings catalog advertisement features the PROTB24, the model that Griffey used.

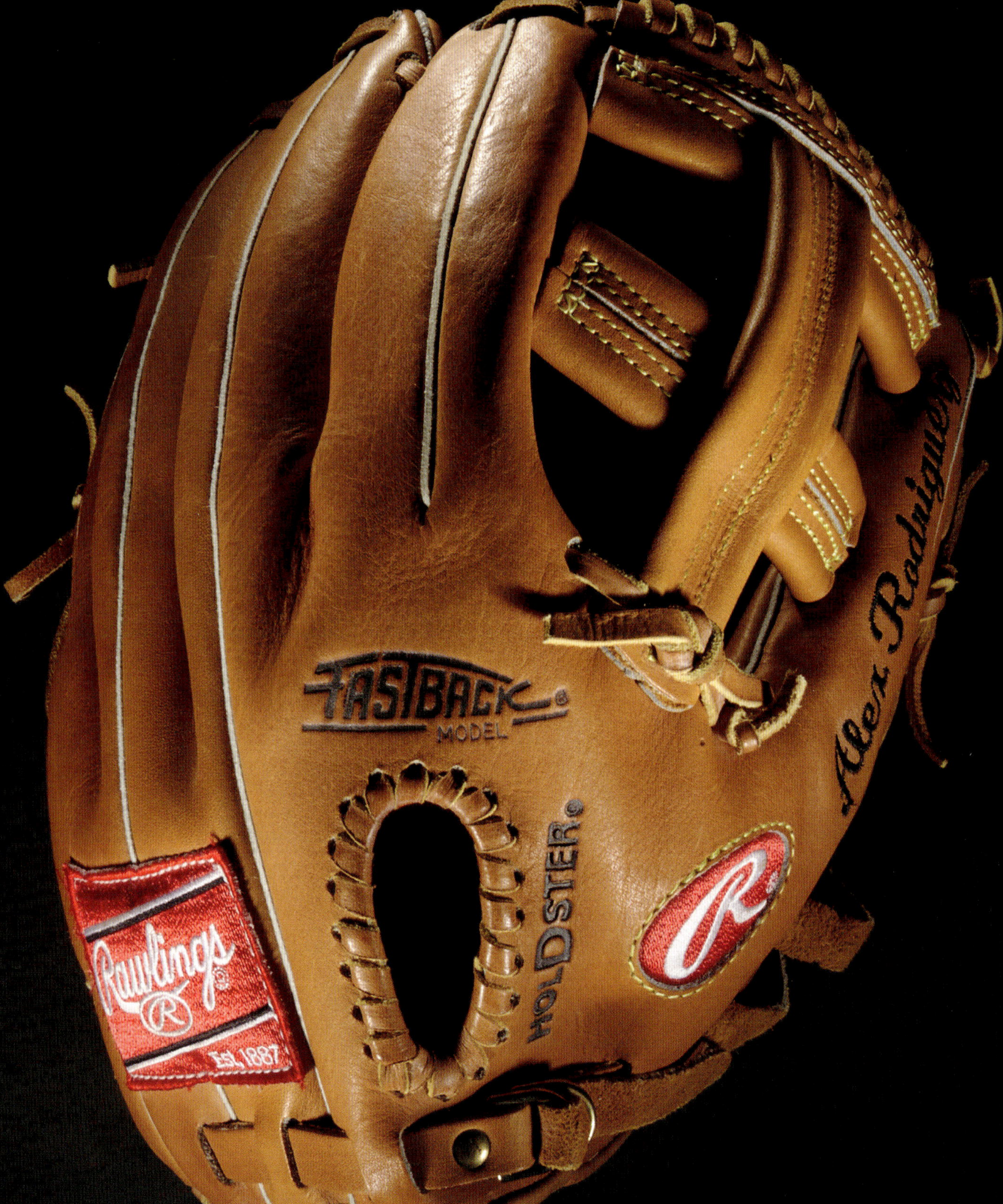
FASTBACK®
MODEL
HOLDSTER®
Rawlings®
EST. 1887
Alex Rodriguez

ALEX RODRIGUEZ

Simply A-Rod

A century ago, the mention of the one-name moniker "Babe" immediately directed fans to a baseball legend named Babe Ruth. The same can be said today—to millions, Alex Rodriguez is simply "A-Rod." He and Ruth each spent most of their careers wearing the pinstripes of the Yankees in the limelight of New York City and garnering sports headlines with their many massive home runs.

Rodriguez has spent over three decades in the public spotlight, making headlines as both a baseball superstar and an outcast. His star shone early as the American Family Insurance ALL-USA High School Baseball Player of the Year. Then he was the first pick in the 1993 MLB amateur draft by the Seattle Mariners. Following the draft, he became a very wealthy 18-year-old after signing a three-year, $1.3 million contract, with a $1 million signing bonus. Rodriguez started 1994 in Seattle's minor-league organization. By July 8, three weeks shy of his 19th birthday, he was in the Mariners' starting lineup. Sent back down prior to the August 1994 MLB work stoppage, he split time the following season between AAA and the big club. In 1996, as Seattle's everyday shortstop, he became baseball's third-youngest player to win a batting title—behind Al Kaline (1955) and Ty Cobb (1907)—with his .358 average.

Rodriguez finished the 1996 season with 36 home runs and 123 RBIs for a slash line of .358/.414/.631. His time split between the minors and the majors in previous seasons had been just enough to make him ineligible (196 vs. 130 at-bat limit) for the Rookie of the Year Award, which went unanimously to his future teammate Derek Jeter, who

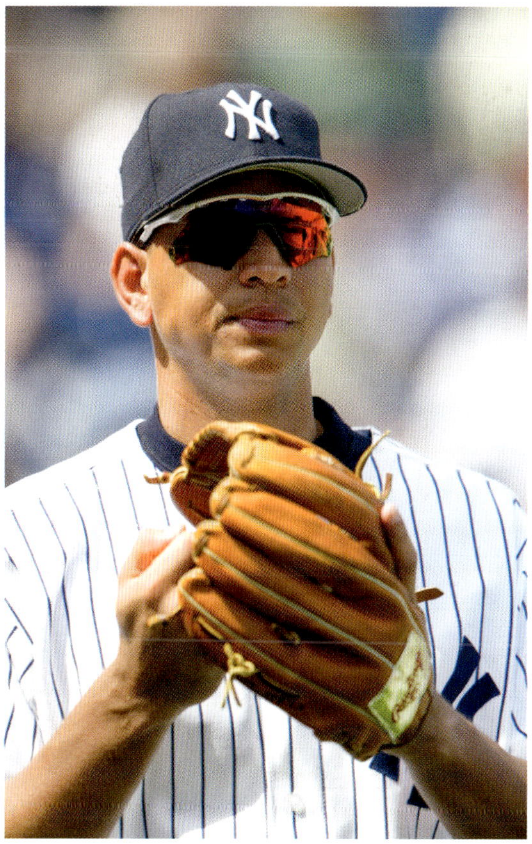

Alex Rodriguez used a Rawlings PRO-6HF model glove (opposite) during part of his big-league career. Rodriguez (right) played shortstop for the Texas Rangers before moving to third base after his trade to the New York Yankees.

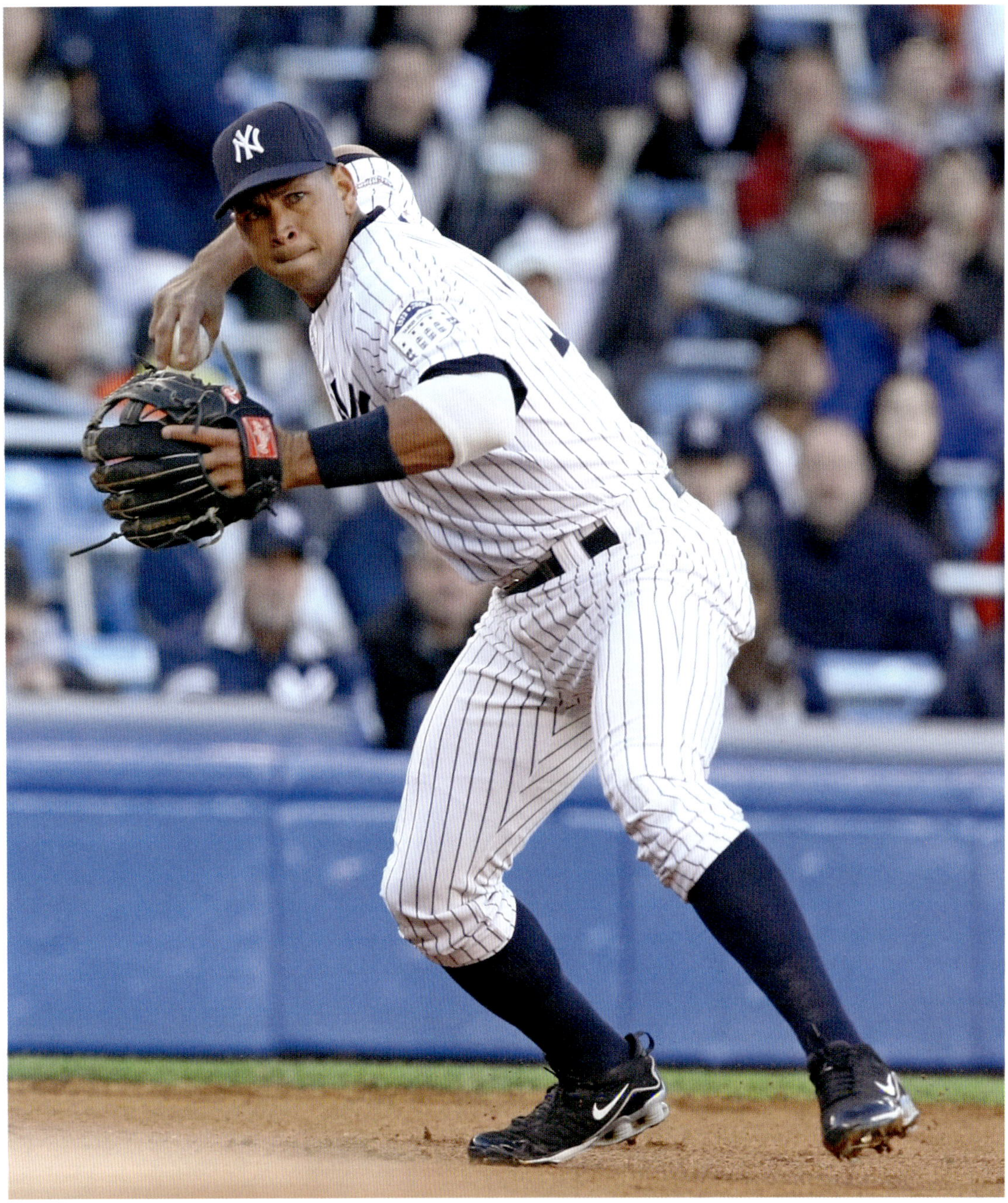

Rodriguez throws to first base against the Baltimore Orioles at Yankee Stadium in 2008.

slashed .314/.370/.430. During that season, Rodriguez set MLB shortstop records for hits, runs, and extra-base hits. That year was also the first of his 14 selections to the annual All-Star Game and when his nickname was born. In her book *A-ROD: The Many Lives of Alex Rodriguez*, author Selena Roberts explained that, during spring training, Rodriguez started writing "A-Rod" on his equipment bags. It soon became the one-word catchphrase used by his teammates and the media.

During his seven seasons (1994–2000) in Seattle, Rodriguez batted .309 and collected 189 home runs and 595 RBIs. He added another dimension to his power and defense when he stole 46 bases in 1998. The Mariners made the playoffs three times but could never get past the ALCS round. Always a good fielder, he became a free agent after the 2000 season and signed with the Texas Rangers. His 10-year, $252 million contract was not just the largest in baseball; it was the largest ever given to any professional athlete.

In the Rangers' uniform in 2001, Rodriguez did not disappoint. He passed the 50-home-run mark for the first time to lead the league, along with 133 runs and 393 total bases. The next year, he launched a career-high 57 home runs to lead the league again, along with RBIs and total bases.

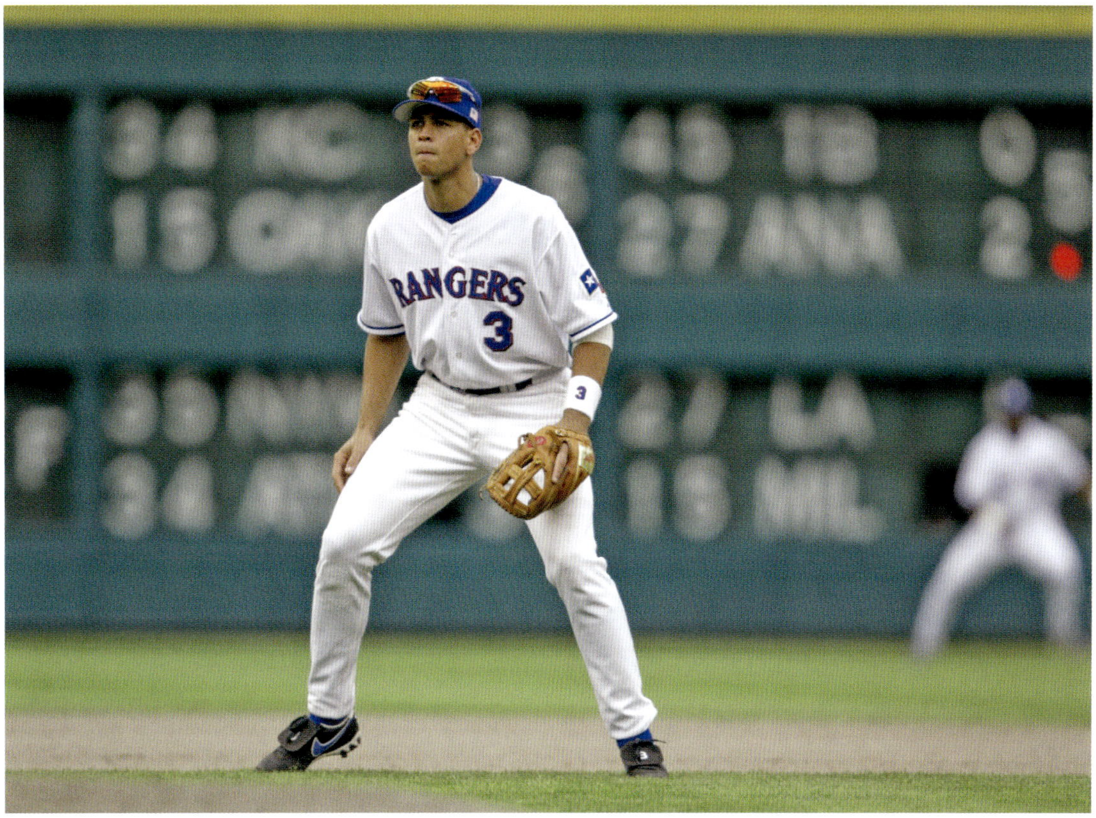

Rodriguez's time with the Rangers brought his first two MVP Awards and two Gold Glove Awards but no postseason appearances.

He also took home the first of two consecutive Gold Glove Awards with a .987 fielding percentage. In 2003, Rodriguez won his first MVP Award after leading the league in home runs, runs, and slugging. Despite his success, the Rangers never exceeded a .500 record or provided a postseason opportunity.

Wanting to rid themselves of his salary, the Rangers traded him to the Yankees in 2004 with the condition that the Gold Glover would move to third base and Jeter would stay at shortstop. It was Rodriguez's ninth full season in the big leagues and his seventh consecutive season hitting at least 30 home runs, 100 runs scored, and 100 RBIs. His new team made it to the postseason but were stopped by Boston's march to break the "Curse of the Bambino."

Rodriguez kept hitting home runs. He became the youngest MLB player to hit 400 home runs in 2005, won his second MVP season, and had another brief Yankee playoff appearance. The following July, Rodriguez got his 450th home run and 2,000th hit on the same swing, and a year later, at age 32, he became the youngest player to reach the 500-homer mark while winning his third MVP Award. He continued to have great seasons in 2008 and 2009 despite tales of substance abuse bubbling up. He helped the Yankees to his one and only World Series appearance and championship in 2009. A year later, on the third anniversary of his 500th home run, Rodriguez parked his 600th drive over the fence at age 35, the youngest and only eighth player at the time to reach the milestone.

The next few years turned into seasons of injuries, operations, and performance-enhancing drug use that eventually led to Rodriguez's 2014 suspension from baseball. He returned in 2015 to play another season and a half and was able to collect his 3,000th hit and 696th home run. Rodriguez's stats rank with the best who have ever played the game. However, his indiscretions off the field cost him more. Would another season of play have enhanced his star power? Or had the ties to scandal dimmed that star so it would never shine in baseball's Hall of Fame?

YADIER MOLINA

El Marciano

For 19 seasons the chant "Yadi, Yadi, Yadi" could be heard throughout St. Louis's Busch Stadium as Yadier Molina displayed his baseball dominance at home plate as both a batter and a defender. The Redbird fans' ovation of love and appreciation was directed toward the man known as "El Marciano." It was a nickname that did not come from the fans but rather his brother, Bengie Molina, a former MLB World Series champion catcher. Translated from the Spanish, and marking the Molinas' Puerto Rican roots, "El Marciano" means "The Martian," and it was given in respect. In speaking about his brother, Bengie said, "He's so good, it's like he's from another planet."

Molina's defensive skills behind the plate have changed the game. He did things no others could. Hall of Fame catcher Ted Simmons called Molina "the best defensive catcher I've seen in my existence." Simmons's claim was supported by not only Molina's nine NL Gold Glove Awards but also his selection as the inaugural winner of the NL Platinum Glove Award in 2011. Molina then went on to win three of the next four selections (2012, 2014, and 2015). The Rawlings Platinum Glove Award, which recognizes the best defensive player in each league, is selected from the pool of that season's Gold Glove Award winners. It represents the best of the best, and Molina received the honor four out of the first five times it was awarded. He was not just the best catcher in the league; he was the best defender in the league—period. As the first to win the award, Molina's play set the standard for all future winners.

Molina came to the big leagues in 2004, when the Cardinals played in their first World Series in 17 years. He was an apprentice to Redbird catcher Mike Matheny, who won his third of four Gold Gloves that year but was traded after the season to make room for Molina as the club's starting catcher. Molina's leadership as the Cardinals' field quarterback helped the Redbirds to another eight division titles, four wild card berths, and three pennants (2006, 2011, and 2013) that led to two world championships. Along the way, until his retirement in 2022, Molina was selected to 10 All-Star Games and hit over .300 five times. He became the complete player, but few playing the catcher position have ever been better defensively.

It is not a stretch at all to say that Molina was one of the best catchers to ever play in the big leagues. His stats support the story. In time, he will likely join the other catchers already enshrined in Cooperstown's Hall of Fame. Compared to them, Molina's contributions over his years behind the plate rank near the top in nearly every category. His fielding percentage (.995) ranks higher than all these inductees. Only Hall of Famers Iván Rodriguez and Carlton Fisk played more games than Molina's 2,184 at the position. And his 18,294.2 innings caught are the

Yadier Molina used this PROSCM41JB model catcher's mitt during his career with the St. Louis Cardinals.

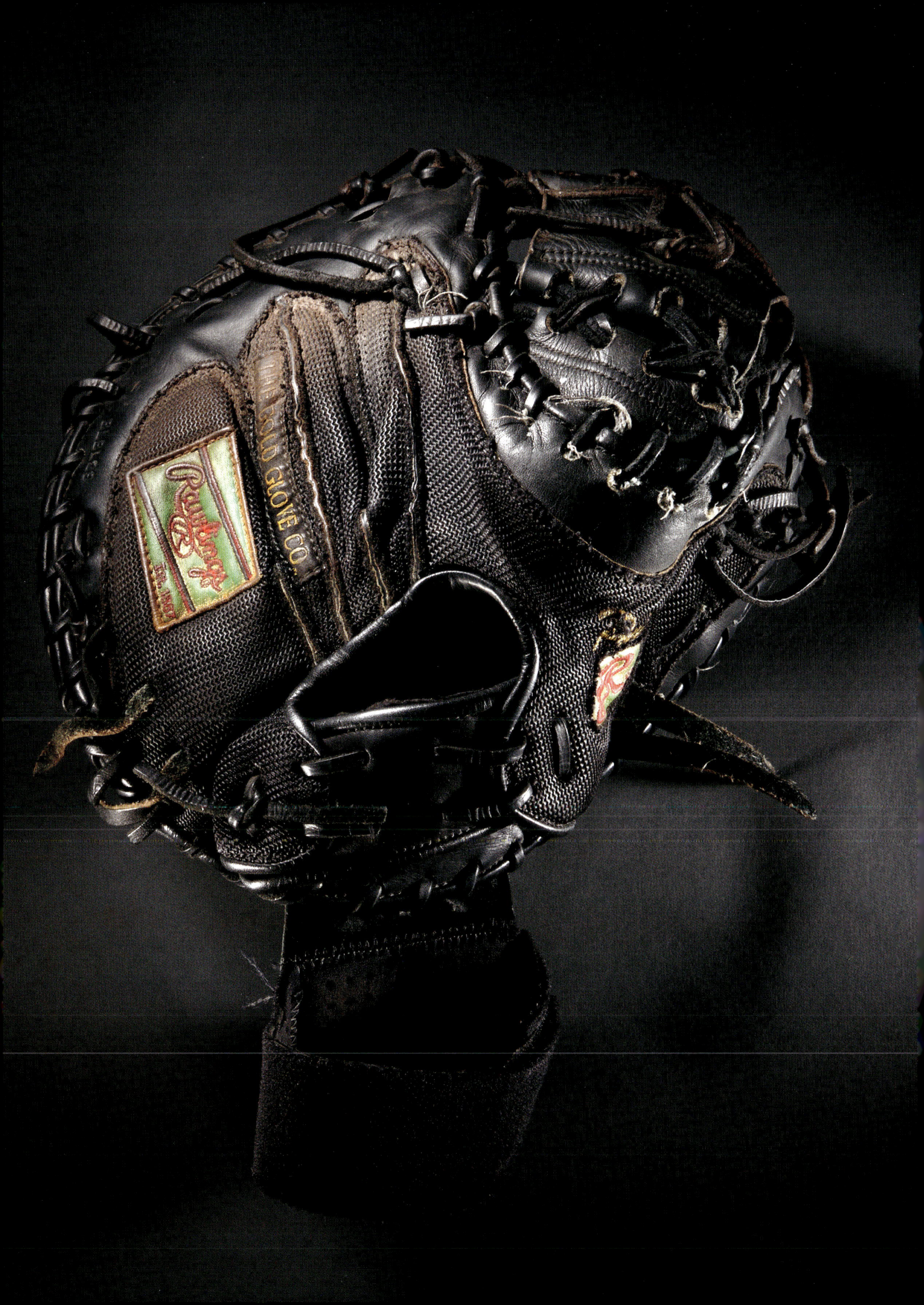
Rawlings
GOLD GLOVE CO.

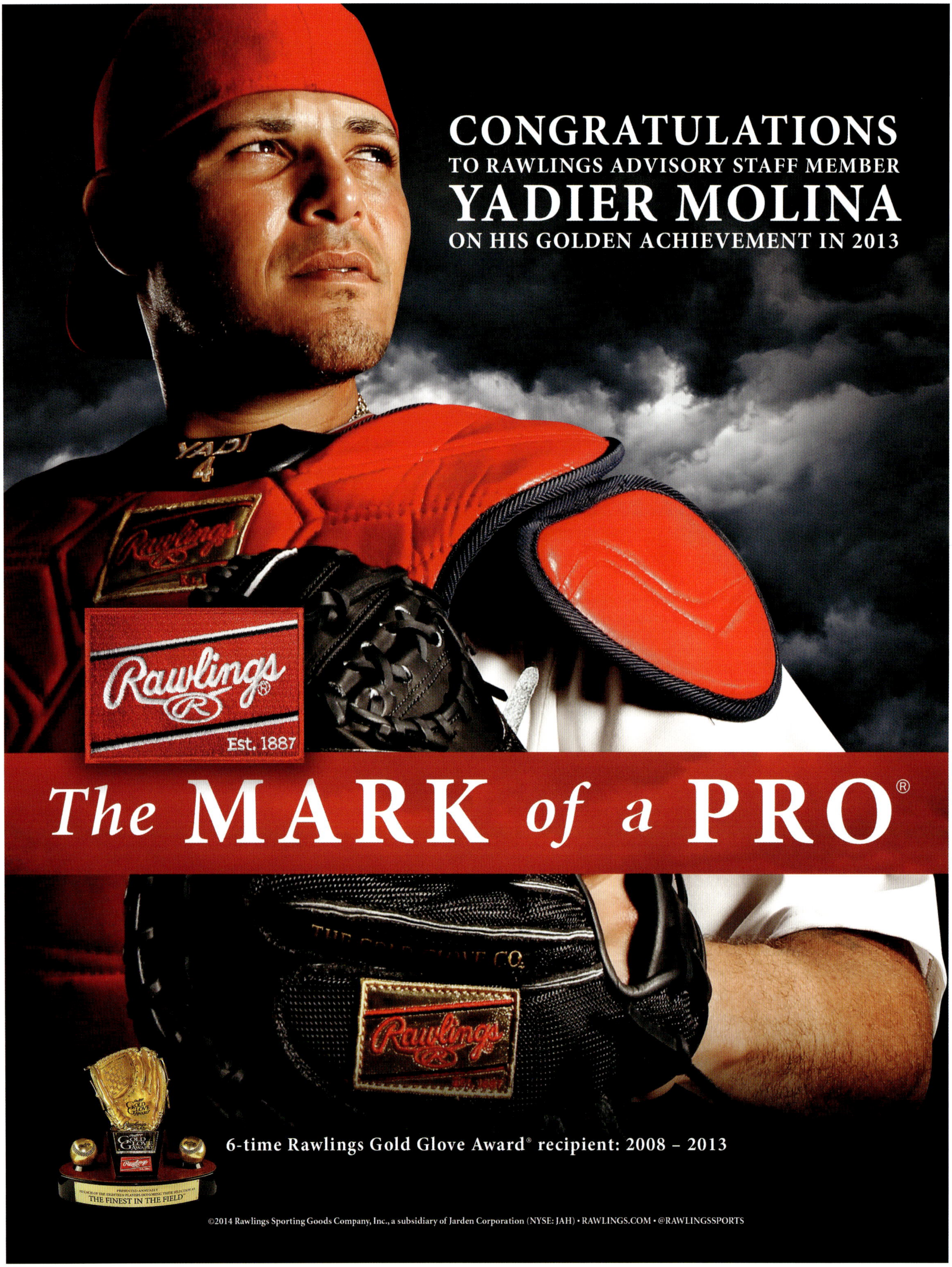
CONGRATULATIONS
TO RAWLINGS ADVISORY STAFF MEMBER
YADIER MOLINA
ON HIS GOLDEN ACHIEVEMENT IN 2013
YADI
4
Rawlings
Est. 1887
The MARK of a PRO®
6-time Rawlings Gold Glove Award® recipient: 2008 – 2013
THE FINEST IN THE FIELD
©2014 Rawlings Sporting Goods Company, Inc., a subsidiary of Jarden Corporation (NYSE: JAH) • RAWLINGS.COM • @RAWLINGSSPORTS

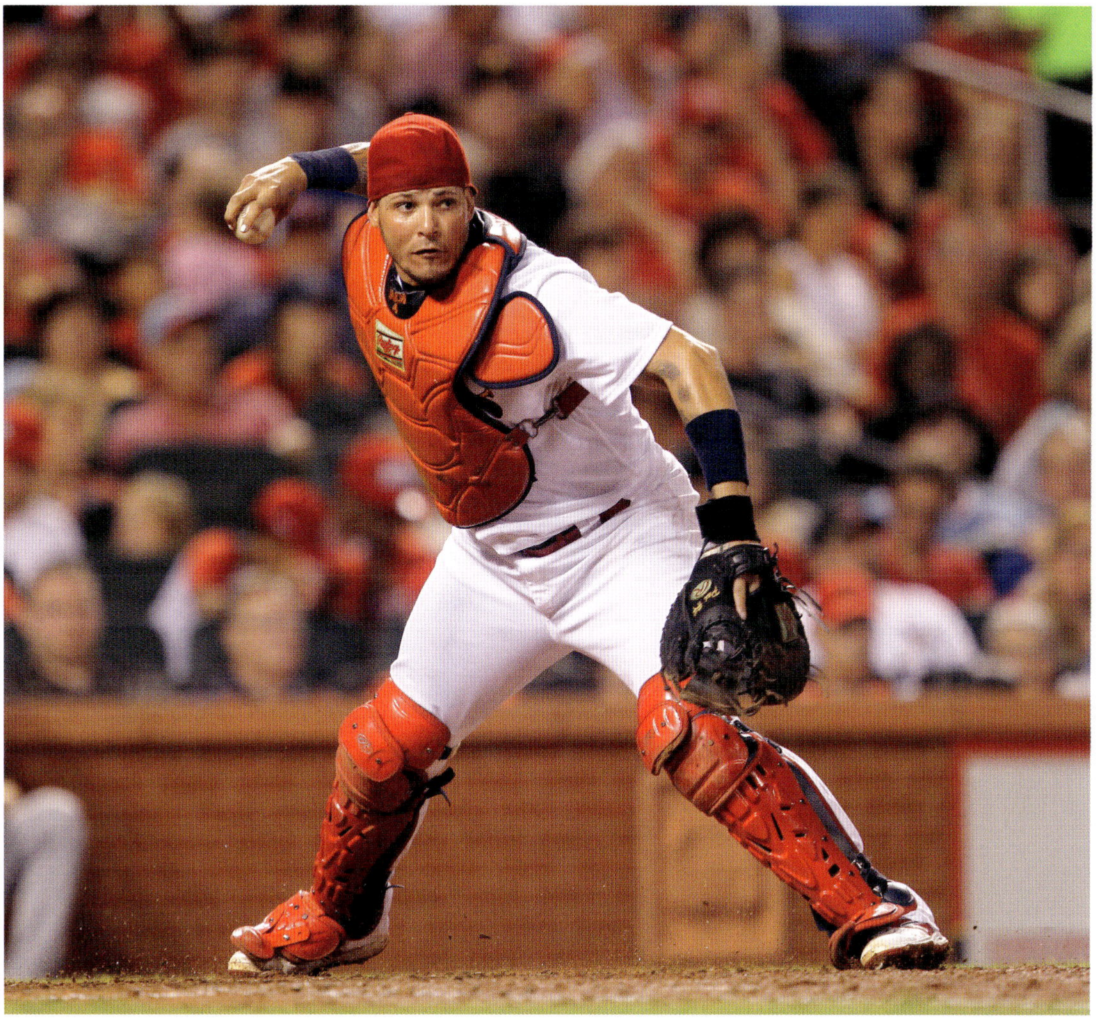

In 2013, Rawlings ran an advertisement to congratulate Molina on his sixth consecutive Gold Glove Award (opposite). He went on to win three more in 2014, 2015, and 2018. Molina (above) showcased his defensive expertise by also winning four Platinum Glove Awards in 2011, 2012, 2014, and 2015.

fourth most in a career and rank third among this group. Across the leaderboard, he recorded more chances (16,267) than any of the catchers in Cooperstown, and his 15,122 putouts are more than any other catcher in the history of the game.

His 40.3 percent caught stealing is only 12th among these inductees, but how much of that number is a product of the fact that base runners had so much respect for—or fear of—his strong arm and throwing abilities that they didn't even try to steal a base? With the advent of hard sliders bouncing at the plate, Molina showed an exceptional ability to quickly move and snag those errant balls in the dirt and prevent runners from advancing. Within those 19 seasons and 2,184 games behind the plate, Molina committed only 83 errors—a remarkable stat that is lower than any of the other Hall of Fame catchers.

TORII HUNTER

Spider-Man

The player who would eventually earn the nickname "Spider-Man" began his career as a standout high school player in Pine Bluff, Arkansas. Torii Hunter's outfield heroics soon led to his selection to the U.S. Junior Olympic baseball team in 1992. When the 16-year-old and his family could not afford the team's $500 playing fee, Hunter reached out to Bill Clinton—then the state's governor—and discovered that he was a fan. A check was soon in the mail, and Hunter's career was aiming for the big leagues.

A year later, Hunter was selected in the first round of baseball's amateur draft (20th overall pick) by the Minnesota Twins. After five seasons of learning the nuances of professional baseball, Hunter made a one-game debut in 1997 as a 21-year-old. (Much of his time before the call-up was spent working on hitting.) Hunter's athleticism offered the Twins an elite defender in the outfield. By 1999, Hunter was ready to stay in the majors, playing center field in one of MLB's most difficult places to play—the Hubert H. Humphrey Metrodome.

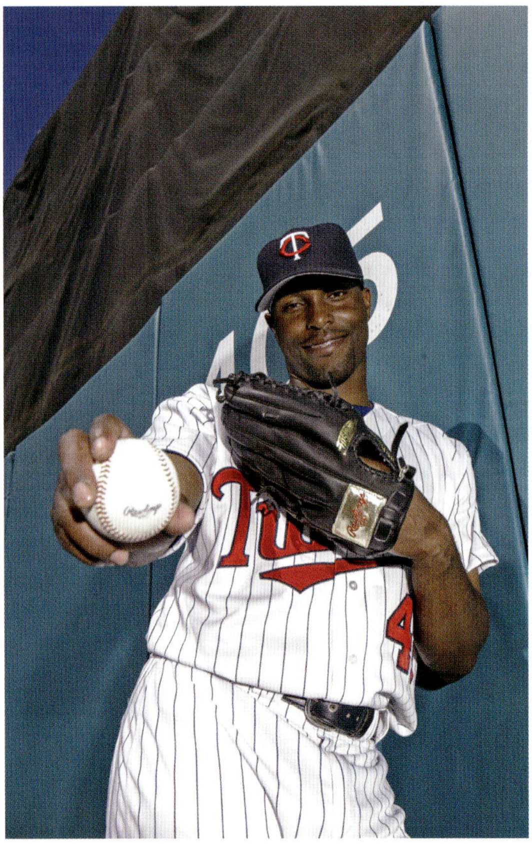

The stadium was a domed building with a Teflon-coated fiberglass-fabric roof that was supported by air pressure. The roof's color made following the flight of the ball off the bat difficult, and sometimes it was impossible to catch. The left-field wall was seven feet high, and over in right to right-center field, there was a 23-foot removable wall of blue plastic stretched between poles that was dubbed the "Hefty Bag" due to its similarity to trash bags. Many outfielders had trouble playing in the stadium, but Hunter was the exception.

Torii Hunter (left) was nicknamed "Spider-Man" due to his ability to climb outfield walls to catch a ball and keep it from becoming a home run. Hunter's PRO-Torii Fastback model glove (opposite) features a popular Spider-Man *catchphrase sewn onto it.*

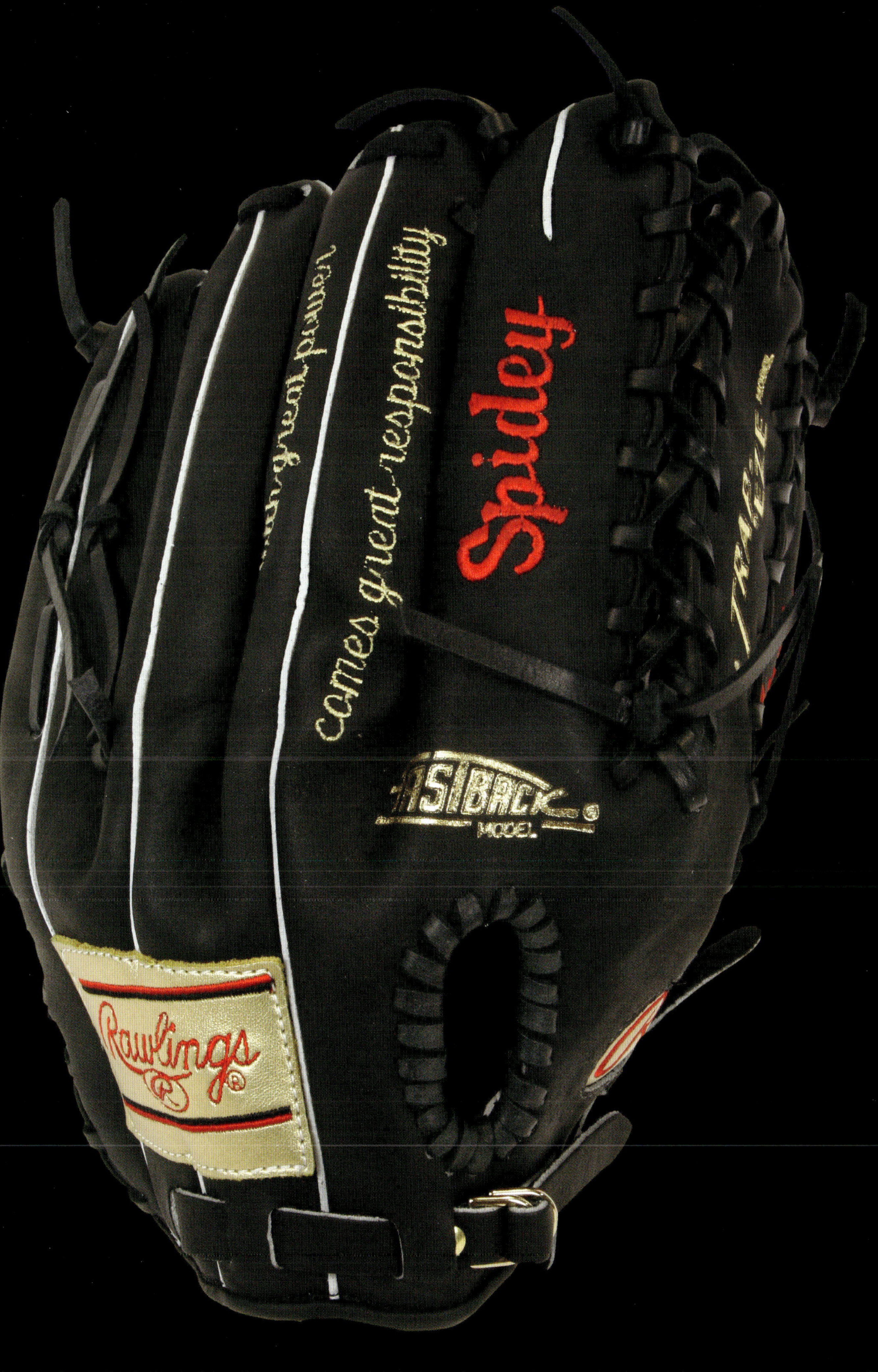
comes great responsibility
Spidey
Rawlings

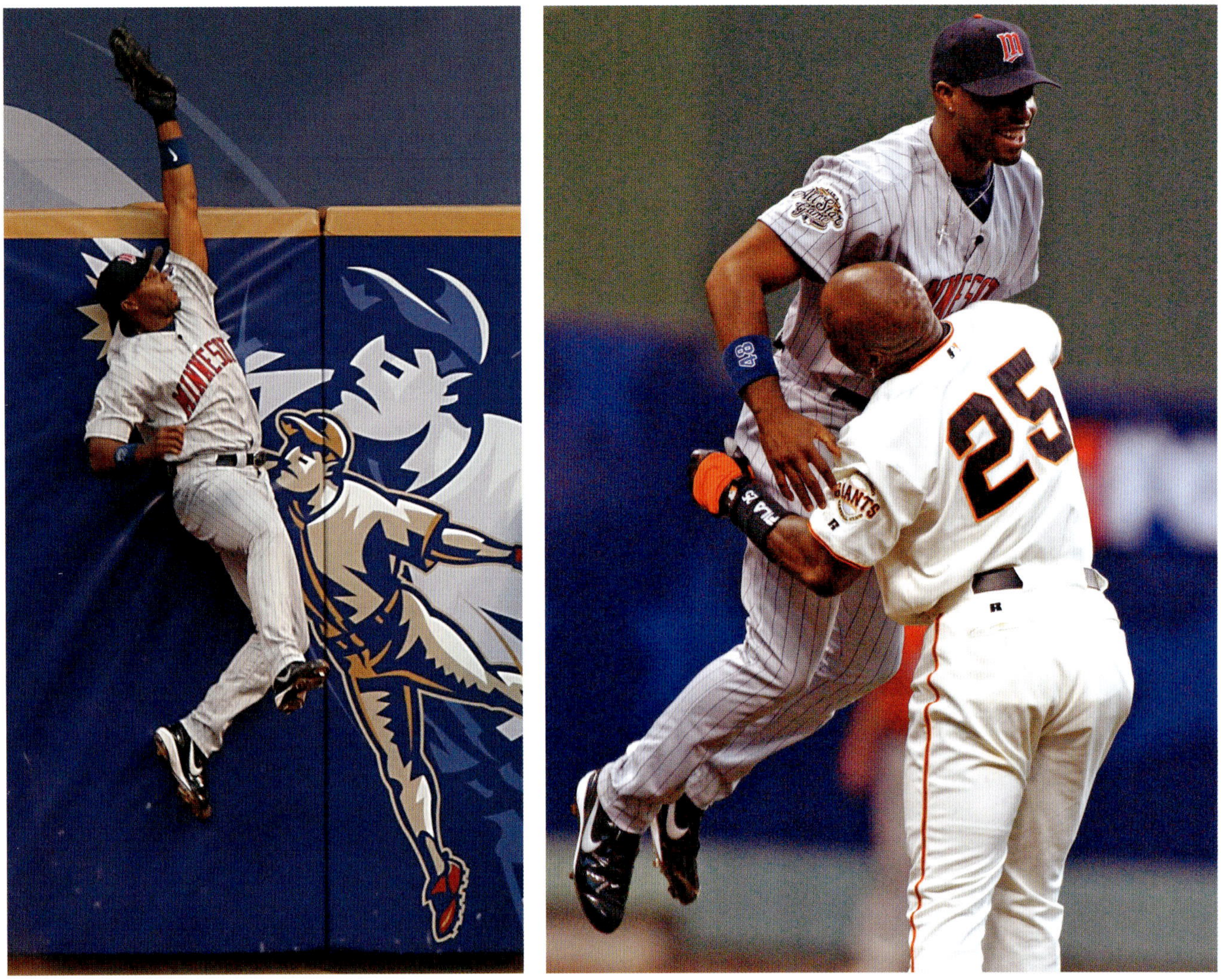

The Minnesota Twins' Hunter leaps to take away a home run from the San Francisco Giants' Barry Bonds to end the first inning of the 2002 MLB All-Star Game at Miller Park in Milwaukee (above, left). To congratulate Hunter on making the catch, Bonds runs and picks him up (above, right).

With his uncanny ability to leap and climb the wall to track down and catch what looked like sure home runs, Hunter became a human highlight reel. He was soon dubbed "Spider-Man" as he regularly saved the day with yet another tremendous catch. How elite was Hunter's play? He won nine consecutive Gold Gloves in center field, and only three other center fielders have won more (Willie Mays, Ken Griffey Jr., and Andruw Jones). Seven of his nine wins (2001–2007) were with the Twins and remain the most by any position player on the team. Only pitcher Jim Kaat has more Gold Gloves with Minnesota than Hunter; he earned 12 of his 16 wins with the team. Hunter's other two Gold Gloves (2008 and 2009) came with the Los Angeles Angels.

Perhaps Hunter's greatest moment came in 2002, when he made one of the greatest catches in All-Star Game history with a tremendous leap and reach over the outfield wall to rob the San Francisco Giants' Barry Bonds of a homer. It was a play in which the game's greatest home-run hitter went head-to-head with one of the game's best center fielders, and the outfielder won. Instead of kicking the infield dirt in disgust, like Joe DiMaggio did after being robbed of a home run in the 1947 World Series, Bonds ran out to Hunter in the outfield and lifted him high over his shoulder as a show of respect for the gem of a play he had just made. Then he returned to the dugout with a smile on his face.

Hunter's success in the field was soon augmented by success at the plate, which led to five All-Star Game appearances (2002, 2007, 2009, 2010, and 2013). His career ended with a .277 batting average, 2,452 hits, 353 home runs, and 1,391 RBIs. Hunter sits with elite company as one of just seven players in MLB history to have at least 350 home runs and at least nine Gold Glove Awards. (The other six are Ken Griffey Jr., Willie Mays, Mike Schmidt, Andruw Jones, Al Kaline, and Johnny Bench.) His .990 career fielding percentage ranks as one of the game's best. Throughout baseball's entire history, only 15 players have had at least 350 home runs, 150 stolen bases, 450 doubles, and 2,400 hits. Hunter is one of them. Ten of the players with these credentials are in the Hall of Fame. The four who have not been inducted were all cast with the shadow of baseball's steroid era—something that has never been pointed in Hunter's direction. Throughout his 19 big-league seasons, Hunter was simply one of the top five-tool players of his era and, like his namesake superhero, he used his powers well. He even had a popular *Spider-Man* catchphrase sewn onto his glove as a reminder: "With great power comes great responsibility."

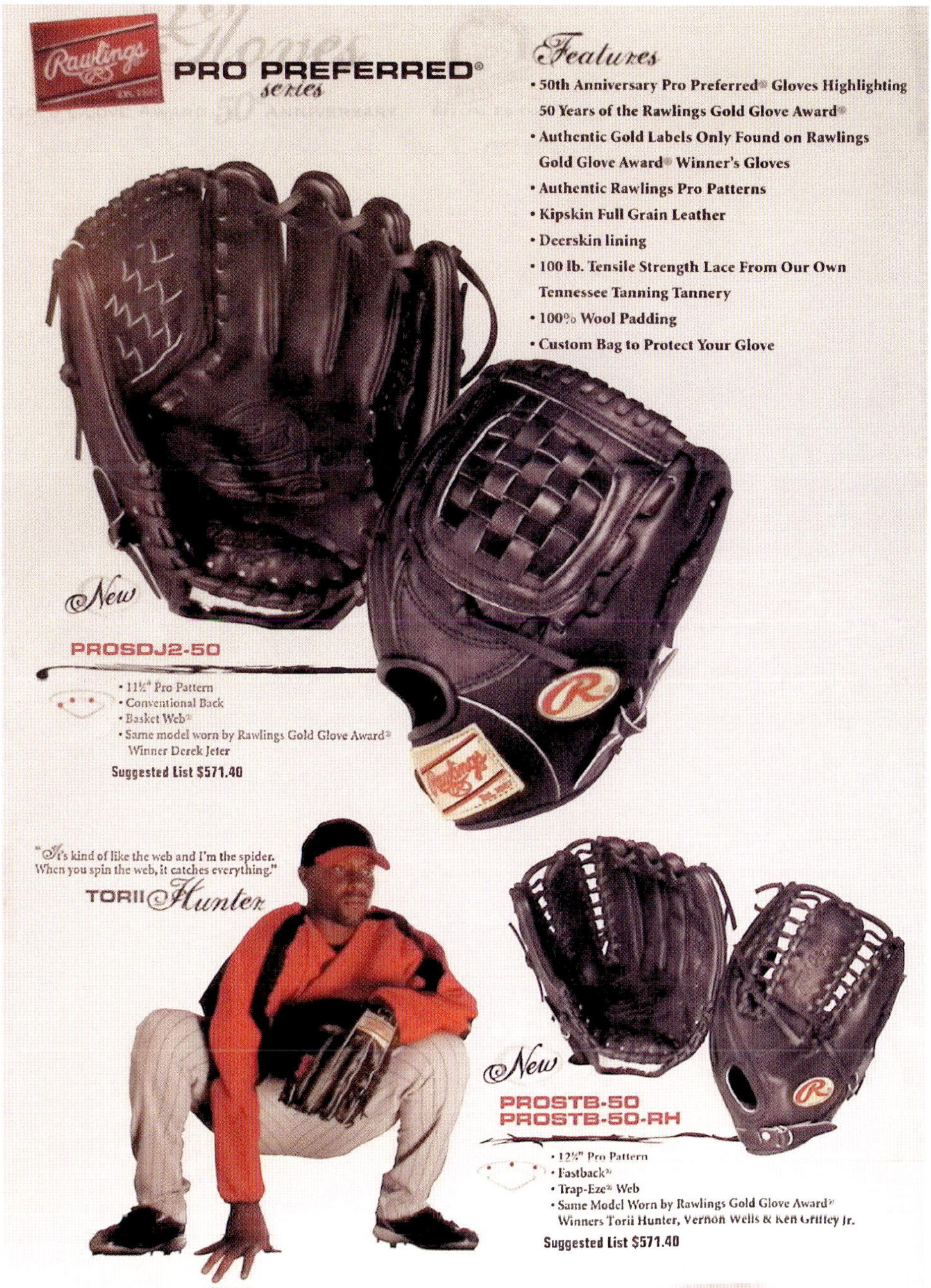

A 2007 Rawlings catalog features Torii Hunter model gloves.

TROY TULOWITZKI

Tulo's Triple on Defense

Troy Tulowitzki's major-league debut with the Colorado Rockies in 2006 continued baseball's transformation at the shortstop position. No longer dominated by small, agile, and quick-fielding players with the byline "good glove, weak bat," teams were beginning to field tall, power-hitting men at the position. The game's stars at the six-hole—Cal Ripken Jr., Derek Jeter, and Alex Rodriguez—had become the dominant prototype. They and others who followed this new and evolving shortstop model exceeded six feet, three inches in height. The big men's athleticism allowed for great range and defensive coverage while they regularly powered baseballs over stadium fences, proving they could thrive as major-league shortstops.

"Tulo," as Tulowitzki came to be known, was following in the footsteps of these players he had grown up watching and worshipping. At six feet, three inches, and 205 pounds, he fit this new mold of major-league shortstops. He was ready to make the leap from his college career at California State University, Long Beach, to join the Rockies as their first-round pick (seventh overall selection) in the 2005 draft. Ahead of the draft, *Baseball America* praised his potential: "He plays with exceptional intensity and an unrivaled passion for the game. . . . He has no holes in his game, and all his tools are close to big-league ready. He is a top defender who has adjusted well to the speed of the game. He has an above-average arm and good footwork. . . . He now projects to hit 25–30 homers a year in the big leagues."

Tulowitzki made it to the majors before the end of the 2006 season and got his feet wet in 25 of the Rockies' final 31 games.

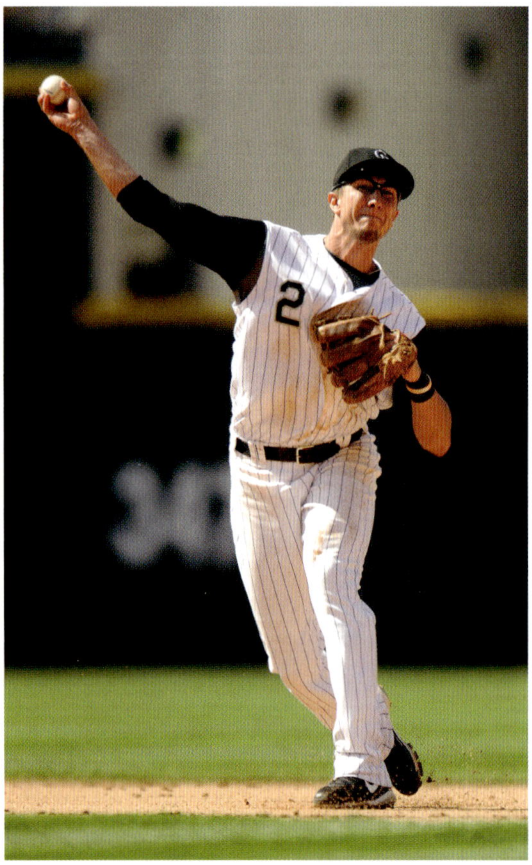

Colorado Rockies shortstop Troy Tulowitzki (left) throws out a runner on the season's opening day in 2009. Tulowitzki used this 11½-inch PROTT2 Heart of the Hide model glove (opposite), which was modeled after the glove of his boyhood idol, Cal Ripken Jr.

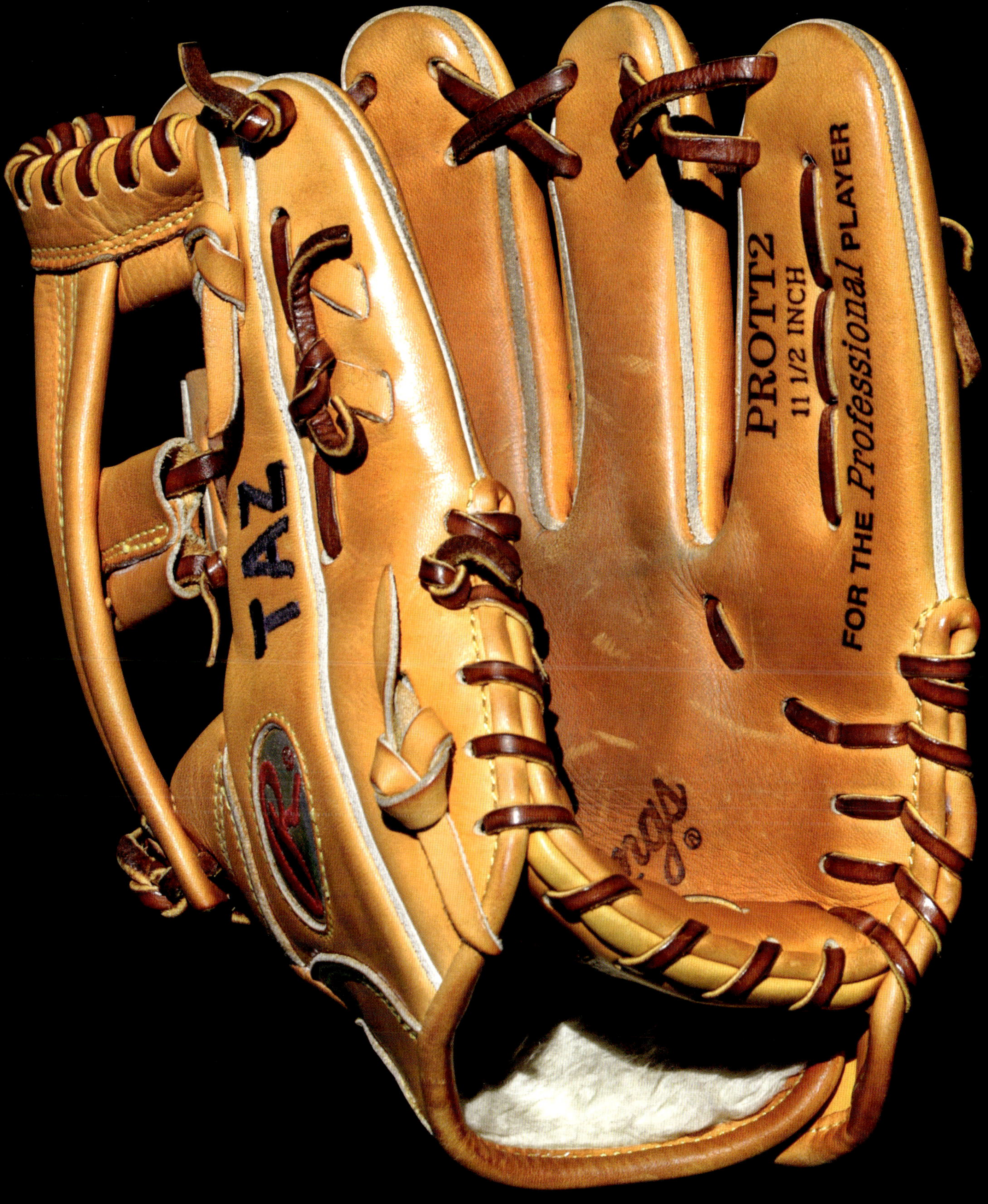
TAZ
PROTT2
11 1/2 INCH
FOR THE Professional PLAYER

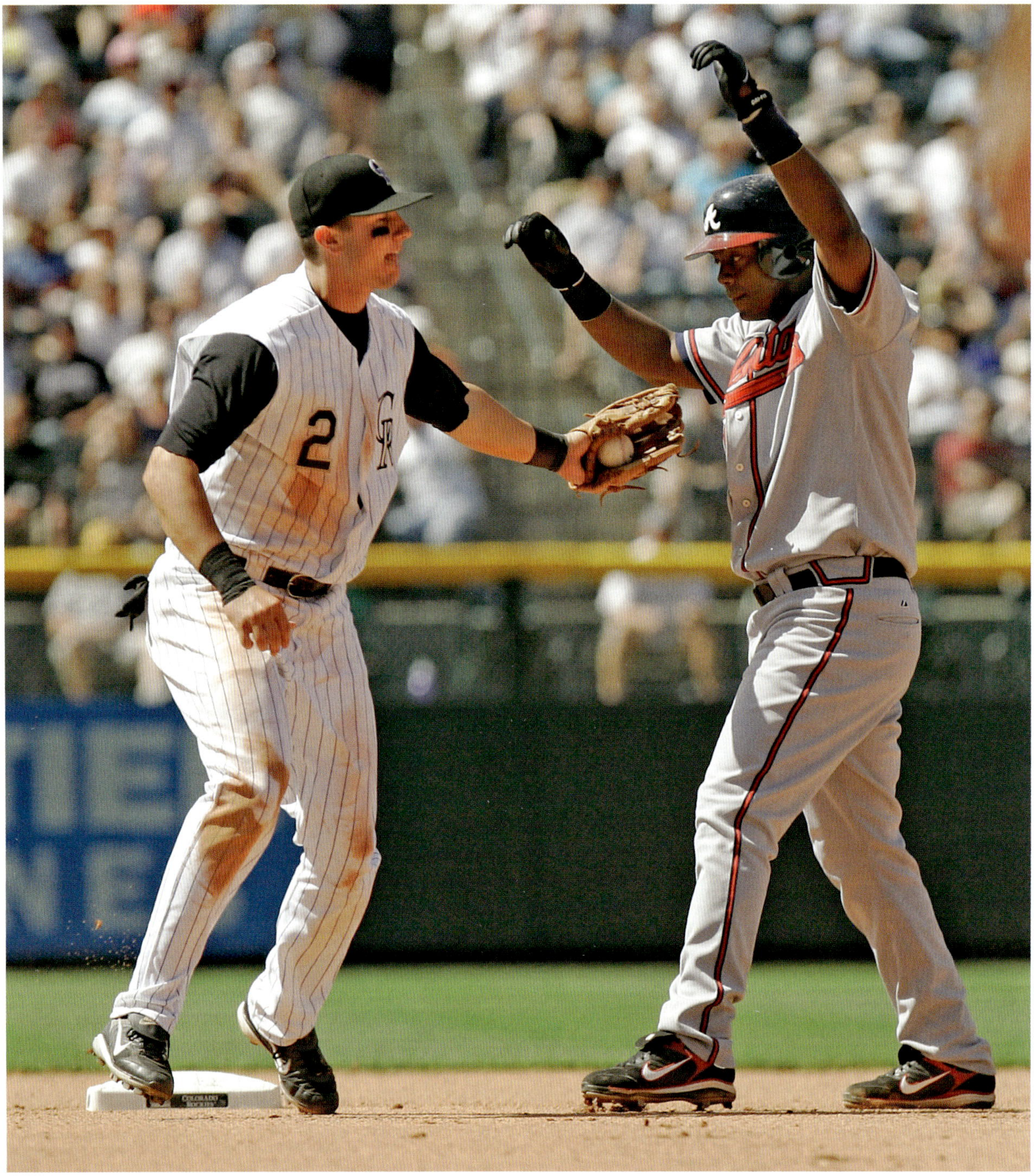

Tulowitzki completes the 13th unassisted triple play in MLB regular-season history by tagging out the Atlanta Braves' Édgar Rentería near second base in the seventh inning of a 2007 game at Coors Field in Denver. The Rockies won 9–7 in 11 innings.

That experience set the stage for a breakout season the following year. He hit .291 and batted 24 homers to eclipse Ernie Banks's 1954 NL record (19) for most home runs by a rookie shortstop. He was quickly becoming the face of the Colorado franchise as the team made their way to their first World Series appearance in 2007 before being swept by the Boston Red Sox. (It was Boston's second Series sweep in four years.) It had been a standout season for the 22-year-old rookie, who finished second in NL voting for the Rookie of the Year Award, a mere two points behind the Milwaukee Brewers' Ryan Braun (128 points to 126).

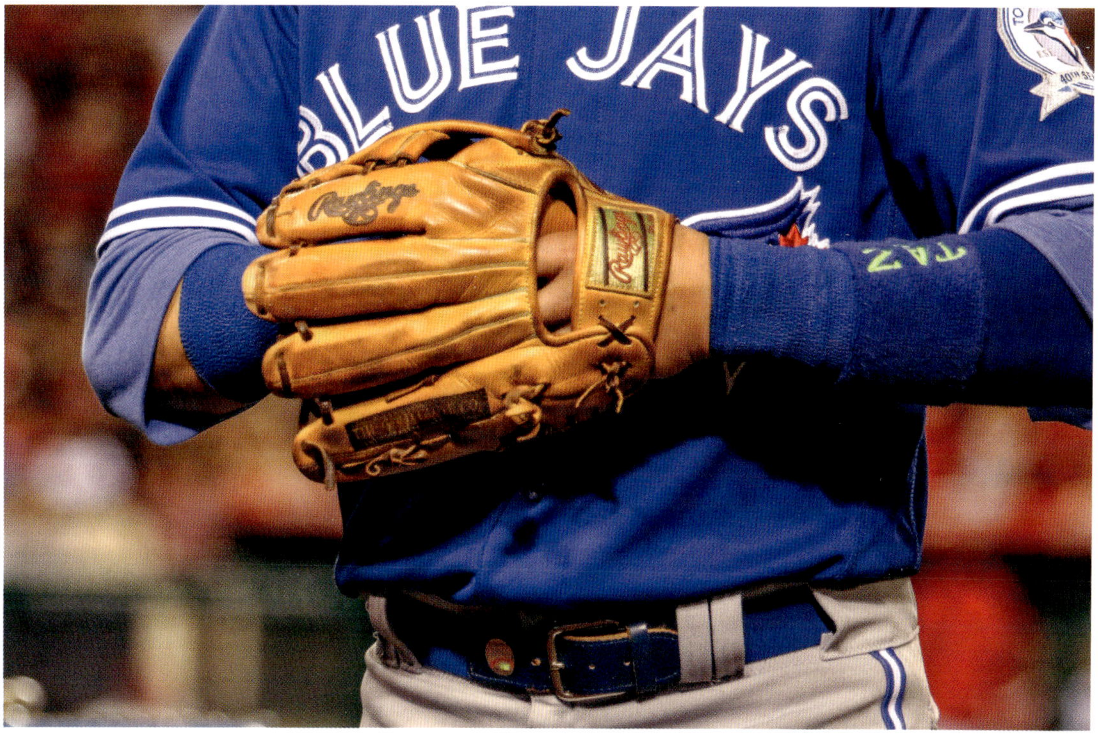

Tulowitzki won two Rawlings Gold Glove Awards (2010 and 2011), which allowed him to wear the gold label on the gloves he used during games.

There was another memorable moment from that 2007 season that would add Tulowitzki's name to baseball's history books. It happened on April 29, in a game against the Atlanta Braves at Coors Field, when Tulowitzki recorded MLB's 13th unassisted triple play. In the top of the seventh inning of a 5–5 game, the visitors had Kelly Johnson on second and Édgar Rentería on first. With a full count on batter Chipper Jones, the runners took off as Jones lined a shot behind second base. Tulowitzki grabbed it in midair, stepped on the base to retire Johnson, and then tagged Rentería out to complete the triple play.

On the field, Tulowitzki became a perennial NL leader on defense while winning two Gold Gloves (2010 and 2011). His name could regularly be found in each season's top 10 leaderboard (and he was often the leader) in putouts, double plays turned, and fielding percentage. His career fielding percentage at shortstop ranks second in MLB history behind only Omar Vizquel, and that is by the slimmest of margins (.9847 to .9846). He hit over .300 four times and wound up with a career batting average of .290 while belting out 24 or more home runs six times (twice over 30) for 225 career homers. In September 2010, he hit 14 home runs in 15 games.

Looking back at his career, the question remains: How good could Tulowitzki have been if injuries had not limited his playing time? There were only three times in his 13-season career that he played more than 140 games. In six seasons, he played 101 games or fewer. However, for those limited seasons that he was healthy, he was on top of his game, powering the ball over the boards and making electrifying jump throws from the hole to live up to the predictions of *Baseball America*'s crystal ball.

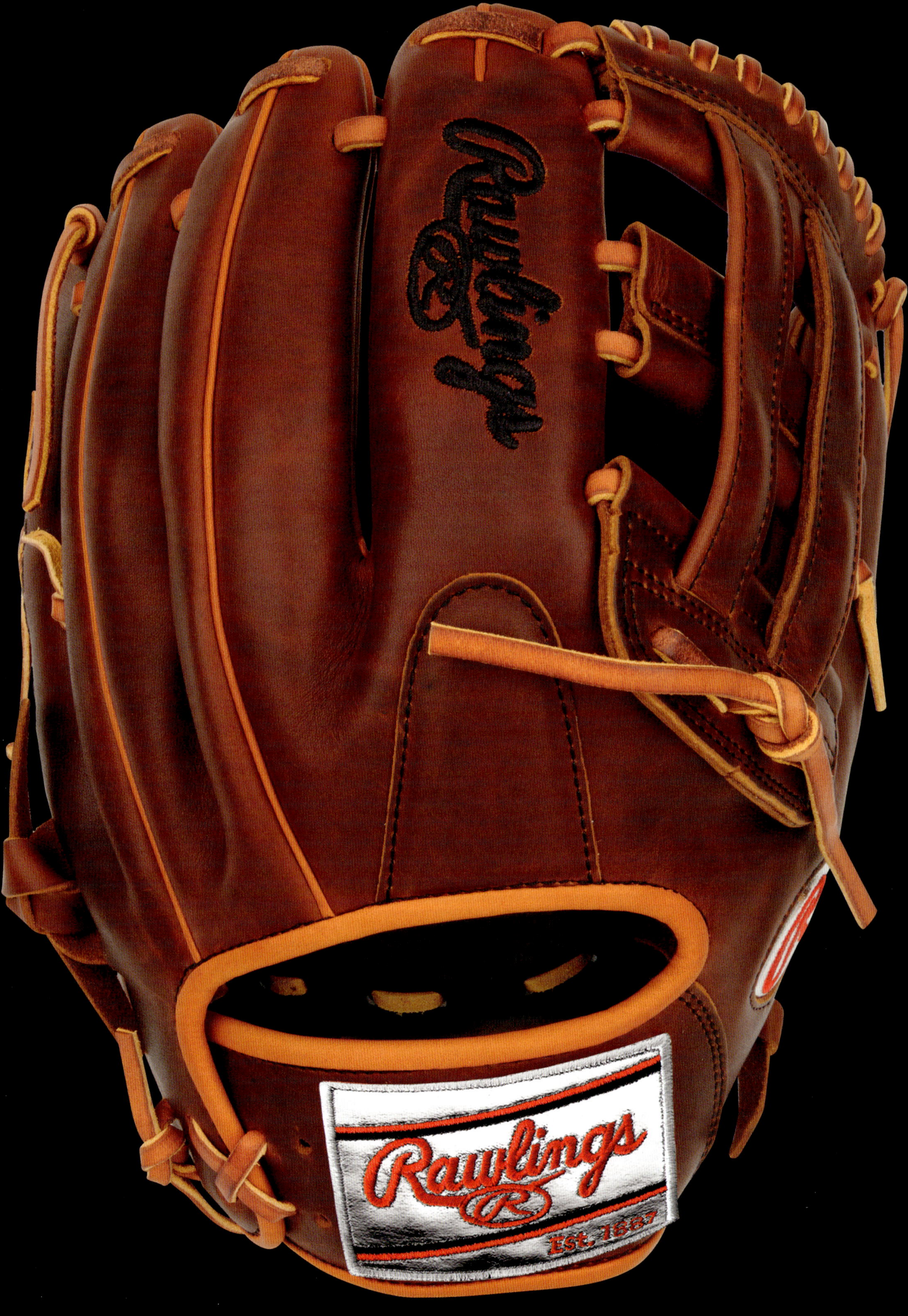
Rawlings
Rawlings
Est. 1887

NOLAN ARENADO

Mr. Platinum

Nolan Arenado's time and résumé at baseball's hot corner may not yet add up to Brooks Robinson's in the record books. There is, however, much to consider when comparing their career accomplishments. The Baltimore Orioles' "Human Vacuum Cleaner" remains the Gold Glove leader at third base nearly five decades after he retired in 1977. His 16 trophies were accumulated during his 23 seasons in the big leagues. Arenado has only played 13 seasons to date, but his 10 consecutive Gold Gloves remarkedly came during his first 10 seasons in the big leagues. He is still playing through the prime years of his career, so it's possible that even more gold will be added to his résumé.

Arenado made it to the major leagues in 2013 with the Colorado Rockies and immediately showed his star power at the plate and in the field. He is clearly one of MLB's impact players. Blessed with a strong arm, quick reflexes, and incredible range at third base, Arenado's playmaking abilities in the field can singularly turn a game around for his team. And he can do it at the plate as well. In his first year, he reached double digits in the home-run department (10) while also flashing leather and winning his first Gold Glove. In his third season, Arenado won his first NL home-run title; he won two more over the next four years to go along with two MLB RBI titles during those same seasons.

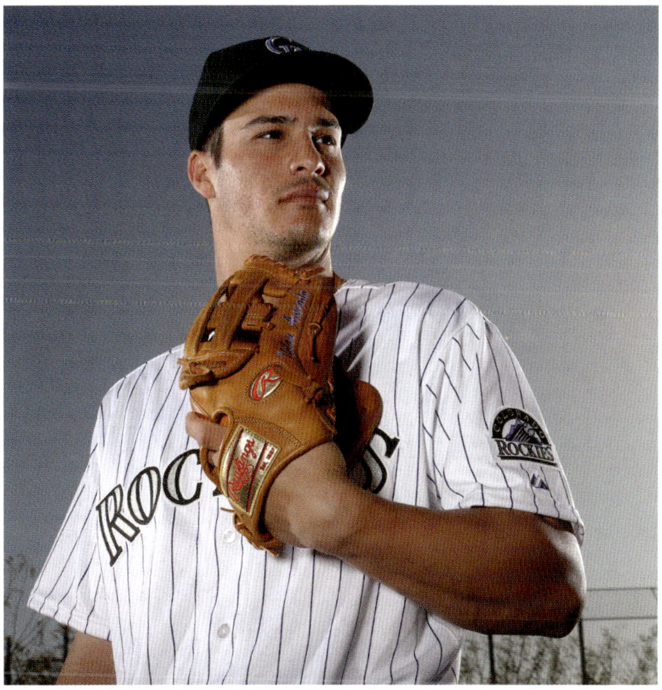

Nolan Arenado preferred using this Rawlings PRORNA28 model glove (opposite), which was adorned with a platinum label to recognize that he won the Rawlings Platinum Glove Award six times. Arenado (above) also won 10 consecutive Gold Glove Awards at third base between 2013 and 2022.

While there may be some who downplay Arenado's hitting prowess due to the fact that he played his home games in Denver's Coors Field, nicknamed the "Launching Pad" due to its high altitude and thin air,

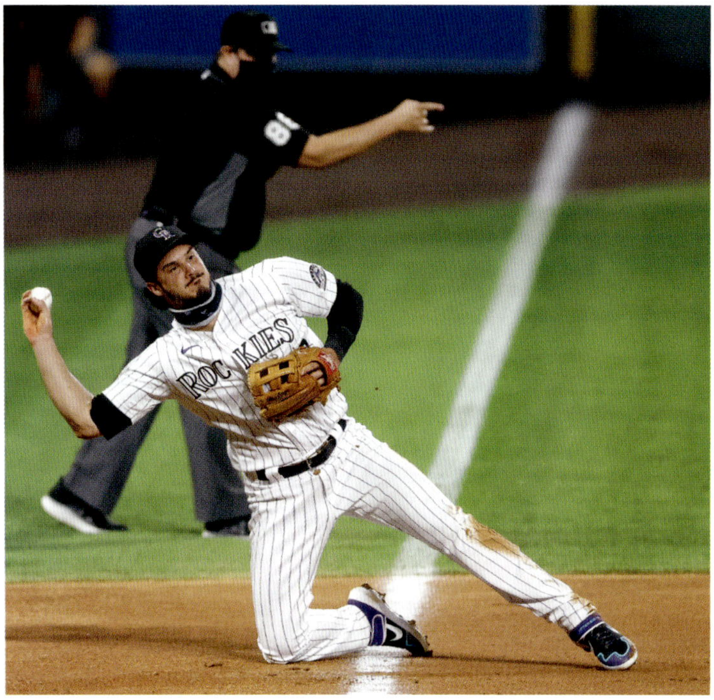

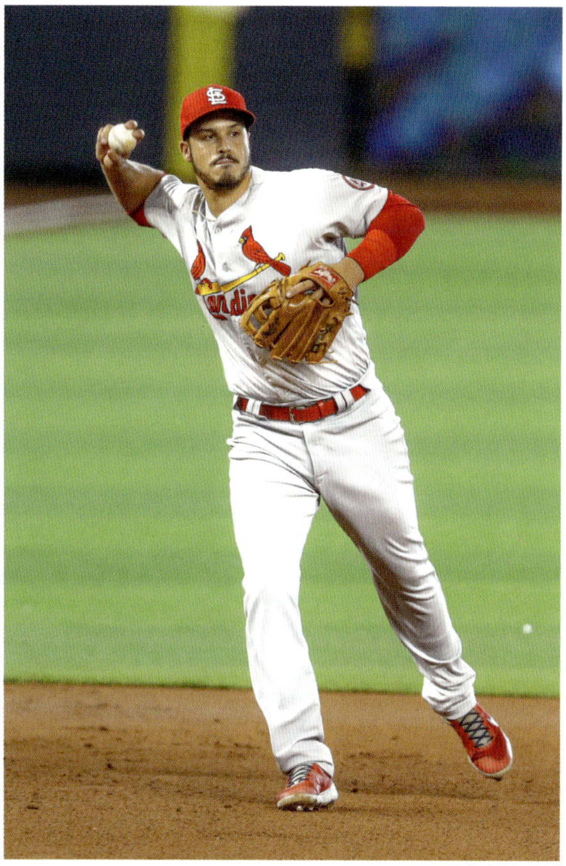

Arenado shows why he is the NL's best defensive player, throwing from his knees during the sixth inning of a 2020 game at Denver's Coors Field as umpire Doug Eddings signals for a fair ball against the Texas Rangers (above, left). Arenado's trade to the St. Louis Cardinals (above, right) in 2021 did not impact his defensive skills; he won Gold Glove and Platinum Glove Awards in his first two seasons with the Redbirds.

there is no denying that—during those league-leading years—Arenado was averaging just three points under .300 at the plate. And, thin air or not, there are no disparagers for the veracity of the difficulty Arenado regularly faced fielding balls hit at him in the hot corner, where, year after year, he added to his Gold Glove collection.

A new lens was focused on Arenado's skills in 2021, when he was traded to the St. Louis Cardinals and forced to play games in Busch Stadium, the team's pitcher-friendly park. In the first two seasons in his new home, he averaged 32 home runs while winning two more Gold Gloves. His relocation in no way deterred Arenado's defensive domination.

In 2011, Rawlings and MLB unveiled the first Rawlings Platinum Glove Award. This new honor was awarded to the best defensive player in each league from that season's list of Gold Glove winners. What a difficult selection to make among each season's roster of defensive greatness! Seven years into the award, in 2017, Arenado was selected for the honor for the first time in his fifth season as a major leaguer. His name was then called as the NL Platinum Glove Award winner over the next six consecutive years (2017–2022) to truly make him the best among baseball's defensive players. His six wins are the most over the history of the award, making him deserving of the title "Mr. Platinum." The next player in line for the most Platinum Glove Awards became Arenado's new teammate after his trade to the Cardinals. That player was the now-retired Yadier Molina, who had claimed the first year's award, plus three more.

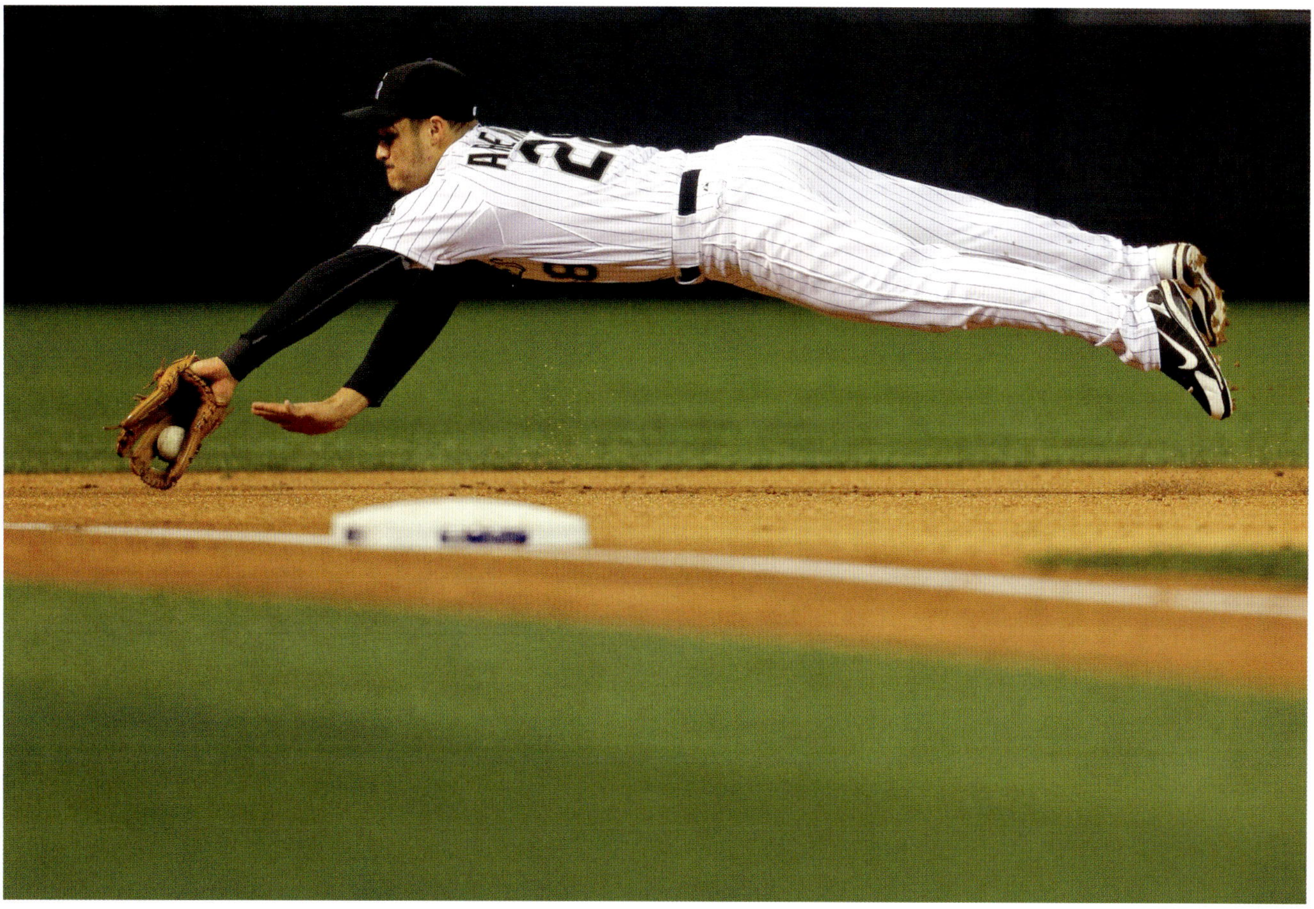

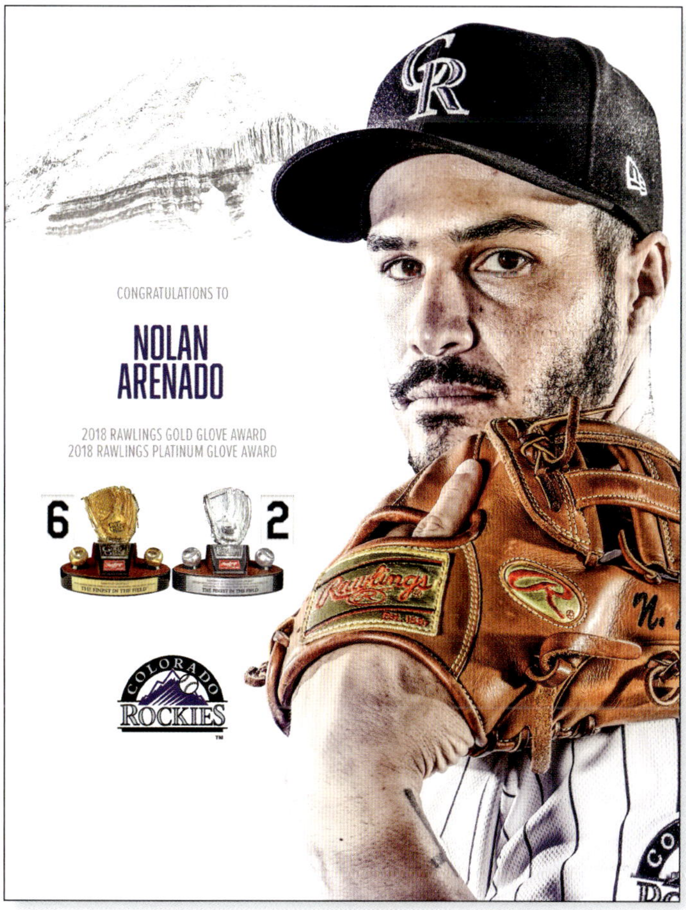

Third baseman Arenado dives on an infield hit by Alex Guerrero of the Los Angeles Dodgers during the first inning of a game at Coors Field in 2015 (above). A 2018 Rawlings advertisement (left) congratulates the third baseman on his six Gold Glove Awards and two Platinum Glove Awards. He has since won four more of each.

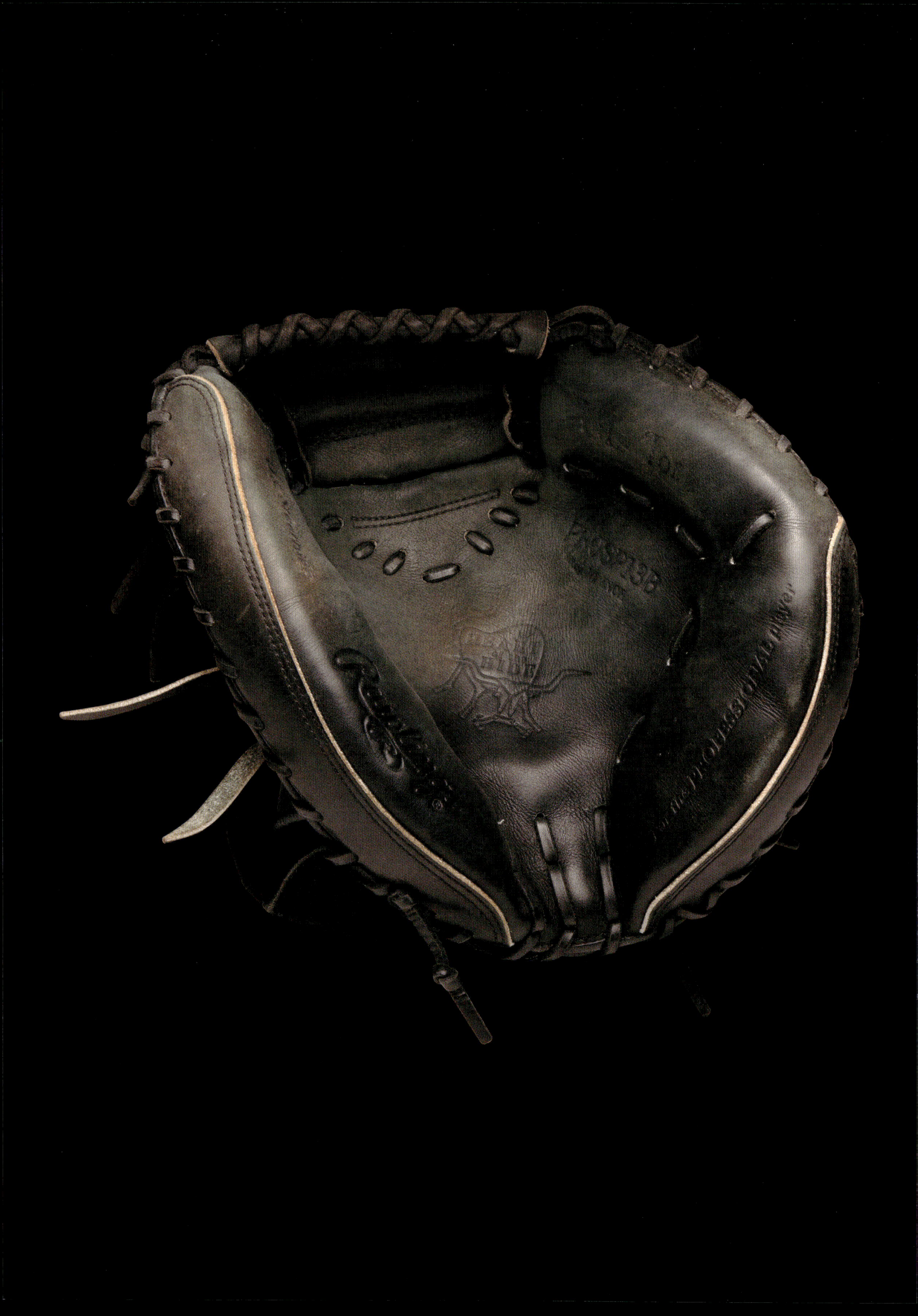

SALVADOR PEREZ

El Niño

Player nicknames have been a part of baseball ever since the game's first ball was thrown. Some are nods to the player's power on the field, like "Hammerin' Hank" Aaron or "Rapid Robert" Feller. Others are references to a specific characteristic, like "Sunny Jim" Bottomley's positive disposition or Mordecai "Three Finger" Brown's missing digits. Over the decades, there have been a "Babe" (Ruth), a "Kid" (Ken Griffey Jr.), and a "Man" (Stan Musial). And today fans cheer on "El Niño," which translates to "The Boy," a nickname earned and then worn by Salvador Perez during the MLB Players' Weekend event, which allows ballplayers to showcase their unique personalities on the field with custom uniforms and equipment.

The nickname was coined by Eric Hosmer in 2008, when Perez was a boyish 18-year-old Venezuelan prospect in the Kansas City Royals minor-league system. Three years later, it became a major-league calling card when Perez joined the parent club, and Hosmer let the Royals fans know they had something special.

And special he became as he undertook the journey from the dirt-floored bedroom of his childhood home in Valencia, Venezuela, to the home-plate dirt of the 2014 World Series. With an everlasting and radiant smile on his face and a passion and drive for success, Perez worked hard to see his dream of playing baseball in the major leagues come true.

The pursuit of that dream began at age four, when his mother's friend, hoping to offer her a respite from long hours of working to support her family as a single parent, asked her if Perez would like to join a baseball team. He did, and was soon expelling all his energy

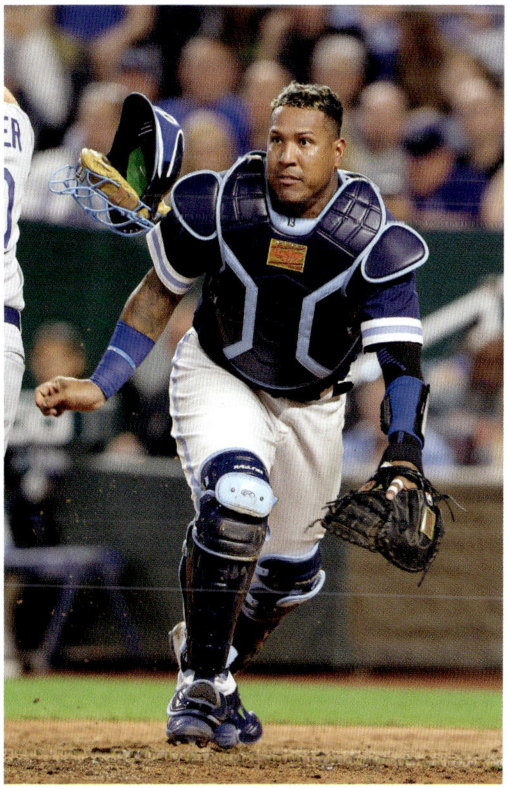

Salvador Perez's glove of choice during his big-league playing career is the Rawlings PROSP13B model (opposite). Perez (right) is a five-time Rawlings Gold Glove Award winner who helped lead the Kansas City Royals to two World Series appearances.

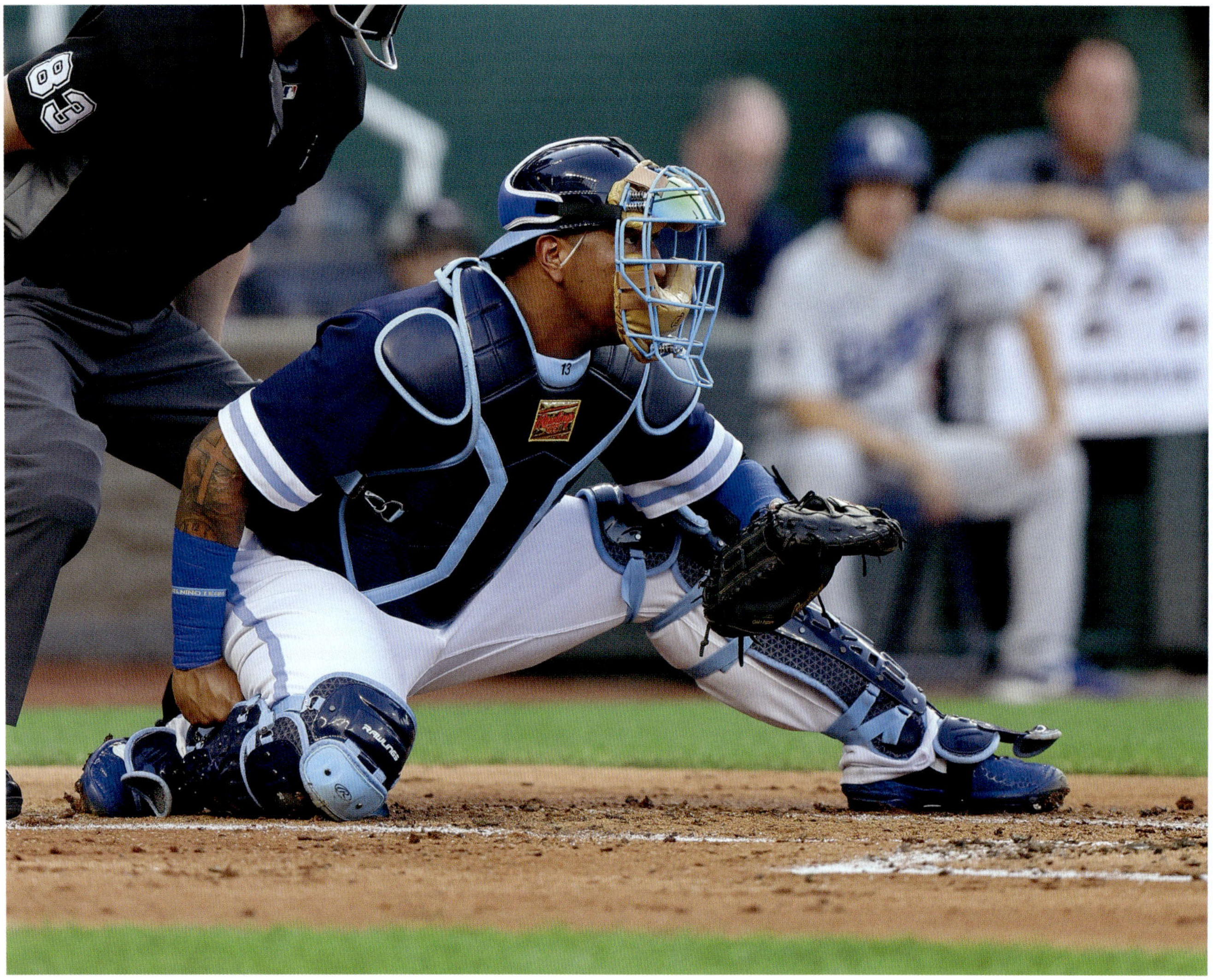

In 2015, Perez was the World Series MVP in the Royals' win over the New York Mets.

running and playing for the team. More importantly, he was learning the game. In time, his size and physical abilities stood out. At age 16, in 2006, Perez signed a professional contract for $65,000 to play baseball with the Kansas City Royals. He joined the organization the following spring and worked his way toward a major-league call-up on August 10, 2011.

Few players have had a debut like Perez. The Royals were visiting the Tampa Bay Rays at Tropicana Field when he was called to the big leagues after hitting .333 in the minors. Catcher Brayan Peña had left the team for parental leave, and the team's reserve catcher was out with a concussion. In announcing Perez's call-up, Royals manager Ned Yost told the newspapers, "We'll get him in there as much as we can. He's got a chance to be really good. He's a young kid, but he's got tremendous tools. Very athletic. He throws as good as any young catcher I've ever seen. Has a real feel for calling a game."

In that first game, Perez showed Yost he had the tools to be good. He had a single in three at-bats to go along with an RBI sacrifice fly. But it was his defense behind the plate that stood out that night. In a stretch of recording seven straight putouts, Perez caught two strikeouts and grabbed five pop fly balls (an astonishing feat for a catcher). He also picked off a runner at first base in the fourth inning, another runner on third base four innings later, and just missed a third pickoff as he made his mark in the big leagues on his very first day.

Those defensive exploits continued. Perez was named to nine All-Star Games and won five Gold Gloves (2013–2016 and 2018). During that 2013–2018 span, only Yadier Molina caught more than Perez's 761 games. Perez's success behind the plate was duplicated when his hitting helped lead his team to two World Series appearances (2014 and 2015), with a world championship in 2015. Perez was named the Series MVP.

Since his second season in the majors, Perez has always been able to hit the ball out of the park. In 2021, he set a new single-season batting mark for a player whose primary position is catcher. His 48 homers (31 as a catcher) that season tied Vladimir Guerrero Jr. for the AL and MLB home-run lead. When Seattle Mariners catcher Cal Raleigh surpassed Perez's home-run mark in 2025, it didn't take anything away from Perez and his career. The backstop's passion and performance made his childhood dream come true. But he went beyond his dream of becoming a major-league ballplayer. He became one of the best all-around catchers in the game.

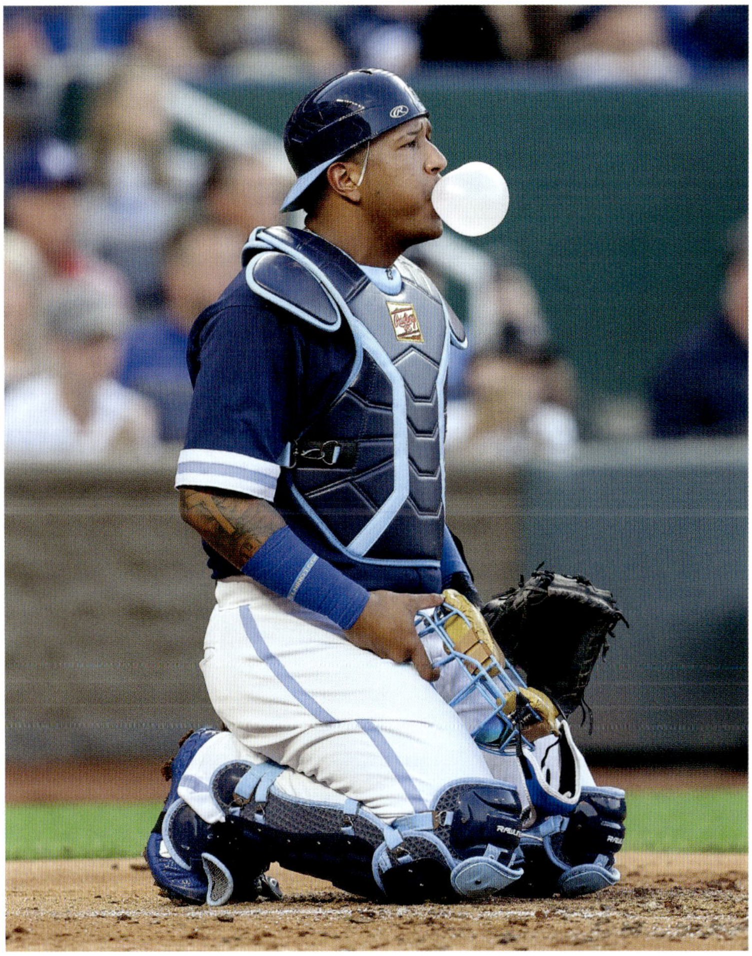

The playful Perez has also been a presence at the plate. He set a new single-season batting record for a player whose primary position is catcher in 2021.

FRANCISCO LINDOR

Mr. Smile

The player nicknamed "Mr. Smile" due to his charismatic personality joined the Cleveland Indians (today's Guardians) in 2015 and quickly established himself as one of the game's premier shortstops. Francisco Lindor had been selected by the team as the eighth pick of the 2011 MLB draft. How ready was he for the big leagues in his rookie season of only 99 games? The switch hitter batted .313 that season while belting double-digit home runs to finish second in a close Rookie of the Year race. His athleticism and speed on the bases led to five straight seasons of double-digit numbers in stolen bases, but it was his elite defense that made Lindor stand out among his peers.

By the end of the 2016 season, Lindor had helped lead the Indians to the AL pennant. But for the young man from Puerto Rico, it was truly about more than the postseason. That year, Lindor was selected to his first of four consecutive All-Star Games. He was also presented with not only his first Gold Glove Award, as the AL's best shortstop, but also his first Platinum Glove Award, as the AL's best defender. His skills in the field were further rewarded with his selection as the Esurance MLB/This Year in Baseball Award winner for best defensive player.

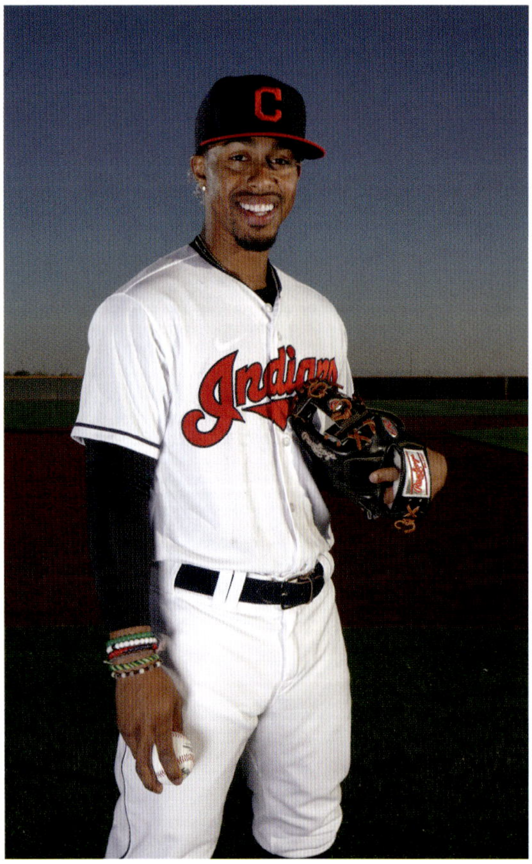

Lindor's Gold Glove in 2016, an award he would receive again in 2019, was the first win by a shortstop from Puerto Rico, and his Platinum Glove is the only one ever awarded to an AL shortstop. Lindor became a symbol of consistency on defense. Dipping into the world of analytics to highlight his defensive skills, Lindor led all MLB players in outs above average (OAA), a range-based metric of fielding skill that accounts for the number of plays made and their difficulty,

Francisco Lindor (left) is known as "Mr. Smile." His personality is reflected in his brightly colored Rawlings REV RL 12 model glove (opposite).

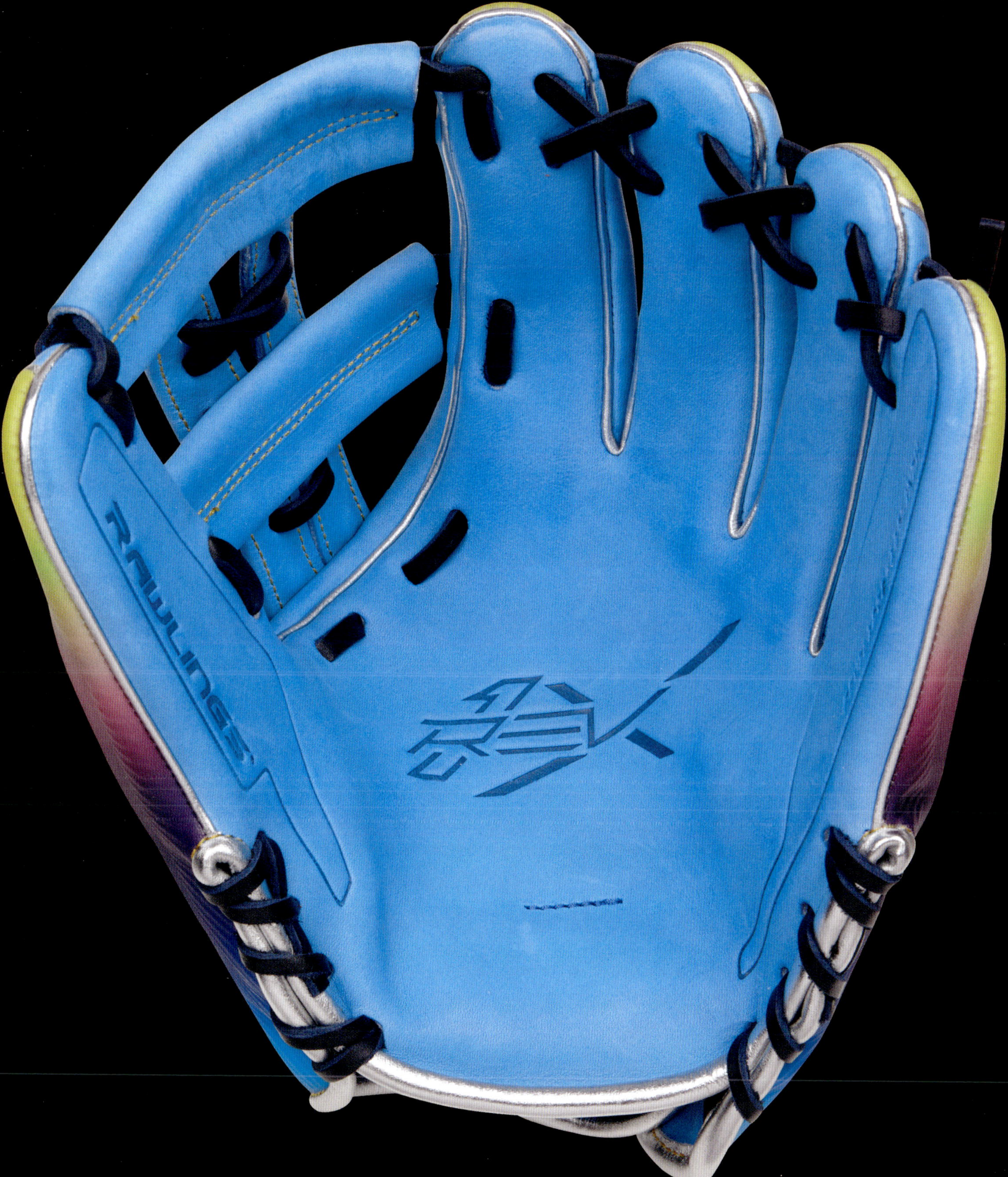
RAWLINGS

between 2016 and 2022. How impressive is Lindor's seven-year average of +117 that topped the majors? To put it in perspective, Nolan Arenado, who won a Gold Glove in each of those seven seasons, as well as six Platinum Gloves, only attained a +92 rating. Lindor's regularity was a product of his father's coaching. "Be consistent," his father always said, "Whatever you do, be consistent." Lindor has the initials "BC" stitched into the leather of his turquoise-colored glove as a constant reminder of this advice.

It wasn't a cannon-like arm that made Lindor a standout at shortstop; it was his agility, instincts, and quickness that created highlight-reel plays game after game and season after season. He has never been in favor of the now-eliminated defensive shifts or laminated coach's cards for positioning players; Lindor's greatness is a product of his own preparation and focus to put himself in position for each hitter, combined with his extraordinary athleticism and range.

As his tenure in the big leagues continued, Lindor's slugging put him in company with baseball's best. In 2024, he became the first shortstop in MLB history to have three separate seasons of at least 25 home runs and 25 stolen bases. He joined Ernie Banks and Alex Rodriguez as the only shortstops in the game to have 20 multihomer games. Now playing for the New York Mets in his 11th season, Lindor has a proven résumé that he continues to build upon each year as one of the best and most productive all-around shortstops in the history of the game.

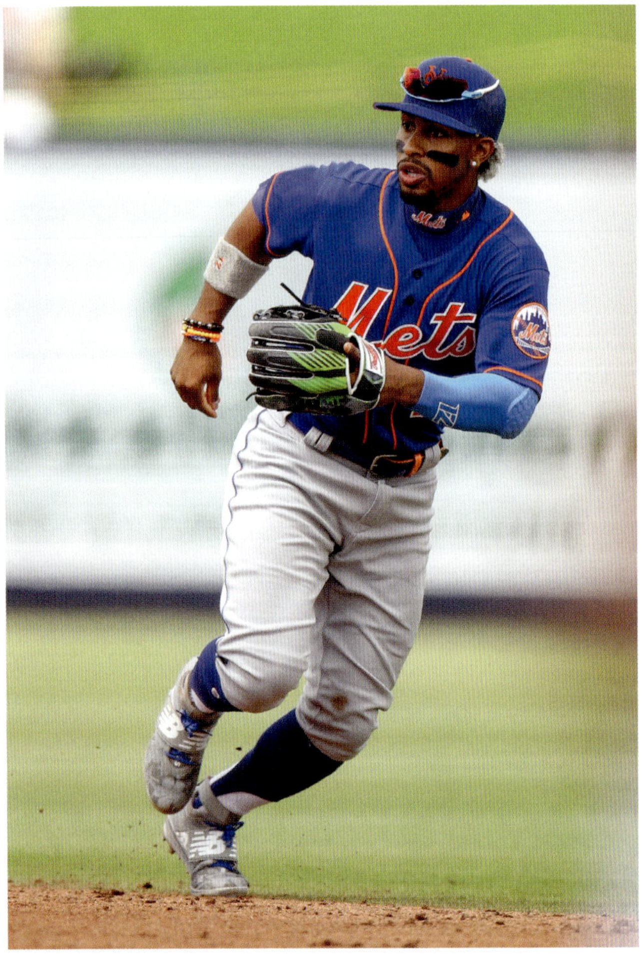

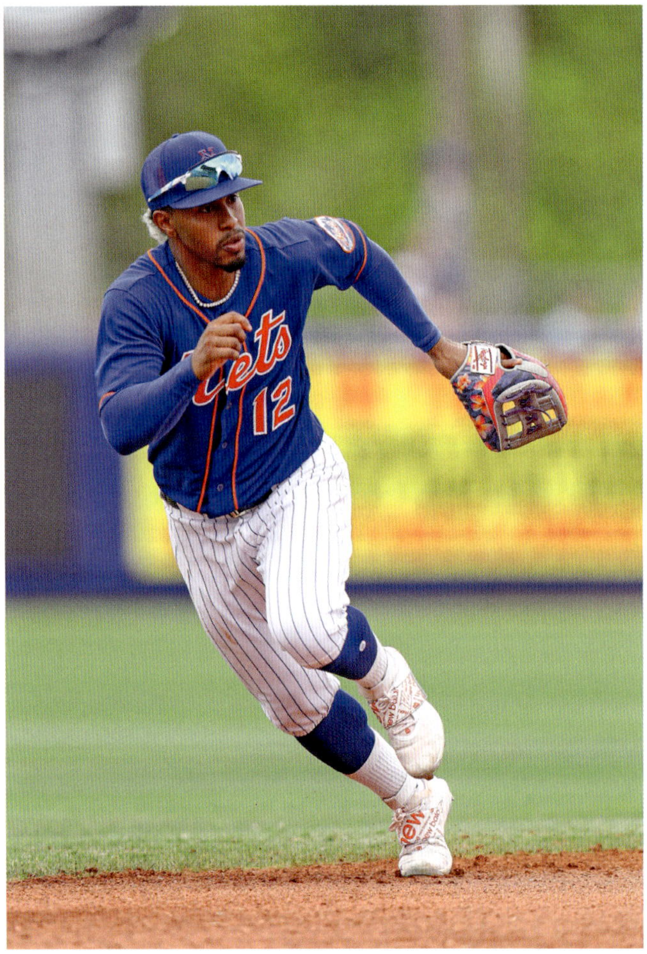

Lindor (above, left and right, and opposite) is known for changing the color of his glove to match his jersey or his mood of the day. His gloves are always decorated with many different designs.

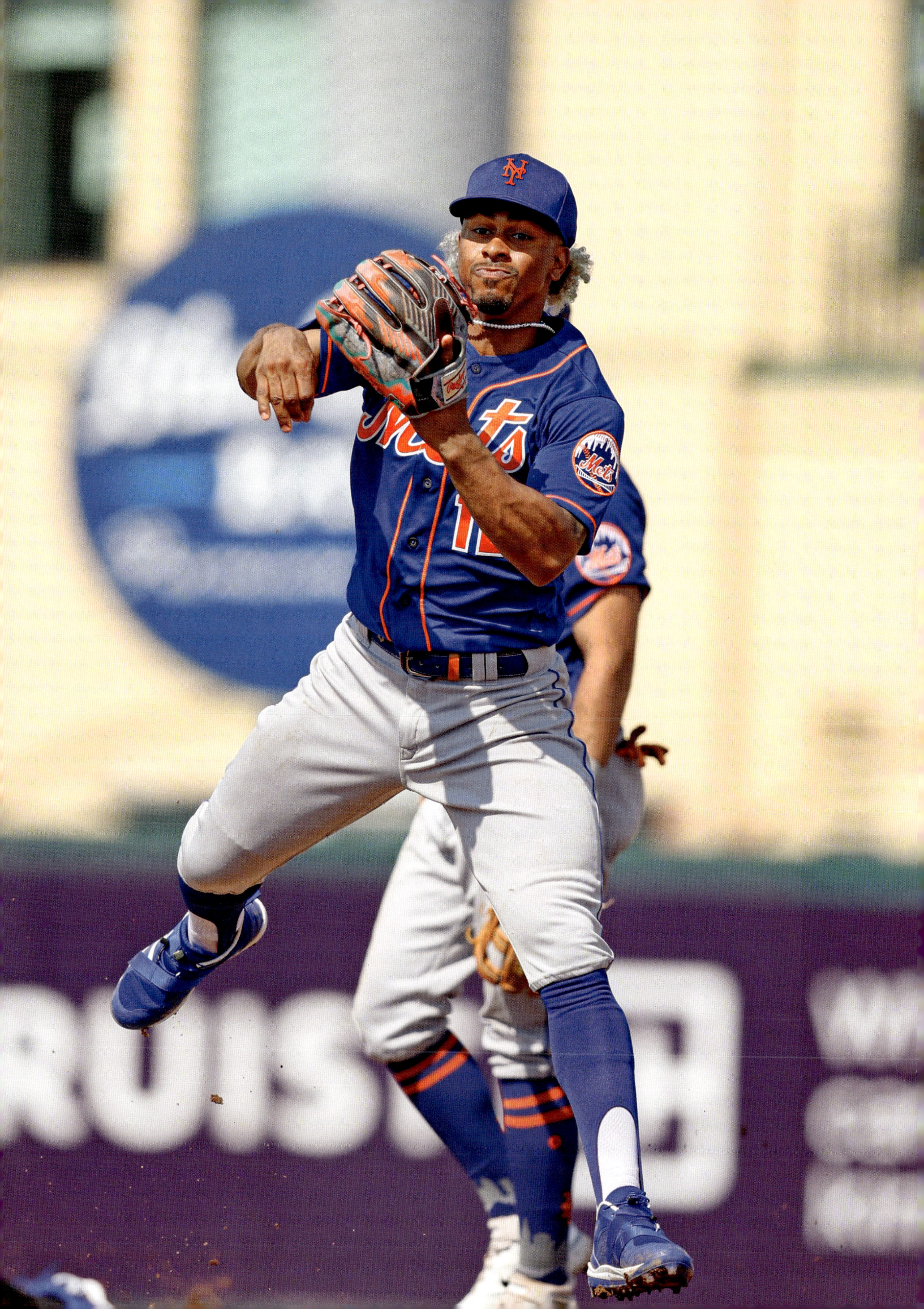

MANNY MACHADO

El Ministro de Defensa

Over the course of 14 seasons, Manny Machado has put together a solid résumé, both at the plate and in the field, that has put him on track for a potential call from the Hall of Fame at the end of his career. This two-time Gold Glove–winning third baseman (2013 and 2015) also picked up a Platinum Glove Award in 2013 as the best of the best defenders in the AL. His skills on the field have earned him the nickname "El Ministro de Defensa," which translates to "The Minister of Defense."

Stellar defense and a strong and accurate arm became a part of Machado's big-league play day in and day out, providing recognition for him and wins for his teams. He has helped his teams get to the postseason seven times. The seven-time All-Star, who has spent his time equally in the AL (Orioles) and NL (Dodgers and Padres), is duly recognized as a five-tool player. Many

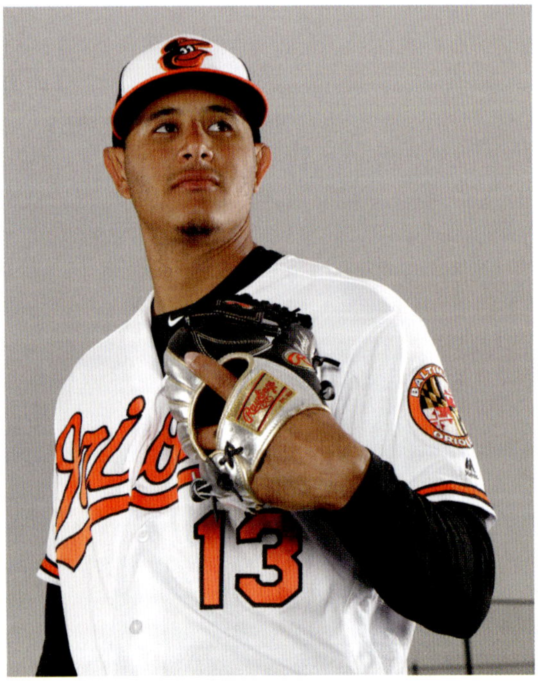

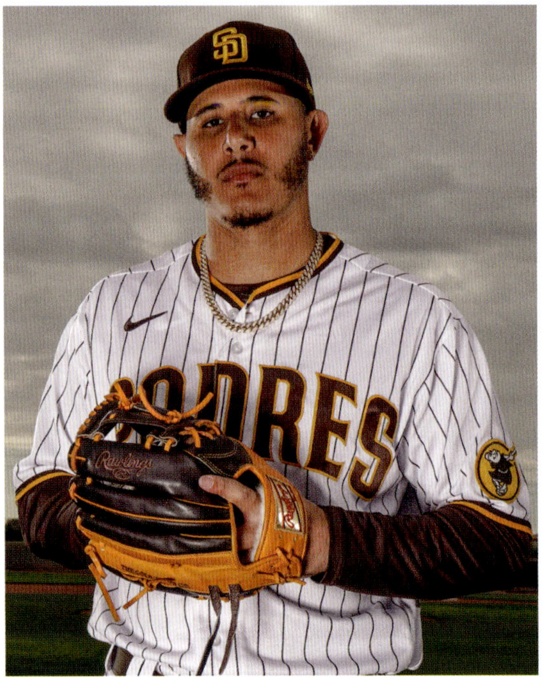

Manny Machado (above, left and right) has anchored third base for 14 big-league seasons with the Baltimore Orioles (2012–2018) and the San Diego Padres (2019–2025), with a brief stop for a half season with the Los Angeles Dodgers in 2018. Machado's PRONP5 (V-Web) multicolored glove (opposite) carries the Rawlings Gold Glove Award label, reflecting his two wins in 2013 and 2015.

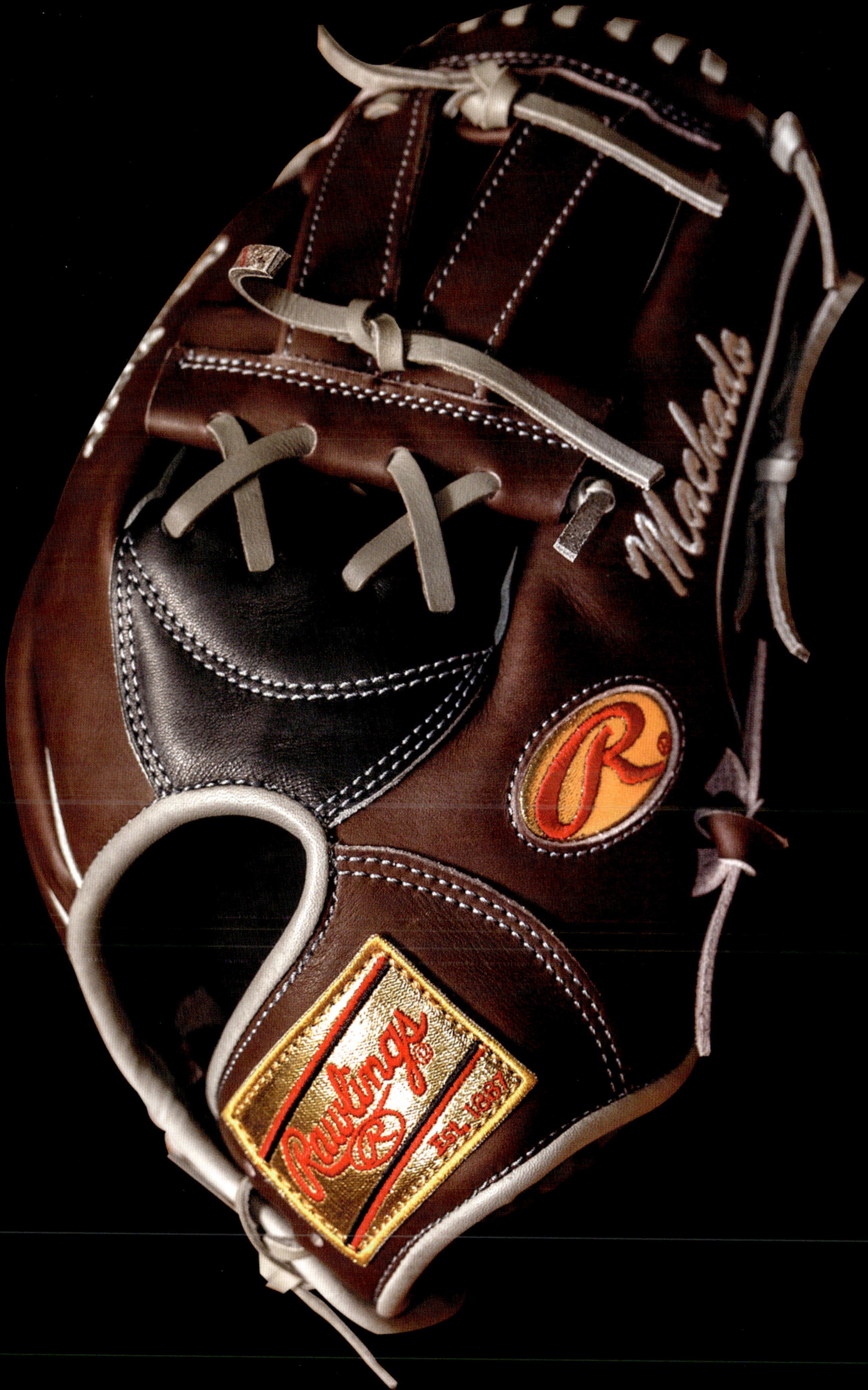
Machado
Rawlings
EST. 1887

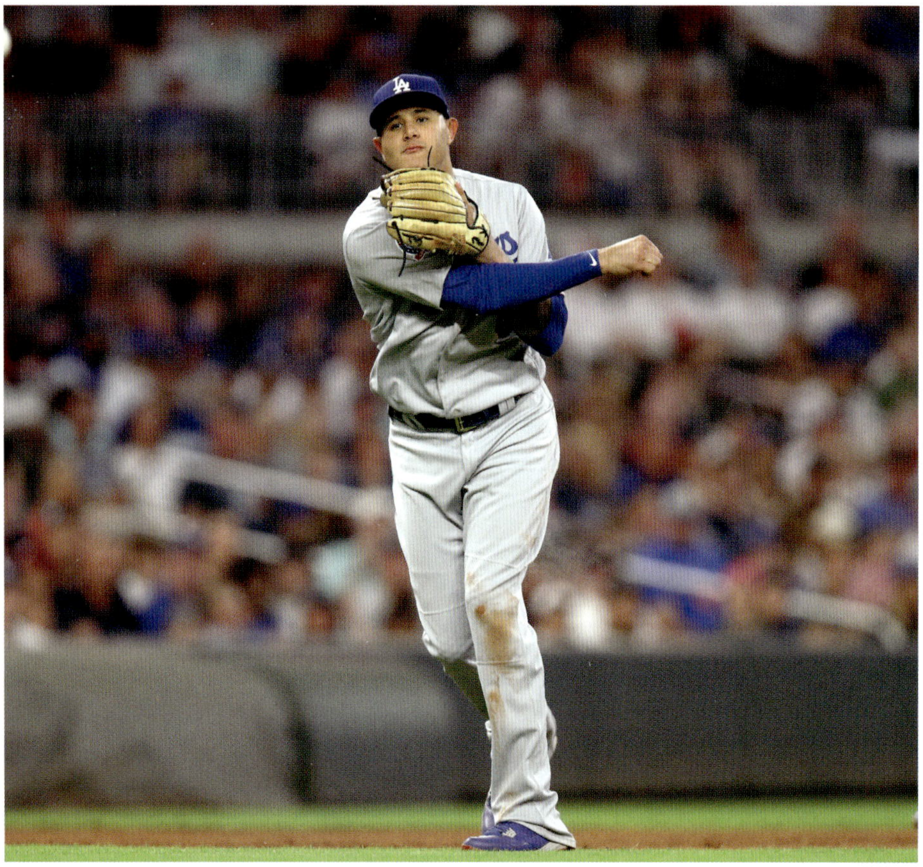

During his half season with the Dodgers, Machado played in his lone World Series to date (left). Since signing with the Padres, the five-tool player (below) has helped get the team to four postseason appearances.

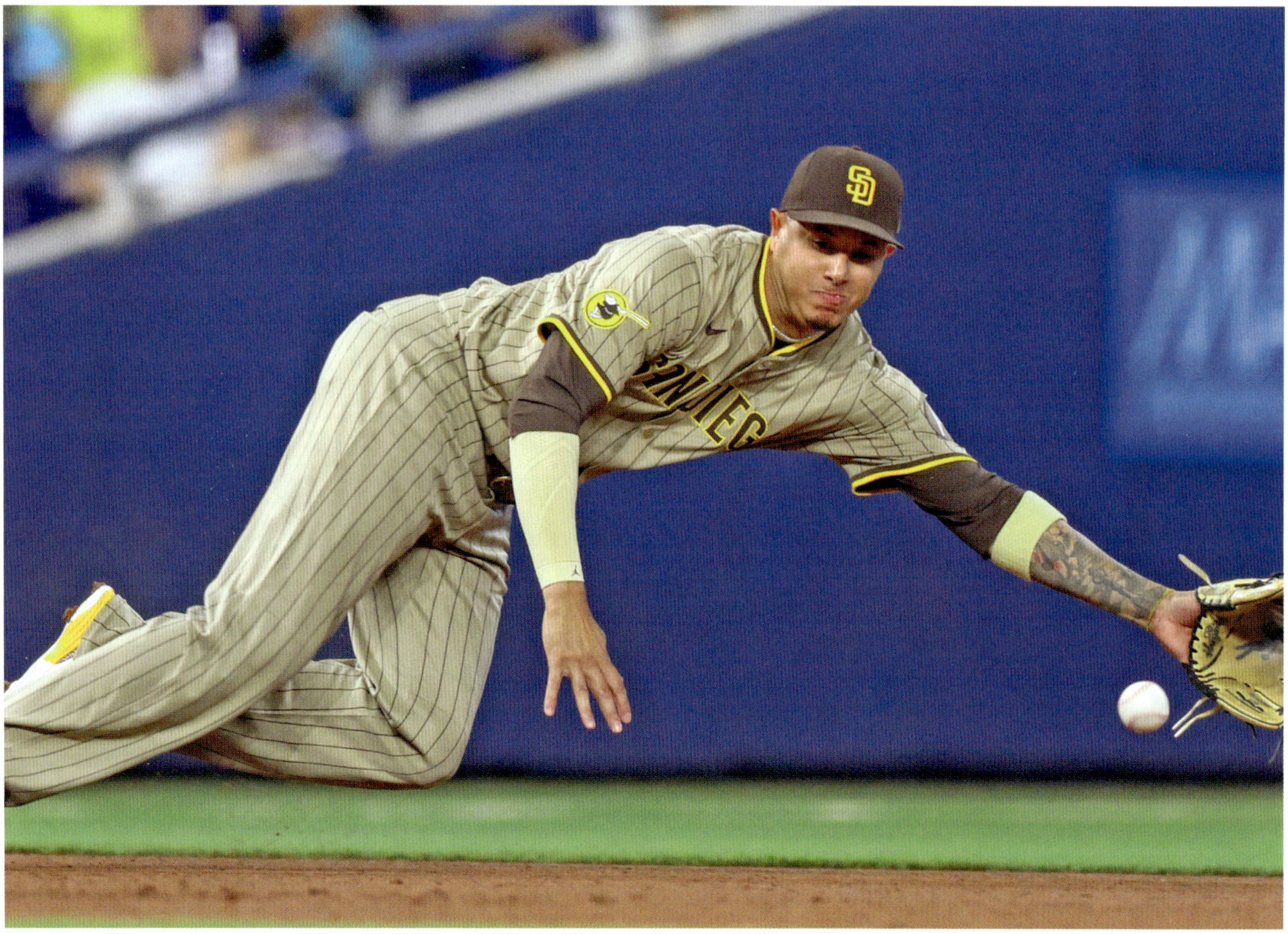

fans believe hitting is his greatest asset, but according to Machado, his glove is best: "Honestly, my glove, since I was a kid, is number one. . . . I always take pride in my glove, for sure. I always take pride in my defense." His smooth and effortless style in the field was born in his youth. "Since I was six, five, maybe four," Machado said, "I was always able to play like that. I would throw tennis balls or racquetballs against the wall for hours, anything that would bounce a lot. I would break windows, just throwing, fielding them barehanded until I got older and got a glove. [I would] work on my hand-eye [coordination], and it just stuck."

Born in Florida to parents of Dominican ancestry, Machado chose to play for the Dominican Republic in the 2017 World Baseball Classic. He did so again in 2023 and 2026. In the 2017 Classic against the Venezuelan team, his play at third base created a social media frenzy and delivered the birth of his nickname. His defense was critical to his team's wins in the first round of play, where he was selected as the pool MVP. In a game in the next round, with the Dominicans holding a slim lead over Venezuela, Machado re-created Brooks Robinson's iconic play from the 1970 World Series. As he ranged deep and to his right to backhand a hard shot off the bat of Miguel Cabrera—the Detroit Tigers star playing for Venezuela—MLB Network announcer Matt Vasgersian exclaimed, "Manny Machado, no way!" The ball was destined for extra bases, but Machado snared it at the foul line where the infield dirt meets the outfield grass. With his momentum pushing him farther into foul territory, Machado twirled and launched an off-balance rocket of a throw that was on target, arriving at first base just before the runner. Machado continued his steady play at the plate and in the field, but the Dominican team lost to the United States team after Adam Jones made a dramatic catch over the wall of a would-be home run hit off the bat of Machado.

Hitting the long ball has always been a part of Machado's offensive arsenal. Nine times in his career he has hit 25 balls or more over the outfield walls. In seven of those seasons, he exceeded the 30-home-run mark. At age 32, and with over 350 home runs, Machado surpassed the 2,000-hit mark to join an exclusive company of players. Only 11 other big-leaguers have attained those marks by age 32 or younger. Eight of them are already in the Hall of Fame—Hank Aaron, Jimmie Foxx, Lou Gehrig, Ken Griffey Jr., Mickey Mantle, Willie Mays, Mel Ott, and Frank Robinson. The other three—Miguel Cabrera, Albert Pujols, and Alex Rodriguez—might one day receive their induction notice as well. As one of the premier players in today's game, Machado and his exceptional defense and power hitting will continue to help his team become a winner.

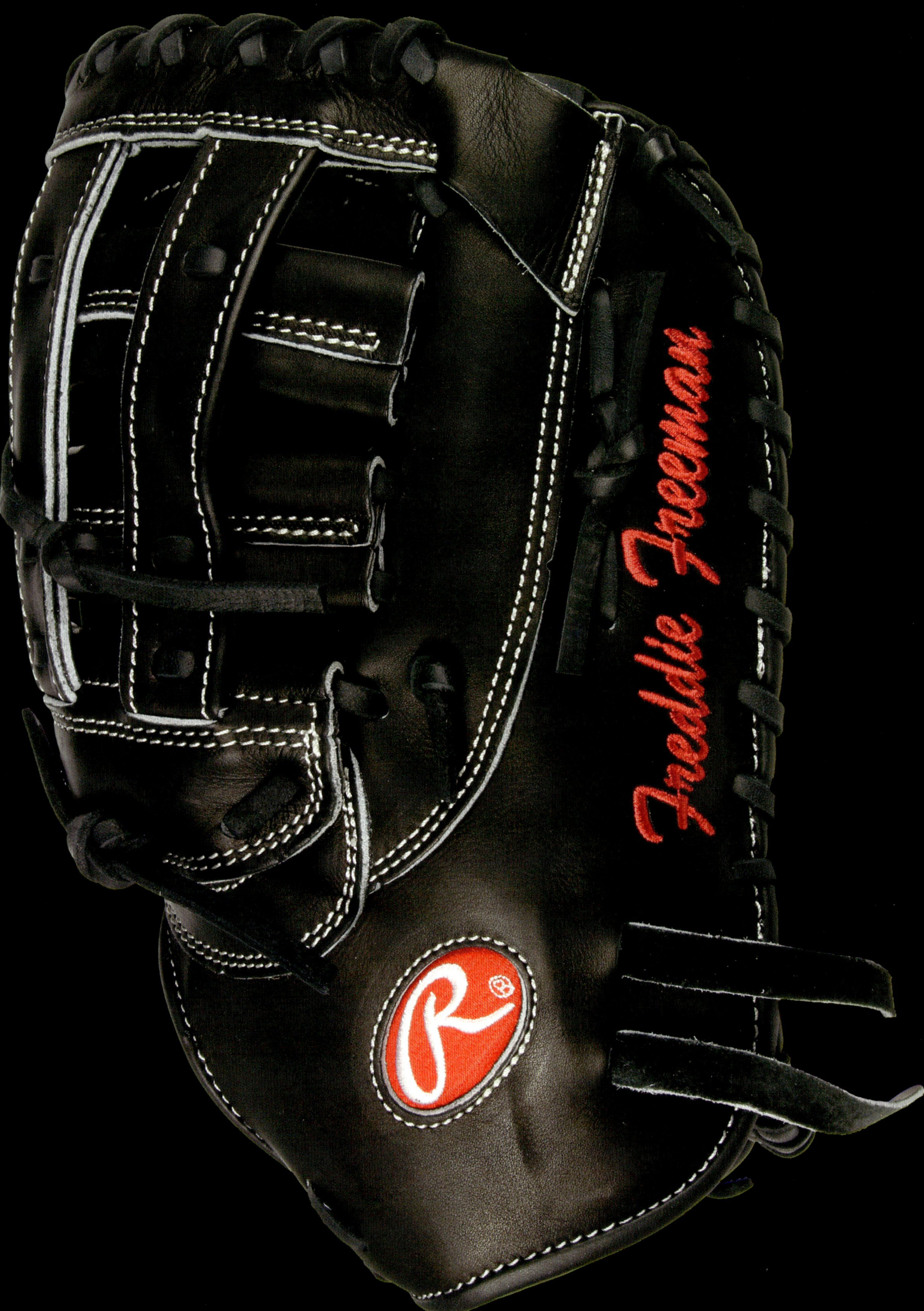
Freddie Freeman

FREDDIE FREEMAN

The Friendliest Man in Baseball

A recent survey by his fellow major leaguers selected Freddie Freeman as "the friendliest man in baseball." They gave him top billing as the nicest infielder to have a conversation with while on base. His teammates and the world of baseball know Freeman as the giver of the biggest bear hugs in the game. Since making his MLB debut with the Atlanta Braves in 2010, Freeman has played at an elite level as one of the game's best all-around players. Unfortunately, during those early years, his talent at bat and in the field was often overshadowed by his teammates.

Freeman got a September call-up in 2010, but baseball's top prospect that year, Jason Heyward, had made his big-league debut with the Braves in April. Heyward's efforts helped the

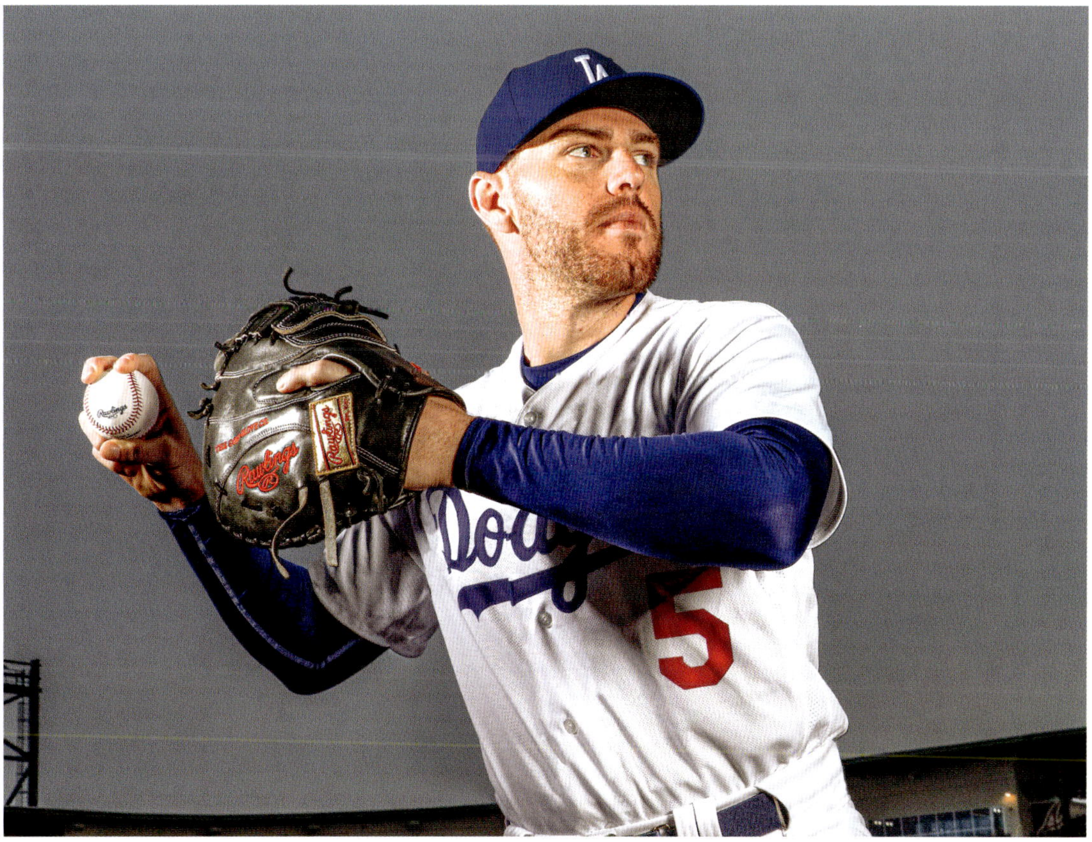

Freddie Freeman used this Rawlings PROSFM20-FF5 model glove with a modified PRO H-Web (opposite). The Rawlings Gold Glove Award winner (above) continues to brandish his 2018 win on his first baseman's mitt while playing for the Los Angeles Dodgers.

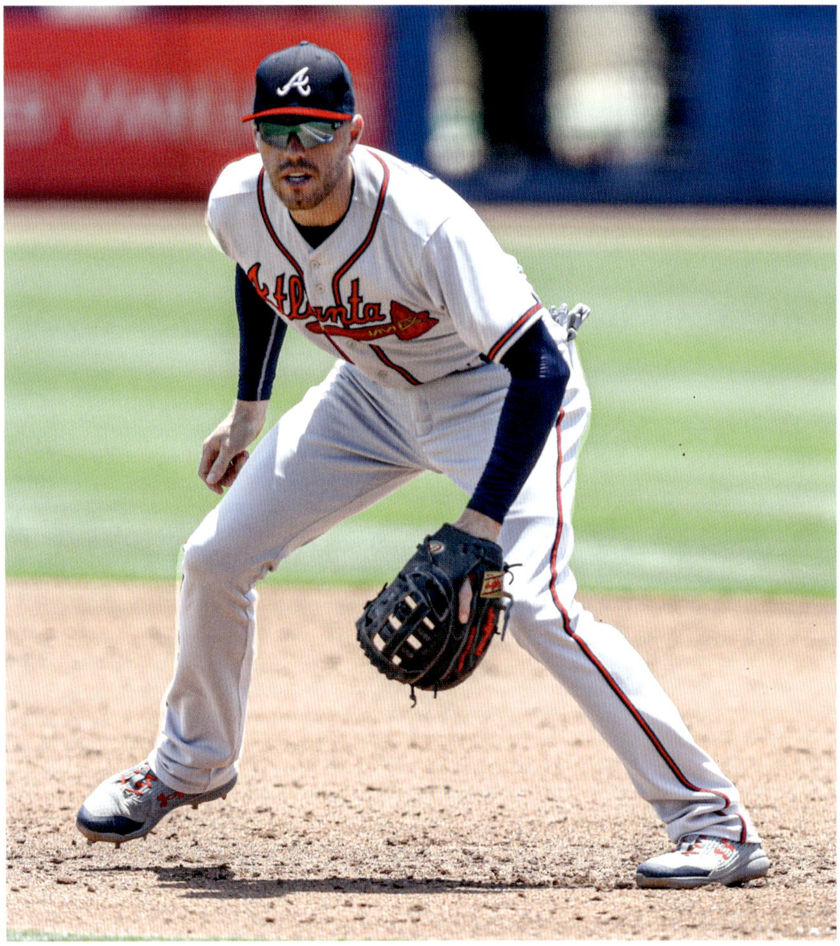

Freeman won his lone Rawlings Gold Glove Award in 2018 while playing first base for the Atlanta Braves.

Overcoming injuries in 2024, Freeman and his outstanding offense and defense helped lead the Dodgers to a World Series win and his selection as the World Series MVP.

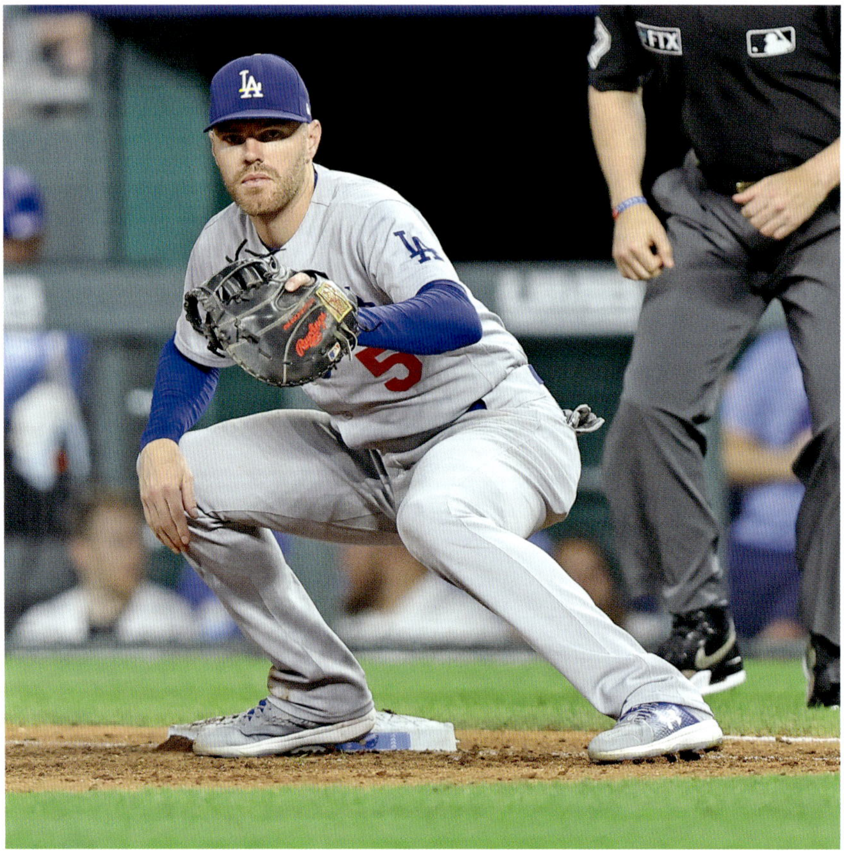

team make it to the postseason for the first time in five years. He was named the NL Rookie of the Year by *The Sporting News* and the MLB Rookie of the Year by *Baseball America*, and he also made the Topps Rookie of the Year All-Star Team. He won every Rookie of the Year honor except the NL award, which went to the Giants' Buster Posey. Freeman played his first full season the following year in the shadow of Heyward but with his rookie eligibility still intact. It was a good season. He batted .282 and began a three-year string of 20-plus home runs. It was good enough for a second-place tally in the NL Rookie of the Year vote, but Freeman was outdone by another teammate—Craig Kimbrel, the team's record-setting closer. In 2013, yet another teammate, Andrelton Simmons, became that season's leader in WAR at 5.8 compared to Freeman's 5.3. Even with his exemplary stats, Freeman remained outside the spotlight.

In the four years that followed, the Braves became an underachieving team, and many of its stars were moved elsewhere. That is, all but Freeman. Mr. Nice became the rock the team was built around. Five times he represented the Braves in the annual All-Star Game. Nine times he helped his team make the playoffs, and in 2021, he helped guide the Braves to their first World Series championship in 19 years. Along the way, he picked up a Gold Glove Award in 2018 for his stellar work at first base, and in 2020 his play was rewarded with the NL MVP Award.

But free agency and a contract dispute in 2022 led to Freeman's departure from the Braves; he reluctantly headed west to join the Los Angeles Dodgers. While this may have been the Braves' loss, it definitely was the Dodgers' gain, as Freemen put together four solid All-Star seasons that saw his new team in the postseason each year.

Heading into the 2024 postseason, Freeman was dealing with physical difficulties (a broken rib and severely sprained ankle), as well as personal worries. His son Maximus was suddenly stricken with the debilitating effects of Guillain-Barré syndrome. The Dodgers made it through the early rounds of the playoffs that year and into the World Series against the New York Yankees, where Freeman fought at the plate and in the field to overcome his obstacles while hoping to lift his team to a world championship. Heading into the Series, Freeman was once more eclipsed by the presence of superstars Aaron Judge and Shohei Ohtani, the eventual 2024 league MVPs. But this time, the Series became Freeman's showcase.

The opening round was reminiscent of a Dodgers moment 36 years earlier, in the 1988 Series—the last time the team won a full-season championship—when an injured Kirk Gibson came to the plate and delivered a Game One walk-off home run. In Game One of the 2024 Series, the injured Freeman came to the plate in the bottom of the 10th inning with two outs and the bases loaded, following an intentional walk to Mookie Betts. Like Gibson, Freeman didn't disappoint the hometown fans; he hit the first World Series walk-off grand slam. He went on to hit home runs in each of the next three games of the Series, adding to the ones he had hit in the final two games of the 2021 Series—an MLB record of home runs in six straight Series games he played in. Freeman's remarkable play finally led him out of the other players' shadows and into the spotlight as the World Series MVP. And who says lightning can't strike twice? In Game Three of the 2025 World Series, Freeman's heroics were on display once more with a walk-off home run to center field for a win in the bottom of the 18th inning. The Dodgers later went on to repeat as World Series champions.

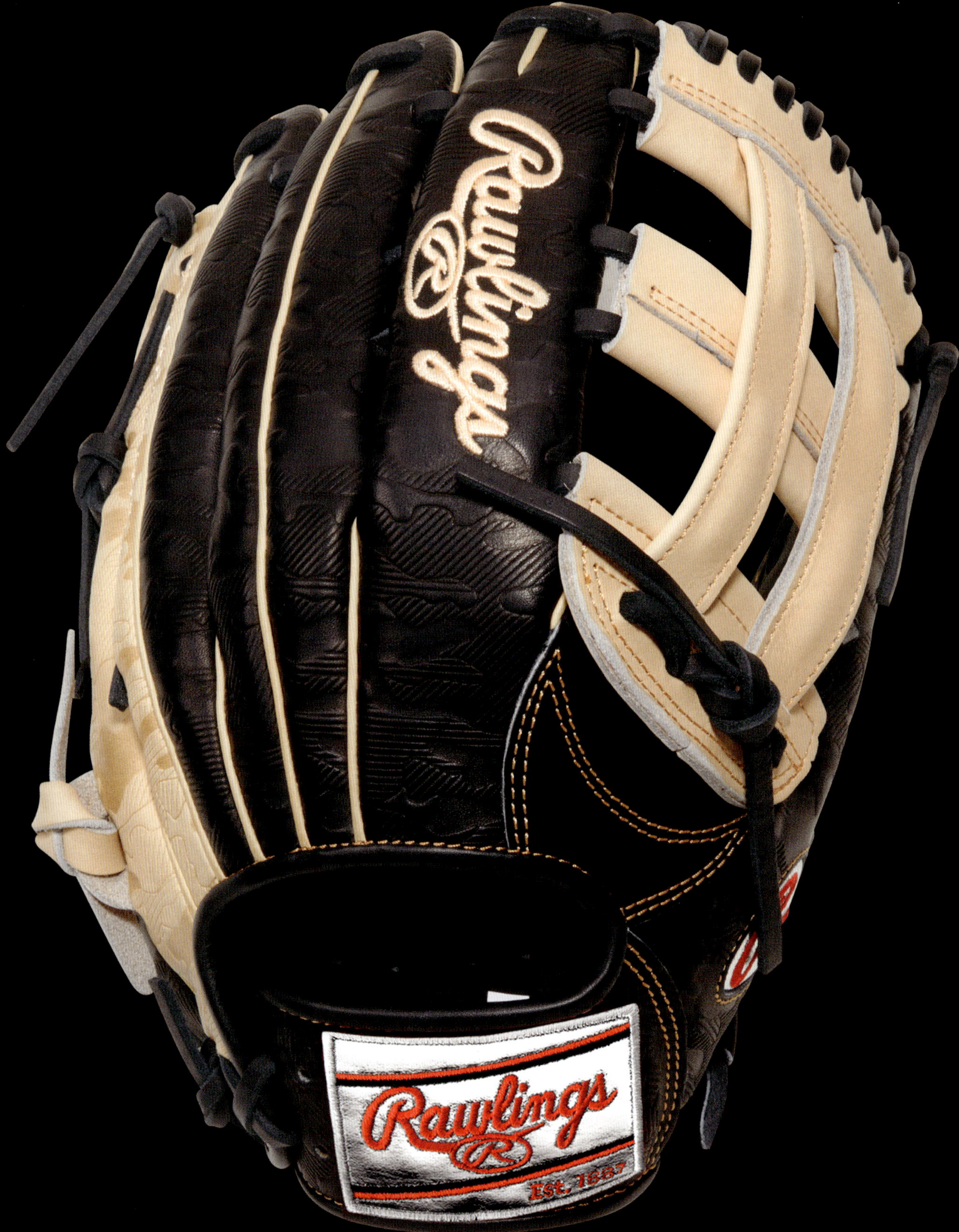
Rawlings
Rawlings
Est. 1887

FERNANDO TATIS JR.

His Own Man

Fernando Tatis Jr. came to the major leagues in 2019 as a 20-year-old from the Dominican Republic with "potential" written all over him. Like many sons of former major leaguers, Tatis had to play in the shadow of his father's past success. But six seasons into his own career, potential is now a word of the past. It has all come together for Tatis, despite missing the 2022 season due to a wrist surgery and an 80-game suspension for using performance-enhancing drugs.

In 2015, Tatis was signed by the Chicago White Sox as an international free agent, but he was traded to the San Diego Padres before debuting in any professional game. He played in the minor leagues for a few years before making his major-league debut in 2019. The Padres believed so

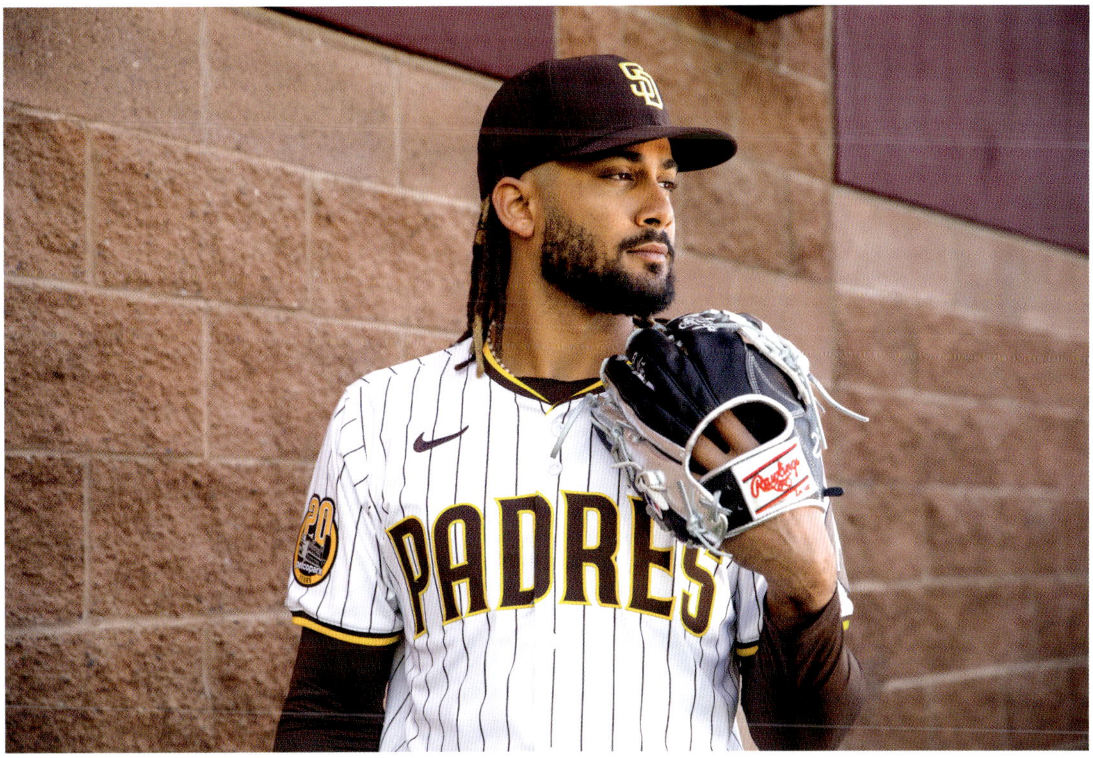

Fernando Tatis Jr. has used this multicolored Rawlings PRO30339-FTJ23 model glove (opposite) throughout his big-league career. The 2023 Rawlings Gold Glove and Platinum Glove Award winner (above) proudly displays the platinum label on his glove.

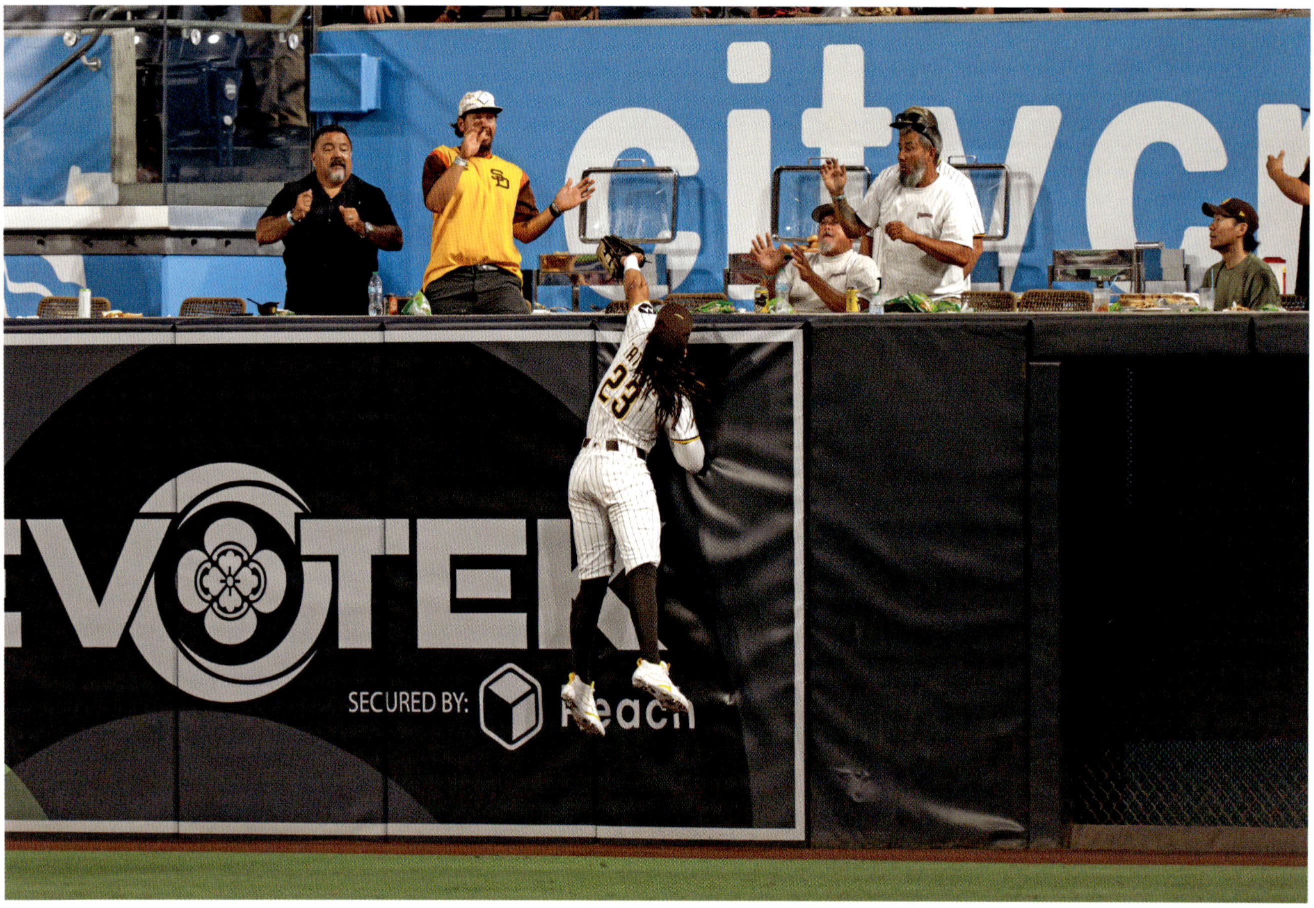

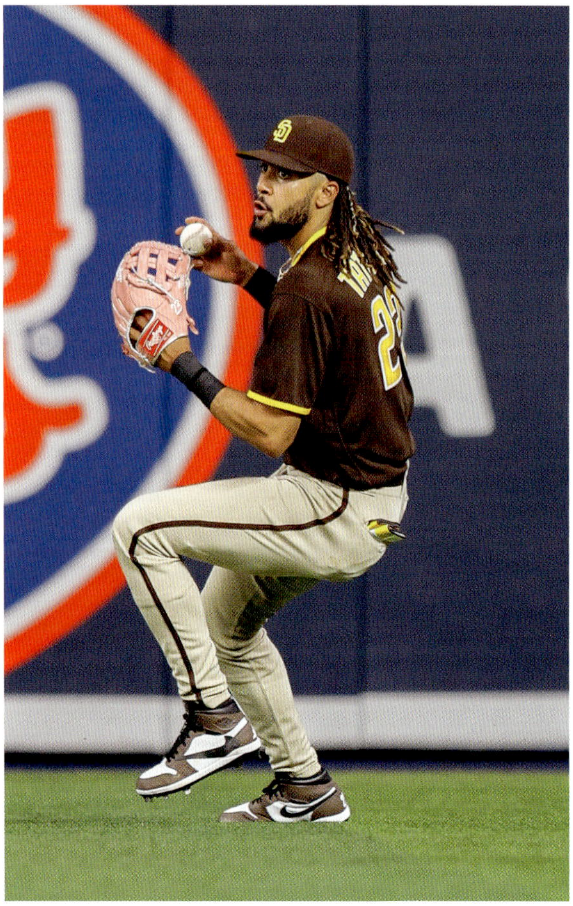

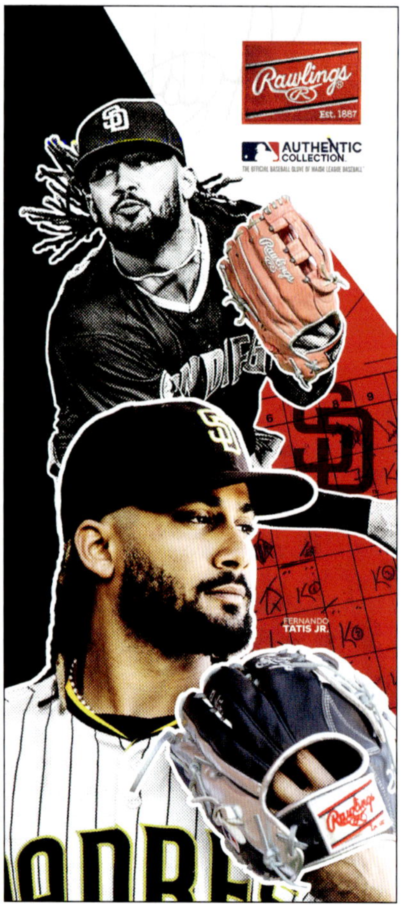

The San Diego Padres' Tatis shows off his defensive exploits with this jumping catch in the fourth inning of a 2025 game against the New York Mets at Petco Park in San Diego (above). Wearing a pink glove in honor of Mother's Day in 2023 (far left), Tatis is ready to use his strong arm after a catch to keep a runner from taking an extra base. A 2023 Rawlings advertisement (left) celebrated Tatis's defensive prowess.

much in his talent that, in 2021, they signed him to a 14-year, $340 million contract extension (the third highest in baseball at the time) after just two seasons in the big leagues. Four years into that deal, Tatis continues to prove his worth.

His father, Fernando Tatis Sr., offered decent defensive skills while playing primarily third base over his 11-year major-league career. Like his son, Tatis Sr. was known to launch a home run or two over the outfield wall. In fact, on April 23, 1999, he hit two out of Dodger Stadium and became the only player in the history of the game to ever hit two grand slams in the same inning of the same game. But Tatis is his own man, playing at a totally different level than his father, who hit 113 homers during his career. In just six years, Tatis has already put more than 140 balls out of the park, with many more to come.

Tatis played as a shortstop during his first three seasons in the big leagues. In 2021, he recorded one of the best offensive seasons of any shortstop who played the game when he was selected to the first of his three All-Star Game appearances. That season he hit 42 home runs, a total surpassed only seven times by two of the game's best—Alex Rodriguez and Ernie Banks. His offense was reaching superstar status, but his defense at the six-hole was just above average. He had the range, quickness, and arm to succeed at a higher level but wasn't up to elite status.

So, after missing the 2022 season, Tatis came back to a new position—right field—and began showing the world of baseball just how good his defense could be. He won not only the position's 2023 Gold Glove Award but also that year's Platinum Glove Award as the best overall defender in the NL. In the outfield, Tatis continues to make dramatic highlight-reel catches every week to prove he may be the best defensive outfielder currently in the game.

People are still talking about the play he made against the Mets in July 2025, when he ran to the outfield wall in Petco Park, 380 feet away from where Mark Vientos had launched the ball, and perfectly timed his jump. Reaching over the wall, with his cheek pressed against it and his body twisting, he made a backhanded catch to take away a sure home run and counter the television announcer's exclamation about the ball being gone the moment it was hit.

A few games into August 2025, he robbed the Giants' Rafael Devers of another sure home run, leading the Padres' skipper, Mike Shildt, to comment to the media, "You're talking about right off the [get-go] again. . . . He makes so many great plays, it's like routine greatness. That was just pure greatness. There [are] a lot of good players in this league, but if you put his body of work together and he's not the Platinum/Gold Glove winner, then I want a recount." Tatis did indeed collect his second Gold Glove and Platinum Glove Awards in 2025. He continues to demonstrate with his bat, glove, arm, and legs why he has all the tools of the trade needed to join just a handful of other players in the game today who have earned superstar status.

AARON JUDGE

The Next Great Yankee

Aaron Judge began his ascension into the big leagues after playing three seasons of college ball. Selected by the Yankees in the first round (32nd overall) of the 2013 MLB draft, he joined their organization in the 2014 season, quickly rose through the system, and made his big-league debut on August 13, 2016, as a 24-year-old rookie.

Was the timing of Judge's debut simply a coincidence or was there a hint of magic tying together Yankee legends since the days of Babe Ruth, Lou Gehrig, Joe DiMaggio, and so on? The day before Judge played his first game with the New Yorkers, another Yankee star, who had belted 696 big-league home runs (the fourth most in MLB history at his retirement), played his last game in pinstripes. Alex Rodriguez made his exit one day, and Judge made his debut the next.

That day, Judge was in the lineup playing right field when he demonstrated in his first MLB at-bat that the torch had been passed. He smashed a monster shot that went an estimated 476 feet to dead center, one of the longest home runs ever hit in the new Yankee Stadium. Welcome to the big leagues! The next day, he went deep again and became only the second Yankee in team history to homer in their first two games (Joe Lefebvre was the other in 1980). But questions arose about whether Judge was really the next great Yankee after he batted .179 with four home runs during that short season, which was made even shorter due to an oblique injury that ended his season.

But the doubters were soon silenced when the 2017 season opened. It didn't happen right away; Judge didn't homer in the season's first game. In fact, it wasn't until the seventh game that he put one over the wall. But toward the end of June, he was leading the league in each Triple Crown category. The untested rookie who had started the season with question marks

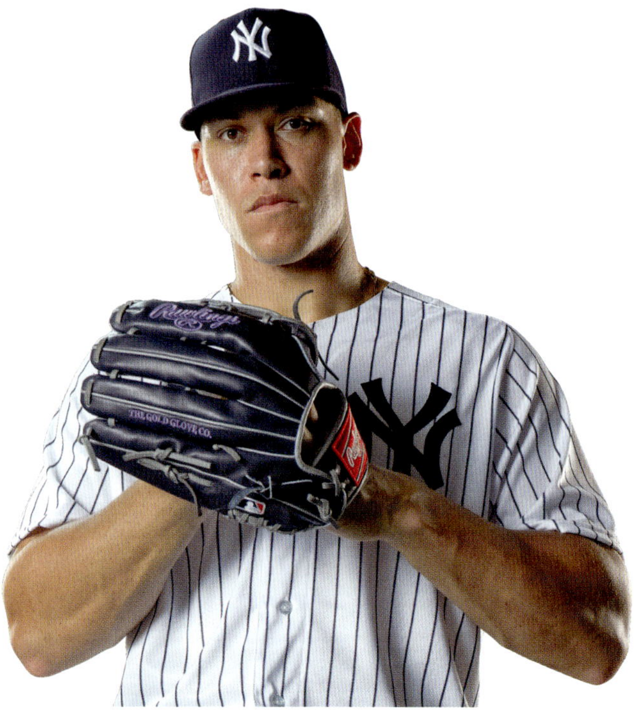

Since his debut in 2016, Aaron Judge (left) has proved that he is equal to all the great New York Yankees of the past. Judge has used a multicolored Rawlings PROSAJ99N model glove (opposite) while playing in the outfield.

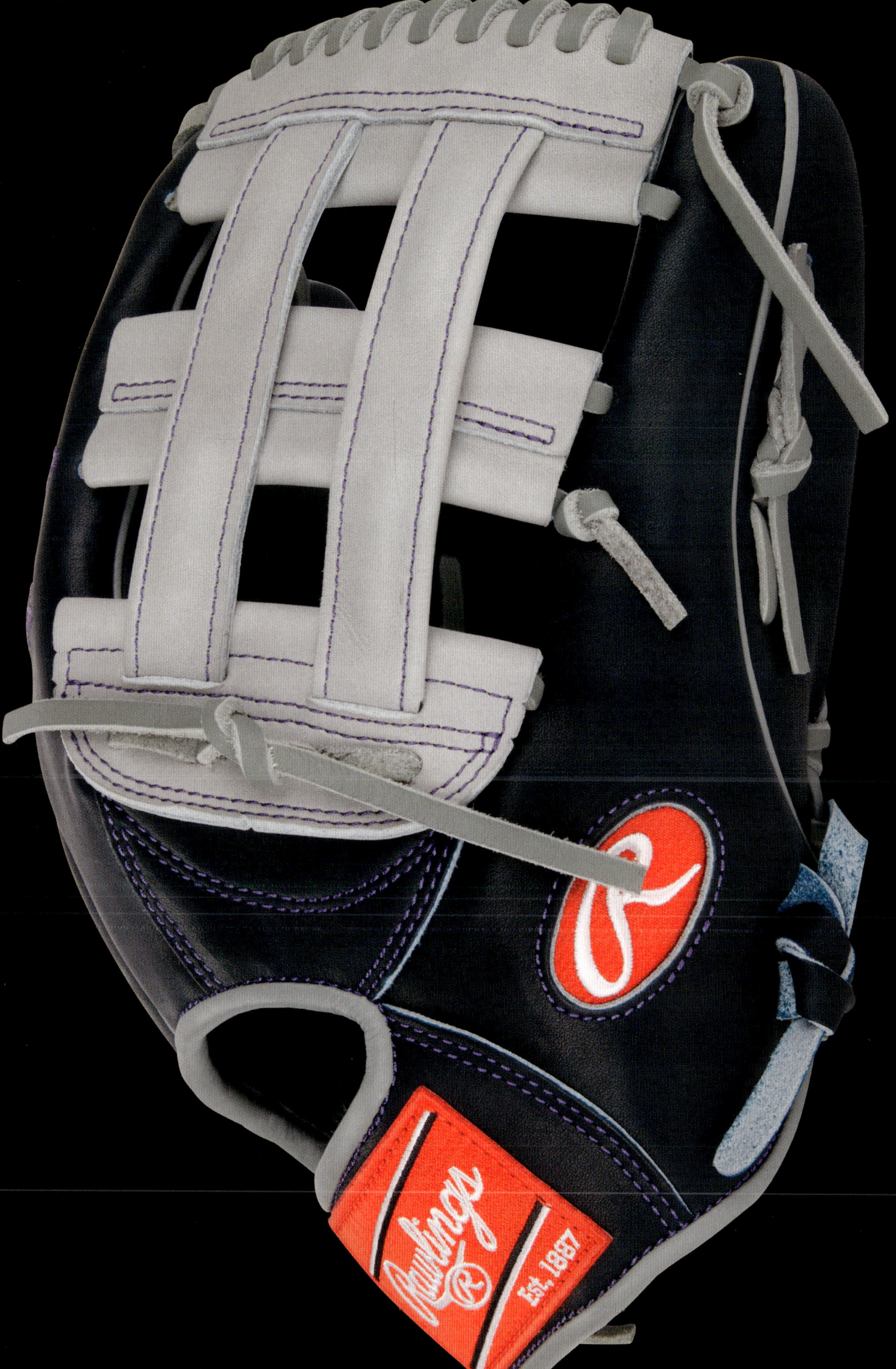
Rawlings
Est. 1887

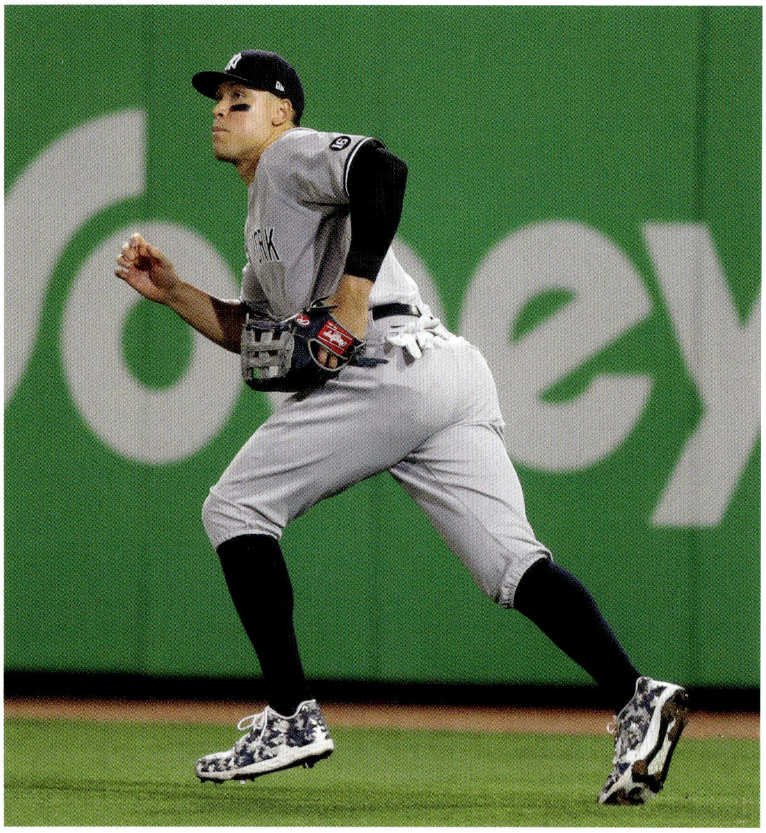

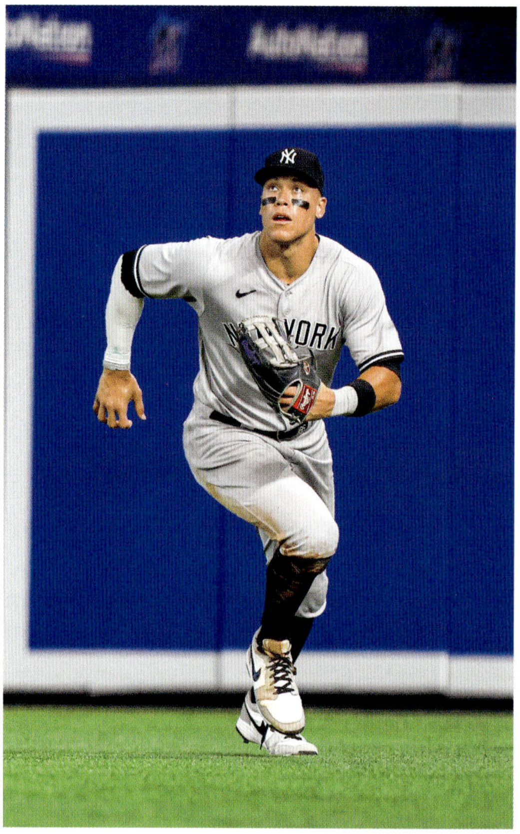

At six feet, seven inches, Judge has highlighted his exceptional defensive skills in both right and center field (above, left and right) while posting a career 62.3 WAR rating.

received more votes to the All-Star Game than any other AL player. When the season was over, Judge's 52 home runs broke Mark McGwire's previous record (49) for the most hit by a rookie, and he unanimously earned the AL Rookie of the Year Award—at the time the ninth Yankee to win the award. The rookie's .284 batting average, 114 runs, and 127 walks led to a runner-up finish in the AL MVP race behind Jose Altuve.

Judge played an exceptional right field in his first two years with the Yankees before necessity—due to player injuries—moved him to center field for the first time. At six feet, seven inches, he joined Walt Bond (1960 Cleveland Indians) as the tallest player to play the position. And there would continue to be more firsts. The next month of that season, another homer made him the quickest player to ever record 60 and then 70 home runs in a career. Despite injuries limiting his playing time and likely his home-run output in 2018 and again the following year, he became the third-fastest MLB player to reach the 100-home-run mark in his 371st game on August 27, 2019.

After hitting only nine home runs in the 2020 season, which was shortened to 60 games by the COVID-19 pandemic, Judge rebounded in 2021 with 39 homers and his third All-Star Game selection. Unable to agree on a contract extension with the Yankees prior to the start of the following season, it seemed as though Judge was determined to show his value. After making his fourth All-Star appearance, Judge surpassed Babe Ruth, Jimmie Foxx, and Ken Griffey Jr. for the most home runs through the end of July and became the second-fastest player (after Ryan Howard) to hit 200 home runs. The world of baseball began focusing on whether Judge would become the third Yankee after Ruth and Roger Maris to homer at least 60 times in a season.

On the day he hit his 60th, his .316 average put him at the top of the batting race and a potential Triple Crown. He passed Maris's 61 round-trippers with his 62nd to set a new Yankee and

AL home-run record. But he lost the Triple Crown (his 131 RBIs were tops) when he sat out the season's last game, allowing Luis Arráez to leapfrog him for the batting title. Judge did, however, take home his first MVP Award that season. Amazingly, his 62 home runs were 16 more than the next closest player, Kyle Schwarber—the biggest gap since Jimmie Foxx's 17-home-run lead in 1932. The season's payoff was a nine-year, $360 million contract extension. Along with it came Yankee captainship, a position that had not been filled since Derek Jeter's retirement in 2014.

While he was picked to his fifth All-Star Game in 2023, he hit only 37 home runs during the season and was limited to just 106 games due to injuries. But healthy once again in 2024, Judge rebounded by getting the most All-Star Game votes for the third time and unanimously winning his second MVP Award. On August 14, Judge became the fastest player to hit 300 home runs and did it in the fewest at-bats as well. There appears to be no stopping the capabilities of a healthy Judge. With 315 home runs after just nine seasons of play, he started the 2025 season with three home runs in the first game, making fans wonder how many more he could have had if so many games hadn't been lost to injuries and the pandemic.

As each week's set of games came and went, Judge's vaunted success seemed to reach yet another milestone or record as he rewrote the history of Yankee greatness. The summer of 2025 was another MVP-like season in which he led in hitting with his .331 average. His 53 home runs gave him his fourth season of 50 or more, and he passed Yogi Berra (358) and Joe DiMaggio (361) to claim fourth place on the Yankees' all-time home-run list with 368—a tally that will continue to rise for seasons to come.

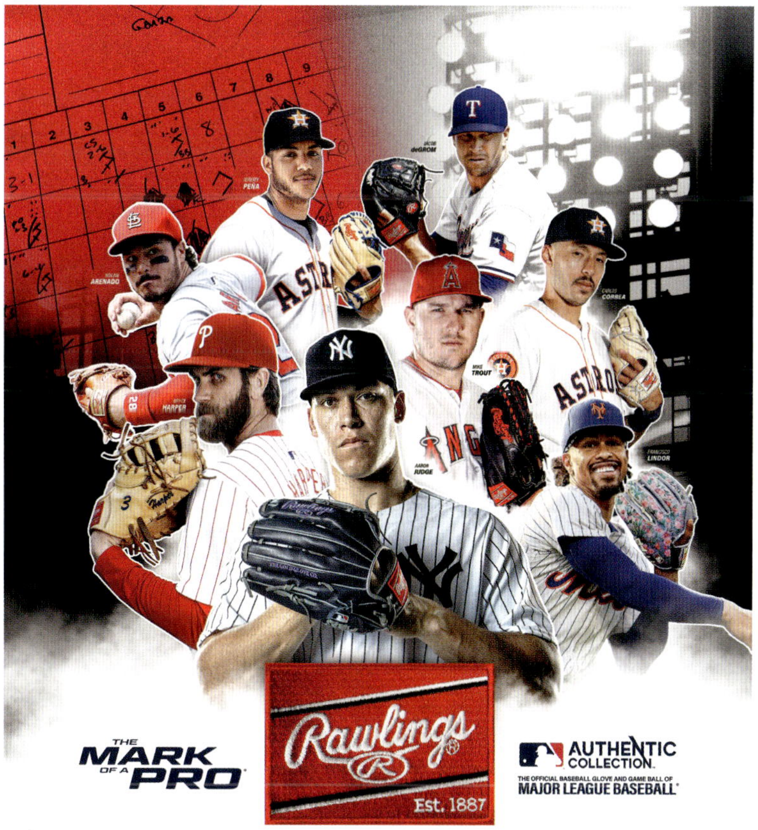

A 2024 Rawlings advertisement shows Judge at the forefront of a collage of MLB baseball greats.

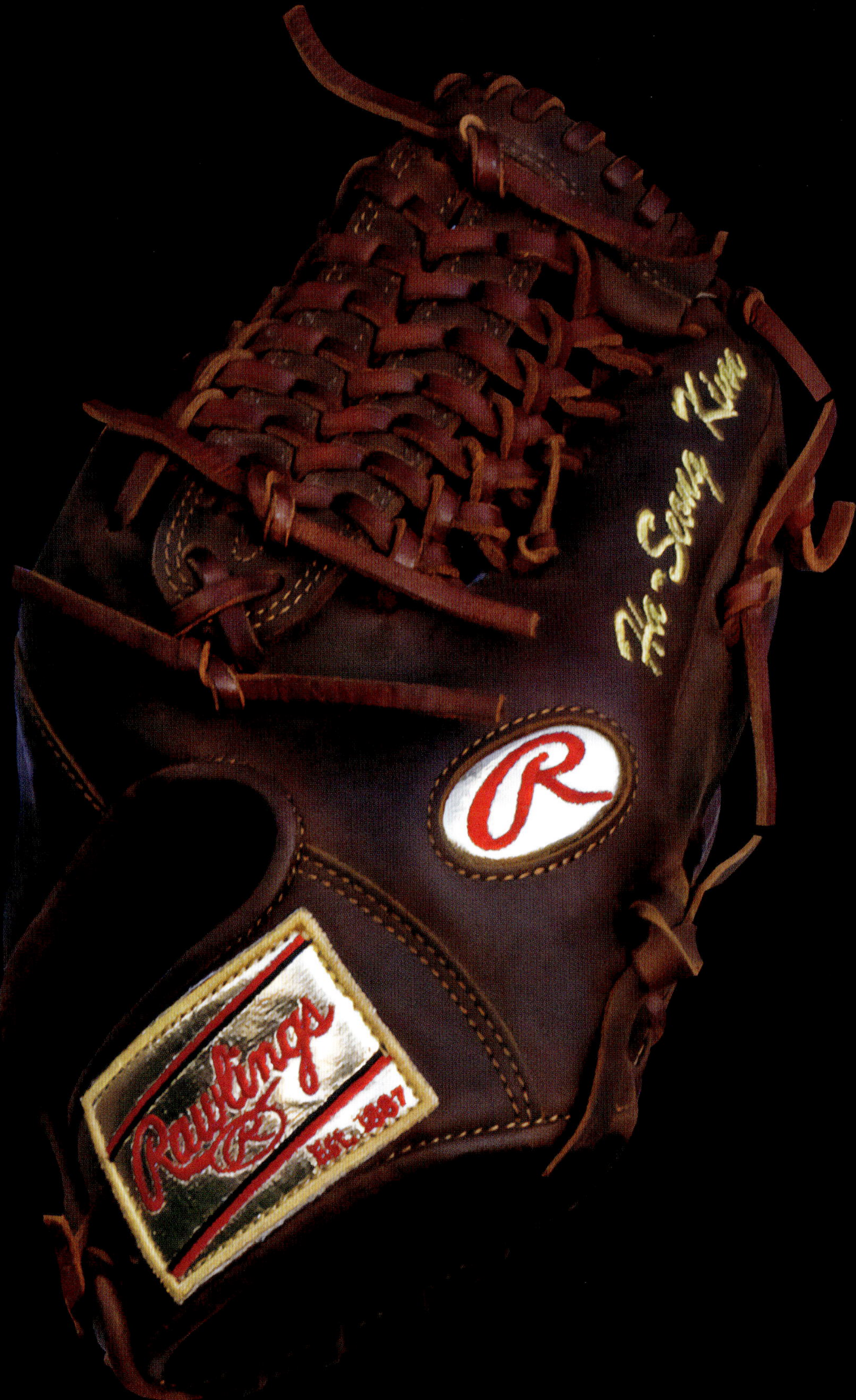
Ha-Seong Kim
Rawlings
EST. 1887

CHAN HO PARK AND HA-SEONG KIM

The Korean Connection

The evolution of baseball in Korea has deep similarities to the growth of baseball in Japan. An American YMCA missionary named Philip Gillett is credited with bringing the game to the Korean Peninsula in 1905, with games first being played in Seoul. There are some sources, however, that document baseball reaching Seoul as early as 1894 or 1896, shortly after the game was brought to Japan by an American professor in 1872. Those few early Korean games consisted of matches between teams of U.S. Marines or American expatriates and the Seoul Athletic Club. The game's expansion was soon limited by the oppression and occupation of Korea by Japanese military forces from 1910 to 1945. Under Japanese rule, restrictions were placed to avoid the potential growth of Korean nationalism evolving from the games. To further control the game, all tournaments had to be sponsored by Japanese companies.

After Japan's defeat in World War II and Korea's liberation, interest in baseball surged. However, ongoing events in the country still limited its growth. In those postwar years, the country was split into two Cold War entities (North Korea and South Korea), followed by years of further warfare during the Korean War (1950–1953). Once the hostilities ceased, baseball became one of South Korea's most popular sports.

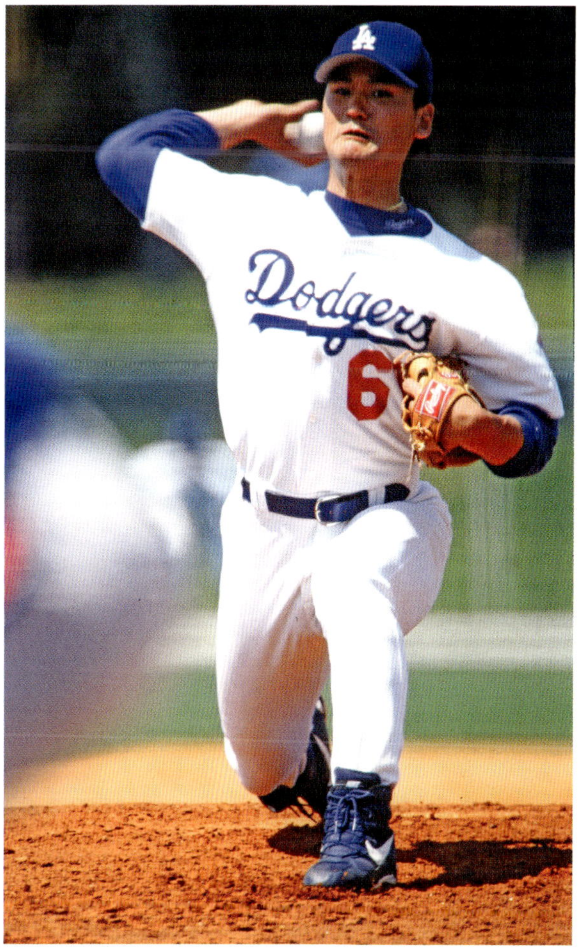

Ha-seong Kim's modified Rawlings Trap-Eze model glove (opposite) has a Gold Glove Award label reflecting his 2023 win as the AL's best utility player. Chan Ho Park (right) took the mound for the Los Angeles Dodgers in 1994—nearly 30 years before Kim's MLB debut—as the first Korean national to play in the major leagues.

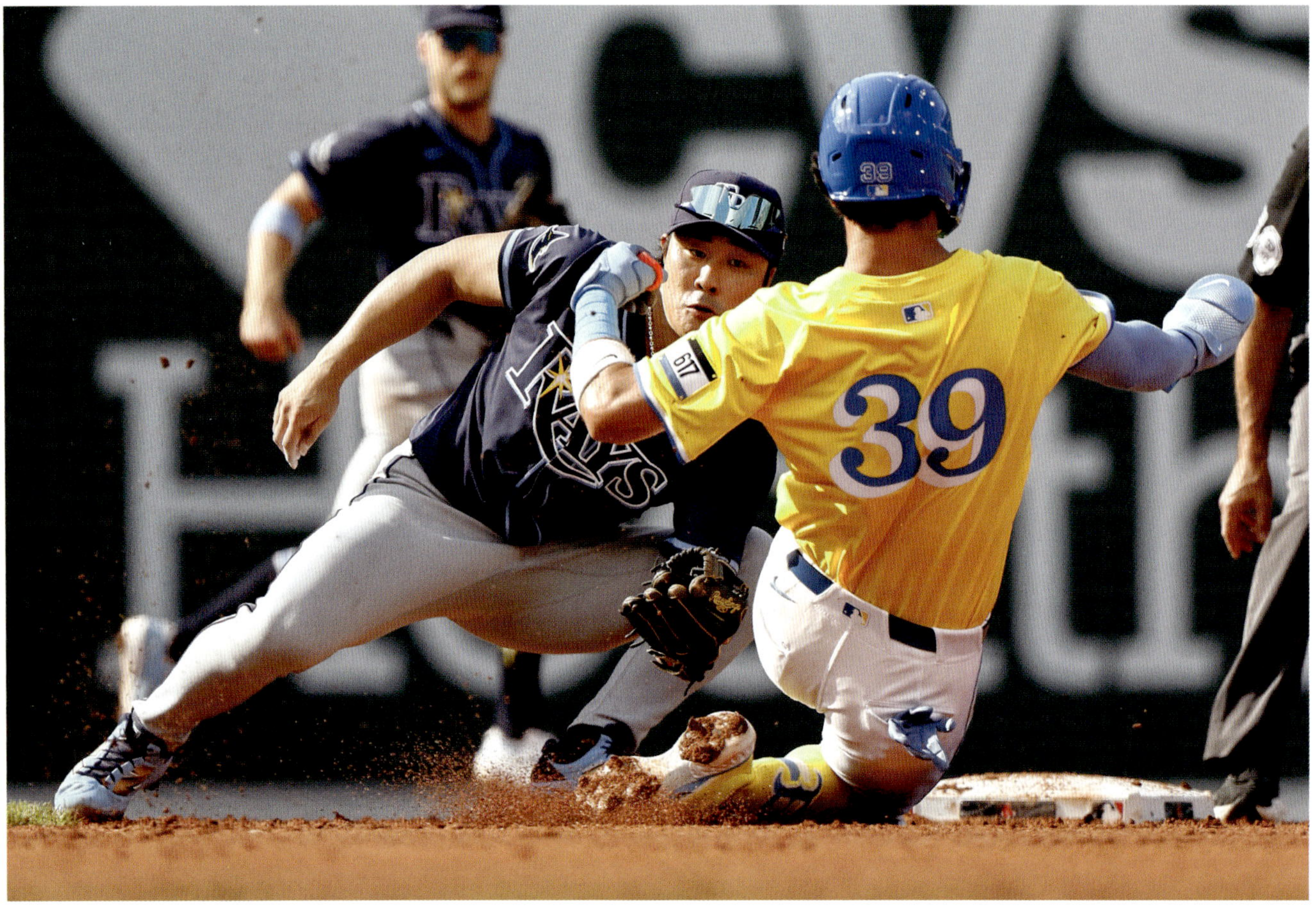

In 2023, Kim, playing for the Tampa Bay Rays, became the first Korean national in MLB history to win the Rawlings Gold Glove Award.

The Korea Baseball Organization (KBO) wasn't founded until three decades later. It originated as a league with six teams that later expanded to 10. The organization's first game was played on March 27, 1982, at Dongdaemun Baseball Stadium in Seoul; the MBC Chungyong defeated the Samsung Lions 11–7.

While MLB never officially restricted Korean players from joining, as it did Japanese players, the perceived lower level of play in the country—somewhere between AA and AAA minor-league levels—delayed a Korean player's entrance into American games for some time. Chan Ho Park became the first Korean to play in the big leagues when he joined the Los Angeles Dodgers in 1994. He stuck around for 17 seasons, pitching for seven different teams, and was selected to the 2001 All-Star Game. Although Park opened the door and created the interest, only 29 Korean-born players have made it to the major leagues in the three decades since his debut.

Shin-Soo Choo, who spent 16 years in the big leagues (2005–2020), may be the best player to come from Korea. Playing for four teams in the majors, the right fielder batted .275 with 218 home runs—the most hit by a Korean player. In 2018, he became the first Korean position player to be selected to an All-Star Game.

In the newest generation of Korean players coming to America, Ha-seong Kim quickly made a name for himself during his rise to the majors. Recognized for his superior defense while playing shortstop for the Kiwoom Heroes in the KBO, Kim won that league's Golden Glove Award three times (2018–2020) based on his offense. Kim signed a four-year contract with the San Diego Padres in 2021. With Fernando Tatis Jr. out for the season the following year, Kim settled in as the Padres' regular shortstop, playing outstanding defense paired with decent offense. He became a finalist for that year's NL Gold Glove Award but did not win.

In 2023, he put together a season of outstanding defense for the Padres and improved his numbers at the plate. He hit .260 with 17 home runs. But it was also a season of change. With the Padres acquiring All-Star shortstop Xander Bogaerts and with Tatis in right field, Kim quickly adapted and showed his athleticism by moving to second base and improving the Padres' overall defense. He also slid back into the shortstop position when Bogaerts was injured and played a little third base as well. Kim was a finalist for not one but two Gold Gloves (second base and utility player). His versatility turned to gold when he was selected as the NL's best utility player. "I am really honored to be the first Korean winner of a Gold Glove," Kim said. "I am also happy that I have inspired and motivated young, aspiring major leaguers." It was an inspiration that crossed two nations, as Kim remains the only player to receive a KBO Golden Glove and an MLB Gold Glove.

Kim switched uniforms and saw action on the field in 2025 after the Atlanta Braves selected him off waivers from the Rays.

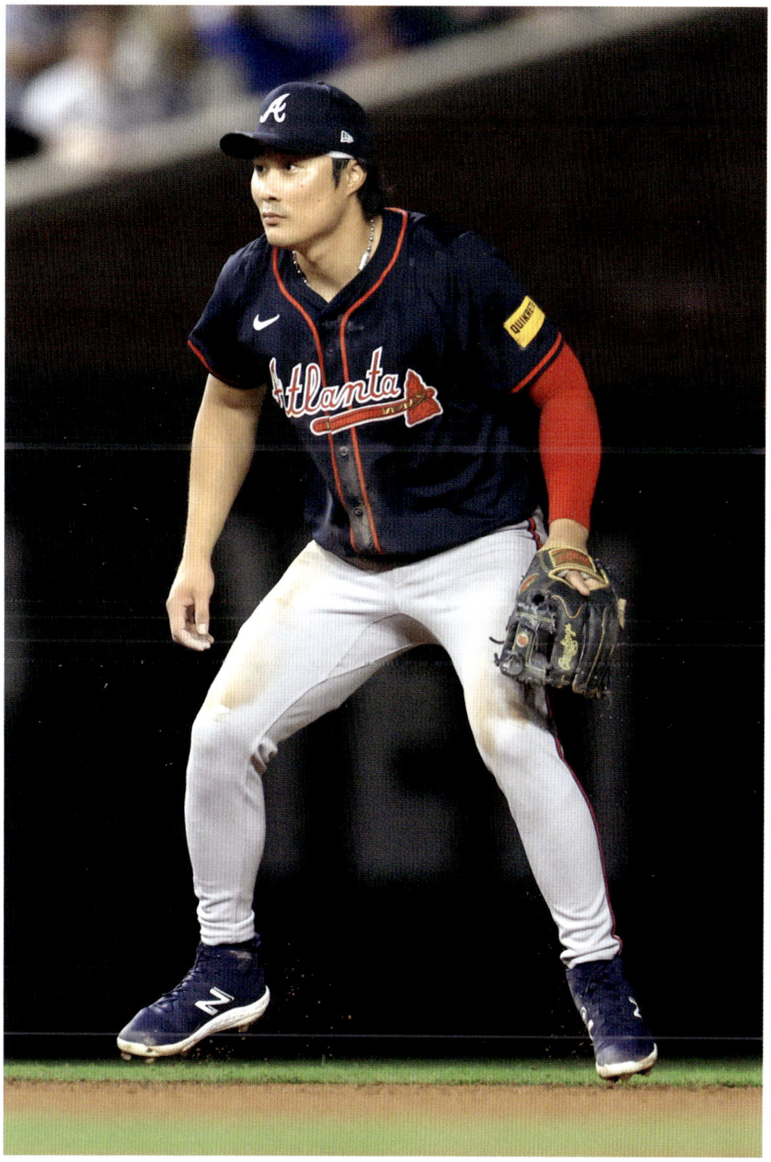

CAL RALEIGH

The Big Dumper

Cal Raleigh's accomplishments in 2025 can't be distilled to a single moment. It was a full season of memorable plays and records. But for many baseball fans, it seemed like the Seattle Mariners catcher came out of nowhere. His winning performance in the All-Star Game's Home Run Derby (the first ever by a catcher) had many fans asking, "Where did this guy come from?" The answer is that he has been around since late in the 2021 season, and his home-run power has always been there. And since his first full season the following year, the switch-hitting catcher has been regularly knocking the ball out of the park. He hit 27 home runs in 2022, followed by three back-to-back seasons of 30 or more.

By 2025, his name was starting to be used in sentences with many of the greatest names to ever play the game. As he approached baseball's Midsummer Classic that year, his 38 home runs were just one shy of Barry Bonds's record of 39 homers hit before the All-Star Game. And his season soon became even more explosive. His 60 home runs that season were the most in baseball, and his 125 RBIs led the AL. The only other catcher to do that was Johnny Bench, when he led the majors in home runs in 1970 and 1972.

In the history of the major leagues, only six catchers before Raleigh have hit more than 40 home runs in a season (Bench, Roy Campanella, Todd Hundley, Javy López, Salvador Perez, and Mike Piazza). Bench and Piazza each did it twice. Weeks after the All-Star Game, Raleigh passed Perez's 2021 record of 48 balls hit over the outfield wall. (Perez had broken Bench's record of 45, which had been set more than 50 years earlier in 1970.) It was the most hit in a season by a player whose primary position is catcher and includes homers while

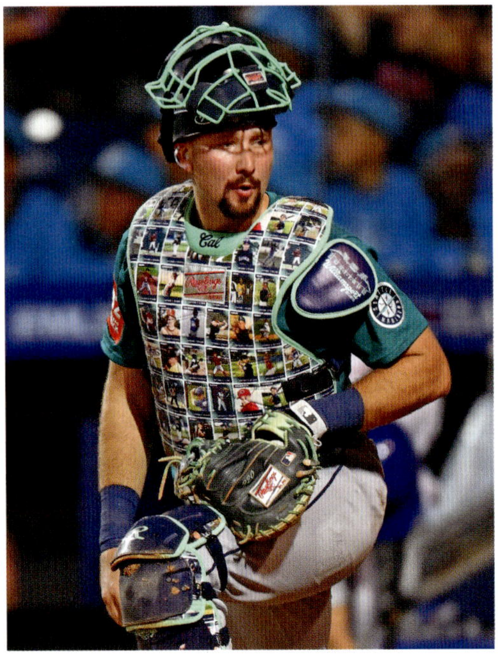

The Seattle Mariners' Cal Raleigh (left) looks on during the 2025 MLB Little League Classic against the New York Mets at Bowman Field in Williamsport, Pennsylvania. His custom-made Rawlings chest protector featured photos of all his teammates during their Little League days. Raleigh has used the Rawlings PROCM33-CR29 model glove (opposite) during his career.

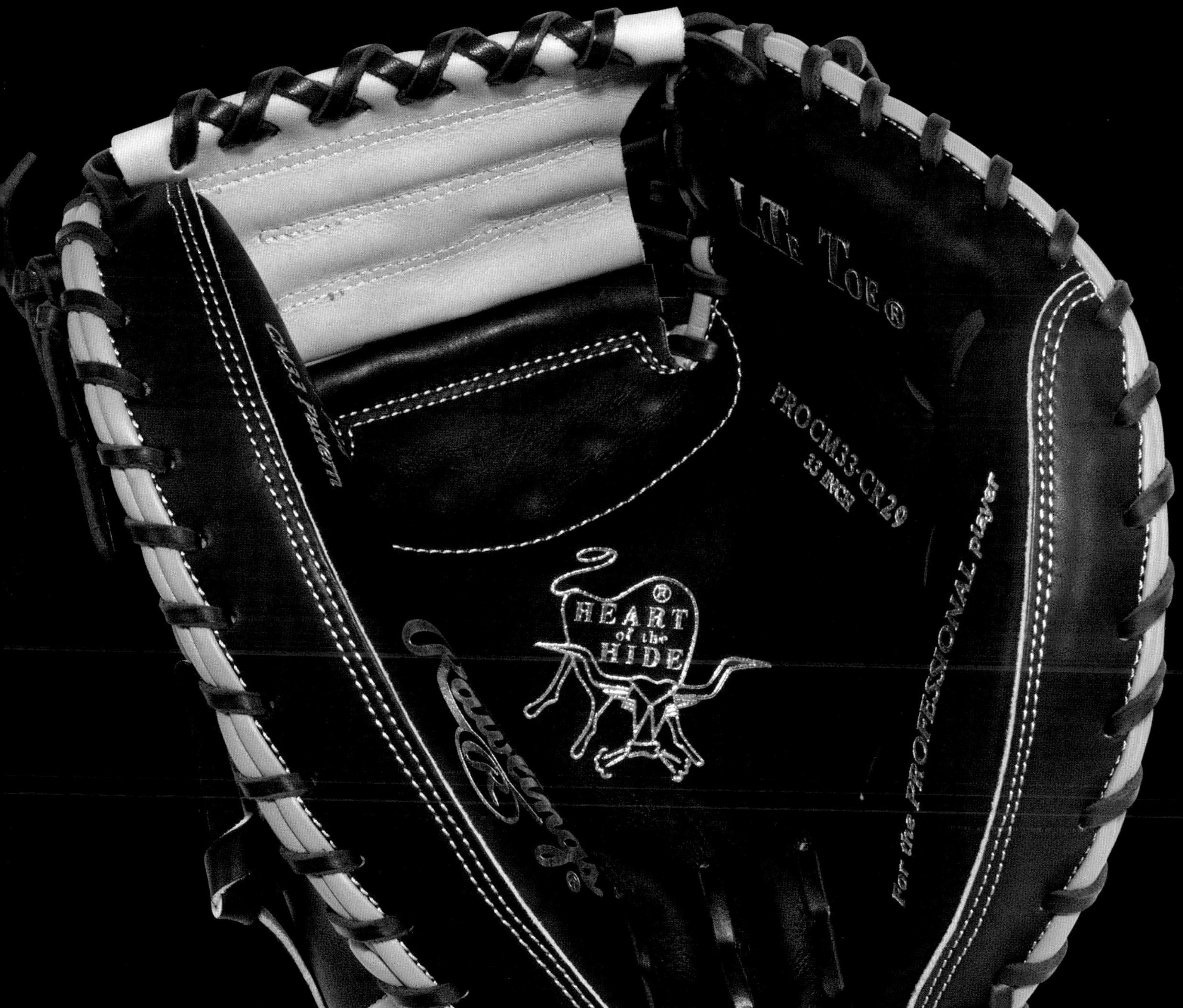
PROCM33-CR29
33 INCH
HEART of the HIDE
Rawlings
For the PROFESSIONAL player

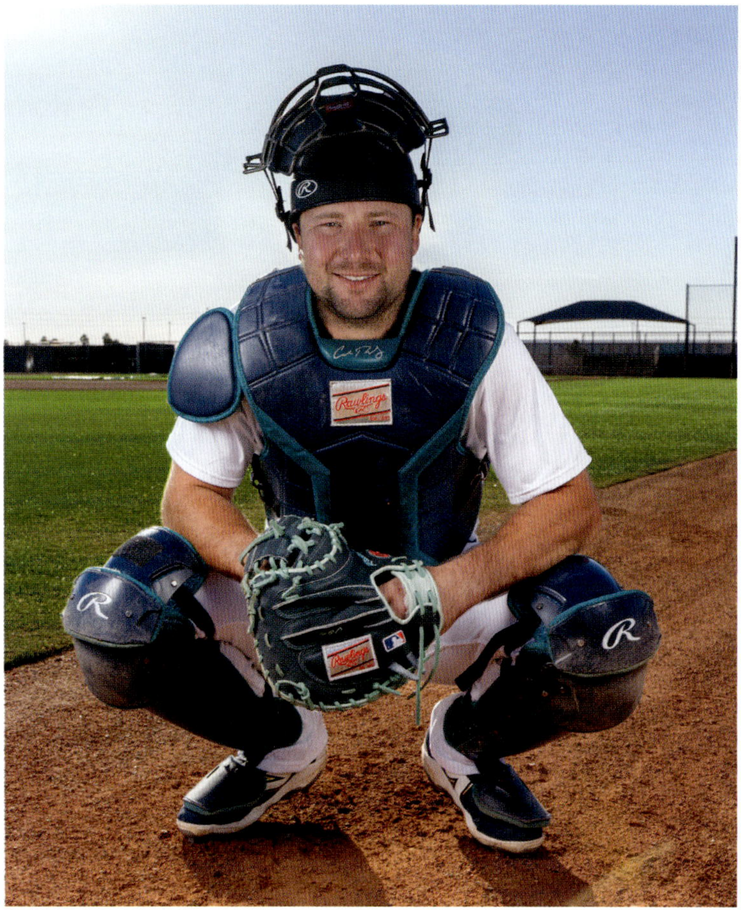

In just his fourth season in the major leagues, Raleigh took home both the Rawlings Gold Glove Award and Platinum Glove Award.

pinch-hitting or as a designated hitter. Raleigh then exceeded López's record of 42 dingers in a season for someone who plays only catcher.

Raleigh tied baseball's great hitters Hank Greenberg, Sammy Sosa, and Aaron Judge for the most games (11) with at least two home runs in a single season. He also became the game's only switch-hitter to hit at least 20 homers from each side of the plate, and with his 55th home run, he passed Mickey Mantle's previous MLB switch-hitting record of 54 balls hit out of the park. He then broke Ken Griffey Jr.'s record of 56 home runs in a season to become the Mariners' team leader.

What is most amazing about the player nicknamed "The Big Dumper" (by a minor-league teammate, due to the enormity of his backside) is that Raleigh's 2025 accomplishments came from the catcher position, the most physically and mentally demanding in the game. He has the résumé to show that he is not simply a one-trick pony, with offense being the trick. Defensively he is one of the best catchers—if not *the* best—playing in the majors. If he wasn't, he wouldn't have been chosen as the 2024 AL Gold Glove Award winner at the position, nor would he have been selected as the AL Platinum Glove Award winner as the best of the best defenders that year.

Raleigh's total performance in 2025 may be looked upon as one of the best seasons ever recorded by a big-league catcher. It was a season of excellence that was among the greatest in the game across all players and all positions. More importantly, Raleigh's accomplishments positioned him for MVP consideration. For the fans in Seattle, Raleigh has energized a team that has only played in the postseason five times since the franchise was founded in 1977. The Mariners are also the only team to have never appeared in a World Series. Raleigh's fifth-inning home run in Game Seven of the 2025 ALCS—his fifth of the playoffs—positioned the Mariners for possibly their first Fall Classic, but it was not to be. The Toronto Blue Jays came from behind to win the game and the AL pennant.

But even in that last game's loss, Raleigh once again put his name among the game's best ever. His 65 home runs from the regular season and postseason combined are now the fourth most ever hit in MLB history, trailing only Barry Bonds (73), Mark McGwire (70), and Sammy Sosa (66). Those 65 dingers also set a new AL record for most home runs (regular season and postseason combined) as he passed Judge (64), Roger Maris (62), and Babe Ruth (62). While the season may have ended on a down note, the potential Raleigh showed in 2025 confirms that his future is only looking up.

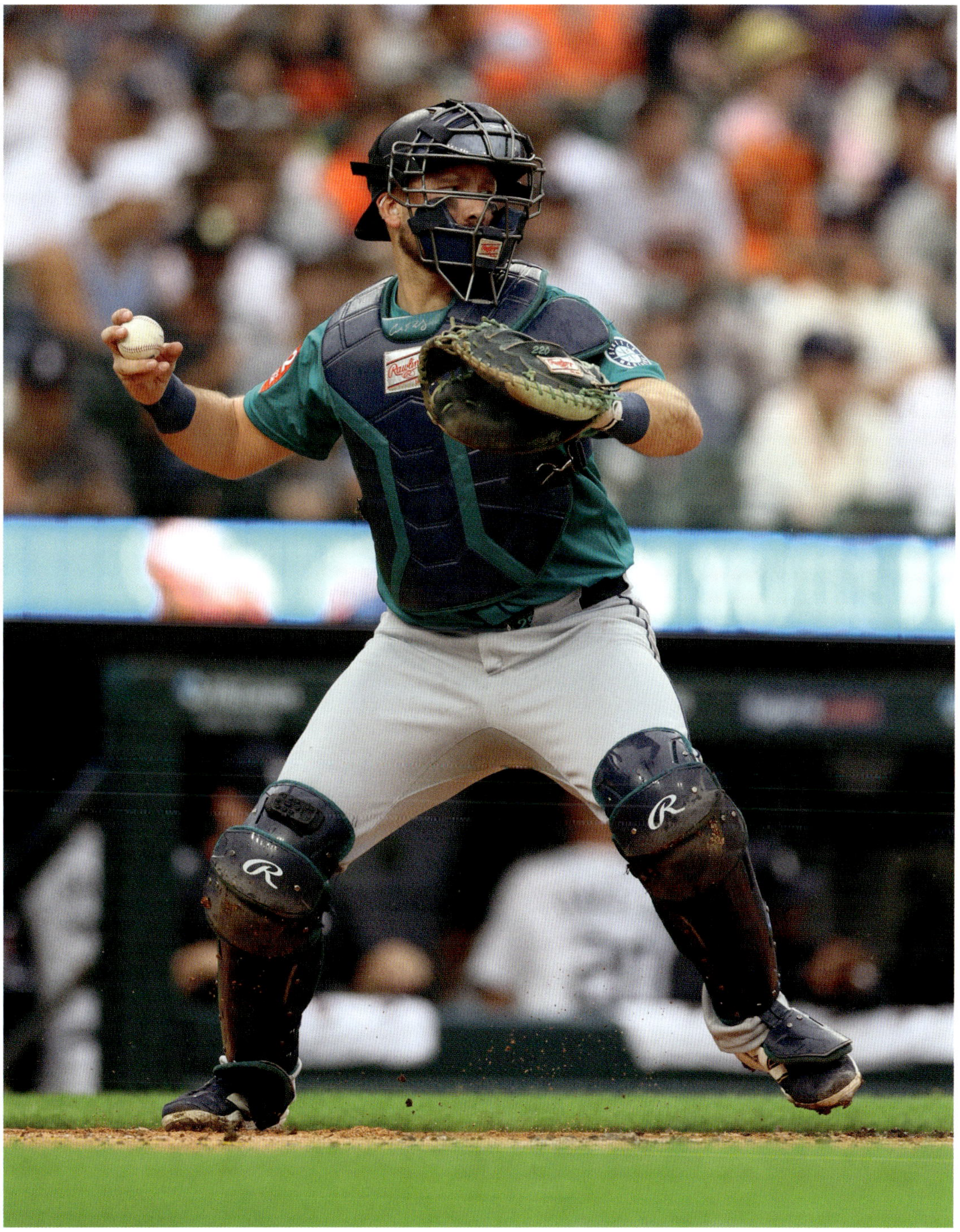

In 2025, brandishing the Rawlings Platinum Glove Award label on his equipment, Raleigh passed many of baseball's greats in the record books to have one of the game's greatest seasons.

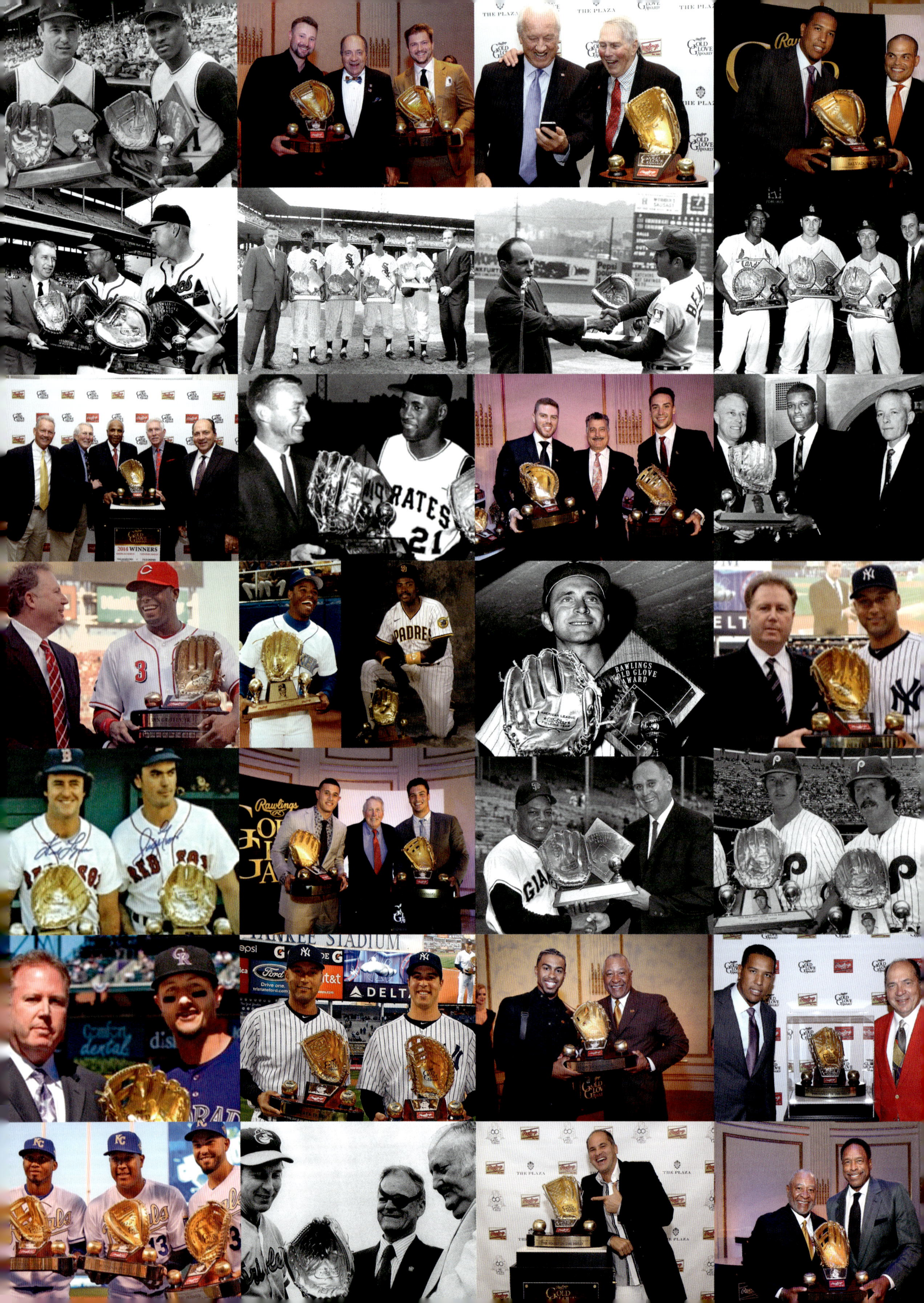
THE PLAZA
2014 WINNERS
RATES
21
RAWLINGS
GOLD GLOVE
AWARD
YANKEE STADIUM
DELTA
Rawlings
GOLD GLOVE

THE FINEST IN THE FIELD: Rawlings Gold Glove and Platinum Glove Awards

The National Baseball Hall of Fame in Cooperstown opened in 1939 to honor the greatest men (and one woman, Effa Manley) who played or contributed to the game of baseball. Their inductions recognize their play on the field or their leadership in the dugout or the front office. In 1957, Rawlings created what became an annual award recognizing MLB's best defensive players. Not all Gold Glove winners wind up with the résumé and credentials for Cooperstown, but—for one or more seasons—those winners are acknowledged as the best in the game. The Gold Glove Award is a testament to their elite defensive skills at their position during a given season. The award has become the benchmark by which all defense is measured, and it continues to be celebrated as the highest symbol of defensive excellence. Managers and six coaches from each MLB team vote on the awards. They cannot vote for their own players and can only vote for players in their own league. Rawlings announced in 2013 that the award would thereafter include a sabermetric component called the SABR Defensive Index, which is an aggregate measure of various advanced defensive statistics, such as ultimate zone rating, defensive runs saved, defensive regression analysis, and total zone rating. The Rawlings Gold Glove Awards have since been calculated based on a combination of managers' and coaches' votes and the SABR Defensive Index. Each year's winners are then proudly looked upon as the finest in the field.

Baseball has undergone many changes since its inception, and so has the Gold Glove Award process. When the award debuted in 1957, there was just one winner for each position across MLB (nine total awards). The following year, it expanded to recognize nine players in both the AL and NL (18 total recipients). There was soon a change to the selection process for outfielders too.

Top row (from left to right): Bill Mazeroski and Roberto Clemente, 1964; Cal Raleigh, Johnny Bench, and Patrick Bailey, 2024; Al Kaline and Brooks Robinson, 2018; Salvador Perez and Iván Rodríguez, 2013. Second row: Unknown, Hank Aaron, and Del Crandall, 1960; Mr. Lee, Minnie Miñoso, Jim Landis, Luis Aparicio, Nellie Fox, and Mr. Bryant, 1961; Unknown and Johnny Bench, 1969; Bill White, Ken Boyer, Bobby Shantz, and unknown, 1961. Third row: George Brett, Brooks Robinson, Frank Robinson, Mike Schmidt, and Johnny Bench, 2014; Unknown and Roberto Clemente, 1960s; Freddie Freeman, Keith Hernandez, and Matt Olson, 2018; Bing Devine, Bob Gibson, and unknown, 1968. Fourth row: Mike Thompson and Ken Griffey Jr., 1999; Ken Griffey Jr., 1990; Tony Gwynn, 1990; Bobby Shantz, 1959; Mike Thompson and Derek Jeter, 2009. Fifth row: Fred Lynn and Dwight Evans, 1978; Manny Machado, Brooks Robinson, and Nolan Arenado, 2013; Willie Mays and unknown, 1959; Jim Kaat and Mike Schmidt, 1976. Sixth row: Mike Thompson and Troy Tulowitzki, 2010; Derek Jeter and Mark Teixeira, 2010; Francisco Lindor and Ozzie Smith, 2019; Salvador Perez and Johnny Bench, 2013. Bottom row: Alcides Escobar, Salvador Perez, and Eric Hosmer, 2015; Brooks Robinson and two unknowns, 1970s; Omar Vizquel, 2019; Ozzie Smith and Dave Winfield, 2023.

Between 1957 and 1960, outfield awards were selected by specific positions—left field, center field, and right field. Beginning in 1961 and lasting through the 2010 season, Gold Gloves were awarded to three outfielders regardless of their specific position. This change allowed, for example, three center fielders to be selected for the award in a given season. But not all outfield positions have the same criteria and characteristics of defensive play. In 2011, the outfield selection process reverted to awarding Gold Gloves to the three independent outfield positions, as had been done years earlier.

As defense continues to win ballgames, an MLB team's success is often a byproduct of its superior defense. In keeping up with the evolving game, Rawlings created two new award categories. In 2020, the Gold Glove Award was expanded to recognize the best team defense during each season. Two MLB teams receive this award each year—one in the AL and one in the NL. In another move to honor versatile players in each league—those who possess the defensive ability to play multiple positions for the good of their team, alongside the nine set positions—an additional Gold Glove Award was established in 2022 to honor the best utility player in each league, increasing the total number of annual Gold Glove Awards to 22.

Baseball has a history built on facts, stats, and trivia. The Gold Glove Awards are no different. While there is much to study within the list of winners from the 68 seasons of the awards, there are some fascinating tidbits of baseball trivia that highlight the history of the game. Are you surprised that baseball's greatest defender is a pitcher? The numbers say so. Pitcher Greg Maddux leads all Gold Glove winners with 18 awards. Another pitcher, Jim Kaat, has the second-most wins; he is tied with the winningest position player, the Baltimore Orioles' Brooks Robinson, with 16. Interestingly, these two players each won their total awards consecutively. Thirteen other players have won at least 10 Gold Gloves in their careers. The sustained success of these multi-award winners often overshadows great defensive performances by other players in a given season or over their career.

And then there is the Los Angeles Angels' Darin Erstad, who in 2004 made Gold Glove history as the only player to win the award as both an infielder and an outfielder. Erstad had won two Gold Gloves in center field (2000 and 2002) before moving to first base and winning the award at that position in 2004. Until 2011, Erstad was the only player to win at two different positions. That changed when Plácido Polanco added a third base Gold Glove to the ones he had already earned at second base in 2007 and 2009. However, Polanco never won in the outfield, so Erstad remains the only player to win Gold Gloves in both the infield and outfield.

Eight times in baseball history a team's battery—the pitcher and catcher—took home the award during the same season, starting with the Minnesota Twins' Kaat and Earl Battey in 1962. The Pittsburgh Pirates' Rick Reuschel and Tony Peña won the award in 1985, and the Kansas City Royals' Bret Saberhagen and Bob Boone won in 1989. Kenny Rogers and Iván Rodríguez won it twice but with two teams, the Texas Rangers in 2000 and the Detroit Tigers in 2006. The St. Louis

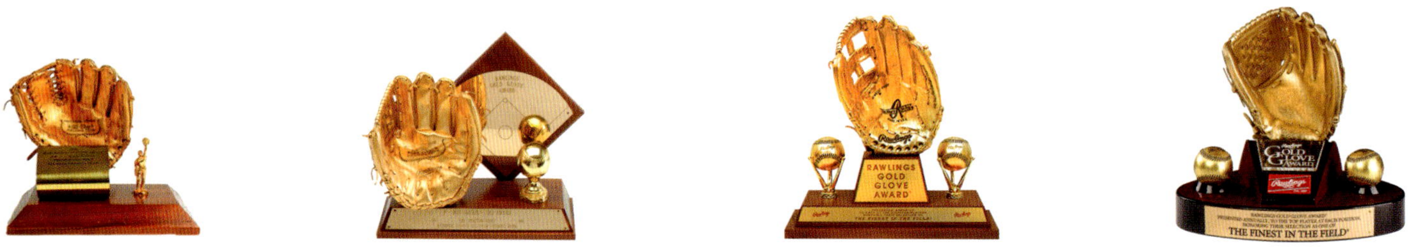

The evolution of the Rawlings Gold Glove Award trophy (from left to right): 1957–1958, 1959–1966, 1967–2006, 2007–present day.

Rawlings Gold Glove Player Awards: Franchise Facts

Excludes the Rawlings Team Award Winners First Issued in 2020

	Arizona	Atlanta (Milwaukee)	Baltimore	Boston
First Winner	Steve Finley - 1999	Del Crandall - 1958 Hank Aaron - 1958	Brooks Robinson - 1960	Frank Malzone - 1957
# of Players	10	23	18	25
# of Awards	22	62	72	52

	Chicago - AL	Chicago - NL	Cincinnati	Cleveland
First Winner	Nellie Fox - 1957 Sherman Lollar - 1957 Minnie Miñoso - 1957	Ernie Banks - 1960	Roy McMillan - 1957	Vic Power - 1958
# of Players	17	22	55	20
# of Awards	40	53	56	44

	Colorado	Detroit	Houston (AL & NL)	Kansas City
First Winner	Larry Walker - 1997	Al Kaline - 1957	Bobby Shantz - 1962	Amos Otis - 1971
# of Players	10	17	15	16
# of Awards	29	44	34	42

	Los Angeles - AL (California/Anaheim)	Los Angeles - NL (Brooklyn)	Miami	Milwaukee (Brewers AL & NL)
First Winner	Vic Power - 1964	Gil Hodges - 1957	Charles Johnson - 1995	George Scott - 1972
# of Players	21	26	10	8
# of Awards	40	47	15	13

	Minnesota (Washington)	New York - AL	New York - NL	Oakland (Philadelphia/Kansas City)
First Winner	Earl Battey - 1960	Bobby Shantz - 1957	Tommie Agee - 1970	Vic Power - 1958
# of Players	16	28	10	12
# of Awards	48	70	20	28

	Philadelphia	Pittsburgh	San Diego	San Francisco (New York)
First Winner	Bobby Wine - 1963	Bill Mazeroski - 1958	Dave Winfield - 1979	Willie Mays - 1957
# of Players	20	21	13	22
# of Awards	50	54	28	49

	Seattle	St. Louis	Tampa Bay	Texas
First Winner	Mark Langston - 1987	Ken Boyer - 1958	Carlos Peña - 2008	Jim Sundberg - 1976
# of Players	17	30	5	18
# of Awards	44	100	9	45

	Toronto	Washington (Montréal)
First Winner	Jesse Barfield - 1986 Tony Fernández - 1986	Mike Jorgensen - 1973
# of Players	17	11
# of Awards	31	23

Since the award's inception, 1,245 players have won the Gold Glove. Nineteen times, players have been traded during their Gold Glove Award season and are therefore counted for each team they played for. Bobby Shantz was traded twice during his 1964 Gold Glove Award season and is counted for all three teams.

Rawlings Gold Glove Awards Leaders by Position

Pitcher	Catcher	First Baseman	Second Baseman	Third Baseman
Greg Maddux - 18	Iván Rodríguez -13	Keith Hernandez - 11	Roberto Alomar - 10	Brooks Robinson - 16
Jim Kaat - 16	Johnny Bench - 10	Don Mattingly - 9	Ryne Sandberg - 9	Nolan Arenado - 10
Bob Gibson - 9	Yadier Molina - 9	George Scott - 8	Bill Mazeroski - 8	Mike Schmidt - 10

Shortstop	Left Fielder	Center Fielder	Right Fielder	Outfielder (1961–2010)
Ozzie Smith - 13	Alex Gordon - 8	Kevin Kiermaier - 4	Mookie Betts - 6	Roberto Clemente - 12
Omar Vizquel - 11	Ian Happ - 4	Adam Jones - 3	Jason Heyward - 5	Willie Mays - 12
Luis Aparicio - 9	Carlos González - 2	Ender Inciarte - 3	Nick Markakis - 3	Ken Griffey Jr. - 10
				Andruw Jones - 10

Between 1957 and 1960, the outfield Gold Gloves were awarded by position (left fielder, center fielder, right fielder). Between 1961 and 2010, outfield awards were not aligned to specific positions. In 2011, the awards reverted back to selections by specific outfield positions. Mauricio Dubon is the only player to win the utility player award two times since its inception in 2022.

Rawlings Gold Glove Award Winners: Selection by Year

AL	1957	NL	AL	1958	NL	AL	1959	NL
Shantz - NYY	P		Shantz - NYY	P	Haddix - CIN	Shantz - NYY	P	Haddix - CIN
Lollar - CHW	C		Lollar - CHW	C	Crandall - MIL	Lollar - CHW	C	Crandall - MIL
	1B	Hodges - BKN	Power - KCA/CLE	1B	Hodges - LAD	Power - CLE	1B	Hodges - LAD
Fox - CHW	2B		Bolling - DET	2B	Mazeroski - PIT	Fox - CHW	2B	Neal - LAD
Malzone - BOS	3B		Malzone - BOS	3B	Boyer - STL	Malzone - BOS	3B	Boyer - STL
	SS	McMillan - CIN	Aparicio - CHW	SS	McMillan - CIN	Aparicio - CHW	SS	McMillan - CIN
Miñoso - CHW	LF		Siebern - NYY	LF	Robinson - CIN	Miñoso - CLE	LF	Brandt - SFG
	CF	Mays - NYG	Piersall - BOS	CF	Mays - SFG	Kaline - DET	CF	Mays - SFG
Kaline - DET	RF		Kaline - DET	RF	Aaron - MIL	Jensen - BOS	RF	Aaron - MIL

AL	1960	NL	AL	1961	NL	AL	1962	NL
Shantz - NYY	P	Haddix - PIT	Lary - DET	P	Shantz - PIT	Kaat - MIN	P	Shantz - HOU/STL
Battey - WAS	C	Crandall - MIL	Battey - MIN	C	Roseboro - LAD	Battey - MIN	C	Crandall - MLN
Power - CLE	1B	White - STL	Power - CLE	1B	White - STL	Power - MIN	1B	White - STL
Fox - CHW	2B	Mazeroski - PIT	Richardson - NYY	2B	Mazeroski - PIT	Richardson - NYY	2B	Hubbs - CHC
Robinson - BAL	3B	Boyer - STL	Robinson - BAL	3B	Boyer - STL	Robinson - BAL	3B	Davenport - SFG
Aparicio - CHW	SS	Banks - CHC	Aparicio - CHW	SS	Wills - LAD	Aparicio - CHW	SS	Wills - LAD
Miñoso - CHW	LF	Moon - LAD	Kaline - DET	OF	Clemente - PIT	Landis - CHW	OF	Clemente - PIT
Landis - CHW	CF	Mays - SFG	Landis - CHW	OF	Mays - SFG	Kaline - DET	OF	Mays - SFG
Maris - NYY	RF	Aaron - MIL	Piersall - CLE	OF	Pinson - CIN	Mantle - NYY	OF	Virdon - PIT

AL	1963	NL	AL	1964	NL	AL	1965	NL
Kaat - MIN	P	Shantz - STL	Kaat - MIN	P	Shantz - STL/CHC/PHI	Kaat - MIN	P	Gibson - STL
Howard - NYY	C	Edwards - CIN	Howard - NYY	C	Edwards - CIN	Freehan - DET	C	Torre - MIL
Power - MIN	1B	White - STL	Power - MIN/LAA	1B	White - STL	Pepitone - NYY	1B	White - STL
Richardson - NYY	2B	Mazeroski - PIT	Richardson - NYY	2B	Mazeroski - PIT	Richardson - NYY	2B	Mazeroski - PIT
Robinson - BAL	3B	Boyer - STL	Robinson - BAL	3B	Santo - CHC	Robinson - BAL	3B	Santo - CHC
Versalles - MIN	SS	Wine - PHI	Aparicio - BAL	SS	Amaro - PHI	Versalles - MIN	SS	Cárdenas - CIN
Kaline - DET	OF	Mays - SFG	Kaline - DET	OF	Mays - SFG	Kaline - DET	OF	Mays - SFG
Yastrzemski - BOS	OF	Clemente - PIT	Landis - CHW	OF	Clemente - PIT	Tresh - NYY	OF	Clemente - PIT
Landis - CHW	OF	Flood - STL	Davalillo - CLE	OF	Flood - STL	Yastrzemski - BOS	OF	Flood - STL

AL	1966	NL	AL	1967	NL	AL	1968	NL
Kaat - MIN	P	Gibson - STL	Kaat - MIN	P	Gibson - STL	Kaat - MIN	P	Gibson - STL
Freehan - DET	C	Roseboro - LAD	Freehan - DET	C	Hundley - CHC	Freehan - DET	C	Bench - CIN
Pepitone - NYY	1B	White - PHI	Scott - BOS	1B	Parker - LAD	Scott - BOS	1B	Parker - LAD
Knoop - CAL	2B	Mazeroski - PIT	Knoop - CAL	2B	Mazeroski - PIT	Knoop - CAL	2B	Beckert - CHC
Robinson - BAL	3B	Santo - CHC	Robinson - BAL	3B	Santo - CHC	Robinson - BAL	3B	Santo - CHC
Aparicio - BAL	SS	Alley - PIT	Fregosi - CAL	SS	Alley - PIT	Aparicio - CHW	SS	Maxvill - STL
Kaline - DET	OF	Mays - SFG	Yastrzemski - BOS	OF	Clemente - PIT	Stanley - DET	OF	Mays - SFG
Agee - CHW	OF	Clemente - PIT	Blair - BAL	OF	Flood - STL	Yastrzemski - BOS	OF	Clemente - PIT
Oliva - MIN	OF	Flood - STL	Kaline - DET	OF	Mays - SFG	Smith - BOS	OF	Flood - STL

AL	1969	NL	AL	1970	NL	AL	1971	NL
Kaat - MIN	P	Gibson - STL	Kaat - MIN	P	Gibson - STL	Kaat - MIN	P	Gibson - STL
Freehan - DET	C	Bench - CIN	Fosse - CLE	C	Bench - CIN	Fosse - CLE	C	Bench - CIN
Pepitone - NYY	1B	Parker - LAD	Spencer - CAL	1B	Parker - LAD	Scott - BOS	1B	Parker - LAD
Johnson - BAL	2B	Millán - ATL	Johnson - BAL	2B	Helms - CIN	Johnson - BAL	2B	Helms - CIN
Robinson - BAL	3B	Boyer - ATL	Robinson - BAL	3B	Rader - HOU	Robinson - BAL	3B	Rader - HOU
Belanger - BAL	SS	Kessinger - CHC	Aparicio - CHW	SS	Kessinger - CHC	Belanger - BAL	SS	Harrelson - NYM
Blair - BAL	OF	Clemente - PIT	Stanley - DET	OF	Clemente - PIT	Blair - BAL	OF	Clemente - PIT
Stanley - DET	OF	Flood - STL	Blair - BAL	OF	Agee - NYM	Otis - KCR	OF	Bonds - SFG
Yastrzemski - BOS	OF	Rose - CIN	Berry - CHW	OF	Rose - CIN	Yastrzemski - BOS	OF	Davis - LAD

AL	1972	NL	AL	1973	NL	AL	1974	NL
Kaat - MIN	P	Gibson - STL	Kaat - MIN/CHW	P	Gibson - STL	Kaat - CHW	P	Messersmith - LAD
Fisk - BOS	C	Bench - CIN	Munson - NYY	C	Bench - CIN	Munson - NYY	C	Bench - CIN
Scott - MIL	1B	Parker - LAD	Scott - MIL	1B	Jorgenson - MON	Scott - MIL	1B	Garvey - LAD
Griffin - BOS	2B	Millán - ATL	Grich - BOS	2B	Morgan - CIN	Grich - BAL	2B	Morgan - CIN
Robinson - BAL	3B	Rader - HOU	Robinson - BAL	3B	Rader - HOU	Robinson - BAL	3B	Rader - HOU
Brinkman - DET	SS	Bowa - PHI	Belanger - BAL	SS	Metzger - HOU	Belanger - BAL	SS	Concepción - CIN
Blair - BAL	OF	Clemente - PIT	Blair - BAL	OF	Bonds - SFG	Blair - BAL	OF	Cedeño - HOU
Murcer - NYY	OF	Cedeño - HOU	Otis - KCR	OF	Cedeño - HOU	Otis - KCR	OF	Gerónimo - CIN
Berry - CAL	OF	Davis - LAD	Stanley - DET	OF	Davis - LAD	Rudi - OAK	OF	Bonds - SFG

AL	1975	NL	AL	1976	NL	AL	1977	NL
Kaat - CHW	P	Messersmith - LAD	Palmer - BAL	P	Kaat - PHI	Palmer - BAL	P	Kaat - PHI
Munson - NYY	C	Bench - CIN	Sundberg - TEX	C	Bench - CIN	Sundberg - TEX	C	Bench - CIN
Scott - MIL	1B	Garvey - LAD	Scott - MIL	1B	Garvey - LAD	Spencer - CHW	1B	Garvey - LAD
Grich - BOS	2B	Morgan - CIN	Grich - BOS	2B	Morgan - CIN	White - KCR	2B	Morgan - CIN
Robinson - BAL	3B	Reitz - STL	Rodríguez - DET	3B	Schmidt - PHI	Nettles - NYY	3B	Schmidt - PHI
Belanger - BAL	SS	Concepción - CIN	Belanger - BAL	SS	Concepción - CIN	Belanger - BAL	SS	Concepción - CIN
Blair - BAL	OF	Cedeño - HOU	Rudi - OAK	OF	Cedeño - HOU	Beníquez - TEX	OF	Gerónimo - CIN
Rudi - OAK	OF	Gerónimo - CIN	Evans - BOS	OF	Gerónimo - CIN	Yastrzemski - BOS	OF	Maddox - PHI
Lynn - BOS	OF	Maddox - SFG/PHI	Manning - CLE	OF	Maddox - PHI	Cowens - KCR	OF	Parker - PIT

AL	1978	NL
Palmer - BAL	P	Niekro - ATL
Sundberg - TEX	C	Boone - PHI
Chambliss - NYY	1B	Hernandez - STL
White - KCR	2B	Lopes - LAD
Nettles - NYY	3B	Schmidt - PHI
Belanger - BAL	SS	Bowa - PHI
Lynn - BOS	OF	Maddox - PHI
Evans - BOS	OF	Parker - PIT
Miller - CAL	OF	Valentine - MON

AL	1979	NL
Palmer - BAL	P	Niekro - ATL
Sundberg - TEX	C	Boone - PHI
Cooper - MIL	1B	Hernandez - STL
White - KCR	2B	Trillo - PHI
Bell - TEX	3B	Schmidt - PHI
Burleson - BOS	SS	Concepción - CIN
Lynn - BOS	OF	Maddox - PHI
Evans - BOS	OF	Parker - PIT
Lezcano - MIL	OF	Winfield - SDP

AL	1980	NL
Norris - OAK	P	Niekro - ATL
Sundberg - TEX	C	Carter - MON
Cooper - MIL	1B	Hernandez - STL
White - KCR	2B	Flynn - NYM
Bell - TEX	3B	Schmidt - PHI
Trammell - DET	SS	Smith - SDP
Lynn - BOS	OF	Dawson - MON
Murphy - OAK	OF	Maddox - PHI
Wilson - KCR	OF	Winfield - SDP

AL	1981	NL
Norris - OAK	P	Carlton - PHI
Sundberg - TEX	C	Carter - MON
Squires - CHW	1B	Hernandez - STL
White - KCR	2B	Trillo - PHI
Bell - TEX	3B	Schmidt - PHI
Trammell - DET	SS	Smith - SDP
Murphy - OAK	OF	Dawson - MON
Evans - BOS	OF	Maddox - PHI
Henderson - OAK	OF	Baker - LAD

AL	1982	NL
Guidry - NYY	P	Niekro - ATL
Boone - CAL	C	Carter - MON
Murray - BAL	1B	Hernandez - STL
White - KCR	2B	Trillo - PHI
Bell - TEX	3B	Schmidt - PHI
Yount - MIL	SS	Smith - STL
Evans - BOS	OF	Dawson - MON
Winfield - NYY	OF	Murphy - ATL
Murphy - OAK	OF	Maddox - PHI

AL	1983	NL
Guidry - NYY	P	Niekro - ATL
Parrish - DET	C	Peña - PIT
Murray - BAL	1B	Hernandez - STL/NYM
Whitaker - DET	2B	Sandberg - CHC
Bell - TEX	3B	Schmidt - PHI
Trammell - DET	SS	Smith - STL
Evans - BOS	OF	Dawson - MON
Winfield - NYY	OF	Murphy - ATL
Murphy - OAK	OF	McGee - STL

AL	1984	NL
Guidry - NYY	P	Andujar - STL
Parrish - DET	C	Peña - PIT
Murray - BAL	1B	Hernandez - STL
Whitaker - DET	2B	Sandberg - CHC
Bell - TEX	3B	Schmidt - PHI
Trammell - DET	SS	Smith - STL
Evans - BOS	OF	Murphy - ATL
Winfield - NYY	OF	Dernier - CHC
Murphy - OAK	OF	Dawson - MON

AL	1985	NL
Guidry - NYY	P	Reuschel - PIT
Parrish - DET	C	Peña - PIT
Mattingly - NYY	1B	Hernandez - NYM
Whitaker - DET	2B	Sandberg - CHC
Brett - KCR	3B	Wallach - MON
Griffin - OAK	SS	Smith - STL
Winfield - NYY	OF	McGee - STL
Pettis - CAL	OF	Murphy - ATL
Evans - BOS	OF	Dawson - MON
Murphy - OAK	OF	

AL	1986	NL
Guidry - NYY	P	Valenzuela - LAD
Boone - CAL	C	Davis - CHC
Mattingly - NYY	1B	Hernandez - NYM
White - KCR	2B	Sandberg - CHC
Gaetti - MIN	3B	Schmidt - PHI
Fernández - TOR	SS	Smith - STL
Pettis - CAL	OF	Gwynn - SDP
Barfield - TOR	OF	Murphy - ATL
Puckett - MIN	OF	McGee - STL

AL	1987	NL
Langston - SEA	P	Reuschel - PIT/SFG
Boone - CAL	C	LaValliere - PIT
Mattingly - NYY	1B	Hernandez - NYM
White - KCR	2B	Sandberg - CHC
Gaetti - MIN	3B	Pendleton - STL
Fernández - TOR	SS	Smith - STL
Barfield - TOR	OF	Davis - CIN
Puckett - MIN	OF	Dawson - CHC
Winfield - NYY	OF	Gwynn - SDP

AL	1988	NL
Langston - SEA	P	Hershiser - LAD
Boone - CAL	C	Santiago - SDP
Mattingly - NYY	1B	Hernandez - NYM
Reynolds - SEA	2B	Sandberg - CHC
Gaetti - MIN	3B	Wallach - MON
Fernández - TOR	SS	Smith - STL
White - CAL	OF	Van Slyke - PIT
Pettis - DET	OF	Davis - CIN
Puckett - MIN	OF	Dawson - CHC

AL	1989	NL
Saberhagen - KCR	P	Darling - NYM
Boone - KCR	C	Santiago - SDP
Mattingly - NYY	1B	Galarraga - MON
Reynolds - SEA	2B	Sandberg - CHC
Gaetti - MIN	3B	Pendelton - STL
Fernández - TOR	SS	Smith - STL
White - CAL	OF	Van Slyke - PIT
Pettis - DET	OF	Davis - CIN
Puckett - MIN	OF	Gwynn - SDP

AL	1990	NL
Boddicker - BOS	P	Maddux - CHC
Alomar Jr. - CLE	C	Santiago - SDP
McGwire - OAK	1B	Galarraga - MON
Reynolds - SEA	2B	Sandberg - CHC
Gruber - TOR	3B	Wallach - MON
Guillén - CHW	SS	Smith - STL
Pettis - TEX	OF	Van Slyke - PIT
Burks - BOS	OF	Gwynn - SDP
Griffey Jr. - SEA	OF	Bonds - PIT

AL	1991	NL
Langston - CAL	P	Maddux - CHC
Peña - BOS	C	Pagnozzi - STL
Mattingly - NYY	1B	Clark - SFG
Alomar - TOR	2B	Sandberg - CHC
Ventura - CHW	3B	Williams - SFG
Ripken Jr. - BAL	SS	Smith - STL
Griffey Jr. - SEA	OF	Van Slyke - PIT
White - TOR	OF	Bonds - PIT
Puckett - MIN	OF	Gwynn - SDP

AL	1992	NL
Langston - CAL	P	Maddux - CHC
Rodríguez - TEX	C	Pagnozzi - STL
Mattingly - NYY	1B	Grace - CHC
Alomar - TOR	2B	Lind - PIT
Ventura - CHW	3B	Pendleton - ATL
Ripken Jr. - BAL	SS	Smith - STL
Griffey Jr. - SEA	OF	Van Slyke - PIT
White - TOR	OF	Bonds - PIT
Puckett - MIN	OF	Walker - MON

AL	1993	NL
Langston - CAL	P	Maddux - ATL
Rodríguez - TEX	C	Manwaring - SFG
Mattingly - NYY	1B	Grace - CHC
Alomar - TOR	2B	Thompson - SFG
Ventura - CHW	3B	Williams - SFG
Vizquel - SEA	SS	Bell - PIT
Griffey Jr. - SEA	OF	Bonds - SFG
White - TOR	OF	Grissom - MON
Lofton - CLE	OF	Walker - MON

AL	1994	NL
Langston - CAL	P	Maddux - ATL
Rodríguez - TEX	C	Pagnozzi - STL
Mattingly - NYY	1B	Bagwell - HOU
Alomar - TOR	2B	Biggio - HOU
Boggs - NYY	3B	Williams - SFG
Vizquel - CLE	SS	Larkin - CIN
Griffey Jr. - SEA	OF	Lewis - CIN
Lofton - CLE	OF	Bonds - SFG
White - TOR	OF	Grissom - MON

AL	1995	NL
Langston - CAL	P	Maddux - ATL
Rodríguez - TEX	C	Johnson - FLA
Snow - CAL	1B	Grace - CHC
Alomar - TOR	2B	Biggio - HOU
Boggs - NYY	3B	Caminiti - SDP
Vizquel - CLE	SS	Larkin - CIN
Griffey Jr. - SEA	OF	Finley - SDP
Lofton - CLE	OF	Grissom - ATL
White - TOR	OF	Mondesi - LAD

AL	1996	NL
Mussina - BAL	P	Maddux - ATL
Rodríguez - TEX	C	Johnson - FLA
Snow - CAL	1B	Grace - CHC
Alomar - BAL	2B	Biggio - HOU
Ventura - CHW	3B	Caminiti - SDP
Vizquel - CLE	SS	Larkin - CIN
Griffey Jr. - SEA	OF	Finley - SDP
Lofton - CLE	OF	Grissom - ATL
Buhner - SEA	OF	Bonds - SFG

AL	1997	NL
Mussina - BAL	P	Maddux - ATL
Rodríguez - TEX	C	Johnson - FLA
Palmeiro - BAL	1B	Snow - SFG
Knoblauch - MIN	2B	Biggio - HOU
Williams - CLE	3B	Caminiti - SDP
Vizquel - CLE	SS	Ordóñez - NYM
Griffey Jr. - SEA	OF	Bonds - SFG
Edmonds - ANA	OF	Mondesi - LAD
Williams - NYY	OF	Walker - COL

AL	1998	NL
Mussina - BAL	P	Maddux - ATL
Rodríguez - TEX	C	Johnson - FLA/LAD
Palmeiro - BAL	1B	Snow - SFG
Alomar - BAL	2B	Boone - CIN
Ventura - CHW	3B	Rolen - PHI
Vizquel - CLE	SS	Ordóñez - NYM
Williams - NYY	OF	Bonds - SFG
Edmonds - ANA	OF	Jones - ATL
Griffey Jr. - SEA	OF	Walker - COL

AL	1999	NL
Mussina - BAL	**P**	Maddux - ATL
Rodríguez - TEX	**C**	Lieberthal - PHI
Palmeiro - BAL	**1B**	Snow - SFG
Alomar - CLE	**2B**	Reese - CIN
Brosius - NYY	**3B**	Ventura - NYM
Vizquel - CLE	**SS**	Ordóñez - NYM
Williams - NYY	**OF**	Finley - ARI
Green - TOR	**OF**	Jones - ATL
Griffey Jr. - SEA	**OF**	Walker - COL

AL	2000	NL
Rogers - TEX	**P**	Maddux - ATL
Rodríguez - TEX	**C**	Matheny - STL
Olerud - SEA	**1B**	Snow - SFG
Alomar - CLE	**2B**	Reese - CIN
Fryman - CLE	**3B**	Rolen - PHI
Vizquel - CLE	**SS**	Pérez - COL
Williams - NYY	**OF**	Finley - ARI
Erstad - ANA	**OF**	Jones - ATL
Dye - KCR	**OF**	Edmonds - STL

AL	2001	NL
Mussina - NYY	**P**	Maddux - CHC
Rodríguez - TEX	**C**	Ausmus - HOU
Mientkiewicz - MIN	**1B**	Helton - COL
Alomar - CLE	**2B**	Viña - STL
Chavez - OAK	**3B**	Rolen - PHI
Vizquel - CLE	**SS**	Cabrera - MON
Cameron - SEA	**OF**	Edmonds - STL
Hunter - MIN	**OF**	Jones - ATL
Suzuki - SEA	**OF**	Walker - COL

AL	2002	NL
Rogers - TEX	**P**	Maddux - ATL
Molina - ANA	**C**	Ausmus - HOU
Olerud - SEA	**1B**	Helton - COL
Boone - SEA	**2B**	Viña - STL
Chavez - OAK	**3B**	Rolen - PHI/STL
Rodriguez - TEX	**SS**	Rentería - STL
Erstad - ANA	**OF**	Edmonds - STL
Hunter - MIN	**OF**	Jones - ATL
Suzuki - SEA	**OF**	Walker - COL

AL	2003	NL
Mussina - NYY	**P**	Hampton - ATL
Molina - ANA	**C**	Matheny - STL
Olerud - SEA	**1B**	Lee - FLA
Boone - SEA	**2B**	Castillo - FLA
Chavez - OAK	**3B**	Rolen - STL
Rodriguez - TEX	**SS**	Renteria - STL
Cameron - SEA	**OF**	Edmonds - STL
Hunter - MIN	**OF**	Jones - ATL
Suzuki - SEA	**OF**	Cruz Jr. - SF

AL	2004	NL
Rogers - TEX	**P**	Maddux - CHC
Rodríguez - DET	**C**	Matheny - STL
Erstad - ANA	**1B**	Helton - COL
Boone - SEA	**2B**	Castillo - FLA
Chavez - OAK	**3B**	Rolen - STL
Jeter - NYY	**SS**	Izturis - LAD
Hunter - MIN	**OF**	Edmonds - STL
Suzuki - SEA	**OF**	Finley - ARI/LAD
Wells - TOR	**OF**	Jones - ATL

AL	2005	NL
Rogers - TEX	**P**	Maddux - CHC
Varitek - BOS	**C**	Matheny - STL
Teixeira - TEX	**1B**	Lee - CHC
Hudson - TOR	**2B**	Castillo - FLA
Chavez - OAK	**3B**	Lowell - FLA
Jeter - NYY	**SS**	Vizquel - SFG
Hunter - MIN	**OF**	Jones - ATL
Suzuki - SEA	**OF**	Edmonds - STL
Wells - TOR	**OF**	Abreu - PHI

AL	2006	NL
Rogers - DET	**P**	Maddux - CHC/LAD
Rodríguez - DET	**C**	Ausmus - HOU
Teixeira - TEX	**1B**	Pujols - STL
Grudzielanek - KCR	**2B**	Hudson - ARI
Chavez - OAK	**3B**	Rolen - STL
Jeter - NYY	**SS**	Vizquel - SFG
Hunter - MIN	**OF**	Beltrán - NYM
Suzuki - SEA	**OF**	Cameron - SDP
Wells - TOR	**OF**	Jones - ATL

AL	2007	NL
Santana - MIN	**P**	Maddux - SDP
Rodríguez - TEX	**C**	Martin - LAD
Youkilis - BOS	**1B**	Lee - CHC
Polanco - DET	**2B**	Hudson - ARI
Beltré - SEA	**3B**	Wright - NYM
Cabrera - LAA	**SS**	Rollins - PHI
Hunter - MIN	**OF**	Beltrán - NYM
Suzuki - SEA	**OF**	Rowand - PHI
Sizemore - CLE	**OF**	Jones - ATL
	OF	Francoeur - ATL

AL	2008	NL
Mussina - NYY	**P**	Maddux - SDP/LAD
Mauer - MIN	**C**	Molina - STL
Peña - TBR	**1B**	González - SDP
Pedroia - BOS	**2B**	Phillips - CIN
Beltré - SEA	**3B**	Wright - NYM
Young - TEX	**SS**	Rollins - PHI
Hunter - LAA	**OF**	Beltrán - NYM
Suzuki - SEA	**OF**	McLouth - PIT
Sizemore - CLE	**OF**	Victorino - PHI

AL	2009	NL
Buehrle - CHW	**P**	Wainwright - STL
Mauer - MIN	**C**	Molina - STL
Teixeira - NYY	**1B**	González - SDP
Polanco - DET	**2B**	Hudson - ARI
Longoria - TBR	**3B**	Zimmerman - WSH
Jeter - NYY	**SS**	Rollins - PHI
Hunter - LAA	**OF**	Bourn - HOU
Jones - BAL	**OF**	Kemp - LAD
Suzuki - SEA	**OF**	Victorino - PHI

AL	2010	NL
Buehrle - CHW	**P**	Arroyo - CIN
Mauer - MIN	**C**	Molina - STL
Teixeira - NYY	**1B**	Pujols - STL
Canó - NYY	**2B**	Phillips - CIN
Longoria - TBR	**3B**	Rolen - CIN
Jeter - NYY	**SS**	Tulowitzki - COL
Crawford - TBR	**OF**	Bourn - HOU
Gutiérrez - SEA	**OF**	González - COL
Suzuki - SEA	**OF**	Victorino - PHI

AL	2011	NL
Buehrle - CHW	**P**	Kershaw - LAD
Wieters - BAL	**C**	Molina - STL
González - BOS	**1B**	Votto - CIN
Pedroia - BOS	**2B**	Phillips - CIN
Beltré - TEX	**3B**	Polanco - PHI
Aybar - LAA	**SS**	Tulowitzki - COL
Gordon - KCR	**LF**	Parra - ARI
Ellsbury - BOS	**CF**	Kemp - LAD
Markakis - BAL	**RF**	Ethier - LAD

AL	2012	NL
Peavy - CHW	**P**	Buehrle - MIA
Hellickson - TBR	**P**	
Wieters - BAL	**C**	Molina - STL
Teixeira - NYY	**1B**	LaRoche - WSH
Canó - NYY	**2B**	Barney - CHC
Beltré - TEX	**3B**	Headley - SDP
Hardy - BAL	**SS**	Rollins - PHI
Gordon - KCR	**LF**	González - COL
Jones - BAL	**CF**	McCutchen - PIT
Reddick - OAK	**RF**	Heyward - ATL

AL	2013	NL
Dickey - TOR	**P**	Wainwright - STL
Perez - KCR	**C**	Molina - STL
Hosmer - KCR	**1B**	Goldschmidt - ARI
Pedroia - BOS	**2B**	Phillips - CIN
Machado - BAL	**3B**	Arenado - COL
Hardy - BAL	**SS**	Simmons - ATL
Gordon - KCR	**LF**	González - COL
Jones - BAL	**CF**	Gómez - MIL
Victorino - BOS	**RF**	Parra - ARI

AL	2014	NL
Keuchel - HOU	**P**	Greinke - LAD
Perez - KCR	**C**	Molina - STL
Hosmer - KCR	**1B**	González - LAD
Pedroia - BOS	**2B**	LeMahieu - COL
Seager - SEA	**3B**	Arenado - COL
Hardy - BAL	**SS**	Simmons - ATL
Gordon - KCR	**LF**	Yelich - MIA
Jones - BAL	**CF**	Lagares - NYM
Markakis - BAL	**RF**	Heyward - ATL

AL	2015	NL
Keuchel - HOU	**P**	Greinke - LAD
Perez - KCR	**C**	Molina - STL
Hosmer - KCR	**1B**	Goldschmidt - ARI
Altuve - HOU	**2B**	Gordon - MIA
Machado - BAL	**3B**	Arenado - COL
Escobar - KCR	**SS**	Crawford - SFG
Céspedes - DET	**LF**	Marte - PIT
Kiermaier - TBR	**CF**	Pollock - ARI
Calhoun - LAA	**RF**	Heyward - STL

AL	2016	NL
Keuchel - HOU	**P**	Greinke - LAD
Perez - KCR	**C**	Posey - SFG
Moreland - TEX	**1B**	Rizzo - CHC
Kinsler - DET	**2B**	Panik - SFG
Beltré - TEX	**3B**	Arenado - COL
Lindor - CLE	**SS**	Crawford - SFG
Gardner - NYY	**LF**	Marte - PIT
Kiermaier - TBR	**CF**	Inciarte - ATL
Betts - BOS	**RF**	Heyward - CHC

AL	2017	NL
Stroman - TOR	**P**	Greinke - LAD
Maldonado - LAA	**C**	Barnhart - CIN
Hosmer - KCR	**1B**	Goldschmidt - ARI
Dozier - MIN	**2B**	LeMahieu - COL
Longoria - TBR	**3B**	Arenado - COL
Simmons - LAA	**SS**	Crawford - SFG
Gordon - KCR	**LF**	Ozuna - MIA
Buxton - MIN	**CF**	Inciarte - ATL
Betts - BOS	**RF**	Heyward - CHC

AL	2018	NL
Keuchel - HOU	**P**	Greinke - LAD
Perez - KCR	**C**	Molina - STL
Olson - OAK	**1B**	Freeman - ATL
	1B	Rizzo - CHC
Kinsler - LAA/BOS	**2B**	LeMahieu - COL
Chapman - OAK	**3B**	Arenado - COL
Simmons - LAA	**SS**	Ahmed - ARI
Gordon - KCR	**LF**	Dickerson - PIT
Bradley Jr. - BOS	**CF**	Inciarte - ATL
Betts - BOS	**RF**	Markakis - ATL

AL	2019	NL
Leake - SEA	**P**	Greinke - LAD
Pérez - CLE	**C**	Realmuto - PHI
Olson - Oak	**1B**	Rizzo - CHC
Sanchez - CHW	**2B**	Wong - STL
Chapman - OAK	**3B**	Arenado - COL
Lindor - CLE	**SS**	Ahmed - ARI
Gordon - KCR	**LF**	Peralta - ARI
Kiermaier - TBR	**CF**	Cain - MIL
Betts - BOS	**RF**	Bellinger - LAD

AL	2020	NL
Canning - LAA	**P**	Fried - ATL
Pérez - CLE	**C**	Barnhart - CIN
White - SEA	**1B**	Rizzo - CHC
Hernández - CLE	**2B**	Wong - STL
Kiner-Falefa - TEX	**3B**	Arenado - COL
Crawford - SEA	**SS**	Báez - CHC
Gordon - KCR	**LF**	O'Neill - STL
Robert - CHW	**CF**	Grisham - SDP
Gallo - TEX	**RF**	Betts - LAD
CLE	**TEAM**	CHC

AL	2021	NL
Keuchel - CHW	**P**	Fried - ATL
Murphy - OAK	**C**	Stallings - PIT
Gurriel - HOU	**1B**	Goldschmidt - STL
Semien - TOR	**2B**	Edman - STL
Chapman - OAK	**3B**	Arenado - STL
Correa - HOU	**SS**	Crawford - SFG
Benintendi - KCR	**LF**	O'Neill - STL
Taylor - KCR	**CF**	Bader - STL
Gallo - TEX/NYY	**RF**	Duvall - MIA/ATL
HOU	**TEAM**	STL

AL	2022	NL
Bieber - CLE	**P**	Fried - ATL
Trevino - NYY	**C**	Realmuto - PHI
Guerrero Jr. - TOR	**1B**	Walker - ARI
Giménez - CLE	**2B**	Rodgers - COL
Urías - BAL	**3B**	Arenado - STL
Peña - HOU	**SS**	Swanson - ATL
Kwan - CLE	**LF**	Happ - CHC
Straw - CLE	**CF**	Grisham - SDP
Tucker - HOU	**RF**	Betts - LAD
LeMahieu - NYY	**UT**	Donovan - STL
NYY	**TEAM**	STL

AL	2023	NL
Berríos - TOR	**P**	Wheeler - PHI
Heim - TEX	**C**	Moreno - ARI
Lowe - TEX	**1B**	Walker - ARI
Giménez - CLE	**2B**	Hoerner - CHC
Chapman - TOR	**3B**	Hayes - PIT
Volpe - NYY	**SS**	Swanson - CHC
Kwan - CLE	**LF**	Happ - CHC
Kiermaier - TOR	**CF**	Doyle - COL
Garcia - TEX	**RF**	Tatis Jr. - SDP
Dubón - HOU	**UT**	Kim - SDP
TOR	**TEAM**	MIL

AL	2024	NL
Lugo - KCR	**P**	Sale - ATL
Raleigh - SEA	**C**	Bailey - SFG
Santana - MIN	**1B**	Walker - ARI
Giménez - CLE	**2B**	Turang - MIL
Bregman - HOU	**3B**	Chapman - SFG
Witt Jr. - KCR	**SS**	Tovar - COL
Kwan - CLE	**LF**	Happ - CHC
Varsho - TOR	**CF**	Doyle - COL
Abreu - BOS	**RF**	Frelick - MIL
Moore - SEA	**UT**	Triolo - PIT
TOR	**TEAM**	MIL

AL	2025	NL
Fried - NYY	**P**	Webb - SFG
Dingler - DET	**C**	Bailey - SFG
France - MIN/TOR	**1B**	Olson - ATL
Semien - TEX	**2B**	Hoerner - CHC
Garcia - KCR	**3B**	Hayes - PIT/CIN
Witt Jr. - KCR	**SS**	Winn - STL
Kwan - CLE	**LF**	Happ - CHC
Rafaela - BOS	**CF**	Crow-Armstrong - CHC
Abreu - BOS	**RF**	Tatis Jr. - SDP
Dubón - HOU	**UT**	Sanoja - MIA
TEX	**TEAM**	CHC

Cardinals' Adam Wainwright and Yadier Molina earned their two Gold Glove Awards together in 2009 and 2013. The San Francisco Giants' Logan Webb and Patrick Bailey won in 2025.

Every player in the major leagues works to be the best at the plate and in the field. Sometimes the best players are all from the same family. The Boyer brothers (Ken and Clete), the Alomar brothers (Sandy Jr. and Roberto), and the Molina brothers (Bengie and Yadier) all took home the Gold Glove, while the father-and-son combo of Bob and Bret Boone each received the award during their playing days.

Interestingly, the team with the most World Series championships is not the team that has won the most Gold Gloves. While the New York Yankees' 27 World Series titles are the most in history, their 70 Gold Gloves fall behind the Baltimore Orioles' 72 wins and the St. Louis Cardinals' 102 Gold Gloves (100 wins by players and two team awards). Perhaps all that gold helped St. Louis to their 11 World Series wins—the second most in history. The Cardinals also have the most wins in a given season. In 2021, five of their players were honored with Gold Gloves.

To further recognize defensive excellence in the game, the first Rawlings Platinum Glove Award was introduced in 2011. The prestigious award was not meant to usurp the Gold Glove honorees. Instead, it sought to honor the decades-long hot-stove and in-season debates over which player was the best of the best. Its presentation goes beyond position-specific defensive skills to honor the exceptional play of the overall best defender in each league.

Since the award's inception, there have been 30 award winners between the two leagues. An old baseball adage says that a strong defense up the middle wins ballgames, but the Platinum Glove Award has been won by only 14 players in the middle positions (six by catchers, four by shortstops, two by second basemen, and two by center fielders). The combined total of these four positions is just three more wins than the 11 total wins at third base. And just like the team leader for the Gold Glove Awards, the St. Louis Cardinals' five selections top the MLB leaderboard for Platinum Gloves.

The Platinum Glove Award winners were initially selected by fan balloting that determined the best defensive player within each league from the pool of that season's Rawlings Gold Glove

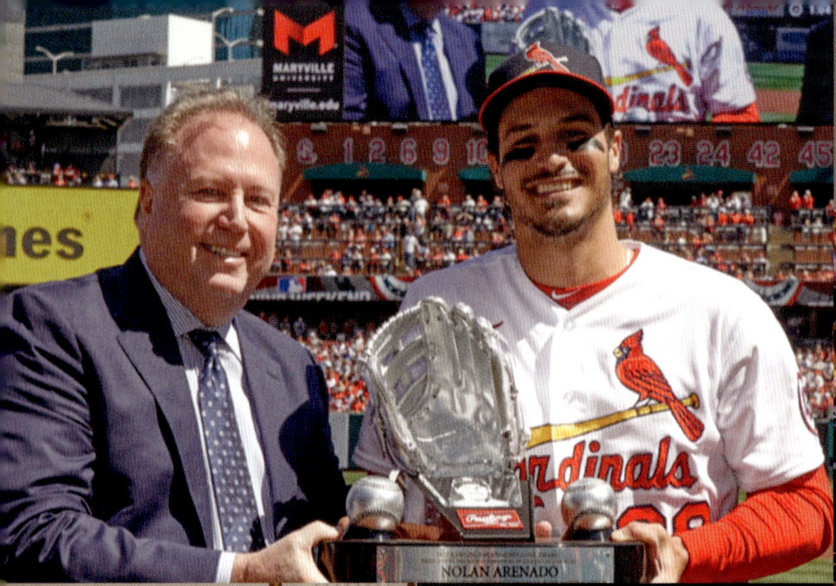
MARYVILLE UNIVERSITY
NOLAN ARENADO

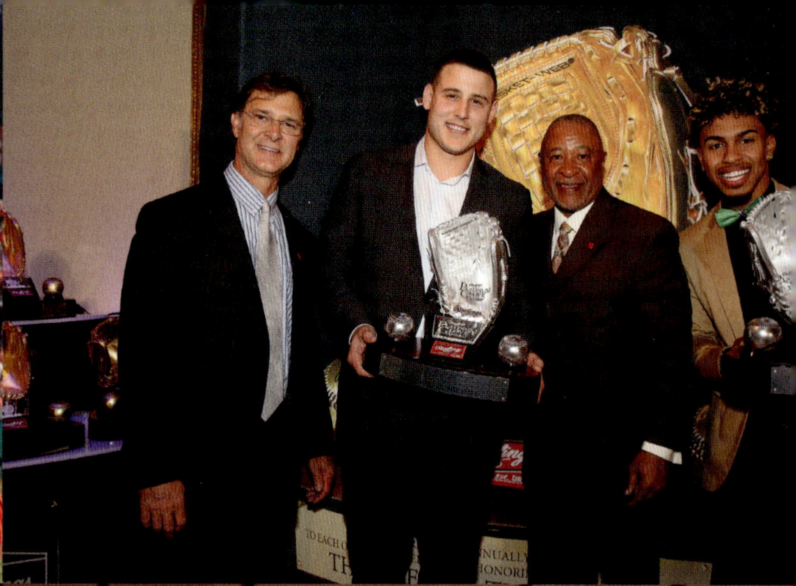

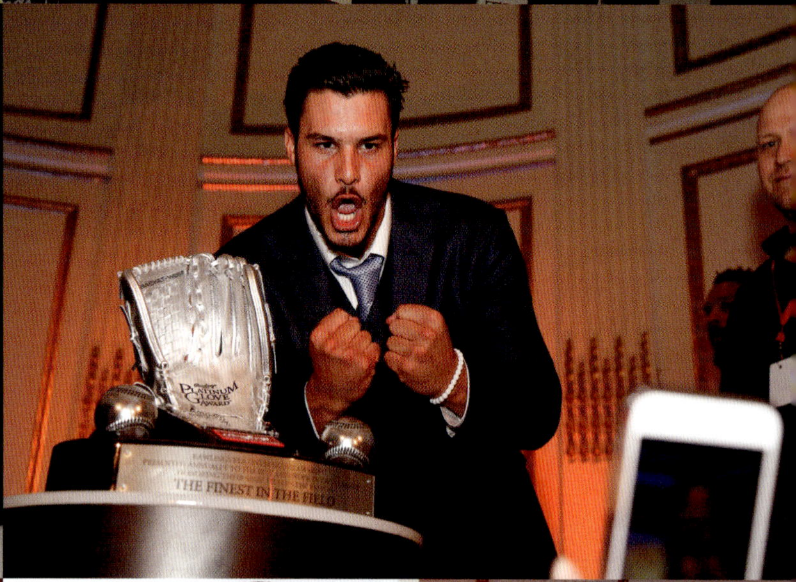
THE FINEST IN THE FIELD

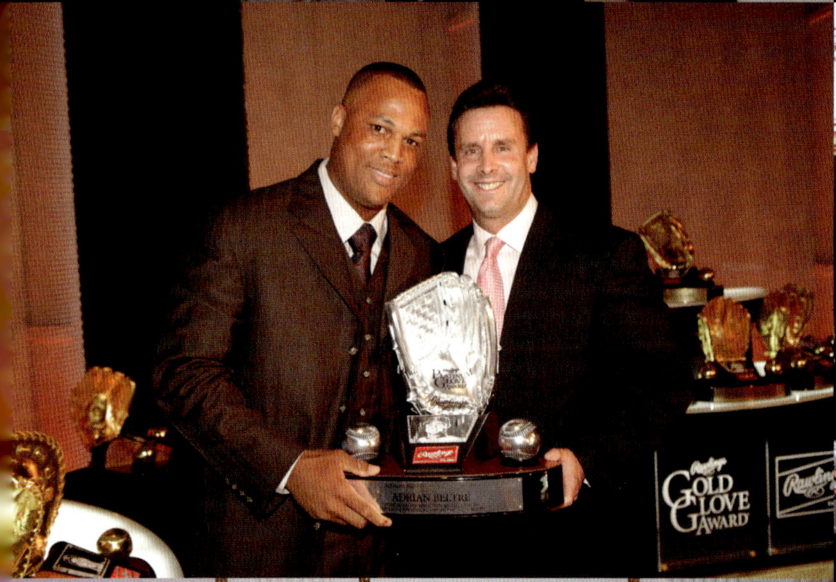
ADRIAN BELTRE
GOLD GLOVE AWARD

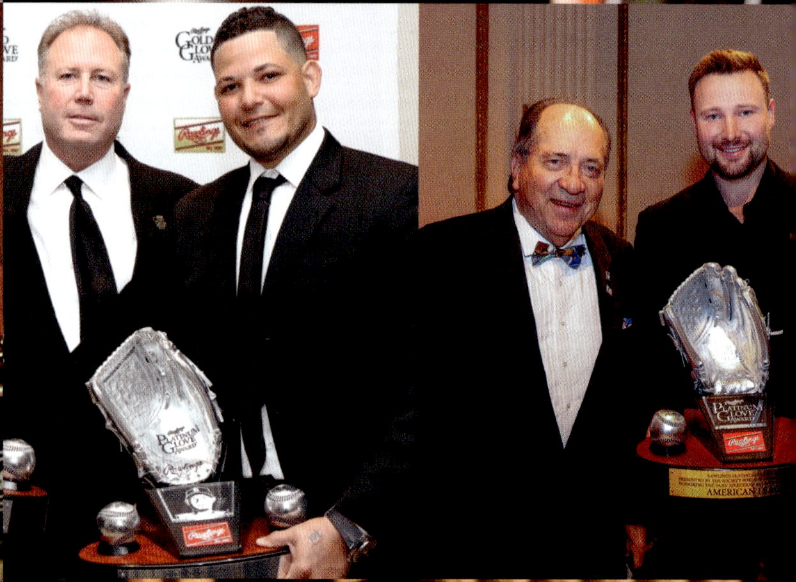

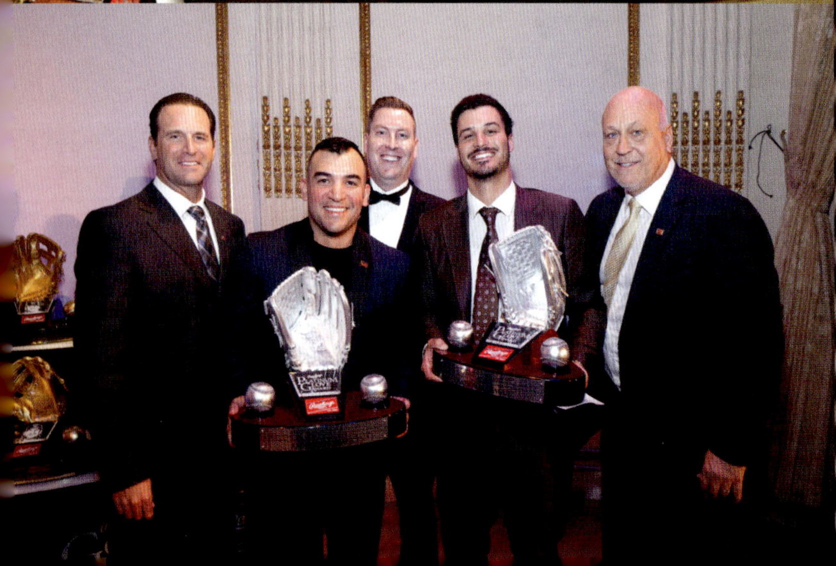

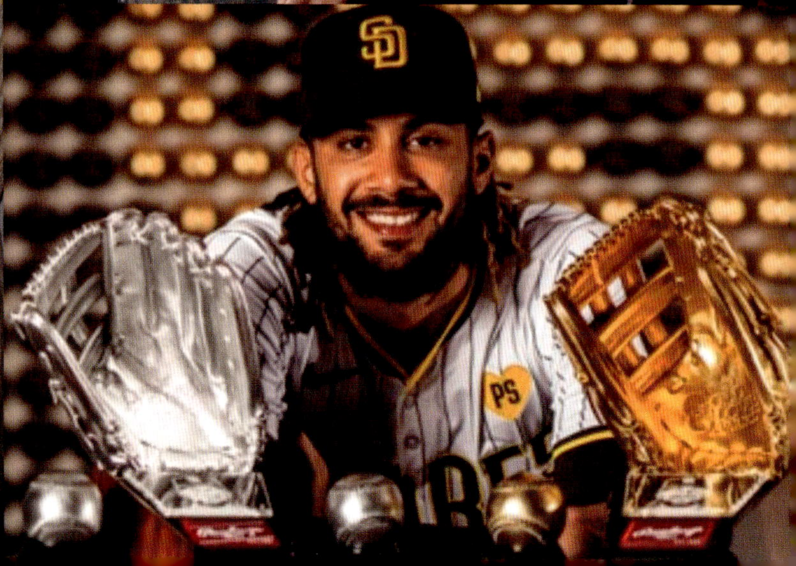

Top row (from left to right): Mike Thompson and Nolan Arenado, 2022; Don Mattingly, Anthony Rizzo, Ozzie Smith, and Francisco Lindor, 2014. Second row: Alex Gordon, George Brett, Yadier Molina, and Johnny Bench, 2014; Nolan Arenado and unknown, 2017. Third row: Adrian Beltré and Karl Ravech, 2012; Mike Thompson and Yadier Molina, 2014; Johnny Bench and Cal Raleigh, 2024. Bottom row: Mike Matheny, Jose Trevino, Scott Bush, Nolan Arenado, and Cal Ripken Jr., 2022; Fernando Tatis Jr., 2023.

Award winners. In 2013, a sabermetric component was combined with the fan vote to enhance the award's integrity by adding objective statistical metrics to the fans' subjective opinions to determine the best defensive player within each league. While this annual award may not fully deter fans from expressing their beliefs in those long-standing hot-stove debates, the Platinum Glove Award provides a documentable and statistical rationale for honoring the single best defensive player in each league during any given season.

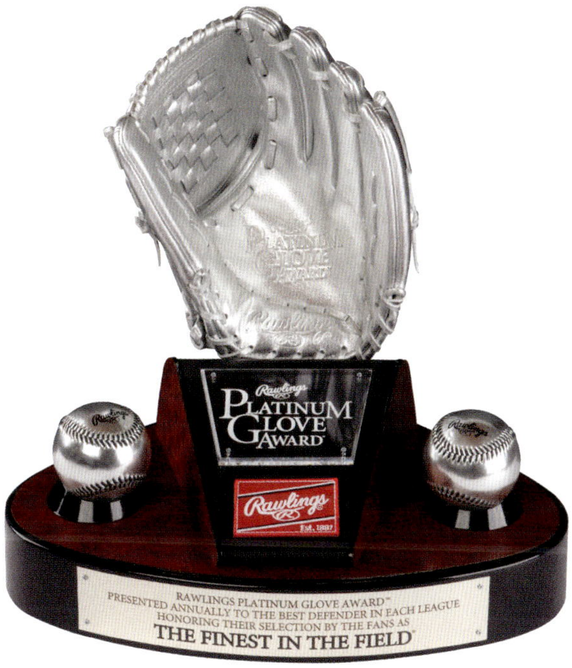

Rawlings Platinum Glove Award Winners: Selection by Year

AL	Year	NL	AL	Year	NL	AL	Year	NL
Beltré - 3B - TEX	**2011**	Molina - C - STL	Beltré - 3B - TEX	**2012**	Molina - C - STL	Machado - 3B - Orioles	**2013**	Simmons - SS - ATL
Gordon - LF - KCR	**2014**	Molina - C - STL	Kiermaier - CF - TBR	**2015**	Molina - C - STL	Lindor - SS - CLE	**2016**	Rizzo - 1B - CHC
Buxton - CF - MIN	**2017**	Arenado - 3B - COL	Chapman - 3B - OAK	**2018**	Arenado - 3B - COL	Chapman - 3B - OAK	**2019**	Arenado - 3B - COL
Gordon - LF - KCR	**2020**	Arenado - 3B - COL	Correa - SS - HOU	**2021**	Arenado - 3B - COL	Trevino - C - NYY	**2022**	Arenado - 3B - STL
Cimónoz - 2B - CLE	**2023**	Tatis Jr. - RF - SDP	Raleigh - C - SEA	**2024**	Turang - 2B - MIL	Witt Jr. - SS - KCR	**2025**	Tatis Jr. - RF - SDP

PHOTOGRAPHY CREDITS

All images courtesy of Rawlings Sporting Goods Inc. (pp. 68, 100, 113, 208, 233, 244, 249, 257, and cover images photographed by Greg Barth), except for the following:

© Archive Films/Editorial via Getty Images: p. 79 (bottom).
© *The Asahi Shimbun*/*The Asahi Shimbun* via Getty Images: p. 135 (top right).
© Brian Bahr/Getty Images Sport via Getty Images: p. 222.
© Al Bello/Getty Images Sport via Getty Images: p. 210.
© Bettmann/Bettmann via Getty Images: pp. 28, 75 (top), 88, 106, 129, 134, 138, and 147.
© Chicago History Museum/Archive Photos via Getty Images: p. 53.
© Diamond Images/Getty Images: p. 162.
© Tom DiPace Photography: pp. 136, 155 (right), 166 (left), 167 (bottom), 170, 178, 180, 183, 184, 185 (both), 188 (top left and top right), 189, 190, 195, 197, 198, 201, 202, 205, 206, 209, 211, 216, 229, 230, 231, 234 (both), 235, 236 (left), 238 (both), 242 (both), 246 (bottom left), 250 (both), 253, and 259.
© Justin Edmonds/Getty Images Sport via Getty Images: pp. 226 (left) and 227 (top).
Courtesy of Dennis Esken: pp. 72 (both), 85 (both), 89 (bottom), 93 (top), 94, 105 (both), 116, and 121.
© Focus on Sport/Getty Images Sport via Getty Images: pp. 117, 120, 168, and 174.
Courtesy of George H. W. Bush Presidential Library Museum: pp. 80 and 83 (top).
Courtesy of Goldin: p. 148 (both).
Courtesy of Tony Gwynn Collection (photographed by Greg Barth): p. 191.
© Hechler Photographers and Rawlings Archives: pp. 260 (all) and 268 (all).
© Hulton Archive/Hulton Archive via Getty Images: p. 102.
© John Iacono/*Sports Illustrated* via Getty Images: p. 173.
© Icon and Image/Michael Ochs Archives via Getty Images: p. 135 (bottom).
© Lelands Auctions, Matawan, NJ: pp. 109, 157, and 164.
Courtesy of Library of Congress: pp. 17 (both), 22 (both), 25 (all), 26, 27, 55, 56, 58, and 66.
© Manny Millan/*Sports Illustrated* via Getty Images: p. 177.
© J. J. Miller: p. 248.
© Peter Read Miller/*Sports Illustrated* via Getty Images: p. 158 (right).
Courtesy of Missouri History Museum: p. 70 (top).
© 2012 MLive Media Group. All rights reserved. Used with permission: p. 200.
Courtesy of National Baseball Hall of Fame and Museum, Cooperstown, NY: pp. 2, 35 (bottom), 57, 59 (top), 62, 64, 67 (bottom left), 71 (top), 73, 74, 76 (both), 78, 86, 89 (top), 93 (bottom), 110, 112, 122, 128, 133 (both), 135 (top left), 139, 144, 146 (left), 149, 150 (top), 154, 158 (left), 160, 166 (right), 187, 196, 203, 220, and 228.
© New York Daily News Archive/*New York Daily News* via Getty Images: pp. 90–91 and 92.
Courtesy of Cal Ripken Jr. (photographed by Greg Barth): p. 182.
Courtesy of Roberto Clemente Museum: p. 119.
© Joe Sargent/Getty Images Sport via Getty Images: p. 256.
© Herb Scharfman/*Sports Illustrated* via Getty Images: pp. 130 (both) and 142.
© Eric Schweikardt/*Sports Illustrated* via Getty Images /Getty Images: pp. 6 and 145.
Courtesy of Ozzie Smith (photographed by Greg Barth): p. 176.
Courtesy of Society for American Baseball Research Archives: p. 79 (top).
© Geoff Stellfox/Getty Images Sport via Getty Images: p. 255.
Courtesy of St. Louis Browns Historical Society: p. 87 (top).
Courtesy of St. Louis Cardinals Hall of Fame (photographed by Greg Barth): pp. 124, 137, and 213.
© Matthew Stockman/Getty Images Sport via Getty Images: p. 218 (right).
Talkin' Baseball® record cover: Words and Music by Terry Cashman; Publisher: PKM Music (ASACP); Record and Cover Copyright © 1981 Lifesong Records, a division of PKM Productions LLC, c/o Publisher's Licensing Corporation, 48 S. Park St., Unit #615, Montclair, NJ 07042: p. 101.
© Matt Thomas/San Diego Padres/Getty Images Sport via Getty Images: p. 246 (top).
© Al Tielemans/Getty Images: pp. 50–51.
© Winslow Townson/Getty Images Sport via Getty Images: p. 254.
© UPI/Bettmann Archive/Getty Images: p. 150 (bottom).
© UPI/Bill Greenblatt: p. 215.
Courtesy of What Pros Wear: pp. 221 and 223.
Courtesy of Ed Wheatley Collection: pp. 42 (top left and top right), 83 (bottom), 101, 146 (right), and 163.
Courtesy of Wikimedia Commons: pp. 15, 16, 23, 32, 71 (bottom), 107, and 141.
Courtesy of Worldpress: p. 199 (all except bottom).
© John Zich/AFP via Getty Images: p. 218 (left).

ABOUT THE CONTRIBUTORS

Ed Wheatley is an award-winning and best-selling author and film producer. His many published books have received national recognition, including a *Sports Collectors Digest* selection as the best book published on baseball and a nomination for the Society for American Baseball Research (SABR) Larry Ritter Award. His multiple films shown on PBS have all received regional Mid-America Emmy Award nominations, including one win. His films have appeared in the National Baseball Hall of Fame's annual film festival and have provided him multiple opportunities to speak at baseball's venerable institution in Cooperstown, New York.

Johnny Bench played his entire MLB career—which lasted from 1967 to 1983—with the Cincinnati Reds, leading the team to six division titles, four NL pennants, and two World Series championships. A 14-time All-Star, two-time NL MVP, and 10-time Gold Glove Award winner, Bench was inducted into the National Baseball Hall of Fame in 1989 in his first year of eligibility. He was named to MLB's All-Time Team in 1997 and All-Century Team in 1999, and ESPN has called him the greatest catcher in baseball history.

ACKNOWLEDGMENTS

This book tells the story of two legacies: The first is Rawlings Sporting Goods, manufacturer of the official glove of MLB and the choice of more major leaguers than all other competitors' brands combined. The second is the gloves themselves—their history, stories, and impacts on the game of baseball.

We want to recognize all the boys and girls who have put on a Rawlings glove and played their way from sandlot games to the major leagues or any of the leagues in between. Without them, there are no stories.

But these stories all revolve around gloves, and we wish to acknowledge the members of the Rawlings team who have been a part of this story for nearly 140 years by making these gloves possible. In particular, we wish to recognize the following extraordinary individuals who have played a special role in the development of the Rawlings glove line over the years: Harry Latina, Rollie Latina, Howard Keene, Akio Aoki, Kan Aoki, Chuck Malloy, Bob Clevenhagen, Denny Whiteside, Scott Keene, Ryan Farrar, Robert Newman, and Justin Hubbard.

We also want to recognize the staff members of the National Baseball Hall of Fame and the various MLB teams who provided insights and guidance as we put this book together. And finally, a special thanks to Amy Berra for her extra effort in helping find additional sources in our search to make this one of the most definitive histories of the game of baseball.

Founded in 1887, **Rawlings Sporting Goods** is the number one baseball brand worldwide and creator of the iconic Rawlings Gold Glove Award® established in 1957. Rawlings gloves are worn by athletes ranging from "Little League to the Big Leagues," as the official glove of Little League Baseball® and Major League Baseball®, respectively. The company is headquartered in St. Louis, Missouri. For more information, please visit www.rawlings.com.

First published in the United States of America in 2026 by
Rizzoli International Publications, Inc.
49 West 27th Street
New York, NY 10001
www.rizzoliusa.com

Rizzoli Team
Publisher: Charles Miers
Associate Publisher: James Muschett
Managing Editor: Lynn Scrabis
Editor: Candice Fehrman
Production Manager: Colin Hough Trapp
Designer: David Skolkin

Rawlings Team
Chief Marketing Officer: Mike Thompson
Vice President, Brand and Sports Marketing: Eric Reinsfelder
Creative Director: Jason McCartney
Senior Director, Brand Marketing: Lindsey Naber
Text and Photo Research: Ed Wheatley

ISBN: 978-0-8478-7657-0

Library of Congress Control Number: Available upon request

Printed in China

2026 2027 2028 2029 / 10 9 8 7 6 5 4 3 2 1

The authorized representative in the EU for product safety and compliance is Mondadori Libri S.p.A., via Gian Battista Vico 42, Milan, Italy, 20123, www.mondadori.it

Visit us online:
Instagram: @RizzoliBooks
Facebook.com/RizzoliNewYork
Youtube.com/user/RizzoliNY

MIX
Paper | Supporting responsible forestry
FSC® C104723

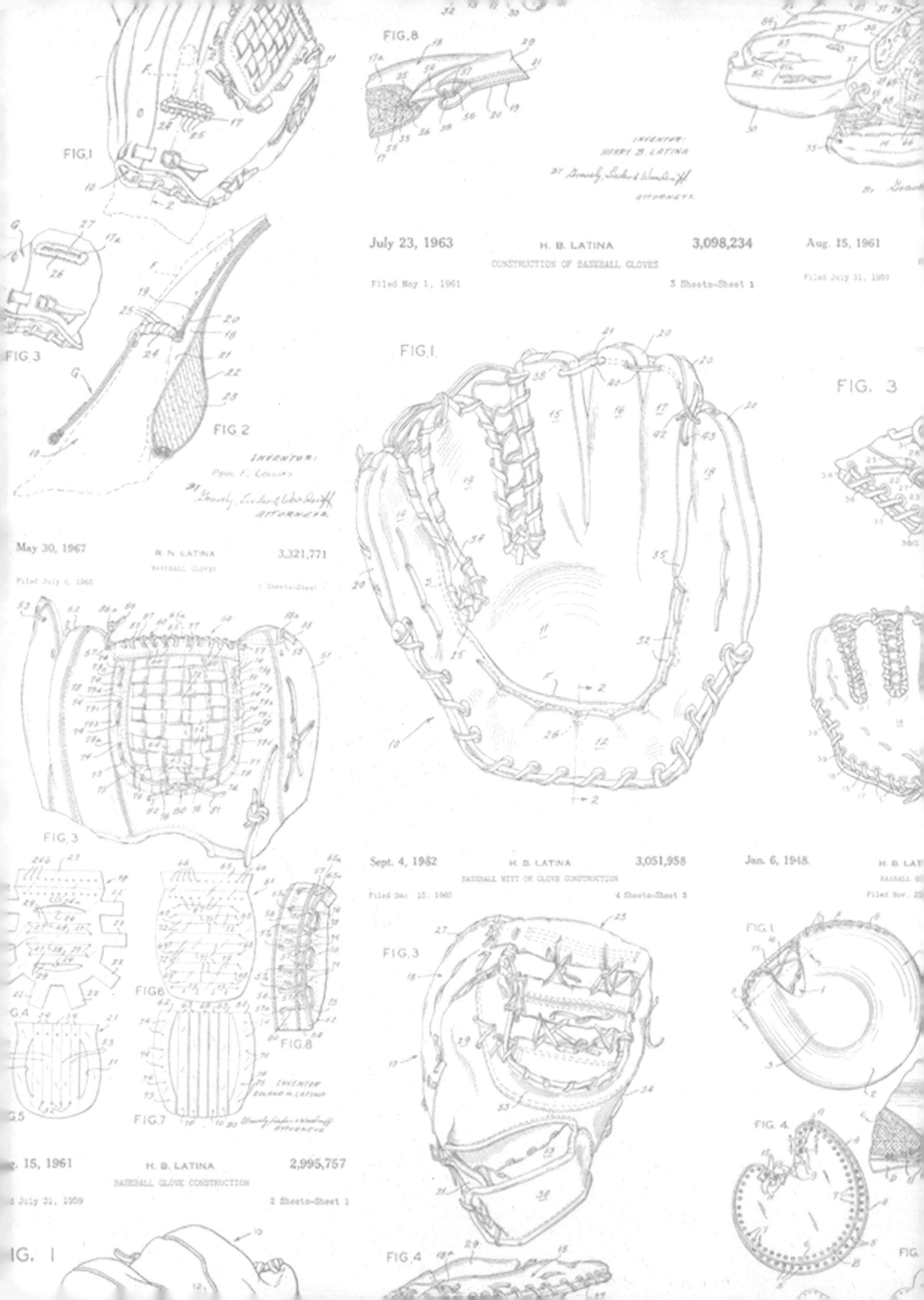
FIG.8
INVENTOR:
HARRY B. LATINA
ATTORNEYS
July 23, 1963
H. B. LATINA
3,098,234
CONSTRUCTION OF BASEBALL GLOVES
Filed May 1, 1961
3 Sheets-Sheet 1
Aug. 15, 1961
FIG.1
FIG.2
FIG.3
INVENTOR:
ATTORNEYS
May 30, 1967
R. N. LATINA
3,321,771
BASEBALL GLOVES
FIG. 3
Sept. 4, 1962
H. B. LATINA
3,051,958
BASEBALL MITT OR GLOVE CONSTRUCTION
Filed Dec. 15, 1960
4 Sheets-Sheet 3
Jan. 6, 1948
H. B. LAT
FIG.6
FIG.7
FIG.8
INVENTOR
ROLAND N. LATINA
ATTORNEYS
. 15, 1961
H. B. LATINA
2,995,757
BASEBALL GLOVE CONSTRUCTION
July 31, 1959
2 Sheets-Sheet 1
FIG. 4
FIG. 1